RETAIL BUSINESS MANAGEMENT
second edition

THE GREGG/McGRAW-HILL
MARKETING SERIES

ADVERTISING IN THE MARKETPLACE
Burke

COLLEGE SALESMANSHIP
Hampton and Zabin

FASHION MERCHANDISING, second edition
Troxell

MERCHANDISING MATHEMATICS
Logan and Freeman

RETAIL BUSINESS MANAGEMENT, second edition
Gillespie and Hecht

RETAIL BUSINESS MANAGEMENT
second edition

Karen R. Gillespie, Ed.D.
Director, Institute of Retail Management
New York University, New York

Joseph C. Hecht, Ed.D.
Professor of Distributive Education
Department of Business and Distributive Education
Montclair State College, New Jersey

Gregg Division
McGraw-Hill Book Company
New York St. Louis Dallas San Francisco Auckland Bogotá Düsseldorf
Johannesburg London Madrid Mexico Montreal New Delhi Panama
Paris São Paulo Singapore Sydney Tokyo Toronto

Library of Congress Cataloging in Publication Data

Gillespie, Karen R
    Retail business management.

    (The Gregg/McGraw-Hill marketing series)
    Includes index.
    1. Retail trade—Management.   I.   Hecht, Jo-
seph C., joint author.   II.   Title.
HF5429.G522   1977   658.8′7   76-25212
ISBN   0-07-023232-6

Retail Business Management, second edition

4 5 6 7 8 9 0   DODO   7 8 3 2 1 0 9

*The editor for this book was Sylvia L. Weber,
the designer was Charles A. Carson,
the art supervisor was George T. Resch,
and the production supervisor was Rena Shindelman.
It was set in Souvenir by York Graphic Services.
Printed and bound by R. R. Donnelley & Sons Company*

CONTENTS

PREFACE

Retail Business Management was first published in 1970 in response to the needs of post-secondary students who were planning careers either as middle managers in large retailing firms or as managers of their own businesses. The authors designed this text to present a comprehensive introduction to retailing principles and practices, incorporating the most up-to-date developments and theories.

Since the publication of this text, the methods that retailers use to promote, distribute, and control merchandise have continued to evolve. The growth of the consumer movement has led to new laws that affect retailers and to voluntary changes in the ways they manage their firms. Technological advances, such as the replacement of cash registers by electronic computer terminals and the introduction of the Universal Product Code, have enabled retailers to serve their customers more quickly. Many retailers have adopted zero-base budgeting, management by objectives, and other systems that improve the efficiency of their management. Changes in the national economy have made franchising a popular form of ownership. Hypermarches, catalog showrooms, and flea markets have increased in number throughout the country. These are among the developments that have prompted the appearance of the second edition of *Retail Business Management*.

Behavioral Objectives

Like the first edition, this second edition of *Retail Business Management* is student-oriented. It provides a foundation upon which students can build an understanding of the activities needed to make a retail business succeed. It not only introduces students to theoretical considerations but also equips them with the skills they will need to succeed in their careers. The larger type, attention to readability, and extensive illustrations of the second edition present the material in a way that is easy for students to read and remember.

Retail Business Management prepares students to meet the performance requirements of retailing positions by providing for the student to develop the following competencies:

- Classify retail businesses
- List and analyze the laws and governmental activities that affect retailers
- Communicate, compute retailing mathematics, and keep records
- Formulate and implement effective merchandising and inventory control plans
- Make decisions, particularly for buying, pricing, advertising, personnel, and career choices

Organization

Retail Business Management is organized into 12 parts that show the role of retail businesses in the national economy and the contributions of the various divisions to individual retailing firms. Part One, "The Wide World of Retailing," presents an historical overview of retailing in the United States and describes the way retailers develop policies and procedures to meet their goals. Chapters also cover the impact on retailing of consumers' buying motives and habits, and the computer's role in modern retailing.

In Part Two, "The Organization of Retail Institutions," stores are classified by ownership and by merchandise categories. The internal organization of retail firms is explained and charted.

The next eight parts discuss the functions of a retail firm. Part Three, "The Personnel Management Function," deals with the hiring and training of employees and with practices concerning store personnel.

Because of the importance of the merchandising division to a firm, in terms of its size and activities, two parts are devoted to this division. Part Four, "The Buying Function," discusses the buyer's job, merchandise sources and classifications, and the relationship of buyer to vendor. Part Five, "The Merchandising Function," explains pricing, stock planning, and inventory procedures.

Part Six, "Store Management and Operation Functions," explores the problems involved in site selection, store planning, and merchandise handling.

Both personal and nonpersonal selling are the topics of Parts Seven and Eight. In Part Seven, "Sales Promotion Functions," the activities of the sales promotion, advertising, visual merchandising, and public relations departments are discussed. Part Eight, "The Power of Personal Selling," presents effective techniques for personal selling and describes the selling continuum from the expert salesperson to the vending machine.

Part Nine, "Customer Operations Functions," treats store services to customers. Financial services, including credit, adjustments, and returns, and nonfinancial services, such as gift wrapping and delivery, are discussed.

Part Ten, "Financial Control Functions," details the financial aspects of retailing, including accounting, budgeting, merchandise valuation, and insurance.

Part Eleven, "Systematic Problem-Solving Techniques," introduces students to the research procedures and areas of investigation that concern retailers in the management of all the divisions of their stores.

Part Twelve, "Looking Ahead," focuses on the student and presents the wide range of career choices and considerations that retailing offers.

End-of-Chapter Activities

To provide practice that will help students develop their skills, each chapter concludes with a series of activities that require review, interpretation, and extrapolation. The first of these activities is "Topics for Discussion," a series of 10 review questions. In "Mathematics for Retailing," one or more questions require students to compute answers from given data. "Communications in Retailing" presents a vignette designed to help the student develop communications skills. "Handling Human Relations" is a management case requiring the student to solve a problem involving subordinates, peers, vendors, or customers. "Decision Making," also a management case, sharpens the student's power to make decisions about retailing problems based on sound logic and analysis of the information at hand. A new end-of-chapter activity, "Career Ladder," invites the student to evaluate various career opportunities, considering the requirements, advantages, and disadvantages of each.

The Instructor's Manual and Key

An Instructor's Manual and Key accompanies the second edition of *Retail Business Management*. This manual contains answers for the end-of-chapter questions and exercises in the text. It also includes specific suggestions for planning the course and for teaching each chapter of the book. It further provides general teaching suggestions, visual aid suggestions, and a reference bibliography. Also included in the manual are ready-to-duplicate midterm and final examinations.

Acknowledgments

A book is the undertaking of many people in addition to that of its authors. In researching and writing *Retail Business Management,* the authors drew on their own backgrounds and experience both in retailing and in the teaching of retailing on the college level. At various times, retail executives and academic colleagues were contacted for information, and they generously responded. Dr. Richard Ashmun of the University of Minnesota, Mr. Randall Carlock of Dayton's, and Mr. Karl Rutkowski of Pierce Junior College, Philadelphia, Pennsylvania reviewed the manuscript and made many helpful suggestions.

The authors also appreciate the cooperation of students in their classes who read portions of the chapters and responded to many of the end-of-chapter materials.

To all others who contributed to the development of this book, the authors are deeply grateful.

Karen R. Gillespie
Joseph C. Hecht

PART ONE

THE WIDE WORLD OF RETAILING

chapter 1

THE DEVELOPMENT OF MODERN RETAILING

Although retailing has changed radically over the years, and even more change is expected in the future, its basic definition remains the same. *Retailing* is the buying and selling of goods and services to satisfy the consumer. In one form or another, retailing dates back to the earliest times. Its history covers institutions and salespeople from trading posts, peddlers, and rural general stores to small five-and-ten-cent stores, mail-order retailers, department stores, mass merchandisers, franchise operations, and catalog showrooms.

In the United States, retailing has grown from simple trade between individuals to a giant industry. The growth of modern retailing has paralleled new advancements in production and transportation. As retailers have adapted to these changes, the consumer has benefited as well.

EARLY RETAILING IN AMERICA

In colonial America, the little retailing that existed was usually conducted through bartering or trade. Most settlers were farming families who built their own homes, grew their own foods, and made their own clothing. However, not all the early colonists were self-sufficient farmers. Some continued to practice the crafts and professions they had learned in their homelands. These settlers established places of business in the seaports of Boston, New York, Philadelphia, and Baltimore and in other populated areas along the coast.

Bootmakers, tinsmiths, and bakers—to name just a few artisans—opened shops along town squares. They made and sold their products in their shops. Eventually merchants set up warehouses on the wharves to sell imported linens, glassware, tools, and many other products. They also supplied merchandise to a special kind of retailer who catered to the frontier customer: the peddler.

Peddlers were a daring and enterprising lot who ventured into the most isolated farmlands and distant frontier settlements with knapsacks and saddlebags full of cutlery, tools, buttons, combs, hand mirrors, and wooden utensils. They were welcome visitors in the hinterlands, for they brought the frontier folks a touch of Eastern life and bits of local news. Trading posts, too, welcomed the peddler—and for the same reasons.

These were the main retailing activities until after the Revolutionary War, when the new government began to improve its land. Roads were carved out of the rugged wilderness, linking outlying settlements with main towns. This was the start of the horse and wagon period.

THE GENERAL STORE

In rural areas, especially where frontier communities were developing into towns, the trading post gave way to shopkeepers who opened stores quite different from those of their city counterparts. Like the peddlers before them, these retailers had to carry a variety of merchandise to satisfy those who could not get to the cities.

The merchandise carried included rifles, tools, rope, china, cooking utensils, ready-made clothing from the East Coast, fabrics, buttons, threads, combs, and a general assortment of foods. The place where this varied collection was sold by retailers was a new type of retailing outlet in America—the general store.

Most shopowners granted credit to their customers. Buying on credit was more of a necessity than a convenience, and owners extended credit freely. There were times when a store owner had to wait for the harvest before customers settled their bills. This situation taxed the storekeeper's resources, but it bound customers to the store.

Limited Mobility

Rural customers traveled to the general store by foot, horse, or horse and wagon. Because neighboring towns were often too remote and difficult to reach, people accepted the local store's merchandise without questioning the prices or the selection. This was their only exposure to retailing.

Limited mobility narrowed the storekeeper's knowledge of goods. The main sources of supply

and information were traveling salespeople from the city, or "drummers" who traveled with their samples and sold merchandise from their stock. The other alternative was for the early storekeeper to go personally to the city and make purchases, but this was often a long, tiresome, and dangerous trip. Later on when manufacturers began distributing catalogs, the shopkeeper was able to order merchandise by mail, but this, too, was a slow and uncertain process.

Limited Productivity

American industry still had to find ways to mass-produce a variety of consumer goods. Besides, the absence of fast, safe, and inexpensive means of transportation limited the distribution of factory-made items. Often the owner of a general store had to purchase the bulk of food products and "homemade" goods from local farmers.

Limited Fashion Influence

Today fashion plays a big role in buying consumer goods, but it played a very small role in the general store. By contrast, in cities where newspapers and magazines carried advertisements of stores, customers were more attuned to fashion. In rural America, however, styles changed very slowly. The popular fashion of one year hardly differed from that of the next, simply because people could not get around to see what better or more popular items were available. In addition, farmers then had to spend most of their income on more essential items.

The general store enjoyed its unique status for many years, but in time, innovative merchants turned an eye to the restricted rural customers who out of sheer necessity had to buy locally. When Montgomery Ward began selling merchandise by mail in 1872, general store owners showed little concern. Their opinion was that smart shoppers would not purchase goods they could not see or touch. But they were wrong. In no time at all, rural customers found they could trust this mail-order merchant. They discovered, much to the local shopkeepers' dismay, that the mail-order system offered a greater variety of merchandise, and often at prices lower than those set by the local merchants. Low postal rates also aided in the growth of the mail-order business. In less than two decades, it was an important retailing outlet for rural consumers.

Local retailers recognized the need to change, and they began to make some necessary adjustments. Progressive merchants attracted to local communities began to specialize. These new merchants devoted entire stores to special products such as clothing, hardware, shoes, feed and grain, or musical instruments. Brand-name merchandise became available, and with the influence of advertising on customer buying, a new retail concept developed—the department store.

THE DEPARTMENT STORE

Department stores differed in two ways from the small shops and country stores before the turn of the century. First, they were much bigger. Second they carried a greater variety of merchandise.

Department stores were a city necessity. The great number of customers and the overflowing stock of consumer goods being produced by American manufacturers required a retail outlet.

A unique feature of the department store was its physical beauty. Typical of city culture and wealth was the great display of home furnishings and fashion. Perhaps the mood of department store retailing was a way of satisfying the demands of the general-store public. Here people found a glittering and abundant array of inexpensive clothing and furnishings for the home in a spectacular setting of marble pillars, great stairways, elaborate lighting fixtures, and exotic plants.

The department store appealed to all types of customers—the extravagant as well as the budget-minded. The main floor usually boasted the most elegant interiors and the finest merchandise. For customers who could not afford the prices there, less-expensive goods were offered in the basement store, or, as it was later to be called, "the budget floor."

Department store organization and methods of buying, promoting, and selling caused many changes in retailing. Some of those changes are still in use today. By setting a policy of "one price for all," big-store management eliminated price haggling and saved clerks' time in making a sale. "Money-back guarantees" also became the order of the day, and the use of newspaper and magazine advertising and elaborate window displays was generally adopted.

Marshall Field, from Chicago, was one of the pioneers in this type of retailing. He understood the importance of women as customers. He made a special effort to cater to women by maintaining an attractive store, complete with doormen who swept the entrance and sidewalks several times a day. To put women shoppers at ease, he hired female clerks for the lingerie department, marking a major change in the male-oriented climate of retailing.

Most of today's giant department stores had their beginnings or were in the stages of development at the turn of the century. Prominent in the retailing evolution at this time were John Wanamaker, J. L. Hudson, Jordan Marsh, and F. & R. Lazarus.

By this time, too, chains of variety stores were strung across the nation. These stores were originated by Frank W. Woolworth and his five-and-ten-cent stores. The Great Atlantic and Pacific Tea Company was the earliest grocery chain. A & P pioneered buying merchandise directly from the producer, reducing the number of middlemen, and thus passing the savings on to the customer. Also at this time, S. S. Kresge, S. H. Kress, J. C. Penney, J. J. Newberry, and Charles R. Walgreen were developing their retailing empires.

This period of vast growth saw a great increase in the country's industrial strength, better systems of transportation and communication, and waves of European immigrants to swell the population. These factors created new business and industrial activity that would open up jobs for a large working class.

In turn, growth created consumer demand.

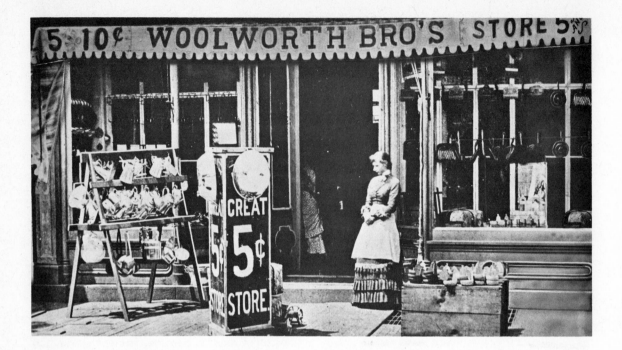

With improvements in communication and transportation, small general stores gave way to large department and variety stores. Woolworth's chain of five-and-ten-cent stores was one of the first to respond to growing consumer demand for a greater array of goods.
Top, courtesy Merchandiser Publishing Company

People had money to spend on purchases other than necessities, and they spent it. Promotional displays in the great department stores whetted the consumer's appetite even more.

Stores came to play an increasingly important role in the lives of Americans. Every major city had its department stores and specialty shops in downtown areas where the trolley lines met or crossed each other. Going into town to shop was an exciting event for the family.

SECONDARY SHOPPING AREAS

Every big city had a dozen or more secondary shopping areas that were located within walking distance of the neighborhood homes. Here in the smaller version of Main Street the self-employed retailer gained a foothold. The grocery store, the butcher shop, the fruit store, the shoe repair shop, the bakery, the delicatessen, the drugstore, the hardware store, and the tailor shop were some of the principal retail establishments of little Main Street during the trolley-car era. A concentrated population made it possible for the specialized neighborhood stores to replace the general store of an earlier time.

People expected shopping to be a multi-stop expedition. One day's shopping might mean a stop in seven or eight different stores. People thought nothing of walking a mile or more and spending several hours shopping. Automobiles were not yet the common means of transportation.

In the 1920s and 1930s self-service retailing developed into supermarkets across the nation. The Piggly Wiggly grocery chain popularized this type in 1916. Eventually self-service retailing joined with the automobile to create a great change in traditional retailing outlets. For a time, the long depression of the 1930s and the war shortages of the early 1940s slowed the buying of automobiles. During this time, retailers continued to ignore the possible effects of the automobile on consumer shopping habits, mainly because roads were poor and few families owned cars. In addition, retailing already had a heavy invest-

ment along the existing public transportation routes.

Discount Stores

The years following the close of World War II were record ones in the country's economy. The United States witnessed its greatest population explosion, a tremendous increase in the demand for and production of consumer goods, and a booming market for private homes. It was also the era of the automobile and the beginning of the third major revolution in retail marketing, the discount store.

At first the discount store specialized in selling brand-name appliances at prices considerably lower than the regular prices suggested by manufacturers. Pent-up demands for these products, caused by wartime shortages, resulted in instant success for these low-priced, no-service retail outlets with their bare surroundings. Through the years, they expanded, selling all types of goods. Specialty discount stores featuring cameras, drugs, and men's or women's wear developed, as did discount variety stores and discount department stores.

Flight To the Suburbs

Whether the great increase in automobile ownership caused or followed the population movement to the suburbs is debatable. Perhaps one development reinforced the other, since no one moved to suburbia without some form of personal transportation. Great numbers of young families left the overcrowded cities to live on the outskirts. They were near enough to commute to work, but distant enough to enjoy living in spacious areas surrounded by trees and grass.

At first the established city retailers remained in the central city's downtown area. They did begin to worry, however, when fewer and fewer shoppers wanted to journey downtown on the bus or streetcar. Traveling by automobile was more comfortable. But as more automobiles came into use, the streets downtown became clogged, and traffic snarled. Shoppers even had difficulty parking their cars. Parking meters were installed as a means of keeping cars moving in and out.

The Hecht Company built this parking facility to attract suburban shoppers to its downtown Washington store.
Courtesy Hecht Company

But it became painfully clear that the old shopping patterns could not continue.

As more people deserted the trolley car and the bus in favor of automobiles, downtown shopping declined. The Saturday downtown shopping excursion was replaced by the Saturday or Sunday family car ride, combined with a visit to the fast-growing newcomer—the suburban shopping center.

Some downtown retailers closed their stores. Others survived by doing business in a new way. They continued to serve the office worker who had to go downtown to work, and they built multi-level parking areas featuring free or low-cost parking for shoppers.

The neighborhood stores on little Main Street also suffered from population shifts. Unable to accommodate the automobile traffic, they had to content themselves with filling the hand-to-mouth food and clothing needs of the immediate neighborhood.

THE SUBURBAN SHOPPING CENTER

Supermarkets, home-furnishings stores, and a few large discount outlets were among the first stores to face the challenge of the car-oriented shopper. The chain stores opened new branches on highways close to the more heavily populated suburban centers. Their immediate success stimulated other stores to do the same. As a result, a radically different retailing idea developed—the suburban shopping center.

Suburban retailers quickly discovered a different kind of patron. More often than not, the suburban family made larger food and clothing purchases than the average city family. Suburban living was less formal, and this was reflected in demands for more casual clothes, backyard and lawn furniture, gardening supplies, and barbecues. Often suburban customers carried these large items home in their cars and station wagons rather than wait for delivery. So the retailers had to keep such merchandise in stock. While limited shopping hours in the city had discouraged family shopping trips, suburban families conveniently shopped during evening and Sunday store hours.

Today shopping centers provide the suburban customer with as many products and services as consumer demand will support. Branch units of mass merchandisers, department stores, specialty shops, and variety stores have joined the giant food stores in bringing all shopping conveniences to the suburbs.

Restaurants, bowling lanes, movie houses, laundries, and other stores and services have located in large suburban shopping areas. The shopping mall was created not only to link this sprawling network of stores but also to shelter the shopper from bad or uncomfortable weather. Completely enclosed malls which are heated and air-conditioned give the shoppers all-weather comfort. In some cases, the shopping mall serves as the center of a suburban community. All the vital elements are there: the post office, police and fire department headquarters, the town hall, and a host of stores and shops.

The giant retail establishments, such as Sears, Roebuck and Company, Montgomery Ward, and J. C. Penney, along with the chain mass merchandisers—Korvette's, Two Guys, K-Mart, Woolco, and the major grocery chains—have prospered because they saw the automobile as an integral part of American life and were able to accommodate its use in shopping.

We have in a sense returned to the general store concept—the customer can shop from morning until night and find almost everything in one center.

THE REBIRTH OF URBAN RETAILING

Though department and chain stores will continue to open units in suburban shopping centers, urban renewal is currently giving city retailers the chance to make a significant comeback. New customers are shopping in the old downtown locations, where old warehouses and tenements are being replaced by high-rise apartment buildings and new offices.

This development may mean a second chance for many intown stores, especially the smaller specialty shops. They can attract new customers and still remain convenient shopping places for the present ones.

Department stores also encourage urban customer traffic because they can expand their merchandise assortments, and also because of their

reasonable prices and many customer services. People who work in the city and those willing to use public transportation will also add to this new traffic. Meanwhile, branch stores in suburban shopping centers will capture the suburban shoppers.

Few events in business are receiving more attention today than minority-group enterprise. Emerging from long years of despair and frustration are men and women who now seek to become successful entrepreneurs. Many are choosing to open small businesses, such as printing services, cleaning services, restaurants, and clothing stores.

Little experience and insufficient capital have made success difficult for some minority-group members. To help alleviate these two problems, the Small Business Administration (SBA) has liberalized its lending policies. It also runs special programs to help minority entrepreneurs. Major corporations, too, have begun to look for ways to help minority economic development.

THE FUTURE OF THE SMALL RETAILER

The greatest victim of retailing changes of the last 30 years has been the small merchant, the one-time backbone of neighborhood retailing. Some merchants have survived, however, and in various ways, such as joining cooperative groups, or becoming franchise dealers. These forms of ownership are explained in Chapter 6. Other retailers survived by extending their business hours, or by offering specialized customer services. Fortunately for the small retailer, it is still convenient for the customer to run to the corner store for a roll of film or a quart of milk.

Some retailers have specialized in a single line of products, such as custom-made draperies and shades. The retailer specializing in this product line will go to a customer's home, measure the windows, carefully explain the variety of shades and draperies and color combinations, and then, having made a sale, expertly install an order. The giant mass merchandiser might sell window trimmings at a lower price, but that same retailer cannot also offer custom fitting.

Most small food stores, hardware stores, department stores, and drugstores have found their larger competitors are moving into the most favorable locations. The competitors are carrying the largest and most diversified inventories, and they are offering easy credit plans.

EFFECTS OF SHORTAGES ON RETAILING

Several factors have contributed to the increasingly rapid pace of retailing in America: the nation's tremendous productive capacity; the growing affluence of the shopper; the influence of fashion; and, for the first time since World War II, the problem of shortages, both in energy and goods. Again retailers are forced to adjust to these changes.

Energy Shortages

The first big adjustment for retailers came with the fuel shortage. Fast-food retail establishments like McDonald's and Burger King were affected immediately because 80 percent of their business is from customers within a 3-mile radius of each outlet. Highway traffic dropped, gasoline became scarce, and customers tended to drive only when necessary. Fast-food retailers adjusted by opening new stores in downtown areas where mass transportation brought customers to the stores. Supermarkets that depended on daily deliveries of goods became vulnerable because they have little bulk storage space of their own. Alternative ways of receiving supplies and storing them are necessary to ease their problem.

Merchandise Shortages

America's era of unlimited resources at its disposal is surely over, and retail buying practices will feel the effects profoundly. Major suppliers are moving toward a new marketing strategy in an era of shortage, forcing retailers to reexamine their purchasing plans.

No doubt manufacturers' shortages will cause problems for retailers. Sellers may find private

The Magic Carpet Service, a shuttle bus run by the city of Seattle, conserves energy and provides free transportation for riders in the city's downtown shopping area.
Courtesy Exxon Corporation

brands difficult to get if manufacturers use their raw materials to produce their more profitable nationally advertised brands. Retailers think manufacturers may increase minimum-order sizes and deliver substitutes when necessary. If shortages continue, shipping dates may become less reliable.

Shortages may also tighten the cooperative advertising budgets that manufacturers allow for retailers. This will raise the stores' advertising expenses. In addition, products in short supply will require great security measures, since obtaining any replacement for out-of-stock merchandise may be difficult. Substitution will be one way to overcome shortages. However, new-product development and quality standards may suffer from the shortage problem.

TOPICS FOR DISCUSSION

1. What were some of the many functions of peddlers other than to sell consumer goods?
2. Where frontier communities were developing into towns, the trading post gave way to a new kind of store. The proprietor had to change the method of retailing. Discuss the changes that took place.
3. What were some of the factors that led to the decline of the general store?
4. What advantages did mail-order retailing offer its customers?
5. What two major factors were responsible for the development of the department store?
6. Explain the statement "The department store appealed to all types of customers."
7. Suburban retailers discovered a different type of customer. What are some of the distinctions between the suburban customer and the urban customer, and what changes did the latter bring about in suburban retailing?
8. How have some of the small neighborhood stores managed to survive the competition of the giants? What does the future hold for the small independent?
9. What steps might the suburban shopping center take to adjust to the energy shortage?
10. Explain why the small retailer may be more affected by merchandise shortages than the larger retailer.

COMMUNICATIONS IN RETAILING

Because of the energy shortage, you have cut down the store hours. The store used to be open from 9:30 a.m. to 10 p.m., but now the hours are 10 a.m. to 9 p.m. A good customer writes to you, explaining that shopping is now inconvenient and charging that the change was made to satisfy union demands that store workers get home early. On a separate sheet of paper, write a one-page letter explaining the facts to this customer.

DECISION MAKING

A merchant wants to establish a new luggage store and finds two vacant stores: one in the heart of the Main Street shopping area, and one in the new suburban shopping center. The rent for the store in the suburban shopping center is the same as the rent for the store on Main Street. However, in the suburban shopping center a 2 percent additional charge will be made on all sales, payable to the shopping center real estate developer. Both stores are similar in size.

The Main Street store is adjacent to both a department store and a travel agency, with the closest competitor two blocks away. The suburban-center store has a department store on one side and a vacant store on the other side. The shopping center developer guarantees that no competing luggage store will be allowed in the shopping center. If you were the merchant, what factors would you consider before selecting the site? Which location would you decide on? List your reasons briefly on a separate sheet of paper, and be prepared to discuss your decision.

chapter 2

DEVELOPING GOALS, OBJECTIVES, POLICIES, AND PROCEDURES

Stores vary in appearance both outside and inside. They vary in size; in the amounts and types of merchandise carried; in the quality of goods; in assortments; in pricing; in the amounts and types of services offered; and in the kinds, ages, and numbers of customers accommodated.

Stores try to create various impressions to attract different kinds of customers. Some stores are elegant and opulent in appearance; some are quiet and dignified; some are bustling and exciting; and some are efficient and well organized, while others are marked by confusion. Some stores aim to satisfy all the customer's product needs, while others appeal only to very specialized demands. Some are service-oriented, while others feature self-service and a cash-and-carry policy.

All these differences are determined by the goals and objectives of the firms, by the policies that are derived from those goals and objectives, and by the procedures used to carry out the policies.

It's not just individuals who set goals and think of ways to achieve those goals. Firms must set long-term goals and more immediate objectives, determine the policies needed to attain the goals, and establish procedures by which the policies may efficiently and profitably be carried out. Periodic evaluation is needed to determine how well the procedures implement the policies and how effective the policies are in helping to attain the goals.

SETTING GOALS AND OBJECTIVES

"If you do not know where you are going, any road will take you there." This is an old saying whose truth is quite evident. To those who watch the retail scene, the saying applies to stores that have no well-defined goals. Many of those stores add to the failure statistics of retail firms. Stores that succeed usually have well-defined goals and work toward those goals. Goals and objectives shape the direction of a firm and enable it to operate profitably as well as serve the needs of customers.

Goals

Goals are long-range plans for the future. Most retailing firms set goals by five-year or ten-year periods. The longer the time assigned to achieve a goal, the more that goal may have to be changed before the end of the time period. However, having a goal in the first place gives direction to all the planning and activity of a firm. Thus, a firm may have a profit-making goal of developing ten stores in suburban areas over the next five years. It will strive to maintain in these newly opened stores its image as a retail establishment that offers high-quality at low prices.

Objectives

Objectives are the more immediate and tangible plans needed to reach the long-range goal. Certain short-term objectives may be set, for example, if the goal of the opening ten stores in suburban

The jewelry department of the mass merchandise store shown above projects a different image from that of the quality jewelry store shown below. What factors contribute to the image of each store? Top, courtesy Korvettes's, Division of Arlen Realty and Development Corporation; bottom, courtesy Zale Corporation

areas over the next five years is to be attained. The first objective that must be set is to maintain profitability, since profit is essential if the firm is to continue to operate. Firms that are unprofitable have no money for improvements, for expansion, or to pay their employees. Unprofitable firms do not have the financial standing that enables them to borrow money for expansion at relatively low interest rates. So profit must be a continuing objective of the firm. Other objectives must be to maintain the level of service and the quality of merchandise that the firm provides for its customers and to develop means by which the organization may prosper and grow. Therefore, for example, additional objectives may be to develop two stores the first year at a break-even level without sacrificing quality.

At the end of the first year, the goal set by the firm will be reevaluated to determine if the eight remaining stores that are planned can feasibly be opened over the remaining four years. The performance of the two newly opened stores will be evaluated to see if a break-even level can be turned into a profit-making level. Constant evaluation, then, of the current objectives must be maintained if the ultimate goal of the organization is to be met.

More specifically, the objectives needed to meet the established goal would be:

1. To continue to operate at a profit

2. To open a minimum of two new stores each year

3. To have each store at least "break even" the first year after its opening and begin to make a profit in the second year of operation

Management by Objectives

Management by objectives, often referred to as "MBO," is the application of systematic thinking to the achievement of predetermined goals and objectives of the firm. Everyone in the firm must be working toward the common goal.

Management by objectives makes the system of bosses supervising subordinates work because:

- Everyone knows his or her job.

- Everyone is accountable for his or her own job.

- The true contribution of each person is measured.

- The processes to achieve desired results are carefully planned.

Through management by objectives, each person is motivated to do a task well because each person realizes how important his or her task is in achieving the firm's goals and objectives.

Establishing a system of MBO requires the following steps:

1. Setting goals and objectives that are considered attainable by people who work in the firm

2. Annually evaluating and updating those goals and objectives

3. Making sure that the goals of individual units or departments match and contribute to the overall goals of the firm

4. Defining the major responsibilities of the firm and outlining each function to be performed in the firm

Through management by objectives, the manager and the people under the manager are working toward the same goal. There is a unified approach to achieving the goal, for each person knows the role he or she is to play. And all workers know how they will be evaluated in their roles.

Thus, if a site were to be selected for the opening of one of the stores that was a partial objective of the five-year plan discussed above, management by objectives might be outlined as follows:

- *Overall objective.* Find a site for a 30,000-square-foot store and build the store.

- *Real estate manager.* By mid-April, a site will be found near or in the center of a suitable shopping area, no more than 50 miles from Central City.

- *Construction manager.* By mid-April, preliminary plans to build a 30,000-square-foot store will be ready for the site found by the real estate manager. These plans will be in final form by May 1. By mid-August, construction will be finished, and the store will be ready for occupancy.

- *Personnel manager.* By July 15, all personnel needs will be determined, and interviews for prospective employees for the new store will begin. By August 10, all needed employees will be hired and ready to begin working.

- *Merchandise manager.* By July 1, all buying plans for merchandise for the new store will be complete.

- *Buyers.* By July 15, all merchandise needed for the first day's opening and for the first week of selling will have been ordered. By August 12, all merchandise will have been delivered to the store.

- *Advertising manager.* By July 1, all advertising plans for the store will be complete. On August 1, the first announcement of the store's opening will be run in the local papers. Merchandise advertising will begin on August 10. Individual articles of merchandise will be advertised twice weekly through the month of September, when advertising will be increased to three times weekly for the remainder of the fall season.

- *Store manager.* By August 10, all employees who will receive, mark, stock, and sell merchandise will be available for initial training. By August 12, employees will be ready to receive, mark, and stock the merchandise. By August 15, when the store opens, the merchandise will be in place, displays arranged, and selling personnel trained and ready for their work of serving the customers.

- *Financial manager.* By April, loans will have been negotiated for the preliminary planning, and for the construction, fixtures, and furnishings needs of the building to be erected. By August, money to be used for paying the store's employees will be available. Also by August, money will be available for planned advertising and for future advertising needs. Money will also be available for the purchase of merchandise.

Such a master MBO plan that is shared by all managers in the firm shows how each managerial role contributes to the overall objective. The plan is effective when all the managers can see how they are working together toward a common objective.

An evaluation is made of each person's actions to determine how well the job was done and how much it contributed to achieving the firm's objectives. The firm determines whether its objectives were attained satisfactorily and considers possible changes in future objectives.

SETTING POLICIES

The goals, objectives, and policies of a given firm together form the business personality or image that the firm projects to its vendors, employees, and customers.

Policies are guidelines for management and employees. They chart the actions to be taken by those responsible for the day-to-day activities of the business. If a firm did not establish policies, it would have to make decisions each time a transaction was handled by an employee. Established policies therefore provide for planned effort, as opposed to haphazard decision making as problems arise.

Following are some examples of policies that might be established to achieve the goal and objectives stated in the case of the five-year plan discussed earlier.

1. To open the proposed stores within 100 miles of the parent store.

2. To open these stores in existing or newly planned shopping areas or centers.

3. To maintain the image of the parent store in each newly opened store.

MAJOR AND MINOR POLICIES

There are two types of policies: major policies and minor policies. *Major policies* are those general guidelines and standards by which the entire firm is run. Thus, a firm may have a "discount policy." This would affect the merchandise bought, the store layout, the store management, the advertising, and all the other activities within the store. *Minor policies* are the policies that apply only to one segment of a firm or that are unique for some reason. For example, a store might have a major policy of granting refunds for merchandise if it is returned within seven days, if the price tags are still attached, and if the customer still has the sales receipt. However, the active sportswear department may have its own special policy of no returns on bathing suits. Or a

J. M. Towne's customer policies, described in this mailing piece, contribute to the total image that the firm presents to the public.

sale may be run with the announcement "All Sales Are Final."

Persons employed by the store are responsible for upholding the policies of the store. If, for example, a buyer in a store that featured a discount policy were to purchase goods and resell them at nationally advertised regular prices, that buyer would not be following the discount policy of the store. He or she would, as a result, be subject to dismissal or some other action. Every person within a firm must be aware of the policies and be guided at all times by those policies.

ESTABLISHING PROCEDURES

After objectives are set and policies to attain those objectives have been formulated, the detailed procedures must be determined. Procedures are the routines necessary to carry out policies. For example, when a store orders merchandise, it might follow the buying procedures listed below:

1. All orders must be confirmed in writing.

2. All orders must be confirmed on the store's own order blanks. The buyer should fill in all information as required.

3. All orders must be signed by the store buyer.

4. Orders totaling over $500 at cost must be cosigned by a store principal.

5. When merchandise arrives in the store, it must be examined by the buyer, the department manager, or the store manager to make sure that it is as ordered. Merchandise not received as specified in the order is to be returned immediately at the manufacturer's expense.

Having predetermined routines assures the store executives that the policies of the store will be enforced by all employees. Routines need to be established for every aspect of store operation. Retailing is a detailed business. Unless every detail is taken care of correctly, costly errors may be made. To ensure smooth, efficient operation of the entire store, procedures must be established in line with the policies of the firm.

EXAMPLE OF GOALS, OBJECTIVES, AND POLICIES

A firm's owners decided to open a store in the town of Arden. It was to be a men's- and boys'-wear center. The town had previously had one high-quality men's specialty store and one discount store carrying men's and boys' wear. The goal the owners established for the new store was to offer customers in the town of Arden and its suburbs fashionable, good-quality men's and boys' wear at regular prices so that the firm would earn a profit yet also provide goods and services needed in that particular town.

The immediate objectives were to select an appropriate site that would be near the center of the shopping area, to construct a store that would have a quality appearance, and to build the store large enough to handle the sales volume the owners expected to achieve over the next five years.

Some of the policies the owners established to achieve these objectives were as follows:

• To establish a reputation for the store as an outstanding men's- and boys'-wear center, it shall be our policy to carry only quality lines of apparel. These lines shall include both nationally branded and nonbranded merchandise made by manufacturers renowned for their high-quality products.

• To maintain a fashion image, it shall be the policy of this firm to carry lines of merchandise shown in leading consumer magazines. It shall also be our policy to feature new items in our windows and to provide fashion information for schools and clubs in the area. This will include lending merchandise to be used for club and school fashion shows.

• In order to inform the families and individuals in the town of Arden and its suburbs about our store and its merchandise, it shall be the policy of this firm to advertise weekly in the local newspaper and to send direct-mail announcements to telephone subscribers in this town and surrounding towns at the beginning of each new season.

• In order to be able to keep fresh, new, complete stocks of merchandise each season, it shall be our policy to charge regular prices for the merchandise carried except for end-of-season clearances, which will be held twice a year.

Since policies must govern every segment of business activity, retail store policies must cover

1 The market area to be served

2 The kinds and qualities of merchandise to be carried

3 The price determinations for the merchandise

4 The handling of the merchandise from the time it leaves the manufacturer to the time it reaches the consumer

5 The services to be provided for customers

6 The way employees, customers, and vendors are to be treated

7 The procedures for accounting and sales control

8 The methods of sales promotion, including publicity, advertising, and display

9 The firm's public relations activities in the community

10 The plans for future development and expansion

WRITTEN VERSUS ORAL STATEMENTS OF POLICIES

Most business philosophers believe that all statements of policies should be written. They cite the following reasons. They believe that:

• The act of writing the policy helps to clarify management's thinking about a problem

• Better direction can be given to employees

• There will be more adherence to management's objectives

• The business can be run more effectively because written statements of policies can be more easily communicated and understood

• Authority can be more readily delegated

• Written policies can be made available to all employees through handbooks, manuals, and store employee publications.

On the other hand, those who oppose written statements of policies say that they are unnecessarily restrictive because situations can be handled as they arise. They say that the many transactions requiring decisions make it impractical to attempt to put all policies in writing and that frequent policy changes make written statements unworkable. They claim that written policies are less flexible; and that the establishment of written policies is very time-consuming.

Many firms have established policies through general practice over the years, and these may have been passed along from the managers to the employees by word of mouth. However, such an offhand method of communicating policy does not ensure uniformity or consistency.

Small firms are usually more negligent when it comes to writing statements of policy than large ones. Most large firms find it essential, if they want to maintain uniform treatment of customers, vendors, and employees, to write their policies and to make them known to all company personnel.

THE POLICY MAKERS

When a firm is established, the owners determine certain goals and objectives for the firm and set the major policies that will aid the firm in attaining those goals. These *major* policies are broad and general. Additional policies are also needed

Form No. 52—NY

White Castle

NEW YORK AREA CASTLE NEWCOMER'S GUIDE

WORK WEEK: The work week ends at the end of the Sunday night shift, and includes Saturday, Sunday, and holidays. Regular days off are assigned for Monday through Friday.

WORK DAY: The regular work day is eight hours, including one 30-minute meal period.

SHIFTS: White Castles are open 24 hours a day, seven days a week. Shifts are assigned weekly by the Castle supervisor.

HOLIDAYS: All full-time employees are paid for six holidays each year: New Year's Day, Memorial Day, Independence Day, Labor Day, Thanksgiving Day, and Christmas Day. Castles are closed only on Christmas Day.

ABSENT OR LATE: When unable to report for work as scheduled, an operator should call the Castle supervisor or shift manager on duty as soon as possible, so arrangements can be made to cover the shift.

Supervisor's   Castle
Home Phone _____ Phone _____
Area Office Phone: 899-8404

(Your future job opportunities depend largely on your conduct and dependability record)

PAYDAY: Regular payday is on Friday each week.

PHYSICAL EXAMINATION: Each job candidate is required to pass a physical examination, including a blood test, at Company expense. Good health is a valuable asset, and White Castle gives its employees every encouragement to protect it.

PUBLIC HEALTH LAW: Physical examinations are required by the New York municipal health department and are given by a medical doctor, designated and paid by White Castle. Food Handler permits are required in some localities, in which case they are issued by the municipal health department.

SICK BENEFITS: Sick benefit payments are available to White Castle employees as provided by New York laws, either through the state or a voluntary agreement. White Castle payments are made through the Travelers Insurance Company upon proper application from a medical doctor.

UNIFORMS: Uniforms are provided by the Company. Employees will provide their own shoes and hosiery of the style and color recommended by the Company. Slips must be white and hairnets must be worn while on duty.

EATS: There is no charge for food eaten while on duty. All food carried out of the Castle must be paid for.

WAGE INCREASES: Individual progress reviews are made at the end of six months, and every six-month period thereafter, dating from the original employment date. Pay increases are based on improvement in personality, personal appearance, conduct on and off the job, in giving fast and courteous service, and in the art of preparing a delicious Hamburger sandwich.

IDENTIFICATION: If a "decision to hire" is made, a job candidate is required to present a Social Security card or take immediate steps to procure one, and is required to present proof of his or her age.

CLEANLINESS: Cleanliness is the responsibility of all those working in the Castle. Cleaning duties are part of the job.

PERSONAL APPEARANCE: Proper grooming, clean shaven appearance, and full uniform dress are required in accordance with company standards, as indicated on "Personal Appearance Requirements" charts.

CONDUCT: Employees are expected to conduct themselves as ladies and gentlemen. Friends and relatives should be discouraged from telephoning and visiting employees while on duty. Loitering around the Castle when off duty is not permitted.

DRESS: Presentable clothing should be worn to and from work.

HOSPITAL AND SURGICAL INSURANCE: Upon completion of three months of continuous full-time service, and if working at time of eligibility, White Castle employees are provided with Hospitalization and Surgical Insurance paid for by the Company. Coverage for eligible dependents is available, if desired, with one-half the cost paid by the Company.

GROUP LIFE INSURANCE: Upon completion of six months of continuous full-time service, and if working at time of eligibility, White Castle employees are provided with a Group Life Insurance policy paid for by the Company. Additional insurance is available, if desired, with part of the cost paid by the employee, and part by the Company.

VACATIONS: After one year of continuous service, full-time employees receive two weeks paid vacation; after ten years, three weeks; after 20 years, four weeks. After one year's service, part-time employees receive a paid vacation as above, with pay based on the average hours worked per week.

EMPLOYEES' TRUST: The Employees' Trust is a deferred profit-sharing fund. A certain portion of the Company's Profits is set aside each year to accumulate for participating employees, and to be increased by investments under the direction of the Board of Trustees. An employee becomes a participant upon completing one full calendar year of service on December 31, and has averaged at least 20 hours per week in that year.

PENSION-INSURANCE PLAN: The White Castle Pension-Insurance Plan provides for benefits after retirement, for death benefits before and after retirement, and for termination benefits, providing age and years of service total 56 or more years. To be eligible for participation an employee must have completed five continuous years of full time service and have attained age 35.

CASH BONUS: The White Castle annual Cash Bonus, paid from a percentage of gross sales and not from profit, is not a guaranteed benefit, but since 1924 it has been paid every year except for three years during the depression of the early 1930's. The amount of payment to each individual is based on length of service, with each six months of employment, beginning January 1 and July 1, constituting a credit, with no limit on how many credits may be accumulated.

SUGGESTION PLAN: The Suggestion Plan provides a means by which employees may submit ideas for improvement of equipment, products, service, safety, and communication. Cash awards are paid for accepted ideas.

CAREER OPPORTUNITIES: White Castle offers excellent food service career opportunities. Without exception, all Castle and Area, Office supervisory and management jobs are filled by promotion from within. Every employee is eligible for these promotions.

All employees should be informed of the firm's policies so that they will know what is expected of them and what they can expect from the firm.
Courtesy White Castle Company

DEVELOPING GOALS, OBJECTIVES, POLICIES, AND PROCEDURES

for the actual operation of the business. Usually the managers in charge of various store activities are responsible for setting the specific operational policies or *minor* policies. The minor policies must be consistent with the ideas expressed in the major policies. Thus, the major policy of "fairness in all dealings" would be interpreted by the personnel division to be "fairness to all employees." Fair treatment would include setting salary scales that are consistent with the amount of work the employee is called upon to do, the length of time the worker has been employed, rank in the organization, and the number of hours of work. The same major policy would be interpreted by the merchandising division to mean "fairness to vendors" and "fairness to customers" in merchandise selection, handling, and selling. The advertising manager would interpret the major policy as "fairness and honesty in all advertising presentations." Thus, every section of the organization would establish minor policies to fit the general or major policy of the firm.

FACTORS THAT DETERMINE POLICY

A retail store exists not as just a separate entity but rather as a part of a complex society. Although the owners of a store may set their own goals and objectives and establish their own policies, many interacting factors determine the policies in addition to those over which the owners or managers have control. Laws, competition, local customs, and customers are among the determining factors to be considered. Some of these are discussed below.

A major factor in determining policy will be the kind of firm the owners or managers have decided to establish. Will it be a discount or regular-price firm? Will it offer minimum, intermediate, or maximum services? Will it cater to an exclusive clientele or to a wide range of consumers? Will the store feature broad assortments and selections, or will it carry limited selections of merchandise? Will the store feature name brands, unbranded goods, store brands, or a combination of these? Will the store employ full-time workers only, or will it also use part-time employees? Will the store advertise? Will the store stage special publicity events?

Laws and rulings of the city, state, and federal governments that affect this retailing organization help to determine policy. For example, civil rights laws affect hiring policies. Wage and salary laws affect employee payment policies. Laws about merchandise affect buying decisions, influence what may be said to the customer about the merchandise both in advertisements and in the store, and determine what information must accompany the products when they are sold.

Competitors affect policy. Retailers must know which other stores will be competing for their customers' trade. The competitors, their location, their merchandise, and the services and prices they offer—these have a direct influence on the policies of a given retailing firm.

Local practices affect policy—legal holidays, religious observances, celebrations, and outings, for example. If an area decorates its streets at Christmas time, most stores will cooperate in displaying decorations. If a local chamber of commerce sets up a community day, most merchants are glad to cooperate to stimulate business. If state laws permit stores to be open for business on Sunday, merchants may find that they have to keep their stores open seven days a week rather than the normal six days in order to serve customers.

Customer needs and wants will determine the policies of a store. If customers prefer to charge purchases rather than pay cash, a merchant may have to extend charge privileges to gain customers. If customers refuse to serve themselves, a merchant may be forced to employ salespeople. If an area changes in character because of new housing, new employment opportunities, or an influx of people from a different ethnic group, merchants may find that they have to change their policies to conform to the needs and wants of the new customers.

Keeping Policies Flexible

Retailing, being a dynamic business, is constantly subject to change. Policies, therefore, must always be flexible. The following incident will illustrate this need for flexibility.

A grocery firm had a policy of providing fresh, quality foods at low prices and of offering no giveaways or trading stamps. A competitor across the street began to offer trading stamps with each purchase. A second competitor a block away also began to offer trading stamps with each purchase. Business dwindled noticeably at the first firm. After several unprofitable months of business, the manager decided that the store policy would have to be changed if the store was to lure its former customers back. Therefore, the policy was changed, and trading stamps were offered with each purchase. Customers returned to the store when the stamps were available, and the other stores found they had gained only a temporary advantage by offering the stamps. After two years, all the stores abandoned the stamp plans, and business once again was conducted by the first grocery firm on the basis of the low-priced, quality, fresh foods that were carried.

New laws, new merchandise, new competition, new customers, or just new demands by customers may affect policies. When policy changes are made, all employees should be advised about the changes.

Carrying Out Store Policies

Every member of an organization is responsible for carrying out the policies of the firm. If, for example, a store has a policy of meeting low prices, the salespeople are expected to report any customer complaints regarding lower prices for identical goods in competing stores. In large stores, comparison shoppers may be dispatched to check prices of comparable products in other stores. Advertisements are also studied to determine what prices are being charged in other stores for similar or identical products. The successful adherence to policy can be achieved only by making all employees aware of the policy and of their responsibility to do their work according to the policy.

In a retail store that charges a full markup for goods, all employees must be informed about the policy and permitted to explain to customers the reason for not meeting the low prices charged in some other stores. Regular-price stores usually offer extensive services to offset the competition of the low-price stores. Regular-price stores may offer charge accounts; time-payment plans; trained, efficient sales personnel; delivery; and gift wrapping. Employees need to know about all these services to explain to customers why their store does not attempt to compete with the mass merchandisers.

While top executives are responsible for establishing general or major policies and store managers for interpreting those policies, every employee is responsible for carrying out all policies of the firm. Since authority and responsibility are greatest at the executive level, those who own and manage the firm have the primary responsibility to maintain policies consistently.

THE MANAGER'S RESPONSIBILITY

Individual store managers are responsible for carrying out major policies and procedures. They are also responsible for establishing some minor policies and the procedures to assure that all policies are followed.

1. Major policies applicable to all stores in a chain or multi-store organization need to be put into effect by the store manager. The manager supervises the staff to make sure the firm's orders are carried out.

2. Minor policies for a particular store that keep it competitive with other retailing firms in its vicinity need to be made by the store manager. The manager may be asked to check these policies to make sure they do not conflict with the overall major policies.

3. Procedures needed to carry out both major and minor policies and to ensure the efficient functioning of the store are under the supervision of the manager.

General Organization Policies

Although store managers may have some control over minor policies and policies that apply just to their particular stores, they are also responsible for carrying out the general store policies that apply to all stores in the organization. For example, an organization had a policy regarding vacations for employees that stated:

Paid vacations will be granted to all employees based on the number of months or years of their continuous employment with the firm. Vacations must be taken within the vacation periods of January 1 to February 28 or June 1 to Labor Day. No vacations with pay may be taken at any other time without prior approval of the central office.

The local manager's responsibility is to carry out this policy and other general policies as stated. The manager gives the employees vacations as earned within the limits of this policy. The manager has no option to change or adapt this policy in any way.

Individual Store Policies

One manager had charge of a single store in a 200-store chain. The organization had a general policy regarding store hours:

It shall be the policy of this firm to have individual stores in the communities in which they are located determine their own store hours to fit the needs and wants of their customers and to meet the hours as established by other competitive firms in the same communities.

The store manager took the following actions in setting the local store policy regarding hours of operation:

- Counts were taken of customers at different hours of the day both in the manager's store,

on the nearby streets, and in competitors' stores. This gave the manager a pattern of shopping hours.

- A questionnaire was handed out in the store. Customers were asked to list what shopping hours they preferred.

- The local chamber of commerce was checked to ascertain the usual business hours maintained in the area and the local ordinance about Sunday openings.

- For a few weeks, the store manager experimented by opening the store one-half hour later in the morning and extending shopping time one-half hour in the evening. Counts of customers before and after the change were made and compared.

- A meeting of the local merchants' group was called to discuss the most favorable store hours for the community.

- After deciding on the best hours to serve customers' needs and wants, the manager posted the store hours so that customers would know when they could find the store open. A notice was mimeographed for all employees so they would know what the store hours were and could answer customers' questions.

- The full-time employees' working hours were scheduled so that each employee worked an equal number of morning and evening hours. This allowed the less-desirable working hours to be shared equally by all full-time employees.

Managers in multi-store firms need to be familiar with all policies of their firms. Usually a handbook containing the policies in writing is available for each manager. It is the manager's responsibility to see that the employees are familiar with those policies that affect them or which they need to know to handle transactions efficiently and in accordance with the standards set by the firm. Some firms make policy booklets available to all permanent employees.

THE WIDE WORLD OF RETAILING

Since stores are no longer managed by their owners but in many cases by hired managers, the establishment of policies has become more difficult and more important. If a multi-store firm is to provide uniform service wherever a branch or another store in the chain exists, its goals, objectives, policies, and procedures must be known, understood, and observed by every employee.

TOPICS FOR DISCUSSION

1. What factors give stores different personalities in their customers' views?
2. What are the differences between goals, objectives, policies, and procedures in a retailing firm?
3. What is meant by "management by objectives"? How may a firm's performance be improved by using MBO?
4. What activities in a business should be covered by policies?
5. Why are policies and procedures needed in retailing organizations?
6. Whose responsibility is it to see that policies are properly observed?
7. What advantages, if any, are there in having written policies? Why don't all firms have written policies?
8. What is the difference between major and minor policies? Who is responsible for making major policy decisions? Who is responsible for making minor policy decisions?
9. Under what circumstances may policies be changed?
10. The store manager has responsibility for policy in two ways. What are they, and what are some examples of each type of responsibility?

COMMUNICATIONS IN RETAILING

Because of increasing costs, a firm has decided to eliminate its policy of giving "incentive days" for good attendance. The present policy reads as follows:

". . . For employees who have been on time and present every working day from January 1 through June 1, a bonus of two days off with pay will be granted in addition to the regular vacation period. These two days, however, are to be taken at a time convenient for the rest of the organization and may not be added to the vacation period nor taken on a Saturday or a Monday."

On a separate sheet of paper, write a notice to be sent to all employees about this elimination of incentive days. Explain why management has taken this action.

MANAGING HUMAN RELATIONS

Refer to the above situation regarding the revision of a store's employee policy. Is it wise for a firm to change a policy that has been in effect for years, especially one of this nature? What is the best way to handle such a situation to minimize employee dissatisfaction? Be prepared to discuss this question in class.

DECISION MAKING

A large discount store opened across the street from a well-established department store in a large city. The department store maintained a competitive price policy. However, it also had a policy of not carrying any manufacturer's nationally branded merchandise that was sold to nearby discount stores. The newly arrived discount store carried Carter towels, which were nationally advertised and had been featured for many years by the department store. In line with its policy of not carrying merchandise featured by competing discount firms, the department store stopped carrying the Carter towels. The department store's customers complained, however. They did not want to buy the towels in the discount house because they wanted the convenience of ordering them by telephone, charging them, and having them sent to their homes. Finally, dozens of customers threatened to close their charge accounts if they could not get the name-brand towels they liked at the department store.

If you were the store manager, what action, if any, would you take? Be prepared to discuss your decisions in class.

CAREER LADDER

A firm had a merchandise vice president, eight buyers, sixteen assistant buyers (two for each buying area), eight merchandise clerks (one in every buying office), forty salespeople to sell to the customers, and eight stock clerks (one for each buying area) to bring the merchandise from the storage areas to the selling floor.

If a person started as a stock clerk, what might the progression on the career ladder be if that person wanted to become a buyer at some time in the future? At what point would the stock clerk have responsibility for carrying out policy? For making minor policies? Be prepared to discuss your point of view in class.

chapter 3

THE CHANGING CONSUMER BUYING MOTIVES AND HABITS

Retailers have found that today's consumer is better educated and more sophisticated than ever before. The byword, and buy word, is *more*. The consumer is more knowledgeable, more selective, and more aware of quality. Consumers' attitudes toward family, work, themselves, their personal needs, and the economy have changed a great deal in the last 25 years. For example, fewer children are being born, more jobs are opening up for members of minority groups, and more married women are seeking careers.

Although an economic recession, like the recession of the mid-1970s, tends to make people feel less secure, many psychologists still claim that the American consumer has developed a psychology of "entitlement," or the belief that "It is right for me to have more of what I want."

These changes have encouraged more spending by consumers on retail goods, a trend only partially modified by the most recent economic recession in America.

UNDERSTANDING CONSUMERS' NEEDS AND WANTS

According to some, Americans no longer rely so heavily on their jobs for life's satisfactions; they look in other directions as well. One of these is the ownership of things they need and want. Alert retailers try to fulfill some of these needs by understanding consumers' buying habits and motives.

By definition, the *consumer* is the ultimate user

of goods and services that satisfy physical and emotional needs. Manufacturers and retailers now base their decisions on two prime considerations: the current and potential needs and wants of the consumer, and the price the consumer will pay to satisfy them.

Everyone who produces or stocks merchandise for sale must consider what merchandise and services consumers are likely to buy or reject. But no matter how skillful the producer and the retailer are at predicting consumer preferences, there is always some uncertainty. To hold this uncertainty to a minimum, marketers try to identify the direction of consumer demands and to influence consumer choices. The producer tries to persuade consumers to want a particular product and retailers to stock it, and the retailer tries to persuade customers to buy. Both aim to market their products successfully by means of sales promotion and advertising, and by making the products widely available. If they can predict accurately, persuasion is easy and sellers are successful. If predictions fail, persuasion will be not only difficult but also costly. Nobody can sell the average person something that is not wanted.

CONSUMERISM

What retailers say about merchandise and how they say it have become very important in the mind of today's consumer.

During retailing's early history, most merchandise was made either in local homes or in nearby

23

communities. Thus it was possible to know manufacturers and their reputations. Today's market spans the entire world, and the consumer has little knowledge of a manufacturer's reputation and only a limited knowledge of the materials that were used.

Rapidly changing markets and changes in technology and social conditions have produced a consumer's dilemma. Shoppers do not make decisions easily, and a certain amount of consumer uprising has resulted. *Consumerism* is a movement in the United States organized by consumers at all levels to ensure that the goods they get are safe, durable, and honestly advertised. They want satisfaction from the items they buy and the agreement that stores will back all guarantees.

Consumerism and the Federal Government

The United States government has responded to consumerism in one way by creating the U.S. Consumer Product Safety Commission, designed to be the consumer's watchdog. The Congress gave tremendous power to the Commission: the right to inspect manufacturers' plants, to remove products from sale, to endorse new safety measures, and in general to give more protection to the consumer.

Among the current federal laws and regulations that help protect the consumer are the following:

- *Textile Fiber Products Identification Act* (*TFPIA*). Requires that the generic names of the fibers included in the article and their relative importance be revealed in labels and in advertising.

- *Federal Trade Commission's Trade Regulation Rule on Care Labeling.* Requires that information on the care of the specific item be provided on the labels of many products.

- *The Fur Products Labeling Act.* Requires that the true English name of the animal be used.

The aim is to protect buyers of fur garments from deceptive labeling.

- *Flammable Fabrics Act.* Prohibits the sale of many textile products that fail to pass standards of nonflammability.

- *Food, Drug, and Cosmetic Act.* Excludes from the market food, drugs, and cosmetics that are of questionable value or that have not yet been proved safe and requires that warnings be affixed to a product to tell users that it may not be safe when used as intended.

- *Consumer Products Safety Commission.* Issues regulations regarding toys and other products that may have a hazard in use. Bans products that are found to be dangerous.

- *Poison Prevention Packaging Act.* Requires "childproof" packaging for hazardous household products, which means that the products must be packaged in containers that children under five years of age cannot open.

- *Truth in Lending Act.* Requires that the annual rate of credit charges be revealed, as well as all the details of the credit agreement.

Retailers are advised to study every description of every product—every label, tag, and catalog advertisement—and then ask themselves, "What will the consumer think about a product after reading this description?" If expectations based on the description could prove false, then the information is considered deceptive. A retailer can't say something is "long-wearing" or "child-proof" unless scientific testing proves this to be so. Retailers must call a product exactly what it is.

According to the Federal Trade Commission, if a retailer runs an advertisement that says "lowest price in town," the store must have substantial proof that the claim is true. The proof must exist before the ad runs, and if evidence—a survey or comparison-shopping report—is lacking, the FTC could bring action against the retailer on this basis alone.

The Textile Fiber Products Identification Act requires that generic names of fibers and their relative importance be revealed in labels.
Courtesy Londontown Corporation

Consumerism and Retailers

Consumerism is not a threatening idea to most retailers who operate legitimately. For years, many stores have been testing merchandise before putting it on shelves. Most have backed guarantees honestly and replaced inferior merchandise because they know this is good business.

With the growth of consumerism, some stores have increased their efforts in teaching salespeople product information so they can answer consumers' questions. The J. C. Penney company has initiated a national consumer program throughout its stores. It has published reams of educational material for consumers, and with the help of local store managers, Penney has begun an annual program for local educators. As a forum for consumer representatives and educators, Penney's program arranges tours of credit bureaus, advertising agencies, factories, and testing laboratories in order to "let the consumer know."

Some food manufacturers have begun to label merchandise with nutritional information. Ninety-five percent of the supermarkets in America now use unit pricing, the marking of merchandise by price per unit of weight or size for easy comparison. The Department of Agriculture says that wise use of unit pricing could save consumers $60 a year.

ANALYZING BUYING MOTIVES

Buying motives are individual and specific. They are the wants and needs that make someone purchase a particular product or shop at a particular store. How well a retailer understands a particular group's buying motives determines important business decisions, such as which merchandise to stock, the range of assortments, the sales promotion approach, and the choice of a location.

In our economy practically all consumers have the means to satisfy their basic material needs—needs for food, clothing, and shelter. But in choosing the form their purchases will take, consumers are moved by a variety of secondary or psychological needs and by a mixture of many motives that are both rational and emotional.

Buying Motives and Maslow's Hierarchy of Needs

In 1954, Dr. Abraham Maslow, the noted psychologist, developed a theory called "Maslow's Hierarchy of Needs." These needs were originally discussed in relation to workers' motivations on the job, but a wide range of day-to-day activities are undertaken to fill these needs. Buying motives may be based on this hierarchy.

Physiological Needs. A human being's first level of needs is the physiological level. People's basic physiological needs are for food, clothing, and shelter. In most cases, these are the easiest needs to satisfy. At this level, people buy only the necessities for survival—clothes to keep them covered, a structure to protect them from the elements, and food to sustain them.

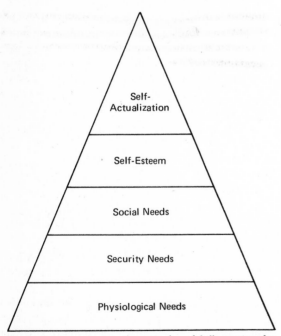

Maslow's hierarchy is a theoretical model illustrating the levels of human needs and their influence on behavior.

Security Needs. As the physiological needs are met, the individual tries to climb to the second level, security. Purchases are made in larger quantities and stored for later use. Among them are better materials for warmth and a more secure home for protection. At this point, the individual moves from the idea of present self-protection to providing for future well-being.

A common way to fulfill security needs is to buy well-known brands. Market researchers have discovered that people actually have rather weak preferences for name brands and will switch from one well-known brand to another within the same price range—for example, from General Electric to Westinghouse. Yet they prefer well-known brands instead of unfamiliar brands or unbranded merchandise. Similarly, national chains give assurance to newcomers in a community. The newcomers feel more secure shopping in a store they know something about.

A rational expression of the need for security is the customer's demands for guarantees of performance, for information about how mechanical products are serviced, and for instructions on laundering and dry-cleaning apparel.

Social Needs. At level three, social needs become very important. They include the need to be accepted into various groups and the need to socialize with people having similar interests. Social needs focus spending and buying habits on things other than basic necessities. At this level, people consider how their purchases will impress others with whom they want to associate. For example, a housewife may use her purchases to win her family's approval of her good judgment and taste. This applies not only to what she buys for the household but also to her personal shopping. The search for romance is also part of the desire to fulfill social needs. It is an important motive in the sale of apparel and cosmetics.

Many consumers conform to the standards of dress and life-style of the group with which they identify. The desire for conformity is particularly strong in young people. Parents are familiar with the clamoring of their children for the toys, clothing, and entertainment that "all the other kids have." Students in college and high school often show conformity as they begin to make their own buying decisions. Retailers who are aware of this social need can take advantage of it by staffing their college shops with college students in the summer. Each student advises the entering freshmen from his or her college about what is being done and worn on campus that year.

Need for Self-Esteem. Style, fashion, and color become more important on level four as people attempt to achieve a feeling of self-esteem. Self-esteem and self-acceptance are important to the individual's psychological health. People will not attempt to fulfill the next higher level of needs before achieving a certain degree of fulfillment at the lower levels. Thus a person will strive for social acceptance before trying to move into a position of social leadership.

Individual personalities and upbringing lead to different sets of values in different people. When people use their purchases as a means of fulfilling the need for self-esteem, they will not all shop for the same items. Some will consider books, recordings, and theater tickets worthwhile purchases. Others will derive more satisfaction from cars, jewelry, or furs. Retailers cannot know each customer individually, but they can understand the ethnic, intellectual, religious, economic, and social backgrounds of the buying community. These factors will influence merchandise selections in the market and the style of promotion. Successful retailers know what items are popular among their customers. They stock these items, but they also select an assortment that is wide enough to satisfy their customers' desire for distinction.

Need for Self-Actualization. The need for self-actualization, level five in Maslow's hierarchy, is the desire to expand on self-esteem. Economic success is apparent on this level, and people want to express things in a personal way in

their decisions and value judgments. Fashion and style leadership are expressions of self-actualization in buying behavior. The achievement of status in the community, which may be derived partly from one's choice of purchases, is an outward sign of self-actualization.

Self-actualization is the highest need level. Having fulfilled their lower-level needs, people who reach this level may spend money for aesthetic, humanitarian, or altruistic causes that benefit others as well as themselves. At this level, consumers spend money on fashions, hobbies, and travel or for other reasons that are not related to their physiological needs.

Retailers' Understanding of Buying Motives

The successful retailer must be able to analyze all the factors that influence buying. First, to make the best selection of merchandise for their stores, retailers must know the basic product-buying motives.

Second, they must understand the extent to which outside influences change the order of priority that customers apply to their needs. One of these influences is advertising—both the manufacturer's and the retailer's own. Retailers must know what kind of advertising will convince customers that a product will satisfy their needs. Retailers must also be able to gauge the extent to which particular customers will be affected by current events, by entertainment trends, by fashion magazines and columnists, by television, and by movies. When placing merchandise orders, retailers must weigh all these influences.

SOCIAL AND ECONOMIC INFLUENCES ON BUYING BEHAVIOR

Customers respond to economic and social changes by altering their living habits and their attitudes toward spending. The marketers' job is to keep close track of these changes. By studying economic and social changes, marketers can predict changes that will occur in buying behavior in their trading area.

HOUSEHOLDS IN THE UNITED STATES, 1960-1985

	1960	1965	1970	1975	1980	1985
Growth (in thousands)	52,799	57,436	63,401	70,001	77,308	84,421

Size of the Consumer Market

The aggregate or sum total of all people who buy goods and services for personal or household use is known as the *consumer market.* In sheer numbers, the consumer market in the United States has grown more rapidly since the end of World War II than in any other period since the early 1900s, when immigration ceased to be an important factor. Today it is estimated that the size of the United States consumer population will approach 241 million by 1985.[1]

What is the significance of this increase to retailers? If business were to maintain the same ratio of stores to people that existed in 1966, it would be necessary to open more than 400,000 new retail establishments in the next 10 to 15 years!

Spending Units—Individuals and Households. Even more dramatic than the population growth is the increase in the number of households. A *household* is a family or other group that shares a residence. Because of changing life-styles in recent years, people who might have lived in the same household in the past are now choosing to live in separate households. Many single people are able to maintain their own homes. These include the widowed and young people just beginning their careers. Many retired couples maintain their own households rather than live with their grown children.

In the 30 years between 1940 and 1970, while the total population increased by about 50 percent, the number of households increased by more than 70 percent. Nearly 6 percent of the 36

[1] Unless otherwise specified, figures quoted in this chapter are from the U.S. Bureau of the Census, *Statistical Abstract of the United States,* 1975. Figures for 1975 and beyond are projected.

million married couples in the country were living with relatives or in furnished rooms in 1950. By 1974 the figure was only 1.1 percent.

The result of this increase in the number of households has been a rise in the sale of durable or household goods. Just as the number of consumers in a market is a measure of the potential demand for apparel, food, and personal items, so the number of households is a measure of the demand for home goods, such as furniture, refrigerators, and floor coverings.

Spending Power of the Consumer Market. A market has two components: the numbers of people and households, and purchasing power—or income available to individuals and households for purchasing goods and services.

Personal income is the money the individual or household receives from all sources of revenue, such as wages, interest-bearing savings accounts and investments, and pensions.

Disposable personal income is the amount the individual or household has for spending or saving after payment of taxes and certain nontaxable payments.

Discretionary income is the amount the individual or household has left to spend or to save after further payment for (1) essential items like food, clothing, household utilities, and local transportation and for (2) major items such as housing, insurance, and debts.

Real income or *real dollars* is an expression of dollar income in terms of purchasing power. It is useful to compare dollar income for one year with dollar income for another. For example, in comparing income for 1959 with income for 1969, it is necessary to allow for price increases during the 10-year period. The 1959 income is stated, therefore, in terms of "1969 dollars."

Specifically, an income of $1,300 in 1959 was equal to $1,600 in 1969 dollars. This is because the cost of living was less in 1959. Real per family income rose 42 percent between 1955 and 1970, and it is expected to rise another 51 percent by 1985. A continued recession can alter these figures significantly, as can a decrease in the inflation rate.

The Increase in Discretionary Income. As an individual's or household's dollar income increases, the percentage required for the purchase of necessities drops, and the percentage available for discretionary spending increases. This raises the standard of living.

Ernst Engel, the German economic statistician, formalized this fact in the four rules called Engel's Laws. These state that as a family's income increases

- The percentage spent for food decreases

- The proportion spent for household operation remains about the same

- The percentage allocated for clothing purchases remains basically static

- Discretionary income, allowing for purchases of nonessentials or for savings, increases

It is important to note that Engel's study of spending patterns by various income levels was first published in 1857 and that his theories are applied to income levels on the average. In other words, the theories are basically sound, but within each income level, some people might spend their money on different items.

The Trend Toward Spending Future Income. The easy access to credit in our society multiplies the number of goods and services a consumer or household can purchase at any one time. The consumer who has $100 of discretionary income in hand does not have to choose between a much-wanted set of golf clubs and a weekend trip to a summer resort. This person can have both by paying "on time." Today people considering purchases of any substantial size calculate in terms of whether they can afford the monthly payments, including interest, rather than in terms of the total price.

The psychological acceptance of buying on credit is one of the many revolutions of our recent history. Fifty years ago buying on credit was not as acceptable as it is now. For many families it was a closely guarded secret. But that attitude has disappeared. The consumer's willingness to commit future income to the payment of today's purchase rests on having confidence in the economy. At the same time, purchases on credit have done much to keep the economy growing and consumer income rising.

Buying on credit, however, has some serious drawbacks. Perhaps most serious is that it destroys cash reserves. A downturn in the economy, when incomes shrink and credit is extended less freely, causes people to pay higher interest rates. Foreclosures may follow, or consumers may return goods they cannot afford.

Business Ups and Downs. When consumers anticipate a national or local recession, or when one actually begins, they are not as willing to buy durable goods. At such a time, retailers reduce their sales forecasts for electrical appliances, furniture, and other big items. At the same time, they also reduce their inventory investment. For consumers, periods of job insecurity and doubts about future income may cause them to cut back on long-term credit commitments.

Similarly, retailers are more cautious about extending credit. When a recession deepens into actual widespread unemployment, short-term credit and cash sales also suffer. The retailer's chance of weathering such a period without too much loss depends on the ability to foresee a downturn and act accordingly.

Social Changes. Retailers today have had to adjust to deep alterations in society which have changed our whole way of living, our product needs, and our shopping habits. Few social changes have been as revolutionary as the growth of a black middle-class buying public.

For special reasons.

Think of it as money.™

Carry a BankAmericard. For your own special reasons.

Black consumers are style-conscious, highly selective, and considerably more loyal to brand names than the general population.

According to market statistics, there are more than 23 million blacks in the United States, representing about 10 percent of the population. Although they tend to live in the major cities and generally concentrate in the downtown areas, blacks are now integrating the suburbs as well.

Spending figures for blacks are revealing. The average black family earning $6,200 to $7,800 annually spends as much on household products and beauty and health aids as white families earning twice these amounts. Few markets can afford to overlook a public that spends $30 billion annually for goods and services.

Urbanization and Suburbanization. The difference between the wants of rural populations and the wants of urban populations has diminished. A number of factors account for this. First, there are fewer rural families, and improved transportation and communication have ended the isolation of farm living. In 1960, in the United States, 30 out of 100 people lived in rural areas; in 1970 the figures were 25 out of 100.

Today good roads link the farm dweller to the city's theaters, museums, and stores. Also important is television, the great leveler of tastes, which brings the same advertising messages to farms and cities.

Differences in spending patterns remain, but they are largely based on differences in income. The median income of urban families is almost twice that of rural farm families.

The most significant population increase of the last several decades has occured in the urban fringe, not in the central city. Differences in spending patterns distinguish the central city from the suburbs. The majority of city families lives in apartment houses, while most suburban families live in single-family or two-family houses. As a result, suburban residents spend differently for household operations. They are buyers of large items such as major appliances, garden supplies, paint and wallpaper, and swimming pools. In fact, the long spending boom for durable goods has depended on suburban purchases.

There is a certain interchange between central city and suburban populations at different ages. A young married couple may start out with an apartment in the city and later move to a suburb to raise a family. An elderly couple whose children are grown and married may leave a suburb for the convenience of a city apartment or retirement community. The result for retailers is that the suburban branch of a department store emphasizes merchandise which is different from that featured in the downtown store.

A larger percentage of the suburban family's budget must go for transportation, both public and private. Some suburban families own more than one car to meet the different needs of their members. The current energy shortage may change this trend, however, and increase the number of one-stop shopping trips.

In sum, smart retailers know their trading areas well and realize the changes they must make to keep up with local or regional changes. The probability, though, is that the spending patterns of suburban shoppers in the East, Midwest, and other parts of the country match each other closely. Any regional differences in spending count less than differences in the style of living.

Regional Differences. Travel, technology, money, and leisure have lessened the differences in buying habits in different regions of the country. Northerners may buy beachwear in January for a cruise. Because of air conditioning, Southerners may wear lightweight wool during a season when only cotton used to be bearable.

However some regional differences, based on local customs and variations in economic conditions and dominant industries, remain. A recent shift in population growth from the North to the

 Buying on credit has become an accepted part of today's lifestyle.
Courtesy National BankAmericard Inc.

South, all across the continent from the East Coast to California, has made the "sun belt" a more influential area in the national economy. The defense, computer, and space technology industries are headquartered primarily in the sun belt, and this area is also important for recreational and retirement centers. Retailers in both the North and the South must be aware of the changes these migrations have made in the makeup of their local populations. They must be prepared to meet the changing needs of their customers.

Educational Differences. Educational differences continue to be influential. They affect the way people spend their discretionary income. At one time educational differences could be predicted almost entirely on the basis of income, since a comfortable income and a good education were so closely linked. There was a quality market composed of the best-educated and most prosperous people, and there was a middle market composed of salaried people. Together these people created a mass market of wage earners. While it is still true that the highest incomes tend to accompany the highest levels of education, the middle-income market has greatly enlarged its boundaries. It now includes blue-collar as well as white-collar workers. A family with an income of $20,000 today may be headed by a law enforcement officer, a plumber, a professor, a journalist, a sales worker, or an auto assembly line worker.

Income no longer serves as the sole index to buying habits as it did when income groups were more alike—or, to use the words of the economist, when most wage earners had very little discretionary income. Thus, successful retailers must know not only the income ranges of their customers but also how to classify them by educational level and occupation. Education and occupation influence the way people buy. They may want the same things, but they have different priorities for them. For some families, owning luxuries now is more important, while for others, savings for future education or travel expenses may take the bulk of extra income.

Having even greater bearing on retailers' success is the fact that differences in education and employment can influence a consumer's choice of stores. The sophisticated image of a store appeals to certain status-minded customers, and many insist on shopping in stores with such a reputation, if only for modest purchases. Still others who before patronized only high-class retail stores buy branded products in discount stores, even though they still shop at high-class stores for clothing and other expensive goods.

There are also many customers with very comfortable incomes who bypass the sophisticated store and spend lavishly in a chain store or discount house where they find the environment more to their shopping tastes. In fact, one of the reasons for the great success of the discount stores is that they began just when the big surge of buying power enriched the blue-collar market. So, no matter how expensive a television set a blue-collar family may plan to buy, the family will probably feel more comfortable buying it in a bargain store, because that is what the members are used to.

Stores whose customers were formerly in low-income groups now show a marked trend toward following them into the middle-income market. They do this by upgrading their *price lines*—lines of merchandise available at fixed prices. This approach of stocking more expensive merchandise of higher quality keeps the customers loyal to the stores, even when their new buying power makes it possible for them to shop where they couldn't before.

Education and Advertising. When retailers choose an advertising style for their stores, they must consider the educational and occupational backgrounds of their customers. Progressive store managers do not make the mistake of believing that an income rise in their trading area necessarily means an increase in buyer sophistication. The journalist and the sanitation worker may have the same spending power. But one may respond to witty advertising copy and artwork, while the other may prefer more direct

THE WIDE WORLD OF RETAILING

appeals. The customer must be able to identify with the store's image, and much of this image depends on advertising style.

Married Women With Jobs. About 40 percent of all American women over fourteen hold paying jobs, and 55 percent of them are married. As long as the employment opportunities exist, the trend for married women to work will continue.

A recent survey found that two-thirds of the women under thirty-five who are full-time housewives intend to go to work in the near future. Many working wives express the feeling that their lives are more challenging and that they may become more financially and socially independent. These feelings affect the buying motives and habits of working women, who shop more often and spend more money on clothing for themselves than married women who do not work for pay.

The family with a working wife will tend to have more spending money, but the family purchasing agent—usually the wife—will have less time to shop. She may want to shop at night and even on Sundays, which means longer selling hours for stores that want her business. She does many shopping errands near her job during lunch hour, and she expects to find the stores near her job fully staffed and ready for service. She is in the market for every kind of labor-saving device, too.

Because of these new employment trends for women, easy housekeeping is a strong motive in their buying habits. Manufacturers found a ready market for work-saving devices, wash-and-wear fabrics, and easily prepared foods.

Change in Clothing Sizes. Each year the retailers in the field of women's apparel increase the proportion of small sizes in their stocks and carry fewer large sizes. Why? Today's emphasis on being slim has reduced the market demand for large sizes. Large sizes for women are in token departments in most large city apparel stores. Some large or tall men and women must shop almost exclusively in stores that cater to their special needs.

Usually, the more affluent customers are the more likely ones to keep a slim figure for life. Better stores carry a larger proportion of small sizes than do those that sell to low-income customers.

One buying problem that suppliers have yet to recognize fully is that while older women may wear the same sizes as eighteen-year-olds, they are often unable to find mature styles in these sizes. The owner of a small apparel store who knows how these older customers shop searches the market for the kind of clothing they like and wins their loyalty.

Store Location and Prices. Many things will influence a customer's choice of a store for buying a particular item. Before they come into play, however, certain basics do limit the number of stores from which a person makes a selection. These are location and price level. Is the store easy to reach? Do its prices fall within the shopper's budget?

Convenience is relatively important, since it depends on what type of purchase the customer is making and also on whether there are few or many stores nearby. But location is a primary factor in retail success.

Store Image. Store preferences, like those for products, are not the same for all people with identical incomes. Disregarding income, store preferences vary according to people's education, occupations, styles of living, and expectations of future income.

Some people want to be chic or very stylish; their attitude is reflected in the items they buy and the things they do. Other people are, or pretend to be, indifferent to changes in fashion. They are usually from families which have been wealthy for generations. The modern store atmosphere and slick advertising that appeals to the first group will alienate the second. These people prefer quiet surroundings with a touch of the old-fashioned in fixtures and decorations. On the other hand, some large stores that are grand in appearance may not attract low-income shoppers, even with bargains and sales.

Important Market Segments

Statistics on current and expected numbers of consumers are important guidelines for all who sell goods and services. This is especially true for those manufacturers who appeal to certain groups. These manufacturers get a better understanding of their markets by dividing the total consumer market into special groups called *market segments*. Thus producers of games and toys for children under five years of age collect and study as much information as they can get on the "preschool market segment." Producers of house paints find out as much as possible about the "homeowner market segment." And publishers of youth-oriented beauty and fashion magazines study the "teen-age market segment."

Though most producers are concerned with national trends, retailers need to have statistics for their own areas. By learning more about special customer groups, they can better plan their selections and promotion activities.

While there has been an increase in the buying power of all groups in general, certain groups have changed more than others. Among them are young people (up to age 24), working women, and the elderly (over age 65). Conse-

quently, these groups have strongly influenced the recent marketing activities of producers and retailers.

The Young. The following table indicates that a large portion of our population is in the under-20 age group. We can easily understand why so much marketing effort throughout the 1960s has been directed to the young by both producers and retailers and why this particular effort has continued in the 1970s.

The 25-to-34 age group, often referred to as the "young adult" segment, will also draw a great deal of attention from marketers into the 1980s. The consumers in this group are spending more money at the retail level than consumers in older groups. In 1975, spending by young adults accounted for a large percentage of almost every kind of retailer's business, despite inflation and recession, while older adults lost confidence and bought less.

The age groups important to retailers moving toward the 1980s are the 10-to-14, 15-to-19, and 20-to-24 age groups. When these groups are combined, they make up a hefty percentage of the consumer population. However, not only the

UNITED STATES POPULATION FIGURES (IN MILLIONS), 1960–1990

by Age Groups and Ratio of each Age Group to Total Population[1]

Age Groups	1960 Population (180.7)	Ratio to Total, %	1970 Population (204.9)	Ratio to Total, %	1980 Population (225.7)	Ratio to Total, %	1990 Population (257.7)	Ratio to Total, %
Under 5 years	20.3	11	17.2	8.4	20.0	12	25.4	12
5–13 years	33.0	18	36.6	18	30.9	11	41.3	11
14–17 years	11.2	6	15.9	8	15.8	9	13.5	9
18–21 years	9.6	5	14.7	7	17.1		14.5	
22–24 years	6.6	4	10.0	5	12.3	8	10.6	7
25–34 years	23.0	13	25.3	12	36.2	15	41.1	14
35–44 years	24.2	13	23.1	11	25.7	10	36.5	12
45–54 years	20.6	11	23.3	11	22.6	9	25.2	8
55–64 years	15.7	9	18.7	9	21.0	9	20.5	6
65 and over	16.7	9	20.0	10	24.5	9	28.9	9

Note: Both population figures and ratio figures have been rounded off to the nearest full number. Population column totals will not agree with column-head figures, and percent ratios will not total 100.
[1] Young Adult Marketing, Inc., Jarzana, Calif., 1975.

size of this market makes it important. There were larger proportions of young people in the early history of the United States. But never before have they commanded such buying power of their own. The approximately 25 million consumers in the teen-age group have buying power estimated between $11 billion and $13 billion annually, and this is over and above what their parents spend on them.

Young marrieds make up another market segment. It includes more than 28 percent of all adults over the age of 18. They already buy more than a third of the furniture and major appliances sold in retail stores. Because of their great number, young homemakers are a vital part of the market for clothing and accessories.

The longer these adults are married, the more likely they are to acquire costlier items, and also the more likely they are to buy on credit.

Senior Citizens. Between 1970 and 1980, the number of people in the over-65 age group will have increased by 4.4 million. Because of their special needs, these older people represent an important market segment for manufacturers and retailers. Experts on the problems of the aging are helping manufacturers to design merchandise especially for this group. For example, the experts have influenced industrial designers to put ovens at waist height, to put storage cabinets on the walls within easy reach, and to put nonskid backing on rugs. Remarkably, every one of these improvements tends to find its way into merchandise for everyone else. What is most comfortable and safe for the elderly is also convenient for the rest of us.

Since the over-65 population is largely retired, it is a good market for travel, and for travel products and services. These older people also buy health and diet products, optical goods, and, in fact, any carefully designed merchandise. Stores with large numbers of customers over 65 are reviewing their services as well as their merchandise. When senior citizens shop, their prime need is for convenience and comfort.

TOPICS FOR DISCUSSION

1. "Consumer demand is complex and changeable." What does this mean, and what significance does it have for today's retailer?
2. How has the Federal Trade Commission come to the assistance of the consumer movement?
3. What changes in advertising and selling can be expected because of the strong consumer movement?
4. List Maslow's "hierarchy of needs," and explain how the needs affect the consumer's buying attitudes.
5. Give one example each of purchases that a college student might make to satisfy the needs listed in Maslow's hierarchy.
6. How do the following terms differ in meaning? (a) personal income, (b) disposable personal income, (c) discretionary income.
7. How has the emergence of the black buying public affected retailers?
8. Explain how working women influence the kind of merchandise sold by retailers.
9. How will today's young adult market affect retailing?
10. How has the growth of the senior citizen market affected retailing?

COMMUNICATIONS IN RETAILING

The buyer in your department has been asked to speak to a high school retailing class next week on the topic "The Advantages and Disadvantages of Consumerism for the Retailer." Since the buyer will be away all next week on a buying trip, you are asked to give the talk. On a separate sheet of paper, prepare a list of advantages and disadvantages (and examples) for this talk.

MANAGING HUMAN RELATIONS

Upon completing your first year of training with a major mass merchandiser, you have been made an assistant store manager in one of the chain's oldest units. The first Saturday in your new position is highlighted by an outstanding sale that is attracting heavy customer traffic. One group of sale items—foreign-made portable typewriters selling for $65.50 each—is moving rapidly. While your store manager is out to lunch, you get a call from the floor urging you to come right out because an argument has started between two people. They are fighting over the last typewriter. When you get there, quite a large number of people have gathered around the two customers who are exchanging rather insulting remarks.

Both have a firm grip on the machine and are being egged on in their fight by several of the spectators. Your first reaction is to break up the crowd and the argument. How might you do it without causing a further disturbance? Be prepared to discuss your answer in class.

CAREER LADDER

Two young women have applied for a position on the college board of a suburban branch of the store where you are a personnel recruitment officer. Sheila is a junior. She is majoring in English at the state university, which is several hundred miles away. Carol is about to enter her second year at the local community college, where she is studying marketing. Both students arrive on time for their job interviews, and both are well groomed. Carol is dressed more casually than Sheila. Both have had some selling experience. Sheila is the campus representative of a cosmetics firm. Carol had been assigned to a local shoe store in her high school cooperative work-experience program, and the retailer had hired her for the summer following her high school graduation. Which student would you recommend for the college board? Be prepared to discuss in class the reasons for your choice.

chapter 4
THE IMPACT OF FASHION

Fashion means many things to many people. Fashion moves merchandise, alters people's thinking, and affects most actions and attitudes. The influence of fashion is seen everywhere. Fashion affects not only clothing and accessories but also automobiles, home decoration, and the way people talk, walk, and think. Even political and social views, travel, entertainment, and participation in organizations may be affected by what is considered fashionable.

What people accept at a given time determines what is in fashion, or what is fashionable. However, most people when referring to fashion are not concerned with its impact on every phase of their lives. Instead, they apply the term primarily to merchandise that they buy and wear.

Fashion is a powerful buying motive and since fashion moves merchandise, retailers are especially concerned with its impact.

Why is fashion so important? Undoubtedly because fashion satisfies the desire for change, the rebellion against monotony, and the desire to be distinctive.

Why do consumers respond to fashion? Simply because people like change. Wearing or owning something new, especially if it is admired by their friends, gives people partial assurance that they are in tune with the times.

FASHION AFFECTS MARKETING

Fashions change faster than most goods wear out. Therefore, fashion encourages people to buy more than they need. The result is that fashion has become a source of recent prosperity. High production in many consumer-goods industries and large retail sales have stemmed from the fact that people have replaced many of their possessions—not because they were worn out, but because they were outmoded. And so, the circle of prosperity: "The more sales, the more production; the more production, the more jobs; the more jobs, the more wages; the more wages, the more sales."[1] On the other hand, when inflation makes products cost too much, people often limit their spending to essential products only, and the circle of prosperity works to the contrary.

THE LANGUAGE OF THE FASHION WORLD

In our everyday language, the words "style," "design," "model," "classic," "fashion," and "fad" have a variety of meanings. The related terms "fashion cycle" and "fashion trend" are also frequently used. For example, people commonly refer to something popular as being "in style" when they mean it is "in fashion." Using these terms loosely when studying the impact of fashion on merchandising can lead to confusion.

A *style* is a general form of a product significantly different from other forms of that product. For example, a bow tie is a style of tie. A dolman sleeve is a style of sleeve. Op art is a style of art. A turtleneck is a style of neckline on a sweater or other garment. Members of different ethnic groups often prefer to wear clothes that represent a style from the country of their origin. Indian women may be swathed in saris and Japanese

[1] Clyde Bedell, *How to Write Advertising That Sells*, McGraw-Hill Book Company, New York, 1952.

women in kimonos and obis, while Africans may wear dashikis. These same exotic influences are also seen in fashionable furnishings for the home, such as Oriental accessories and furniture, African prints and art objects, and paisley, batik, and madras fabrics. When certain styles prevail, they become the fashion for that time.

A *design* or *model* (usually referred to by a number in a manufacturer's line) is a particular variation of a general style. For example, there are many sizes, shapes, colors, and patterns of bow ties, or dolman sleeves, or op art, or saris, or dashikis.

A *classic* is a style that is in demand from year to year. There may be minor changes, such as changes in length, color, or decoration. Examples of classics are the shirtwaist dress, the barrel-cuffed shirt for men, oxfords for children, and blue jeans for all young people.

A *fashion* is a style that is accepted by a considerable number of people at a particular time or place for a certain length of time.

A *fad* is a short-lived fashion that characteristically springs into overwhelming popularity and then suffers a sudden end. In apparel and accessories, the life of a fad may be no more than one month for a seasonal item. A fad that is less seasonal in nature may last several months. In home furnishings, the life of a fad may be a year or more. Fads are often confined to particular age groups—usually the young—and restricted to relatively inexpensive products. Wide-legged pants and 3-inch platform shoes were recent fads. Typical fads, they were short-lived but greatly in demand.

A *fashion trend* is the direction in which a given style is moving, whether upward or downward with regard to demand. A trend may involve more than just the shape of an item. The trend may have to do with fabric, texture, color, or decoration. Dishes, for example, often are plain when a new shape is introduced. Yearly, new decorations are added to the shape until a rather ornate product has been developed. Then, the direction of the decoration may be reversed if that shape is still in demand. Thus, the buyer can chart the trend for that particular product.

FASHION AFFECTS RETAILING

When department store or chain store retailers refer to departments as "fashion departments," they mean departments that sell outer apparel and accessories for women. In all these departments, with the exception of fur departments, merchandise is bought for several short seasons in the year and is often completely replaced by new and different merchandise within a season. A selection of merchandise is not carried over by the retailer either from one season to another or from one year to the next.

The term "fashion department" is a narrow one. It does not imply that other departments and other items are not strongly influenced by fashion changes. The other departments differ from the so-called "fashion departments" in that fashion changes in their items occur less quickly. Also, the seasonal factor may not be present, and the risk of being too late or too early in presenting a new fashion is not quite so great. Examples of garments which are found in departments or stores not referred to by the term "fashion" are men's clothing, children's clothing, and intimate apparel. However, all these garments are coming closer each year to being true "fashion" articles because of accelerating fashion changes and increasing fashion consciousness.

As noted earlier, fashion influences not only apparel but also almost everything else the consumer purchases, such as furniture and household equipment, automobiles, food and drink, education, sports equipment, and even medical

THE WIDE WORLD OF RETAILING

THE IMPACT OF FASHION

services. The influence of fashion on buying behavior is expressed in many ways.

Fashion Creates Obsolescence

Fashion may lead people to discard a product that is still useful but is no longer in fashion. This commonly happens with dresses, suits, shoes, and handbags, and it occurs with other types of merchandise, too. The custom of replacing an automobile long before it stops running well has become the classic example of making a purchase because of fashion obsolescence. *Style obsolescence* is the outmoding of an article by fashion change before its usefulness is exhausted.

Fashion Adds a Competitive Advantage

Fashion gives many so-called "staple" products a competitive advantage. A common staple is a screwdriver. But a person choosing a screwdriver at a hardware counter will be attracted by one with a contoured handle of bright plastic rather than by a standard model that has not changed in generations. One manufacturer, by streamlining a stapler and producing it in a range of colors, multiplied sales fourfold.

Depending on the item, the average person may not replace a primarily utilitarian article until it is worn out or lost or until a technically superior version appears on the market offering considerably more convenience or efficiency. But when that purchase is made, elements of fashion may help determine the choice between two competing products.

American consumers tire of what they are wearing, using, or doing and seek something different that will spark their interests and make them feel a sense of change and renewal. Fashion provides this change. Consumers may not discard their white bed sheets just because colored sheets are fashionable. But when they replenish their supply, the influence of fashion may be strong enough to make them buy colored, floral-printed, or striped sheets, even though they are more expensive and offer no more utility. A retailer who sold white sheets only would lose sales to more fashion-minded competitors.

Fashion Creates New Needs

Introducing a new style is like dropping a pebble into a pool. The new style creates many ripples of new needs. When skirts are lengthened, for example, it is not only dresses that are affected. The perfectly good slips the customer owns must be replaced by longer versions. Low-heeled shoes no longer look right. And hosiery fashions change, too. Short gloves or long gloves are in or out of fashion with short sleeves or long sleeves. The popularity of white coats or white wool dresses greatly improves the dry cleaner's business. Wigs require wig stands and wig boxes. The fashion for long hair on boys adversely affects barbershops but boosts hair stylists' business. The fashion for jazz music causes a boom in record sales and in sales of phonographs and stereos, and it develops an entire generation of rhythmic-beat music lovers.

Thus, the vitality of modern production and marketing is largely dependent on the influence of fashion. All retailers need to keep up to date on fashion developments, even though new developments seem at first glance to be far removed from their sphere of operations.

FASHION CYCLES AND FASHION LEADERS

What causes fashion changes? Why does one style go out of fashion and another style come into fashion? Social historians point out that fashion in apparel, home furnishings, and other products reflects in some way the economic and political situation and the social spirit of a given period.

Successful fashion designers are tuned in to the world around them and sensitive to the signs of change in the spirit of the fashion world. A fashion is by definition *popular*. Designers create styles, or variations of styles, but people create fashions by accepting them.

Fashion is generally evolutionary in character. The changes that people desire evolve slowly from one concept to another. Thus when the brims on men's hats began to get narrower, the

Fashions change in response to social, political, and economic trends. There are fashions in the display of apparel and other merchandise as well as in the merchandise itself. Compare these lingerie displays; one is in a turn-of-the-century department store, and the other, a modern mass-merchandise store.
Top, courtesy Younkers Brothers, Inc., Iowa; bottom, courtesy *Chain Store Age General Merchandising Group*

THE IMPACT OF FASHION

change took place slowly and almost imperceptibly from year to year until the 3-inch brim had been reduced to as little as 1 inch. And then, just as slowly, the brims started to get wider. Only by looking at pictures of hats some years before could a startling change be observed. Similarly, women's sleeves or skirts are usually shortened or lengthened slowly until a reverse in the direction is desired.

Occasionally, however, fashion becomes revolutionary. This is particularly evident during or after times of great change. When World War II ended, for example, women revolted against the short skirt lengths that had resulted from government restrictions on the use of fabrics. Skirts suddenly became almost ankle-length and very full. But such revolutionary changes are rare.

Fashion Cycles

Every fashion has a life cycle. In its first, or rising, phase, it is taken up by the pacesetters, the people who are always first with the new. In this phase it is called "class fashion." It appeals to customers whose primary buying motive is the desire for distinction and change.

In the second phase, the fashion reaches its peak of popularity. It is called "mass fashion" and is adopted by average people—those who conform rather than lead in accepting the new. In this phase, the fashion is purchased in large volume.

In the third, or "declining fashion," phase, the fashion is left to those who, by choice or necessity, are slow to accept new products and ideas or who must buy job-lot or reduced-price goods.

The cycle of fashion is the same for all products, although the speed of that cycle may vary radically. First the leaders—manufacturers, retailers, and consumers—introduce and accept a product. Then the followers in all three fields adopt it, and it enjoys its peak of mass production and mass acceptance. At this stage, the leaders have already disassociated themselves from that particular fashion and are beginning a new cycle. In the final stage, only a few manufacturers, retailers, and consumers are making the product, selling it, or using it.

Feminine apparel and accessories have a *high fashion velocity*. The whole cycle of a fashion may be completed in a few months. Men's suits, decorative home furnishings, and home accessories, as well as children's wear, have a *medium-velocity cycle* which may extend over one, two, or more years. Luggage, umbrellas, floor coverings, china, silverware, and upholstered furniture have *low-velocity fashion cycles* which may last several years.

The higher the velocity of a product's fashion cycle, the greater the business risk for both the manufacturer and the retailer. Yet the rewards of good fashion merchandising—being neither too early nor too late in introducing a fashion product—are so great that there is constant pressure to introduce more fashion velocity into traditionally staple products.

Fashion Leaders

At one time the three phases of the fashion cycle roughly represented degrees of affluence among consumers. New styles appeared first among the wealthy and then slowly reached those in middle- and low-income groups. Today, however, fashion by and large no longer wears so obvious a price tag, although quality does. The system of marketing fashion designs and the techniques of mass production are so well developed that it is not necessary to be wealthy to wear the newest fashions. Fashions once filtered through from the wealthy to the poor. Nowadays fashions start in the young teens-to-twenties group and are then taken up by older people. Those who design for and sell to women in the 12-to-20 size range are likely to be guided by what is already selling in the 3-to-13 size range. In men's apparel, the source of a popular fashion is in the college-age group. Middle-aged men are slower than middle-aged women in following the lead of younger people.

Designers, manufacturers, and retailers who desire the quick acceptance of fashion leaders must range widely in their search for clues to what these leaders will adopt. Fashion designers and marketers have always found inspiration in the printed news of the world. People in the films inspired the Gatsby look of the mid-1970s. Nowadays designers must keep an eye on what is happening among the inventive young of Chelsea and Greenwich Village in New York City and among their counterparts in other cities and countries. They watch the affluent college students who spend their Christmas holidays skiing in Switzerland. They also watch the equally imaginative young people who mass at country music concerts or go to see Shakespeare's plays in Central Park. Wherever the young get together, a new fashion might well be brewing.

Fashion Seasons

The demand for new merchandise determines how many seasonal openings will be held to show new lines of goods. Most accessories, men's and children's wear, and home furnishings have only two major showings each year: in January for spring and summer goods, and in June for all fall and winter lines. Millinery, however, has many more seasonal openings, since almost every month there is a change in millinery fashions.

For women's coats, suits, and dresses, there are three major seasonal openings and three minor ones. Cruise, ski, and beach items are sold during two minor openings. During the major openings, most manufacturers are showing their lines, and buyers are flocking to the showrooms. Fewer manufacturers and fewer buyers participate in minor openings.

The following chart shows the calendar for the openings. Major seasons are noted in capital letters and minor ones in capital and lowercase letters.

Increasing or decreasing the number of manufacturers' openings tends to accelerate or slow down the speed of the fashion cycle. The fewer the new lines of merchandise, and the less frequently they are introduced, the slower the change in the fashion cycle. It is the demand of the customer, however, that determines how many lines the manufacturer shows each year.

THE PARIS COUTURE AND OTHER EUROPEAN INFLUENCES ON FASHION

Paris, to many, has long been synonymous with fashion leadership. Copying Paris styles has for many years been a multi-million-dollar business in America. Other European countries also affect

CALENDAR OF READY-TO-WEAR SEASONS

Season	Manufacturer's Opening Dates	Retailer's Selling Season	Merchandise Mainly Shown
SPRING*	November	March–April	Coats, suits, dresses
SUMMER*	February	May–June	Coats, suits, dresses
Transitional	April	July–August	Specialty dresses
FALL*	May & June	August–December	Coats, suits, dresses
Holiday	August	November–December	Formal dresses, cocktail dresses, jackets, formal coats, dressy suits, sportswear, ski clothes, bathing suits
Cruise & Resort	October	February–March	Dresses, sportswear, bathing suits, casual clothes

*Major season.

fashion to a large extent. When discussing the world of Paris and European fashion, certain terms need to be understood.

Couture (koo-tour) is the French word used to refer to the French fashion industry. Instead of saying "the French fashion industry," one says simply, "the French couture" or "the Paris couture."

Haute couture (oat-koo-tour) refers to the leading French fashion manufacturers who create original styles. Since the firms are small and are housed in lovely homelike structures, they are referred to as fashion "houses." Christian Dior, Chanel, Balenciaga, St. Laurent, Cardin, and Givenchy are leading designers whose firms are members of the select haute couture.

Couturier (koo-tour-ee-ay) is the term for the individual designer. Thus, one may refer to the work of the couturier who creates a style with "fabric, labor, and imagination."

Prêt-à-porter (pret-ah-por-tay) refers to ready-to-wear garments that are mass-produced in France. Ready-to-wear clothes in France are a relatively new development. The manufacturers are members of the Federation Francaise des Industries du Vetement Feminin. Approximately 1,700 firms belong to this organization, and they have two showings annually, in April (for fall) and in October (for spring). Italy and other European countries also offer ready-to-wear merchandise.

Line-for-line copies are the exact copies of dresses from France, Italy, England, and other countries. These copies are made for retail stores. Manufacturers examine every detail of the French (or English, or Italian, or other country's) original and reproduce it for the American market in either identical or similar fabrics by modified mass-production techniques.

Retailers or manufacturers from the United States may visit the French couture houses twice a year to purchase models. For fall and winter clothes, Paris houses show in July, and for spring and summer clothes they show in late January and early February. The price of each dress or coat purchased at a showing may be $1,000 or

Parisian fashion houses, such as St. Laurent, show their new designs to buyers and manufacturers twice a year. Spring and summer models are shown in January or February, and fall and winter models, in July.
Photograph by Bill Cunningham

more. When an American firm purchases a garment, it also purchases the right to copy the garment or adapt it for its customers. By the time the private customers of the famous French houses are making their selections from the originals in Paris, line-for-line copies and adaptations are in production in New York and other cities. Within a couple of weeks they will appear in American ready-made collections in both expensive and inexpensive versions. The original garments, which were brought into this country "in bond" to avoid payment of costly duty, are sent

THE WIDE WORLD OF RETAILING

to South American countries after being copied. There they are sold to wealthy clients.

The manufacturers and the stores that send buyers to the Paris showings—and to those in London, Rome, Madrid, and elsewhere—represent ultimate consumers at all income levels.

THE RETAIL STORE BUYER'S ROLE IN FASHION DEVELOPMENT

While accepting the risks in fashion merchandising—for they are justified by the profits—both the manufacturer and the retailer do their best to minimize these risks. One way they do this is by carefully noting the trends and then testing the acceptance of a style or design before going into heavy production or full-scale marketing.

The manufacturer's first testing comes when the new line is shown to the retail customers—the store buyers. A *line* is a collection of styles designed for a particular season. The typical manufacturer who shows a new line to the buyers is still uncommitted to the production of all models in it. That depends on the reaction of the buyers. If a large number place orders for a particular model, it goes into production. If orders for a model are not large enough to make the cutting profitable, the model is eliminated.

This is the first crucial screening of a new season's fashion ideas. It is accomplished by a process of evaluation and decision making for which buyers are prepared by training and experience. Buyers are also guided by (1) their store's fashion policy, (2) sales data accumulated during the preceding season, (3) personal observation of the scene in their own community and elsewhere, and (4) information received from buying offices, fashion reporting services (including that of the fashion coordinator, if the store employs one), and the fashion press.

The Store's Fashion Merchandise Policy

The buyer's selections must be compatible with the store's fashion image. Customers may look to this store to be the innovator, the first in town to announce and display what is new. Or the store may be in the middle of the fashion scale—more an adopter than an innovator, one that waits to see which styles the retail fashion leaders present and which of these the customers accept.

This fashion policy rules the buyers in their choice of manufacturers to deal with and in their selection of the various models shown by the manufacturers. The buyers who represent a store that is a fashion leader are quick to investigate new fashion resources, and they may make a point of doing so every season, particularly checking on small houses where young designers are experimenting.

The more firmly established and clear-cut the store's fashion image is, the more confidently the buyer operates. Some stores are so completely accepted as fashion authorities that their approval is almost enough to assure that a style will be accepted as a fashion.

Fashion Trends Noted from Accumulated Sales Data

Fashions of one season are generally predicted by the experts, for they can see how fashions evolve from those of the previous season. A fashion buyer constantly analyzes unit control records to chart developing and declining customer preferences. The unit control system (to be described in Part Five) provides a history of the progress of every model, usually referred to for easy identification by a number. The sales history of each piece that comes into stock tells whether it moved fast or slowly, was reordered frequently, sold out, or was marked down. When preparing for a new season, the buyer analyzes sales results to uncover whatever characteristics the best sellers have in common. The buyer searches particularly for the characteristics that may not be very obvious. For instance, all soft, natural, loose-fitting dresses in stock may have sold quickly. But perhaps the fastest seller was a manufacturer's dress that had metal link belts. A study of coat sales records, model by model, may lead the buyer to look for fewer fitted coats for the coming season and more of the belted styles. Analysis of the slow sellers will determine which styles are no longer popular.

In addition to having unit control records, the buyer in a well-run department or store also has records of things customers asked for which were not in stock, or perhaps not on the market. These records may suggest, for instance, that the store's own customers wanted all the brown garments they could buy, even if brown was not considered a fashionable color elsewhere.

All this information has been accumulated from day to day. It makes up a memory bank of customer preferences that the buyer draws upon when searching the market.

Fashion Trends Noted from Personal Observation

The buyer is very much a part of the scene in the community and a shrewd observer of what goes on. Sometimes, in a large store, the buyer's own observations are backed up by reports from market research people. Store buyers know about new-home developments and the occupants. Buyers have the season's social program in mind: symphony concerts, the opening of a new theater, weddings, and college and high school activities. Buyers are also aware of customers' travel plans. And they know the local economic situation. If there is a loss of jobs or even a threat of unemployment, many customers may be less adventurous in their fashion purchases.

Since buyers are also travelers and vacationers, they are aware of trends in fashion centers and resorts around the country and of what is being worn in those places. What is seen in Miami Beach in February and March might be purchased in the home town in May and June.

Fashion Trends Obtained from Fashion Reporting Services

Buying offices in the market cities send out bulletins to their subscriber stores, and buying office staffs brief store buyers and guide them when they come into the market. Stores also subscribe to fashion reporting services that alert them to each sign of a new trend, to fads as well as fashions. These services use sketches and photographs as well as word descriptions. Retail trade papers and magazines keep buyers aware of fashion trends in all types of merchandise. The many consumer magazines are read by buyers for direct news of fashion. But even more important, buyers can assess the demand for particular styles which these magazines create among consumers by means of their editorial and advertising pages.

Sampling and Timing as Further Tests of Fashion Trends

All the factors noted above are weighed by the buyers when they make initial selections. Some models are seen as obviously safe and sure answers to customer preferences. Others will be ordered in sample (small) quantities for testing. Some of the styles may be ahead of customers' fashion acceptance but will be important later on, perhaps the following season. The buyer may order a few of these, if only to give prestige or an air of fashion authority to the store, or to create excitement in the window displays. The buyer's problem is timing. Open-to-buy money (discussed in Part Five) must not be tied up too early in fashion innovations before the customers are quite ready for them, even though in a matter of weeks they will be purchasing the new styles. Even worse, however, would be to miss the tide of customer acceptance at its peak.

In-Store Testing of Fashion Trends

Models ordered from the manufacturer for sampling come into the stock early in the season, and unit control records are closely examined to see how the models are accepted. This is the crucial testing period of new fashions. Buyers are learning in February, for example, what styles will be most in demand two weeks before Easter. On the basis of the reorders the stores place, the manufacturers will know on what models they will concentrate their mass-production efforts. During the sampling and reordering period, a manufacturer will drop some more models from the line originally shown. Of the 100 to 200 models with which a manufacturer opened the season, no more than 40 or 50 may be produced for reorder, and perhaps 20 of these will be the genuine volume and profit producers.

THE RETAILER'S PROMOTION FUNCTION FOR FASHION

The retailer minimizes fashion risks as far as possible by trying to predetermine customer acceptance. Having made their selections, buyers make great efforts to guarantee customer acceptance. The promotional machinery of the store is put to work. Now customers are assured that the store endorses completely the styles and models its buyers have selected. Early in a season a store may show in its windows, in fashion shows, and in advertisements some models it has selected. This is done more for prestige reasons than to stimulate heavy sales. At mid-season, the promotional effort is concentrated on proven best sellers. These best sellers will differ among the fashion-leader stores, the fashion-follower stores, and the ultraconservative stores. But within its sphere, each store and each manufacturer goes through the same cycle: (1) preseason or early-season testing; (2) mass acceptance, when advertising dollars and sales efforts are concentrated on proved best sellers; and (3) clearance of fashions that have had their run in order to make room for new ones.

FASHION'S IMPACT ON OTHER MERCHANDISE

The same process that has been described for fashion departments or stores happens with all other merchandise a store sells in which any fashion element is present. But what happens in the course of weeks or months in a dress or suit department or store occurs at a much slower rate in other departments or stores. As a result, somewhat less risk is involved, for there is more time to get rid of declining fashions without loss. Manufacturers of nonapparel lines face less risk, too. Nevertheless, the fashion approach is in-creasing in most types of manufacturing and retailing. With it come the problems of sampling, reordering, and timing. By and large, retailers welcome these problems because nothing matches fashion appeal for inspiring purchases. And nothing so enhances a store's image with customers as the evidence that it is fashion-conscious in every department.

THE CUSTOMER'S ROLE IN FASHION

Designers, retailers, and customers, as you have noted, interact with each other in creating fashions. Retailers' reports guide manufacturers, and retailers' selections and promotion efforts guide customers. Nobody can say which group has the most important influence on fashion. Consumer fashion magazines glorify the designers, while the trade press and the whole retail world are inclined to believe that certain elite buyers for important stores are the true fashion dictators. But to confound both schools of thought, consumers periodically prove all over again that they have minds of their own and can stifle a so-called fashion before it has been fairly started. The fact is that designers, manufacturers, and retailers are successful in direct proportion to how well they interpret the spirit of the times. And they do this by being deeply involved in the scene around them.

The importance that retailers attach to fashion testing may seem to suggest that the customers are the dictators of fashion. In fact, the customers themselves are limited in their choice to what is actually offered them. Customers cannot register, when making a purchase, a preference for dark blue-greens when only yellow greens are available. During a period when all prints are large and sharp-colored, a person cannot buy a print that has muted and gentle tones. In short, the customer can choose among variations of a fashion, but none of the variations may be particularly desirable. Thus, the retailer must carry on direct fact-finding research among the customers. The buyers need to know what customers are asking for that they cannot find at all. In relaying customer preferences to the manufacturer, the buyer plays not only a reporting role but also a creative role in fashion development.

THE STORE MANAGER'S ROLE IN FASHION

The store manager is mainly responsible for co-ordinating the various segments of the store with regard to the store's fashion image and for coop-erating with the buyers and merchandisers of fashion goods. The store manager works with the fashion buyers in planning the store windows, displays, advertising, and allotment of space for special seasonal selling. The manager sees that there are enough trained personnel to receive, mark, stock, and sell the merchandise. In some chain stores, a manager is also responsible for unit control records and reorders. Thus, store managers are deeply involved in any part fashion plays in their stores.

TOPICS FOR DISCUSSION

1. Some people believe that fashion is just a form of frivolity. What arguments can you give to show that fashion is an important force in our economy?
2. Explain the difference between the terms "style," "fashion," and "fad."
3. Explain what is meant by the statement that fashion is usually evolutionary.
4. Explain the fashion cycle.
5. What is meant by the velocity of fashion? How is the retailer affected by this factor?
6. What are the major seasonal openings in women's apparel lines? When do the manufacturers hold these major openings?
7. What is meant by the Paris "haute couture"? By "prêt-à-porter"?
8. Explain the manner in which fashion trends are determined within a retail firm.
9. What role does the retailer play in the development of fashion?
10. What role does the customer play in the development of fashion?

MATHEMATICS FOR RETAILING

A retail-store buyer in the misses' fashion department placed the following initial order for dresses. On a separate sheet of paper, compute the cost and retail totals for each separate style number and the total cost and total retail value of the entire order.

Quantity	Style No.	Description	Color	Size	Unit Cost	Total Cost	Unit Retail	Total Retail
6	132Y	Belted dress	1 blue 1 pink 1 white 2 green 1 black	10	$8.75	xxx	$16.95	xxx
6	132Y	Belted dress	Ass't. as above	12	8.75	xxx	16.95	xxx
6	132Y	Belted dress	Ass't. as above	14	8.75	xxx	16.95	xxx
6	442P	Side-button/belt	4 green 2 blue	10	6.75	xxx	12.95	xxx
6	442P	Side-button/belt	Ass't. as above	12	6.75	xxx	12.95	xxx
6	442P	Side-button/belt	Ass't. as above	14	6.75	xxx	12.95	xxx
					TOTAL	xxx		xxx

COMMUNICATIONS IN RETAILING

You are the manager of a specialty store in a medium-sized town located in the Midwest. You have a buyer in the New York buying office who takes care of special orders on occasion for your customers. You have a very good customer who is attending a formal ball to be held in three weeks, and she wants a special gown for the occasion. She wants to be sure that no other woman at that ball will have a gown like hers. She wears a size 12, and she prefers a turquoise blue and gold combination in the latest fashion. She is willing to pay up to $150 (retail) for the dress. She is 5 feet 5 inches tall and has no figure problems. What instructions would you give the buyer about this order? Outline these on a separate sheet of paper.

MANAGING HUMAN RELATIONS

The customer for whom you ordered the dress in the previous exercise went to the ball wearing her new gown. She looked and felt very elegant in it. To her dismay, however, the identical dress, in a different color, was worn by another socialite in the town. The next morning your customer called you to complain about this fact and to advise you that she will never again purchase anything in your store. She was very angry. You then checked with the manufacturer of the dress and found that another had been sold to a retailer in a large city about 80 miles from your town. What explanation would you give to the customer? Be prepared to discuss this in class.

DECISION MAKING

Assume you are the buyer for the misses' dresses as ordered in the "Mathematics for Retailing" exercise. These dresses represent the newest styles, and you bought them in small amounts and in assorted sizes and colors. When you saw the dresses in the showroom, they were modeled by attractive young women. Hanging on the hangers in your store, the dresses appear very ordinary, and the salespeople have not been recommending them to customers. None have been sold in the week since they arrived in the store. What steps would you take to spur the sale of these dresses? Be prepared to discuss your answer in class.

CAREER LADDER

The person interested in fashion may choose a job from many different areas—styling, designing, buying, coordination, or promotion, for example. A person may begin by working in the stock room or in the alterations department. A person may also start by working as a merchandise clerk, by selling fashion merchandise, or by displaying goods in departments or in store windows. As one moves ahead, one may become an assistant buyer, a fashion department manager, a fashion buyer, a store manager, a fashion coordinator, or a merchandise manager of fashion goods. Make up a career ladder from a beginning position for yourself or for someone interested in fashion. (Use a separate sheet of paper.) How long do you think it would take to get into a fairly important position?

chapter 5

POINT-OF-SALE SYSTEMS
THE IMPACT OF THE COMPUTER

Merchants sleeping, as Rip Van Winkle did, and awakening 100 years later to see a store in the 1970s or '80s would be astounded by what they would see. Salespeople would be recording transactions, using small electronic terminals with lighted dials that would confirm the input. Instantaneously, that information would be transferred to central processing units, to be recorded as a sale and charged to a customer's charge account. The purchase would be subtracted from the total of merchandise on hand; noted on the buyer's records as no longer in stock; and added to the salesperson's sales total, the manufacturer's list of goods sold, and the store's total sales for the day. As a result of the enormous capacity of the computer, awakening merchants would see fewer employees taking care of larger numbers of customers. Details would be handled with a minimum of error and handwork, and everything would be so speedily processed that the managers would have difficulty keeping up with the latest printouts! This is the picture of retailing recordkeeping in the last quarter of the twentieth century.

Do you know how much detail is needed in the average retail store? Even the smallest store carries hundreds to thousands of items, and each item must be recorded and accounted for either as a sale or in the form of merchandise on hand at inventory time. Each transaction made with customers must be recorded. All records of vendors' bills and returns of merchandise to vendors must be accurately noted. Employees' work schedules; their rate of pay; their commissions, if any; and the withholding for taxes and other deductions must be accurately computed and recorded.

The larger the store, the more items it carries, the larger its work force, and the more customers it has, the greater the recordkeeping tasks will be. In large organizations where computers are not used, large staffs of employees spend their time recording transactions, keeping track of customers' accounts, and taking care of payrolls and the accounts that are payable to vendors.

Until the mid-1950s, all these records were entirely kept by hand or simple machines. Slowly, since that time, various retailers have been investing in computers or have paid to share time on a computer (known as "time-sharing") with other firms to lessen the burden of recording and collecting details needed so that the business can function properly.

Modern-day computers, which can count in billionths of a second and can print reports at speeds faster than anybody can read, have provided a solution to the retailer's recordkeeping problems.

THE LANGUAGE OF COMPUTERS AND DATA PROCESSING

Retailers who once used manual or mechanical processes to record facts about their business now record the same facts through electronic computers. *Data* is the plural of the word "datum," which means "a fact." A fact is used as a basis of counting, computing, calculating, or reckoning. The word "data," therefore, refers to many facts assembled for reckoning or computing. *Processing* refers to manipulating or handling, and a synonym for the manipulating or handling of facts is *data processing*.

Hardware refers to the machines or devices—the electronic computer equipment—used in gathering, recording, computing, summarizing, and visually displaying or printing out data.

Software refers to the explanations that direct the computers in their operations. These sets of directions are known as *programs*. For example, an electric stove may be programmed at the push of a button to heat only to a given temperature, to maintain that temperature for a given period of time, and then to turn off automatically at a pre-set time. Computers are directed by programs that are written by *programmers* to record, compute, store, summarize, and exhibit or print out data on command.

A *binary code* is a two-symbol code (1 and 0) used by the computer. Electrical paths or circuits are *on* or *off* to represent the 1 or the 0 in the processing of data. A *bit* is a binary digit, either a 0 or a 1.

A *flow chart* is a diagram of the step-by-step instructions that the programmer preparing the program must develop.

A *computer* is an electronic machine that differs from ordinary calculating devices in at least four ways:

- To program the machine, logical step-by-step analyses of the problem at hand must be developed. This is helpful in later decision making.

- Calculations are done with lightning speed.

- Computations are invariably accurate.

- In addition to adding, subtracting, multiplying, and dividing, the computer can compare, sort, arrange, rearrange, select, combine, store, and print out data.

Computer terminals are devices that may be placed at any point where data can be entered into a computer or reported out of a computer. For example, stores use terminals in place of cash registers to enter records of sales and, when necessary, to receive information about the credit rating of a customer.

USING THE COMPUTER

The steps needed to process data are known as origination, input, processing or manipulation, and output. The first step does not involve the computer directly. *Origination* is the collection of data on a source document, such as a payroll form or a price ticket. It is when this information is organized for input that the computer comes into use.

Input

When using an ordinary adding machine, the operator depresses the keys to record the amounts to be totaled. In computer language, the amounts would be referred to as *input*. Data placed into the computer represent input. A charge bill for a customer is input; a vendor's bill to be paid is input; an employee's hours of labor used to determine his or her pay are input.

The difference between input for an adding machine and input for an electronic computer has to do primarily with the speed with which the machine can be fed the data and absorb or read the data.

Since the computer can read the data so fast, methods of input must match the reading speed of the computer. Input, therefore, may be in the form of punched cards, punched tape, or magnetic tape and may be handled by optical readers or scanners or by terminals.

Punched Cards. One of the best-known input devices is the punched card. Information is key-punched onto cards with a typewriterlike machine. The machine makes round or oblong holes on the cards that activate electrical impulses when wires brushed over the holes make contact with a metal roller. The electrical impulses are the language of the computer. A high-speed computer can read in a minute the holes punched in hundreds of cards.

Punched Tape. Another popular input device for electronic computers is punched tape. The punched-tape reader receives electrical impulses through the holes punched into the tape and allows the computer to receive data at remarkable speeds.

Both punched cards and punched tape do rely, however, upon some manual punching of the holes before being fed into the computer. These devices, therefore, are not as sophisticated as the newer ones that are being introduced and used to a greater extent.

Magnetic Tape. Banks use a common language called "magnetic ink character recognition" (MICR) to enable them to process quickly the millions of checks written daily and to keep abreast of their customers' accounts. The ink they use on the specially designed numbers that appear on individual checks has been given small charges of electricity. These magnetic ink figures can be used to sort the checks according to individual account numbers so deposits can be properly recorded. A machine called a MICR reader can read the electrical impulses from the magnetic ink numbers and transmit these data to the computer.

Retailers can use magnetic tape, similar to tape for sound recordings, that has magnetized bits which can be used for input. These act in the same manner as the magnetic ink on checks.

Optical Reader or Scanner. The newest input device is the optical reader, which is capable of scanning characters written in special shapes and then translating those characters into electrical impulses that the computer can process. Since optical readers can use conventional language as well as special computer language, records that never before could be used directly by computers have now become acceptable input. Thus, adding machine tapes, cash register tapes, tags, labels,

and codes stamped on cans, bottles, and cartons may be used directly as input. Special hand-held wands may be passed over a tag to read it, or the coded merchandise itself may be passed over a stationary optical scanner. The information is relayed to a computer that flashes each price on a screen and automatically rings the price up on the cash register. The cashier then takes the money from the customer and makes change. Speeding the customers through the checkout counters saves their time as well as the employees' time. Accuracy is also improved by this method of recording data about purchases.

Visual Display Terminals. Terminals have become familiar machines on the selling floor of retail stores. In place of a cash register, the terminal is used to record sales, and since the terminal is linked to a computer, the data are immediately recorded and computed with other data previously entered into the machine. Thus, a customer's charge may be added to previous charges, the amount of the sale added to previous sales, the item of merchandise sold deducted from the total merchandise on hand, and the amount of the sale added to the salesperson's total sales—all virtually simultaneously.

Processing

In processing as well as receiving input, computers operate much more quickly than any human could, and thanks to technological developments, succeeding generations of computers continue to improve in speed.

In everyday English, the word "generation" refers to a group of people of approximately the same age. In computers, the word "generation" refers to the advancement in computer technology. The *first generation* of the electronic mechanisms known as computers used vacuum tubes that heated up and wore out quickly. These computers could figure in thousandths of a second, or in *milliseconds*. The *second generation* of computers used solid-state transistors that did not heat up and that did not burn out like vacuum tubes. These computers were able to figure in

Renting Equipment

The high cost of renting equipment may be justified only if the equipment can be kept in almost constant use. Even though the retailer rents the equipment, the store must hire and train its own personnel to run the machines. Rental plans usually include service charges for "down time" repairs.

Using Service Plans

For smaller firms that cannot afford to purchase or rent the costly equipment, and for those firms that cannot keep the machines in constant use, service centers are available where material may be processed for a service charge. The service center provides the personnel needed to do the processing of the data, including the programming, and certain time periods are assigned for each firm being serviced. By this means, even small retailers who need detailed records may have computer recording available.

PROBLEMS OF CONVERSION TO ELECTRONIC DATA PROCESSING

When a retailing firm plans to convert from a manual system to a computer system for the various activities within the organization, a number of important steps must be taken.

- The firm must create a conversion calendar, which will serve to set the plans for the activities to take place. This must be adhered to as closely as possible.

- The firm must propose that major changes coincide with periods when the store personnel are not overburdened with routine store activities. Periods when business is slack are generally best for conversion.

- The firm must select a clerical staff that can work on both manual and, later, computer facilities.

- The firm must hold frequent meetings so that every person understands what is taking place. Those directly concerned should meet daily.

- All plans should be written out so that there can be no misunderstanding, no omission of any important detail, and no chance to forget the agreements made.

- The firm should carry out every planned activity. Forms must be ordered; step-by-step programs must be planned; personnel must be trained. Everything must be accomplished.

- The manual and computer systems should be tested simultaneously to make sure that everything is working correctly. The manual system has to be checked against the computer system and the computer system against the manual system to make sure that complete data are present and correct as the new system takes over.

THE IMPACT OF THE COMPUTER ON RETAILING

Electronic data processing has potentials for use wherever counting, computing, and recording must be done. Every division of retailing firms can make use of EDP. Accounts receivable, accounts payable, merchandising unit and dollar control, and payroll are all divisions that lend themselves to speedier and more accurate recordkeeping through EDP.

Supermarket Checkout Using the Universal Product Code

Some mass merchandisers and supermarkets across the country use the newest, speediest, most accurate method of registering supermarket merchandise sales available. Merchandise is premarked by manufacturers with a *Universal Product Code,* (UPC)—inked lines of different widths and lengths that represent numbers. These numbers tell all about the product: its size, weight, color or texture, and manufacturer, and what the item itself is. Only the price is not included in this code. The operator moves the coded merchandise across the surface of an optical scanner. Immediately the scanner reads the inked lines on the product and relays the facts to

```
HOMETOWN FOOD MART
STORE 123    04/20/7-


GRO    .54F  CEREAL
NFD   3.90H  WINSTON
GRO    .57F  CHILI
MT    1.13F  T BONE
NFD    .43C  KLEENEX
PRO    .47F  BANANA
NFD    .19C  DOG FOOD
NFD    .35C  GLAD WRAP
GRO    .07F  KOOL AID
GRO    .07F  KOOL AID
GRO    .06F  KOOL AID

       .06   TAX

      7.84   TOTAL

     10.00   CASH

      2.16   CHANGE

0007 02   4   4.22PM
```

As the optical scanner (top) reads the Universal Price Code (bottom left), the price is flashed on a screen and is recorded on an itemized sales slip (bottom right).
Courtesy NCR Corporation

the computer. The computer matches the price to the code. Prices may be changed as frequently as desired simply by putting new price information into the computer. As the code on each piece of merchandise is read by the scanner, the price is flashed on a screen for the customer to see, just as a cash register shows a price. At the conclusion of the sale, an itemized sales slip is issued from the machine for the merchandise purchased, and the cashier either rings up the customer's money and makes change or records the total against the customer's charge account. Through the use of the Universal Product Code and the fixed scanner (a movable wand scanner may also be used), customers move through the lines faster. This means that fewer cashiers and baggers are needed and the costs of doing business are reduced—resulting in lower prices for goods.

Integrated Data Processing

The ideal EDP system is the one in which data are captured at the *point of sale* from the price tag attached to the goods or from the Universal Product Code printed on the label. The data thus obtained are used repeatedly throughout the store's recordkeeping system. This is known as *integrated data processing.*

The information taken from the price tag or the UPC is either punched into the cash register terminal or scanned by a wand or a fixed scanner. The following information is retrieved and computed or recorded:

- The item, and its style number, size, and color

- The season letter of the item (representing the month or week it entered the store's stock)

- The manufacturer of the item

- The retail price of the item sold

- The department or area where the item was sold

- The identification of the salesperson who sold the item

- The tax on the item, if any

- The type of sale, such as cash take, cash send, charge take, charge send, or COD

- If a charge sale, the name and account number of the person to whom the merchandise is charged

The information about the merchandise sold will be sent automatically to the merchandising division, which will update the unit-control records to show that those particular items were sold. The merchandising division will refigure the totals to determine the number of articles of that style, color, and size, for example, that now remain on hand. When the number on hand reaches a preset low point, an order will automatically be printed for the vendor, and a new on-order total will be entered in the unit-control records for that merchandise. Simultaneously, other records will be adjusted to indicate what dollar amount remains in that period for purchases. Accounts payable records will be updated when the new merchandise arrives so that the store will know what it owes to the vendor.

Similarly, the records for the customer's account for charge sales will be updated. The records of the salesperson's sales will also be adjusted. If the salesperson sells on commission, the new amount owed to that person as a result of this sale will be computed.

EXCEPTION REPORTING

The computer, as you have learned, can supply large amounts of information rapidly. Thus, for example, if a firm wanted to update customers' charge accounts daily, the computer could do this. However, no person in the firm would be able to read the daily reports about some 20,000 or more customers. Nor would customers want to receive bills on a daily basis. Consequently, the large amounts of data that can be poured out of the computer need to be handled selectively. If a situation is unusual or needs the immediate attention of a manager, the necessary information should be available immediately. *Exception reporting* that selects only problem areas, critical items, or unusual activity at a given time, while holding ordinary reporting for periodic output, has proved to be immensely valuable to retailers.

For example, assume a customer's credit rating allowed charges on his or her account up to $300 per month. Suddenly this customer makes a large number of purchases in one day totaling over $300. The computer would print a report about this account alerting the store's manager to this sudden flurry of activity. The manager could then determine what action is necessary, or the computer would signal that further credit would not be granted.

For the unit control of merchandise, exception reporting is ideal. If, during a normal period, sales for an item were 24 units weekly, the machine could be programmed to issue no report for sales activity for the item if between 18 to 30 units were sold weekly. If, however, 31 or more units were sold during one week, or if fewer than 18 units were sold, the machine would issue a report to alert the buyer to the unusual situation occurring in the sales of this item. The buyer could then take the necessary action to ensure adequate stock for the department or to get rid of the surplus.

THE MANAGER'S ROLE IN HANDLING COMPUTERIZED POINT-OF-SALE RECORDS

While an integrated data processing system eliminates much of the tedious recordkeeping that used to be done by hand, it does not reduce the decision-making workload of the executives or the management team. The computer merely counts, stores data, tabulates, and does routine ordering. Making special decisions, selecting new merchandise, changing merchandise lines, determining which customers' accounts are poor or questionable risks, deciding which salespeople are doing the best job—these tasks and countless others continue to be the responsibility of the management team in retailing.

TOPICS FOR DISCUSSION

1. Why have retailers turned to electronic data processing for recordkeeping?
2. Explain briefly the steps necessary in processing data.
3. What is the advantage of the internal memory of a computer?
4. What is meant by the term "alphanumeric output"?
5. What is the role of a programmer?
6. Why do some retailing firms use EDP service plans instead of purchasing or renting EDP equipment?
7. Why should both manual and computer systems be maintained simultaneously during conversion to electronic data processing?
8. What two types of optical scanners are available?
9. Why is point-of-sale computer recording being used increasingly?
10. What is meant by "exception reporting"? Why is it used?

MATHEMATICS FOR RETAILING

On a separate sheet of paper, write the following numbers in the binary system: (a) 374, (b) 55, (c) 8906.

COMMUNICATIONS IN RETAILING

You are the manager of a store that recently converted its charge accounts (accounts receivable) to electronic data processing. This speeded all operations but caused some billing problems. One customer, Mrs. Walters, previously received several bills that were incorrect. You had promised her that she would find this new system far more accurate. With that promise in mind, she ordered a refrigerator-freezer and was told it would be delivered in one month. She had it charged to her account. Mrs. Walters expected that the amount due for this purchase would not appear on her bill until some time after the refrigerator-freezer had been delivered and installed in her home. The week after she placed her order she received a bill that included the price of the refrigerator-freezer. It would not be delivered for at least three more weeks. Her irate letter about this premature charge, which she considered to be a new kind of error was turned over to you for answering. On a separate sheet of paper, compose a letter in which you explain the reason for the charge. Your aim is to keep this customer.

MANAGING HUMAN RELATIONS

Miss Joplin, a buyer in the stationery and supplies department, did not like the idea of having her department's merchandise control placed into the store's computer system. She disliked the necessary record analysis need for the conversion, and she was sure that her job would no longer be needed once the ordering and record-keeping of stationery and supplies were done by the computer. How would you, as the store manager, handle this problem? Be prepared to discuss your answer in class.

DECISION MAKING

A general merchandise firm was expanding rapidly by adding branch stores. The owners believed that they could not afford computer processing of data because they estimated the purchase and rental costs to be prohibitively high. However, with nine branches plus a main store, they found that the buyers were unable to make frequent visits to the branches. They also found that each store kept getting further and further behind in updating its orders for merchandise. Even the most basic items, such as men's white shirts, were often out of stock in some sizes and styles. What recommendations would you make about this matter? What arguments would you present in favor of your recommendations? Be prepared to discuss your recommendations and supporting arguments in class.

CAREER LADDER

A store with approximately 500 employees was considering conversion to electronic data processing. Since the firm was planning initially to rent the equipment, store employees would be needed to run the machines and program them. All other personnel would need to be trained to read the machines' output. You were recently hired, as a community college student, by the firm.

The managers of the firm planned to give an aptitude test to all employees who desired to know if they had potential for data processing work. The firm urged all interested employees to take the test on company time. Would you plan to take the test? Be prepared to explain your answer in class.

If you took the test and showed a promising aptitude for such work, what types of work related to computers would you like to do? Be prepared to discuss your ideas in class.

PART TWO

THE ORGANIZATION OF RETAIL INSTITUTIONS

chapter 6

STORES CLASSIFIED BY OWNERS

To the casual passerby, retail stores in shopping centers and on America's main streets may appear very much alike. The differences seem to lie in the categories of merchandise sold and the way the merchandise is presented. Some stores have modern display fronts, up-to-date interiors, and shelves stocked with vast supplies of merchandise. By contrast, other stores don't follow the modern changes taking place in retailing and prefer instead to keep their old traditions. Yet there are many differences in retail stores more important than differences in appearance. One difference has to do with the various forms of store ownership. Some stores are individually owned or partnerships; some are part of corporate chains; and still others combine these forms of ownership in various ways.

THE NEED FOR CLASSIFICATION

There are seven major store ownership categories. These were set up so that both government and private agencies could compile retailing statistics in the same way. Government agencies and retailers use these statistics to keep abreast of marketplace activities and better watch over America's giant retailing industry.

The term *retail establishment* means any single outlet where merchandise is sold to customers. A recent survey estimates that there are approximately 1.8 million retail establishments of all types and sizes selling a great array of goods and services to Americans. Total store numbers fluctuate each year, but industry economists and others have noted a growing trend toward fewer new-store openings and more enlargement of existing facilities.

Keeping track of what goes on in more than 1.8 million stores is a big job, but economists and business people must do it. Facts and figures help retailers and manufacturers analyze their own sales and those of their competitors. In this way, they learn what products are most in demand, which models and colors are increasing in popularity, and which are declining. Reports also show in what kind of store sales of specific products are going up and where they are going down. Retailers must be constantly alert to changing trends in all the merchandise they carry.

Such findings may indicate, for example, that a

certain manufacturer's men's hosiery is selling best in self-service stores rather than in stores where customers rely on salespeople for help. This information might move the producer to change the packaging to something more eye-catching and to suggest that all retailers buying the product line set it up in a self-service arrangement.

When retailers need information on sales and profits, they use any number of sources, such as the U.S. Department of Commerce; the Federal Reserve Bank; the U.S. Department of Labor; research departments of large business organizations, both manufacturing and retailing; banks; trade associations; and business magazines and newspapers.

Marketing Decisions

All these data—and remember, this is a sum total of events occurring in about 1.8 million stores every day—make up the body of information on which businesses base their marketing decisions. Manufacturers plan their production and distribution according to this information, and retailers use it when they make changes in their selling methods, add new lines of merchandise, or even change the character of their merchandising. Bankers are guided by this information as they decide who should or should not receive retail financing, and city planners learn where retail activity is greatest.

Retail Store Classifications

Classifying retail establishments is difficult because stores often mix their selling methods as well as their merchandise. Therefore classifying stores by form of ownership is more reliable, for the kind of ownership is less subject to change. The seven basic categories of retail stores are as follows:

1. *Independent store.* A one-unit enterprise privately owned and managed by a single person or a partnership—or, in the case of a larger establishment, by a corporation

2. *Corporate chain.* A group of two or more stores under single ownership, managed by a central headquarters

3. *Manufacturer-owned chain.* Often single-line stores, owned and operated by the manufacturer and selling the manufacturer's products

4. *Leased department chain.* A merchandise or service firm that rents selling space in stores and operates under its own management

5. *Franchised dealership.* A single-line or service store that purchases exclusively from a sponsor or uses the name of a sponsoring organization

6. *Leased dealerships.* An establishment leased by a dealer from a sponsor

7. *Consumer cooperative.* A store owned by its own customers

THE SMALL INDEPENDENT

Independent stores range in size from the tiny one-unit enterprise, individually owned, to the colossal corporate organization. Also, the internal makeup of independent stores ranges from the simple to the very complex, depending on each store's size and sales volume.

The small retailer, in addition to being the owner, wears the hats of manager, buyer, salesperson, stockkeeper, custodian, and bookkeeper. This retailer usually operates one store and almost always puts in a longer-than-average workday and workweek.

If you consider the entire range—including hardware stores and groceries—about half of all independents are run entirely by one or two people—the owner and a spouse, a partner, or a hired salesperson. Nearly half of all apparel and apparel accessories stores in the country employ fewer than three workers per store. In sheer numbers, the single-store independents take first place in American retailing. In terms of volume, however, this is not the case.

Advantages of Being Small

Retailing provides more opportunities than any other field for the ambitious, small-scale entrepreneur whose dream is to own a business. Opportunities for the small store are widespread. Small independents can flourish in locations considered unprofitable by chain companies.

Having a Convenient Location. Small independents are everywhere. You can spot them in a small town or on a neighborhood shopping street in a large city, in a hotel lobby, in subway station arcades, and in suburban shopping centers. To compete with the lower prices and the bigger assortments of the giants, small retailers offer convenience and service to neighborhood customers.

Selling One Item. Convenient location is not the only factor that makes small stores a vital force in our economy. Some small stores capitalize on their distinctiveness, serving markets that are big enough for them but not big enough to interest their larger competitors. For example, the market for unusual seashells that are expensive and beautiful is obviously a limited one. But a tiny shop in downtown New York City draws enough customers from all around town to keep its business flourishing—with no advertising or publicity. Just as prosperous is a tiny neighboring

The small independents make up the largest portion of American retail establishments.
Photograph by Fern Logan

shop, about 10 feet wide, that sells nothing but baskets.

Imaginative people constantly find retailing opportunities in the weaknesses of big stores. That was the case with a piece-goods buyer, a textile expert employed by a large department store. He knew that women who make their own clothes admire good fabrics. But his department, like fabric departments in other stores, was a constant bother to these women because of its emphasis on price and bargains. Believing that women make their own clothes because they want distinction and quality, too, he opened his own quality fabric shop, and he proved his merchandising ideas were right.

Offering Personalized Shopping. Several other advantages for the owner of a small-scale independent store are as follows:

- The opportunity to develop a warm, personal relationship with customers and to learn their personal preferences. This has caused many customers to ignore the big stores and return often to the small shops.

- The opportunity to do buying, pricing, and selling by oneself. The independent retailer can change buying procedures, drop certain lines and acquire others, or change the method of advertising—all without having to get the approval of a board of directors or a central headquarters.

- The opportunity to save customers' time. Many customers who value their time find it more practical to pay a slightly higher price in a small store rather than spend their time going through a large one.

Purchasing Methods of Independents

Another reason for the success of the small independent is that in the fields most pressed by chain store competition—foods and staples—the retailer can achieve some of the efficiencies enjoyed by the chains. They do this by purchasing goods through buying pools, or as cooperative or

voluntary chains, or through buying offices. There are tradeoffs, however. Most of these buying methods force the owner to give up some measure of independence.

Buying Pools. By combining into buying pools, several neighboring stores that sell the same merchandise can place a single order for all member stores at the same time. By placing a bulk order instead of small, separate ones, they get a better price from their wholesalers and from the manufacturers. Each store keeps its independence, since the buying pool is not involved with a central authority. But the advantages of pooled buying are limited to stores that sell identical items and brands. Furthermore, the members must be concentrated in a relatively small area, since each store must pick up its own portion of the order from the point of delivery.

Cooperative Chains. Some independents have gone beyond the pool system of simply ordering merchandise as a group. They have organized their own wholesale company with warehouse and offices. Discounts for large orders are available through this method of buying. This arrangement involves cooperative ownership, and the stores make up a cooperative chain. Despite the implication, the member stores are not chain stores at all, since each is still owned independently.

Voluntary Chains. Groups of independent stores that are served by a governing wholesaler are known as voluntary chains. Although member stores remain independent in ownership, they surrender some of their operating freedom when they agree to operate under the chain name and feature the wholesaler's private brands of merchandise. In return, the stores receive better wholesale prices, advertising copy, store displays, and help in merchandising and management. The wholesaler may even provide the financing for new stores or store expansions. Usually the retailer pays a nominal fee for these continuing services.

Thus the small independent members of a

voluntary chain can enjoy the assistance that is available to big corporate chains. This assistance puts them in a better position to compete because it results in greater buying power, promotional and management know-how, and financial strength.

Cooperative chains and voluntary chains are most prevalent in the food, drug, and hardware fields. Examples of voluntary chains are the Super-Value and Red Owl food stores, the Ben Franklin variety stores, and the Rexall, Walgreen, and Snyder drugstores.

Buying Offices. Some retailers, like the independent fashion retailers, cannot adapt well to the principles of pooled buying. Fashion stores that compete in the same trading area cannot pool purchases of identical items because their main goal is to offer unique items. Furthermore, they do not buy fashion merchandise through wholesalers. Their purchases are spread among the large number of fashion producers who give this field its diversity.

These retail stores, and other independents, often use the services of resident buying offices. These are purchasing agencies located in important market areas. The agencies shop the markets and advise their clients (the retail stores) about available items and upcoming trends. They will then place orders for the same merchandise at the same time for noncompetitors. Large chains and department stores often have their own buying offices, which purchase exlusively for the company.

The store that uses such a service sends weekly sales and inventory reports to the buying office and lets the buying office decide what merchandise to order and how much. This system is very much like the chain store system except that there is no central warehousing, and the method generally applies to lower-priced merchandise. This service saves the store owner time because it means fewer trips to the market for the owner. Secondly, every store using the service enjoys the advantage of having the sales trend information that is gathered by all the stores in the group. The

final advantage is savings. The volume of pooled purchases is large enough to win some price concessions from the manufacturer, even though the manufacturer must make separate shipments to each store.

THE LARGE INDEPENDENT

The main differences between the small and large independents have to do with size and internal organization. Ownership is still by an individual, a family, a partnership, or a corporation. If the establishment is large and is incorporated, policy may be governed by a board of directors.

The larger retailers, of course, have the advantage over smaller ones in buying power, merchandise assortment, and promotional budgets.

Multi-Unit Organization

Large independent stores may carry on their business in only one retail outlet or have one or several branches, and their operations may closely resemble those of centrally controlled chains. The retail trade, however, does not refer to the branches of large stores as chain stores. Branches do not go as far as the traditional chains in standardizing merchandise assortments, and they do not make any point at all of having a standardized appearance. They are much more flexible in fitting their merchandising policies to the places where they operate. Within the retail trade, department stores that operate branches are generally described as *multi-unit organizations* rather than being called chain store organizations.

Ownership Groups

During the past decade, giant corporations have been very active in buying up the independents. The trend probably had its roots in the depression years of the 1930s. At that time, manufacturers bought some of their client stores to help keep them from going bankrupt, but they still allowed the stores to operate as independent enterprises. Today many manufacturers and other nonretailers are acquiring ownership of small chains and multi-unit stores. For example, Abraham & Straus in New York City and Bullock's in California are both owned by Federated Department Stores, Inc. However, each is independent in its merchandising and planning. In the retail trade, corporations that own many department stores but do not operate them on chain store principles are called *ownership groups* rather than chains. Examples of ownership groups are Federated Department Stores, Inc., Allied Stores, and the May Department Store Company.

THE CORPORATE CHAIN STORE

A *chain store* is one of a string of stores under single ownership, with a central headquarters that manages and buys merchandise for all stores in the chain. Headquarters decides what merchandise the stores will carry, what kind of service they will offer, and what kind of advertising they will do. The key to success is keeping the merchandise assortments and store operation standard throughout the chain.

By buying identical merchandise for many stores, the chain has the advantage of mass buying power. The biggest national chains can and do buy up the complete output of certain manufacturers and may sell these products under the stores', rather than the manufacturers', brand names.

The cost of chain store management, buying, and promotion is spread over many units instead of only one. As a result, each store can have the services of experts in different fields and pay less than an independent store might pay for even mediocre help. For example, the chain store will not have to hire its own display designer or window trimmer. At central headquarters a highly professional staff designs the displays for all stores. Working sketches, which the store manager or assistant manager can easily follow, go to the individual stores, along with the actual props, posters, and signs.

Many other things become standardized. Advertising copy and art are mass-produced. Personnel specialists at headquarters prepare sales training courses for the chain store managers. The layout and fixtures of the stores may be the same. The retailer who operates a small store learns by trial and error which location is the best display place for each item. The chain store manager gets this advice from headquarters.

Small-store owners have to count and analyze their own sales tickets to determine what goods to order and when. Chain store managers have this done for them by a central office that is probably equipped with computers which total and analyze sales records and place reorders for some merchandise automatically. The central office can also compare the sales figures of all its

The advertising staff and art department at central headquarters provide all the stores in the chain with advertising art and copy.
Courtesy J.C. Penney Company

THE ORGANIZATION OF RETAIL INSTITUTIONS

units and quickly detect national or regional trends. All stores in the chain benefit immediately from this exchange of information.

Diversity of Merchandise

The chain system of retailing applies to almost every type of merchandise and service. There are grocery store chains, variety store chains, and drugstore chains. There are chains of stores that specialize in a single line or a single family of merchandise: shoes, men's clothes, candy, jewelry, and sporting goods, for example. There are also chains that carry a larger and more varied assortment of merchandise. Stores in these chains include the bigger units of such retail organizations as Sears, Roebuck and Company; Montgomery Ward; and J. C. Penney.

Originally, the advantages associated with shopping in a chain store were all practical ones. The appeal of the first chain stores was thrift. Because of low operating costs and mass buying power, the food chains, variety store chains, and general merchandise chains could sell at lower prices the same merchandise or similar items carried by the independent merchant. Since this advantage depended on mass purchasing, chain stores concentrated on merchandise that had a steady, predictable demand. Thus high-fashion merchandise and expensive foods were not carried. The early chain stores cultivated the mass market for low- or medium-priced staple goods, and this accounted for their early success.

While purchasing inexpensive or moderately priced goods is still a common characteristic of chain stores, it is not always so. Today general merchandise chains are stocking higher-quality goods and broadening their customer appeal. Sears, Roebuck and Company is one of the leading retail organizations that recognizes the demand for better-quality merchandise, and particularly for leisure-time goods, such as ski equipment and ski clothes. Other examples of items in demand are fine art and, most recently, fashions that keep up with the changing tastes of young people. While Sears is in a class by itself,

many of its successful ventures are being copied by other chain store organizations.

Manufacturer-Owned Chains

Many chains of single-line stores are owned and operated by manufacturers. Best known of this type are the shoe store chains, which are responsible for most of the business done by all shoe stores.

Invisible Chains—Leased Departments

Some departments in department stores are not owned or operated by the stores themselves. Instead, the store leases space to specialists in particular types of merchandise or service. Rents are based on a percentage of the sales or on a percentage plus a fixed charge.

Many of the specialists are chain organizations, operating departments in a number of stores. Some chains are national. They conform to the definition of chain store organization in that they are centrally owned and operated and sell merchandise according to a standard formula. They operate almost every type of retail business, although their names are not generally known to customers. Some of the departments most often leased out to chains carry millinery, photographic equipment, shoes, books, optical goods, jewelry, pets, or automotive supplies. Other leased departments may take the form of beauty salons or repair shops.

Usually the responsibility for locating and training a specialist for the leased department belongs to those who are leasing the space rather than to the store. But before a store rents space, it may require some evidence of special training.

Mass merchandisers use leased departments even more than department stores do. Usually department stores sign leases with outside chains in order to gain the advantage of having specialized management in a few fields where there are merchandising problems. On the other hand, discount stores often use leasing as an investment-free way to expand. Many discount houses operate the majority of their departments through leasing, and some lease out all their departments. This is not a general rule, however. The most successful discount chains are those that operate most of their departments themselves, leasing only a few when specialists are needed. Discounters have complained that stores run entirely by leased departments often lose their identity, since each renter may have a different way of operating.

FRANCHISED DEALERSHIPS

A franchised establishment is essentially the same as a store in a voluntary chain. The wholesalers who sponsor voluntary chains often describe their stores' owners as franchise dealers. In a narrow definition, the franchise dealer runs a single-line store or service establishment that does all its purchasing from a sponsoring manufacturer or wholesaler in return for the use of a well-known name. The franchise dealer will also contract to follow a completely standardized pattern of operation.

The contract of the voluntary chain store, in contrast, may require the owner to do only some business with the sponsoring company, thus allowing more freedom and flexibility of opera-

tions. The franchiser—the person holding the franchise—usually enters the business with a cash investment. The amount of this investment depends on the contract.

There are a number of franchised operations in existence today, selling such goods and services as automotive products, construction and remodeling materials, specialty foods, fast food services, paint and decorating supplies, laundry and dry-cleaning services, hotel and motel accommodations, and recreation and entertainment facilities.

Developing most recently is a new type of dealership in which the franchise holder pays a percentage of sales to the owner but has no obligation to buy franchise merchandise. In promoting its merchandise, however, the franchised store still uses the franchise name and stands to reap the benefits from advertising campaigns that the owner usually conducts. One retail furniture store became so successful because of its discount policy and unique advertising that it franchised its name to other furniture retailers for a fixed percentage of total sales.

This new kind of franchised organization is moderately successful. One obstacle for some retailers may be the franchise fee of 8 to 10

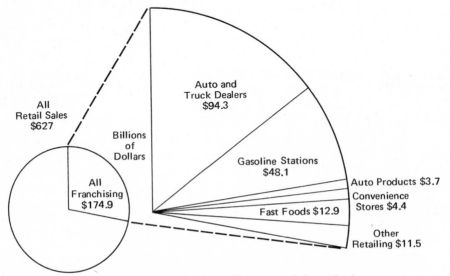

Franchise dealerships make up 28 percent of all retail sales.

THE ORGANIZATION OF RETAIL INSTITUTIONS

percent of sales, which is about double the usual advertising budget for a store. But very often, the increase in sales more than makes up for the fee.

LEASED DEALERSHIPS

The leased dealership is a variation of the franchised dealership. The dealer does not own the establishment but leases it from the company whose franchise he or she holds. The best-known example of the leased dealership is the service station. In most cases, service stations are owned by oil companies. An oil company rents the land, buildings, and major equipment to dealers. Each dealer then agrees to follow the oil company's operating policies and buys the gas and oil from the oil company.

The oil company maintains the property as well as the major equipment. The dealer's rent is usually a percentage of gasoline sales.

The major advantage of a leased dealership for the entrepreneur is that only a small investment is needed. With enough capital to buy the initial stock of merchandise, tools, and equipment, the leased dealership has many of the advantages that an independent business does.

CONSUMER COOPERATIVES

Stores that are owned by consumer groups are called *consumer cooperatives.* Each member of a co-op invests in the enterprise by buying shares. Each investment provides the capital needed for merchandise and operation. The consumer cooperative sells to all comers. But only those who have invested in the enterprise share in an annual distribution of the profits. Their share is based on the amount of their yearly purchases.

Most American cooperatives sell farm supplies. Others operate restaurants and groceries. Today members of minority groups are involved with food cooperatives in ghetto areas around the country. This experience opens up new opportunities in retailing and involves the whole community in alternative ways of buying. In some cases, a co-op venture may counter discrimination in hiring or pricing policies.

On a whole, though, cooperatives are not a significant force in American retailing. They have the same operating expenses that other stores have, and they remain unable to undersell their competitors by any significant margin. As long as the gap stays small, consumers will shop at more attractive stores with larger stocks.

The dealer in a leased dealership rents the land, buildings, and equipment, and buys the gas and oil from the oil company.
Courtesy Cities Service Company

TOPICS FOR DISCUSSION

1. How does the classification of stores benefit the retailing and manufacturing industries? What other enterprises besides the two mentioned here have an interest in store classification reports?
2. What are the basic differences between a corporate chain, a manufacturer-owned chain, and a leased department chain? Are there any similarities?
3. What advantages does the small independent have over larger retailing outlets?
4. Describe a cooperative chain and a voluntary chain. How does each operate? How do they differ?
5. Name at least three advantages the large independent has over the small independent store.
6. What are the major differences between an ownership group and a corporate chain? How does each work?
7. How can chains offer the expert knowledge of high-salaried display, advertising, and merchandising executives to their individual units?
8. Explain the operations of a leased department. What advantages, if any, does the leased department offer the store in which it operates?
9. How does the franchised dealership differ from the leased dealership?
10. How does the consumer cooperative differ from other types of retail outlets? Is the cooperative a significant competing force? Explain why or why not.

MATHEMATICS FOR RETAILING

A leased department in a large store sells high-priced jewelry. The department pays the store a flat $7,000 a year for rent plus $1\frac{1}{2}$ percent of its sales. Supplies used by the leased department are charged at the rate of .005 percent of sales, while the advertising and delivery costs are charged according to actual cost incurred.

If the leased department's sales were $80,000 a year, what would be the total amount, excluding advertising and delivery costs, it would have to pay the store?

COMMUNICATIONS IN RETAILING

You have confirmed your suspicion that some of the full-time salespeople in your department, who receive a commission on their sales, have been asking the part-time salespeople, who do not get commissions, to let them record their sales. You recognize the ethical problem as well as the fact that you will not be able to evaluate fairly the efficiency of your part-timers. Before the matter gets further out-of-hand, you decide to send each member of your department a memo. What points would you make in the memo, and how would you present your points?

MANAGING HUMAN RELATIONS

A leased-department owner in your store signed an agreement that he would abide by all the policies and regulations of your company. He agreed to place advertisements in the local paper to equal ten full pages a year. In addition, he said he would comply with the store's liberal return policies and participate in any seasonal sales announced by the store. He has kept to all points of his contract except the one about complying with the store's return policies. The leasing arrangement has been very profitable for both of you, yet you are uncomfortable about the number of steady customers who have expressed annoyance over his refusal to accept returned merchandise.

How would you handle this problem and encourage him to adjust his policy without alienating him? Be prepared to discuss your answer in class.

DECISION MAKING

You decide to go into the retail business and feel that a franchise arrangement offers you more opportunity than any other type of store ownership. You must decide between two different franchise plans.

One company's owners insist that you must purchase the bulk of all your merchandise through them. Prices will be set at a competitive level. All franchise holders of this company handle the exact same merchandise and sell it at similar prices. Training, store policies, and merchandise displays are arranged by the company, and each building houses the merchandise in exactly the same way. Payment of the franchise fee is based on store volume, and rent is paid to the company, since all franchisers must operate in a building owned and built by the company.

Another company's owners make no demands on you with regard to purchasing. You are allowed to buy in the open market and select the type and quality of merchandise you want for your particular store. Payment of the franchise fee is based on a percentage of sales only. The company provides no training or other assistance and does not require you to open your business on a specific site. Franchisers may set up business wherever they wish.

From which company would you choose a franchise? On a separate sheet of paper, list the advantages and disadvantages of both plans, and explain your reasons for choosing one over the other.

CAREER LADDER

Not all career opportunities in a retail store are the same. To determine the career outlook in both the franchised dealership and the corporate chain, follow the steps listed below. Report your findings to the class.

1. Choose both a specific local store that is owned by a franchisee and one owned by a corporate chain.
2. After making an appointment with the store manager, visit each store.
3. For each store, obtain a listing of jobs that covers all positions, from entry-level positions up to store manager.
4. List the duties and requirements (educational and other) for each position.

chapter 7

STORES CLASSIFIED BY MERCHANDISING CATEGORIES

Besides being classified by type of ownership, retail stores may be identified by the merchandise they carry. These outlets form two main groups: general merchandise stores and limited-line merchandise stores. Those selling general merchandise carry a wide variety of goods. The limited-line stores, however, restrict themselves to just one category or a few closely related lines. No merchandise specialty is too narrow to support some kind of store, but, on the other hand, there are few items so restricted that a general merchandise store will not consider selling them.

Retailing is a dynamic business that must adapt to changes in consumer demand. One of the greatest changes, which resulted from the demand for convenience shopping, is the trend to mix or scramble merchandise lines. Since World War II, more and more stores find it both necessary and profitable to expand their merchandise mix. Drugstores, service stations, and some neighborhood meat markets are just a few of the smaller retail establishments that have added nontraditional and impulse items to their shelves.

Today drugstores offer prepackaged clothing articles, toys, and gift items along with drugs and cosmetics. Service stations have vending machines that dispense soft drinks, candy, ice cubes, milk, bread, and other convenience items. Butchers sell limited assortments of canned goods and frozen foods, along with fresh meats. Some major department stores have crossed their traditional boundaries by adding full-scale meat markets, bakeries, and auto accessory shops. This enables them to compete with the supermarkets and discounters who have excelled in scrambled merchandising for years.

Expanding, reducing, or adding sections causes changes in the boundaries that divide stores into types. What may appear to be a rigid system of classification is not really so rigid after all. The edges tend to blur as one type of store enters the domain of another. However, the traditional categories still exist, and there are distinguishing characteristics for each category.

THE TRADITIONAL DEPARTMENT STORE

The traditional department store sells all kinds of merchandise for the individual and the home and offers a variety of items in each category. The broadest definition of a department store is that used by the Department of Commerce in classifying retail sales statistics:

An establishment normally employing 25 or more people and engaged in selling some items in each of the following lines of merchandise:

1. Furniture, home furnishings, appliances, radio and television sets

2. General apparel for the family

3. Household linen and dry goods

An establishment with total sales of less than $5,000,000 in which sales of any one of these groupings is greater than 80 percent of total sales is not classified as a department store.

An establishment with total sales of $5,000,000 or more is classified as a department store even if sales of one of the groupings described above is more than 80 percent of total sales, provided that the combined sales of the other two groups is $5,000,000 or more.

Competitive Position

One-stop shopping for the entire family has been the boast of traditional department stores for years. Along with this distinction, department stores have developed a policy of carrying full assortments of well-stocked merchandise, including items on the fringe of customer demand. Department store management believes that generating a large volume of sales depends on its ability to meet every customer need.

Events have proved the theory sound. In time, other types of stores tend to change into department stores. For example, the variety store grows up to become a "junior" department store. It, too, aims at becoming a one-stop shopping center. Soon the wider range of merchandise makes it desirable for the store to move into a busy high-rent location. Gradually, the growing variety store competes with the large department store not only in price but also in the services offered and in appearance.

The experience of meeting the discounters' competition has been difficult but healthy for department stores. They have learned from discounters that some of their services could be dropped, modified, or made optional. They have introduced self-service into appropriate departments, such as drugs and housewares, and many have changed their free-delivery policies. Many of them have kept their expense-to-sales ratio stable, in spite of the pressure of mounting costs and discount-price competition.

Locations

Because of its nature and size, the traditional department store is located in the main shopping area of the city, serving customers from many neighborhoods. In the past, the presence of a department store actually created the main shopping area, for smaller retailers and chain stores clustered around it in order to benefit from its customers. The arrangement was mutually advantageous. The department store gained as well by the presence of the other stores, for they helped to assure a steady stream of traffic.

Today the attraction of the department store in its downtown location has not been strong enough to overcome the inconvenience of shopping downtown. So department stores have been forced to follow their customers to the suburbs by building branch stores. The typical department store today is not a single retail establishment but a multi-unit organization, doing business in at least two—and often in several—locations. In recent years, department stores have been doing about half of their total business in branch stores and half in their main, or downtown, stores. This is an average figure for all department stores. Thus, while the smallest were still making most of their sales downtown, the biggest were making most of theirs in branch units.

Many of the shopping centers which contain department store branches are owned by one department store. This store leases space to other retail stores, including its competitors, and to other tenants, such as restaurants, banks, and service establishments. In this way, the department store re-creates the competitive downtown shopping environment in which it thrives—without adding the inconvenience of downtown shopping.

Branch and Twig

Branch stores have grown dramatically in the past 10 years. The typical department store branch is a trimmed-down version of the main store. The "high-ticket" departments, such as furniture and furs, may be eliminated. Within the branch-store departments, the selections may be just as wide as those of the main store's departments, somewhat narrower, or very much narrower. This is because the customers in any one suburban trading area are much more alike than the people who shop downtown. A department store branch, for example, may have a children's department that is as large as the one in the main store because it has so many young mothers among its customers. But a branch located in a retirement community will offer a smaller selection of children's wear than the main store.

The *twig* is a small branch that carries only one line of merchandise or a few related lines. The department store builds a twig when its site-selection experts see a special opportunity for a particular kind of business in some trading area, but not for a full-department branch. The twig may be either in a shopping center or in a special location off a highway. Its particular merchandise line might be children's clothing, shoes for the family, auto supplies, or garden equipment.

THE DISCOUNT DEPARTMENT STORE

Cut-rate retail stores sell merchandise that includes major appliances and hard goods (durable items) as well as apparel and other soft goods (perishable goods). Discount stores have a rela-

tively short but exceptional history. Though a few were in existence during the 1930s, their full impact did not hit traditional retailing circles until 20 years later. Most of the early discounters specialized in the cut-price retailing of national-brand electrical appliances, major kitchen equipment, television sets, and other hard goods. In the late 1950s and early 1960s came the soft goods discounters, offering bargains in apparel and textile merchandise. Many discounters of both types have expanded into the general merchandise field and have become discount department stores or junior department stores.

Mass Merchandising Policies

A discount department store sells both home furnishings and apparel. Like the traditional department store, it operates as a one-stop shopping center for all family needs.

While the discount department store has the wide variety of merchandise associated with a department store, it generally does not have the same broad assortment in each category. One reason is that some national-brand manufactur-

In today's mass merchandise store, a self-service policy reduces costs for the retailer, who passes the savings on to the customers.
Courtesy *Chain Store Age General Merchandise Group*

THE ORGANIZATION OF RETAIL INSTITUTIONS

ers do not want to have their merchandise sold in discount stores. Those that deal directly with retailers, rather than through wholesalers, can enforce this policy. Another reason, equally important, is that the discount store does not meet the department store ideal of having everything in stock at all times. The discounter concentrates on the fastest-moving merchandise and shops carefully for special buys of all kinds, even though these may throw the store's assortments out of balance.

Price Policies

The discount store sells nationally advertised brands below list prices. Discounters have largely defeated the efforts of brand-name manufacturers to set the prices at which retailers must sell. From the beginning, discounters ignored list-pricing requirements and frustrated manufacturers' efforts to close their sources of wholesale supply. They argued convincingly in the courts that if they could make branded products available to customers at prices lower than those set by other stores, they had the right to do so.

Today's Image

The discounters of the early 1950s went into business with little capital and limited credit. They rented in low-cost locations away from the mainstream of shopping. They sold their merchandise in self-service, supermarket style. They could not afford anything more than basic service and a bare, undecorated shopping place. All purchases were made with cash. As a rule, they counted on low prices to overcome what they frankly regarded as shopping inconveniences.

Price appeal certainly was and is their strong point. But, more than that, customers did not find the stores inconvenient. They liked them. However remote they were from regular shopping districts, the discounters were still handier for suburban shoppers than the crowded downtown sections. They offered plenty of parking space, and their evening and Sunday hours met a need that had been largely ignored by traditional stores. Over time, supermarkets had conditioned

customers to accept, and often prefer, self-service. Indeed, the national brands which they featured were presold by national advertising. All the customers wanted to do was compare the selling price with the advertised list price.

Today's discount department stores carry a variety of merchandise in the lower price ranges and offer it in attractive surroundings. For these stores, the descriptive term "discounter" is now disappearing. In fact, there are many customers who do not think of stores such as E. J. Korvette, Arlan, Vornado, and Miracle Mart as anything but regular department stores that have lively ideas about promotion and shopping.

Expenses and Margins

Competition in pricing has its limits. The natural tendency of successful discounters is to emphasize services, such as credit and delivery. Their new stores are often as attractive as those of their neighbors in the suburbs, the department store branches, and the new stores are just as expensive to build and maintain. The discounters have sought high-traffic locations, which means higher rent. With their expansion to department-store-type businesses, they have increased buying and management expenses as well. All this means compromising their original goal of offering low prices.

Discount department stores have kept their price-cutting practices with regard to well-known national brands. But increasingly they are turning to private brands and unbranded merchandise, which yield higher margins. By carrying these items, discounters avoid the risk of direct price comparison.

Some of the major retailers have opened discount chains of their own. Allied, Bell/Nugent, Federated, J. C. Penney, May, Strawbridge & Clothier, Kresge, Woolworth, and Food Fair are just a few. Learning from the mistakes of their predecessors, many of them have done a better job of fashion merchandising and improving their assortments to attract younger customers and a greater variety of customers.

As a group, however, the discount retailers

have experienced a substantial decline in earnings. Several major stores have reported high deficits, probably due to overexpansion and the failure to build strong management teams to support the new stores.

Future mass merchandisers will follow one of two different paths. Some will be built on a small scale, about one-half to one-third the size of today's stores. Others will be built on a grand scale, patterned after the huge stores now operating in parts of Europe. An example in this country is America Meijer Incorporated of Grand Rapids, Michigan, which covers a staggering 5 acres, or more space than two football fields! Designed after the hypermarkets of France and Germany, it sells merchandise at a discount, right from the original packing cases.

THE SUPERSTORE—HYPERMARCHE

The superstore is designed to serve all the needs of a customer including those now served by the supermarket. It is designed to be a place where people can make all types of routine purchases. The first hypermarche (high-per-mar-shay) opened in France in 1963. It covered over 5 acres of floor space and offered a staggering quantity of food and nonfood products, selling at about 15 percent below regular store prices. There are over 1,000 hypermarche stores in Europe, and several are operating in Canada. In the United States, such firms as Jewel in Chicago and Great Scott Supermarkets in Detroit have introduced the superstore. It is expected that in the 1980's the phenomenon will be widespread in metropolitan areas across the country.

The original store, called "Carrefour" (Crossroads), is based in Paris and boasts sales of $70 million to $90 million per outlet. This is much more than the $20 million to $30 million earned by United States supermarket outlets. Merchandise is stacked 10 feet high; stocks are replenished by forklift trucks. Superstores have 50 to 60 checkout counters to handle their customer traffic. The biggest items are groceries, which are

The hypermarche carries an enormous variety of merchandise which is usually stacked from the floor to ceiling in aisle after aisle. There may be as many as 50 checkout counters to serve the large number of customers.

bought directly from farmers and producers. This makes warehousing unnecessary.

Experts predict that the American superstore will measure about 150,000 square feet and be located in an area that can be reached by car by 80,000 people within 15 minutes. Should a serious economic crisis develop, the experts say that hypermarkets will be less affected than other distributors because they sell practically nothing but staples.

THE DEPARTMENTIZED SPECIALTY STORE

The *departmentized specialty store* is one that follows the same plan of organization as the department store but does not carry as complete a range of merchandise. Usually it does not sell large electrical appliances, furniture, hardware, or housewares, unless one of these lines of merchandise is its main specialty. In its apparel divisions, however, the departmentized specialty store does have the same variety and wide assortments as the department store.

Examples of large departmentized specialty stores are the I. Magnin stores on the West Coast; Julius Garfinkel, Washington, D.C.; Neiman-Marcus, Dallas; Filene's, Boston; and the Saks Fifth Avenue stores.

The departmentized specialty store is so much like the department store in its policies and carries such a wide range of merchandise that its customers generally regard it as a department store. However, it does not meet the Department of Commerce definition of a department store.

The Supermarket

The supermarket is a departmentized food store, usually self-service, selling groceries, dairy products, meats, and fresh produce, along with nonfood items. The supermarket defies precise definition because of the popular trend to mix food and nonfood products. The giant supers have crossed merchandise boundaries so much that, along with their traditional produce, they now offer customers small housewares, books, phonograph records, toys, toiletries, drugs, plants, hardware, and apparel. In short, today's supermarkets are a combination of food and variety stores, and because of their tremendous size, they are not unlike departmentized specialty stores. With this in mind, some analysts have described the supermarket as "a departmentized retail store having annual sales of $1 million or more in a variety of merchandise, and in which the sale of food, much of which is on a self-service basis, plays the major role."[1]

The supermarket's ability to return a satisfactory profit out of a small gross margin depends on a large volume of sales in one location. The supermarket must draw customers from a wide trading area, as in a regional shopping center, or else the store must be in a high-population center, such as a neighborhood with large apartment houses.

[1] Charles F. Phillips and Delbert J. Duncan, *Marketing Principles and Methods,* Richard D. Irwin, Inc., Homewood, Ill., p. 218.

In recent years supermarkets accounted for 76 percent of the grocery sales in the country, although they represent only 10 percent of all the retail establishments that the Department of Commerce describes as food stores.

Corporate chains dominate the supermarket field. Not more than 20 percent of the supermarkets are independently owned, and many of these belong to the voluntary chains described earlier.

The Appeal of Self-Service

Supermarkets, the pioneers in self-service, showed department and discount stores how to reduce expenses by getting customers to serve themselves. More than that, they demonstrated that with proper displays customers serving themselves will buy more than those who have to ask for an item or rely on someone to suggest it. Supermarket retailers know what locations, what display levels, and what positions are most valuable for their products. National brands compete with store brands for the best shelf space.

Supermarkets also apply the principle of self-service to nonfood merchandise. The variety of these items sold in supermarkets increases each year. Nonfood merchandise is often supplied to supermarkets and to food stores by rack jobbers. *Rack jobbers* are wholesalers who sell on consignment. That is, they receive payment only for the merchandise consumers buy. Jobbers choose the assortment, stock the shelves, and replenish them when the merchandise runs out.

While price appeal is the strong point of the supermarket, the convenience of well-organized self-service and one-stop family marketing is equally important to customers. But since many areas cannot support large supermarkets, small grocery stores and other food stores are still thriving. Their customer appeal is not based on price or merchandise assortment but on convenience. In addition, some kinds of food retailing do not lend themselves to mass handling. Delicatessens, pastry shops, and health food shops can and do flourish in the shadow of the supermarket.

Competing with the supermarkets are the big general mass merchandise stores. They have set up food stores of their own, just as the food supermarkets have branched out into other fields.

Today supermarkets sell for cash. But we are rapidly approaching cashless buying in all areas of retailing. Very likely supermarkets will get into the credit business. Some experiments with using credit plans are already taking place. Credit is strictly limited to 30 days. This development may raise prices to cover the expense of financing and billing. But it will further cut down the competitive advantage of the small neighborhood groceries, many of which have always offered the service of buying on credit.

THE JUNIOR DEPARTMENT STORE

In trying to describe the general merchandise store that is almost but not quite a full department store, the retail trade has come up with a classification called the *junior department store*. The junior department store carries a considerable variety of merchandise and has a departmentized organization. But while the departmentized specialty store is strong in apparel and generally carries higher-priced merchandise, the junior department store is likely to have grown from a moderate-price family apparel store, a dry goods store, or a variety store.

J. C. Penney stores are examples of junior department stores that evolved from dry goods stores and are on their way to becoming full-line department stores.

THE VARIETY STORE

The variety store was once popularly called a five-and-dime in the United States because its merchandise was limited to inexpensive items. The variety store has a definite merchandising policy: it sells whatever lends itself to a quick sales transaction, generally with no exchange at all between the customer and the salesperson. This means that the merchandise must be rela-

tively minor items in the customer's budget. Within these limits, the variety store is truly a general merchandise store, stocking such items as pots and pans, lipsticks, novelty jewelry, and inexpensive curtains and linens.

High Visibility Display

To make sales transactions as quick and simple as possible, the variety store has developed its own style of merchandise display. Packaging is designed so that merchandise will be easily visible to the self-service customer. Stock is arranged on binned tables and shelved fixtures from which the customer makes a selection. A cashier then wraps or bags the item and takes the customer's money.

Only the supermarket can match the variety store in setting up efficient displays that make selecting easy. Bright lighting is often used. It doesn't glamorize the merchandise, but it does give the items high visibility.

In the variety store merchandise is arranged on binned tables and shelves so that the customer may easily make a quick selection.
Photograph by Fern Logan

Most variety stores are chain stores. The stores of any one chain look alike from the outside. On the inside, they all follow the same pattern of display. Again, the purpose is to make shopping quick and easy. A customer who has shopped in one Woolworth store will feel at home in any other.

Because so little time is spent on any one transaction, the customer is likely to stop at several counters and may wind up making quite a lot of purchases. This makes it very worthwhile for the variety store to operate in high-rent locations, whether downtown or in the suburbs. Once the variety store drew its customers from nearby department and specialty stores. People ended a day's shopping by dropping into a variety store for small items because it was tiresome to hunt these items down in the department store. Today the variety store, with its wider range of merchandise, generates customer traffic of its own. It remains the first choice of many customers for items such as stationery, cosmetics, kitchen gadgets, hair goods, small hardware, and a quick lunch. Among shopping-center developers, the variety store is a highly valued establishment in the center's complex of stores.

Expanded Merchandise Lines

In developing its business, the variety store is likely to experiment with merchandise types and merchandise price lines that allow it to compete directly with the department store. For example, the variety store's toy section may branch out from small pickup toys into an assortment of larger wheel toys. But as price limits edge upward, shoppers do not select merchandise so quickly. Consequently, the variety store needs more selling time and may require an informed salesperson rather than a clerk.

A few variety store chains have expanded their merchandise lines to the point where they now call some of their units junior department stores. J. J. Newberry is an example. F. W. Woolworth, however, draws a sharp line between the variety store and department store types of operation. It has established a separate chain of junior dis-count department stores called Woolco Department Stores. The Woolworth stores themselves keep their variety store character. The K-Mart stores form the discount division of the familiar S. S. Kresge variety chain.

THE GENERAL STORE

The general store described in Chapter 1 survives today only in isolated rural areas. Particularly in towns with summer visitors, it enjoys a special appeal, and often its summer business may be enough to keep it going for the entire year. The general store still carries groceries, housewares, and a wide selection of other goods, though the variety of merchandise depends on customer demand and competitors.

LIMITED-LINE STORES

Retail establishments that sell only one kind of merchandise or a selection of closely related goods are *limited-line stores*. Limited-line stores deal in all kinds of merchandise: apparel, foods, home furnishings, electrical appliances, automobiles and accessories, hardware, lumber—the list is endless. Limited-line retailing is mostly a field of small independent enterprises, although many national chains have limited-line stores, too.

That all these specialized retailers flourish in America today is proof that retailing is as diverse as the society it serves. In spite of all the advantages of one-stop shopping, the customer is not bound to it.

Apparel and Accessories Stores

Even though a limited-line store specializes in a particular type of merchandise, the retail trade does not call it a specialty store or a specialty shop. A *specialty shop* is an outlet for women's apparel and related lines of accessories. At one time, a specialty shop meant high fashion, like that of Bergdorf Goodman, Bonwit Teller, or Hattie Carnegie. Nowadays the term refers to apparel shops in all price ranges. These include popular-price stores such as those of the Lerner chain, discount-type shops such as those of the Virginia Dare chain, and the middle-to-high-price stores such as I. Magnin.

Other limited-line apparel stores are called specialty shops. They are defined by the name of the merchandise in which they specialize, such as men's clothing, infants' and children's wear, shoes, millinery, corsets, and lingerie. There are also family apparel stores. And there are some very narrow specialty shops that sell only handbags and costume jewelry, or only sweaters and skirts, or neckties, or hosiery, or maternity clothes.

Home-Furnishings Stores

There are over 90,000 limited-line stores that sell home furnishings, radios, television sets, and electrical appliances. Like the apparel stores, they are quite diverse and range from the big departmentized store to small shops such as those that sell china and glassware. Although there are relatively few limited-line home-furnishings stores, they can be quite large.

Retailers who sell electrical appliances, radios, and television sets deal with merchandise that is presold by national advertising. The only competition is in terms of price, and so the chains of appliance and radio and TV stores that buy in quantity have an advantage over the small independents. The independents who compete best are those who offer custom work, such as built-in television and music systems and specially designed kitchens.

Some capital investment is necessary to start a limited-line home-furnishings store. To sell furniture, rugs, and related lines and to compete successfully, the store must extend credit, and extending credit requires capital. In addition, investment in inventory is large—much larger than for an apparel store with the same annual sales volume. A dress shop, turning over its inventory six times a year, can realize sales of $200,000 with an average merchandise inventory of only $33,350 in retail value, or about $18,000 in wholesale value. To realize the same sales total, a furniture store will need an average

inventory of as much as $100,000 in retail value, or $50,000 to $60,000 in wholesale value.

In narrower home-furnishings specialties, however, for which the capital investment requirements are not as great, small enterprises can be very successful. Small china and glassware shops and upholstery and drapery shops are good examples. These shops are appealing to customers because they carry so much in limited categories. Very often the owners' tastes even match their own.

Automobile Dealers

So far the automobile dealers—about 100,000 throughout the country—have their field to themselves. As yet scrambled merchandising has not brought department stores or chain stores into competition with them. This is not true of the limited-line outlets, usually associated with service stations, that sell tires and other auto accessories. The general chains, discount stores, and department stores are invading the auto accessories market by leasing shops.

Lumber and Hardware Dealers

Like the automobile dealers, the retailers of lumber and building supplies compete with each other rather than with general merchandisers. They deal with a knowledgeable class of customers who require specialized service. Although hardware stores do a good part of their business in small everyday items and housewares, they must also meet the needs of carpenters, builders, and other tradespeople, as well as serious do-it-yourselfers.

SERVICE ESTABLISHMENTS

American consumers spend more than $6 billion a year on automobile services and automobile rentals; $4 billion for the laundering, cleaning, and repairing of their clothes and shoes; $5 billion in beauty salons and barbershops; and $1 billion for radio and television repairs. These and similar nonprofessional services are sold in about 650,000 specialized establishments. Many of these services are also available in department stores, chain stores, and discount stores.

Department stores have always included some service departments, which gave the independent service establishments moderate competition in a few areas. Among them are beauty salons, furniture upholstery, rug cleaning, photography, fur repair and cleaning, and lending libraries. Many department stores offer medical services as well, such as an eye clinic.

Although department stores regard the service departments as a means of attracting customers for their merchandise departments, some are also beginning to regard service departments as a potential source of profit. These stores are branching out into entirely new fields: automobile servicing; fuel-oil deliveries; home-improvement services; classes in dancing, driving, and good grooming; and theater-ticket service. Some have counters for selling mutual funds and life insurance. But this list only skims the surface. There is hardly any paid service—from renting lockers to landscaping gardens—that is not for sale in some department store, discount store, or chain store.

Consumer interest in the service business indicates the growing importance of purchased services. Some advisers to big retail stores consider the service business so important that they recommend a position for a top-level merchandise manager who will supervise all service departments. They suggest that these stores consolidate all service departments into big service centers in one wing of the store or in an annex.

Surely these big outlets can cut into the business of small independent establishments. But the average service business is a convenience to neighborhood residents who are likely to shop nearby. In this field, as in so many merchandise fields, the independent worries mainly about the growth of chain-owned competition.

Rental Services

One of the newest types of service, which marketing experts say will become a common part of American living, is the rental of merchandise and equipment. The same reasons that make automobile rental sometimes more desirable than ownership apply to many other items as well. United Rent-All, with more than 300 franchised outlets, has built a successful business on the premise that people don't want to pay for or keep things that they use only occasionally.

This assumption applies to a considerable variety of merchandise, including wedding gowns and evening clothes, furs, floor sanders and waxers, every kind of equipment for the ill and disabled, playpens and beds, power tools, and party equipment.

As all renters of equipment know, more is required to open a service business than just money. Skilled maintenance and repair work are necessary. This is why department stores and discount stores will probably continue to lease store space to specialists rather than manage the services themselves.

Catalog Showroom Stores

In the early 1970s, the idea of a catalog showroom store showed great promise, but by 1975 growth had slowed considerably. This type of store relies almost entirely on catalogs, heavily financed by vendors, to sell the merchandise. The customer shops either in the store or at home, with a catalog. In some catalog stores the merchandise listed in the catalog is on display. Displayed merchandise is limited to just one of a kind, but a hidden storage area may hold the stock in quantity. Orders are filled in just a few minutes, and sales are on a cash-and-carry basis. Most catalog showrooms honor national credit cards, although few, if any, extend in-store credit.

Catalog showrooms are usually located away from the high-rent districts, most often along highways, and they usually occupy only a single floor. They have a small staff of order takers and cashiers. Prices are usually below those of the traditional retail stores.

The catalog showroom's decline can be traced to its inability to offer merchandise at prices substantially lower than those of discount stores. Further problems relate to the number of showrooms opening up and crowding an already crowded discount scene. Inflation has caused catalog prices to become obsolete by the time the showroom makes goods available. Some showrooms have announced a 10 percent addition on prices listed.

NONSTORE SELLING

Not all retailing goes on in stores. Some merchandise and services are ordered by customers from catalogs, mailers, or newspaper and magazine advertisements. Other forms of nonstore retailing are in-the-home selling, manufacturers' salesroom selling, and selling from vending machines.

Catalog Retailing

Much of what used to be called the mail-order business is more accurately called catalog selling today. For example, Sears, Roebuck and Company earns over $1.5 billion of its more than $13 billion annual volume from the orders from its catalogs. But less than one-quarter of these orders are placed by mail. About 30 percent come over the telephone, and the rest are placed in person by customers who visit catalog sales office or the catalog order desk in a Sears store.

Catalog-order business in the big general merchandise chains is increasing, although the mail-order portion of it is declining. Sears had seven catalog offices in 1938. Today it has more than a thousand. Montgomery Ward has almost tripled the number of its catalog stores. And as further evidence that the catalog business is considered to have a good future, the J. C. Penney Company began to publish catalogs in the early 1960s. By 1974 catalog sales had begun to show a profit for this company.

The catalog sales office doesn't stock any merchandise, although it does display some. Catalogs are at the counters for customers to use. Clerks help customers make selections and then fill out the order forms for them. Next the order forms are forwarded to the nearest warehouse so the orders can be filled. After the merchandise is sent to the catalog sales office, the customers are notified that the items have arrived. When the customers return to the office, they may inspect the merchandise to make sure everything is satisfactory.

Advantages and Disadvantages. Selling by mail order from a catalog means that merchandise can be stored in an inexpensive warehouse instead of in a busy store location. Order clerks, kept steadily busy, are less of an expense than salespeople who are rushed at peak shopping hours and idle during slower periods. There are no walkouts by customers who cannot get a salesperson's attention or who see long checkout lines. Delivery costs are usually paid by the customer.

Disadvantages of mail-order shopping are the chores of filling out the order form and computing the charges, as well as being unable to see the merchandise until it has arrived at home. The help of a clerk and the chance to reject merchandise upon its delivery make ordering through a sales office a better system for customers. They can examine a huge assortment of merchandise, either at home or in the catalog office, and this is a considerable advantage. The Sears semiannual catalog, for example, shows over 150,000 items.

On the other hand, catalogs are expensive to produce. They must be very precise because the text and pictures must substitute for an examination of the merchandise itself. Also, items returned by customers may be damaged, and, by nature, catalog retailers must be liberal in their return policy. Finally, a catalog may have a very long life once it is in the customer's hands. So catalog businesses must calculate very carefully how much merchandise must be kept in stock and for how long. By issuing catalogs in the spring and in the fall, they can more or less set a limit on the amount of stock kept on hand.

The "big four" in the catalog business, which account for 75 percent of the trade, are Sears, Ward, Spiegel, and Penney's. In addition, there are about 2,500 other mail-order houses, most of them specializing in apparel, gift items, home

Some catalog retailers offer their customers the convenience of telephone order service. These people take orders and compute charges for customers who prefer to remain at home while making their selections from catalogs.
Courtesy Sears Roebuck and Co.

furnishings, novelties, and other limited lines. These companies have more serious inventory-control problems, although many become successful by specializing in merchandise that doesn't go out-of-date.

Some of the nation's leading department stores offer the convenience of catalog buying through special promotional mailers. These are usually geared to seasonal buying periods, such as Thanksgiving and Christmas, and to special events, such as spring home-furnishings sales. Often these miniature catalogs are included with monthly mailings to charge customers, who are invited to write or call in their orders and charge their purchases.

Telephone Order Service. Catalog retailers operate at an advantage when they have trained clerks who accept phone orders and also compute charges. Not only mail-order houses but also most big department stores are introducing this convenience. Department stores offer Sunday phone order service and toll-free calls to encourage phone orders. This is a form of catalog retailing, although the catalog in the case of the department store is probably an advertisement in the Sunday papers. The Bell Telephone System refers to those who order by phone as the "locked-in shoppers"—customers who remain at home because of bad weather or illness, or because they have no babysitter.

In-the-Home Retailing

There are over 66,000 business organizations that use door-to-door selling methods. Their annual sales are in excess of $2.5 billion. This figure does not include money earned through in-the-home selling activities of established retail stores. Increasingly, department stores and home-furnishings stores are offering customers the service of selecting floor coverings, upholstery, custom draperies, and other home furnishings at home. For merchandise that involves measurement, estimating, and choosing colors and fabrics, at-home service is a convenience. For the store that has developed good salesworkers, it is profitable. In addition, selling at a customer's home gives the smart salesperson an idea of what other home furnishings the customer might need.

Stores may use outside sales representatives to sell storm windows and kitchen equipment. Customers of a food-plan organization shop at home, using special lists to order food items to store in the freezer purchased from the organization.

House-to-house selling accounts for more than one-fifth of the 2 billion dollars' worth of cosmetics sold each year. Leaders in this method of direct selling are Avon Products and Helene Curtis. Other well-known businesses are the Fuller Brush Company and the Electrolux Corporation. Magazine publishers, encyclopedia publishers, some manufacturers of cooking ware, and even producers of custom-tailored clothes, who sell from pictures and fabric samples, use house-to-house selling.

Some house-to-house salespeople are order takers, operating on a generous commission, but many are really independent, franchised dealers in their own right. They actually own the merchandise they sell. A major drawback to house-to-house selling is getting access to customers. They may be afraid of intruders or inhospitable to uninvited visitors.

Route salespeople for food distributors are like house-to-house salespeople. They provide a convenient service for "locked-in shoppers." The route sales staff of one firm that sells in 42 states reportedly takes orders for some 300 food items and more than 26,000 types of general merchandise.

Automatic Vending

Improvements in vending machines over the last 20 years have resulted in many new locations for selling merchandise and services through machines. Because they are automatic, vending machines can operate 24 hours a day. The four leading items sold through automatic vending machines are candy, coffee, cigarettes, and cold drinks, but many other foods are available through these machines: hot foods, sandwiches, fruit, milk, cookies, and ice cream. Among the successful additions to automatic vending are stockings, handkerchiefs, combs, aspirin, toiletries, paperback books, newspapers, and railroad tickets. There are automatic shoeshine machines, copying machines, and dollar-bill changers.

Many retailers now sell shopping bags from machines located all around their stores, and several have experimented with vending machines to sell their merchandise. In Stockholm, Zurich, and other European cities, banks of vending machines greet customers at the main entrance of some stores after they close. The machines dispense a variety of small convenience goods—items that are purchased frequently for immediate use.

To date, the vending of foods has proved most profitable in the United States, where more than 6,000 vending service companies together realize total sales of close to $5 billion annually.

Of course, the key to the vending machine's success now and in the future is convenience. In the minds of some retail prophets, the store that is one big vending machine is always just around the corner. In Germany, Austria, and Switzerland, huge vending machines which dispense as many as 1,000 different items are already quite popular.

Syndication

Holders of credit cards from various oil companies such as Exxon and Texaco are not always aware of the tremendous business that results from the merchandise advertisements included in the monthly oil company bill. These four-color advertisements are the result of the efforts of *syndicators*—companies that sell merchandise directly to customers who hold credit cards. The business has grown significantly in the United States. It began in 1955, when for the first time syndicators used credit-card mailing lists to sell their programs. The liberal credit policies of companies like American Express and Diner's Club enhanced the appeal of the syndicators' direct-mail promotions. By the early 1960s, syndicators had encouraged the petroleum companies to enter the field, too. Syndicators operate by giving a percentage of sales to the credit card companies for the items sold.

Manufacturers usually retain ownership of the merchandise and perform the jobs of stocking items and filling orders. They also handle all returns from the customers. Syndicators are most often responsible for printing promotional material, mailing, test-marketing programs, and initiating the direct-mail promotion itself. The credit card company assumes the responsibility for billing customers, financing the accounts, and paying for the test-market run.

Oil companies and credit card businesses use syndication because they find that it not only activates old accounts but also gives them additional income and profit. According to many, syndication has increased their sales as well as the number of times customers see the firms' names.

For customers, syndicate retailing offers an easy, convenient way to shop for merchandise they often cannot get in traditional retail stores. They order through the mail or on an easy check-off form that often entitles them to free gifts, free trial periods to use and examine the merchandise, and easy payment plans.

TOPICS FOR DISCUSSION

1. According to the Department of Commerce, what types of merchandise must a store carry to qualify as a department store?
2. What are "twigs," and why do parent stores establish them? How do they differ from branch units?
3. Trace the history of the discount store from the early 1950s to today. Comment on changes in its line of merchandise, and on its overall image.
4. What effects have discount stores had on traditional department stores?
5. What are the advantages and disadvantages of the superstore?
6. What is the appeal of self-service to the customer? In what kinds of stores is it used?
7. What are limited-line stores? What are some of the merchandise lines they carry?
8. What is the predicted trend in service retailing? Do you agree or disagree with the prediction? Why?
9. What are the advantages and disadvantages of catalog retailing for the consumer? For the company?
10. Why have some credit card companies accepted the programs of syndicators?

COMMUNICATIONS IN RETAILING

You are the sales manager in a retail catalog store whose policy is to accept returned merchandise within 14 days after purchase. A customer complains in a letter that one of your clerks refused to accept some merchandise, even though it was returned within the time limit. The customer was so irritated by the incident that she threatened not to shop in your store again. You must now take action to pacify the customer and win her back. You must also find the clerk who refused to accept the merchandise and get that clerk's side of the story. All your clerks are busy, and the number of customers looking through your catalogs indicates that it will probably be a very busy day. You decide to contact the customer immediately. Although you don't know why the clerk refused the customer's returned merchandise, you feel you must uphold the company's integrity. On a separate sheet of paper, write a short reply to the customer that will regain her loyalty.

MANAGING HUMAN RELATIONS

During a lull in business one afternoon, you find time to ask your clerks if they have ever refused returned merchandise. One of your clerks informs you that he had done so just the other day because this particular customer has made a habit of returning about half of her purchases. After reading the letter from the customer described in the previous exercise, the clerk recognizes the customer's name and continues to give you all the details. "She was so insistent," the clerk explains, "and it was the third purchase she had returned in the last two weeks. I really felt that if I refused her just once, she would learn to be a more responsible shopper." You realize the clerk was sincere, but you must correct his attitude. How might you do this without making him lose confidence or causing him to become inefficient? Be prepared to discuss your answer in class.

CAREER LADDER

A young woman, graduating from a community college with a marketing major, is planning a career as an apparel buyer. There are several retail establishments near her suburban town where she is considering applying for her first full-time job. These include:

• A large department store. The main store and two of its five branches are nearby. The store has a management-training program.

• A unit of a national mass-merchandise chain. This company also has management training programs.

• A departmentized specialty store selling high fashion merchandise. The main store, downtown, and the branch are within commuting distance.

• An independently-owned boutique selling middle-to-high price junior sportswear.

What advice would you give this young woman about the pros and cons of applying to each of these stores for a position?

chapter 8
INTERNAL ORGANIZATION OF FIRMS

A customer walking into a retail store usually observes only the functions of those people who provide service—salespeople, cashiers, wrappers, or order takers. To such a customer, the functions of retailing appear simple to perform and few in number. To the person who is knowledgeable about retailing, its functions are many and quite complicated.

A retail store, like any other business, must make a profit if it is to continue in business. To achieve this end, the retailer must sell merchandise at prices greater than the original costs. In selling at a profit, a number of different activities are involved, some of which are only remotely connected to buying and selling. For the people who perform these activities to contribute to the efficiency of the operation, each store develops an organization plan relating the various functions to each other.

THE BASIC FUNCTIONS OF RETAILING

Regardless of size, all retailing firms have several basic functions. Assume, for example, that you wanted to start a soft-drink stand. First, you would need to decide where your stand should be located, how large it should be, and what storage and sales space it should have. This is usually classified as part of *store operations.*

Next, you would need to determine what soft-drink brands to carry; how many to buy; where to buy them; how much to pay for them; and how much to sell them for in order to cover the cost of the drinks, the cost of the selling and storage areas, and the cost of your time and labor. This is known as *merchandising* and *buying.*

Third, you would need to obtain the money to cover the initial costs, either from your own savings or by borrowing from family, friends, or a bank. You would also need to keep detailed records of sales, sales taxes, costs of goods, and payments made to the firms from which the soft drinks were obtained. These tasks are part of the *finance* and *control* function.

Fourth, you would need to let people know that you were open for business. You might put up signs, distribute leaflets, advertise in a local paper, or just shout your wares as customers walked by. These activities are part of *sales promotion.*

Division of Work by Functions

The *organization* of any firm is the grouping of related jobs according to the basic or main functions to be performed. A *function* is the actual work purpose that different jobs have in common. The basic-four function plan described above, known as the "Mazur plan," has been recognized by retailers since 1927, when Paul M. Mazur recommended it to the National Retail Merchants Association. The four functions— (1) merchandising and buying, (2) finance and control, (3) sales promotion, and (4) store operations—are basic because they occur in *every* retail enterprise, regardless of the size of the firm or the number of people employed.

Some firms find it necessary to divide these functions in various ways. *Personnel* activities, for example, which include hiring, training, and firing people, may be part of the store operations function, or they may be classified as a separate function. Similarly, subfunctions concerning real estate, credit, and catalog preparation may be so important in some firms that they are classified as independent functions.

Responsibility and Lines of Authority

In a small store, all functions may be performed by one person—the owner or manager. In a partnership operation, the four basic functions may be divided between two people: one may be in charge of merchandising and sales promotion, while the other takes care of finance and control and store operations. As a store grows, a manager may be placed in charge of each function.

In a large store, each function may be given the status of a division, with a division manager in charge. The division manager may report to a general manager. If the general manager is not the owner of the store, that person is in turn responsible to the owner or president. If the store is a publicly owned corporation, the president is responsible to a board of directors and to the stockholders.

The Line Organization and the Staff Organization

As soon as more than one person must be hired to do a certain job, lines of authority need to be established. Thus, if you hired a person to sell in your soft-drink stand, you would need to arrange the times that individual would work, explain the rate of pay, discuss the way to treat customers, and show how to handle the money and record the sales. You would establish a *line* of authority, and the person you employed would report to you.

Similarly, within each major function in a store, a line from the manager of the work area extends to those at each lower level who assist in performing the work. Thus a merchandise manager may need help from a buyer, who, in turn, needs

help from an assistant buyer, who needs a merchandise clerk to do detail work. A line of command is formed, and orders usually pass from the top to the bottom of such a line. Reports of work accomplished go from the person with the lowest rank, known as the *subordinate,* to those above, known as the *supervisors.*

Staff functions are work performed by persons outside the line of command to aid the division. For example, if a merchandiser in a large firm wished to have the research staff determine the number of customers who might buy a new type of product, such a request would be made to the head of the research department. The research personnel would serve as consultants in performing this service for the merchandising division. They may also perform research services for the finance, store operations, and sales promotion divisions.

Within the research department itself, a line of command would extend from the research director to the assistant and then to the research workers.

The Organization Chart

An organization chart shows how the operation of the business is divided into functions and subfunctions—that is, divisions and departments—and how lines of authority and staff functions relate to each other.

Even though many firms have elaborate organization charts, few companies have grown entirely according to a plan. In most stores there are both executive and nonexecutive jobs which, having been built around particular individuals, combine activities that are not functionally related. For that reason, firms should reanalyze their organization charts whenever personnel changes are contemplated.

The organization chart in large firms is often supplemented by a job-classification manual. Such a manual describes the activities of each job and is used as a guide for hiring.

All organization plans for retailing companies resemble each other, since the general objectives and the basic functions are all the same. Retailing

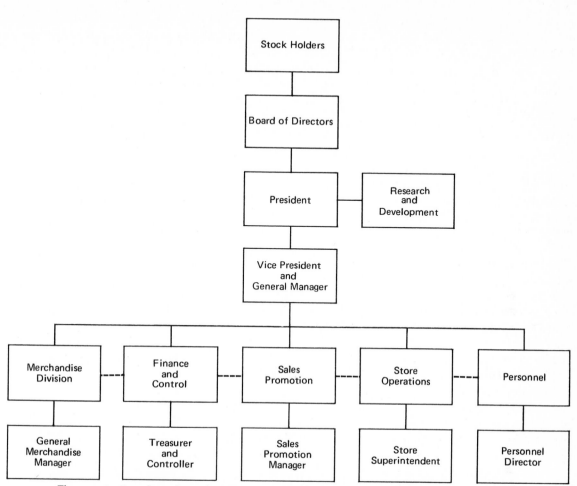

The organization chart shows how the operation of a large retail business is divided and traces lines of authority for the executive in the divisions.

companies, however, differ in size, being either single-unit or multi-unit enterprises; in complexity, being either single-line stores or multi-purpose stores; and in their operating policies. The following description of the organization of a departmentized store provides an overview of the subfunctions of the divisions.

THE MERCHANDISING DIVISION

The merchandising division performs the following functions:

• *Planning for Sales Growth.* With the aid of staff members, the division director sets up long-

term annual and seasonal sales goals for the store. These goals are based on sales plans for individual merchandise departments, and for merchandise classifications within departments.

• *Budgeting.* With goals for planning and sales growth in mind, the division decides on a buying plan and budget to achieve the sales goal. The budget is then divided among the different classifications of merchandise.

• *Buying.* The division staff determines as accurately as possible what customer demand will be for the various merchandise items. Buyers then select the right items and order them for delivery at the proper time.

- *Pricing.* Using cost information and profit factors, the merchandising division sets the selling prices for items and decides when they should change.

- *Managing Inventory.* Merchandisers must maintain accurate sales and stock records. This is because buying plans are revised continuously according to what these records say about customer demand. In some stores, preparing merchandise control records is the responsibility of the control division, but interpreting and using these records is always a merchandising job.

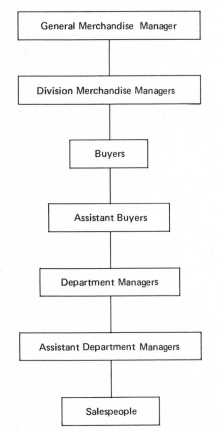

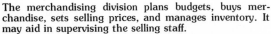

The merchandising division plans budgets, buys merchandise, sets selling prices, and manages inventory. It may aid in supervising the selling staff.

- *Maintaining a Profit.* Sales goals are important, and the planned gross margin—or the difference between cost and selling price—is necessary for maintaining a profit.

- *Selling.* This division shares with the store operations division the tasks of supervising selling-floor activities and training a sales staff.

- *Promoting Merchandise.* The merchandising division plans merchandise promotions with the help of the sales promotion division.

Department Organization

The general merchandise manager is head of the merchandising division and reports to the general manager of the store. The general merchandise manager determines merchandising policies, subject to the general manager's approval, and is responsible for the satisfactory performance of all merchandising functions.

The division merchandise manager heads a group of related merchandise departments, such as all those selling home furnishings or all basement departments. In large stores there may be eight or more merchandise divisions, and in small stores there might be none at all. The division merchandise manager also sees that buyers do their work in accordance with policies set by top management and helps them along the way.

A merchandise department is a unit in which one line or a few closely related lines of merchandise are sold, such as lingerie, shoes, or floor coverings. Each department maintains a separate accounting record. At the head of the departments are buyers who vary in number from store to store, depending on the volume of business. For example, there may be just one dress department in which all types and sizes are sold. Or there may be separate departments for juniors', misses', women's, petite, and tall sizes. There may be separate departments for low-priced, medium-priced, and high-priced dresses, or for evening dresses, daytime dresses, and sportswear. A large department store will have a hundred or more departments and keep separate sales, expense, and profit records for each.

Buyers are important members of the merchandising division staff. After getting approval from their division merchandise manager, they select merchandise, place orders, choose merchandise for promotion, and supervise selling and stockkeeping. The assistant buyer aids the buyer in all activities.

In cases where department stores have branches, each branch has department managers who run one or more departments. The department manager assists the buyer in determining what merchandise would be best for the local branch. Branch department managers may also have assistants who are training for a manager's position.

Usually, salespeople are part of the store operations division, but they report to the merchandising division for the handling of merchandise.

Staff Services

Large stores employ a number of staff specialists who provide information and advice to guide various merchandising activities. For example, people in the comparison shopping bureau check to see that the merchandise and prices are in line with those of competing stores. Fashion coordinators help buyers plan their purchases along a selected fashion theme, which all related departments will follow. Some stores have their own merchandise testing bureaus, which buyers can use before they buy an item. The merchandise control office keeps sales and stock records for all departments and writes regular, sometimes daily, reports for the buyers. In smaller stores, the buyers and assistants do the recordkeeping themselves, usually with the aid of a clerk.

Outside Services

Practically all department stores and departmentized specialty stores use the help of buying offices to supplement their own buyers' work. These services are purchased for the merchandising division. Also, stores may use independent testing agencies, fashion consultants, and consumer research agencies that study shoppers' preferences.

THE FINANCE AND CONTROL DIVISION

The finance and control division performs functions related to the following:

- *Money Management.* The division prepares budgets and payroll; supervises investments, insurance, taxes, and loans; and helps to prevent inventory shortages.

- *Accounting.* The division handles all accounting, bookkeeping, and auditing services and prepares the store's financial statements.

- *Statistics.* The division prepares statistical data on which executives throughout the store base their budgets and buying. It compares plans with actual performance and prepares departmental operating statements.

- *Systems.* The division develops uniform office procedures and also expense control systems for the entire organization.

- *Credit.* The division approves customer credit, recordkeeping, billing, collections, and credit promotion.

Department Leadership

The controller is head of the finance and control division. In many stores, the controller and company treasurer are the same person. In many large department stores, the controller's authority extends beyond just gathering financial statistics. Controllers may be asked to interpret all figures and recommend actions with regard to financing, merchandising, and promotion. The controller may be in charge of planning and research for the company's future.

The Credit Office and the General Accounting Office

Often, the finance and control division is divided into two separate offices. The credit office handles all requests for customer credit, while the general accounting office sets the store's accounting procedures.

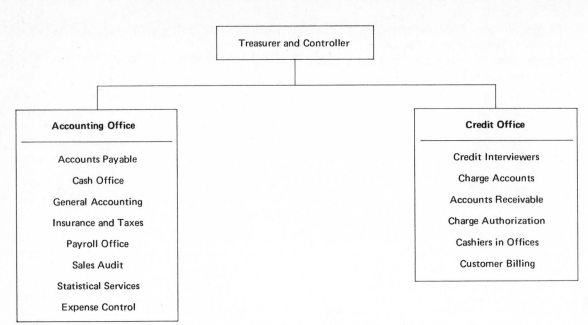

```
                    ┌─────────────────────────────┐
                    │   Treasurer and Controller  │
                    └─────────────────────────────┘
```

Accounting Office	Credit Office
Accounts Payable	Credit Interviewers
Cash Office	Charge Accounts
General Accounting	Accounts Receivable
Insurance and Taxes	Charge Authorization
Payroll Office	Cashiers in Offices
Sales Audit	Customer Billing
Statistical Services	
Expense Control	

The finance and control division supervises the store's internal financial affairs, such as investments, taxes, bookkeeping, payroll, billing, customer credit, and accounts payable.

Duties of the Credit Office. Besides supervising authorization, billing, and collections, the credit manager is responsible for increasing the number of charge accounts and the use of accounts. Therefore the job requires skill in promotion as well as financial control. The executive should be able to handle direct-mail appeals expertly. In many cases, the accounts receivable section of the credit department will be the first to use electronic data processing (EDP). As a result, the credit manager may be the ranking expert in the store on EDP installations.

Duties of the Accounting Office. On the other side of the division, the accounting office strictly audits all department expenses and reviews certain expense responsibilities assigned to each department. Employee payrolls, accounts payable, and insurance and taxes come under the authority of the accounting office. These are called "payout accounts." Accounts payable refers to all the money due suppliers of goods and services for the store. The suppliers' bills are usually paid by set deadlines in order to get the traditional cash discounts.

Stores must pay federal, state, and local taxes on the products they purchase and sell. The accounting office pays these taxes as well as premiums on insurance policies that protect the store, its employees, and its customers during the operation of the business. Also, the accounting office must keep adequate records for the cash office, which supplies cash for all registers and offices that need it. In addition, the accounting office records the costs of operating the four or five store divisions mentioned earlier.

THE SALES PROMOTION DIVISION

Occasionally the sales promotion division is called the publicity division. Its functions include the following:

- *Merchandise Promotion.* In cooperation with the merchandising division, the sales promotion division plans and executes merchandise promotions by using a variety of media: newspapers, displays, radio and television, direct mail (catalogs, fliers, bill inserts), and billboards.

- *Institutional Promotion.* The division creates an advertising style and executes a publicity program that aims to produce a favorable image for the store.

- *Promotion Budgeting.* The division assists the merchandise manager and controller in determining the percentage of department budgets to be used for advertising.

The sales promotion manager of a store coordinates all the activities that carry the store's message to the public.

The advertising manager supervises a staff of copywriters, scriptwriters, and artists in the preparation of advertising. The manager also deals with media representatives with regard to production and advertising rates. The promotion staff may be organized according to the media they use or according to merchandise divisions within the store.

The display manager and display staff create window and store displays. The special-events manager coordinates special promotional events, such as fairs, holiday parades, fashion shows, and branch store openings.

The public relations manager writes press releases for the print media and develops contacts with community organizations and store-sponsored clubs.

THE STORE OPERATIONS DIVISION

The functions of the store operations division include the following:

- *Merchandise Handling.* The division is responsible for transporting merchandise to the store, receiving and checking merchandise, and price marking. It also handles packaging and delivery for the store.

- *Customer Service.* The division supervises departments selling services and handles

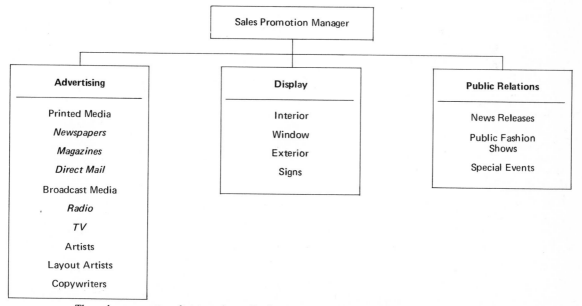

The sales promotion division plans all advertising, display, and public relations activities.

adjustments, returns and complaints, mail orders, and telephone orders. It also supervises parking facilities.

- *Building Management.* The division operates, maintains, and repairs utilities and equipment. It maintains the store and the warehouse.

- *Store Security.* The division protects the merchandise as well as the premises.

- *Workroom Activities.* The division operates alteration, repair, and manufacturing workrooms.

- *Restaurant Management.* The division operates food services for customers and employees.

- *Purchasing.* The division places orders for fixtures, supplies, and operations equipment.

Department Organization

The store operations manager, sometimes called the store superintendent, is the manager who heads the store operations division. This person handles directly some of the functions listed above, particularly those connected with modernizing the store and making building plans, ongoing activities for most large retailers. The store operations manager also directs those functions connected with designing improved systems for handling merchandise in the store and the warehouse.

The traffic manager is responsible for getting merchandise to the store on schedule and at the best transportation rates. The manager must worry about merchandise claims arising from damage in transit or failure to follow transportation instructions. Whether or not a traffic man-

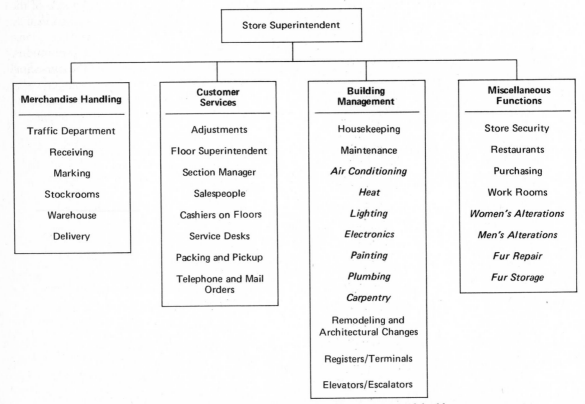

The operations division coordinates all merchandise transportation and building management. It may supervise the selling staff.

ager directs the receiving and marking room depends on the store. Some stores have a receiving and marking manager who reports directly to the head of the store operations division, as does the traffic manager.

The service manager oversees selling service and adjustments. At the supervisory level, section managers do this job in each merchandise department. They report to floor or area superintendents or, in smaller department stores, directly to the service manager.

Other executives reporting to the store operations manager are the security manager, delivery manager, warehouse manager, restaurant manager, building superintendent, and purchasing agent.

Outside Services

The store operations manager may buy many outside services that the store needs. Engineers and architects, system planners, packaging designers, and fixture designers all work with the store operations manager. Although some store services—for example, restaurants, parking garages, and delivery service—are leased to outside specialists the store operations manager must see that all services are satisfactory.

THE PERSONNEL DIVISION

In a four-function organization plan, personnel management is a subfunction of store operations. In a five-function plan, personnel is a major division, and the personnel manager reports to the general manager rather than to the store operations manager.

The personnel division performs the following functions: recruiting, selecting, and placing full-time and part-time employees; training employees in systems and sales techniques, and sometimes giving merchandise information; handling employee recordkeeping, evaluation, and job review; supervising employee welfare and counseling; and publishing company news.

The personnel manager is assisted by an employment manager, who directs a staff of interviewers and test administrators, as well as by a training manager. Depending on the size of the store, there may be other assistants who evaluate employee fringe benefits, such as pension plans, and rating systems for raises and promotions.

According to store policy, either the personnel manager, the store operations manager, or a special labor relations manager may carry on negotiations for contracts with labor unions.

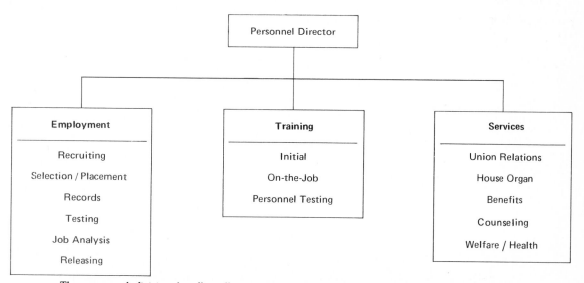

The personnel division handles all recruitment, selection, training, and release of employees.

BRANCH STORE MANAGEMENT

In the early years of multi-unit stores, any branches were considered simply extensions of the main store. At that time, a branch store manager reported to five executives. But later on, some firms devised a new line of authority in which branch store managers reported directly to the general manager or to a single executive in charge of branches. The merchandising, sales promotion, and finance and control functions were still handled in the main store, but the store operations function, some personnel activities such as hiring and training, and some record-keeping duties were delegated to the branch store manager.

Within the branch store there is no standard organization of functions. In general, the branch store manager acts as a sales manager and advises the main store's merchandise manager and buyers on merchandise needs. The branch store manager also prepares store budgets and is responsible for expense control within the branch.

He or she represents the store to the community and deals with the management of the shopping center in which the store is located. The assistant branch store manager is usually assigned responsibility for personnel management, merchandise-handling operations, and office activities such as handling cash and extending credit.

As the chart on page 99 indicates, the branch store manager in the equal-stores concept no longer has four or five bosses but reports instead to one general branch stores manager. Each branch store has its own selling and operations organization. The merchandising division of the main store buys for the branches, but it no longer has the responsibility for branch store selling.

The heads of the main divisions are still in charge of their operations at the main store, where the merchandising division continues to share responsibility for selling with the store operations and personnel divisions.

The chart on page 99 shows a plan of organization that abandons completely the concept of a main store with branches. Now the parent store,

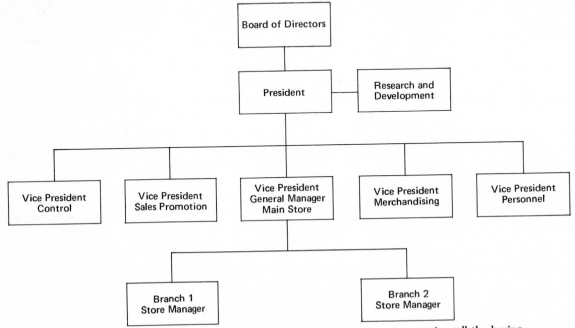

In some multi-unit stores, the merchandising division of the main store supervises all the buying and selling for the branch stores.

THE ORGANIZATION OF RETAIL INSTITUTIONS

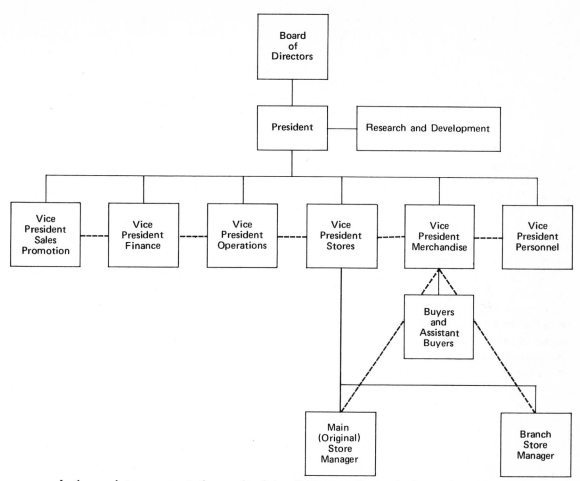

In the equal-stores concept, the merchandising division coordinates the buying for the original store and the branches, all of which have an equal voice in merchandise selection.

like the branch stores, has its own store manager, who is responsible for all store activities. The main division managers become a headquarters staff, formulating policies and procedures but not executing them, except for those that are related to buying.

CHAIN STORE ORGANIZATION

As the departmentized stores adopted the equal-stores type of organization, they moved closer to chain stores in their activities. Chain organizations have long used the headquarters idea for the major functions except for selling. The economies provided by this method of doing business have allowed many of them to pass savings on to customers and to establish reputations that have led to national or even international fame. In the typical chain organization all the major activities—managing store operations, planning for and buying merchandise, hiring and training managerial personnel, selecting sites for new stores, handling finance and control functions, keeping records, and supervising sales promotion efforts—are performed through the central or home office. Each store that is part of the chain is planned, stocked with merchandise, and controlled and publicized through the efforts of personnel in the home office. Each store is headed by a store manager who reports directly to a supervisor from the home or regional office. This is the line of command in the typical chain organization.

Differences Among Chains

It is hard to generalize about chain store organization because chains are so complex. Chain organizations differ from one another in many ways. First, they differ in the number of stores they have. Some chains have two or three stores, while others, such as Kresge, Sears, Montgomery Ward, and J. C. Penney have hundreds. The number of stores is only one aspect of the size of chain organizations, for size is also affected by the sales volume of the individual units. Some chain stores may take in a few hundred dollars a week, while others may take in approximately one million dollars a week.

A second way in which chain organizations differ from one another has to do with the kinds and assortments of merchandise carried. Chains that carry general merchandise lines require more complex organizations than those that specialize in limited lines of merchandise, such as shoes, jewelry, and men's hats.

Third, chain organizations differ according to the extent of their geographic distribution. Chains that are located in just one city, one state, or one region may be organized differently from national or international chains, which need regional offices to supplement the home office.

Fourth, chain organizations differ by type of ownership. Some chains own outright all their units, while a growing number have units that are franchised to owner-managers who, although they own the individual units, are subject to the rules and regulations of the central organization.

All the basic functions described above for the departmentized stores are also performed in chain organizations. However, for most chains the complexity of the operations requires that the basic functions be divided. No one organization chart would be typical for more than the one chain it represented, but basically, the chain store has a headquarters organization and a field organization.

Headquarters Organization

In the *home office* or *headquarters* office of a large national chain, the *president* is usually the top executive who is in charge of the entire operation. The president reports to and is a member of the board of directors. Major executives for both line and staff functions report to the president.

Staff Functions. The following staff functions are typical in the headquarters office of a chain organization:

- The general counsel and his or her staff do legal advisory work. They check all contracts and advertising and selling claims and make sure that other members of the organization observe government laws and rules in all their activities.

- The general secretary and a staff keep all the records of meetings of the president and board of directors, and they assist in various ways in the running of the organization.

- The research and development staff analyzes every detail related to buying and selling and suggests changes that should be made to improve the effectiveness of those activities.

- The corporate planning staff makes analyses that help the president and board of directors make plans for the next five- and ten-year periods. Annual checks are made to determine what progress the organization is making toward its goals.

Line Functions. The line functions of a chain organization usually include the following:

- Public relations personnel are in charge of all display planning, advertising, public relations, and image building for the organization.

- Catalog merchandising personnel are in charge of coordinating merchandise, assigning catalog space, taking pictures, writing copy, publishing the catalog, and distributing it to customers.

- Merchandising personnel plan sales goals, search out sources of merchandise, and buy the merchandise to be sold throughout the entire chain. This function may be divided according to type of merchandise.

- Personnel executives employ and train managers for the entire organization. They are responsible for ratings and evaluations, and they set wage and salary scales. They also produce employment and training manuals to be used by the rank-and-file employees hired locally for each unit. In addition, the personnel executives handle unionization problems and contracts.

- Physical distribution personnel are in charge of moving merchandise to individual stores, either from a warehouse or directly from the manufacturers. They must move goods in the least-expensive way. These employees may also be in charge of warehousing goods and reordering staple merchandise that is stocked in the warehouse.

- Treasury and control personnel are in charge of all the financial dealings and of the financial records, including records of amounts to be paid to vendors (accounts payable), records of amounts owed by customers (accounts receivable), and payrolls. In addition, these people must make financial reports for other members of the firm and for the government.

- Credit personnel are in charge of establishing and maintaining a credit system for the firm and of collecting amounts owed by customers.

- Data processing and computer personnel are newer additions to the ranks of those involved in chain organizations. These people are in charge of all the recordkeeping done by computer concerning merchandise purchases, merchandise on hand, merchandise sold, credit customers, and payrolls. Increasing amounts of data are being stored in computers to increase the scientific management of retailing organizations.

- Real estate personnel decide on sites for new stores, contract for the erection of new stores, and advise about the zoning regulations in the areas under consideration.

Field Organization

The *field organization* for a large national chain usually includes personnel who are in charge of all the individual stores and their activities. In a large firm, there may be several regional supervisory offices, each headed by a manager. He or she assigns people to visit the local stores and check to see that all policies of the firm are being observed; that merchandise is well stocked, properly displayed, and priced according to company policy; and that the stores are being run efficiently.

The various supervisors and their staffs oversee the individual stores and offer help in running them. Each store, in turn, is run by a store manager who reports to the local field office supervisor. The store manager has a staff that takes care of displaying goods according to the plans of the home office. The staff also takes care of selling, stocking the shelves, handling cash, and record-keeping. The store manager is in charge of hiring and training these employees. In a large store, the manager may have one or more assistant managers, floor supervisors, office managers, and other supervisory personnel in addition to the sales and stockroom employees.

Thus, the chain store organization is seen as a complex web in which each person reports to someone who has broader job responsibilities. Much paper work is required to keep track of the merchandise that is being sold and the merchandise that needs to be replaced. Records must be kept of the customers to whom the goods are delivered and of the employees who are handling the merchandise, money, and orders. The detail and need for accuracy in these reports require personnel who are prompt, well organized, and precise in their work. Yet chain store and branch store organizations leave ample room for the creative person to succeed. Two similar stores set in almost identical communities often show entirely different performances because the manager and the assistants in one store are far more imaginative than those in the other store.

Chain store organizations and departmentized stores are constantly interested in expansion and growth. They offer young people excellent job opportunities in a field with unlimited potential.

TOPICS FOR DISCUSSION

1. List and discuss the basic functions that exist in all retailing firms. How and why do the jobs of persons in a firm often differ from the basic functions to be performed?
2. Explain how the five-function plan differs from the four-function plan. In your opinion, what effect might each plan have on nonmanagement employees in a large store?
3. What are the main tasks accomplished by merchandising personnel?
4. What are the main tasks accomplished by finance and control personnel?
5. What are the main tasks accomplished by sales promotion personnel?
6. What are the main tasks accomplished by store operations personnel?
7. What are the main tasks accomplished by the personnel division?
8. Explain the difference in organization between a branch store whose manager reports to four or five division heads and one whose manager has the same status as the division heads.
9. How does the "equal-stores concept" of store organization differ from the "main store with branches" concept with respect to the role of the branch manager?
10. Compare the functions of a chain organization with the functions of a store with branches using the equal-stores concept of organization.

MATHEMATICS FOR RETAILING

A chain store manager had a store with five cash registers, and all five were needed to check out customers' purchases throughout the day. Six full-time cashiers were employed. Each worked five days a week, $7\frac{1}{2}$ hours each day. A half hour was allowed for lunch. In addition, each cashier had a 15-minute coffee break in the morning and in the afternoon. When a cashier was not running a cash register, that person would help out with the stock work or with the recordkeeping.

The store was open five days a week from 10 a.m. until 6 p.m. and one day a week from 9 a.m. until 9 p.m. When the full-time cashiers were not on duty, the manager used high school and college students, who worked part-time. Each student worked only 4 hours a day and had no lunch period but was allowed a 15-minute coffee break. How many of these part-timers would be hired by the manager to handle all five cash registers when the full-time cashiers were not on duty? Do your calculations on a separate sheet of paper.

COMMUNICATIONS IN RETAILING

A large multi-store organization had a policy of paying the minimum wage to students who worked part-time. Some of the managers of the various units complained that they were not able to hire good student help because competing stores in their areas paid above the minimum wage. Full-time employees were paid considerably more than the minimum hourly wage. The central office of the organization decided to revise its policy and allow individual store managers to meet competition in the payment of part-time student help, but without paying as much as full-time employees earned. On a separate sheet of paper, write a memo to the store managers explaining the new policy.

MANAGING HUMAN RELATIONS

There are several salespeople who have worked for many years in the department to which you are assigned as assistant buyer. The buyer for the department has been rather lax in enforcing the employee regulations regarding lateness, extended lunch hours, and coffee breaks, and the salespeople have been taking liberties for quite a while. You know that this has created a temporary shortage of salespeople on the floor, and on several occasions you have had to serve customers yourself, rather than have them go unattended. You want to maintain good relations with the salespeople in your department, and you certainly don't want to antagonize the buyer. Yet you feel the situation has gotten out of hand. Be prepared to discuss in class what you might do to improve matters.

CAREER LADDER

Upon graduating from a two-year college, you receive several job offers. One is from a large department store chain. You can begin as a trainee and work your way up to a position as store manager. Another offer is from a large department store. You can begin as a trainee and then become a junior assistant buyer, an assistant buyer, and, finally, if you are successful, a buyer. Each firm pays the same beginning salary. Which offer appeals to you more? Why? What advantages and disadvantages can you think of in each opportunity? Be prepared to discuss your answers in class.

THE PERSONNEL MANAGEMENT FUNCTION

chapter 9

PERSONNEL FUNCTIONS EMPLOYMENT AND TRAINING

Although retailing is called a business of buying and selling, it is in reality a business of people. Every store gets its character from the people who work in it. The merchandise they buy, the policies they develop, and the work they do all shape the personality of the store. Therefore, the management of employees is crucial to the success of the entire business.

THE DEVELOPMENT OF PERSONNEL MANAGEMENT

Personnel management is the direction or administration of people to achieve the objectives of the organization. This particular function of retailing was one of the last to be recognized as a separate and distinct area of management. As long as the work of employees was not costly and their work was regarded as a "commodity" to be bought and sold, little attention was paid to managing the employees. As people have come to be recognized as individuals with unique abilities and interests, managers of personnel have been needed to select employees, analyze their work, evaluate them, counsel them, and aid them.

Many large retailing organizations today consider the personnel manager to be as important as the merchandise manager, the store operations manager, the controller, and the sales promotion manager. Each reports to the president of the firm, and each has full authority for the operation of a division. Having a personnel manager in an important position assures the employees that they have a direct line of communication to the president or general manager. It also assures them that their interests and concerns will receive attention.

THE FUNCTIONS OF THE PERSONNEL DIVISION

The personnel manager and others in the personnel division are concerned with all factors involved in establishing and maintaining an adequate work force. Personnel functions are complicated and diverse. Personnel managers and their assistants are responsible for:

- Recruiting and selecting employees, using affirmative action standards

- Training employees and retraining them when necessary

- Evaluating employees

- Transferring, promoting, and discharging employees

- Keeping accurate records about employees

- Providing for the welfare of employees

- Maintaining labor relations with unions that represent employees

- Establishing wage and salary scales

- Developing job specifications

The Personnel Division in Relation to the Size of the Organization

When a retailing organization is small, the owner is responsible for all major functions. As the organization grows, the owner may continue to buy the merchandise and do the recordkeeping but may hire and train other employees for stockkeeping, store maintenance, and selling. The owner supervises the workers in these activities. Small organizations of this type have little need for performing any of the usual elaborate routines of the personnel division, since it is possible for face-to-face discussions with the boss to take place many times a day. Usually a mutual feeling of concern for the success of the enterprise exists when employees work directly with the owner.

As stores become larger, or when managers replace owners, or when stores are located far from the main store or central office of the firm, there are fewer opportunities for face-to-face discussions with the owners or executives. Under such circumstances the establishment of personnel policies and the assignment of specific persons to manage personnel become a necessity.

In large firms, one person may be assigned to handle the personnel function. Very large organizations may have complete staffs who devote their entire time to personnel work.

In multi-store operations, the personnel function becomes more complicated. Local store managers may hire employees for their store. However, the management personnel are usually hired by the personnel department of the main store or central office and are sent to the local stores for on-the-job training. Promotion in such firms is usually achieved by being transferred from smaller stores to larger stores, where there is greater responsibility. Managers may be promoted, for example, from a small store selling $250,000 a year to one selling $500,000 a year. This larger volume means that the manager has greater responsibility, as well as a chance to earn a larger income if the store is run successfully.

Recruitment of Personnel

If a retailing firm is to be successful in attaining its objectives, the employees of the firm must perform their jobs efficiently. If a firm has devoted, loyal, hard-working, energetic, imaginative employees, it has a far greater chance for success than another firm that has indifferent, lackadaisical, bored, lazy workers. The people hired to work in a firm will consequently determine to a large extent the success of that firm. Since the personnel division is responsible for the caliber of the employees hired, employment becomes one of the division's main responsibilities.

To reach as wide an audience as possible and to employ people in accordance with affirmative action policies and guidelines, the personnel or employment manager will recruit from many sources. Most retailing organizations need to seek new employees throughout the year. Employees are needed to replace those who have left for better jobs, those who have retired, those who have left to return to school, and those who have been dismissed. Employees are also needed to fill temporary positions at the Christmas or Easter season, to staff temporary departments such as the College Shop or Garden Supplies, and to staff an expanded organization. When employment managers need new employees for specific jobs, they seek them both inside and outside the organization, keeping in mind the requirements of the Civil Rights Act of 1964—which includes Title VII, "Equal Employment Opportunity." This part of the act prohibits discrimination in hiring and other conditions of employment because of race, color, religion, sex, or national origin. Since 1972, Title VII has given the Equal Employment Opportunity Commission direct access to courts in cases of grievances.

Insiders. New personnel are frequently recruited from within the organization. These people, called *insiders,* may be employees currently working in other positions, former employees, or people recommended by friends or relatives employed in the firm.

- *Transfers.* A person doing a job in one section of the organization may be *transferred* to a new position. Transferees usually perform similar tasks in their new jobs and therefore are rarely given more than minimal raises on their new assignments.

- *Promotions.* If a person accepts a newly opened job that is better than the one previously held, the person is in effect *promoted* to a new position. It will require greater responsibility and more difficult work. The personnel or employment manager will usually search through the ranks of the employees to find the one who most deserves promotion and whose capabilities match the demands of the new job. Promotions mean increased status as well as increased pay.

- *Recommendations.* If no one currently employed in the firm can be transferred or promoted to a new job, employees may be asked to recommend friends or, in some cases, relatives who might fill the job.

- *Former Employees.* On occasion, former employees might be asked if they wish to return to work or if they know anyone who might fill a particular job.

Outsiders. A growing and expanding organization cannot long exist by relying solely on insiders to fill new jobs. Consequently, *outsiders,* those who have never worked for the firm and who are not friends or relatives of employees, must be sought. Outsiders may be obtained through applications, through advertising, through schools and colleges, or through employment agencies. At times specialized firms, such as black personnel agencies, or foreign-language newspapers may be used to recruit members of specific ethnic groups.

- *Recruitment Through Applications.* Most large firms attract some applicants almost daily. These people may just stop in during the day and ask if they can be interviewed. If they meet the minimum requirements for employment by the firm, they may be asked to fill out application forms. These applicants then become potential employees for any jobs for which they are qualified.

  In addition, stores often receive letters and telephone calls from those seeking appointments for interviews. These inquiries are also sources of potential employees.

  People who applied at some previous time and whose applications were filed may also be interviewed if they are still available for employment.

- *Recruitment Through Advertising.* Growing firms can rarely depend only on those applicants who drop in, telephone, or write for positions. The personnel or employment managers must actively promote their employment needs by advertising for people. Advertising in store windows, in newspapers, and through radio, television, and other communications media is used to inform people that jobs are available. Newspapers are the most convenient media for this purpose. Open and blind advertisements may both be used.

  The *open advertisement* explains the employment needs, lists the name of the firm and its address, and tells readers how to apply for the job. Such an advertisement may draw anywhere from a few applicants to several hundred. As a result, the store may need to have many interviewers available the day following the advertisement just to screen applicants. This could be costly and time-consuming for both applicants and store personnel. The *blind advertisement,* by contrast, does not give the name or address of the firm. A post office box number or a number assigned by the newspaper is included in the advertisement. All applicants must respond by mail. The mailed replies may then be screened before any applicant is informed about the position or told where to apply for it. This eliminates the need to interview large numbers of unqualified people for any one job.

Some applicants dislike answering blind advertisements. They fear that they may be applying to the firm for which they are currently working and thus possibly jeopardize their present position. To alleviate this problem, most blind advertisements state, "Our employees have been advised about this advertisement."

• *Recruitment Through Schools and Colleges.* A more personal method of recruitment is having a personnel recruiter visit schools and colleges to meet with groups of students and their advisers. In a general talk about the firm they represent, these recruiters may give background information about the organization and its employment needs. Interview time is then scheduled for those students who are interested in applying for jobs. Through this type of recruitment, stores may attract young men and women who otherwise would not have been drawn to them. People for training programs are very often obtained in this manner.

• *Recruitment Through Employment Agencies.* In order to get experienced personnel, as opposed to young people on the threshold of their careers, recruiters may turn to employment agencies and, in some cases, to professional organizations. *Private employment agencies* are valuable sources for executive-level personnel or for people with technical knowledge or skills. A private employment agency may be paid a fee by the retailers for each person employed upon its recommendation, or it may be retained on an annual basis to recruit personnel for the retailers. Free *public employment services,* often run by state governments, are proving increasingly to be good sources for obtaining retailing workers. The head offices of *professional organizations,* such as buyers' clubs and advertising groups, may, through their membership lists, be able to match experienced personnel with jobs.

These various sources may be used to find qualified persons for employment. It is, however, the favorable overall image of a store or the impression it makes in the community that will best aid its recruiters in attracting desirable personnel. If a store has a reputation for having good hiring practices, for giving fair pay, for offering adequate employee services, for maintaining good employee relations, and for promoting from within, it has a far better chance of being sought by both young people and those with experience than a store that does not project such a favorable image.

EMPLOYMENT PROCEDURES

Employment procedures differ according to the size and complexity of the store. In the small store the owner may interview the applicant; take down pertinent information, such as the address, telephone number, and social security number; and ask for the names of a few references. In large multi-store organizations, however, employment procedures are usually more structured and controlled.

Employment managers in large stores work from employee "requisitions" when they seek people for jobs. For example, if a salesperson has left the firm, a "requisition to fill the vacancy" will be filed with the employment office by the manager of the department in which the salesperson worked. If more salespeople are needed, then a "requisition to add personnel" will be filed. The employment office is charged with the responsibility to fill those positions.

No store can afford to hire new people every time a few extras are needed. To take care of emergency situations, large stores maintain "flying squads"—groups of people with no permanent departmental stations. They may be assigned as needed throughout various sections of the store. For example, if a sudden cold spell caused a horde of customers to rush to the coat and suit departments, the trained people from the "squad" would be assigned to sell in those areas. They also cover special sales.

In multi-store and chain operations, salespeople as well as assistant managers are sometimes transferred temporarily to other stores in the same firm that have serious personnel shortages. Also, chain organizations often have extra personnel in training for management positions to cover emergency openings on short notice.

The Application Form

Most retailing firms require applicants to fill out application forms. Although these differ according to the needs of each organization, in general they include requests for the applicant's name, address, telephone number, and social security number; height, weight, marital status, and status as a citizen; background education (including degrees received, major courses studied, extracurricular activities, and achievements in school); and previous work experience and salary received. Some application blanks also include space for giving information about military service classification, for indicating job preferences, and for listing the names of persons who may be used as references.

Matching the Applicant to the Job

The employment requisition that the recruiter has received gives details about the qualifications needed by the person who is to fill the job opening. The employment manager matches these requirements with the information provided on the application filled out by a person seeking the job. If the application is neatly and completely filled out, and if the information indicates that the applicant may be suitable, the applicant will be interviewed by someone in the personnel department. Further information about the applicant is obtained through the interview. The interviewer will be able to determine the applicant's interests and personality characteristics and judge the applicant's grooming, behavior, speaking voice, vocabulary, and ability to listen, answer questions, and think under pressure. The interview may even be so structured that the applicant will reveal his or her abilities to analyze situations and make decisions.

For some firms the interview is the final determinant in considering the fitness of the individual for the opening to be filled. In other firms additional information about the applicant is sought through records and tests. Records of an applicant's previous employment, recommendations from previous employers, and records of school grades and achievements may be obtained. Testing is used in large firms that have the personnel to evaluate and interpret the test results. Smaller firms that do not have facilities to do their own testing and analyses may use the services of testing bureaus.

Tests for various jobs may include:

- *Physical examinations.* Persons who are not physically fit can rarely be employed in retailing jobs unless they have special, limited assignments. Most retailing jobs require a good deal of physical effort. Therefore, no one would be hired who was not physically able to perform the tasks assigned.

- *Tests of manual dexterity.* Applicants for such positions as wrappers, packers, and markers may be tested on their ability to work quickly and deftly at manual tasks.

- *Tests measuring clerical abilities.* Applicants for such positions as clerks and stenographers may be given clerical aptitude and ability tests.

APPLICATION FOR EMPLOYMENT

IN THE EVENT YOU ARE EMPLOYED THIS BECOMES PART OF YOUR PERSONNEL RECORD,
THEREFORE IT IS IMPORTANT YOU ENTER ALL INFORMATION NEATLY, ACCURATELY AND COMPLETELY.

☐ MISS ☐ MRS. ☒ MR.	LAST NAME (PRINT CLEARLY) Fong	FIRST NAME Arnold	MIDDLE NAME Henry	MAIDEN NAME

ADDRESS — NUMBER AND STREET 732 W. 116th Street CITY New York, STATE NY ZIP CODE 10027 TELEPHONE NO. (212) 555-1234

HEIGHT 5 FT. 7 IN. WEIGHT 140 LBS. AMERICAN CITIZEN YES ☑ NO ☐ DATE OF BIRTH 1/18 – – AGE* 21 SOCIAL SECURITY NO. 987-65-4321

* APPLICABLE LAW PROHIBITS DISCRIMINATION IN EMPLOYMENT BECAUSE OF RACE, COLOR, RELIGION, SEX, NATIONAL ORIGIN OR AGE.

SCHEDULE PREFERRED: ☑ FULL TIME ☐ PART TIME ☐ EVENINGS AND SATURDAYS | OTHER | POSITION DESIRED ☑ SALES ☐ OFFICE | OTHER

HAVE YOU BEEN EMPLOYED BY MACY*S BEFORE? ☐ YES ☑ NO IF YES | UNDER WHAT NAME WERE YOU EMPLOYED? | POSITION, DEPT. AND STORE | DATES EMPLOYED FROM ___ TO ___

EDUCATION

	SCHOOL ATTENDED	NUMBER OF YEARS	DATES ATTENDED FROM	DATES ATTENDED TO	GRADUATED YES	GRADUATED NO
HIGH SCHOOL	NAME OF SCHOOL Hilldale High School — NUMBER AND STREET 241 North Avenue, CITY AND STATE Hilldale, N.Y.	4	MO. 9 — YR. / – –	MO. 6 — YR. / – –	✓	
COLLEGE	NAME OF SCHOOL Watson Community College — NUMBER AND STREET 1993 Second Street, CITY AND STATE Layton, N.Y.	2	MO. 9 — YR. / – –	MO. 6 — YR. / – –	✓	
OTHER	NAME OF SCHOOL — NUMBER AND STREET CITY AND STATE		MO. — YR.	MO. — YR.		
OTHER	NAME OF SCHOOL — NUMBER AND STREET CITY AND STATE		MO. — YR.	MO. — YR.		

PREVIOUS EMPLOYMENT

PLEASE ACCOUNT FOR THE LAST FIVE YEARS EMPLOYMENT AND PERIODS OF UNEMPLOYMENT.
STATE IF ANY OF THESE EMPLOYERS ARE RELATED TO YOU.

BUSINESS NAME AND ADDRESS	DATES EMPLOYED FROM	DATES EMPLOYED TO	JOB TITLE AND DUTIES	REASON FOR LEAVING	SALARY
LAST OR PRESENT EMPLOYER Harvey's Sporting Goods — NUMBER AND STREET 98 Post Street, CITY AND STATE Layton, N.Y.	MO. 9 — YR. / – –	MO. 6 — YR. / – –	part-time Salesperson	end of school year	$3.50/hr
PREVIOUS EMPLOYER Pizza Palace — NUMBER AND STREET Route 9E CITY AND STATE Layton, N.Y.	MO. 6 — YR. / – –	MO. 9 — YR. / – –	Salesperson	return to school	$3.50/hr
PREVIOUS EMPLOYER	MO. — YR.	MO. — YR.			

The application form provides the employment manager with pertinent information about the applicant's personal data, work experience, and education.
Courtesy Macy's

- *General intelligence tests.* Applicants for management positions and for positions as executive trainees may be given general intelligence tests. Some arithmetic tests may also be given to prospective salespeople and other prospective employees who will handle money and perform calculations.

- *Personality tests.* In some firms applicants for management positions are given personality tests to determine whether they have characteristics similar to those of management personnel already in the firm who are considered successful in their jobs.

When tests are used, the test results are usually only an additional guide for the interviewer in determining the ability of the person to do the job. For those looking for management positions, a battery of interviews may be scheduled in addition to tests. The interviews are with executives in several divisions of the firm. If the prospective managers pass the tests and make a favorable impression on the different executives, they are considered to be good prospects for achieving successful careers in the retailing field.

Résumés
Individuals applying for management-level positions may send résumés when they write for an appointment, or they may bring their résumés to supplement the information on their application forms. Résumés summarize one's background and achievements more dramatically than application forms. The preparation of a résumé is discussed in Chapter 39.

TRAINING RETAIL EMPLOYEES

After new employees have been hired, they need to be trained. Every retailing firm finds it necessary to train new personnel to some extent. In small stores, training is limited to on-the-job instruction by the store owner or manager and is usually given as the need arises. In larger organizations, training may be conducted both through

meetings and on the job and may take from a few hours to many months. Some firms also supplement training sessions with booklets, manuals, tapes, and film loops prepared to aid the beginner in a retailing job.

Kinds of Training
All firms need to teach their incoming personnel basic rules, regulations, and procedures. This is known as *initial training.* Many firms also provide *ongoing* training for the continuous updating of personnel duties. Some firms conduct *promotional* training for employees who are being prepared for job advancement. For those whose performance is not satisfactory, *retraining* is usually provided. Training includes giving information about policies, systems, merchandise, selling skills, and human relations.

Centralized and Decentralized Training
Training in most retailing organizations is both centralized and decentralized. *Centralized training* refers to training that takes place in a classroom or other area separate from the place where the job is actually performed. Centralized training is usually given by personnel executives or others specifically assigned to teach particular topics. *Decentralized training* is given on the job by the person's immediate supervisor or by a more experienced worker.

Training is usually provided for selling and nonselling employees, often referred to as "rank-and-file" employees. Training is also provided for management trainees. *Selling employees* are those who sell merchandise to the customers. *Nonselling employees* include receiving clerks, markers, checkers, stockkeepers, merchandise handlers, office clerks, wrappers, packers, telephone-order clerks, billers, computer operators, recordkeepers, bookkeepers, and accounting clerks.

Most salespeople remain in centralized training somewhat longer than nonselling personnel. Salespeople must learn the background information and rules and regulations explained to all new employees. In addition, they need to learn how to fill out the various kinds of sales checks and forms used in selling; how to handle both cash and charge sales; how to manipulate a cash register or computer terminal; and how to sell merchandise to customers. Teaching these skills in the store's classroom may take several hours or as much as a week or more.

Decentralized training for both selling and nonselling employees is given by the immediate supervisor. The purpose is to make the new employees familiar with the special systems unique to their particular areas of work and to make the salespeople familiar with the location of stock, the kinds of products carried, and the nature of those products. Decentralized training may continue for many weeks until the new employees are thoroughly familiar with all routines in their departments.

Management trainees may also receive both centralized and decentralized training. Chain organizations, however, provide little, if any, training in central locations, since travel to the home office or centralized area is too time-consuming. Therefore, many chain store employees are trained almost entirely on the job by the immediate supervisor. Training manuals, tapes, film loops, and tests distributed from the home office may supplement on-the-job training.

The Importance of Training

Training that is done effectively leads to many desirable results.

- The employees learn the objectives, policies, and procedures of the firm and can therefore present a unified image of the store to customers and the public in general.

- The trainee is prepared to do the job efficiently and effectively. The trainee learns the necessary skills so that time will be saved and errors avoided as he or she undertakes the job.

- The need for close supervision of the employee is eliminated. Thus the supervisor is free to perform other duties.

- When employees have learned to handle customers properly, there are fewer complaints and returns, as well as more satisfied customers who purchase again and again at the store.

- The well-trained employee becomes confident about his or her own abilities. The confident employee enjoys his or her new job and helps improve company morale.

- The trainee acquires greater respect for the organization and its owners or managers, for the job to be done, for the merchandise to be sold, and for the customers to be served.

Methods of Training

Many different methods of training people are used by the various retailing organizations. The situation, the people to be trained, the material to be learned, the teaching aids available, and centralization or decentralization of training determine the most appropriate method or methods to be used.

Lectures. Certain types of instructional material are most quickly and easily transmitted to new employees by telling them about it directly. For example, if the history of an organization was to be presented, the lecture method would prove speedy and effective. Similarly, explaining rules and regulations is often accomplished quickly in this way. The lecture method might also be used to explain store policies or philosophy, or to introduce an all-store promotion. Guest speakers such as manufacturers' representatives, store principals, and representatives from the Better Business Bureau may present ideas through lectures.

The lecture method allows training to be accomplished quickly, especially with large groups of people. The speaker can easily adjust the length of the speech to the time available. The speaker is also in control of the subject under consideration.

Some firms have lectures taped so that employees may listen to the information at the time they are hired. Thus a formal lecturer and special

Dear Co-worker:

Welcome to Hess's! We want to do everything possible to make your first days at Hess's happy and comfortable as well as full of new learning experiences.

As soon as your training classes are completed, you will be taken to your department. An experienced co-worker will be assigned as your sponsor. He or she will show you the things you will need to know about your new department.

Please give this checklist to your sponsor who will be responsible for completing and returning it to your Store Manager within three days.

We wish you a happy beginning of your career at Hess's.

PERSONNEL OFFICE
HESS'S

SPONSOR CHECKLIST
FOR
NEW SELLING CO-WORKERS

SPONSORED IN _____

Dept.   (Issue Date)

RETURN TO STORE MANAGER BY_____

(Return Date)

_____ /

CO-WORKER'S NAME   #

SPONSORED BY_____

(Name)

DEPARTMENT SPONSOR MUST COMPLETE
CHECKLIST AND RETURN TO THE
STORE MANAGER WITHIN
3 DAYS FROM DATE OF ISSUE.

- [ ] Show where to put personal belongings.
- [ ] Show where nearest restrooms and water fountains are.
- [ ] Introduce to department personnel and Floor Supervisor.
- [ ] Show Department Manager's office location.
- [ ] Explain lunch time and location of weekly schedule.
- [ ] Give a tour of your department(s) to show stock by type, brands, sizes, reserve stock location.
- [ ] Ask Buyer or Sales Manager to assign specific stock responsibility.
- [ ] Explain PRICE tickets in detail and, if you STUB, go over this thoroughly.
- [ ] Show where supplies are kept and how they may be ordered.
- [ ] Show location of department bulletin board.
- [ ] Get selling supplies needed.
- [ ] Explain delivery procedure.
- [ ] Show how to handle gift wraps.
- [ ] Tell how to answer department phones, take messages and transfer calls.
- [ ] Review how to call Security.
- [ ] Explain alteration procedures if applicable.
- [ ] Show location of fitting rooms.
- [ ] Explain telephone and mail order procedures.
- [ ] Show how to handle co-worker package.
- [ ] Take person to location for depositing register media, keys, etc.
- [ ] Go over dress standards, grooming, selling, floor conduct, etc.
- [ ] Review co-worker's part in accepting bank checks.
- [ ] Show location of numbers to call for charge authorization.
- [ ] Show list of wanted charge plates and list of checks which are not to be accepted.

Hess's department store pairs new employees with co-workers ("sponsors") who explain store regulations and procedures. The store provides sponsors with a check-list of useful information to ensure that each new employee is thoroughly familiarized with the store's layout, policies, and personnel.

PERSONNEL FUNCTIONS: EMPLOYMENT AND TRAINING   113

class sessions can be eliminated. Film loops and audiovisual presentations are also used increasingly to present lectures for training main store, branch store, and chain store employees.

Question-and-Answer Sessions. When the instructional material to be taught is not just background information or directives, the instructor may use the question-and-answer method. This method permits two-way conversations between the learners and the teacher. For example, in teaching employees how to write sales checks, the teacher might ask, "Why is it necessary to get the customer's name and address on a charge transaction if the customer is going to carry the item from the store?"

The trainees are also able to ask questions about procedures to clarify them in their minds. Question-and-answer sessions are often allowed after a lecture so that the listeners can ask questions about points that weren't clear to them. At the conclusion of the study of a problem, question-and-answer sessions may be valuable.

Discussions. One of the most democratic methods of training is the discussion procedure. This is used when employees are being urged to think about a problem, when the firm is attempting to build morale, and when employees are being trained for more responsible positions. Discussion is, however, time-consuming. Discussion is also difficult to control, since it may take many directions depending upon the interests of the people participating.

Informal discussions take place frequently on the job and during breaks and lunch periods. They may take place between rank-and-file employees only, between these employees and their managers, or between managers only.

Seminars. In the seminar method, one person in a group presents the topic assigned for a meeting and gives the pertinent background information. Each person in the group then presents a point of view. Each person eventually gets a chance at subsequent meetings to introduce

another topic and lead a discussion. Since people are not equally skilled, however, these presentations are not equally effective. Such a method is time-consuming, and much of the information obtained from sharing viewpoints may be of little value. In departmentized stores, where salespeople sell in more than one department, seminars held by knowledgeable head salespeople enlighten the entire sales force about each area of merchandise.

Personal Conferences. One of the most effective training methods is holding personal conferences between the employee and the immediate supervisor. Conferences may be held at any time during employment. The personal conference method permits the employee to be instructed without embarrassment. It permits discussion of any pertinent problem.

Demonstrations. Teaching by demonstration is particularly useful when people are being taught how to do a specific task. For example, showing salespeople how to record a sale and make change by using a cash register or a computer terminal, showing shoe salespeople how to fit shoes, or showing yard goods salespeople how to measure fabric can be effectively accomplished through demonstration. Film loops and audiovisual tapes of demonstrations eliminate the need for repeat performances and enable personnel in all units of a chain or other retail organization to receive identical training.

Practice. For many retailing jobs, skills need to be made virtually automatic. Constant practice will help to ensure that employees will accomplish their tasks quickly and accurately. Repeated practice will generally improve the way employees use machines—for example, adding, calculating, and marking machines; switchboards; cash registers; terminals; and computers.

Brainstorming Sessions. One of the most entertaining methods of training is the idea-gathering method known as "brainstorming." A group of employees, preferably with no supervisor present, is encouraged to express any ideas, no matter how "wild" or "offbeat," about the matter being discussed. These ideas are all recorded by a secretary appointed from the group. Following the session, the ideas are screened and evaluated. During the brainstorming session, however, no one is allowed to say "That won't work" or to express any negative thoughts. One person's ideas often spark those of others. (This is called "hitchhiking.") An array of challenging new approaches to a problem results.

One store used this method in training its salespeople. On one occasion, an ordinary kitchen mop was used as the item of merchandise to spark the salespeople's creative thinking. Each person was asked to think of at least one unusual use for the mop. Thirty-five different uses were listed, including wiping cobwebs off walls, propping open a basement window, and washing a car.

Skits. A playlet that relates to the ideas to be learned is written. This skit may then be performed by members of the training group. The audience consists of the members of the group who do not have roles in the skit. Skits may be used to demonstrate various tasks, such as "handling difficult customers," "handling more than one customer at a time," "making an exchange for a customer," and "showing managers how to evaluate employees."

Role Playing. The main difference between role playing and acting in a skit is that in role playing, the people playing roles speak extemporaneously. People in a skit have prepared lines. Usually, the training manager sketches out a situation and then asks members of the training group to play roles and ad lib their parts. For example, one person might be assigned to play the part of the salesperson in a given area of the store; a second, to play the part of the domineering customer; a third and a fourth, to play the parts of customers in a rush to buy; and a fifth, to be the manager who is responsible for seeing that customers get good, quick, courteous service.

Following the role playing, the various actions of the participants are analyzed by the entire group, and suggestions for improvement in handling the situation are made.

Case Study Method. One method of developing the ability to analyze problem situations and arrive at solutions is the case method of teaching. A difficult problem that has to be solved is presented either orally or in writing to the class. The class members are then asked to study the background of the problem, analyze the situation, discuss it with others who can answer some of their questions, and finally suggest a solution based on their analyses. This method is used primarily to develop managerial personnel.

Programmed Instruction. Programmed instruction is effective for many types of classroom situations. Through programmed instruction, individuals may be trained at their own speed and with a minimum of supervision during the training period. A detailed training manual must be drawn up which provides a small amount of learning within each page or section, called a *frame*. The employee reads the frame and writes the answer that is called for. This answer is immediately checked for accuracy in the following frame, and the trainee does not proceed to more advanced bits of learning until the one bit at hand has been mastered. Any routine learning where answers must be exact can be programmed. For example, a new salesperson may be taught to read price tickets, to write sales checks, to operate the cash register, and to give simple sales talks by this method.

Once the program has been developed, it may be used repeatedly for individual instruction at little additional cost, since only limited supervision is needed.

Sensitivity Training. Sensitivity training is designed to develop managerial abilities in those who have not been managers before. It is also used to enhance these abilities in people with experience on the job. This kind of training has

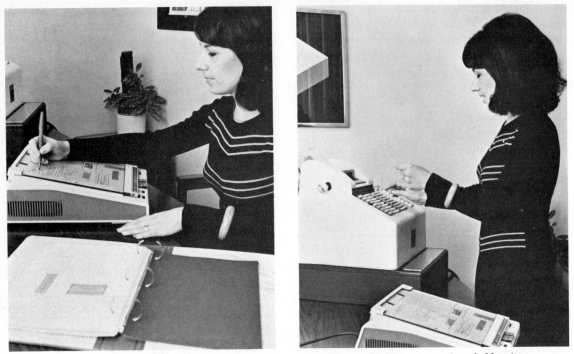

Some stores use programmed instruction to train their salespeople. Here, a new Joseph Magnin employee learns how to use a computerized sales register. First, she completes the questions provided in each frame of the training manual (left); then she tries practice exercises on the register (right).
Courtesy 3M Company, Visual Products Division

been used increasingly by industry and by retailers. The purpose of this method is to help the participants become aware of their behavior patterns and of their ability to relate to other people and to their environment. It also helps the people know how others relate to them. Sensitivity training is often used in firms where people with many different ethnic backgrounds are working together.

A group of managerial personnel is invited to attend five or more training sessions. The group is presented with a problem for discussion and resolution. An outside adviser meets with the group members, not as a leader but merely to see that they stick to the purposes for which they are meeting. The adviser also observes the behavior of the individuals present. Sessions may be taped for later playback and analysis. The manner in which people respond to problems and to each

other is subsequently evaluated and then discussed with each participant.

In-Basket Training

Decision making is difficult to teach. Managers, especially, must make decisions about all matters referred to them. Methods of developing this ability are open to constant experimentation. One method of helping managers learn how to decide the order of importance of tasks and how to make decisions about ways to accomplish the tasks is "in-basket" training. The employee is given a number of problems which theoretically occur during the business day. The employee then suggests how and in what order he or she would resolve the problems. When the problems are solved, in theory, they move across the employee's desk from the "in basket" to the "out basket." Thus, a branch store manager-in-train-

THE PERSONNEL MANAGEMENT FUNCTION

ing might find the following in-basket problems when arriving at 9:15 a.m. for work:

- One employee has telephoned that he is ill and unable to come to work today. No one else has been assigned to cover his area in the store.

- A customer has telephoned to complain that she did not receive an article she bought a week ago. She had asked that it be sent to her home.

- The boss has called a meeting of all department managers for 10:15 a.m., just 15 minutes after the store opens for business.

- Some merchandise is stacked in a wheeler in the department. The wheeler needs to be unpacked, but the stockkeeper who usually does that work will not arrive for another half hour. In the meantime, the wheeler is blocking the main traffic aisle.

- An order form needs to be completed and sent to the main store by 10 a.m. Getting the information for that form and filling it out will take at least a half hour.

What decisions does the manager-in-training make about the various problems? How does that person handle all the unexpected problems, get the work done, get to the boss's meeting on time, clear the floor, and have all the selling areas properly covered?

Practice in resolving such problems on paper helps the manager-in-training when that individual finally has to meet actual daily challenges that are similar.

Selection of Training Methods

No retailing organization needs or uses all the methods listed above. Each firm selects those that best suit its needs and budget allotments for training. Organizations that are interested in successful training constantly experiment in attempting to find the quickest, most effective, and least costly means of making employees ready for the job they are to do.

TOPICS FOR DISCUSSION

1. Explain the differences in personnel activities between a small, single-ownership store with a few employees and a large retailing corporation with hundreds of employees.
2. Why is it necessary for large retailing firms to recruit employees almost constantly?
3. What information is requested on an application form?
4. For what positions might the following tests be used, and what might the interviewer learn about the applicant from the results of each test? (a) Physical examination, (b) Test of manual dexterity, (c) General intelligence test.
5. Why do most retailing organizations use both centralized and decentralized training?
6. What can effective training achieve for an organization?
7. Which method or methods of training might be used most effectively to teach the following subjects to new employees? (a) Store history, (b) Dress regulations, (c) Behavior on the selling floor, (d) How to ring up a sale and make change, (e) How to approach customers quickly and courteously.
8. If you were to plan a skit for all employees to see as part of training for an all-store chinoiserie (Chinese) promotion, what preparations for the skit would be necessary?

9. What advantages might be expected from using such a skit for an all-store promotion?
10. In determining which training methods to use in a store, what are some of the criteria you would use?

MATHEMATICS FOR RETAILING

Miss Fulmer, a department manager, is opening a back-to-school shop that will be in existence for only four weeks. She has a budget of $1,000 for salespeople's salaries. While she need not use all the money, her expenses may not exceed that budget. Full-timers receive $2.75 an hour and work 35 hours a week. Part-timers are paid $2.30 an hour and work 8 hours a week in 4-hour shifts. Since full-timers do much more work and are more dependable, the manager prefers them. Therefore, she will allocate the larger portion of her budget for them. What is the maximum number of full-timers she will be able to hire? How many hours a week will be left for part-timers? Work out this problem on a separate sheet of paper.

COMMUNICATIONS IN RETAILING

A store that dealt only in cash sales had 500 salespeople. The store manager had received many complaints from customers about misaddressed sales checks that resulted in delayed delivery of merchandise that had already been paid for. Since the salespeople reported for work at different hours, it was impossible to find a time when they could all be assembled. Can you suggest a quick, inexpensive, yet effective way of informing the salespeople about their errors? Can you suggest how they can improve their way of addressing sales checks? Be prepared to discuss your ideas in class.

MANAGING HUMAN RELATIONS

The main store of a retailing organization was in the downtown section of a large city. Its four branches were located in the suburbs within 5 to 20 miles of the parent store. Main-store employees were loyal workers, and most of them had been with the company for 25 years or more. Business in the main store had been dropping off noticeably. The management decided to remodel the parent store and transfer to the branches all the more mature employees who wanted to make the move.

The suburban branches that had been built over the past 10 years were modern and were staffed mostly by relatively young employees. The more mature main-store employees who lived closer to the branches than to the main store were urged to transfer to the nearest branch store. They all chose to stay with the main store, however, preferring the inconvenience of travel to learning the ways of new managers and the routines of the newer stores.

What steps could the personnel department take to make transferring to the branch stores more appealing for the more mature workers? Be prepared to discuss your answer in class.

DECISION MAKING

The employment department was asked to suggest a replacement for the assistant buyer in the jewelry department. Two salespeople in the jewelry department were available for the position, and both were interested in it. Jane Brown had been in the department for 15 months. She was a pleasant person who did an adequate job, but she resented having to do anything other than sell merchandise. She was also a "clock watcher"—always in on time, but always leaving the exact minute that she was supposed to be through. Jill Black, the other salesperson, had been in the department for 12 months. She, too, was a pleasant salesperson. In addition, she was always in the store about 10 minutes early each day to help open up the department, and she frequently stayed a few minutes after closing to help do the final chores of the day. What are some of the facts the employment department would have to consider before arriving at a decision? Be prepared to discuss your answer in class.

CAREER LADDER

A young man graduated from a community college with an AAS degree (Associate in Applied Science). A large chain organization offered him a job as a trainee and said that he would be able to move up to store management positions. On a separate sheet of paper, list the kinds of jobs he would have and the order of their importance, from trainee to manager of one of the largest stores.

chapter 10
PERSONNEL PRACTICES AND CONCERNS

Today, when people are employed, they expect to be told what work they will do, what hours they will work, what payment they will receive for their work, what additional benefits they will get, how the performance of their jobs will be judged, what prospects they have for promotion, and how their interests will be protected. All these are the personnel concerns of the management of the firm. They extend beyond hiring and training people to do jobs. In addition to these concerns, certain theories about the basic needs of people and how people are motivated to work are of interest to all management personnel in retailing.

JOB CLASSIFICATIONS

What is the scope of the job for which the individual has been hired? This is a question every new employee wants to have answered and one that every manager must be able to explain. Since retailing has never been highly routinized, retailers have often been remiss in establishing job classifications and in specifying what each job entails.

Job classification, also called "job analysis," is the determination of the duties, responsibilities, and requirements for each job in an organization. *Job specification,* also called "job description," is the recording of this analysis or classification in writing. When the scope of a job has been analyzed and defined, it is possible for the manager to observe the person on the job, know what additional training, if any, is necessary, and judge how well the person is doing the job.

Initially, establishing job classifications and specifications entails various activities. The most effective way to develop job classifications is first to observe experienced personnel as they perform their jobs, then record their activities and the time they devote to each type of task. Next, the workers are interviewed in order to study the analyses in detail. Finally, the job specifications are written up. The write-ups may be reviewed with other management personnel and then rechecked with the persons doing the jobs. For the analysis, a check sheet may be helpful. This guide might include the following:

1. The job title

2. The location in the store where the job is performed

3. Actual work performed
   a. The percentage of the person's time devoted to each task
   b. The importance of each particular task in relation to other tasks performed by that same worker

4. Performance requirements on the job
   a. Responsibilities of the worker
   b. Machine or tool skills needed
   c. Knowledge needed
   d. Physical activities the worker will perform, such as lifting, standing, pushing, or walking
   e. Working conditions, such as temperature, kind of activity (group versus isolated), or

environment (crowded quarters versus open work areas)

5. Minimum hiring requirements for the job
   a. Experience needed
   b. Education needed

6. Training that will be needed after employment
   a. Centralized
   b. Decentralized

7. Supervision that will be needed for the person during the performance of the job

8. Relation of this job to other jobs in the organization
   a. Promotion from previous jobs in the organization
   b. Promotion to other jobs in the organization

After completing the job analysis, the personnel division can write up the job specifications. These need to be reviewed and updated every two or three years. New machines, new skills, new and speedier methods of doing things, new routines and systems, and better-educated employees all affect the tasks and the way the tasks will be performed. No job specification can, therefore, be static. It needs to be analyzed and rewritten periodically.

WAGE AND SALARY ADMINISTRATION

How much does the job pay? Every new employee wants to know the answer to this question, and every manager must know what each job is worth. What a job is worth is determined by a number of complex factors. A wage or salary is determined by the demands of the job, by the skill of the individual worker, by the general cost of living, by competition, by the available supply of workers, by the hours of work, by the previous experience of the applicant, and by the profit-making ability of the organization. If a firm is unionized, the union will seek contracts that set certain wage levels. In addition, the United States government, through its Fair Labor Standards Act (Federal Wage-Hour Law), has set minimum

wage and salary scales that affect most businesses.

The final determination of a wage and salary policy is the responsibility of top management in any firm. This policy, however, may be somewhat flexible to allow individual store managers to meet competition in local areas.

The Low-Wage Myth in Retailing

Retailing has long been characterized as a business that pays low beginning wages and salaries but that rewards its managers and executives rather handsomely. Competition for workers from nonretailing organizations, the Wage-Hour Law, collective bargaining, and—in some cases—the threat of unionization have changed the beginning wages in most retailing firms. While some beginning jobs may still offer minimum pay, those retailing workers who have demonstrated particular abilities or talents and those who have received promotions are usually compensated as well as or better than their peers who hold positions in nonretailing firms with similar educational requirements and responsibilities.

The Wage-Hour Law

The federal government's Fair Labor Standards Act of 1938 (amended in 1961, 1966, and 1974) has increased minimum salaries and decreased hours of work per week for employees in retail businesses whose annual gross volume is at least $250,000. The minimum hourly wage was set at $2.30 as of 1976. The basic workweek is 40 hours, and $1\frac{1}{2}$ times the regular rate of pay is given for hours worked beyond 40 by nonexempt personnel (those in nonsupervisory positions). Those who are in supervisory categories or who have special jobs come under the exempt rule and are not paid overtime for hours worked beyond the usual workweek. Management personnel usually work 40 to 45 hours per week on a year-round basis.

The Fair Labor Standards Act calls for equal pay for both men and women for equal work. That is, both men and women must receive the same pay for "jobs requiring equal skill, effort and responsibility which are performed under similar working conditions."

This act also requires that certain records be kept on wages, hours, and other data. These records must be preserved for three years. Since recordkeeping is simplified if full-time employees are paid a set weekly salary, this law has caused many retailers to put the majority of their non-managerial employees on weekly salaries. Some employees, however, are still paid by other methods that require more complex computations than set weekly salaries do.

Wage and Salary Plans

Wage and salary plans that can be computed easily, that are clear and understandable, and that provide good control of operating costs are the most efficient. In addition, some plans provide incentives for employees.

Wages usually applies to payments to employees who work at hourly or daily pay rates. For example, people holding "blue-collar" jobs as truck drivers or helpers, furniture finishers, sign makers, porters, painters, wrappers, and packers may be paid by the hour or by the day. Most wage plans have set hourly rates for a given number of hours per day or per week. Time and a half—or in some cases double time or even triple time—may be paid for overtime or for holiday or Sunday work.

Salaries refers to payments to employees who work at weekly or monthly or yearly pay rates. So-called "white-collar workers" come under this category. However, many department store salespeople are paid by the hour.

Salary Plans

The usual plans found in retailing organizations are straight salary, salary plus commission, salary plus bonus, straight commission, and quota bonus. Each of these plans has specific merits.

Straight Salary. The method of payment easiest to administer and the one most readily understood by the employees is the straight-salary plan. Full-time nonmanagerial retail workers usually work from 35 to 40 hours a week. The weekly salary, therefore, may be easily divided to determine the hourly rate for overtime pay.

Many employees like the straight-salary plan because it gives them a fixed number of dollars for each payment period and allows them to budget their expenditures for that time span. The main disadvantage of the straight-salary plan is its inflexibility. It neither rewards unusually fine performance nor penalizes poor job performance. Straight-salary methods of payment therefore require frequent evaluation to assure that workers are being compensated equitably for the jobs they are doing. Merit increases must be given, or there is little incentive for workers to improve their performance. Other methods of salary payment reward workers more directly in relation to their efforts and do not require such frequent analysis.

Salary Plus Commission. A method of payment that provides incentives to selling personnel to sell more goods is the salary-plus-commission plan. This plan assures the employee a basic weekly salary, and it also offers an incentive in the form of an additional small percentage of sales. This commission usually ranges from one-half of 1 percent to a maximum of about 2 percent. When this plan is available, the weekly salary is usually somewhat lower than that of employees receiving straight salaries, but this difference is offset by the added percentage of sales. Thus, if a person's base salary were $125 per week and that person had, during one week, net sales of $2,000 at 1-percent commission, the additional payment for the week would be $20. The total salary for the week, therefore, would be $145. *Net sales* refers to the total sales made by the individual during a given period, minus the price of any merchandise returned by that salesperson's customers during that same period.

The salary-plus-commission plan has most of the advantages of the straight-salary plan. In addition, it provides a reward for good performance in the form of the commission. This plan, however, requires more elaborate recordkeeping plus additional computations that are necessary for figuring taxes and other deductions.

Salary Plus Bonus. A method of payment used when a firm decides to give some money in addition to the regular salary at certain times of the year is known as the salary-plus-bonus plan. For example, in addition to receiving a regular salary, an employee may get $10, or $25, or even as much as a week's salary as a bonus. Bonuses are often given to regular employees at Christmastime.

Straight Commission. The method of payment that provides the greatest incentive for salespeople in large-ticket departments is the straight commission plan. In departments or stores that carry, for example, shoes, furs, coats, furniture, carpets, hard-surface floor coverings, better dresses, men's suits, and fine jewelry, the employee may work entirely on a commission basis. The commission is usually based on a percentage of net sales and ranges from around 3 percent to as much as 11 percent. If a person sold three sets of furniture during a week at a total retail price of $6,500 and that employee received a $4\frac{1}{2}$-percent commission on the sales, the salary for that week would be $292.50.

Under this plan of payment it is possible for some weeks to run considerably above average in sales and for other weeks to run below average. Many salespeople therefore like to have a *drawing account,* which provides them with a definite amount of dollars each week. A salesperson's drawing account is charged against his or her total yearly commissions, and the remainder may be paid at the year's end in one lump sum.

Recordkeeping for such a system is complicated. The ambitious salesperson who is paid under this plan, however, has an incentive that keeps her or him working at peak performance. Many salespeople selling large-ticket merchandise make salaries comparable to those of executives in other fields.

This method has a major disadvantage in that the salesworker might be put under high pressure to perform well. Also, it is possible that the "just looking" customer could be neglected.

Quota Bonus. In the quota-bonus plan, salary is based on the weekly quota set for each salesworker. For example, each person may be expected to have total sales of at least $2,000 each week. Each person whose sales total $2,000 will receive 8 percent, or $160. Those whose sales exceed $2,000 will be given a bonus—3 or 4 percent of the amount over $2,000. Thus, if the person's sales are $300 over the quota and the bonus rate is 4 percent, the person makes $12 more, or a total of $172 for the week.

Quotas must be reestablished every month, since fluctuations in sales would cause salaries to range widely. For periods of high sales activity, quotas are set at higher figures. For periods of low sales activity, quotas are lowered. On occasion the bonus may be shared by several employees rather than given for individual sales effort. This may promote team activity but may also discourage individual initiative.

Because this system is complicated, for both the employee and the employer, it is not used as often as the other salary payment methods.

Salary Supplements

In addition to receiving salaries according to different types of salary plans, retailing employees may have chances to make additional money through salary supplements. These may take the form of *spiffs,* or *P.M.s* (premium money), or *prizes.* Supplements are usually paid for selling new merchandise that manufacturers are trying to get customers to buy or high-priced products that move slowly.

Profit Sharing. Another inducement offered employees by some firms is profit sharing. At the end of the year, a certain percentage of the profit is divided among employees in proportion to their salaries.

Managers' Salaries. Managers are compensated in different ways by different firms. Some firms pay managers a straight salary. Some pay managers a straight salary plus a bonus based on the success of the store or the department. Others pay managers a salary plus a percentage of the net profit. Another method of payment is to give the manager a percentage of the net profit at the end of the year but to provide a monthly drawing account during the year. The total amount of the drawing account is subtracted from the manager's percentage of the net profit before final payment is made. Some grocery firms base the manager's salary on the net sales of the store instead of on net profit. The manager receives a small percentage of the net sales.

To attract and keep outstanding managerial personnel, some firms offer stock-option plans that allow certain people to buy stock in the firm at relatively low prices. These plans, in addition to profit sharing and bonus-payment plans, may help to make the total incomes of managers quite substantial.

FRINGE BENEFITS

Although most employees do not consider the fringe benefits they receive to be part of their salary or wage, fringe benefits may actually amount to 10 percent or more of their total pay. In addition, many fringe benefits are not taxed as pay and therefore add even more value to the overall income of the individual. Following is a list of fringe benefits available in many retailing firms.

- *Employee discounts* are offered in most stores. These often amount to 10 percent on regular purchases and as much as 20 percent or more on personal clothing items.

- *Medical coverage* for employees, such as that provided by Blue Cross and major medical plans, is entirely paid by some firms and partially paid by others.

- *Unemployment insurance,* designed to protect a person against loss of earnings should that person be unemployed for a certain period of time, is offered by most firms.

- *Pension plans* are available in many firms today. Some are funded entirely by the firm. Others are contributory plans—funded partially by the firm and partially by the individual worker. Under the Employee Retirement Income Security Act of 1974, if a firm has a pension fund, employees are eligible to join when they are 25 years old or older or when they have completed one year of service with the firm.

- *Group life insurance premiums* may be wholly paid by the firm or paid by both the firm and the worker for the benefit of the worker's beneficiaries.

- *Vacation and holiday pay* are additional bonuses that regular salaried workers receive.

- *Miscellaneous benefits* may include low-cost loans through mutual benefit associations or credit unions, sick pay, accident insurance, and dismissal pay.

EMPLOYEE RATINGS AND EVALUATIONS

All employees want to know what their job entails, how much their job pays, and how well they are performing their job. Judging job performance requires ratings and evaluations. An employee's work may be rated both formally and informally. *Formal ratings* occur in most large and well-organized retail businesses after the first two or three months of employment and every six months thereafter. In some small retailing firms no formal ratings are ever made. *Informal ratings* take place as often as the supervisor has reason to consider the work of the subordinate.

Formal ratings usually follow guidelines. The ratings are used to determine what the worth of the individual is to the firm, how well that person is doing the job, how satisfactory the person's attendance and promptness are, how effectively the individual works with other people, how high the overall production is, and what the person's potential is for promotion. Ratings are usually

NAME..Grochowski....Elizabeth.....A.........Beth........... SOCIAL SECURITY NUMBER 014-45-6591 ....
       (Last)   (First)   (Middle)   (Nickname)

PLACE
BORN ....New Haven, Conn..........: DATE.........10/6/--......HEIGHT....5ft.9in...WEIGHT ....120 LB....
              State or Country

EDUCATION ....University of Connecticut.. B. S. ....
                                                                       Degree—If any

MARRIED ☒ SINGLE ☐ DIVORCED ☐ WIDOWED ☐ SEPARATED ☐

DATE EMPLOYED....9/6/--....BY WHOM.....J. Brown.........WHERE......Milford.........Conn.........
                                                         CITY   STATE

RATING SUMMARY

NAME E. A. Grochowski

POS. ____Mgr.____   STORE Westfield, Ma.   VOL. ____1,950,000____   PER.END. 1/31/--

PERSONAL CHARACTERISTICS:

| 1. PLUS | Motivates people, has drive, is cooperative, and works well under pressure. Above average in self-expression. |

| 2. MINUS | Should develop greater ability to plan and organize, delegate and hold her people accountable, follow up on all projects, and should be more prompt in completing assignments on time. |

MERCHANDISING AND STORE OPERATION:

| 1. PLUS | Has good knowledge of merchandise, promotes aggressively, and follows new items well. Gives good customer service. |

| 2. MINUS | Needs to control inventory shortage better, be more concerned with operating details, and more profit conscious. Can improve markdown handling and record keeping. |

____C. Smith____   ____F. Jones____ | Summary ____2____ |
PREPARED BY   REVIEWED BY

EXPERIENCE

DATES FROM	POSITION	LOCATION	SALARY	BONUS		TOTAL COMPENSATION	FISCAL YEAR
				SPRING	FALL		
9/6/--	Mgmt. Trainee	Milford, Conn.	$135.00				
2/14/--	Div. Merchandiser	Milford, Conn.	$140.00				
8/22/--	Div. Merchandiser	New Haven, Conn.	$145.00				
2/17/--	Asst. Manager	New Haven, Conn.	$150.00				
12/1/--	Asst. Manager	Bristol, Conn.	$175.00				
1/2/--	Asst. Manager	Willimantic, Conn.	$200.00				
2/1/--	Manager	Westfield, Mass.	$275.00	$500.00	$2,000.00	$14,600.00	19--

(CONTINUED ON REVERSE SIDE)

Evaluations should be reviewed with the employee.

worked out at a meeting where records of the person's production, attendance, willingness to work, attitudes, and appearance, for example, may be discussed. Usually present at the meeting are personnel executives, the person's immediate supervisor, and other members of the management team under whom the individual works. In a smaller store one or two management executives might rate the person's performance. Some firms provide the employees with rating forms and ask them to rate themselves. These forms are then discussed with the supervisors, who indicate what points are incorrectly evaluated, in their opinion. Each rating is then corrected by a supervisor, signed by both the employee and the supervisor, and forwarded to the personnel office.

Subsequent to these evaluation meetings, raises or promotions may be given to those whose records indicate that they deserve such rewards. Those who do not receive raises may need counseling to help them receive merit raises after the next rating period. Following an evaluation session, each employee should receive either praise for a job well done or an explanation of his or her faults in performing the job. Even between evaluation sessions employees should be made aware of any unsatisfactory performance.

Informal evaluations, which are continuous, may also result in discussions of ways to improve performance.

Most retailing firms give full-time employees raises twice a year for the first two or three years but only once a year as workers progress to higher salary levels. If a person does not get an anticipated raise, that individual should check to see if he or she is actually doing everything that should be done to merit a raise.

SCHEDULING EMPLOYEES

A question just as important as "What do I do?", "How much will I be paid?", and "How well am I doing?" is "When do I work?" This is a complex question in retailing organizations because stores are usually open much longer than the number of hours any one employee will work. A store open daily and five nights a week might have an open-hour time of 62 hours per week. Yet no employee would work more than 40 hours, and some might work fewer hours. Grocery stores, stationery stores, drugstores, gasoline stations, and restaurants may be open from 72 to 168 hours each week. Employees, however, will work only a fraction of the time that the firms are open for business. Having adequate store coverage during all those hours, requires rather complicated employee scheduling procedures.

Stores need sufficient staffs for open hours. In addition, they try to accommodate customers by having service at its peak during hours that customers favor for shopping. To do this, stores work with several categories of employees. *Permanent employees* may be either full-time workers or part-time workers. *Temporary employees* may be seasonal employees; contingents on call as needed; or employees who work whenever they have time after school, on Saturdays, or during other busy periods. Temporary employees work during the Christmas, back-to-school, and Easter seasons, for example, or when special promotional events bring many customers to the store.

Full-time and Part-time Workers

Full-time employees work 35 to 40 hours a week. In most stores these hours cover a five-day workweek, often including Saturday. One day during the week is the "day off." If the store is open evenings, full-time employees may have their hours adjusted to include at least one evening of work a week.

Part-time employees are used extensively in retailing. Coverage for those periods of the day when buying activity is at its peak necessitates a large staff, which may then not be needed for several hours until another buying peak occurs. For example, stores in downtown areas may have an influx of shoppers between the hours of 11 a.m. and 2 p.m. Office workers like to browse through the stores and make purchases during their lunch hours. Yet this is also the lunch-hour period when regular, full-time employees of the stores need time off to eat. Hiring part-time sales workers who work from 11 a.m. until 3 p.m. daily permits regular employees to have a lunch period while providing needed coverage for the stores. Other part-time workers might be scheduled during the late afternoon and evening hours (4 p.m. to 8 p.m.) or at other hours as needed.

Two-Platoon and Three-Platoon Systems

Some large stores that are open two or more nights a week have experimented with a two-shift or a three-shift schedule instead of juggling people's hours daily to arrange different schedules. On these shift schedules, known as *platoons*, workers have fixed daily hours that they work. One shift leaves, and another shift is ready to step in and continue the work. Thus, one platoon might work from 9 a.m. to 5 p.m. daily, Monday through Friday. A second platoon might arrive to work from 5 p.m. to 9 p.m. daily, while a third platoon might take over on Saturday. Some stores have each platoon of workers on a part-time schedule of 20 hours a week.

Stores using platoon systems may also hire assistant managerial employees to work on these shift schedules. This relieves full-time managers who would otherwise find it difficult to provide supervision when stores are open so many hours during the week.

Platoon systems enable stores to hire more able employees than they might otherwise find for part-time or split-schedule work. Many housewives and high school and college students, and even some teachers and other professional workers, have some free hours each day for part-time work. The result is that stores using platoon systems often attract a high caliber of applicants for the part-time schedules.

EMPLOYEE SERVICES

The services that firms provide are valuable aids in attracting and holding desirable employees. These services may include employee lounges, eating places, health services, recreational activities, counseling for personal problems, and grievance procedures.

Lounges, Recreation Areas, and Lunchrooms

Most stores, even those that are rather small, assign some area of space for lounges where employees may sit to eat, read, or relax during their rest breaks and lunch periods. Large stores may have rather elaborate areas for such purposes. These may include lounge chairs, library books, racks for magazines and daily papers, and vending machines for food and drink. Some large organizations also have sun decks, auditoriums, and ping-pong, billiard, and card rooms in addition to regular lounge rooms. Such facilities enable employees to remain in the store during their relief and lunch or supper periods. These facilities also give employees an opportunity to relax or to socialize with other employees.

In small stores the lounge is often the lunchroom where employees gather to eat and relax. Larger stores may have separate employee lunchrooms equipped with cafeterias that sell food at low prices.

Health Services

Health services are often provided by retailing firms. Some stores have a doctor to whom they refer employees for initial physical examinations and to whom they send employees for any emergency that might arise during working hours. Other firms may have some facilities for physical examinations and limited treatment on the premises. Large firms may have well-equipped medical departments where care can be provided for customers as well as employees who need emergency treatment during store hours.

Counseling

Large firms usually have some provisions for employees to air grievances, either against other employees or against supervisors. In addition, counseling for personal problems may also be available on the premises. In small stores, the manager is often the only person available to provide counseling.

COMMUNICATIONS

The larger a firm becomes, the more difficult it is for employees to know one another and for the owners and managers to know all employees individually. In large firms communication becomes complicated. Three types of communication are considered important: *downward vertical*, which spreads from managers down to their own subordinates; *upward vertical*, which originates with subordinates and progresses to management levels; and *horizontal*, which is exchanged on the same employee level (managers talking to other managers, salespeople talking with other salespeople, and so forth). Some *diagonal* communications also exist that spread downward from managers to employees who do not report to them or that are initiated by subordinates and progress to management personnel to whom the subordinates do not report.

In very large firms verbal communications, except with people with whom one works directly, may be impossible. Various other methods are therefore used to keep people informed about what is going on and what needs to be accomplished. Memos, bulletins, letters, meetings, handbooks, and house organs are among the communications devices used. *Memos*, which are just short notes, may be sent by a manager to a subordinate to remind that person to do a job. Memos may also be sent by one manager to another manager, or they may originate with a subordinate and be sent to the manager to remind the manager that a job needs to be done or that a promise needs to be kept.

Bulletins are quick ways of informing people in the organization of some event, activity, or change in rules. When a very important announcement needs to be made, a bulletin may be issued for all employees.

General meetings, when possible, are effective means of face-to-face communication. However, staggered hours for employees make this method less suitable.

Handbooks are made available for new employees by most large retailing firms. These handbooks summarize rules and regulations, explain historical beginnings of the firm, and tell employees about fringe benefits they can expect.

House organs are distributed to employees in most large firms several times a year. These newspapers or magazines contain news of importance about the activities and the personnel of the firm; they tell about changes that have taken place; they list promotions and certain anniversaries of service with the firm; and they give other personal news of interest to readers. Most house organs have reports from each unit of an organization. This requires the appointment of a reporter from each store or branch. These publications may also provide space for letters written by employees. Such means of communication from management to employees and among employees serve to make those who work in a firm feel that they are a part of a community. Through such papers the organization often fosters pride among its employees.

Since people are the most important part of any organization, the manner in which the retailing firm arranges for communication among its employees will determine to a considerable extent the success of that firm in competition with other well-run firms.

LABOR UNIONS AND RETAILING

Retailing was developed by individuals who believed in working hard for long hours and who expected their employees to do the same. Since pay in the early days of retailing was relatively low and the hours were long, employee discontent with conditions often existed. This attitude paved the way for the "Early Closing Societies," which were the forerunners of the unions that have made headway in some segments of the retailing field. Both union activity and labor legislation have contributed to the modest growth of unionization in retailing. Although many unions have persisted in trying to unionize retailing firms, most retailers have resisted such union activities.

There are several unions that solicit membership among retailing employees. The oldest of these was organized in 1889 in the Midwest and was known as the Retail Clerks International Protective Association. In 1947 its name was changed officially to Retail Clerks International Association, better known as RCIA, and its membership is now national in scope.

A second union, The Retail Wholesale and Department Store Union, became firmly established in 1937, with employee groups mainly from the New York City area. Other unions that claim some retail membership among their lists include the Building Service Employees International Union, the Amalgamated Meat Cutters and Butcher Workmen of North America, the Amalgamated Clothing Workers of America, and the International Brotherhood of Teamsters, Chauffeurs, Warehousemen & Helpers of America. A few large stores also have independent unions of their employees.

Legislation and government decisions that have particularly affected retail unionization include the following:

- 1914—The Clayton Act, which gave labor greater legal protection.

- 1933—The National Industrial Recovery Act, which encouraged labor union growth.

- 1935—The National Labor Relations Act, better known as the Wagner Act, which guaranteed the right of employees to "self-organization to form, join, or assist labor organizations. . . ."

- 1965—The decision of the National Labor Relations Board that unions could "splinter" employees of stores into separate units for organizing purposes. This permitted selling, nonselling, and restaurant employees in the same store to be organized separately by interested unions.

In general, unionization of retailing employees has been only modestly successful. Fewer than one-half million people out of some 10 million employed in retailing hold union membership. The reasons why some retailing employees have turned to unions as their representatives are as follows:

- Labor legislation in the United States has generally favored unionization.

- The increasingly impersonal nature of modern industry and inadequate communication have caused personnel to turn from the management of the firm to the union representatives for understanding and attention.

- The increased activity on the part of the unions in some parts of the country in enrolling members has resulted in some membership growth.

- The reluctance of some retailing managements to take forward steps in modernizing their personnel practices has made some employee groups seek union strength to obtain benefits granted by other firms.

- Some unions have not only won wage and salary increases for their members but have also introduced medical plans and other fringe benefits to aid workers.

Offsetting these reasons for joining, however, are the reasons why vast numbers of retailing employees have never considered unionization. These include the following:

- Most retailing workers have little interest in unionization.
  a. Many consider themselves to be "white-collar" workers and associate unions with the representation of "blue-collar" workers.
  b. Large numbers of part-time and seasonal workers who are employed in retailing have no interest in joining unions.
  c. Employees who hope to be promoted to management positions are usually not interested in joining unions.

- The variety of jobs available in retailing is not conducive to unionization.

a. Workers in retailing are often difficult to classify under exact job titles.

b. Many retailing jobs require only short training periods. This makes it easy to hire replacements. Striking employees, therefore, can easily be supplanted.

c. There is little loyalty among different groups of workers. Salespeople, for example, are usually not concerned with the attitudes and interests of stock, warehouse, or office personnel, and vice versa.

• To avoid unionization, stores have decreased working hours and increased salaries and fringe benefits. Therefore unionization would no longer offer workers important advantages.

• Many retail stores are small, or the units or branches of large organizations are small. When employees know their supervisors well and work closely with them, unionization rarely has an appeal.

If a store wishes to avoid unionization, it should make sure that its salary policies, fringe benefits, and hiring and dismissal policies are fair and equitable and that its working conditions are good. If a store has not established job classifications and specifications, it should do so, since one of the first activities of the union is to determine the limitations of the various job categories. Probably the most important element in keeping a store nonunion is the attitude of managers toward the employees. If the managers are interested in the workers and willing to listen to their work problems and to adjust unfair practices or policies, and if they are thoughtful in praising employees for good work, the employees will probably have little interest in forming or joining a union.

MOTIVATION OF EMPLOYEES

How are people induced to work well, efficiently, and imaginatively? No topic concerning working people has been discussed and analyzed more than that of the motivation of people to work and to enjoy their work. Books on management instruct would-be managers on how to help develop employees, and books on psychology talk about the motivation of the worker. Work itself is regarded as an integral part of life, as is indicated by the book *Working, People Talk About What They Do All Day and How They Feel About What They Do* by Studs Terkel.

Retailing is a business that deals with both goods and people. Buyers (people) buy goods from vendors (people) and sell to customers (people). Therefore, to be in retailing is to be involved in working with people.

Although motivation of employees is the concern of everyone in a retailing firm, the personnel division, being most responsible for the hiring and development of people, is generally credited with preparing managers to deal with the many aspects of employee satisfaction and motivation. What makes people enjoy a job and work hard at it has been the concern also of psychologists and educators.

Many theories exist about people's attitudes toward work and about what motivates them to want to work and to excel in their work. Three theories that are popularly discussed are McGregor's Theory X and Theory Y concepts,[1] Maslow's Hierarchy of Needs theory,[2] and Herzberg's Motivation-Hygiene theory.[3]

McGregor's Theory X and Theory Y

According to McGregor, managers view people in one of two ways, and he named those ways Theory X and Theory Y. Managers who accept Theory X, he said, believe that people are basically lazy and that they will avoid work, if possible. Such managers, therefore, think people need direction in their work and that workers are motivated to do a job right only by fear. Workers, according to Theory X, seek security mainly through work, but they do not like responsibility, and they have little ambition.

[1] Douglas McGregor, *The Human Side of Enterprise,* McGraw Hill Book Company, New York, 1960.
[2] Abraham H. Maslow, *Motivation and Personality,* Harper & Row, Publishers, Incorporated, New York, 1964.
[3] Frederick Herzberg, *Work and the Nature of Man,* New American Library, Inc, New York, 1973.

THE PERSONNEL MANAGEMENT FUNCTION

By contrast, managers who accept Theory Y believe that people like to work as well as to play. They think that people control their habits and actions in the best interest of the job they are doing; that they accept and even seek responsibility; and that they enjoy using their imagination and creativity to do a job well.

According to McGregor, a manager's ideas about the way people react to work affect the way that manager treats the people under his or her direction.

Maslow's Hierarchy of Needs Theory

In Chapter 3, we considered how people use their buying activities to satisfy the five needs that make up Maslow's hierarchy. Now let us apply Maslow's theory to the motivation of workers.

Employment, in retailing and other jobs, provides the financial means to satisfy the physiological needs for food, clothing, and shelter. A steady job also contributes to the fulfillment of the need for safety. Job security is an important factor in a worker's sense of well-being. If the security of an employee's job in a company or the future of the firm is in doubt, the employee may find the need for security unsatisfied. Such insecurity could have profound effects on the employee's attitude and performance.

The social needs can be well satisfied in a people-oriented business such as retailing. Helping customers and working and socializing with other store personnel can foster a sense of belonging for a salesperson or a manager.

Whether a retailing job satisfies a person's need for esteem depends on how well the person performs the work. Precise job classifications and specifications help both workers and their supervisors to evaluate job performance. A worker who performs well and whose efforts are rewarded by merit raises, bonuses, and promo-

tions, for example, can satisfy the need for self-actualization through work.

The managers and the personnel executives who understand this hierarchy of needs will know that even high pay and short hours will not make people work well. They must believe that the work they do is appreciated and that their particular contribution makes a difference on the job.

Herzberg's Motivation-Hygiene Theory

Dr. Herzberg's theory has been tested in many job situations. His concept shows that certain policies and actions on the part of the management of a firm will be hygienic but will not motivate the workers, while other factors will serve to motivate them. Among *hygienic factors,* Dr. Herzberg includes company policy and administration, supervision, salary, interpersonal relations, and working conditions. If these are not satisfactory, workers may rebel, quit their jobs, or do their jobs poorly. Therefore, all these factors must be satisfactory. In themselves, however, they will not either singly or collectively create the desire in employees to work harder or to do a better job.

The true satisfiers or *motivators,* according to Dr. Herzberg, are achievement on the job; recognition of a job well done; the work itself, which many people find rewarding; responsibility for the work being done; and promotion to positions of even greater responsibility. Thus, motivation cannot be achieved in ways that serve only to keep the worker from being dissatisfied. It must come from the achievements and satisfactions of and responsibility for the work itself.

The knowledge and application of these three theories of attitudes toward work, needs of workers, and motivation to work should help managers to supervise employees in a firm effectively.

TOPICS FOR DISCUSSION

1. Explain why retailing firms have lagged behind industrial firms in making job specifications.
2. Why do job specifications have to be revised frequently?
3. Discuss the factors that must be considered in planning a salary or wage for a given job.
4. Discuss the advantages and disadvantages of the straight-salary method of payment.
5. How do fringe benefits aid the worker?
6. Explain the procedures to be followed when an employee's formal rating is only "fair."
7. Explain the advantages of the platoon or shift method of scheduling employees as opposed to the more usual method of using part-timers and Saturday helpers and staggering the hours of full-timers to give coverage for busy periods.
8. What is the function of a house organ? What advantages does it offer retailers and their employees?
9. Explain why retail firms have not been more generally unionized throughout the country.
10. Discuss, in relation to the manager's supervision of employees, the following concepts: (a) Theory X and Theory Y, (b) Maslow's hierarchy of needs, and (c) Herzberg's motivation theory.

MATHEMATICS FOR RETAILING

A salesperson in a men's shirt department was paid a straight salary of $185 for a five-day workweek. In the store during the year he bought clothing for himself at a total retail value of $250 and also household goods, presents, and clothing for his wife valued at $500. For these purchases, he received the usual employee's discount of 20 percent for personal clothing and 10 percent for all other items. The store paid his medical insurance premiums, which totaled $11 per month, but 5.85 percent of his salary went for Social Security deductions. Another $1\frac{1}{2}$ percent went for unemployment insurance, and 5 percent was taken for his pension plan. That year the salesperson enjoyed a two-week vacation with pay plus seven paid holidays. What percentage of his annual salary was used for fringe benefits? Work this out on a separate sheet of paper.

COMMUNICATIONS IN RETAILING

A store manager thought it would be a good idea to remind the firm's employees how much above and beyond their salary was being paid in fringe benefits. On a separate sheet of paper, outline an effective method the manager might use to get this information to the employees.

DECISION MAKING

A salesperson's work was evaluated during the formal rating period. Everyone agreed that she was a very capable worker, since she had the highest sales total in the department week after week. However, the rating discussion revealed that her poor housekeeping in the department irritated all the other salespeople. She had a bad habit of leaving out all the merchandise that she had been showing customers. Her co-workers were forced to do her stockkeeping for her in order to know where goods were. This kept them from making as many sales as they otherwise might. The friction has created arguments and impatience among the other salespeople. What action should the department manager take? Be prepared to discuss your answer in class.

CAREER LADDER

A young woman graduating from a local two-year college decided to apply to a chain store's headquarters office for a position in the large personnel department. On a separate sheet of paper, outline the jobs she might have as she works her way up from the position of preliminary interviewer to the position of personnel vice-president over a period of 15 years.

PART FOUR

THE BUYING FUNCTION

chapter 11

BUYING AND THE BUYER'S JOB

A newly constructed retail store in the suburbs was to be opened on August 20 in time for back-to-school selling and fall home-furnishings sales and well before the festive Christmas selling season. Three days before its scheduled opening, the entire store was complete and ready to have the merchandise moved in. A stroll through the store at that point was like a walk through a cavernous jungle of wooden, glass, and metal shelves, cases, and racks. No customer would be induced to enter such a place.

Three days later, when the merchandise had been moved in, the store was a riot of color and excitement. There were signs about the merchandise; mannequins; displays of room settings; racks of dressy clothes and blue jeans; and stacks of back-to-school bags, paper, and pencils.

People swarmed through the store, enthusiastic about the appeal of the goods—their textures, colors, shapes, and varieties. Merchandise, then, is the catalyst that brings the customers and the retailers together.

A store may feature merchandise that is mass-produced or all handmade. The store may offer goods made locally, manufactured throughout the United States, or imported from the four corners of the earth. Shoes from Italy, gloves from France, and woolens from the British Isles may be among the featured merchandise. Stainless steel from Scandinavia; watches from Switzerland; cameras, radios, and television sets from Japan; artifacts from Africa, Mexico, and South America; clothing from Hong Kong; carpets from Iran; jewelry from Thailand; and brassware from India may fill the shelves, racks, and storage areas. Stores are wonderful places filled with the things people need and want as well as the things they dream about and hope to buy someday.

Since retail stores are in business to buy and sell any or all of these varieties of goods, some person or people within each retailing organization must decide what merchandise to buy, when to buy it, how much of it to buy, where to buy it, what price to pay for it, and, finally, what price to ask for it.

THE BUYING FUNCTION

Retailing was defined earlier as the buying and selling of merchandise to satisfy the needs and wants of the ultimate consumer. Although a modern retailing organization has important functions to perform in areas such as personnel management, financial management, store operations, and sales promotion, its primary functions are buying and selling. These two essential functions are the hub around which all the other activities revolve. The selling function will be discussed in detail in later chapters. The following list indicates the many kinds of work that the buying function involves:

- Forecasting the needs and wants of the customers likely to purchase from the firm

- Planning the kinds and amounts of merchandise to buy

- Selecting the sources of supply of the merchandise

- Negotiating the contract for the sale of the merchandise

- Pricing the merchandise initially for sale to the customers and repricing at a later date any merchandise that has not sold

- Keeping records about the merchandise while it is in the possession of the store

- Reordering merchandise that is continuing to be in demand

The person in retailing who is responsible for most of these tasks is known as a *buyer*. The person assigned to aid the buyer in performing these tasks, and who is often in training for the more responsible position, is known as an *assistant buyer*. The executive to whom the buyer in a large organization reports is known as a *merchandise manager*. The merchandise manager supervises the work of several different buyers in related departments.

The Relationship of the Buying Function to Other Major Retailing Functions

The buyer works closely with the managers of finance and control on all the records of the merchandise that is on order, in the store, and sold. The buyer consults with the personnel managers about the personnel needs for the buying activities and about the training of personnel who will sell the products of the buyer's department. With the managers of store operations, the buyer determines space needs and the proper shelves, bins, racks, and display areas. The buyer and the store operations managers also discuss any special problems concerning protection of the products carried. With the sales promotion managers, the buyer discusses and plans the advertising, displays, and general image building for the department.

How Retail Buyers' Jobs Differ

Buying functions are the same for all retailing organizations, but the division of work among individual buyers may vary considerably. The work of any one buyer depends on many factors. Stores range in size. Therefore, the tasks of buyers in small stores may differ from those of buyers in larger organizations who purchase the same kinds of goods but in much larger quantities. Within one store, the buyers for large departments may have tasks to perform that are quite different from those of buyers for small departments. The merchandise can range from staple goods to fashion goods, from mass-produced items to handmade items, and from goods for daily consumption to articles purchased once in a lifetime. There can be little similarity in the activities of the buyers who cover such different types of products.

The two basic kinds of buying are known as market buying and specification buying. In *market buying* the buyers go to the manufacturers' showrooms or use a catalog to view the merchandise. The buyers then select from those goods that are available the products they think their stores can sell profitably. These are the products that the manufacturers' designers and stylists have developed. Retailers all over the country will be able to purchase these products. Therefore, competitive retailers may have the same merchandise on their shelves. In market buying the quantities purchased by the retailer

Buyers often go to the manufacturers' showrooms to inspect the merchandise and place orders.
Photograph by Bill Cunningham

may be small or large depending on the needs of the retail firm and the capacity of the manufacturers to produce the goods. Some buyers arrange to franchise the lines of certain manufacturers. This means that they negotiate contracts for exclusive sales of certain items or lines of merchandise on a regional basis so that no nearby competitors will carry the same items of merchandise.

Specification buying, by contrast, gives the retailers unique merchandise. The retailers develop the products for their own stores and then seek manufacturers to make them for their exclusive use. In many cases, through specification buying, the retailer is able to develop a product that is superior to one carried in other stores at a similar price. Sometimes the merchandise produced to the retailer's specifications sells at a lower price than comparable nationally branded lines. Since

the individual retailer has developed the product, he or she has it exclusively, and no competitors carry that identical product.

The main disadvantage of specification buying is that if there is any investment necessary for tools, dies, or skilled labor, no manufacturer is willing to make up a product exclusively for one firm unless that firm places a sizable order. Consequently, in most merchandise lines, only rather large retailing firms can purchase in the volume necessary to have their own private-label or privately developed products.

DIFFERENT KINDS OF BUYERS' JOBS

Buyers' jobs differ not only because of the size of the retailing organization or department and the kinds and price ranges of merchandise carried but also because of the type of firm for which the

THE BUYING FUNCTION

buyer works. Buyers are employed by retail stores, by chain or central buying offices, and by service organizations known as resident buying offices. Again, the character of these organizations varies, and many of the buyers have different responsibilities and duties. Examples of each of these organizations and the buying jobs existing within them will illustrate the various aspects of the buying function.

The Retail Store Buyer

In a small retail store, the owner or manager may be responsible for purchasing all the merchandise to be sold. That person would, therefore, be the "buyer" for that store. In that capacity, the manager would determine what the store's customers would need and want for the coming period of time, visit manufacturers or have their representatives call, and place orders for goods. Such a person is usually in the store most of the day and also supervises the activities related to handling the goods within the store and oversees the selling of the products to the customers. The owner or manager would perform all functions of the buyer in addition to those other tasks for which he or she has assumed responsibility, as a jack-of-all-trades.

In Large Single-Unit Stores. In a somewhat larger store, one individual may be assigned to do the buying for the entire store. If this necessitates that person's being out of the store a large part of the time, others, such as the store manager, may take care of the activities that pertain to handling and selling the merchandise within the store. In departmentized stores, a buyer may be assigned to be in charge of the merchandise for one department only. That buyer may, however, need to travel to obtain the goods and may, therefore, be aided by an assistant buyer or a department manager who handles the activities within the department itself. Still, the responsibility for spending money for the merchandise and for the success of the department in selling the goods is still the buyer's. Each separate department is like a small store for which the buyer

assumes responsibility for financial and operating success. A buyer is compensated in relation to the volume and profit which that department or area of merchandise produces for the retailing organization. The greater the sums of money involved, the more the buyer is paid.

In Stores with Branches. When branches are added to a store, the main store's buyer may also handle the buying for the added stores. In many cases, this merely means that the buyer computes the additional merchandise needed to stock the branch stores and makes the necessary larger purchases. Assistants or department managers in the branches then oversee the actual handling and sale of the merchandise in those stores. Some buyers, however, find their buying activity complicated because the demands of the customers in the branch stores vary from those of customers in the main store. If the branch stores are very large, or if they are at a considerable distance from the main store, some firms assign *associate buyers* to the branch stores. These people work with the main store's buyer on general purchases of goods, but they also place individual store orders for special kinds of goods desired by their particular customers. The main store's buyer continues to have the responsibility for the financial success of the entire department, including the branch stores' departments.

The advent of increasing numbers of branch stores has complicated the buyer's job in other respects. As more branches were added, and as distances of these from the main store became greater, the buyer found the branches less accessible. Increasingly, supervision of selling was delegated to those people whose full time was spent in the branch stores. Store management began more and more to separate the work of the buyer from the selling activities of the department. Some stores even isolated the buyer physically from the main store by providing the buyer with an office in a separate building. The buyer could then concentrate exclusively on procuring merchandise and on balancing the flow of goods to all the branches according to their needs.

Buyers who had previously been able to oversee the salespeople as they served customers, to hear customers' expressions of approval or disapproval of merchandise, and to observe directly the daily movement of merchandise believed that the divorce from the selling floor would detract from their buying ability. However, with new and speedier methods of obtaining information, buyers are finding that their computer records give them adequate knowledge about their customers' wishes. And buying can be done effectively even without actually seeing customers or supervising the selling of the goods. Thus, large stores with branches have, in some instances, changed to a method of central buying that chain stores have used for many years.

The Chain Organization Buyer

When chain stores were first organized in the United States, their managements found that centralizing their activities was economical. Today chain organizations maintain central buying offices which employ buyers who perform the buying for all the stores controlled by the chain. Each chain has its own way of handling its buying activities, but all have an overall concentration of buying.

In chain organization buying, the buyers' responsibilities may range from total control in central merchandising, to control shared with store managers through central distribution, to little control under price agreement. These three kinds of control are described below. In addition, committees, also described below, may advise buyers.

Buying Through Central Merchandising. Some chain organizations control all retailing functions through the central office except the actual running of the individual stores. In such organizations, the buyer plans what to buy, investigates the market to select the best sources, prices the goods, controls how much is bought, and allocates specified amounts to the individual stores. The computerized sales records of the stores are sent regularly to the central office, and replenishments of stock are made on the basis of these records. The individual store manager does not know what merchandise will be arriving until it actually is unpacked for sale at the store.

Display plans and advertising are similarly developed in the central office. The store manager follows display plans, prices the merchandise as directed by the buyer, and sells the merchandise. This type of tight central control is frequently used by specialty store chains.

Both increased competition and the speed and efficiency of computerized recordkeeping have expanded this method of central buying. Fashion departments that are highly competitive and that require a new look every week or two to remain leaders in their areas are efficiently stocked by central merchandising.

Let us examine this method used by a chain organization with 200 stores across the country. There are many types of merchandise bought and sold by this chain. One buyer is assigned to buy only handkerchiefs for ladies, men, boys, and girls. This buyer has an office in the headquarters of the chain, located in a large office building in the downtown area of New York City. The buyer of handkerchiefs gets weekly records of the sales of handkerchiefs from each of the 200 stores. This buyer knows how many and what kinds, sizes, and colors of handkerchiefs each store usually sells during a given period of time. Keeping in mind the sales figures of previous years and current trends, the buyer visits the handkerchief manufacturers often. The buyer places the orders, and has the handkerchiefs shipped to a central warehouse or directly to the individual stores. If one of the stores has some special needs, the store manager or department manager in that store sends a request to the central office's buyer. One store in the Southwest, for example, had customer requests for bandana-type handkerchiefs. When this information was transmitted to the central office, the buyer, searched for a manufacturer who made such bandanas at a reasonable price. The buyer then ordered the desired quantity and had the bandanas shipped directly to the Southwest store.

In this way the chain can gain the economies of central buying as well as recognize the diversities of individual stores in different locations. This is a simplified explanation of the complex central buying activity. Because a central buyer buys vast quantities of merchandise and has responsibility for the success of all stores of the chain in selling that merchandise, the buyer is well paid for his or her ability and knowledge.

Central Distribution. Some chain organizations, primarily variety chains and food chains, give their store managers more latitude in the selection of merchandise. Through the central buying office, the buyers purchase the merchandise and have the stocks of goods shipped to centrally located warehouses. The individual store managers then requisition the goods as they need them from the central warehouse. Lists of the items appear on check sheets, which the buyer has filled out and sent to the warehouse. Economies are realized for the entire chain by the buyers' placing of large orders for merchandise for all the stores at one time. The individual store manager, however, selects those items that meet the local customers' needs. Perishable and seasonal items may be shipped directly to the individual stores (this is called *drop shipment*) instead of being sent to the warehouse. For products such as plants, fresh foods, baked goods, and candy, the manager may do the buying locally.

This method gives the store manager considerably more autonomy and responsibility for the merchandise than exists under the central merchandising plan. The buyer's responsibility, by contrast, is slightly reduced.

Catalog Price-Agreement or Listing Plan. Central buying by catalog price agreement gives the store manager the fullest authority over the goods carried in the individual store. The central buyers visit manufacturers and select merchandise that is shown in catalogs. The prices for which those goods can be obtained and the terms of purchase are listed in the pages of the cata-

logs. The central buyers' responsibilities are to search the marketplace for the best available goods for the price; to arrange for their purchase; and to plan the speediest, most economical delivery procedure for each store to use. The buyers then notify the store managers of the availability of the goods listed in the catalogs, which are issued frequently. Each store manager decides which goods to carry, how much of them to order, and when to buy them. Store managers are also free to find their own sources of merchandise if they can locate better products at lower prices. However, since the buyers spend all their time searching the marketplace for the best merchandise at the lowest prices, only rarely does a store manager find a buy superior to that suggested by the central office. This freedom of the store manager to select the merchandise from local sources becomes a challenge, however, to the central buyer to search for the best buys to recommend to the stores. The buyers who work under the price-agreement plan have less responsibility and authority than buyers working under the plans already discussed.

Some of the large junior and regular department store chains use this method of central buying. Because of competition and the growing use of computerized records, however, this method is increasingly giving way to central merchandising.

Committee Buying. As chain organizations have grown in size, buyers have had increasingly large sums of money to expend for merchandise. This has been accompanied by greater responsibility for making successful buys. Since wrong decisions could be extremely costly to the firm, an aid to the buyer in the form of *committee buying* has developed. This started first in the grocery field, where buyers made purchases for supermarkets involving many thousands of dollars. Later committee buying was adopted by other types of firms.

Committee buying aids the buyer by ensuring proper consideration of all factors before the buyer embarks on plans to introduce a new line

Buyers keep abreast of fashion trends by attending fashion shows given by designer houses.
Photograph by Bill Cunningham

THE BUYING FUNCTION

or a new item. The committee is composed of executives within the central office who are designated to review the work of the buyer. To illustrate this method of buying, let us visit a buyer of children's shoes for a large chain, Mr. Walters, who is about to create a new infants' shoe line.

After checking the competitors' footwear offerings and those of stores carrying higher-priced lines, Mr. Walters decided to develop a white leather shoe for infants that could be priced at about $3.98. First he bought six different pairs of infants' shoes from various competing stores. These shoes ranged in price from $3.59 to $5 a pair. The shoes were then analyzed for quality, comfort, attractiveness, ease of care, safety for the child while wearing them, support for the child's feet, and durability. Following this analysis, the buyer drew up specifications for the infants' shoe to be carried by every store in the chain.

A search of the market was undertaken to find which manufacturers would be interested in developing the shoe the buyer had decided upon at a price that would permit the shoes to retail for $3.98 a pair. Several manufacturers cooperated by making samples of shoes for him from his specifications. He distributed these sample shoes to employees in his firm who had infants in their families so that the shoes could be tested for wear and comfort.

At the end of a two-month period, he obtained the shoes from the employees, interviewed them about the wear and comfort features, and analyzed the way the shoes had held up in use. Then the buyer discussed desired changes from his initial specifications with each of the manufacturers. Finally one manufacturer was selected; the price the firm would pay for the shoes was established; and the schedule of delivery dates for the quantities necessary to stock the 270 stores in the chain was fixed. The buyer was then ready to submit his findings to the committee assigned to review this large initial order, which amounted to over $25,000.

Every aspect of the proposed merchandise was scrutinized by committee members, and the entire planned purchase was analyzed. The committee agreed that the buyer had developed, with the aid of the manufacturer, a good, salable, competitive product. The committee thought, however, that the buyer had not sufficiently considered the kind of packaging that would best showcase this product when it was displayed on store counters throughout the country.

After the committee's suggestions were submitted, the buyer worked out further details with the manufacturer. He tried to figure out how he could include the package in the cost which he had set as the maximum for this item.

When the shoes were finally purchased, they were packaged in clear vinyl containers tied with pink and blue ribbons with tiny bells attached. The shoes, so attractive in these containers, sold in tremendous quantities. The see-through containers exposed the merchandise to view and, at the same time, protected the shoes. The gift look of the package with its bells and ribbons appealed to customers.

The sales success of the product proved the value of having a knowledgeable management team review the work of the single buyer in developing a product for which both the initial order and the repeat business would represent a large monetary investment.

The Buyer in a Resident Buying Office

The resident buying office is primarily a service organization that helps retail store buyers, although it is sometimes also used by chain organizations. Retail stores are often located at considerable distances from the goods their buyers purchase. The stores, however, may have constant market representation through the services of resident buying offices. These enable the store buyers to visit the market only periodically but to have an advisory service available at all times for assistance.

Resident buying firms exist to serve the individual retailing organization's buyers. Since resident buying offices are located in the center of the market from which goods are bought, these

When the buyer writes up an order, fabrics, colors, patterns, and other information must be supplied.
Photograph by Bill Cunningham

firms offer a valuable on-site service for their member stores.

Buying offices charge an annual fee for the assistance each provides its member stores. The resident buyers employed in the resident offices scout the market daily and keep store buyers informed about new merchandise, where it can be obtained, and what the prices are. On order from the store buyers, the resident buyers may actually make purchases of goods. Since resident buyers rarely make purchases except when instructed, they have less responsibility than store or chain buyers and receive smaller salaries.

There are currently four main types of resident buying offices: independent or salaried, private, associated, and syndicate. Although they perform many of the same functions, their relationships to their member stores affect their responsibility and authority for the merchandise they buy.

The buyers in these different resident offices are compensated according to their total responsibility for actually purchasing merchandise. Those who merely inform store buyers about merchandise have the lowest salaries, but those who act as central buyers in their responsibility for buying goods for their member stores receive the highest salaries. In between are those who have some responsibility for purchases.

Independent Buying Offices. Stores in any area of the country may belong to independent buying offices. They pay the office of their choice a set percentage of purchases on an annual contract basis. This fee covers all the services provided by the buying office. Some of the resident offices represent large department stores, while other smaller offices represent specialty apparel stores, home-furnishings stores, and other types of stores that require the services of market contacts. The resident office has member stores with similar interests, so that one buyer in the office for a given line may scout the market for as many as 200 or more stores carrying similar goods.

No competing stores, of course, are members of the same resident office. This enables the resident buyer to work also with groups of buyers from the member stores to develop privately branded items that all the stores agree to carry and for which sizable group orders are placed. This group buying helps to reduce costs and makes the participating stores better able to compete with chain organizations. It also permits these stores to offer their customers exclusive merchandise, broader assortments, and sometimes additional price lines.

Resident buyers not only scout the market each day but also send out daily and weekly "flashes"—announcements of new and interesting items available, as well as information about items that have proved to be best sellers in stores in other parts of the country. Both this constant exchange of information and market representation give each store ready access to the newest and most salable products at a low buying cost.

Resident offices also serve as headquarters for member-store buyers when those buyers come to the market. They are able to have a desk for their records, a phone for their calls, and a meeting place for holding discussions with manufacturers' representatives and other buyers.

Additional services provided for member stores may include help in planning group promotions, advertising layouts, training aids, and executive recruitment.

Private Buying Offices. A few very large retailing organizations maintain their own private buying offices in market centers such as New York City. The buyers in these offices perform the same functions as the buyers in the independent office, but they restrict their activities to the one retailing organization to which they belong.

Associated Buying Offices. Associated buying offices are established by a group of stores, which own, operate, and control them. Such offices lack the flexibility of choice of members that the independent offices enjoy, but they have the advantage of being able to develop a greater assortment of brand-name goods and to operate wholesaling and other activities that are more difficult for the independent offices to maintain.

Member stores have complete autonomy in their individual store activities, but they may use the facilities of the buying office for any advantages it offers. Group buying, promotional buying, and the opportunity to exchange important data about store operations are the main advantages these offices offer their members. In addition, all other services provided by independent resident firms are available to the members of the associated offices.

Syndicate Buying Offices. In contrast to the associated offices that are owned by their member stores, the syndicate buying offices own the stores that they represent. This ownership gives the buying offices more control in setting merchandise policies and in buying merchandise for their member stores. Although some degree of autonomy is granted to the individual stores, certain merchandise promotions and controls are established and maintained by the syndicate offices. In certain merchandise lines, therefore, their operation resembles that of a central buying office in a chain organization. All other services provided by buying offices are available to member stores in the syndicate group.

TOPICS FOR DISCUSSION

1. Explain in what way buyers' jobs are related to the other major functions performed in retailing.
2. What methods may a retail organization use to provide merchandise for branches that are some distance from the main store?
3. Discuss the advantages of central buying for chain organizations.
4. Explain how central merchandising, central distribution, and the catalog price-agreement plan affect the job of the buyer in the organizations that use each.
5. Explain the ways in which committee buying may help in important buying decisions.
6. Under what circumstances would a buyer want to use the services of a resident buying office?
7. Explain the differences between an independent buying office and a private buying office.
8. What are some of the services provided by resident buying offices?
9. Explain the function of an associated buying office.
10. In what ways do associated offices differ from syndicate buying offices?

COMMUNICATIONS IN RETAILING

You are the buyer for the central office of a large variety store chain. A new policy has just been put into effect that will permit individual stores to make up Easter baskets to sell to their customers. The baskets will range in price from 98¢ to $5.98 each. They will come in assorted sizes and contain cellophane grass, candy, and small Easter toys. The baskets will be covered with green glassine paper and tied with ribbons. In your position as buyer, you must supply all the materials except the toys and candy. Since this is the first time this promotion has been tried, you do not know how many stores will want to participate, how many will have the personnel to assemble and decorate the baskets, and how many baskets each store believes it can sell. On a separate sheet of paper, prepare a short memorandum asking the store managers for this information. Provide space on your memorandum for replies.

DECISION MAKING

A small store's owner served as the buyer for the merchandise carried. She had good taste and was able to select merchandise that appealed to many customers. As she became busier, she employed several salespeople. Eventually she added three branches, and these were run by managers she employed for the task. She continued to do the buying for the stores. As her stores grew, she found that she was often too busy to go to the market showings in a nearby city. She did see merchandise when sales representatives from manufacturers came to call, but that left her without the competitive advantage of getting the newest goods in her stores first. How might she solve this problem and thus be able to get the newest goods into her stores quickly? Be prepared to discuss your answer in class.

CAREER LADDER

You have been working as an assistant buyer of teen ready-to-wear clothing in a retail store. You have heard that a chain store has some openings in its headquarters office for assistant buyers. When you apply, you are given your choice of two positions: one as an assistant in a department that uses the catalog price-agreement plan for its stores, and one as an assistant in a department that uses the central office for merchandising the line of goods directly for all stores. The salary is $10 a week higher for the second position, but you will have to work harder, and you will have much more responsibility. Previous assistants have left because of the pressure of the job. Which position would you take, and why? Be prepared to discuss your answer in class.

chapter 12

MERCHANDISE CLASSIFICATIONS, SOURCES, AND METHODS OF BUYING

Many ways exist for the grouping of merchandise in stores. Grouping merchandise is known as *classification*. Merchandise may be classified by type (men's wear, women's wear, children's wear, home furnishings). Or it may be classified by whether it consists of fashion goods or staple goods; by the way customers think about goods when seeking to purchase them (casual shoes, dressy shoes, active sport shoes, slippers, boots, rubbers and galoshes); by special selling seasons of the year (Easter, Christmas, back-to-school); and by the frequency of purchase. The demands customers make in their selections (convenience goods, shopping goods, specialty items) may also be a way of classifying the merchandise.

Store buyers have many sources among which to choose and several different methods of buying merchandise.

MERCHANDISE CLASSIFICATIONS

In the early days of retailing, a buyer would classify merchandise by the manufacturers' lines. Manufacturers usually made goods in one type of material, for example. A manufacturer of stainless steel items would make just stainless steel pots and pans, and the buyer could make an entire grouping or classification around that manufacturer's stainless steel line. Still another manufacturer would make only aluminum pots

and pans. A third would produce iron skillets. Classifications were simple when they were based on manufacturers' lines and when manufacturers were specialized in their production.

Managers of stores, however, in analyzing the amounts and frequency of purchases, began to realize that customers did not buy goods by manufacturers' lines. Furthermore, manufacturers themselves began to make additional items, and their product mix became more complex. A manufacturer of aluminum products, for example, would make, in addition to pots and pans for cooking, utensils for storing food, for picnics, for throwaway, and for ornamental purposes. Thus, classification by manufacturers' lines became less usable.

Classification by Customer Purchasing Patterns

Meanwhile, to make planning for future buying easier, retail store owners and managers urged their buyers to classify goods according to the way customers bought them rather than according to the way manufacturers produced them. When customers want pots and pans, they want to see samples made of stainless steel, aluminum, porcelain enamel, iron, ceramic, and glass and to have the opportunity to choose among all those types.

As merchandise becomes more complex, as

more types of merchandise are produced, and as manufacturers mix their product lines, classification of merchandise according to customer selection becomes more useful than classification by the manner of production. From the customer's point of view, items of merchandise within a classification may be substituted, one for the other. If the stainless steel pot in the right size and shape is not available, a pot made of aluminum may serve instead.

Classification by Staple Goods or Fashion Goods

Merchandise is categorized as being either staple goods or fashion goods. *Staple goods* are those items in all classifications of merchandise that customers buy year in and year out and that a store carrying that kind of merchandise is expected to have in stock at all times. *Never-out-goods* is a synonym used by many retailers for such staples. For example, nails, screws, hammers, screwdrivers, paint, and wallpaper are staples, as are housewares, stationery, sheets, pillowcases, men's white shirts, underwear, and the thousands of other items that people buy continuously. Any store or department carrying these types of products is expected by customers to have these articles on hand and ready for sale at all times. The buyer of staple goods can estimate demand rather easily by checking on the sales of the previous years and by noting the trend in sales for the present year. Orders can therefore be placed with little fear that the merchandise will not be sold within a reasonable period of time.

Fashion goods are those articles that appeal to customers for a limited period of time. Fashionable merchandise is usually demanded rather suddenly. After a point of highest demand, sales drop abruptly.

Reorder Formula for Fashion Goods. The following experience of one buyer illustrates the differences in the buying of staple and fashion goods, especially in relation to reordering these goods.

Ms. Jones was a successful buyer of notions—needles, pins, threads, hair goods, buttons, closet accessories, sewing aids, and protective shields for clothing. For years she had kept splendid records of thousands of these items and ordered them so that customers could always find what they wanted. The store observed her steady sales increases and determined that the way to reward her was to transfer her to a department having a considerably bigger volume. Her salary would be much higher. When there was an opening in the handbag department, Ms. Jones was promoted to the position of buyer in that department.

Again she kept careful records of sales of merchandise, stock on hand, price lines, sizes, and styles. At the end of the winter season, there was a surplus of suede handbags, and she had no money left in the department's account with which to purchase spring goods. She could not understand what had gone wrong. Her records had been kept meticulously, and she had followed the buying pattern that had been so successful in the notions department. What had caused the disastrous results?

Ms. Jones found black suede handbags to be in demand during November and December. Her orders reflected the tremendous volume of sales she was doing during those months. However, the demand for black suede handbags stopped suddenly at Christmastime, and in January customers were looking merely for marked-down goods. In February the demand was for different styles of handbags in springlike materials and colors. The black suede bags she had ordered, based on the extraordinary sales of November and December, were therefore left untouched in the stock room. By the following fall, styles, sizes, and shapes of handbags would have changed so that those leftover suede bags would have little sales appeal for customers. In the meantime, the department's allotted money was tied up in this winter merchandise that had no chance of being sold for many months, and then only if substantial markdowns were taken.

According to the formula for reordering fashion goods, when the first shipment of fashion apparel or accessories is received, the items are closely watched for customer response. The good sellers are reordered immediately in reasonable quantities which the buyer determines, drawing on past experience and knowledge. As the season progresses, the buyer places fewer and fewer reorders.

The buyer of fashion merchandise must be alert to what is new and fashionable and to what colors are of interest. This buyer must buy the merchandise, have it ready for sale during the peak selling periods, and then reorder that merchandise only in quantities that can sell quickly. The abrupt ending of selling periods for fashion merchandise can be a disastrous trap for the unknowing buyer.

Fads are subject to even more changeable buying and selling patterns than fashion goods. *Fads* are items that burst suddenly into demand, reach points of peak demand quickly, and then have permanent "sudden death" sales cutoffs. Even substantial markdowns will not move fad merchandise once it has lost favor with the customers. Fads may occur in record albums, children's toys (for example, hula hoops) or clothing and accessories (three-inch platform shoes).

Any item may become a fad. The retailer who stocks it quickly and who determines accurately the point when it will lose its popularity may successfully make a profit on it. The retailer who enters the race late or who reorders just before the demise of the article may carry over stock for years without ever selling it.

Reorder Formula for Staple Goods. Since staple merchandise is to be kept on hand throughout the year, merchants use formulas that may be computerized to assure that those staple goods are never out of stock.

The simplest formula is to add three quantities: the amount sold in a given period, the amount needed to cover the time when the goods are being reordered and received from the vendor, and a *safety factor*. This safety factor is an amount of goods to cover any unusual purchasing activity on the part of customers or any delay in receiving goods from the manufacturer.

For example, normal sales are two dozen per week, goods are ordered monthly, vendor delivery time is two weeks, and the buyer plans one week's supply as the safety factor. The buyer would want to use 14 dozen as the standard quantity against which to determine the reorder. Sales multiplied by lead time plus reserves equals items needed on hand, as shown below.

The buyer uses 14 dozen as the gauge for buying that article. If stock counts showed 6 dozen on hand (OH), the buyer would subtract those 6 dozen from 14 dozen and place an order for 8 dozen (OO means "on order"). The OH and the OO would total 14 dozen.

Constant recordkeeping would assure that increases or decreases in customers' purchases would be reflected in the counts each month.

The buyer has to consider the vendor's selling unit. If the vendor packages by the gross (12 dozen), for example, the buyer might order less frequently and carry larger stocks of those goods.

Classification by Seasonal Merchandise

Some merchandise is in demand only at certain times of the year or for special events during the year. For example, Christmas cards sell primarily from October through December. Certain fresh vegetables, groceries, flower seeds, bulbs, and bushes have seasonal selling periods. Toys may sell in limited amounts during most of the year, but in the last three months of the year sales expand greatly.

$$4 \text{ weeks' supply} = 2 \text{ dozen per week (anticipated sales)} \times 4 = 8 \text{ dozen}$$
$$\text{Delivery time} = 2 \text{ weeks} \times 2 \text{ dozen sold per week} = 4 \text{ dozen}$$
$$\text{Safety factor} = 1 \text{ week's supply} \times 2 \text{ dozen per week} = 2 \text{ dozen}$$
$$\text{TOTAL} = \overline{14 \text{ dozen}}$$

THE BUYING FUNCTION

Seasonal goods may be classified as staple goods during the period of the year in which they sell. Christmas cards unsold in one year may be held and sold at the regular price in the following year. However, the money the store has paid for them has been invested in this unprofitable merchandise for nine months before any return on the investment can be obtained. Perishable goods, by contrast, must be marked down at the close of the normal selling period. Some seasonal goods are also fashion goods—bathing suits and ski wear, for example—and therefore it would be doubly hazardous to carry them over for a year.

Convenience, Shopping, and Specialty Goods Classifications

Still another way to classify merchandise is by its availability or convenience, its frequency of purchase or shopping aspects, or its uniqueness or specialty features.

Convenience Goods. Items of merchandise that the customer expects to have readily available at handy locations are called *convenience goods*. These are usually inexpensive. Examples of convenience goods are groceries, hardware items, newspapers, candy, automotive supplies, paperback books, special occasion cards, notions, drug items, and small housewares. Convenience goods are either articles for which there is an immediate need or items which are bought on impulse because they are so appealing.

Shopping Goods. More costly, less frequently needed merchandise requires more careful selection by the customer. These items are called *shopping goods.* They are not bought as casually as are convenience goods. The customer, in buying a new suit, for example, might visit several stores, examine the various articles for sale, and compare prices and styles before deciding on a particular suit. Similarly, the purchase of furniture, bedding, and other large household items; major clothing articles; and products such as camping supplies and other leisure-activity mer-

Would you classify the merchandise in this store as convenience, shopping, or specialty goods?
Photograph by Helena Frost

chandise might necessitate careful comparison and evaluation.

Specialty Goods. Products for which the customer will accept no substitute are known as *specialty goods.* These are articles for which there is no replacement or alternative in the customer's mind. For example, if a bride had purchased a set of chinaware and wished to enlarge the set, she would want to have the same pattern for her new dishes. She would go from store to store in search of that particular pattern. Some brand-name items, watches, expensive shoes, pianos, chinaware, glassware, silverware, and furniture are examples of specialty goods. If the customer is willing to consider another brand or a similar item, the product is classified as shopping goods rather than as specialty goods.

Reasons and Need for Merchandise Classifications

As goods have multiplied in both type and sales volume, classification of goods by the merchants who handle them has become essential. The reasons for classification are as follows:

1. To help customers find the things they seek

2. To help customers find suitable substitutes if the items they seek are not in stock

3. To give the retailer permanent categories that can be used for ordering, reordering, and recordkeeping

4. To simplify coding for data processing

5. To enable a store to exchange data with other stores about sales and pricing

6. To enable stores to assemble merchandise for selling in boutiques and small branch stores, known as twigs

SOURCES OF MERCHANDISE

In addition to all the classifications of merchandise, the buyer must consider the market and the ways to buy goods there. Buyers may go to the market themselves, have the representatives come to them, or buy through intermediaries.

Buying at the Market

When buyers actually purchase goods at a showroom or factory, they are said to be "in the market." This is a phrase that has many meanings depending on the kinds of goods for which the buyers are responsible, the kinds of firms with which they deal, and their distance from the primary sources of supply. Manufacturers of merchandise may sell directly to retailers in a variety of ways. Manufacturers may present merchandise to buyers in special rooms set up at the factory where the goods are manufactured. Since manufacturers of similar kinds of products are frequently located near one another, the buyer can visit several manufacturers during one buying trip.

Markets for home furnishings are found in the Southern states and in Chicago's Merchandise Mart. Markets for women's coats, suits, and dresses are concentrated in a relatively small area in New York City and in the Fashion Mart in Dallas, Texas.

Buying Through Manufacturers' Representatives

Some buyers, because they represent small stores or are a great distance from the market centers or from the factories, may buy their goods through *manufacturers' representatives*. These representatives call on stores or set up displays in local hotel rooms and invite buyers to see their lines of merchandise. Some present the lines of more than one manufacturer. Thus the market is literally brought to the buyers, who select from displays that are smaller than displays available to those who can go to the market themselves. Many small firms must use this type of local buying.

Buying Through Catalogs or Price Lists

Bulky merchandise or staple goods can be bought through catalogs or price lists. Thus some manufacturers of furniture, household goods, and hardware may carry only catalogs to show their lines. The buyers will receive catalogs from the manufacturers showing the products and listing the prices at which the goods may be bought. The buyers may select items at their leisure.

Buying Through Market Representation

When buyers are unable to visit the market centers frequently, they may use the services of a resident buying office as described in Chapter 11.

Buying Through Wholesalers

Some retailers buy in such small quantities or are so far from the manufacturers that they purchase their goods from wholesalers who serve their area. A *wholesaler* is a dealer who purchases goods in large quantities directly from manufacturers and sells those goods in smaller quantities to local retailers. Local drugstores, for example, commonly purchase from wholesalers, who supply as small a quantity as desired and deliver a day or two after the order is placed. Buying is done from a catalog or price list supplied by the wholesaler. Because the wholesalers purchase in large quantities to supply many local retailers, they usually buy at a considerable discount over the local retailer's cost. Wholesalers' charges to the retailers are therefore only slightly higher than the retailers would pay if they bought directly from the manufacturer.

Since the retailers have the advantage of being able to buy from the wholesaler in small quantities—often called "from hand-to-mouth buying"—they consider this an economical way to purchase goods.

Buying Through Rack Jobbers

In the supermarket field, the expansion into non-food lines created problems for the store managers. They were inexperienced in buying toiletries, housewares, hosiery, and stationery supplies, which customers liked to purchase while doing their grocery marketing. The rack jobbers meet the needs of these supermarket operators by supplying the goods needed and filling the racks or shelves assigned to their line either weekly or more often. Since they service many stores, the rack jobbers can buy goods in amounts large enough to obtain quantity discounts. They resell the goods to the retailers at prices only slightly above those which the retailers would pay in dealing directly with the manufacturers. By using rack jobbers, retailers are relieved of record-keeping for nonfood merchandise, and they are also relieved of the problem of selecting seasonal products. The rack jobbers maintain the stock, arrange it, and see that the store is stocked with the items that sell.

Using Leased Departments

When a store wants to relinquish all responsibility for a certain line of merchandise and yet wishes to have that merchandise available for its cus-

The rack jobber supplies the display rack, orders the necessary stock, and keeps the racks filled.
Courtesy L'Eggs Products Inc.

tomers, it may rent space to another firm. The use of leased departments is discussed in depth in Chapter 6.

Buying From Foreign Sources

Stores may want to have the prestige of carrying foreign merchandise. They may want to have goods that are noncompetitive with other retailers' merchandise, and particularly with the discounters in their area. Or they may be seeking merchandise that is unique or lower in cost than similar goods made in America. For any one of these reasons a store may want its buyers to purchase foreign goods.

Buyers who go directly to England, France, Italy, Spain, Japan, Hong Kong, or the hundreds of other less frequently used foreign markets usually have foreign market representatives to assist them. Many problems arise in buying in foreign countries. A buyer has to know where to buy, what the rate of exchange is, how to figure duty, how to have merchandise packed for the long voyage, what arrangements to make for shipping in the most economical way, and other details for dealing in a foreign language and in a foreign country.

American buying offices may have representatives in a foreign country. If a store uses the services of such a buying office, the foreign representatives can assist the buyers in their purchases while they are abroad. If the buyers choose, they may select instead a *commissionaire,* a native foreign buying office, which charges a percentage of the net cost of the purchases it helps the buyers make, in a manner similar to that of the American buying representative.

If a store does not want the expense of sending its own buyers abroad, the buyers may select goods from foreign importers based in the United States. These importers purchase in large quantities, much as wholesalers do. They then sell their foreign merchandise to local retailers. The retailers purchasing from the importers are, however, not as likely to get exclusive merchandise as they are by purchasing abroad. While the store pays the importer a higher cost than if the merchandise were purchased directly, the travel costs and costs of accommodations incurred when buying in person are saved. Thus, the total cost of the goods may be somewhat less than if the store buyers actually visited the foreign country themselves.

SOURCES OF INFORMATION TO AID BUYERS

No buyers make all the buying decisions for their departments by themselves. Various individuals, agencies, departments, and outside firms aid them in their work. Within the store the buyers have the help of the following people:

Salespeople
Department and store managers
Merchandise managers
Sales promotion experts
Research specialists
Fashion coordinators
Comparison shoppers
People from the bureau of standards and testing

People from the training department
People from the data processing or unit control department.

Some stores also have consumer panels, college boards, and teen-age boards that serve as advisers to buyers.

Outside the store organization, the buyers may look for help from manufacturers, trade associations, the trade press, and the consumer press. The buyers act as magnets to attract ideas from these various people and groups. They analyze the ideas and interpret them in making their buying decisions.

Within the Organization

Research specialists within the organization may keep the buyers knowledgeable about the trading areas from which their customers come. Buyers receive information about the average income of the customers and the average family size. Different kinds of customers may be recognized according to their ethnic backgrounds, religious or political affiliations, occupations, levels of education, habits, customs, and leisure activities.

Fashion or home-furnishings coordinators, who travel extensively, attend fashion openings, and keep abreast of fashion changes, can help buyers learn about the total fashion picture and about changes and new developments in their specific merchandise areas. In addition, they can help to plan coordinated color and style promotions in which individual departments participate. Fashion and home-furnishings coordinators also put on fashion shows to publicize the merchandise the store is featuring.

Comparison shoppers inform buyers about competitive activities in their merchandise lines. They analyze complete stocks of merchandise among competitors for type, assortments, and price and advise the buyers about those selections. When comparison workers find competing products, they show them to the buyers so that the buyers can determine whether comparably attractive and similarly priced merchandise is in their own stocks.

A bureau of standards and testing is charged

with the responsibility to see that merchandise meets the size standards set either by the United States government or by the retailing organization itself. Entire lots of dresses, for example, will be tested to see if the size 10 dress measures up to the specifications for a size 10. The testing bureau will test to see that merchandise is properly labeled, that content statements are correct, and that merchandise is not hazardous. Outdoor materials must be sufficiently fadeproof to give service, and goods marked "water repellent" must adequately repel water. Sheets listed as 200-count percale must really have 200 threads to the inch. The bureau of standards and testing acts as the consumer's protector by ensuring that merchandise performs as the manufacturer claims it will. In a small firm, this service might be provided by an outside agency.

The training department prepares manuals or plans meetings to inform employee groups about new products and new materials and to help develop good sales presentations for merchandise.

The unit control center or data processing center provides buyers with daily reports about the sales in their departments. In modern, large-scale buying, the buyers know as soon as they enter the store that they will have complete reports of the previous day's sales available. If they buy for stores located at some distance from the office, reports from all the stores in the group will be available usually on a weekly basis. Analysis of these reports gives buyers a total picture of stock on hand and on order and of the best-selling and the poorest-selling items. This information is broken down by classifications of style, size, and color, as well as by manufacturer.

Consumer advisory groups and college and teen boards may be formed in some retailing organizations to aid the stores in various ways. Buyers may find such groups helpful in analyzing new styles they are considering, especially for college groups and high school students. Such boards are formed from members of interested local groups, who serve also to promote the store among their organizations.

Outside the Organization

In addition to seeking help from those within their organizations, buyers look to impartial, outside agencies for assistance in making buying decisions.

The manufacturers or wholesalers with whom the buyers deal can be especially helpful, since they know how their merchandise is selling in different stores.

METHODS OF BUYING

Buyers must consider still another factor beyond those already discussed. In addition to the types of merchandise they buy and the many sources from which they may buy or obtain information, they also have numerous methods of buying that affect their planning and, in some cases, the prices that they pay for merchandise.

Regular Price Line Buying

For staple goods and fashion goods, the majority of orders the buyers place are for regular price line merchandise. Normal delivery for such merchandise takes from two weeks to a month. The buyers order the amount of goods that they believe will sell during a given period and then place reorders as quickly as they consider necessary to keep an adequate supply of the merchandise on hand.

Advance Buying

When buying staple goods for which there is a steady, continuous demand, buyers may place advance orders, and this results in economies for the manufacturer. These economies are then passed back to the buyers. Instead of placing frequent small orders, the buyers estimate their needs for a period of several months. Although they place the orders in advance, permitting the manufacturer to schedule work during slack periods, the buyers may have the merchandise delivered to the store at various staggered dates to avoid having to handle large quantities of goods at one time. Christmas goods, for example, may be ordered shortly after Christmas for delivery the following October, or for delivery in October, November, and December.

Promotional Buying
Many stores feature special events, sales, and general store promotions. Buyers must make special purchases for these occasions. For example, a men's-wear buyer may be asked to find related merchandise to feature during a store-wide South American promotion. A special-price sale requires a buyer to locate merchandise that can be sold at lower-than-usual prices. The buyer must also calculate the amount of merchandise needed for this event. Previous sales may give a clue, but the buyer cannot rely wholly on previous experience, as is possible with regularly priced goods.

Job Lot Buying
At the end of a season, manufacturers have odds and ends of merchandise left over, usually in incomplete size, color, and style assortments. To get rid of these unwanted goods they offer *job lots* to retailers at very low prices. The unusually low prices may be very appealing to the retailers, but they must consider how these odds and ends of goods will fit into their present stock. What are the chances that their customers will buy these goods at the end of the season and what markup can they make on those goods that do sell to offset the markdowns on the merchandise that will be left at the end of the selling period?

Consignment and Memo Buying
When articles are very costly, when they are new and the buyers do not care to risk purchasing them, or when the buyers consider the price for the merchandise to be higher than they think it is worth, the vendor may suggest taking the merchandise *on consignment* or *on memorandum*.

These forms of buying allow retailers to return any or all of the goods to the vendors if they have not been sold within a given period of time. These methods also permit the vendors to showcase their merchandise in the stores, while the

stores are merely using the space allotted without any financial loss if the goods do not sell. If the goods are sold, the stores take title to them and pay the vendors. If the goods remain unsold, the retailers have risked very little. However, since merchandise ordered in this way usually costs more than goods ordered by other methods, the stores do not usually gain the same markup that is obtained on merchandise purchased outright for resale.

Specification Buying
When a buyer buys for a large department, or when a store is a member of a buying office where group buying is done, or when a central buyer buys for many stores, the store or chain may urge the buyer to do *specification buying* instead of using nationally branded merchandise. Through this method, the stores are able to have merchandise comparable to, or better than, nationally branded lines. Stores can sell under their private brand names at prices considerably lower than those of the nationally branded lines. Thus the customers benefit. Stores particularly seek private or store-branded lines in the hope of establishing customer loyalty.

In order to do specification buying, buyers must know the product, study the market, and analyze the merchandise sold by other stores. They must search the market for vendors willing and able to produce the products they specify in the quantities they need and at the prices that they are willing to pay. Large national firms have been so successful with specification buying that some of their brands have become more famous than the national brands of well-known manufacturers.

The store takes a normal or near normal markup. The manufacturers sell a large quantity of goods and often can keep their employees working the year round because the large orders are placed well in advance of the selling season.

Special Order
When stores do not carry full stocks or have come to the end of a season and are out of some

sizes or colors; when odd sizes are in demand; or when odd items in open stock lines are desired, customers may be served through "special orders." These are orders placed by the buyer just to satisfy the needs of individual customers. This is a costly service, since it takes the time of the staff to place the order and to check and receive the merchandise, and often there is an extra charge paid to the vendor for handling a small order. Stores that are not "full-service" stores therefore do not attempt to handle special orders.

Sometimes stores can carry fewer colors, fewer odd sizes, or less open stock and yet make almost as many sales by using special orders as by carrying larger stocks of goods. The overall savings may more than compensate for the small extra cost entailed in providing this service for the occasional customer who has special needs.

Franchised Lines

Two types of franchising exist. One is the franchising of an entire store's merchandise—typified by the fast-food chains that have sprung up across the United States. The second type is the franchising of individual product lines. If stores carry brand-name merchandise, or if they select merchandise to be made by a vendor to specification, those firms may want to establish franchises with the manufacturer who supplies the goods in order to have that merchandise exclusively in their communities. The franchise agreement with the manufacturer binds the store for a given period of time to carry and display the manufacturer's line of merchandise and, in turn, restricts the manufacturer from selling this line to competing retailers within a given geographic area. For example, a store in a given city might agree to buy, display, and promote a certain silverware line. The manufacturer would agree not to sell the silverware to any other retailer in that city. However, a store in an adjacent city or town could have the merchandise. Noncompeting stores also may be permitted to carry the product. A department store might feature a special line of glassware but not consider a small jewelry store in the same city to be a threat to its sales. The jewelry store could therefore carry the same glassware products.

Franchise agreements bind the buyer to purchase the manufacturer's stock for the period covered by the franchise. The buyer may, of course, also carry other lines from other manufacturers, but must give certain stipulated space, display, and attention to the franchised line. If the line does not sell well, after a given period of time the manufacturer can withdraw the merchandise and establish a franchise with another retail firm.

TOPICS FOR DISCUSSION

1. Explain how staple goods differ from fashion goods.
2. Explain how the buying of fashion merchandise differs from the buying of staple goods.
3. Differentiate between convenience goods, shopping goods, and specialty goods.
4. What is meant by the statement "The buyer is in the market"?
5. Under what circumstances do retailers find buying from wholesalers to be helpful?
6. Explain the role of the rack jobber.
7. Why do firms sometimes have leased departments?
8. In what ways does a commissionaire serve a United States firm?
9. What are the advantages for the store buyer of being able to obtain merchandise by placing a special order? Why do some stores refuse to order goods this way?
10. What are the advantages of franchised lines to a store?

MATHEMATICS FOR RETAILING

A jewelry buyer served four branch stores which received merchandise on a weekly basis from the main store. Counts of merchandise were taken once a week in the morning and telephoned to the main store. The buyer then determined the needs of each branch store for the coming week, and the merchandise was assembled and shipped by truck that same day.

A new line of jewelry had been shipped to each store one week before. The amounts shipped at that time were as follows: necklaces, 3 dozen; earrings, 2 dozen; bracelets, 1 dozen. Although shipments are made by dozens, counts are taken of single items. On a separate sheet of paper, record the amounts of merchandise you would recommend that the buyer ship for the coming week in light of the counts shown below. Keep in mind that the merchandise is packed in lots of a dozen and that the buyer ships it from the main store in those lots. Each store is to have just the merchandise needed for the one week of selling. OH stands for "on hand" and OO for "on order."

Item	Price	Store A OH	OO	Store B OH	OO	Store C OH	OO	Store D OH	OO	Totals OH	OO
Necklaces	$1.98 ea.	6		3		13		3		25	
Earrings	1.00 ea.	3		1		11		4		19	
Bracelets	1.98 ea.	3		0		12		8		23	

1. What is the total dollar amount to be ordered at retail for the necklaces?
2. What is the total dollar amount to be ordered at retail for the earrings?
3. What is the total dollar amount to be ordered at retail for the bracelets?

MANAGING HUMAN RELATIONS

A buyer, Mrs. Martin, worked with one resource whose goods during the past several years represented one-fourth of the sales of her department. She was very pleased with the manufacturer of those goods. The vendor, Quality Line, however, had recently had several serious problems. Quality Line had just lost, through illness and an accident, two of its most valued designers. As a result, the line this year was just average in appeal. If Mrs. Martin suddenly bought no goods from this vendor, the manufacturing firm would be in serious financial difficulty. What would you suggest Mrs. Martin consider doing under the circumstances? Be prepared to discuss your ideas in class.

DECISION MAKING

A woman who owned a small women's shoe store with her husband decided that they could build their volume if they added hosiery, handbags, a few jewelry items, and some cosmetics. She assured her husband that she would take entire charge of this new branch of the business. However, she had no knowledge of the market resources for those products. Suggest how she might go about finding firms from which to buy these goods. If she had to spend her days in the store, how could she arrange for the selection and purchase of those goods? Be prepared to discuss your answers in class.

CAREER LADDER

Since buyers, like other people, have distinctive personalities and abilities, they gravitate toward the kinds of goods they like best and which they are qualified to buy because of training. On a separate sheet of paper, make a list of the lines of merchandise you think you would enjoy buying. Break the list down into staple goods and fashion goods. Which would you prefer to buy? Give reasons for your answer.

chapter 13

THE BUYER AND THE VENDORS

Buyers work with and purchase goods from *vendors* (sellers). These vendors may be manufacturers, wholesalers, jobbers, or importers.

The relationships and rapport between the buyer and the vendor are affected by the authority of the buyer, the buyer's obligations to the vendor, and negotiations that take place between them. The terms of the orders, the handling of the orders by the vendor and the extra help the vendor gives the buyer to sell the products profitably also affect buyer-vendor relationships.

In the early days of retailing, there were no rules to govern activities between buyers and vendors. Some buyers canceled orders at will, shipped merchandise back for no reason, or neglected to pay for goods as promised. On the other hand, some vendors overcharged for goods, undershipped on orders, refused to accept return goods even when products were not as ordered, sold to competing retailers at different prices, and substituted inferior goods on orders.

Chaotic conditions of this type could not continue if distribution in the United States was to grow, prosper, and serve the constantly increasing population. An agreement on trade practices was therefore inevitable.

In 1948 the Vendor Relations Committee of the National Retail Dry Goods Association (later renamed the National Retail Merchants Association) and the Apparel Industries Inter-Association drew up the Basic Trade Provisions agreement. This document required the vendor to notify the buyer within 10 days if order terms were not acceptable. Cancellations were limited to orders undelivered after specified delivery dates. And

returns of merchandise to the vendor were restricted to defective merchandise or merchandise not made to specification. Vendors who could not deliver were required to notify the retailer immediately, and claims and controversies were to be settled by arbitration. The Basic Trade Provisions agreement, as updated in 1973, is still in effect today.

THE AUTHORITY OF THE BUYER

In the relationships between the vendor and the retail store or organization, the buyer plays an important part. If the buyer has the authority to place orders, he or she acts as an agent for the firm and, as such, represents the firm in all the dealings with suppliers. If, however, as is the case in many firms, the buyer's orders must be countersigned by the merchandise manager, the buyer is not, in fact, the agent for the retail firm. That role is assumed by the merchandise manager, who has the ultimate authority to contract for merchandise and to place orders.

When buyers are authorized agents, they represent the firm in dealings for their respective departments. Their authority, however, is limited to the purposes stated. For example, if they are hired to buy stationery, they cannot place orders for food or drugs for the store. In the agreement between the retail firm and the buyer, there must be mutual consent—the buyer must agree to buy goods as designated, and the retailer must agree to compensate the buyer for that work.

Once a buyer has been appointed, that person represents the retailer under the authority given to him or her, and the retailer is required to accept the orders for goods that the buyer places. Understandably, the retailer wants to be sure the person being employed for such an important job is responsible and capable.

THE OBLIGATIONS OF THE BUYER

Buyers accept certain obligations to the firm when they accept the authority vested in them by the retailer. They must be loyal to their company and act in good faith in their dealings for that company. If they delegate any part of their work to others, they must still be responsible for that work. They must observe lawful instructions in all their actions for the company. All money made through their dealings for the company must be accounted for, and they must not accept personal gifts or make a personal profit outside their arrangements with the company on any work done as buyers for the firm. Once the buyers are appointed as agents for the firm, they hold their responsibility until their appointments are canceled or until their resignations are accepted.

PLACING ORDERS FOR MERCHANDISE

Although legally orders for small amounts of merchandise up to $50 may be placed orally, it is unlikely that most stores would permit a buyer to place oral orders. Orders should be written. If orders are placed orally by telephone, the order number should be given to the vendor, and a written *confirmation* should follow as soon as possible.

The buyer should observe the following rules in writing orders:

1. Always use the retail firm's order form. If you have placed a telephone order, confirm it by a properly signed written order.

2. Always write the order yourself. Do not have the manufacturer's representative do so.

3. Check the order carefully before signing it.

4. If any specifications are needed, be sure they are written out precisely.

5. Put every agreement in writing on the order. For example, if money is to be available for advertising, or if other special services are to be provided (demonstrators or free samples), those must be designated on the order.

Since every detail of a transaction must be present on the order form, it is the single most important document with which buyers work. They must understand every factor that is entered on the order, and they must also make sure that they have considered every line and subdivision on the form. The carbon copies of the order form provide records for the buyers, for the merchandise control department, and for the accounts payable department for checking with the invoices. The same order forms are used for initial orders and for reorders.

ACCEPTING ORDERS FOR MERCHANDISE

Vendors who offer goods for sale and who accept orders complete the cycle that forms the contract. An offer must be made and an order must be accepted before a contract has taken place. The laws of making contracts require that the order and its acceptance:

1. Be established for a lawful purpose.

2. Be made by parties competent to draw up a contract. Both must be over age 21, sane, competent, and not enemies.

3. Entail payment for the merchandise and/or services provided.

4. Reveal a meeting of the minds and agreement by the buyer and vendor that the order is reasonable and acceptable. Mere announcements, notices, catalogs, and advertisements published by vendors are not considered to be legal offers. When merchandise is so offered, the offer may be withdrawn at any time before it is accepted. After an offer is accepted, however, it cannot be canceled except by the express consent of both parties.

VENDOR NUMBER: 66-4

FILL IN NAME AND ADDRESS OF SHIPPER AS GIVEN ON PRICE LIST

Walter Verne Company
1113 Broadway
New York, N.Y. 10025

SHIP TO: STORE NO. 11

Balder & Sons, Inc.
326 Great Neck Rd.
New York, N.Y. 10036

IMPORTANT
ORDER NO.
SUBDIVISION
MUST APPEAR ON ALL
PACKAGES, INVOICE AND
CORRESPONDENCE.

ORIGINAL

HOW SHIP — CHEAPEST WAY — IF NOT OTHERWISE SPECIFIED
WHEN SHIP: 3/25
AT ONCE IF NOT OTHERWISE SPECIFIED
ORDER No. 6-70-3641

TERMS
ORIGINAL TO VENDOR: DUPLICATE ✓ N.Y. DAL. L.A.
ORIGINAL AND DUPLICATE TO VENDOR: ✓ N.Y. DAL. L.A.
ORIGINAL AND DUPLICATE TO WAREHOUSE: ✓

UNIT CONTROL — BOOK NO. 213 PAGE NO. 3
EST. WEIGHT — SECTION — LBS.
ORDER DATE: 3/15
SUBDIVISION

CANCEL DATE: 4/15

VENDOR: SEE REVERSE SIDE FOR PACKING, SHIPPING AND BILLING INSTRUCTIONS
WRITE A SEPARATE ORDER FOR EACH DEPARTMENTAL CLASS

LOT NO. OR ITEM	ORDERED QTY.	UNIT	QTY. SHIPPED	WIDTH, COLOR, PATTERN, ETC.	S 8-9	M 10-11	L 12-13	QUANTITIES BY SIZE	COST PRICE	COMPANY RETAIL
Knee High Hose 66214X	6	doz.	@ 7.50	Camel cable stitch	2	2	2		45 00	99
— "	3	"		Brown	1	1	1		22 50	
"	3	"		Red	1	1	1		22 50	
"	3	"		Navy	1	1	1		22 50	
									112 50	

WRITE SPECIAL INSTRUCTIONS HERE:

Bill Atkinson
MANAGER'S SIGNATURE

DATE BILLED — TAB AND PRICE — FILLED — CHECKED — NO. PIECES
TOTAL COST — TOTAL RETAIL

MANAGER DO NOT WRITE IN THESE SPACES

TEAR OFF THIS STRIP ON ORDERS TO OUTSIDE VENDORS

FORM 9017

WATCH TRANSPORTATION COSTS. SPECIFY "CHEAPEST WAY" IF YOUR TIME NEEDS PERMIT.

The buyer's order form is not just a request for merchandise, but also a record of purchases for the buyer, for the receiving department, and for the accounting department.

THE ORDER FORM

Although order forms differ in general appearance from one retailing firm to another, all basically contain the same information. Both the front and the back of the order form constitute the legal contract when signed by the authorized store agent and accepted by the seller.

On the front of the order form are spaces for the following:

• The name and address of the firm from which the buyer is ordering merchandise

• The order number

• The date of the order

• The unit, department, or store ordering the merchandise

• The delivery date

• The cancellation date for nondelivery. An order may not be canceled before the due date (except as noted previously). The vendor has three working days to ship the merchandise after the stated cancellation date.

• Terms and dating

• Transportation method

• FOB (free on board) point

• Style number, quantity, description of merchandise, unit price, and total price

• Signatures of those empowered to act as agents for the firm

On the back of the order form are the stipulations concerning legal arrangements and agreements by which the vendors are bound when they accept the order. The following are representative of such statements:

- The contract shall be deemed breached if any of the terms, conditions, or warranties, express or implied, are not complied with by the vendor.

- Routing instructions must be followed precisely.

- The vendor protects and indemnifies the retailer against any claim of infringement of any patent, trademark, or copyright, or claim of unfair trade, or litigation with respect to the merchandise delivered under the contract.

- The price shall not be increased by the vendor without written consent of authorized persons in the retailing firm.

- The title for the merchandise does not pass until the merchandise has been inspected and accepted as being as ordered by the retailer.

- The invoice is to be mailed or delivered the same day the shipment is made, but it is not to be included with the merchandise.

In addition to these specifications on the front and back of the order form, the buyer usually details the method of invoicing and packaging the merchandise, and the method of labeling cartons for distribution to the various departments, stores, or units of the firm.

NEGOTIATIONS FOR MERCHANDISE

The interchange between buyer and vendor before the order is written and signed is extremely important to each. The buyer must attempt to obtain the best price, terms, and delivery arrangements possible from the vendor. The vendor wants to hold the buyer to prices, terms, and delivery arrangements that will give that manufacturer or wholesaler the best profit potential. Only a certain amount of negotiating can be done

without violating the laws that are aimed at protecting both the buyer and the seller.

One important law is the Robinson-Patman Act of 1936. It requires that vendors charge the same price for identical merchandise to all retailers except when quantity buying or the method of buying (cash and carry, for example) demonstrably saves money for the seller. This law provides that vendors must not discriminate among competing customers when concessions are granted. It further requires that differences in price may not be extended if the price differences substantially lessen competition, or tend to create a monopoly, or injure, destroy, or prevent competition. The law also makes it illegal for a retailer to seek knowingly or receive discriminatory prices.

The Federal Trade Commission Act has provided for the establishment of a body to interpret the laws. Thus, when questions arise under such a law as the Robinson-Patman Act, members of the Federal Trade Commission judge the problems of price concessions and competition, and their findings are binding on parties concerned.

TERMS AND DATING ON ORDER FORMS

Various accounting practices that permit reducing payments in return for prompt payment of bills aid the buyers in showing a profit in their stores or departments. These practices are referred to on the order form as "Terms and Dating." *Terms* refer to the cash discount the vendor allows for early payment, and *dating* refers to the amount of time the retailer has to take the discount and pay the bill in full.

Cash Discount Terms

One type of discount almost universally used is the *cash discount*. This is a form of price concession written on the order and permitted if the store pays its bill promptly. Usually, if the store pays within 10 days from the date of the invoice, a cash discount may be subtracted from the total amount due the vendor. This discount varies, depending on the kinds of merchandise being sold, from as little as 1 percent to as much as 8 percent. The usual cash discount on the majority of merchandise is 2 percent.

Dating

The buyer, after reaching an agreement with the vendor, includes the terms and dating on the original order form. Thus, the term "2/10 net 30" written on an order means that a 2-percent deduction on the total invoice may be taken by the store if the bill is paid within 10 days from the date of the invoice. If the bill is not paid within that 10-day period, no cash discount may be deducted, and the entire bill must be paid within 30 days. If the invoice were dated November 1, the cash discount could be taken at any time that the invoice was paid until and including November 11. If the bill was not paid by November 11, it would have to be paid by December 1, since that would be 30 days after November 1, the date of the invoice. No cash discount would be permitted after November 11.

Some large retailing firms, whose prompt payment policies are known, prefer to negotiate with the vendor to obtain the cash discount as a lowered price for the goods, rather than as a separate discount for paying promptly. Thus, the buyer would negotiate to buy at $2.45 net goods that would normally cost $2.50. In this way the retailing firm would be assured of the 2-percent discount whether or not the bill was actually paid within 10 days.

Various dating methods are encountered for cash discounts on buyers' orders.

Net. If no discount is listed and just the term *net* appears, this indicates that no discount will be permitted for early payment. The term is usually accompanied by the number of days in which the bill must be paid—for example, *net 30*.

Advance Dating. Buyers may arrange to purchase merchandise ahead of the time when it will be sold in their store and agree to let the manufacturer make and ship the goods early. This aids the manufacturer in keeping the plant running during slack periods and permits the manufac-

turer to ship the goods and not provide storage for them. The retailing firm, through the grace of advance dating, however, does not have to pay for these goods until the date specified on the invoice. Thus, an invoice, for an assortment of Christmas tree ornaments shipped on August 1 could be dated August 1 as of October 15. If a cash discount of 2/10 were specified, the 2 percent could be deducted at any time that payment was made until and including October 25.

Extra Dating. Another method of extending the time period for payment is allowing extra days beyond those normally specified. For example, "2/10—30 extra" on an invoice dated September 1 would mean that the cash discount could be subtracted any time the bill was paid up to and including 40 days from the date of the invoice. The bill would be due on that date, but a grace period of 20 days without cash discount privileges is extended before payment must be made.

Receipt of Goods Dating (ROG). If a store is located a great distance from the vendor's shipping point, the merchandise may arrive weeks after the invoice. To save the store from paying for merchandise not yet received, the buyer may request ROG dating. Thus, if an invoice dated August 1 specified 2/10 ROG, and the merchandise was received August 20, the store would receive the cash discount if the bill was paid on or before August 30.

End of the Month Dating (EOM). Another method of delaying payment for merchandise is EOM dating. An invoice dated August 1 carrying the notation "2/10 EOM" would not be payable until September 10, ten days after the end of the month of the date of the invoice.

Invoices Dated on or After the 25th of the Month. Many manufacturers automatically treat invoices dated on or after the 25th of the month as though they were dated the 1st of the following month. Thus, an invoice dated August 27 specifying terms of 2/10 would be entitled to the cash discount if paid by September 11.

THE BUYING FUNCTION

Invoices with EOM dating that are dated on or after the 25th of the month permit extension of payment until the end of the following month. If additional days are allowed, they are noted also. For example, an invoice dated August 27 stating 2/10 EOM would earn the cash discount if paid on or before October 10, ten days after the end of September.

LOADING

Some retailers are not satisfied with the amount of cash discount obtained from the vendor because, they believe, it does not provide enough "cushion" to assure profit. To encourage store buyers to try to get larger cash discounts, these retailers may resort to loading invoices. This requires that they increase the amount of the charges for the goods to the individual department or store by an amount equal to the difference between the percentage of the actual cash discount and the amount of the cash discount that the retail firm wants maintained.

Computations for loading invoices are done as follows:

Assume an invoice from a manufacturer is for $50, and a cash discount of 2 percent is allowed if the bill is paid within 10 days. The store, however, has set a standard rate of 8 percent for cash discounts. The formula shown below is used.

Loading is used to force the buyer to work for larger cash discounts. It is also used in some cases where different departments in a store have different cash discount rates. Through loading, all discount rates can be equalized throughout the store. Another reason for loading is to get additional money to use for advertising for the store.

Loading is particularly important when a manufacturer decreases the cash discount but maintains the same price for the goods. For example, if the manufacturer decreased the cash discount to 1 percent from the 2 percent listed above, the new cost of the goods would be $49.50. If the markup were not similarly increased, the buyer would be making less on the sale of those goods. By loading, the price of the goods would be increased, and the buyer would be forced to increase the markup to maintain the usual amount of difference between the cost and the retail price for that merchandise.

ANTICIPATION

Another form of saving money for the retailer is deducting *anticipation* when paying invoices. As explained above, the retailer is often given a cash discount for paying a bill within a certain number of days from the date of the invoice. This technique is used by the vendor to obtain prompt payment of bills. Some retailers, however, pay even before the final date at which the cash discount may be obtained. A retailer may have an invoice dated August 1 with terms of 2/10 net 30. The buyer receives, checks, and marks the goods by August 4 and passes the bill to the

Regular Method
Manufacturer's cost − 2% cash discount = amount paid to manufacturer
$50 − $1 = $49

Loading Method
Cost (from regular method) = $49
Loaded cost − 8% cash discount = $49 paid to manufacturer
$49 = 92% of loaded cost
$49 ÷ 92% = $53.26 loaded cost billed to store or department
$53.26 × 8% = $4.26 cash discount
$53.26 − $4.26 = $49 paid to manufacturer

accounts payable section for payment. Payment is made on August 5, which is 6 days ahead of the deadline for the cash discount period. The store, therefore, believes that it is entitled to deduct interest on this money paid to the vendor for the period between the time of actual payment and the deadline for receiving the cash discount.

Traditionally, anticipation has been figured at the rate of 6 percent for each year. However, as rates for lending money have increased, some retailers have sought as much as 8 percent for anticipation. At 6 percent, a bill for $2,041 first has the 2-percent cash discount subtracted. (Some retailers deduct anticipation from the bill before the cash discount is subtracted.) Anticipation of 6 percent for 6 days would be figured on the remaining $2,000.18 as follows:

$$6/360[1] \times 6\% \text{ of } \$2,000.18 = \$2$$
$$\$2,000.18 - \$2 = \$1,998.18 \text{ paid to vendor}$$

Even though $2 may not appear to be much of a saving on $2,000, such interest deductions may add up to many thousands of dollars a year on total purchases.

Large firms deduct anticipation on all bills possible. Small firms, however, sometimes consider the mathematics too involved to take advantage of this form of discount. And some manufacturers specifically refuse to allow anticipation to be deducted from their invoices because it reduces profit and ready cash.

Cash discounts and anticipation should be understood by the buyer. The buyer needs to use the cash discount as a bargaining feature in securing the lowest price possible on every order. However, the buyer does not actually compute the cash discount or the anticipation. The calculations are performed by the bookkeeping or accounting department that handles the actual payments to the vendors. The discounts are not reflected in the merchandise markups but in the net profit of the department or store.

[1] The base for figuring anticipation is 360 days for the year.

CHARGES FOR LATE PAYMENT OF BILLS

As interest rates have increased and money has become more difficult to borrow, some manufacturers have begun to charge interest ranging from $7\frac{1}{2}$ percent to as much as 9 percent for late payment of bills. This action has forced stores to be more prompt in their payments for goods.

SHIPPING CHARGES

An important designation by the buyer on the order form concerns the shipping charges for the merchandise. The vendor pays transportation charges for goods purchased by a retail firm as far as a place known as the FOB point. Goods are "free on board" from the vendor to that designated point. From that point, the retailer takes title to the merchandise and pays all transportation charges.

Most FOB points are the factory or local shipping point where the vendor is located. Ideally, the buyer seeks to purchase goods with "prepaid" freight charges or an FOB point near the store, charging all transportation and insurance costs to the seller of the goods. This, however, is not the usual practice.

The Robinson-Patman Act requires that the FOB point be the same for all retailing firms dealing with a given vendor if the goods are identical. If two vendors are competing, however, and one is a local vendor, the one at a distance may meet the local vendor's competition by adjusting the FOB point so transportation charges for the goods are not charged to the retailer.

Shipping Charges Increase the Cost of the Goods

The cost of transporting merchandise to the store is traditionally considered to be a cost of the merchandise itself. Thus, if a buyer purchased goods from local manufacturers, the costs of transportation would be negligible. Dresses costing $10.75 bought from a manufacturer located across the street from the retail store would cost

$10.75 delivered. They would be sold for $21.50 each if the markup was 50 percent. The same dresses, however, if bought from a manufacturer at some distance from the store, might cost $10.75 plus 50 cents each to deliver. This would bring the cost of each dress to $11.25 and lower the markup on the dress, if it still sold for $21.50, from 50 percent to 47.67 percent. Similarly, all kinds of merchandise may have their cost substantially increased by these transportation charges.

In some cases, where the costs of transportation are very high, those costs may be passed on to the consumer. Thus merchandise manufactured in New York may retail for $1 more in states west of the Mississippi River than the identical goods sold in Eastern states.

Buyers Must Provide Shipping Instructions

Since any transportation charges must be added to the cost of the goods bought, the buyer wants to be sure that the merchandise is shipped by the least expensive method consistent with the store's delivery needs. Four factors must be considered: the size of the shipment, the carrier to be used, the route to be followed, and the packing materials to be used.

The size of the shipment should be considered to eliminate excessive charges for small shipments. If the goods, such as furniture and major appliances, are large and bulky, carload lots are much less costly per item to ship than less-than-carloads lots (LCL). Small-town retailers sometimes group orders for shipment to obtain carload lots and reduce freight charges. Shipments that are insufficient in weight to fill a freight car cannot qualify for a carload rate, and therefore their costs are increased considerably.

The type of carrier also affects costs. Parcel post for some items may be less costly than freight shipments, for example.

The route the merchandise will take to arrive at its destination may affect the costs. Goods shipped by water routes, for example, usually are less costly than those that travel by land routes.

The weight of packing cases may affect trans-

portation costs. Light-weight modern materials may prove to be as safe as bulkier, heavier materials. Furniture, for example, in cardboard cartons is usually as well protected as it was in the heavy wooden crates that were used in the past. The buyer needs to investigate the various materials and the methods used for packing to make certain that the lightest and safest materials are being used. All these details must be specified on the order form.

AREAS OF FRICTION BETWEEN RETAILERS AND VENDORS

Although the Basic Trade Provisions previously mentioned and the order form provide for fair dealing, many problems may arise between the vendor and the retailer. Since amicable relations are important for good future business activities, each vendor and each retailer must attempt to adjust any differences that arise.

Returns and Adjustments

The Basic Trade Provisions explicitly state that "no returns of merchandise shall be made except for defects therein, or for nonconformity with some material provision of this Order" and further that "the Purchaser shall send the Seller a separate written notice, setting forth the nature of the defects or nonconformity claimed, prior to or simultaneously with the return." Still, many retailers return merchandise without meeting either of these stipulations.

Some retailers may, without the vendor's consent, return unsold goods at the end of a season for credit. Some may return goods rather than take markdowns on them. Some may return goods that are damaged not in transit but in the store by rough handling. Retailers may return goods purchased by the customer and then brought back to the store for a refund. Since the goods are slightly soiled, the retailer wants the manufacturer to replace them. These types of returns, as opposed to those permitted because of late delivery or wrong merchandise, are a loss to the manufacturers, since they cannot resell

NRMA VOLUNTARY VENDOR TRADE GUIDELINES

Adopted by NRMA Vendor Relations Committee November 8, 1973, the following voluntary guidelines are offered to retailers for possible use in whole, in part, or not at all, in their individual dealings with vendors. NRMA offers these guidelines on a completely voluntary basis, reminding its members that they are free to alter or vary any of its terms.

SELLER'S ACCEPTANCE OF PURCHASE ORDER

It is mutually agreed and understood that all the terms and conditions set forth in this order are satisfactory and that the seller will make complete shipment of this order unless seller notifies purchaser to the contrary not more than 10 days after receipt of this order. If seller so notifies, buyer must confirm any changes of this purchase order in writing. Seller will not ship before the beginning delivery date or after the completion date specified herein, without prior written approval of the purchaser, unless otherwise specified herein.

CANCELLATION OF ORDER BY PURCHASER

Purchaser may not cancel this order before date for completion of delivery, unless seller consents thereto, or unless a cancellation date is specified on the purchase order, in which event this order, or any unshipped portion thereof, is automatically cancelled upon that cancellation date, unless purchaser authorizes further extension in writing.

RETURNS OF MERCHANDISE TO SELLER

Merchandise received from seller that is defective, or shipped beyond cancellation date, or not specifically ordered, or otherwise in violation of the terms of the purchase order may be returned to seller, and shall be accepted by the seller, at seller's expense, F.O.B. buyer's store, within a reasonable time after receipt, and without requirement for return authorization. Seller shall bear the risk of loss with regard to such returned merchandise. Merchandise not immediately discovered defective may be returned at time of discovery and will be accepted by the seller.

INTERRUPTION OF BUSINESS

In the event of the material interruption of the business of either the Seller or Purchaser by reason of fire, war, Act of God, governmental action, or strikes which materially affect the performance of this contract, the party so affected may cancel the order for such merchandise as has not been delivered, upon notice to the other party, notwithstanding any other provisions herein.

PARTIAL SHIPMENTS BY SELLER

In the event that the seller shall not be able to manufacture or deliver any part of this order, after having shipped part of this order, purchaser must be notified immediately. Seller shall not be liable for non-delivery of such merchandise except that purchaser has right to cancel and/or return any remaining portion of the order whose saleability may be affected because of non-shipment of the remainder of the order.

LIMITATION OF CREDIT

Seller shall have the right to limit credit extended the purchaser; however, seller shall inform purchaser in writing of any limitation.

SELLER'S INVOICE

Seller's invoice shall:
1. include statement(s) of conformity with all existing State and Federal laws;
2. not be dated prior to actual date of shipment;
3. follow format of NRMA Standard Invoice wherever possible.

MODIFICATION, WAIVER, AND DEFAULT

No modification of the terms of this agreement shall be effective unless stated in writing, and no waiver by either party of any default shall be deemed a waiver of any subsequent default.

such goods. The retailer is not justified in making such returns unless there is an agreement with the manufacturer in writing that such goods will be accepted for credit.

If the retailer is a good customer otherwise, the vendor may agree to take back such merchandise for full or partial refund rather than risk losing future orders. But the relations between vendor and retailer in such situations become strained.

Vendors, likewise, sometimes refuse to accept legitimate returns or to make adjustments when they are at fault. Such practices cause friction and result in poor retailer-vendor relations.

Premature and Split Shipments

Manufacturers, when they have storerooms filled with merchandise, like to get that merchandise out to make room for newer goods. The vendor may therefore ship an order earlier than specified. Retailers with limited storage space may find it impossible to accept those goods until the time designated for shipment on the order. If the retailers cannot accept the goods except at the time specified on the order, they should state this in writing on the order form: "Do not deliver before Sept. 1," for example.

Since invoices are sent when shipments are made, the early shipment will require earlier payment by the retail firm unless the manufacturer provides for extra dating. This would allow the retailer to pay for the merchandise at the later time as originally noted.

Sometimes manufacturers are not able to fill an entire order as specified. They therefore make partial shipment on time with a notation that the remainder will be shipped later. It may happen, however, when they ship the rest of the merchandise, that some retailers may refuse to accept it, although they had not previously notified the manufacturers of their intention to reject it. The courtesy of a telephone call or letter can prevent such problems.

Split shipments often work an unusual hardship on retailers. A store may plan an advertisement for men's suits, for example. When the order arrives from the manufacturer containing only some of the sizes to be advertised, the store must cancel the advertisement, since it would be unable to accommodate all its customers with only some of the suit sizes available. Such advertising cancellations may be costly for the retailer.

Overcharges on Shipments

For most orders, the retailer pays the shipping costs. When shipments are split, added charges are incurred. This results in higher costs to the retailer than would occur if the shipments were made as specified. Manufacturers should be willing to absorb these added costs.

Minimum Orders and Special Orders

Some buyers order merchandise "from hand to mouth," meaning that they buy in small quantities those goods they can sell within a short period of time. Special orders for single customers also are placed frequently by some buyers, who thereby are able to carry limited stocks of goods. Such small orders are as costly for manufacturers to handle as larger orders, and manufacturers therefore dislike working on them. They prefer that the retailers assemble their orders and place less frequent but larger orders. Some manufacturers charge extra for minimum orders to reduce this problem. Retailers, of course, object vehemently to these extra-handling charges.

Price Maintenance

Some buyers order merchandise from vendors who will sell their merchandise only if the retailers agree to maintain the manufacturer's suggested retail price, except for end-of-the-season clearances. In this way the manufacturers protect all the retailers of their goods from the price cutting of a few. If a retailer does cut prices, manufacturers take recourse by refusing to sell to that retailer in the future. In the meantime,

◁ The NRMA voluntary vendor trade guidelines provide a model of fair business dealings between retailers and vendors.

however, a vendor may lose several other accounts because the price agreement was violated by one retailer.

Order Cancellation

Once an order is submitted by the retail firm and accepted by the vendor, it cannot be canceled except by mutual consent. Some retailers, after placing an order and having it confirmed, change their minds about wanting the goods, and without the consent of the manufacturer, they cancel the order. Such practices cause difficulties between retailer and vendor. Similarly, once the manufacturers have agreed to accept an order, they should not expect the retailers to wait beyond the time of promised delivery for the goods.

Exclusive Agency Agreements

To showcase their wares in certain stores and to be sure of full coverage of their lines in those stores, some manufacturers franchise their lines to certain retailers by geographic area. A retailer may violate a franchise agreement by purchasing merchandise and then shipping it to another retailer in a noncompeting area. Thus, Retailer A of silverware, for example, may have an exclusive agency contract with the manufacturer of a nationally branded line. A jeweler in another town, Retailer B, may be unable to get that line because it is already franchised to a competitor. Retailer B therefore arranges with Retailer A to ship the goods as needed for Retailer B's customers. The manufacturer who is able to track the shipments cancels the agreement with Retailer A. Both retailers consequently lose access to the goods.

In still other cases, the manufacturer may observe that Retailer A, who has the contract for those goods in a given territory, is not showcasing them properly, is giving priority to competing goods from other manufacturers, is selling very little of those products, or is permitting practices such as demonstrations for other lines that cause unfair competition for the manufacturer's goods. In such cases, the manufacturer may wish to seek another outlet for those goods at the termination of the contract.

Sometimes Retailer A is the exclusive agency for goods that Retailer C in an adjacent geographic area also carries. Retailer C establishes a branch store in Retailer A's territory. Now the customers of Retailer C's branch store have access to the goods that were previously carried exclusively by Retailer A. This causes friction between Retailer A and the vendor, and the vendor must find some way for this problem to be resolved.

Displays such as this one are frequently supplied or sold to retailers by the manufacturer to feature a particular brand of merchandise.
Courtesy Westvāco Corporation

THE BUYING FUNCTION

Competition from Nontraditional Retailers

To increase sales volume, a manufacturer may sell identical merchandise to firms other than those traditionally associated with those goods. For example, a dinnerware or glassware manufacturer may sell a line of dishes or glassware to soap or detergent manufacturers to include in their boxed products or to be available in return for the coupons attached to the boxes.

Some manufacturers sell items to be used in banks as premiums or "giveaways" for people who open new accounts. Some stamp-plan stores carry lines identical to those of nearby retailers. The retailers see such competition as a threat to their product lines, and they consequently seek products from manufacturers who do not practice such selling of identical goods. They may also seek to have agreements established preventing the selling of identical goods to these nontraditional retailers.

Dealer Aids

Some vendors promise to help retailers sell their products through dealer aids—showcase or window display stands, mounted copies of national advertisements, specially made sign cards, brochures for customers, and so forth. Some of these aids are of inferior quality, while others are too large or too small, or too unattractive for use. Manufacturers should be sure that the aids they develop can be used and are really helpful for showcasing the products.

Cooperative Advertising

Although the Robinson-Patman Act requires that all vendor services provided for one retailer be provided for all, certain services are available only to those retailers who can comply with the stipulations for their use. Cooperative advertising, which provides that the manufacturers absorb a portion of the cost when their goods are advertised by the retail store, is usually available and depends either on the total amount of goods ordered or on the frequency of ordering stipulated amounts. Thus, only large users of the products can usually earn the cooperative advertising money. The small retailers believe that they are not given an equal opportunity to benefit from this concession. This is another reason for friction between vendor and retailer.

TOPICS FOR DISCUSSION

1. Explain how buyers' jobs today differ from buyers' jobs that existed before regulatory legislation.
2. Explain the buyers' authority and obligations in placing orders for their firms.
3. Why is a retail firm careful in selecting its buyers?
4. What are the rules buyers should observe in placing orders?
5. What role does the Robinson-Patman Act play in aiding the buyer?
6. What is meant by the "terms and dating" on an order?
7. Explain the role of anticipation. Why are many manufacturers refusing to allow anticipation on orders?
8. If an order stated "FOB factory," what would it mean?
9. Why is it to the buyer's advantage to specify shipping instructions?
10. What are some important areas of friction between vendors and retailers?

MATHEMATICS FOR RETAILING

1. An invoice dated June 1 carries terms of 2/10 net 30. By what date must the bill be paid in order to receive the cash discount? When must the invoice be paid to avoid its becoming overdue? If the bill was for $250, and it was paid within 10

days, what would be the net amount of the bill? Do your calculations on a separate sheet of paper.

2. An invoice dated March 26 carries terms of 2/10 EOM. When does the cash discount period expire?

3. An invoice for $100 is subject to terms of 2/10—30 extra. Anticipation is taken at 6 percent per year. If the invoice is dated December 4, and the bill is paid on December 14, how much should be paid to the vendor?

COMMUNICATIONS IN RETAILING

You have received a shipment of sweaters in only three of the four colors you had ordered. An advertisement planned for three days later specified all four colors. The manufacturer's plant is 200 miles away, and delivery of goods would take a minimum of four days. You must attend a meeting in 5 minutes, and your assistant is out to lunch. You have just a few minutes to outline directions to the assistant about calling the manufacturer. On a separate sheet of paper, briefly list the information you would want your assistant to obtain for you.

MANAGING HUMAN RELATIONS

At Christmastime, Ms. Farrar, an assistant buyer of silverware, was sent an inexpensive gift of jewelry by Mr. Ward, one of her store's silverware suppliers. Mr. Ward had served the store for many years. She disliked accepting the gift, so she simply left it in the box in which it came. But since she did not want to offend the vendor, she did not return it to him. Later, he urged her to reorder larger quantities of the product line he represented, and when she refused, he reminded her of the gift he had sent her. What should the assistant buyer's response be to Mr. Ward? Be prepared to discuss your answer in class.

CAREER LADDER

A local store in your area runs a special "college promotion" in the spring each year. During this time, college students are invited to compete for the job of buyer-for-a-summer for the college shop. The person chosen gets to select merchandise, run the shop during the summer months, and receive a better-than-usual salary.

The store owner uses a contest in selecting a college student for this unique opportunity. Applicants have to write about the current fashions for college students and suggest a back-to-school wardrobe for entering freshmen in their respective colleges. Assume you are a contestant. On a separate sheet of paper, list the items you would write about.

PART FIVE

THE MERCHANDISING FUNCTION

chapter 14

PRICING PRINCIPLES AND POLICIES

The successful buyer is one who buys the right goods at the right time in the right quantities at the right price and who then retails those goods at the right price.

The big questions for the buyer are: What is the right price, how is it arrived at, and what determines what it should be?

Everyone who has gone from store to store looking for an article has had the experience of finding identical merchandise at different prices in different stores. Why would the same item be priced so differently in those various stores? The buyers or department managers responsible for setting prices have many controls they must observe and many factors they must consider before they set the prices at which goods will be sold. They must, of course, consider the expenses to be covered in the buying and selling of those goods and the profit the store hopes to make by selling them. In addition, store policies, federal and state laws, and pricing principles affect pricing decisions.

STORE POLICIES AFFECT PRICE

Store policies that affect the image the store projects to its customers will help to determine what prices are charged for goods.

One-Price Policy

Most stores today have a one-price policy. This means that the price is visibly marked on the goods, and all customers pay the same price for goods. If any change in the price of an item is made, all the identical goods are changed to the newly designated price. The one-price policy assures all customers of being fairly treated, reduces the time needed for selling, and makes self-selection and self-service in stores possible. One-price policies were introduced by food merchants and department stores in the mid- and late 1800s.

Variable-Price Policy

Some stores in the United States and many stores in some foreign countries continue to mark prices in code and to allow the individual salesperson to determine a retail price for each customer. If the salespeople meet price resistance, they can lower the price from the one they first quoted. Different customers, therefore, could buy identical merchandise for different prices in the same store at the same time. The customer who was shrewdest at bargaining would gain the greatest advantage in the sale. This variable-pricing method gives less assurance to the customer of receiving fair treatment, requires a salesperson to handle the sale, is more time-consuming, and prevents self-selection or self-service.

Some small stores, even though they price goods openly, may, if the customer appears interested but objects to the price, offer to sell the item for less money to secure the sale. Thus a variable-price policy is actually in effect. Some stores also vary a price on goods if services, such as alterations, are included.

Trade-in Allowances

In certain lines of merchandise—such as tires, typewriters, office machines, appliances, automobiles, and fine jewelry—firms may accept trade-ins and place a certain dollar value on those items turned in when new products are purchased. Since all trade-ins have different values depending on their original cost, their age, and their condition, the trade-in becomes a lever in the hands of the customer to obtain a lower price on the new item from the retailer. The harder the customer bargains, therefore, the lower the price may be in such a transaction.

Noncompetitive Price Policies

Nonpromotional stores do not attempt to compete with stores that feature discounts or low prices. These nonpromotional stores, regardless of type and size, consider the customers whom they attract to be more interested in the image of the store, the services it provides, or the assortments of merchandise available than in the prices of the goods. These stores may seek unique and exclusive merchandise not carried by most other stores, or they may cater to customers who can afford better-quality products not commonly found in the lower-price firms. Sometimes stores that do not compete on prices are open longer hours, are located in neighborhood areas, or give more services, thus offering conveniences for which customers are willing to pay higher prices.

Competitive Price Policies

Some stores do not initiate low prices, but they have a policy of meeting any prices of competing stores on identical merchandise. Thus a department store with a competitive pricing policy may meet the lower price of a local mass merchandiser on identical merchandise. If the department store provides services, such as delivery, which the mass merchandiser does not, additional charges are made for those extra services for the repriced product.

Low-Price Policies

Some mass-merchandising firms establish low-price, discount, or underselling policies. These firms consider price to be an important buying motive and believe that large numbers of cus-

Syms is a mass-merchandising firm whose policy it is to offer nationally branded merchandise at a discount in order to attract customers and ensure fast turnover in stock.

tomers will seek the firm that has identical or equal-value goods at low prices. When such firms are new, they usually rely upon nationally branded merchandise to use for comparisons to prove that their prices are low. After they have established their reputation for offering low prices, however, they may introduce their own private-branded goods and nonbranded lines that may be accepted by their customers as reflecting the same low-price values they initially offered.

Product Quality Policies

Some retailing firms have a policy of handling first-quality products only. Others may have such a policy for their upstairs store, but the downstairs or basement store may carry *seconds*—merchandise with slight manufacturing defects. The merchandise is usable, but because of the defects it sells at a price that is lower than the price of first-quality products made by the same manufacturer. Some stores may carry seconds, mill ends, and even used goods. Buyers who feature first-quality products rarely find stores that carry seconds or low-quality items to be competitive.

Policies on Giveaways

To attract new customers and hold regular customers, some retailers have had policies of offering trading stamps, gifts with purchases over a certain amount, or special games customers can play that involve prizes for winners. The first firm in a locality to establish such methods of attracting customers usually enjoys an immediate increase in business. As competitors add these attractions, however, the initial advantage is lost, and the retailers then have the job of keeping their regular customers from being lured to other firms for these giveaways.

All these plans cost the retailer money. Stamps, for example, cost from about two-tenths to three-tenths of a cent each. Added volume would offset this cost, but competition usually keeps this added volume to a minimum. This added cost must be considered in the buyer's pricing of goods.

Single-Price Policy

Small specialty shops that deal in single items, such as millinery, costume jewelry, decorative posters, small housewares, or men's ties, may have just one single price at which all their merchandise is sold. Thus a millinery shop may retail all its hats at $7, or a dress shop may have dresses at the one price of $9.95, or a tie shop may carry ties for $1.50. Housewares and a limited line of cosmetics items may sell in one store for 88 cents. This pricing policy limits the variety of merchandise buyers for such stores may select. The buyers may, of course, buy some goods that are priced somewhat higher and average the

This store offers all its merchandise at a single price; the merchandise varies from small housewares, to cosmetics, to costume jewelry. The single-price policy is an effective stimulus to consumer buying.

PRICING PRINCIPLES AND POLICIES

prices of those goods with the prices of lower-priced merchandise to arrive at the one uniform price.

Multiple-Price Policy

Drugstores, food stores, and some general merchandise stores may price goods in *multiples*—such as 2 for 15 cents, 3 for $1, or 6 for $1.98. Multiple pricing has a psychological effect on some customers by suggesting that they purchase the larger number at which the merchandise is priced. Also, multiple pricing makes it more costly for the customer to buy only one item or a smaller number than the multiple suggested. Since selling in larger quantities is economical for retailers, multiple pricing permits them to pass some of the savings on to the customer who buys, in the suggested quantities.

Some firms run 1-cent sales as a method of multiple pricing. They advise the customer to buy one product at the regular price—for example, 99 cents—and to make an additional purchase of the same article at only 1 cent more. This is a form of discount price, but again it encourages the customer to purchase in larger numbers.

Multiple pricing makes price comparisons between stores more difficult unless the same numbers of articles are grouped in each store into the multiple pricing unit.

LAWS MAY AFFECT PRICE

Many kinds of laws, such as wage and hour laws, affect price by increasing the cost of selling goods. The laws of concern to the buyer, however, are primarily those that deal specifically with the pricing of goods.

Unfair Trade Practices Acts

About half the states have laws that require a certain minimum percentage to be charged by the retailer above the total cost of the goods plus transportation charges. These small percentages, commonly from 2 percent of the cost price to 6 percent of the retail price, are designed to protect small retailers from ruinous competition. Other-wise some larger firms might choose a product to be a loss leader and sell it below cost for a certain period of time. For a small, limited-line store where this product (cigarettes or milk, for example) is an important part of its business, such competition for an extended period of time can be disastrous.

Robinson-Patman Act

The Robinson-Patman Act, referred to in Chapter 13, ensures that all retailers pay the same amount for goods, with exceptions only that permit the seller to save money in production costs. The buyers then are free to price those goods according to their stores' policies.

The Sherman Antitrust Act

The Sherman Antitrust Act of 1890 sought to prevent conspiracies to monopolize or restrain trade. Retailers who conspire to fix prices are fined and may even be imprisoned for violations of this act. Three prominent New York stores were fined in price-fixing cases in 1975. In addition, some of those stores' charge account customers brought class action (group) law suits against them.

PRINCIPLES OF PRICING

Buyers are guided in pricing not only by the policies of their stores but also by certain principles that have long been known about pricing.

Store Image Affects Price

Some customers are willing to pay for certain advantages offered by some stores. The fame of a store, the well-known designers it features in its advertising, the services it offers, the convenient location, or the genial atmosphere provided by the store's employees may all attract customers. Other customers may be drawn to a store by its low-price policies, by its bargain days, by its wide assortments, or by its self-service methods of selection. Since services and elaborate fixtures, excellent employees, and central locations all cost money, stores with these features usually charge higher prices for their goods.

THE MERCHANDISING FUNCTION

Limited Customer Loyalty Affects Price

Some customers may be loyal to a certain store because it carries goods for which the label or the services of the store are important. Those same customers, however, when shopping for nationally advertised, mass-produced merchandise, may seek another store that offers a lower price. Customers who want to buy coats or suits, for example, may purchase only in certain exclusive stores. For phonograph records, books, photographic supplies, radios, and television sets, however, those same customers may happily shop in discount houses. A store may have to price some products competitively with off-price retailers if it wishes to maintain the customers' business in all its departments.

Weather Affects the Price of Goods

The price of bathing suits, snowsuits, skis, umbrellas, raincoats, winter coats, spring suits—in short, the price of any items whose wear or use is dependent on the weather—may be adversely affected if the weather is not conducive to their use. Ski outfits in a snowless winter, spring suits during an unusually warm or cold spring, and bathing suits during a cool or rainy summer are examples of goods whose sales will suffer because of customer resistance. Only if the prices of those goods are substantially reduced will they sell under such weather conditions.

The Rate of Sale Affects Price

Charging a high price for articles does not automatically result in a high profit from the sale of those items. If more of an item can be sold by reducing its price, a greater profit may result. For example, if a buyer decided that a fur coat that cost $600 should retail for $1,000, and just one coat was sold, the amount made to cover all costs would be just $400. If those same $600 coats were priced at $700, and 12 of them were sold, $1,200 would be available to cover expenses.

Price Lining Affects Price

Establishing definite price lines within categories of merchandise helps customers and aids the buyer in pricing those goods. If a store, for exam-

ple, carried handbags for $5, $5.25, $5.50, $5.75, and $6, customers would be confused by such minor price variations. What advantage, the customer might want to know, is there in the $5.25 handbag over the $5 one? Such small price differences make it difficult for the customer to make decisions. Retail stores, therefore, usually select certain price lines that allow customers to observe recognizable differences among products. If handbags were priced at $5, $7.50, $10, and $15, the customer would have an opportunity to select one at a price that would reflect obvious advantages over the ones in the lower price line.

Price lining reduces confusion in shopping, permits customers to have a basis for making definite comparisons among merchandise, aids the store in recordkeeping and marking goods, and allows buyers to plan their purchases according to established price lines. Most stores

Price lines help the customer discern differences in quality between similar products.
Photograph by Fern Logan

consider a minimum of three price lines desirable: a low-price line, a medium-price line, and a high-price line. Those stores with wider assortments may carry many more price lines. Sales reports on previous sales activity help a store to establish its price lines by showing customers' preferences for certain price lines. Price lines are also determined by competitors' prices, by manufacturers' suggested retail prices, and by experimentation.

Certain kinds of merchandise do not lend themselves to price lining. Small items in the staple category and convenience goods such as drugs, foods, toiletries, housewares, notions, hardware, and small stationery items cannot be priced in this manner. Customers expect small price variations for such merchandise.

Customer Psychology Affects Price

Various reasons are given for odd prices such as 99 cents and $1.98. These may have been initially established to give the customer the illusion of a bargain or to give the impression that pricing and profits were figured in pennies. Before sales taxes were imposed, these prices may have been established to keep salespeople honest by forcing them to record each sale in order to give customers the odd pennies in change. Odd prices may also have been used initially to hold customers in the store longer so they could be exposed to merchandise while the sale was recorded and change was made.

Regardless of the reasons for use, many stores have adopted the policy of using these odd price endings, and buyers find this affects their markups on merchandise. Some firms price all merchandise with odd price endings. Some firms use odd prices up to a stated amount, such as $25,

and use even prices above that amount. Some quality stores believe their image is better reflected in even amounts, and therefore, they use prices such as $1, $2, $3.50, and $5.

Although odd prices appear to be negligibly different from even prices—99 cents being only 1 cent less than a dollar—such small differences multiplied by a large sales volume may have a significant effect on the overall profits of a store.

Value Affects Price

Customers who buy merchandise frequently can quickly notice any slight change in the price. A grocery shopper, for example, usually knows to the penny the prices charged for milk, butter, or cans of certain often-used foods. When merchandise is not commonly purchased, however, the customer has little real basis for judging its price as being low, average, or high. Surprisingly, if the price appears to be too low, the customer may resist products just as much as when the price appears to be too high. Retailing at too low a price results in customer resistance because customers think something is wrong with the goods. For example, in one store a 16-piece Japanese chinaware dinner set priced at $6.45 did not sell. When the price was raised to $10.95, several sets were sold.

The cost of some collectors' items and antiques has no relationship to the retail price if those items have become rare or sought after by customers. Old comic books, for example, that initially cost 10 cents to 25 cents each may be selling for $1.50 to $10 or more. Old coins, stamps, antique automobiles, rare musical instruments, and old manuscripts are other products whose value may be reflected in very high prices.

TOPICS FOR DISCUSSION

1. Explain the statement "A merchant is not a free agent in establishing prices."
2. What is meant by a one-price policy? a single-price policy?
3. What are the disadvantages of a variable-price policy?
4. Why can some stores be noncompetitive in their pricing policies?

5. Differentiate between stores that have competitive price policies and those that have low-price policies.
6. What are the advantages to the retailer of a multiple-price policy?
7. What is the purpose of the Unfair Trade Practices Act? the Robinson-Patman Act?
8. Explain why customers are willing to pay higher prices for some goods while seeking bargain prices for other goods.
9. Explain what is meant by price lining. What kinds of merchandise are suitable for price lining?
10. How may the customer's view of the value of merchandise affect the price of those goods?

MATHEMATICS FOR RETAILING

1. A buyer has a price line of $3.25. He can buy some goods to sell at this price for $1.65 each. If he wants to have approximately $175 worth of goods at cost, how many of these items can he buy? Do your calculations on a separate piece of paper.
2. A buyer had been used to pricing goods in round numbers—$1, $2, and so forth. Price endings were changed by store policy to 98 cents, $1.98, and so on. On 500 items priced to sell at $1.98, what is the difference between the total value at the previous retail price the buyer used and the total value at the new price?

MANAGING HUMAN RELATIONS

As assistant manager in a busy self-service supermarket, you are in charge while the manager is out to lunch. A customer approaches you with a 1-pound can of coffee marked 99 cents and a 2-pound can of the same brand of coffee marked $2.09 and asks which is the correct price. Obviously, if the 99 cent price is correct for 1 pound, the 2-pound can should cost no more than $1.98. However, if the $2.09 price is correct for the 2-pound can, the 1-pound can should cost at least $1.05. You check your price list and determine that one of the markers incorrectly priced the 1-pound cans at 99 cents when they should have been marked $1.09. Although you explain the error to the customer, she insists that she should be allowed to purchase the coffee as marked. Be prepared to discuss the ways you might handle this situation.

DECISION MAKING

A buyer, Miss Caraballo, found that customers had enthusiastically accepted handbags priced at $7.95. She had sold them during the months of September and October. On November 1, the manufacturer offered her an exceptional buy on the identical bags. This permitted her to retail them at a normal markup for $5.95, or sell them at a slightly better than normal markup for $6.95, or continue to sell them at $7.95 at a much higher markup than her department ever had. What would you suggest she do about pricing them? Be prepared to explain your answer.

CAREER LADDER

The store you have joined has two paths to management positions. On one path you do clerical work in a buyer's office initially, then progress to the positions of junior assistant, assistant, associate, and, finally, buyer. On the second path you become a stockkeeper, then a salesperson, a junior department manager, a department manager, and, finally, a group department manager. The first route involves mostly working with figures and merchandise and those who sell the merchandise. The second route involves mostly working with store personnel and with customers. Which route would you prefer, and why? Be prepared to discuss your answer.

chapter 15

DETERMINING
THE PRICE OF GOODS

Profit is the lifeblood of the retailing business. Since profit is dependent upon the pricing of the goods, determining the right price for the products that have been selected is the key to the success of the retailing business.

Using the knowledge of policies and principles of pricing as explained in Chapter 14, and keeping in mind the laws regarding pricing, the buyer in most stores writes the price at which the ordered goods are to sell on the store's copies of the order form. This is known as *preretailing* the order. This retail price reflects the usual price at which such goods are sold. The buyer, in marking this price, considers the competitors' price lines and the expenses this price must cover. The buyer also considers how this price fits into the store or department's price lines and what price the customers are willing to pay for such goods.

MARKUP

The retail price at which the goods are marked determines the markup that is obtained by the merchant on those goods. *Markup* is the difference between the cost of merchandise, including the charges for transporting the merchandise to the store, and the selling price of such goods. The formula for markup may be stated in three ways:

Retail = cost + markup (R = C + M) or
Cost = retail − markup (C = R − M) or
Markup = retail − cost (M = R − C)

Thus, if an item costs $2.75, and transportation charges are 25 cents, the total cost of the merchandise is $3. If those goods retailed at $5 each, the markup would be $2 each.

Markup may be stated in three different ways. It may be stated in dollars and cents as noted above. It may be stated as a percentage of the retail price ($2 ÷ $5 = 40% markup on retail price). In some cases it may be stated as a percentage of the cost ($2 ÷ $3 = 66.7% markup on cost).

What Markon Means

Some retailers use the term "markon" interchangeably with "markup." For others, however, "markon" refers only to the initial or first markup given to an item. Others believe that "markon" refers only to additional markups taken after the initial markup. Since "markon" has several different meanings, the universally accepted term "markup" will be used throughout this book. Markup is the more commonly used term in retailing and in retailing literature.

What Cost of Goods Means

Buyers work with the vendor's cost of goods and apply their markup percentage to determine the retail price. The terms and dating on the buyer's order state that certain discounts, both cash discount and anticipation, may be obtained for early or prompt payment of bills. Although these early payments reduce the total cost of the merchandise, such early payments are not due to the buyer's skill but to the availability of the firm's cash at the time the invoice is submitted. The cash discount is therefore not subtracted from the cost of the goods when computing markup. Similarly, anticipation, if taken at the time of payment, is considered to be an accounting device and does not become part of the markup consideration. If a store is in a financial position to take these discounts, they become insurance against losses due to theft, spoilage, or fashion obsolescence of merchandise.

The costs of transporting the goods into the store and getting them ready for sale are, however, considered to be legitimate costs. If retailers did not have to pay the transportation charges, the manufacturers or wholesalers would; thus, their charges for the merchandise would increase by that amount. The costs of transporting goods to the store or warehouse are accepted as a portion of the total cost of the merchandise. Therefore, the billed cost of goods plus transportation charges equals the total cost of the goods ($5,000 for goods + $75 for transportation = $5,075 total cost of the goods).

How Markup Is Determined

In addition to all the factors that determine price—such as the principles of pricing, the policies of the store, laws, competition, and agreements with the vendor—buyers must consider their costs of doing business and the potential profit that the store hopes to make. The buyers may know, for example, that overall costs amount to 37 percent of retail sales. If they wish the merchandise to contribute to the profit of the store, they add another 3 percent of sales, making a total of 40 percent of the *selling price* of the goods. It is at this point that a common error is often made in figuring markup. Note the results of the two following examples.

The merchant multiplies $3 (cost figure) by 40% (markup percent) and arrives at $1.20 (markup percentage of cost). Assuming that cost plus markup (as a percentage of cost) equals the retail price, the merchant figures the problem this way:

$$\$3 + \$1.20 = \$4.20$$
$$(\text{cost}) \quad (\text{m.u.}) \quad (\text{retail})$$

In reworking this problem, you will notice that the merchant has shortchanged the department. If you multiply $4.20 (retail price) by 40% (markup percent), you get $1.68 as the markup figure. By subtracting this $1.68 (markup figure) from $4.20 (retail price), you are left with $2.52 as the cost of the item. But you know that the cost of the item was $3. Thus there is a 48-cent shortage. The reason for this error was that the merchant calculated the markup on the cost when it should have been figured on the retail price.

In order to figure the markup correctly, the buyer must apply all percents to the same base. Since in almost all firms expenses and proposed profit are based on the retail price, markup should also be based on the retail price. The following example shows the correct formula which explains this:

$$\text{Retail} - \text{markup} = \text{cost}$$
$$100\% - 40\% = 60\%$$

This cost percent is referred to as the *complement* of the markup. Since 60 percent of the retail price equals $3, then $3 divided by 60 equals 1 percent of the retail price; therefore, 100 percent multiplied by the 1 percent amount would equal the actual retail price. Mathematically it would look this way:

$$\text{Cost (which is 60\% of the retail price)} = \$3$$
$$1\% \ (\$3 \div 60) = .05$$
$$100\% \ (\text{retail price}) = \$5$$

Refiguring this to determine if the costs and proposed profit are covered adequately shows:

$$\text{Retail (100\%)} - \text{markup (40\%)} = \text{cost (60\%)}$$
$$\$5 \quad - \quad \$2 \quad = \quad \$3$$

THE MERCHANDISING FUNCTION

COMPARISON OF PERCENTS OF RETAIL PRICE AND COST MARKUPS

The equivalent percents of retail price markup and cost markup are determined by figuring the percent of markup on the retail price and dividing it by the remaining cost percent (the complement of the markup). Thus,

Retail (100%) − markup on retail price (40%)
= cost (60%)
Markup on retail price ÷ cost
= % markup on cost
40% ÷ 60%
= 66.7% markup on cost
40% markup on retail price
= 66.7% markup on cost

Because expenses and profits or losses are based on retail prices, few stores today use the cost method of figuring markup. A few small stores that have variable-price policies, some drugstores, and some independent stores whose owners have never bothered to study markup methods still price goods by using markup on cost. Manufacturers also refer to markup on cost, and this keeps the tradition alive. Modern merchants, however, use the method of figuring markup on the retail price almost exclusively.

There are many reasons for using figures at retail instead of at cost:

- Reporting by trade associations and other firms is done on retail figures. Comparisons, therefore, with other comparable firms are easier to make when figures are based on retail prices.

- Markdowns, additional markups, employee discounts, and allowances to customers are calculated on the retail price.

- Goods (except in variable-price stores) are marked at retail, and so this figure is readily available.

- Expenses and profits are figured on retail sales.

- Cost markups are larger figures, which psychologically leave a negative impression.

Markup tables may be used to translate retail markup percent to cost percent and vice versa.

Markups on cost may exceed 100 percent. Markups on retail price, which is represented as 100 percent, may never exceed nor even equal the retail percent figure; therefore, these markups are always less than 100 percent.

TABLE OF EQUIVALENT COST AND RETAIL PRICE MARKUP PERCENTS

Percent Markup on Cost	=	Percent Markup on Retail Price
5.3		5.0
11.1		10.0
14.3		12.5
15.0		13.0
17.7		15.0
20.0		16.6
25.0		20.0
30.0		23.1
33.3		25.0
40.0		28.6
42.9		30.0
50.0		33.3
53.8		35.0
60.0		37.5
66.7		40.0
75.0		42.9
100.0		50.0
150.0		60.0
200.0		66.7
300.0		75.0

Marking Goods at Cost

Although the retail price of goods sold in one-price stores is openly marked on the goods, those retailers who base their records on cost or who use variable-pricing policies or who do not mark their goods with a retail price must use a code. Often, such merchants select words that include 10 different letters and translate these in price-coding their goods. For example, a merchant's price code might be established as the following example shows:

Code words: T R A D E   Q U I C K
Meaning: 1 2 3 4 5   6 7 8 9 0

A price of $2.50 then would be coded on the price ticket as REK. An "X" or other letter may be added to represent a decimal point. In this case, the $2.50 price would read RXEK, and a $25 price would read REXK, and a $250 price would read REKX.

Marking goods in code and translating those code prices always subjects the retailer to more errors than occur when the price is clearly marked on the merchandise.

FORMULAS FOR PRICING

With the formula Retail = cost + markup, it is easy to derive any one figure once the other two are known.

Retail Price from Cost and Markup

A retailer whose total cost for an item is $2 wishes to obtain a 45% markup on the retail price. The retailer subtracts the markup percent from 100%, the unknown retail price, and has $2 remaining.

100% = Retail price
 45% = Markup on retail price
 55% = Cost, which is $2

By dividing the cost by the percent of the total that it represents, the retail price is automatically determined. Thus,

C ÷ C% = Retail price
$2 ÷ 55% = $3.64

This retail price can now be checked by applying the markup percent and subtracting the answer from the retail price. Thus,

$3.64 (R) × 45% (M) = $1.64
$3.64 (R) − $1.64 (M) = $2 (C)

Cost When Retail Price and Markup Are Known

If the retail price and the markup percent on the retail price are known, the cost can be determined readily. For example,

$5 = 100%, or the retail price
    45% is the markup
    ____
    55% is the cost

Since 55% represents the cost, 55% of $5 will be $2.75, the cost of the goods. The formula is C% × R = C.

Markup Percent When Retail Price and Cost Are Known

A buyer may be purchasing an item for $3.20 which must retail for a $5.75 price line. This buyer wishes to know what the markup percent on the retail price will be. The formula is as follows:

Retail price − cost = markup
$5.75 − $3.20 = $2.55

To figure the percent of the markup on the retail price, divide the retail price into the markup amount ($2.55 ÷ $5.75 = 44.3% markup).

Retail Price When Retail Markup Dollars and Markup Percent Are Known

If retailers know that their markup on an item is $3 and that this markup is 25 percent, they can find the retail price by dividing the markup dollars by the markup percent: $3 ÷ 25% = $12.

In determining the retail selling price of this dress, the buyer must cover the manufacturer's cost of producing and the store's cost of selling it; consider the competitors' price on comparable dresses; and estimate what the customer would be willing to pay for it.
Copyright © 1974 by the New York Times Company. Reprinted by permission.

Behind the Price Tag of a $110 Summer Dress

Cotton and polyester dress: Wholesale price $59.75
Retail price $110.00

Manufacturer's Cost

Fabric
($2^{11}/_{16}$ yards
at $1.60)   **$4.30**

Lining
($1\ ^3/_4$ yards at .75,
plus interlining,
$^3/_4$ yards at .60)   **1.54**

Belt
(Including covered
snaps, elastic)   **2.28**

Labor, wages
(Operator, finisher,
presser)   **21.03**

**Labor,
fringe benefits**
(Health and welfare,
Social Security,
vacation, pension)   **6.73**

Overhead
(Rent, insurance,
utilities, salaries,
costs of samples,
trade discounts, etc.)   **19.87**

Total cost   **$55.75**

Taxes   **2.00**

Profit   **2.00**

**Wholesale cost
of dress**   **$59.75**

Retailer's Cost

$59.75 less discount for
prompt payment   **$55.00**

Markdowns
(Averaged over all
dresses in stock)   **$11.00**

**Shortages,
pilferage, etc.**   **2.00**

Alterations
(Cost of maintaining
department
averaged out)   **2.00**

Salaries
Sales staff   **5.00**

**Merchandising and
buying staff**
(Including expenses)   **3.00**

Clerical and stock room
(Receiving, marking,
deliveries, etc.;
including expenses)   **3.00**

**Advertising, display,
sales promotion**   **4.00**

Administrative
(Executives, credit and
accounting offices,
including expenses)   **8.00**

**Employe fringe
benefits**   **2.00**

Overhead
(Rent, insurance, utilities,
cleaning, security)   **9.00**

Miscellaneous   **2.00**

Total   **$106.00**

Taxes   **2.00**

Profit   **2.00**

Selling price   **$110.00**
(plus tax)

Once the retail price and the markup are known, the cost can also be determined:

Retail price − markup = cost
$12 − $3 = $9

Retail Markup Percent When Cost Markup Percent Is Known

Mr. Filbert, a manufacturer, told Miss Margulies, a retailer, that she should get an 80-percent markup on some goods he was showing her. Miss Margulies knew Mr. Filbert referred to a percent markup on the cost of the goods. To determine the markup percent on the retail price, she figured as follows:

Markup on cost + cost = retail price
80% + 100% = 180%
80% ÷ 180% =
44.4% markup on retail price

Translated into dollars and cents, if the cost of the item was $3, the figures would be as follows:

Markup on cost (80% × cost) + cost (100%)
= retail price (180%)
$2.40 (80% × $3) + $3 = $5.40
Markup on cost ÷ retail price
= retail markup %
$2.40 ÷ $5.40 = 44.4%

MARKUPS AND MARKDOWNS

Retail prices are marked on goods when those items arrive in the store. These prices may change upward or downward, however, during the time the merchandise remains in the store.

Initial Markup

When goods arrive from the manufacturer and are checked against the invoice (bill) received from the manufacturer or wholesaler, they can be marked at the buyer's preretailed price as indicated on the store's copies of the order form. This retail price, which is also marked on the invoice and recorded in the books of the firm, is then placed on the price tags attached to the goods. This is known as the *initial markup*. The term "initial" indicates that some changes in price may occur later.

Additional Markups

Buyers may have many reasons to change the initial price placed on the goods. They may have bought the merchandise for a one- or two-day special sale and had to change the price of any goods left over after the initial days of selling. They may have brought the goods in at a low price and found that competitors had similar goods selling at a higher price. They may, after receiving the merchandise, have compared the new goods with those already in the department and decided they looked as good or better, and therefore they raised the price so the new goods could compete favorably with other merchandise for sale. Additional markups, then, may have to be taken on some goods. These must be duly recorded, and new price tickets must be made to reflect the higher price.

Markdowns

Prices on goods are more commonly lowered than raised. After receiving the goods, the buyer may decide to have a sale and to use those goods on hand but at a lower price. The buyer must therefore take a markdown on those items. If the buyer originally estimated the markup just to cover expenses and yield a small profit, a markdown may negate any chance for a profit when those goods are sold. Comparable goods may be selling at a lower price. After a reasonable period, the merchandise may still be unsold, and it may become soiled or shopworn. Setting a lower price may be the way to make these goods attractive to customers.

In each case, a price change form must be filled out indicating the former retail price and the new lower price, the style number, the kind of article, the quantity undergoing a price change, and the reasons for the price change.

If the goods when marked down do not sell, further markdowns may be necessary. In some cases, merchandise may be marked to "zero" and then given away.

Initial Markup versus Maintained Markup

What buyers plan initially as their markups may bear little relationship to the actual markup obtained when customers decide whether or not to buy the goods at the prices charged.

For example, one firm bought 100 sets of stainless steel flatware (knives, forks, and spoons) and set an initial retail price of $60 a set. Twice during the year, the sets were put on sale for $40 a set. The cost of $30 a set yielded a 50-percent markup on the initial retail price but only a 25-percent markup on the sale price. The firm sold 6 sets at the regular price and 94 sets at the sale price. The initial markup, therefore, was quite different from the actual markup obtained. The initial markup is what the buyer hoped for, but the actual markup, which was *maintained* for the entire selling period, was considerably lower:

Initial markup
100 sets bought at $30 = $3,000 cost
  100 sets sold at $60 = $6,000 retail
        Markup = 50%

Maintained markup
  6 sets sold at $60 = $360
94 sets sold at $40 = $3,760
Totals: 100 sets sold
Total cost—$3,000; total retail price—$4,120
$4,120 (R) − $3,000 (C) = $1,120 (M)
$1,120 (M) ÷ $4,120 (R) = 27.2% (M%)
Maintained markup percent = 27.2%

The buyer would now need to determine if the maintained markup yielded sufficient dollars to cover the costs of doing business on those products.

Although the illustration above showed the maintained markup figure for one group of items, this figure is usually based on the activity of an entire department or an entire store for a given period of time. For example:

	Cost	Retail Price	Markup
Goods on hand	$22,000	$40,000	45 (initial)
Markdowns		3,000	
Sales	22,000	37,000	40.5 (maintained)

The lower maintained markup on the goods sold was due to the markdowns needed to move the merchandise.

System of Averaging Markups

As you have seen, not all goods bring the retail prices at which they are initially marked. The merchants must constantly reevaluate the stock and consider how they can obtain the overall markup needed to cover their costs and yield the desired profit. Since all goods cannot provide the same markup, some must produce more to offset the loss of markup on others. Thus a system of averaging markups becomes necessary. This is done by purchasing additional merchandise, buying merchandise with several different markups, buying merchandise with several different costs, and buying job lots of goods.

Merchandise Added. Goods on hand plus purchases commonly have to be averaged. Mrs. Furness, a buyer, needed to have a stock amounting to $50,000 at retail of bathing suits for the summer season to do the amount of business she had planned. She wanted to obtain an overall markup of 40 percent on her stock. At the beginning of the season she had $20,000 worth of merchandise at retail with a markup of 38 percent. On the $30,000 worth of stock at retail which she planned to buy, she therefore needed a higher markup in order to have an average markup of 40 percent. Her figures were as follows:

	Cost	Retail Price	Markup, %
Total planned purchases	$30,000	$50,000	40
Goods on hand	12,400	20,000	38
Needed to buy	$17,600	$30,000	41.3

To determine what prices she could afford to pay for goods to fit into the remaining category, she simply subtracted the cost and retail price of the goods on hand from the planned purchases totals. She found she needed $30,000 worth of goods at retail for which she could pay $17,600 to yield a 41.3-percent markup. Her entire stock would therefore have an average markup of 40 percent.

Merchandise With Several Markups. Initial purchases with different markup percents also need to be averaged to assure the desired overall markup percent. A buyer, Mr. Alt, had $5,000 to spend for Christmas ornaments. He wanted to obtain an initial markup of 50 percent on these items. In one wholesale firm he placed orders for $2,500 worth of merchandise, which he believed was so attractively priced that he could retail it for $5,500. His calculations to determine what he had left to buy were as shown in the following table:

	Cost	Retail Price	Markup, %
Planned purchases	$5,000	$10,000	50
Purchases to date	2,500	5,500	54.5
Balance to purchase	$2,500	$ 4,500	44.4

On the final $2,500 worth of goods at cost, the buyer figured that he need only achieve a markup of 44.4 percent to reach his goal of an average markup of 50 percent. He could there-

fore offer his customers an attractive low price on the second purchase of ornaments.

Merchandise With Several Costs. Pricing articles with different costs which must, however, fit into one price line also entails averaging markups. A buyer of leather goods articles, Mr. Levy, had a $2.98 price line. He wanted to obtain a 39-percent markup in his department. He had one vendor who offered leather goods at $1.75 each, which could be retailed for $2.98. Another vendor's goods to fit into that price line, however, cost $1.95 each. If he wanted $500 worth of merchandise at cost, how many goods at each vendor's price could he buy to obtain the 39-percent markup?

This problem would be figured in the following way:

$$\$500 \text{ (C)} + 39\% \text{ (M)} = R$$
$$61\% \text{ (C)} + 39\% \text{ (M)} = 100\% \text{ (R)}$$
$$61\% = \$500$$
$$100\% = \$500 \div 61\%$$
$$= \$819.67 \text{ (\$820 in rounded figures)}$$

He now knows that his total purchases will cost $500 and be priced to bring in $820 to yield a 39-percent markup.

At a retail price line of $2.98, a 39-percent markup will yield an average cost of $1.82 ($2.98 × 61%).

Now, taking the two price lines, he observes the following:

$1.95	$1.82
− 1.82	− 1.75
$ .13 over	$ .07 under

The 13 cents above the average cost for a 39-percent markup is almost twice as much as the 7 cents under the average cost for the $1.75 merchandise. He therefore just reverses these ratios! If he buys almost twice as much of the $1.75 goods as he does of the $1.95 goods, he should come out with an average markup of 39 percent:

	Cost	Retail Price	Markup, %
Total purchases	$500	$820	39
$1.95 items	177	270	34.6
$1.75 items	323	550	41.2

Since they are figured on a different base, the percents themselves cannot be averaged. Only if each percent figure represented exactly half of the purchases could they be averaged.

Job Lots. Job lots of merchandise bought at the end of a season containing various qualities, styles, and values of merchandise need to be examined carefully when they arrive at the store to see what retail prices can be obtained for these goods. Job lots represent a good example of the importance of averaging markups on goods.

A buyer, Miss Meltzer, bought a job lot of 300 pairs of draperies for $399. She hoped to retail them for $650, at a 38.5-percent markup. In sorting the draperies for pricing when they arrived in the stores, she decided she could probably sell them as shown in the table below.

To realize the original markup she had planned, the buyer would have to raise the price of each pair of draperies by 20 cents. The buyer decided that her chances of selling them were increased by keeping the retail price at the lower amount quoted.

ADDITIONAL PRICING FACTORS

Several other pricing factors must be considered. These are dollar markups, trade discount off list price, keystone price, industry practices, discount price policy, exclusive merchandise, and leaders and loss leaders.

Dollar Markups

Some costly merchandise is priced by adding dollars or cents to the cost rather than by computing the markup in percent. For example, a buyer may consider that $100 added to the cost of a diamond ring is sufficient to cover costs and permit a reasonable profit. A ring costing $1,000 is therefore retailed for $1,100. This price reflects only a 9-percent markup, but if several rings are sold at this price, the store makes sufficient dollars to provide a handsome profit on the sales. Dollar markups are becoming more popular as merchants observe their effect upon volume selling of high-ticket goods.

Trade Discount Off List Price

Some vendors suggest the retail price at which they believe their merchandise should be sold. This suggested retail price is known as a *list price*. When a list price is given, discounts from that list price may be stated to determine the cost for the store. Such discounts are known as *trade discounts* or *functional discounts*. These trade discounts may be stated as 1 percent or more off the list price. For example, a trade discount may simply be written, "less 40%." It may also be written as "less 40% and 5%." Notice that this does not mean 40 percent plus 5 percent, or 45 percent. Rather, it means that 40 percent may be deducted from the list price, and then an additional 5 percent may be deducted from the remaining figure.

Mr. Barker, a manufacturer, listed his flatware sets to sell for $20 each. He offered them to a store "less 40%." The buyer figured 40 percent

Total Cost of Draperies		Retail Price per Pair	Total Retail Price	Markup, %
$159.60	120 prs.	$1.50	$180	11.3
26.60	20 prs.	2.00	40	33.5
172.90	130 prs.	2.50	325	43.7
39.90	30 prs.	3.00	90	55.6
$399.00			$635	

$635 (R) − $399 (C) = $236 (M) or 37.2%

THE MERCHANDISING FUNCTION

of $20, which equals $8, and subtracted this from $20 to arrive at a cost of $12 for each set.

If retailers were to purchase a large number of these sets, the manufacturer might grant the stores an additional 5-percent discount. The buyers would then reduce the $12 cost by this added 5 percent, which is 60 cents. The new cost, therefore, would be $11.40. This results in a 43-percent markup for the store.

Offering a trade discount is a flexible method used by manufacturers or wholesalers to determine the cost of goods. The vendors can reduce the price further if they have a surplus of goods that they want to sell. If prices are rising, the vendors can easily drop some of the additional discounts. If competitors are underselling them, they can easily add more discounts to reduce their price. The manufacturers can also easily add special discounts for wholesalers. The flatware listed above might be quoted to a wholesaler as "less 40-5-3." The wholesaler's cost, therefore, would be figured as follows:

$20.00 less 40% = $12.00
$12.00 less 5% = $11.40
$11.40 less 3% = $11.06

In turn, the wholesaler might sell the sets to a retailer at a trade discount of "less 40 and 5" or a cost of $11.40.

Keystone Price
A manufacturer may have a suggested retail price that is double the cost. This is known as a *keystone price*. Buyers may be making a purchase of jewelry which is quoted at a keystone price. A necklace, therefore, quoted at a keystone price of $4 will cost the stores $2. If the buyers do not want to retail the necklace for the keystone price, they will reduce their markup percent. Note that a retail markup of 50 percent is available if the retailers price the goods at the keystone price.

Industry Practices
The practices followed by the majority of retailers in the industry may dictate the retail price. Dresses, for example, which cost $10.75 may retail for $22.50, providing a 52-percent markup for the retailer.

Discount Price Policy
If a store has a "discount policy" for pricing merchandise, a different standard may be used. The $10.75 dresses referred to above might be priced at $18.85 to produce a 43-percent markup.

Exclusive Merchandise
The buyer may make an unusual purchase and be able to price the goods above the normal store markup but still at a price competitive with the prices of other retailers. One buyer, Mr. Jackson, for example, purchased some foreign-made stainless steel place settings, each consisting of a knife, fork, salad fork, soup spoon, and teaspoon. The cost was $3 a unit. He decided to retail the place settings for $8.99 each, a price below the $9.95 price for comparable goods in other stores, but still at a markup of 66.5 percent, which was far in excess of the normal markup for his department.

Leaders and Loss Leaders
The buyer may want to draw customers to his or her store or department with unusual bargains. Or because of the competition, the buyer may have customers demanding merchandise with a very low markup. Thus, for example, some items costing $3 might be retailed for $3.25, reflecting a 7-percent markup. Such "leaders," however, must be maintained to keep traffic in the store.

Loss leaders are items that are sold at or below cost, often as attractions for store openings or for special sale days. Because of the Unfair Trade Practices Act, such loss leaders are rare. Since it is difficult to police these acts, some firms

A store's policy of allowing trade-ins offers the customer the advantage of a variable price in that the allowance the customer receives when trading in the item reduces the price originally paid for it. The trade-in allowance depends, of course, on such factors as the age and condition of the item, and the potential for resale.
Courtesy The Singer Company

continue to use loss leaders to attract customers. Since these customers usually also buy goods at the regular markup, the losses are offset by the added volume in regular merchandise. Loss leaders advertised as "below wholesale cost" may have been purchased at special bargain prices from the vendors.

MERCHANDISE MANAGEMENT ACCOUNTING

Retailers have long observed that certain items sold more rapidly than others; that certain items were more profitable in terms of dollars than others; and that some items were slower-selling and produced less profit. *Merchandise management accounting* is a merchandising device developed to enable managers to price goods for maximum sales and turnover. It allows the merchants to use accounting techniques to provide information on which merchandising decisions can be made. To make these decisions, the merchants need to examine their stocks and to determine what costs are associated with the selling of each classification of merchandise. Two factors are especially important considerations: the costs of handling individual articles and the turnover of those articles.

Costs of Handling Certain Types of Goods

In their analyses, merchants might discover that certain goods arrive in the store, are checked and marked, and then move to the selling floor in the same packages in which they arrived from the manufacturer. Subsequently, these products move to the customer without any advertising and with a minimum of handling.

Other items, by contrast, must be unpacked when they arrive, repacked for storage in the stock room, advertised to attract customer patronage, again handled when being sent to the selling floor, repackaged for display on the floor, and again handled and repacked before being sent to the customer. The cost of handling each of the first items might be 10 to 15 cents, while the cost of handling each of the second items

might be almost $1. If items in both these groups sold for 50 cents over their cost, the first group would make a 35- to 40-cent contribution to profit in the store, while the second would cost the store money each time its items were handled and sold.

Turnover of Articles

If items sell steadily and quickly, they may be replaced frequently, thus making money each time they are bought and sold. Imagine, to illustrate this principle, that two young men each have $20 with which to buy and sell merchandise. One buys 100 pocket combs at 20 cents a comb and sells these combs for 30 cents each. In just one week, he sells these products as shown in the table:

Day of the Week	Number of Combs	Cost	Retail
Monday	100	$ 20.00	$ 30.00
Tuesday	150	$ 30.00	$ 45.00
Wednesday	225	$ 45.00	$ 67.50
Thursday	337	$ 67.40	$101.10
Friday	505	$101.00	$151.50
Saturday	757	$151.40	$227.10

By the end of the week, he had a return of slightly more than $207 over the original investment—a return over 10 times the amount of $20 with which he began.

The second young man invested his $20 in a pair of trousers to be sold for $40. By week's end, he finally sold the trousers. Thus, he had $20 over the initial investment—or a return 2 times the original investment.

Profit Potential of Goods

The amount of space an article occupies, the ease with which it is sold, the frequency of sale, and the amount of money above cost realized on the sale will all contribute to the total value of that product in analyzing its profit potential. Items such as cigarettes, candies, and soft drinks may be extremely profitable even though they are low-cost, low-margin goods.

THE MERCHANDISING FUNCTION

On the other hand, expensive dresses, coats, or suits may require expert sales consultants, spacious areas with elaborate decor, and special handling—all of which add up to high costs in the selling of those goods. A high markup, therefore, may be sought by the retailer, yet this high markup may reduce the rate of sale of these goods. Merchandise management accounting is a way of pricing the goods for optimum sales at a profit.

Problems Incurred

A great deal of time is usually needed to solve the problems associated with analyzing each category of merchandise to determine the rate of turnover and fixed and variable costs. Time is also needed to use the answers to determine the markups on goods. Computers, when properly programmed, can supply the necessary cost and selling information speedily and accurately.

Some chain store organizations have studied the rate of sale of certain products and entered the facts into a computer. They then determined what total amount of that merchandise should be in stock at a given time, how frequently it should be ordered, what lead time is needed for merchandise to arrive at each store, and what reserve amount of that merchandise should be in stock at a given time for emergency selling. When additional facts about direct and indirect costs were added to the computer-stored knowledge, stores moved toward an analysis that helped to eliminate the concept of a similar markup on all goods. They were able to employ some of the more advanced thinking represented by merchandise management accounting.

TOPICS FOR DISCUSSION

1. Explain what is meant by preretailing an order. Why do most buyers handle orders this way?
2. Explain what markup is and in what ways markup may be stated.
3. Explain the relationship of cash discount and anticipation to the markup on the retail price.
4. Why is markup on the retail price used by most retailing firms instead of markup on cost?
5. Explain the difference between the initial markup and the maintained markup.
6. Under what circumstances might a firm use a dollar markup instead of a percentage markup on goods?
7. What are the purposes of trade discounts?
8. What is meant by a keystone price?
9. What is a loss leader? Why do some stores price goods to be loss leaders? What law must be observed in all discount pricing?
10. How does markup under merchandise management accounting differ from list price markup?

MATHEMATICS FOR RETAILING

If a buyer must purchase goods for one retail price line and there are two different costs for the items which are to be sold at the same retail price, how does the buyer arrive at the markup needed on those goods? On a separate sheet of paper, illustrate this with the following figures: costs of goods—$3.18 and $2.75 each; retail price— $5 each; overall markup—40 percent.

COMMUNICATIONS IN RETAILING

The merchandise manager of your men's-wear department has asked you to explain why you have priced men's ties at $2.98 each when there are two different costs—$1.50 and $1.75. Your price lines for ties are $1, $1.98, $2.98, $3.98, and $5. On a separate sheet of paper, draft a memorandum explaining your reason.

MANAGING HUMAN RELATIONS

A buyer had an agreement with a vendor to purchase an exclusive line of merchandise at a discount off the list price that brought a 55-percent markup for the store. The buyer found, however, that as soon as the merchandise was displayed for sale at the list price, a competing retailer was selling the same goods—and at a lower price. What courses of action are open to the buyer in this matter, and how might those actions be carried out? Be prepared to discuss your answers in class.

DECISION MAKING

1. Miss Syms, a domestics buyer, carries sheets and pillowcases, towels, and other linens in her department. She wants to maintain a 35-percent markup on her stock. She makes only 30 percent on her sheets and pillowcases, which represent 50 percent of her sales, and 33 percent on the towels, which represent 35 percent of her sales. If you were the buyer, what markup would you have to make on the other linens to average 35 percent in the department? Be prepared to show your calculations in class.
2. A jewelry buyer purchases goods quoted at a keystone price and marks them at the manufacturer's suggested retail price. The volume of sales, however, is rather low. What suggestions about pricing could you make that might help to increase the sales volume? Be prepared to discuss your ideas in class.

CAREER LADDER

A young person hopes to become a buyer in a retail store someday. What subjects would you advise that person to study in college to prepare for such a career? Be prepared to discuss your suggestions in class.

Rate (from "1" for highest to "7" for lowest) the importance of the following aptitudes and knowledge for a buyer:

Knowledge of textiles and nontextiles

Ability to write creatively

Ability to get along well with people

Ability to add, subtract, multiply, divide, and figure using decimals and fractions

Ability to remember important facts and figures

Ability to listen

Knowledge of customers' tastes

THE MERCHANDISING FUNCTION

chapter 16
STOCKTURN
AN IMPORTANT CONCEPT

How fast merchandise is sold, replenished, and sold again is an important factor the merchant watches carefully in trying to make a profit. If, for example, $500,000 worth of goods is sold in a year and the stock turns once, $500,000 of working capital at retail would be tied up in that stock. If, however, that stock turns over five times, only $100,000 of working capital invested in merchandise would be needed. The formula for this is as follows:

Retail sales	÷	*average retail stock*	=	*stockturn*
$500,000	÷	$500,000	=	1
$500,000	÷	$100,000	=	5

One very valuable lesson for any retailer is to learn the importance of stock turnover.

WHAT IS STOCK TURNOVER?

Stock turnover, also called "stock turnover rate," is the number of times the average stock is sold during a given period of time in relationship to the sales for that same period. Stockturn may be figured on the retail price, on cost, or on units of merchandise. It may also be determined for any period of time—a week, a month, a season, three months, six months, or a year. In general, when a stockturn figure is specified, it refers to a period of one year.

Stockturn at Retail

Mrs. Radom, a merchant, wanted to know her stockturn for one month's time. Since she kept her records at retail, her stockturn could be figured on that basis. To get the stockturn figure at retail, both the sales and the stock must be based on retail value.

Mrs. Radom had $3,000 worth of stock at retail on hand at the beginning of the month (BOM) and $4,000 worth of stock on hand at the end of the month (EOM). Her sales for the month totaled $7,000. How would she find her stockturn at retail? First, she would need to figure her average stock for the month: $3,000 + $4,000 = $7,000; $7,000 ÷ 2 = $3,500. Then she would divide her total sales, $7,000, by her average stock. By doing this, she would find that she had 2 stockturns for the month.

Average Stock

The *average stock* for any period is the stock at the beginning of that period, plus stock for similar parts of the period, plus the stock at the end of the period divided by the total number of stock listings. For a month, as noted above, this included stock at the beginning of the month and stock at the end of the month divided by 2—the total number of stock listings.

For a six-month period, the average stock would include stock at the beginning and end plus the beginning-of-the-month stock for each month. This would produce seven stock figures, so the total stock would be divided by seven to arrive at the average stock.

For the period of one year, which is the commonly used figure in stating the rate of stockturn, the beginning stock for the year plus each

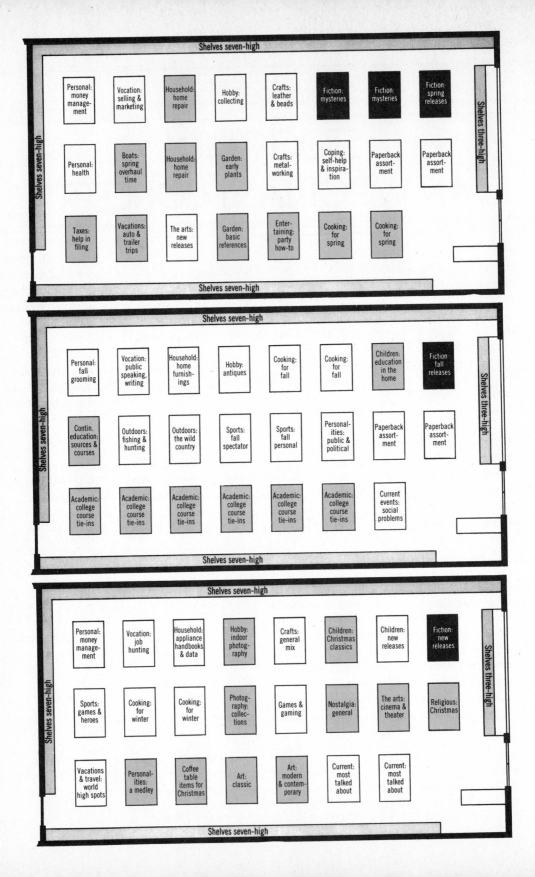

month's beginning stock plus the last month's end-of-month figure would total 13 stock figures. This divided into the total stock for all the months listed would produce the average stock for the year.

STOCK FOR ONE YEAR

Month	Stock in Dollars	Month	Stock in Dollars
February 1	$4,000	September 1	$ 8,000
March 1	6,000	October 1	9,000
April 1	7,000	November 1	10,000
May 1	6,000	December 1	15,000
June 1	5,000	January 1	8,000
July 1	4,000	January 31	3,000
August 1	5,000	TOTAL	$90,000

Year's Stock		Number of Listings		Average Stock
$90,000	÷	13	=	$6,923

If total sales for the year were $31,153, the stockturn would be 4.5 and would be called the *rate of stockturn* or *stock turnover rate*.

To determine more precisely what the average stock is, especially in those departments where stock tends to peak during the month but be low at the end of one month and the beginning of the next, the stock may be taken on a weekly basis. Over a year's time, with the closing stock figure for the last week, this would produce 53 weekly figures by which the total would be divided.

Stockturn at Cost

If merchants keep their records at cost, they may wish to figure their stockturn on a cost basis. To do this, they must use all computations at cost. Thus, sales figures must be translated to cost, and stock figures must be figured at cost.

The following illustration shows how the stockturn on the same goods is figured at retail and at cost.

Stockturn at Retail
Sales $7,000 ÷ average stock, $3,500 at retail = 2 stockturns

Stockturn at Cost
Sales $7,000 at retail at a 40% markup = $4,200 cost of goods sold
Average stock at cost = $2,100
$4,200 ÷ $2,100 = 2 stockturns

Although this illustration shows both stockturns to be the same, stockturns at cost are usually slightly larger than stockturns at retail because the average stock cost is figured at the regular markup, while the retail sales are figured on the maintained markup, which includes markdowns and shortages.

Because the majority of retail firms value their merchandise at retail and compute their sales at retail, the cost method of figuring stockturn is little used.

STOCKTURN BY UNITS

It is possible in computing stockturn to figure it by units sold rather than by dollar sales. For most merchandise categories, this would be an almost impossible task. A hardware merchant would find it difficult to count all the nails, screws, and electric light plugs sold, for example, in order to compute their unit turnover. Many retailers, therefore, use the average dollars of stock on hand and compute stockturn by using dollar sales figures. However, for costly items of merchandise, such as pianos, major appliances, diamond rings, or automobiles, it is possible and sometimes desirable to compute turnover by using units instead of dollars.

Thus, if at the beginning of the year a firm had 100 pianos which cost $300 each and which

These layouts show how a bookstore can cater to customers' seasonal reading interests by monthly stock rotation. In March (top) outdoor and social activities are featured as spring begins. College course tie-ins get a large proportion of the shelf space in September (center). Coffee-table books and children's Christmas classics are among the items highlighted in December (bottom). Reproduced from an article by Paul D. Doebler in *Publisher's Weekly*

	Cost	Retail	Unit
Opening inventory	$30,000	$ 50,000	100
Closing inventory	15,000	25,000	50
Total	$45,000	$ 75,000	150
Average inventory (total divided by 2)	22,500	37,500	75
Cost of goods sold	60,000	100,000	200
Rate of stockturn	$\frac{60,000}{\$22,500} = 2.7$	$\frac{100,000}{\$ 37,500} = 2.7$	$\frac{200}{75} = 2.7$

were marked to retail at $500 each, the total stock would equal 100 units, $30,000 at cost and $50,000 at retail. If the firm at the end of the year had 50 pianos at the same cost and retail price, the figures would be 50 units, $15,000 at cost and $25,000 at retail. If sales for the year were $100,000, the figures would be 200 pianos sold at a cost of $60,000. The three ways of computing turnover for these pianos as shown above.

Stockturn, whether figured at cost, at retail, or on units bought and sold, is NOT the average number of times that a given stock is bought and sold. It is based on the average amount of stock on hand in relation to sales for the same period.

CAPITAL TURNOVER

Another way to measure the efficiency of an organization is to check the relationship between retail sales and the average stock at *cost* rather than at retail. This results in a figure that is always larger than stockturn. This relationship of sales to cost of average stock is known as *capital turnover*.

Using the retail sales of $100,000 and the average stock at cost as listed above, $22,500, the capital turnover for the year would be 4.4.

Capital turnover measures the number of times the cost of the average investment in merchandise turns in relation to sales during that same period. This figure, however, is little used by merchandisers. It is a figure commonly used by investors and financial analysts.

VARIATIONS IN STOCKTURN BY MERCHANDISE

An examination of different types of retail firms reveals a wide variation in the stockturns depending on the kinds of merchandise carried. The following chart indicates the approximate stockturns that are commonly found in different kinds of firms.

Type of Retail Firm	Approximate Number of Stockturns Yearly
Meat stores	50
Stores selling fresh fruits & vegetables	40
Gasoline service stations	21
Supermarkets	17
Budget millinery stores	11
Liquor stores	6
Paint & wallpaper stores	5
Ready-to-wear stores	4
Drugstores	4
Infants'- & children's-wear stores	4
Men's-wear stores	3
Furniture stores	3
Retail shoe stores	2
Fur stores	1.5

To some extent, the stockturns vary with the frequency of purchase by customers and the need to keep stocks of fresh goods on hand. Food items, gasoline, and confections are replaced often and have high turnovers. Less frequently bought items, such as furniture, yield a much lower turnover. Shoes and clothing, which must be carried in a wide range of styles, colors,

and sizes, represent a relatively low turnover, even though they are items that must be purchased rather frequently.

VARIATIONS IN STOCKTURN BY METHODS OF BUYING

In addition to the kinds of merchandise and the way customers buy them, the way the store buyers purchase the goods can affect turnover. For example, upholstered furniture, complete with outer cover, was once stocked in large quantities. The buyer purchased the goods and placed them on the selling floor, where the customers selected them. The buyer had to stock many styles, sizes, and colors to have the assortments the customers sought. This method of stocking merchandise,

The rate of stockturn depends on the price, customer demand, and perishability of the goods. For these reasons, cut flowers have a higher rate of stockturn than furniture.
Photograph by Charles Gatewood

with its resulting slow turnover, was changed, however, by *in-muslin* buying. Now the buyer of upholstered furniture may stock only sample pieces. The stock is expanded, however, by the use of extensive samples of covering materials from which the customer may select. Even shapes and sizes of furniture may be changed by such custom orders.

Upholstered furniture selected in this way never reaches the selling floor but is delivered instead by the manufacturer directly to the retailer's warehouse and then shipped to the customer's home. Twice a year the floor samples are reduced in price and sold before new floor models are brought in. The turnover in upholstered furniture departments has increased many times since the introduction of this method of buying and selling.

STORE POLICIES AFFECT TURNOVER

If a firm has a policy of carrying many styles of merchandise and all sizes and colors in each style, turnover is likely to be quite slow, since some sizes and styles will not sell as well as others. If, however, the policy is to carry only fast-moving goods, turnover will be higher. If, instead, the policy permits *hand-to-mouth buying* (buying merchandise just sufficient to meet the needs for a short period of time), turnover may be high, but lost sales may be great also. If customers are disappointed too often in their search for merchandise, lost sales may drive business away to the competitors and keep the firm from increasing its volume.

STOCK CONTROL AFFECTS TURNOVER

Firms that institute detailed recordkeeping of stock and rapid reorder systems find that they can reduce the amount of stock on hand, keep turnover high, and yet, by careful planning, have the merchandise the customers want when they want it. Variety firms have, by instituting such controls, increased stockturns on some staple merchandise from 3 or 4 a year to 11 to 13.

SLOW-SELLING MERCHANDISE

In a discussion concerning merchandise that had been held over since the previous inventory period, a merchandiser said, "True, those men's shirts have been in stock a year, but if we reduce them to sell them, we just have to place another order for identical goods. That makes no sense, since we must have those goods in stock."

This, unfortunately, is the attitude of many merchants. Merchandise in stock beyond the average period in which such goods normally sell will make a department look dowdy and give the impression of being shopworn. Even if the shirts are identical to those which would replace them, just having moved the shirts around several times in the normal course of handling would have caused them to become less than bandbox fresh.

No precise definition of slow-selling merchandise can be given that encompasses all kinds of goods. Products are considered to be slow-selling if they do not sell as quickly as the average of those same products. For example, candy and furniture cannot be compared because people select these items in different ways and expect different performances from them. Certain kinds of candy can, however, be compared to other kinds of candy for rate of sale.

Stores place *season letters* on price tickets. In this way, the date of arrival of all goods is known. Bread that is one day old is slow-selling and has to be reduced for sale the second day. In most stores, ordinary goods, except for fashion goods, are not considered to be *prior stock,* a synonym for overage stock, for one year. In fashion departments, of course, slow-selling goods might be in stock only a few weeks and, if not sold, have to be marked down. The same goods kept for a year would probably be unsalable unless prices were greatly reduced.

The merchants must therefore know the goods they carry and how well the goods are accepted by the customers, and they must be ready and willing to take prompt markdowns on items that do not sell at the expected rate. In this way they will increase their stockturn; keep their departments full of fresh, new-looking goods that lure customers; and be able to purchase new merchandise when it is available.

CAUSES OF LOW STOCKTURN

If merchandise is turning too slowly in a store, any one of several factors, or a combination of those factors, may be the reason.

- *Assortments needed may be very broad.* A department with limited styles, colors, and/or sizes may have a relatively high stockturn. Conversely, by increasing the number of styles, colors, and/or sizes, the stockturn will become much slower. Sheets, for example, used to come in one color—white—and in three or four different qualities—200 percale, 180 percale, 144 muslin, and 128 muslin. Sizes of sheets varied by bed size—crib sheets, cot-size sheets, single-bed size, twin size, three-quarter size, and full size. With a limited number of items, stockturn could be fairly rapid. Then fiber, construction, and size changes and, ultimately, fashion came to the sheet industry. In addition to stocking the white sheets, it became necessary to carry a variety of colors and designs. In addition to flat sheets, contoured sheets to fit over mattresses, half-contoured sheets to be used on top, and pillowcases in varied sizes and designs became popular. Nylon, Dacron, permanent press, and a variety of other materials and finishes entered the sheet market. Beds became, in addition to the regular sizes, queen-size, king-size, and extra-long. All these changes necessitated an increase in the size of the stock needed to do business.

  The increased fashion emphasis on sheets resulted in additional business in these items because of their new and varied appeal. Stockturn was therefore not slowed as much as it might have been had the merchants simply had to increase their stock severalfold without additional sales. However, the added size of the stock needed could not be entirely offset by the increased sales volume.

- *The merchandise selected may not be the right merchandise.* There are many reasons why merchandise selection may be wrong. The styles the buyer selected may be out of date, or they may represent too much high fashion for the community, or the styles may not be the ones the customers want. Local interests, customs, and habits determine merchandise preferences, which must be understood by the buyer. Even within one locality, tastes of customers can vary widely from one section to another; therefore, mistakes in selecting merchandise can easily be made.

- *The merchandise may not be available at the right time.* The buyer may be slow in stocking seasonal items. He or she may wait to order merchandise until customers start to ask for it. By the time it arrives, the customers may have found the goods elsewhere.

- *The merchandise may not be priced right.* The prices of the goods may not be conducive to sales. Items that do no represent good values in the eyes of the customer may not sell. The buyer might put off making price changes on merchandise, thus retaining the stock too long.

- *The merchandise may not be available in the right quantities.* Buyers may not have correctly anticipated the sales of an article. A school book store, for example, was asked to purchase 30 books for a class and to have them on hand by September 15. The store buyer ordered only 15, thinking to reorder if 30 were needed. The demand was for 30 books, but the reorder arrived too late, since the books were to be read by the third week of the term.

- *The store may not be doing an effective sales promotion job.* Even if the right merchandise has been bought at the right time and at the right price, the customers must be informed that the store has the goods. If the advertising is not telling them, or the displays are not promoting sales, or the salespeople are indifferent, or the general atmosphere of the store is not attractive, the merchandise may not be sold.

- *Poor stockkeeping may be reducing sales.* If salespeople cannot find goods readily, if goods are not kept in view on the selling floor, or if items are not filled in from stock-room supplies, sales may be lost even though the right merchandise is in the store. Poor stockkeeping is responsible for many lost sales.

- *Miscellaneous factors may be reducing sales.* Such uncontrollable things as adverse weather conditions or poor economic conditions in the area can also affect sales and turnover. Unfortunately, these happenings can reduce sales as drastically as any other factors.

ADVANTAGES OF INCREASING STOCKTURN

Increasing the stockturn in a department or store leads to many desirable results.

- Rapid stockturn of merchandise reduces the number of markdowns necessary due to outmoded merchandise or soiled or damaged goods.

- Small stocks of fast-moving merchandise require less space. If merchants are buying just the goods their customers want and will buy within a certain period of time, they do not need excess storage space for that merchandise.

- Interest charges on money owed for goods and insurance charges on merchandise in the store are both reduced by having small stocks that turn over rapidly.

- Merchandise that is being replaced frequently always looks new and fresh. The appeal of such merchandise is greater than for soiled or shopworn goods. Thus, customers are induced to buy more when the merchandise has more eye appeal.

- If sales increase and the amount of stock decreases there is a corresponding increase in the return on the investment. The capital of the firm is used more productively.

STOCKTURN CAN BE TOO HIGH

Excesses in stockturn can be disadvantageous.

- Buying in small amounts can result in lower quantity discounts for the merchant and higher costs for the goods bought.

- Added transportation charges for merchandise shipped in small lots may increase the cost of goods.

- Handling charges for several small shipments may be higher than for one large shipment, thus increasing total merchandise costs.

- Clerical and recordkeeping charges increase when several small orders are placed instead of one large order.

- A rapid stockturn may mean that the buyer is buying in too small amounts and losing sales because goods that are in demand are often out of stock.

STOCK-SALES RATIO

To get an overall picture of sales in relation to the dollar value of stock at retail, retailers may use a stock-sales ratio. This shows the relationship that exists between the stock on hand at a given period and retail sales for that same period. A month is the period of time commonly used, although for fast-moving stocks the retailer may prefer to use a weekly figure. Some analysts prefer to use an annual figure for the stock-sales ratio.

To determine the stock-sales ratio for a month's time, the beginning-of-the-month (BOM) stocks at retail are divided by the retail sales for that month. If stocks at the beginning of the month were valued at $30,000 retail and sales for the month totaled $20,000, the stock-sales ratio would be 1.5. If, however, this were figured for the week, note that the ratio of stock to sales would be higher. Stock at the beginning of the week, $30,000, divided by sales for that week, $5,000, equals a stock-sales ratio for the week of 6.

THE MERCHANDISING FUNCTION

In figuring the stock-sales ratio for a period longer than a month, average stocks and average sales are used. Thus, a store may have annual sales of $240,000 and an average stock of $30,000. The average monthly sales are $20,000. The average stock of $30,000 divided by the average monthly sales indicates that the stock-sales ratio is 1.5. The monthly figures are easily compared to determine the relationship between the amount of stock carried and sales in that same period.

TOPICS FOR DISCUSSION

1. Explain under what circumstances a store would do the following: (a) figure stockturn at retail, (b) figure stockturn at cost, (c) figure stockturn by units.
2. How is average stock for a year's period derived if weekly figures are used?
3. Why is capital turnover always a larger figure than stock turnover?
4. Two apparel shops with similar sales volumes report stockturns as follows: store A claims 4 turns annually; store B has 2 turns annually. In which store would you expect to see new merchandise more often? Which store would usually carry a larger selection of colors and sizes? Give reasons for your answers.
5. How may store policies affect turnover?
6. Explain what is meant by slow-selling merchandise.
7. Explain how fashion in staple goods might slow their turnover rate.
8. What are some causes of low stockturn?
9. List and explain at least four advantages of increasing stockturn.
10. Explain at least three problems caused by stockturn that is too high.

MATHEMATICS FOR RETAILING

A men's-wear store had the following stocks at retail: BOM $30,000 and EOM $14,000. Sales for each of the four weeks were $12,000, $8,000, $8,000, and $10,000. On a separate sheet of paper, determine the answers to the following questions: (a) What was the stockturn for that month? (b) If a 40-percent markup at retail was maintained on both stocks and sales, what was the capital turnover for the period? (c) What was the stock-sales ratio for the month?

COMMUNICATIONS IN RETAILING

Mr. Johansen, a buyer, was recently transferred to a men's shirt department that had a very heavy inventory of prior stock and a low stock turnover. The merchandise manager asked Mr. Johansen to write a memorandum explaining what he planned to do to increase the turnover in the department without taking excessive mark-downs. On a separate sheet of paper, list a few suggestions that the buyer might find helpful. Be prepared to explain your suggestions.

DECISION MAKING

Mr. Helfant, a women's shoe store owner, had a policy of trying to please all his customers. Therefore, he carried a wide assortment of colors, sizes, and styles at all times. However, his stockturn was only 1.5, lower than that of most women's shoe stores. At the end of each season, he found he had a lot of odd sizes and colors on hand. The leftover sizes were mostly for the very wide, very narrow, longest, or shortest shoes carried, and the leftover colors were usually those that were least commonly worn. What are some changes that you would suggest to improve stockturn in his firm? Be prepared to discuss your suggestions.

chapter 17

DOLLAR PLANNING AND CONTROL OF STOCKS

Mr. Temple was an independent men's-wear store owner who was successfully increasing his annual sales. He was proud of his ability to select merchandise that his customers liked to buy. He noticed, however, that he had more and more stock left over every year after a successful Christmas season. His inventories of merchandise became larger and larger and his turnover, less and less. He examined his past four yearly records which are shown below.

Mr. Temple observed that although his sales had not doubled, his end-of-year stock had doubled. His turnover, which had been 3.2 the first year, was reduced to 2.3 during the most recent year. He asked his accountant what he was doing wrong.

Questioning revealed that Mr. Temple enjoyed going into the market to buy goods. But he disliked recordkeeping and planning. He bought by judging what he had on hand and by thinking about what might sell well. As his business grew, his investments in merchandise became larger and larger. He made few plans to mark down old goods—in fact, he disliked taking inventory so much that he usually omitted that chore altogether. His only controls were "eyeball controls"—looking around and judging what he needed by estimating the stock on hand. Many businesses that have eventually failed have been managed in this manner.

MERCHANDISING

The term "merchandising" is used by some people to mean all the activities relating to the buying and selling of goods. *Merchandising,* as used in the more definitive manner, is the term applied to the planning and control of the merchandise offerings of a retail firm in conformance with the policies of that firm. This planning and control are essential for the successful buying and selling of goods on a continuing basis.

	Three Years Ago	Two Years Ago	One Year Ago	This Year
Beginning stock at retail	$ 30,000	$ 47,000	$ 59,000	$ 67,000
Yearly purchases at retail	150,000	180,000	205,000	225,000
Total stock at retail	$180,000	$227,000	$264,000	$292,000
Sales	125,000	160,000	189,000	192,000
Markdowns and shortages	8,000	8,000	8,000	6,000
Stock at end of year at retail	$ 47,000	$ 59,000	$ 67,000	$ 94,000

According to the Committee on Definitions of the American Marketing Association, *effective merchandising* aims to provide "the right merchandise at the right place at the right time in the right quantities and at the right price." To achieve these five "rights," it is necessary to chart a course. Tied in with charting or planning, however, is the other necessity, control. Every step along the way, plans must be checked to see that they are being followed and that they are thereby achieving the desired goals.

Control of merchandise involves collecting and analyzing the facts about the buying and selling of goods and the stocks of merchandise necessary to achieve sales. This planning and control may be done in terms of both dollars and units of merchandise.

Many of the facts the merchant needs are obtained through the taking of *physical inventory.* That means counting the merchandise at certain times during the year to know exactly what is on hand and what merchandise is to be classified as prior stock and marked down so it may be sold. Inventory is discussed in detail in Chapter 18.

DOLLAR PLANNING AND CONTROL

The analysis and forecasting of stocks of merchandise in terms of the amount of dollars that need to be invested in order to achieve a certain amount of dollar sales of goods is called *dollar planning. Dollar control* is a method of checking on the progress of the dollar plans.

Dollar Planning

If a firm wants to have $100,000 in sales of merchandise, it must plan to have the amount of merchandise available that will produce those sales. If the firm does not set goals toward which to work, and if it does not plan intelligently what merchandise it needs to achieve those goals, it is unlikely to be very successful.

In general, the smaller the organization, the less formal will be the plans needed. As firms become larger and more decentralized, more extensive and more formal planning must be done. Factors other than the size of the organization also affect the amount of needed planning. If merchandise is staple, and if a great deal of the same kind of merchandise is carried the year round, as in hardware stores, drugstores, and grocery stores, planning is simplified. Where fashion and seasonable changes in merchandise are extensive, it is more difficult to keep stocks and sales balanced. Another important consideration necessary in planning is the amount of time it takes to get merchandise replacements.

Dollar planning or budgeting requires estimates of sales and of stocks essential to achieve those sales. It also requires a knowledge of markups needed so that expenses, markdowns, and shortages will be covered, and so that some profits can be realized.

Most dollar planning is done twice a year. Such plans are known as *six-month plans.* The plans may be based on the calendar year, January through June and July through December, or on the fiscal year, February through July and August through January. The fiscal method of planning provides stores with a clearance period before taking a physical inventory at the end of the summer and following the Christmas selling period. The sales and merchandise plan on page 205 is an example of a six-month plan.

Although planning is done for a period of six months at a time, most firms keep the planning flexible so that changes can be made as conditions warrant. If sales increase, purchases of stock may also need to be increased. Conversely, if sales decrease, smaller amounts of stock may be advisable, and markdowns may be needed to stimulate sales.

Plans made on a six-month basis are divided by months and plotted against plans for the same months of the previous year. Since comparisons cannot be made on a day-to-day basis, some firms find such monthly planning inadequate. For example, if Christmas falls on a Sunday one year and on a Tuesday on the following leap year, an extra day of selling is provided. This would cause a modification of the figures on which the plans are based. Similarly, some months end on a

SALES AND MERCHANDISE PLAN

SEASON _FALL_ STORE # __3__ DEPT. # __56__

BASIC MERCHANDISE PERCENTAGES

INITIAL MARKUP	MARK DOWN	GROSS PROFIT	SEASONAL SALES	BASE FORMULA	BASE STOCK	STOCK TURN
42.5 %	7.5 %	37.7 %	$30,000	%	$9,400	3.1 TIMES

		AUG. FEB.	SEPT. MAR.	OCT. APR.	NOV. MAY	DEC. JUNE	JAN. JULY	TOTAL	FEB. AUG.
S A L E S	LAST YEAR	3,500	4,500	6,500	6,000	5,000	4,000	29,500	
	PLAN	4,000	5,000	7000	6,500	5,500	4,500	32,500	
	REVISED PLAN	5,250							
	ACTUAL	4,225							
	INCREASE + %	+.056							
B. O. M. S. T.	LAST YEAR	7,000	9,000	13,000	12,000	10,000	8,000	9,400	
	PLAN	8,000	10,000	15,000	13,000	11,000	9,000	10,600	
	REVISED PLAN	10,500							
	ACTUAL	7,775							
P U R C H	PLAN	5,000	7,000	6,500	6,000	5,000	4,000	33,500	
	REVISED PLAN	7,500							
	ACTUAL	5,000							
M. D.	LAST YEAR $	175	305	415	485	490	595		
	PLAN $	200	300	400	500	500	600		
	ACTUAL	215							
M. U.	ACTUAL %	43	42.9	42.8	41.5	40	38		
	LAST YEAR %	42.5							
	PLAN	44	44	45	45	42	38		
	ACTUAL	42.8							

In planning future sales, the retailer must consider last year's sales, stock, purchases, markdowns, and markups.

Sunday and leave one less selling day in that month than in the comparable month a year before.

Because of this uneven comparison on a day-to-day basis, some retailers prefer to plan on a 4-5-4 basis. In place of the calendar months, they use alternate months with four and then five weeks each. Keeping these four-week months and five-week months consistent from year to year eliminates many problems of planning associated with the traditional calendar months. By using these 13-week periods, four quarters with equal time periods result to make the 52-week year.

Information Needed For Planning

To plan knowledgeably, a retailer must assemble analyses of all available facts plus information about business conditions, trends, competition, and changes planned within the organization. Once these analyses have been gathered and all the forecasts have been considered, actual planning for the period ahead can begin. Dollar merchandise planning or budgeting includes information on the following:

- Planned sales

- Planned stocks

- Planned purchases

- Planned markups

- Planned markdowns

PLANNED SALES

In considering the sales for the forthcoming six months, merchants review past sales records, check the general sales trends throughout their stores or departments, and determine trends in customer demand. They consider also their planned advertising and promotions for the period, their competition, advice from the trade, and forecasts of local business conditions. Once sales for the six-month period have been planned, these figures can be reconstructed to

show what sales for each month should be. Weekly sales figures can then be forecast.

A retailer's analysis may show that his or her sales for a fall period will be $100,000. Next, the proportion of the fall business that will be done in each month can be determined. Relying on previous years' experiences, the merchant might budget the sales as follows:

SIX-MONTH SALES PLAN

Month	Percent of Total Fall Business	Planned Sales for Month
August	9	$ 9,000
September	10	10,000
October	12	12,000
November	20	20,000
December	42	42,000
January	7	7,000

PLANNED STOCKS

Planned stocks are directly related to planned sales. Stocks may be determined on the basis of a reasonably anticipated stockturn and on the basis of stock-sales ratios. Thus, if planned sales for a six-month period are $100,000 and stock for the department or store turns on the average of two times a half year, the average stock needed for each month of the half year would be $50,000 at retail. This $50,000 multiplied by 6 months equals $300,000 worth of stock at retail needed to realize $100,000 worth of sales.

If the merchant now knows from previous records the stock-sales ratio at retail for the months being planned, he or she can determine what stocks are needed at the beginning of each month (BOM).

BOM STOCK SALES RATIO FOR SIX-MONTH PERIOD

Month	Ratio	Planned Sales	Stock Needed
August	4	$ 9,000	$36,000
September	4	10,000	40,000
October	5	12,000	60,000
November	4	20,000	80,000
December	1.5	42,000	63,000
January	3	7,000	21,000

THE MERCHANDISING FUNCTION

PLANNED PURCHASES

The figure for planned purchases indicates the amount of merchandise needed in the store or department in addition to the stock on hand for a given period to achieve the sales desired for that period. It also includes a certain amount of merchandise to be on hand at the end of the period. The planned purchases include merchandise already on order and due to be received during the period under consideration, plus the amount of money left open for the buyer to spend for that period. This sum is known as the *open-to-buy*, and it is an important sum for the person in charge of purchasing for the store or department. This figure may be adjusted as frequently as needed throughout the month. Thus, if a buyer has $6,000 at retail for planned purchases and $2,000 worth of merchandise on order at retail to be delivered this month, the remaining open-to-buy is $4,000.

Planned Purchases at Retail

The formula for figuring planned purchases at retail for a given month or other period is as follows:

Planned sales + planned EOM stock − planned BOM stock = planned purchases
$10,000 + $8,000 − $12,000 = $6,000

Retail sales for the period plus end-of-period stock at retail minus beginning-of-period stock for period equals planned purchases.

The amount of money for the planned purchases is the amount that can be spent at retail for merchandise to be received within a given period of time.

To determine the amount of money which can be spent at cost, this retail figure needs to be adjusted by the amount of initial markup planned. If the initial markup is 52 percent, the $6,000 for retail purchases is multiplied by the cost complement of the retail markup, 48 percent, to determine that $2,880 worth of goods at cost can be purchased.

Planned Purchases at Cost

If a store uses the cost method of analyzing sales and stocks, the formula will be the same, except that cost figures will be used.

Sales at cost + EOM stock at cost − BOM stock at cost = planned purchases at cost
$5,200 + $4,160 − $6,480 = $2,880

The open-to-buy at cost for the period under consideration would be $2,880.

Open-To-Buy

One of the most important figures that dollar planning provides is the amount of money that is available to be spent on new merchandise for a given period. If careful planning has been done and the inventory and sales figures are according to plan, the buyer should have the amount of money needed for new merchandise in the department. If, however, something has gone wrong—if the inventory is larger than planned, or if sales have not been as good as planned—this open-to-buy amount will be reduced.

If a buyer has no money available for new goods, he or she may be unable either to take advantage of special merchandise that is offered by a manufacturer at a given time or to purchase a "hot" item that is selling well in the competitors' stores. The buyer may not have the money to fill in stocks to maintain complete assortments.

Buying and selling goes on daily. Therefore, plans must be checked and frequent adjustments made, with the goals constantly in sight. Through dollar controls of open-to-buy, the total investment in goods can be regulated, and a balance can be maintained between the amount of inventory on hand, the amount of sales that are made, the amount of goods on order, and the amount to be ordered.

Records kept in the controller's office and made available keep the buyer informed about the money allotted for purchases. Sometimes, for unusual buys or situations, modifications are made in these totals. For efficient dollar control of a department or store, however, it is essential that these exceptions be kept to a minimum.

Although the term "open-to-buy" is commonly used throughout the retail industry, a better term is "open-to-receive." The buyer may have outstanding orders due during a given open-to-buy period that would equal the amount of money available to be spent for that period. That buyer is therefore open to receive that specified amount of goods.

PLANNED MARKUPS

Once merchandisers know their sales plans and their stock plans, they must determine what markup they need to cover the costs of goods sold, expenses, reductions, and anticipated profit. The methods of determining that markup were discussed in Chapter 15.

The merchants are concerned with initial markup, which will be the amount they hope to achieve by the sale of the merchandise. On some merchandise, they may find that additional markups may be taken. This happens especially in times of rapidly rising prices, or when some pieces of merchandise brought in for a special sale still remain after the sale period is over. Reductions from the retail price in the form of either markdowns or discounts can also be planned. Unless these reductions are excessive because of overbuying on the part of the merchant or underbuying on the part of the custom-

ers due to unforeseen conditions, they should not cause the maintained markup to change significantly from what is planned. Shortages, however, over which the merchandiser has little control, may cause the maintained markup to be considerably lower than the planned figure.

The term "initial markup" is used to identify the first markup taken for individual purchases of goods. For the entire department or store, the difference between the cost of all merchandise on hand and the retail price of that merchandise at any one time is known as the *cumulative markup*.

Cumulative markup is illustrated below. The cumulative markup represents the markup of goods on hand plus the initial markup on current purchases.

PLANNED MARKDOWNS

Markdowns on merchandise may be taken for many reasons. Overbuying is a common markdown cause. The buyer may have purchased too much of an item. When it is apparent that all the goods will not sell within the normal sales period, a markdown may be needed to move the goods.

Some beginners in retailing can see no reason for marking goods down that might be sold the following year during the same season. Boxed Christmas cards, they reason, can be sold next year at the regular price. Consider the following, however: money is tied up in the Christmas cards. Until they are sold, this money is not released for the purchase of new goods. For an entire year space will be occupied by this unsalable merchandise. Rarely do cards kept for a year look as fresh and appealing as those just bought from the manufacturer. Personnel must be used for boxing and storing the leftover cards.

Everyone agrees that fashion merchandise

	Cost	Retail	Markup, $	Markup, %
Beginning inventory	$ 7,200	$12,000	$4,800	40
Purchases	3,000	6,000	3,000	50
Total	$10,200	$18,000	$7,800	43.3

must be marked down promptly if it has not sold. The items must be watched carefully to be sure they move at the marked-down price. Otherwise, even more substantial reductions may be necessary.

Merchandise may become soiled as it hangs on a rack or rests on a shelf or counter. If merchandise has been in a window, it may have faded slightly. If customers have tried garments on, lipstick smears or soil may have marred the appearance of the garments. Buttons or belts may be missing, or the goods may have minor damages that cause them to be less desirable in the eyes of the customers. For any or all of these reasons, goods may need to be reduced in price.

Sometimes buyers plan to mark down regular goods just for a few days for special sales. Following such sales, any remaining goods are again sold for the original retail price. This second change in price is known as a *cancellation of a markdown.*

Policies on Showing Markdowns

Retailers have different policies on whether or not the markdown is to be evident to the customer. Some firms want the customer to know that the merchandise has been marked down, believing that many customers seek such goods as "bargains." They have a policy of showing the original price crossed out and the new price written in. Some retailers, on the other hand, believe that goods not sold at the initial price were probably overpriced and that the new price tags should not, therefore, indicate the reduction. In such a store, the customer cannot tell which items have the initial price and which have the marked-down price.

Automatic Markdowns

Some firms have a policy that goods in the store for a given period of time are marked down automatically. This markdown may be figured on a designated percent basis. Goods may also be marked down to the price line below the present one or to a price between the two price lines.

These automatic markdowns continue at the periods set until the merchandise is sold, or until it is marked to zero, at which point it is given to charity.

Figuring of Markdowns

Markdowns reduce the sale price of goods. Therefore, the markdowns are expressed as a percentage of the reduced price, not of the initial price marked on the items. If an article originally sold for $5 and the new price is to be $4, the markdown is 25 percent, since that markdown is expressed as a percentage of the new retail price. Markdowns are figured according to the following formula:

$$100\%, \text{ the new retail price} = \$4$$
$$\$1, \text{ the markdown} = \$1 \div \$4 = 25\%$$
$$100\% \ (\$4) + 25\% \ (\$1) =$$
$$125\%, \text{ or } \$5, \text{ the original retail price}$$

Determination of Markdowns

The size of the markdown differs depending on the merchandise and the original price. The customer should be able to see an advantage in making the purchase at the reduced price. If, for example, an article selling for $4.95 was reduced to $4.90, the reduction would be so slight that it would have little, if any, effect on the movement of the merchandise. If, however, the product was marked down to $4.69, the reduction might be sizable enough to interest the customer in buying the product. This amount of reduction on a garment selling for $24.95, now reduced to $24.69, would undoubtedly have no effect on sales. A dress initially priced at $24.95 might be considered a bargain at $19.95, however. It is the percentage of the markdown that influences customers.

The reason for a markdown also affects the size of the markdown. If the markdown is taken to meet competition, the initial price may only have to be reduced to the price set by that competition. The markdown may amount to only a few cents. If it is taken to speed the sale of slow-selling goods, it must be large enough to attract the customers interested in such merchandise at bargain prices. If the customer must be made to see a great advantage in purchasing at a given time, the markdown may need to be sizable. After Christmas, prices of Christmas cards must show sizable reductions so that customers will buy them 11 months before they can use them.

Timing of Markdowns

Markdowns taken too late in the season have less drawing power than those that are taken while there is still considerable interest in the purchase of the goods. For example, if summer bags are marked down immediately after July 4, a substantial number of customers may still be in the market for them.

In general, it is better to take markdowns on large quantities of fashion goods and seasonable goods before all interest in these goods has waned. If large stocks of the articles are on hand, an effective way to sell them is to make them available at reduced prices while demand still exists. Clearance sales for odds and ends of small quantities of merchandise may be held at the end of a season, but such sales rarely move large purchases of merchandise unless reductions are substantial.

Markdown Variations

Markdowns vary noticeably by merchandise groupings. The more the merchandise is affected by fashion, usually the greater the markdown problem. A few examples taken from the "Merchandising and Operating Results" section of the annual report of the Controllers' Congress of the National Retail Merchants' Association showed that overall markdowns averaged about 7.5 percent but that individual categories showed wide variations: dresses, 14.2 percent; women's coats and suits, 13.5 percent; women's and children's shoes, 12.8 percent; piece goods, 8.4 percent; men's sportswear, 7.4 percent; women's neckwear and fashion accessories, 7.5 percent; costume and fine jewelry, 5.0 percent; notions, 3.5 percent; candy, 2.9 percent; books, 1.8 percent; patterns, 0.7 percent. Depending on the category

of merchandise, therefore, markdown planning will vary widely.

Using previous markdown records from their own store and markdown information based on records of similar stores, merchants can plan the dollar markdowns just as sales are planned. They can thereby plan their purchases with these markdown limitations in mind.

Recording of Markdowns

If records in a firm are kept at retail, all markdowns and other reductions, such as discounts to employees, must be recorded, since these change the maintained markup attained on the merchandise. In addition to telling retailers about their maintained markup, records of reductions help them to analyze profits and to know where merchandise trouble spots exist. If records are kept at cost, such records of reductions are not needed.

Recording of Employee Discounts

Employees in most retail firms receive reductions of 10 to 20 percent or more on goods they buy within the firm. These reductions appear on the individual sales check rather than on a form made out by the buyer or department manager. Total reductions are then compiled from these checks and recorded in the accounting office.

Some stores grant special discounts to church or synagogue groups, charity groups, clubs, and schools. These discounts also appear on the sales check at the time of the sale and are subsequently recorded by the accounting department.

Recording of Shortages

Thefts of merchandise and errors in charges for merchandise also cause reductions when physical inventory is compared to book inventory. Good planning therefore includes an allowance for such shortages. If shortages are larger than planned, they can cause the department or store to show a loss instead of a profit on sales.

Overages also occur through errors in counting merchandise, in charging customers for goods, or in bookkeeping. If errors in counting merchandise or in bookkeeping are the causes of overages, those reported in one year are usually balanced by an offsetting shortage of goods the following year.

DOLLAR CONTROL

Planning means charting the course that the business hopes to take. Control means checking on that charting to be sure the business is keeping on the right course. Control also aids in the determination and direction of future plans that need to be made.

Dollar control is a method of regulating the amount of money invested in goods needed to achieve the desired sales. A balance between the amount of inventory needed and the amount sold must be maintained to achieve planned sales.

To maintain dollar control of stocks, having a book inventory system that tells the retail dollar value of the following is necessary:

- Beginning stocks

- Stock on order

- Stock received

- Additional markups and reductions

- Merchandise returned to the vendor

- Merchandise that has been returned to the store by customers

This book inventory figure will differ from the actual inventory figure because of shortages or overages. The book inventory figure is adjusted whenever an actual inventory is taken. In between inventory periods, however, the book inventory provides a running record of dollar investment in stocks.

With the exception of the figures for reductions, dollar control at cost requires the same figures as those listed above under retail control, but at cost. Markdowns and discounts do not enter into the computations in cost control.

MERCHANDISING BY STORE, DEPARTMENT, OR CLASSIFICATION

In a small store, the owner can plan the assortments, sales, and purchases for the entire stock that is carried. In larger stores, to facilitate recordkeeping and to be able to check events in the various parts of the store, merchandise is usually grouped by departments, and planning, sales, stocks, and other figures are all recorded by these departmental groupings.

When individual departments are very large, the merchant may wish to divide them. Merchandise may be grouped by classification.

Classification Merchandising

There are various methods for grouping by classification. Kinds of merchandise, size, price zones, materials, and sources are used under different circumstances to develop classifications of goods.

In grouping by *kind of merchandise,* natural divisions may be used. In a notions department, for example, all sewing aids and accessories may become one classification, while hair goods may make a separate classification, and sanitary goods, a third. The buyer, by using these classifications, is able to determine where the largest volume of business is, what the stock-sales ratio is, what the turnover is, and where further sales development is needed.

Size differences in merchandise often provide natural groupings. Dress departments, for example, have dresses in misses and junior sizes, half sizes, tall-girl sizes, and junior petite sizes. By keeping records by these groupings, merchants can determine their stock needs quite accurately.

Price zones in many lines of merchandise provide handy classifications. Handbags, for example, might be grouped by taking all those up to $3 at retail, then those priced from $3.01 to $6, those that sell from $6.01 to $10, and those that sell from $10.01 and up.

Materials are also used for classification. Dishes may be grouped by chinaware, earthen ware, ironstone, or stoneware or even more

A store may use several methods for grouping merchandise. This toy department is divided according to types of merchandise: dolls; stuffed animals; mechanical toys. This glassware department is grouped by manufacturer.

Top, photograph by Ezra Stoller Associates, courtesy Neiman-Marcus; bottom, photograph by Virginia Hamilton definitively divided by bone china and feldspathic china, or by fine china and casual china.

The source of manufacture, either by country or individual company, may also be used for classification of goods. Foreign merchandise may be classified in one grouping and domestic products in another. In such lines as cosmetics, goods may be grouped by manufacturer.

Recording Merchandise by Classification

Once the groupings of merchandise have been decided, the necessary arrangements must be made to record the merchandise according to the divisions planned. If goods are not to be grouped, the detailed records are not necessary. Division by departments requires that all price tickets, sales checks, invoices, and other records be kept by department number. Classification merchandising requires that in addition to the department number, the classification of the merchandise also be noted on the price ticket and all other records concerning those goods. Since more detail is needed, classification recordkeeping is more costly than recordkeeping by department only, and both of those are more costly than keeping just all-store records.

TOPICS FOR DISCUSSION

1. What is meant by "eyeball control of stocks"? Explain why merchants may get into trouble by using this type of control.
2. Explain the two meanings of merchandising. Which is the more definitive meaning? Why?
3. What are the differences between dollar planning and dollar control?
4. Which type of store has a greater need for dollar planning and control, assuming both stores do the same volume of business: a stationery store or an apparel shop?
5. How do calendar year and fiscal year plans differ? What is the reason for using the fiscal plan? What is meant by the 4-5-4 plan? What are its advantages?
6. What merchandise is represented by the dollar planned-purchase figure?
7. What does the term "open-to-buy" mean? Why do some people believe the term "open-to-receive" is better?
8. What is meant by cumulative markup?
9. Discuss the factors that have to be considered in determining the amount of markdowns to be taken on merchandise.
10. Explain why discounts to employees are not treated like regular markdowns and recorded by the buyer or store manager as markdowns.

MATHEMATICS FOR RETAILING

1. Mr. Jones, a merchant, planned markdowns on his retail stock. The initial retail price for the lot of merchandise was $200. He planned to mark down the goods to sell for $175. What was the percent of the markdown? Do your calculations on a separate sheet of paper.
2. Mrs. Diaz, a store owner, had planned sales of $25,000 for a certain period. Her planned BOM stock for that period was $18,000, and her planned EOM stock for that period was $19,000. What were her planned purchases for that period?

COMMUNICATIONS IN RETAILING

As an assistant buyer in a large department store, you have been required to help your salespeople serve customers during peak selling periods. One morning you inadvertently overhear one of your salespeople telling a customer who apparently is a friend or relative that she will purchase the merchandise the customer had selected and get her employee's discount on it. In checking through, you find that though this practice is against company policy, the majority of salespeople in your department admit that they often use their discount benefits on behalf of a friend or family member. When you bring this to the buyer's attention, he asks you to handle the matter with the sales staff. You can get the word to the salespeople through a memo, a poster, or a brief talk at the next preopening meeting. Select one of these three methods of communication, and on a separate sheet of paper outline the points you would stress to the staff regarding the misuse of their discount rights.

DECISION MAKING

Two days before Easter, Mr. Koch, the manager of a variety store, found he had an excessive stock of Easter candy, Easter greeting cards, Easter baskets with candy and Easter novelties, and large, white, furry toy Easter bunnies on hand. Mr. Koch believed he could sell some of these goods during the next two days if they were reduced in price, but he disliked marking anything down that could be stored and sold the following year. What merchandise should he mark down immediately? Why? Be prepared to discuss your answer in class.

CAREER LADDER

Two jobs with identical salaries were open in a sweater buyer's office. One job required clerical tasks: recording invoices (the total cost and the total retail price), checking that those figures were accurate, and then comparing them with figures on computer printouts. Keeping records of stock numbers, writing orders and reorders as assigned, computing markups, and other general clerical tasks were included.

The second job involved handling the merchandise: examining a small portion of each shipment to see that it met order specifications; checking for size, color, and style accuracy; placing the merchandise in bins ready for selling; and seeing that a representative amount of each item was constantly on display and that signs and tags correctly identified the products. If you were an applicant, which of those two jobs would you prefer? Why? Be prepared to discuss your reasons.

THE MERCHANDISING FUNCTION

chapter 18

UNIT CONTROL AND PHYSICAL AND BOOK INVENTORY

A new buyer, Miss Farber, was employed on June 1 to buy for a blouse department. She was scheduled to go into the market on June 15 to purchase fall merchandise. Her merchandise manager had allotted $12,000 at cost for the purchase of $25,000 worth of goods at retail. With her dollar controls established, Miss Farber now had to analyze the styles, colors, sizes, and prices of blouses she had to buy. She had to determine how many should be tailored and how many should be dressy, how many should be white and how many should be in other colors, and how many should be purchased to fit into each price line. Miss Farber found her preplanning was essential to the wise expenditure of the open-to-buy money for the department.

UNIT CONTROL

Dollar control reveals how dollars have been apportioned. *Unit control* shows how the physical units of the stock have been allotted. Unit control is not a substitute for dollar control, but it is an important supplement to it. The merchandise manager works closely with the buyer and the controller in developing the dollar controls. The buyer or store manager, however, usually controls the units of goods ordered and maintained. The larger the firm, the more varied and the more sizable the stocks of goods carried. Because of the larger number of people involved in the handling of the stock, unit control becomes a necessity.

In small stores, unit control may not be necessary if the merchant can check the merchandise frequently.

Information Provided by Unit Control

Although information recorded for unit control varies by firm and by merchandise category, records usually include sales by style number, color, size, and material; stocks on hand; and stocks on order. Some unit-control systems also include returns from customers, markups, markdowns, rate of stockturn by price, merchandise classification, and vendor.

Advantages of Unit Control

Unit control provides a great deal of essential information for the buyer. Properly kept controls show when goods are needed; what goods are slow-selling; when stocks are well balanced with respect to styles, colors, and sizes; and when out-of-stock conditions will adversely affect sales. Unit control is especially important for high-cost items, such as ready-to-wear, men's suits, furniture, fine jewelry, televisions, and major appliances. The faster the merchandise moves in and out, as it does in fashion departments, the more unit controls help to keep stocks on hand and balanced.

Since the advent of automatic controls, even low-cost staple items have successfully been put on unit-control systems. By using electronic computer recording methods, buyers now know what merchandise is in stock, on order, and sold.

This information may be available in either daily or weekly reports. Automatic reorder systems speed the fast-selling items to the store. Through these methods of reporting and ordering, stock-turn has been increased, providing newer merchandise more frequently and yielding an increased profit.

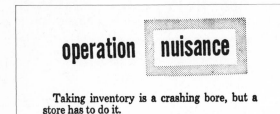

operation nuisance

Taking inventory is a crashing bore, but a store has to do it.

Wallachs will be taking inventory at their twenty-four stores July 27th and 28th.

• • •

The following twelve stores will be closed at 4 P.M. on Tuesday, July 27th:

Fifth Ave. (46th St.)	Manhasset
Empire (350 5th Ave.)	White Plains
253 Broadway	Bridgeport, Conn.
Newark	Pru Center, Boston
Jamaica	Worcester, Mass.
Flushing	Braintree, Mass.

• • •

The other twelve stores will be closed on Wednesday morning, July 28th until 2 P.M. They are:

Kings Plaza	Menlo Park
Roosevelt Field	Garden State Plaza
Huntington	Willowbrook Mall
Smith Haven Mall	Natick, Mass.
Nanuet Mall	Peabody, Mass.
Cross County Center	Warwick, R.I.

• • •

Wallachs calls it operation nuisance, but we try to do it when it will cause you the least inconvenience and get it over with as quickly as possible.

In addition to the store's computerized inventory records, a physical count of inventory is taken every year. Taking physical inventory turns up shortages due to theft or breakage, reveals the age and condition of stock on hand, and serves as a general housecleaning for the store.

Reasons for Nonuse of Unit Control

Some firms dislike using unit control for several reasons. First, controls are costly. People are needed to help keep the records, to check the stock, and to make notations on formal record-keeping forms.

Second, controls are time-consuming for those who perform the necessary tasks if extra people are not especially hired to do the work. Some salespeople who are asked to count and keep records when they are not waiting on customers keep right on counting and recording when customers enter the store, thus losing sales for the department. Sometimes salespeople even have to be taken from the selling floor to make counts of goods or to record receipts of merchandise in stock rooms. This further reduces their availability to serve customers.

Third, some buyers do not use the records or use only a small portion of the information they receive from unit control. This has been particularly noticeable since the advent of electronic data processing. The printouts of figures available to the buyers are sometimes so extensive that the buyers do not want to take the time needed to read through these lengthy records.

Fourth, some buyers believe such records may reveal their buying errors and may be used to check up on them.

Fifth, some buyers fear that if unit controls are used, they will not be needed, or they will be replaced by control clerks.

Sixth, some buyers prefer to use their own personal methods of control, such as looking over their stocks, remembering what has been ordered, and then, by intuition, deciding what will be needed.

Unit-Control Planning

Retailing firms have different reasons for the kinds of controls they institute. Some firms may use all three of the following planning and control measures. Others may use just one or none of them.

Model Stock. Merchants who believe that they should have available the variety of styles, colors, sizes, materials, and prices wanted by their customers when those customers are interested in buying find model-stock planning a good method of determining all these factors.

To plan model stocks, merchants must first have unit information about stocks of goods and sales for previous seasons. They must also know how often their stock counts are taken and the length of time it takes to place orders and receive merchandise from the manufacturers of those particular items. With this information, they are able to determine the number of items they should have on hand and on order to cover the needs of their merchandise categories for a given period of time. For example, buyers know that black cocktail dresses sell during October and November. They also know that they sell a certain number of 8s, 10s, 12s, 14s, and 16s. Even though styles change from year to year, they must have a minimum number of black cocktail dresses in the correct size range if they are to maintain their customer following. They therefore set up a model-stock plan for such dresses. Once such a plan is made, it needs to be updated yearly or even by season to account for changes in customer buying and for increases or decreases in the total volume of business done by the department. A model stock is a guide to the actual buying done for the category of merchandise under consideration.

Basic-Stock List. For staple goods, which are constantly replenished to meet sales demands, basic-stock lists are often used. A basic-stock list identifies each item exactly by brand name, size, color, or any other specific factor that characterizes it. Merchandise that is carried in stock at all times is particularly suitable for basic-stock lists.

In determining their basic-stock lists, buyers are guided, as they are in model-stock planning, by the previous year's sales. The basic-stock items may be reordered by a formula. This includes:

- The rate of sale of the items, which is obtained from past records.

- The length of time between counts that will be made for this merchandise. Counts may be taken once a month, every two weeks, weekly, or even daily.

- The length of time it takes under normal conditions to obtain this merchandise from the manufacturer.

- The amount of reserve stock needed in case of unusual fluctuations in sales, slow delivery from the manufacturer, or ordering errors in the store. This is called the "safety factor."

Reorder formulas were shown in Chapter 12.

Merchandise categories for which basic-stock lists are used include drugs, housewares, groceries, clocks, notions, books, stationery, china and glassware, curtains, silverware, hosiery, and tires and automotive accessories.

Never-Out Lists. For use in checking to see that staple merchandise is on hand at all times, buyers or department managers prepare "never-out lists." These are checklists of merchandise by specific style, color, size, and price that may be used either by the comparison office or by the superintendent or district manager of a chain organization during a visit to the store. With such a list in hand, the checker can quickly be shown the actual item in stock to determine if customers will be properly served when they seek that item in the store. These lists are so important that chain organizations expect store managers to have above 95 percent of listed merchandise on display at any time. Managers who cannot do that are considered to be inefficient in their store operation.

Large stores are expected to have more extensive assortments on their never-out lists than small stores, besides having a greater number of each item on display and in the stock room.

Through periodic checks, the buyers or managers responsible for merchandise are kept alert to the condition of their stock assortments, and customers are assured of getting the products they seek on each visit to the store.

Never-out lists may also contain seasonal items during the time those articles are in demand.

Methods of Recordkeeping for Unit Control

Once it is determined that controlling stocks by units is desirable, a store manager or buyer must decide how the recordkeeping for those stocks will be done. Some stores keep book records, called perpetual or book sales-analysis systems. Others prefer to count merchandise on hand periodically and to place orders following these periodic counts.

Perpetual Sales-Analysis System. Perpetual controls may be kept through a set of books or by computer. Sales made, goods on order, and goods on hand are noted. This book or perpetual inventory advises the buyer about the condition of the stock at any time. It is an instant reference for the purpose of unit control.

Even though controls might be accurately kept, shortages may occur. These shortages are not revealed until an actual physical inventory record advises the buyer about the true condition of the stock. A perpetual inventory could thus indicate that merchandise is in stock when, in reality, because of error or theft, no merchandise is actually in stock.

Perpetual inventory has increased in importance as branch stores have been added and as chain stores continue to use central distribution systems that allot merchandise to different stores on the basis of their prior sales records.

Originally all perpetual controls were hand-recorded. Even today tallies are kept for a main store with branches. Full-time unit-control clerks are needed to keep such records up to date so that they give useful information on the stock condition in any category of merchandise at any time as needed.

Automatic recordkeeping systems using punched cards, precoded price tickets, cash registers, and optical readers to feed data into computing machines reduce the amount of labor needed to keep these records.

Physical Counts to Provide Control Data. Periodic counts are used extensively in retailing to reveal the actual amount of stock and kind of stock on hand. These periodic counts may be taken daily, weekly, or at some other regularly specified interval. The merchandise found to be *on hand* must be checked against goods *on order* in determining what needs to be purchased.

Since no records of goods on hand between these periodic counts is available, some merchandise could be completely sold between counts and no other merchandise ordered until the count revealed its out-of-stock condition. However, for merchandise that usually sells at a steady rate, this method of control is often adequate.

The physical counting of goods is time-consuming, but it may be done during periods when no customers are in the store and thereby use time when the salespeople are not busy. Physical counting systems are usually less costly to maintain than perpetual inventory systems, which require constant updating of the records.

Some firms use *tickler controls* to remind buyers that certain classifications of goods are to be counted. This is used in categories of merchandise for which periodic routine counts are not necessary.

Some firms use systems of *warehouse control* by placing tags on goods displayed on the selling floor. One tag or gummed label is provided on the display piece of merchandise for each identical item in the warehouse. As a salesperson sells an article from the floor samples, he or she removes one of the tags or labels and attaches it to the sales check. Each time this article is sold, one less item is indicated by the control.

Stock Location Used for Control. If complete controls of goods are maintained, they cover all locations of the merchandise within the store. Thus, merchandise on the selling floor and stock in adjacent stock rooms (known as *forward stock*) plus stock in reserve stock rooms and stock, if any, in warehouses must be accounted

THE MERCHANDISING FUNCTION

for. When merchandise sells quite rapidly, a firm might record any goods leaving the reserve stock room or the warehouse as "sold" and place reorders for those goods at the next reorder period. For fast-moving items such as drugs, cosmetics, notions, hardware, and paints this is a satisfactory method of recordkeeping. Control cards placed in packing cases are used by some manufacturers to help retailers to record this information automatically.

Methods of Obtaining Unit Information

To establish unit-control systems, several factors must be considered:

- What information is needed by the buyer and others in the firm?

- Can that information be obtained by perpetual control or by physical counts?

- How often will summary reports be needed?

- What will be the source of information—sales checks, cash register stubs, price-ticket stubs, salespeople's records or tallies, control cards kept on each item (such as diamond jewelry), tags on the floor sample stating the amount of goods in stock, or something else?

- Who is to be responsible for actual record-keeping?

- What report form will be used?

- How can the buyer or department manager obtain data from the unit-control system?

In setting up any controls it is wise to keep them brief, simple, and clear and to provide an explanation of how controls are to be used when they are available.

Various methods of obtaining information on units of merchandise are used depending on the system established by the store, the kinds of merchandise being sold, and the frequency of selling those goods. Unit control is obtained by manual sales recording, by automatic sales recording, and by physical stock counting.

Manual Sales Recording. At the point of sale, the salesperson may make a record of the sale of each item. There are many ways in which this information may later be retrieved.

- *Price-Ticket Stubs.* Information on sales may be supplied by price-ticket stubs. Each time an item is sold, a stub from the price ticket—which contains information such as the style number, color, size, manufacturer, and retail price—is placed in a container. These stubs are then sorted manually by a merchandise control clerk and tallied on a form supplied for this purpose. After recording the data, the buyer can make notations for the necessary orders to be written. This method does not always provide accurate counts, however. Failure to tear off the stub and deposit it, loss of stubs during handling, and errors in recording information on stubs result in incorrect counts of merchandise sold and merchandise on hand. Physical counts taken from time to time may correct the inaccuracies.

- *Tallies at the Point of Sale.* The salesperson may tally at the point of sale instead of tearing off a stub from the price tag. This is necessary because some merchandise cannot have a large price ticket and stub attached. Fine jewelry, for example, would not look attractive with large price tickets attached. Each sale of such merchandise must therefore be tallied by the salesperson. Tallying saves the extra work of sorting and counting and recording information from stubs. As with providing information from stubs, errors may occur through omissions in tallying and mistakes in totaling.

- *Cash Register Stubs.* As each sale is rung up, the salesperson tears off the stub from the customer's receipt and deposits it in the appropriate container for unit-control data. This provides accurate records if the ringing up of the sale is correct and if the stub is properly deposited.

- *Sales Check Copies.* Information on styles, sizes, and colors may be gathered by a control clerk for unit-control data and recorded for the buyer's use. Unless copies of the sales checks are misplaced, these provide accurate data.

Automatic Sales Recording. As stores have grown, as stocks have become larger and more varied, and as employees' salaries have become higher, mechanical methods of tallying sales have increased.

- *Punched Stubs.* Sales information from punched stubs may be retrieved by data processing machines. Perforations on the stubs permit electronic impulses to process the unit-control facts needed.

- *Cash Registers.* Records from cash registers may be used for input of control data. Special reading devices may be fitted to the machines, or a punched tape may be printed and then processed by an electronic data processing machine.

- *Sales Checks.* Required unit-control data may be obtained from sales checks, and these may be used as the basis for punched cards that are fed into the computer for subsequent data retrieval. Some restaurants record the orders of customers directly onto punched cards or pressure-sensitive machines with order forms that double as sales checks.

- *Control Cards.* Some manufacturers place punched cards into boxes of merchandise to identify the products, their color, and their size, and to show other pertinent data. When the products are sold, the cards are filed in the department. Periodically, the cards are sent to the vendor, who feeds them into a data processing machine to activate the refill order from the store.

- *Terminals.* Used in place of cash registers, terminals transmit data directly to the computer as the salesperson or cashier depresses the keys on the terminals.

- *Universal Product Code.* When the Universal Product Code marked by the manufacturer on the box or container for the goods is read by an optical scanner, accurate instant data is given on price, size, number of articles, color, and manufacturer.

RECONCILING UNIT AND DOLLAR OPEN-TO-BUY

Once buyers have the data on sales, stock on hand, and stock on order, they are ready to plan their open-to-buy. Now they must reconcile their available dollars with the number of units of merchandise they need. If their sales have been balanced according to plan, they will find that they will have little difficulty in adjusting their order plans by units to their available dollars. If, however, they have spent the dollars for merchandise for special promotions or for categories of goods for which they did not initially plan, they will have no money for the products they need to purchase to keep a balanced stock. They therefore must not only plan carefully initially but also adhere to their plans as made. For special savings and for unique but unplanned buys, buyers should attempt to secure additional open-to-buy money or they will be out of stock on regular merchandise.

Unit open-to-buy is calculated in much the same way as dollar control. The planned sales for the period and the planned ending stock are added, and the stock on hand at the beginning of the period and merchandise on order are subtracted to obtain the open-to-buy for the period.

UNIT PLANS FOR OPEN-TO-BUY

Planned sales for the period		600 items
Planned ending stock	1,160	
Total		1,760 items
Minus stock on hand, beginning of period	620	
Merchandise on order, beginning of period	720	
Total		1,340
Open-to-buy for the period		420 items

THE MERCHANDISING FUNCTION

PHYSICAL INVENTORY

In addition to all the records about items of merchandise and the counts needed to record the items on hand, a physical inventory is taken at least once a year in retail firms. The primary purpose of physical inventory is to determine the profit or loss for the firm during the past year and to report that profit or loss for income tax purposes. For those firms reporting on the basis of the calendar year, the inventory is taken during the last day or two in December. Those reporting on the basis of the fiscal year take inventory during the final days of the period that ends their fiscal year.

For fashion items, inventory at least twice a year is desirable. Some fashion departments, such as millinery departments, may take inventory once a month. Perishable merchandise also requires frequent inventories.

The annual or semiannual physical inventory of every item in stock serves several other purposes besides the primary one of determining the firm's financial status.

• It shows the relationship of the physical inventory to the book inventory, thus revealing any shortages due to theft, breakage, loss of goods, or errors in bookkeeping entries. It may also reveal overages caused by faulty recordkeeping. Book inventory is then adjusted to the figures as determined by the physical inventory.

• Records of physical inventory not only show the number of each item in stock. They also reveal the age of the stock on hand, the various price lines, style numbers, and general condition of the stock. This type of information is not available from stock counts as taken for unit-control purposes.

• Taking a complete and accurate physical inventory necessitates checking all areas where stock might be, including windows, display departments, interior displays throughout the store, stock rooms, safes, workrooms, photo-graphic studio, and advertising department. Thus it promotes a roundup and housecleaning for the entire store.

Inventory Procedures

To assure that every item of merchandise is included in the inventory, firms do the following:

1. Plan definite inventory procedures.

2. Use forms for recording each item of merchandise. These forms also help to guide the actions of those who are responsible for the counts.

3. Calculate the value of the merchandise at both retail and cost, except where records are kept only at cost.

4. Issue reports to management employees for study and analysis.

Inventory procedures include methods for recording data and also the use of geographic charts showing areas where merchandise is to be found. If any case, window, shelf, or room is overlooked, the inventory count will be inaccurate.

Care in the correct use of the inventory forms is essential. If boxes of merchandise, for example, are being counted, the recorders must be sure that the units within the box are accurately counted and recorded. When single items are mixed with pairs or with other items in boxes, the danger of miscounting or incorrectly recording is always present.

Inventory forms on which counts are recorded are numbered consecutively. Every sheet must be accounted for to ensure the most complete and accurate record possible. Most counts are taken by having one person do the physical counting of the goods and a second person serve as a recorder. Still another person serves as a checker. The checker comes around frequently to observe the procedures and to count a sample of the goods already counted to double-check the accuracy of the reports.

Some chain organizations, to assure the completeness and accuracy of the counts and to assure that only salable merchandise is included in the inventory, have store managers assigned to stores other than their own for the inventory period. This method, they believe, ensures a more accurate inventory of salable merchandise.

When the final records of the inventory are available for the buyer or manager, the figures indicate the age of various stock classifications and reveal imbalances in the various categories of merchandise. Stocks that are too large or too small or that are overage (prior stock) or that have unbalanced sizes show up in the final tallies. The inventory also reveals any shortages against book inventory and calls the attention of the store manager to problem areas.

TOPICS FOR DISCUSSION

1. If you were planning to buy candy worth $100 at retail to sell at your school store during the Christmas selling season, what facts would you want to obtain before you invested the money?
2. Explain how unit control differs from dollar control.
3. What information is available through properly kept unit-control records?
4. Why do some firms choose not to use unit control?
5. Explain how model-stock planning differs from basic-stock planning.
6. What is the purpose of the never-out list?
7. Explain the reasons for keeping perpetual book inventories.
8. Why do some firms use physical counts instead of perpetual book inventories to tell them what merchandise is on hand?
9. What are the disadvantages of using price-ticket stubs for obtaining unit-control data?
10. What advantages are obtained in unit control through the use of (a) electronic data processing? (b) the Universal Product Code?

MATHEMATICS FOR RETAILING

Mr. Wills, a buyer, made plans for sales of gloves during February, March, and April. How many pairs is he open to buy based on the following data for these three months? Do your figuring on a separate sheet of paper.

Sales for February	64	April planned ending stock	80
Sales for March	70	On hand	64
Sales for April	100	On order	126

COMMUNICATIONS IN RETAILING

The small ready-to-wear firm for which you are a buyer has just opened two additional stores. Buyers will now be expected to purchase for all three stores instead of for one as in the past. You have decided that unit control would be a great aid to you in planning sales and in knowing what was in stock in the three stores. On a separate

THE MERCHANDISING FUNCTION

sheet of paper, outline a brief memorandum to the president of the company setting forth your position on this matter. Indicate why you believe unit control would be helpful and how the records could be kept without incurring considerable expense.

DECISION MAKING

Having checked the unit-control sheet for February in the men's hat department for style "Corporal" hats, you compile the following information:

1. Of the original purchase of $1\frac{1}{2}$ dozen brown hats containing one hat in size $6\frac{3}{4}$, two in $6\frac{7}{8}$, four in 7, five in $7\frac{1}{8}$, three in $7\frac{1}{4}$, two in $7\frac{3}{8}$, and one in $7\frac{1}{2}$, you now have in stock only two in size 7, two in $7\frac{1}{8}$, two in $7\frac{1}{4}$, one in $7\frac{3}{8}$, and one in $7\frac{1}{2}$.
2. Of the original order of $1\frac{1}{2}$ dozen charcoal hats containing one hat in size $6\frac{3}{4}$, two in $6\frac{7}{8}$, five in 7, four in $7\frac{1}{8}$, three in $7\frac{1}{4}$, two in $7\frac{3}{8}$, and one in $7\frac{1}{2}$, you now have in stock all but one in $6\frac{7}{8}$, one in 7, and one in $7\frac{3}{8}$.
3. Of the original order of 1 dozen green hats that included one hat in size $6\frac{7}{8}$, two in 7, three in $7\frac{1}{8}$, three in $7\frac{1}{4}$, two in $7\frac{3}{8}$, and one in $7\frac{1}{2}$, you have sold one in size 7, one in $7\frac{1}{8}$, one in $7\frac{1}{4}$, and one in $7\frac{3}{8}$.

On a separate sheet of paper, indicate which color sold best. Give a tally of sales by sizes, and tell which color(s) and sizes you would reorder if your open-to-buy allowed for $1\frac{1}{2}$ dozen more hats in this style. Also, suggest at least three ways in which you might push the sale of the slow-moving colors.

CAREER LADDER

Two sales employees were considered for promotion to the position of unit-control clerk in the furniture department. Both employees were well groomed and reliable. One was vivacious and enjoyed talking to everyone. She had a following of customers who came to visit her frequently and to shop in the section of the store where she worked.

The second employee was a quiet but diligent worker. She liked to tally sales and frequently offered to help the assistant buyer compile records and fill out forms. Which one would probably enjoy the job of unit-control clerk and be most satisfactory in that position? Be prepared to give reasons for your decision.

PART SIX

STORE MANAGEMENT AND OPERATION FUNCTIONS

chapter 19

SELECTING RETAIL LOCATIONS

Since the earliest days of retailing and up to today, a store's ability to remain in the same place for many years has been a sign of its reliability and the loyalty it enjoys from many satisfied customers.

Although a steady location is certainly the ideal, each year many merchants are forced to move. Often this is due to conditions beyond their control. Countless communities in the United States are building or rebuilding. New population centers are growing up, and urban renewal plans are changing others. New roads, new neighborhoods, and new shopping centers, integral parts of our economy, all affect the way retailers locate and relocate.

DETERMINING A GOOD LOCATION

The location needs of a store depend on the type of its operation, its merchandise, and its customers. What would be a prime spot for a self-service supermarket might be a poor one for a gift shop. Regardless of size, type, or customers, the loca-

tion of any store must satisfy three basic requirements:

- The location must be easy to reach by a sufficient number of customers who will buy the merchandise that is for sale.

- The location must be in a suitable shopping environment.

- The location must be economical in terms of cost, compared with sales volume.

With regard to location, several terms need to be defined. The city, town, or urban complex (city and suburbs) in which the store operates is the *community*. The *district* is the immediate shopping area of the store—for example, the downtown area, a neighborhood area, or a suburban shopping center. The *site* is the exact spot where the store is located. This might be the southwest corner of Fourth Street and Shirley Avenue, the ground floor of an apartment house, or the space between Woolworth's and Penney's at the shopping center.

The Trading Area

Another important term in any location study is *trading area*. In general, the trading area extends to that point in each direction where another store or shopping district becomes more convenient for customers. So the trading area is the area from which the store draws its many customers.

Since convenience is relative, the trading area of a food store may extend for only a few city blocks, while a downtown department store may draw customers from a trading area stretching 50 miles or more in several directions. One of the essentials of location analysis is to determine the probable boundaries of the trading area and decide if there are enough potential customers there to make a new store profitable.

The Search for a Location

The best way to select a store location is to start with a large geographic region. For example, choose an urbanized area that includes several cities with densely settled suburbs between them. Then narrow your choice to a community, district, and site. More or less, this is what a large chain store organization or a multi-unit department store will do when it plans to open a new store. For most medium-size stores and all small stores, the process of selecting a location is much less elaborate and time-consuming.

When most retailers start a business, move, or add a branch store, they do not have freedom of choice over a wide area. Yet many do not give themselves as much freedom of choice as they might. This is because they consider only one aspect of a possible location—the rent—and do not study other factors seriously enough.

Circumstances or personal choices may limit owners of small stores to the home community or even to the immediate neighborhood. For them, the fact that equal or better opportunities are available elsewhere may be of no practical interest. Yet even if they accept these general limitations, very often a helpful comparison can be made between different districts or between different sites in a particular shopping district.

WHY RETAILERS DECIDE TO MOVE

New retail businesses must spend some time studying possible location sites, but from time to time established stores may want to do the same. Because of unexpected social or economic changes inside the trading area, or for other reasons, these stores will reevaluate their locations and think about moving. Here are some examples.

Lease Expiration

The lease on a dress shop doing a satisfactory business is running out. The property owner offers renewal on a 10-year basis. Besides evaluating the terms of the new lease, the retailer must decide whether the present location will remain satisfactory for the next 10 years or whether a new place will offer a better opportunity. To look ahead 10 years, the retailer must examine how and where the community is growing. This includes any expected changes in highways, transportation, and parking areas; changes in the character of the population and of nearby stores; and the growth of new shopping districts that might shrink the present trading area of the store.

In short, the retailer must weigh every known factor: convenience, suitability of the shopping environment, and the ratio of rent to probable sales. If the retailer decides to remain, there is still the question of whether the present site is the best. Does it offer room for expansion that may be necessary? Is there a nearby site available that offers advantages this one does not have? Whenever it is time to renew a lease, retailers start shopping around for locations.

Modernization

A men's-furnishings store has become shabby and crowded. The owner is considering modernizing it to utilize the space more efficiently and make it more attractive. But because of the expense involved, the owner will do a location and site analysis before going through with the plans. Is the shopping district declining or doing well?

Will the store be too expensive to modernize? Would the owner do better in a newer building nearby?

Changes in the Neighborhood

Changes in the character of a shopping district often pose a choice between new merchandising policies and a new location. In a neighborhood with a large Eastern European population, a grocery store owner learns that blocks of houses will be demolished to make way for a large city housing project. The majority of the tenants in the new project will be Puerto Ricans. Should the grocery store owner relocate so that the store can continue to serve present customers or customers like them? Or should the retailer study Puerto Rican tastes in food, hire a Spanish-speaking clerk, and be ready to welcome the new people when they arrive?

Decline of the Downtown Area

In a city where population and income levels have increased markedly, a small department store finds that its sales do not reflect the new prosperity. If this situation is storewide, rather than just in one or two selling departments, the store must reappraise its location. Is it still conveniently accessible to a growing number of customers, or is it losing customers to a new shopping district or a new large store on the outskirts of the city? Has the immediate shopping environment changed—become less attractive or too crowded for easy movement? Actually, this is a very prevalent situation, and it has caused downtown department stores also to open suburban branches. For one reason or another, some old locations are no longer convenient for large numbers of customers. So the stores may follow the customers to new locations.

Decline of a Planned Shopping Center

What has happened in the past to downtown shopping areas is happening now to some planned suburban shopping centers. Where they once were dominant, they are now overshadowed by larger or more attractive centers equally convenient to large numbers of customers.

A real estate consultant for large retail companies advises stores to check constantly to see if their locations are convenient for as many customers as possible. Retailers can do this by taking a map of the city or area and plotting the homes of their present customers. They can obtain information about customer locations from charge account lists and delivery records or just by asking customers when they visit the store. By doing this from time to time, store owners will know if the number of their customers is declining or not.

Competition

Although retailers prefer to select sites for whatever advantages they offer, some take drastic action to prevent competitors from moving in. For example, a shopping center may have two chain stores belonging to the same company. The second store was opened to prevent a competitor from renting it. In a small town, a merchant may rent a costly retailing facility to prevent a competitor from moving in and threatening the business.

SELECTING A COMMUNITY

When retailers begin their site selection process, they must decide on a community. The four main types of communities are as follows:

- *The Large Industrial-Commercial City.* Within the city limits, there is one major downtown shopping district, or possibly several of equal importance, a number of secondary shopping districts, and many neighborhood shopping districts.

- *The Suburban Community.* Outside the city limits are the suburban towns. Some of these communities may have well-developed downtowns of their own, as well as neighborhood shopping districts. Those developed within the past 20 years or so have their major retail facilities in planned regional shopping centers and in smaller community shopping centers.

Occasionally, there are several regional shopping centers competing with each other for the business of surrounding towns. They also compete with the downtown district of the neighboring central city.

- *The Medium-to-Small City or Town.* Relatively smaller cities or towns, which are in the majority, have their own industries and still have room to grow within their boundaries. They usually support one main downtown shopping area but often have secondary shopping centers on the outskirts. In addition, there are small clusters of convenience stores that correspond to the big-city neighborhood shopping districts.

- *The Rural Town.* This is the business center of a primarily agricultural or vacation area and is sparsely settled compared with other communities. Besides convenience stores, the center may support a few apparel shops, but major purchases are probably made at a city within a few hours' driving distance.

What a retailer should know when considering a community as a store location is whether now and in the future it can support profitably the kind and size of store the retailer has in mind. To make this judgment, the owner needs information about several aspects of the community and its residents.

The Population and Its Trends
Very important, of course, is how many people there are in the community and how many households. The kinds of households that predominate directly affect buying patterns, so retailers must distinguish from among newlyweds, young parents with growing children, older families, and single people. Characteristics such as age, education, race, and nationality are significant as well. If the community is home to any colleges or large boarding schools, hospitals, or other institutions, their personnel will form sizable nonhousehold population centers. Thus the retailers may also regard them as consumers.

Retailers will look at population trends over a period of time: five years ago, five years from now. They will make other studies as well. Quarterly sales figures are good gauges of business ups and downs, particularly if the community is a resort area and enjoys a seasonal tourist trade. Other factors that influence sales are convention and meeting halls, hotels, and tourist attractions.

All these considerations will determine whether or not a community is a good location.

Buying Power
Retailers need to know several things about income in any given community—the average income, the approximate number of families at each income level, and where the concentrations of families are at different income levels. Real estate values are good indicators, too. But more important, retailers should know the number of families at the income level they will appeal to and whether that number is increasing or decreasing. The central city of large urban areas tends to have a concentration of families with very high incomes and very low incomes, as the number of middle-income families steadily drops. The middle-class flight to the suburbs is a well-known occurrence in our major cities, but perhaps urban renewal movements will stem this process somewhat. In many smaller cities, the suburbanization of middle-income families is just beginning.

Community Economy
Retailers often examine the main sources of community income. This is an important activity because the sources of income, too, affect buying. Some communities are dependent on one or two major industries. If one fails, towns become blighted and poor. A one-industry city, such as Flint, Michigan, with its automobile industry, can experience sharply curtailed buying power for months at a time in the face of a strike or an economic recession. In general, retailers can safely conclude that the more diverse the sources of income in a community, the more stable its future is likely to be.

Retail Competition

For average small-store owners, the question of direct competition comes into focus when they narrow their choices to just a few shopping districts. With specific sites in mind, retailers can study their markets more effectively.

But the large department store or chain store wants to make an entire community or even a cluster of communities its trading area. Consequently, the owners will examine the community from another point of view, that is, overall opportunity. For example, one department store chain will build a new branch only in an area that supports a store of 160,000 square feet. In sales terms, that means that within its first year or two, the branch must reach an annual volume of about $10 million.

With such requirements, retailers must be assured that their business ventures will be successful. The new store may do well for a number of reasons. Perhaps the growing population has only a few stores to choose from. Or maybe the new store's location is more convenient than that of the existing stores. In cases where there are many factors at work, retailers will do highly technical market research before making a decision. Their success depends on knowing in advance what share of the market they can expect to get in each major line of merchandise.

In other cases, retailers may not set any minimum volume requirements. To some degree, the store will alter in size in view of what the market may offer. Among some large department stores today, the trend is to build small limited-line stores.

Supporting Services

Whether entering a small community or a large one, retailers need to be sure that they can get the services they need to operate efficiently. Among these services are professional accounting, reliable deliveries, and advertising facilities. The retailers must also consider the means and costs of transporting merchandise to the community. If retailers sell on credit, they need the services of a credit bureau to obtain local credit information.

Local Laws

Retailers will check carefully the zoning laws, tax rates, and general land values of the community. If the tax rate is favorable for now, retailers will try to learn whether or not it will continue to be favorable. A growing small city or suburban town may offer fine customer potential, but it may also have to face heavy expenditures for new schools and other facilities, which increase taxes considerably. Also, there may be city ordinances that will affect merchants' plans. For example, in some locations Sunday openings are permitted; in others, they are not. In addition, some places may have a city ordinance or a retailers' agreement concerning night openings.

Sources of Information

Bureau of the Census publications give basic facts about population, population trends, industrial character, and income by regions and states, metropolitan areas, counties, and cities. Within the community, sources of information are chambers of commerce, real estate boards, planning commissions, newspapers, and often business research departments of local universities. Utility companies know the number of new and planned residences and their location, as well as the planned industrial developments that will bring new customers into the area. School boards can report the number of children in each sector of the community and tell where new schools will be built.

SELECTING A SHOPPING DISTRICT

There are six categories of shopping districts, and any one of them could be very profitable to the retailer looking for a new location. These include the neighborhood shopping district, the specialized shopping district, the highway shopping district, the downtown or major shopping district, the secondary shopping district, and the planned shopping center. Retailers evaluate each of these possibilities in view of their merchandising and their special needs.

Neighborhoods

Generally, neighborhood areas support only convenience stores. These stores sell goods or services that customers buy often, but with little comparison shopping. The food store, drugstore, and laundry are examples of convenience stores.

The trading area of these stores is generally within walking distance or, in the case of the suburban or rural customer, a few minutes' driving time. However, many convenience stores are equally suited to locations in nonresidential areas, such as the downtown shopping districts or places where there are many large office buildings. Convenience stores draw their customers from the pedestrian traffic that other stores and businesses generate. Drugstores are the outstanding example of convenience stores that flourish in places other than neighborhood districts.

Specialized Districts

A cluster of limited-line stores that compete directly with each other is called a *specialized shopping district*. The stores that thrive in this setting are those where people can browse over hobby-type merchandise or closely compare special merchandise or price offers. A good example of a specialized shopping district is the concentration of antique shops in one section of a city. Other stores that seem to find only their direct competitors as neighbors are cut-rate record shops, office-furniture stores, and second-hand bookstores. Some cities have similar concentrations of shoe stores, fine jewelry stores, and millinery shops. Any location in a community may house this type of cluster, and its trading area is the whole community.

A form of retailing that has many characteristics of the specialized shopping district is the flea market. Here vendors specializing in small, unique items sell their wares. Antiques; craftware, such as pottery, hand-tooled leather goods, and jewelry; and art works are commonly featured.

The diamond exchange in New York City is an example of the specialized shopping district. The jewelry stores in this area thrive because their customers prefer to browse in shop after shop, looking for the best buy.
Photograph by Fern Logan

Individual vendors pay a fee for the use of an assigned space. The stalls or tables may be set up in an empty lot, vacant building, or street that has been temporarily closed to traffic. Flea markets frequently open for limited periods of time, for example, summer weekends.

Flea markets have the appearance of a return to the early days of retailing, when the artisans who produced goods often sold them directly to their retail customers. Today's flea markets, however, may be major business enterprises. There are buyers who serve flea market vendors in much the same way buying offices represent other retailers. Furthermore, an individual vendor may rent selling space in many flea markets. Some antique dealers and other vendors who operate stores sell in flea markets to introduce customers to their main retail establishments.

Highway Shopping Districts

Strings of stores that extend for miles along the highways are known as *highway shopping districts*. They cater entirely to automobile traffic. Once the stores along the highways were mainly diners, produce stands, gas stations, and, in some areas, antique shops. Nowadays, relying correctly on the willingness of people to drive a long distance for a bargain, retailers have opened highway discount stores, furniture stores, and even apparel stores and shoe stores. Price is their main appeal, but another important factor is avoiding downtown traffic congestion and the difficulty of parking downtown or even in some of the older planned shopping centers.

The Downtown Area or Main Street

Some stores that sell specialty items and shopping goods (goods that are purchased only after

The flea market is similar to the specialized shopping district in that the merchants offer similar goods in a limited area.
Photograph by Virginia Hamilton

STORE MANAGEMENT AND OPERATION FUNCTIONS

the customer has compared price, quality, and style in more than one store) are concentrated downtown or along Main Street. When customers want to buy such merchandise, they make a special trip for shopping. In most cases, they choose areas where they can compare the assortments and prices of different retailers. Department stores and apparel stores prefer an environment in which there is a mixture of competitive and complementary stores. And this is exactly what the downtown shopping district provides.

Department stores and larger specialty stores use advertising and their well-established reputations to generate customer traffic. When they are close together, each store benefits by the ability of the others to draw customers. Those small specialty shops and variety stores that don't advertise also benefit, and without cost. Their trade is the result of promotion activities by their neighbors. From the department stores' viewpoint, having these smaller shops and variety stores nearby adds convenience and a buying atmosphere to the district that makes it attractive to shoppers.

A city may have more than one downtown shopping district. Higher-price stores and bargain-type stores may be concentrated in sections away from the big medium-price department stores. Thus they create complete shopping areas of their own. Retailers take this into account when they look for a suitable shopping environment. Their immediate neighbors must have prices and an image that are compatible with their own.

Some larger cities have developed new major shopping districts that are competing with the traditional downtowns. In a city where the core is choked with traffic and lacks good parking, new retail concentrations are taking away some of the traffic coming in from outlying districts and suburbs. Retailers shopping for a location will chart these developing districts on a city map, because one of them may be the downtown of the future.

The most visible signs that a traditional downtown shopping district is declining are the num-ber of empty store sites and the absence of new construction. Evidence that the district is successfully fighting off downtown decay is the construction of new stores and the remodeling of old ones. Other positive signs are the building of parking garages, widening of streets, and construction of belt streets to carry through traffic around instead of into the shopping area, as well as new pedestrian malls.

Secondary Locations

Smaller downtowns are secondary shopping districts. A secondary shopping district competes with the main downtown area because of its convenience for some segment of the community, even though it lacks the completeness of the major downtown district. The trading area of a secondary shopping district is not the whole community. Rather, it extends to the point in each direction where another shopping district becomes more convenient to the customer. Such a trading area may well offer all the customer potential the retailer needs, and probably at rents much lower than those in the main downtown district.

Planned Shopping Centers

The planned shopping center is still almost entirely a suburban experience. No doubt, one day there will be many urban shopping centers. Forerunners of the planned downtown shopping center already exist in Rochester, New York; Boston, Massachusetts; Salt Lake City, Utah; and several other cities. There are plans for others as well.

Usually a planned shopping center is controlled by one developer or owner. The owner may be a large chain or department store with a branch that dominates the shopping center. There is a predetermined number and mix of stores designed to generate customer traffic and provide an excellent shopping environment.

A shopping center may be planned to serve a large region or a smaller community.

Regional Shopping Centers. A widespread or densely settled suburban area that often includes a number of communities is served by a regional shopping center. The center has one or more major department store branches, chain stores, variety stores, specialty stores, and convenience stores. Besides providing the advantages of the downtown district, the regional shopping center offers these additional advantages:

- Controlled competition—that is, enough stores of each kind to let customers shop around, but not enough to saturate the market

- An attractive environment

- Plenty of parking space and traffic-free walkways

- The presence of convenience stores, making it possible for the customer to buy several kinds of merchandise at once

Community Shopping Centers. The community shopping center resembles the secondary shopping district but has the advantages of a preplanned environment, plenty of parking space, and convenience stores.

SELECTING THE SITE

Generally, retailers have a wide selection among communities and districts in which to do business. This choice narrows sharply, however, when it comes to selecting the best site available within the district. At this point, retailers may call in an architect who is going to design the store. Because of previous experience in store planning, the architect can be an important adviser on site selection. Before final commitments are made, retailers most often ask an attorney and an insurance adviser to give their opinions, too.

In the City

Retailers who wish to locate their stores in a city shopping district, whether major or secondary, must consider several site factors. Among them are the immediate retailing neighbors, for stores do best in related groups. A department store makes a good neighbor for most other kinds of stores carrying similar price ranges. A dress shop, a shoe shop, and a lingerie and corset shop provide a natural shopping sequence, and a children's wear shop rounds it out. A men's shop would do better near other men's shops than in a row of female apparel stores. As noted before, some stores prefer to be elbow-to-elbow with dozens of direct competitors.

Equally important are the density and type of pedestrian traffic that passes a store. In fact, retailers often do traffic counts at the site before they make their move. A traffic count can be a good index of potential business.

Other factors that retailers will consider are location and structure. A corner rates high, even though it is more expensive, because it has traffic from two streets, larger window display areas, and often two entrances. What a building looks like is important, too, because the inside and outside must give the store the selling, operating, storage, and display facilities it needs, as well as the image it wants.

Even though the premises are rented and the landlord will remodel to suit the tenant's wishes, these costs are bound to be reflected in the lease terms. So the retailer will calculate these expenses. On the other hand, if the merchant is building a store rather than renting one, this retailer will select a site with few obstructions, because these raise construction costs considerably.

At a Shopping Center

In judging the potential of a shopping center, retailers get out their maps again and chart the trading area from which they can expect business. Included in their study are the population and income characteristics. The geographic area or the driving distance from which they expect customers varies widely in different sections of the country. There are densely settled sections where several regional centers thrive within 2 miles of downtown. The shopping center management will provide information retailers need on population and the competition at other centers. Retailers always make sure that they have all the data they need before reaching a decision.

Transportation is another key consideration. What are the existing and planned roads and bus lines? Shopping center retailers must know this because their business depends on auto and bus traffic. New roads and new lines now in the planning stage may increase the accessibility of the center, but they may increase the accessibility of competing centers and downtown areas as well. In addition, increased transportation could indicate where new competitive shopping centers will be built in the future. Retailers want to make sure that their trading area does not shrink.

With regard to other stores in the center, retailers must frequently negotiate for space while a center is still being planned. The character and drawing power of the center depends on its anchor stores, that is, the large department store branches and chain stores. Smaller retailers do not make a commitment to space in the center until the anchor stores do. Next retailers will want to know the total number of stores planned and how many will be direct competitors.

Some centers impose restrictions on their tenants that prevent them from selling certain kinds of merchandise. For instance, a luggage shop with plans for a sideline of sandals may find that the center restricts the sale of shoes to the department stores and shoe stores.

If the center is already established and operating, the management can provide potential renters with volume figures for the entire complex and its key stores.

Nonretail businesses often enhance the popularity of a center. These are banks, professional and business offices, restaurants, and recreation facilities. Promotional activities keep the traffic coming, too, as do facilities such as auditoriums for community activities. Most retailers like contracts that commit all the stores in the center to giving financial support to centerwide advertising and special events.

Financing is a necessary ingredient for getting started in business. Retailers are most likely to consider those centers which offer financing of various types. Frequently centers will induce stores they consider attractive tenants to open in their locations by offering good financing terms.

There are two other items retailers will consider before deciding on a shopping center. One is the design limitations the center may impose on the tenant stores. For example, all stores may have to look similar. The other is store hours. Retailers might prefer to set their own trading hours but discover that they can't because there is a mutual agreement among tenants to open and close at the same time.

TOPICS FOR DISCUSSION

1. Why do merchants try to choose a permanent store location?
2. What are the forces at work that are changing the value of retail locations?
3. What are the three basic requirements of any store location?
4. Differentiate between community, district, site, and trading area.
5. The text gives a number of reasons why retailers should periodically reappraise their present locations. Select any two. What are some of the considerations retailers must weigh during the reappraisal?
6. What are the four principal types of communities? If you were opening a limited-line convenience grocery store, which community would you select? Give your reasons.
7. What is meant by "community economy," and of what importance is it to the retailer contemplating a move?

8. What supporting services should a retailer look for when choosing a new location for a store?
9. Name three sources from which a retailer can obtain local statistical data that are pertinent to moving to another community.
10. What are the six categories of shopping districts? If you were opening an avante-garde fashion boutique for young working women, which district would you select? Why?

COMMUNICATIONS IN RETAILING

You are contemplating opening a second family apparel store in a town 15 miles from your present location. You already know you will face little competition from other stores in the area. However, you are a bit in the dark regarding the economic and population picture of the town. You hope to be able to obtain enough statistical information to support your belief that your store would do very well in that community. You decide to write to the town's chamber of commerce and its main bank. On a separate sheet of paper, draft a letter to either one of these institutions. List the kinds of information you would be specifically interested in obtaining.

MANAGING HUMAN RELATIONS

Assume three weeks have passed since you mailed the letter written for the previous exercise. You have yet to receive a reply from either the chamber of commerce or the bank. Understandably, you are becoming concerned, because your final decision to open the second store in that town will be based largely on the information you requested. You are a bit distressed that the institution has not shown the courtesy of at least acknowledging your letter. In spite of your irritation, you realize that you must handle this situation with great diplomacy, for you do want the information, and you do not want to alienate those who might prove to be your future business allies. Would you phone, visit, or write the chamber of commerce or the bank? Be prepared to explain your choice and how you would go about handling the matter.

DECISION MAKING

Your "Modern Homemakers' Shop" has been open for business only three weeks in its new location across town from its original site. Business has been exceptionally good, and the sale of many high-priced small appliances and unusual items for the home has bolstered your confidence that moving to this high-rent location was a wise decision. The first visitor to the shop this morning is a young woman who wants to return an electric egg cooker for a cash refund. She has no sales check to prove the purchase had been made in your shop, and upon checking your stock of egg cookers, you find you still have the six you opened your store with. You explain this to the young woman, but she insists that she had received the item as a wedding present just two weeks ago and was told that it had been purchased in your store. You are hesitant to refund her the $23.95 for a purchase you know was not made in your store, yet you realize your refusal might cause her, and possibly her friend, not to patronize your shop in the future. If you give her the refund, you will be adding an item of merchandise to an obviously slow-moving stock. What would be your decision in this case? Be prepared to explain how you arrived at it.

CAREER LADDER

Find a store in your local or nearby community that has just opened, either in a shopping center or in the downtown area. Visit the manager and find out how this person became manager. What characteristics does this person think made the company choose him or her over other applicants?

chapter 20

STORE PLANNING AND MODERNIZATION

A good-looking, well-designed store plays a major role in keeping customers happy and satisfied. It helps the retailer to attract shoppers, boost sales and profits, and build a good reputation. By planning their departments and modernizing the inside and outside of their stores, retailers can add greatly to their success.

How do retailers plan and modernize? A New York City branch of Macy's wanted suburban shopping comfort in the big city, so it built a circular store with a parking area around the retail hub. I. Magnin in Beverly Hills has main entrances at the front and back for customer convenience.

These are good examples of comfortable exterior design. But the store's interior design and layout are equally important elements of planning. Shoppers want to make their purchases quickly and easily. So to accommodate their customers, stores will do everything they can to assign space among the departments in the most convenient and profitable way.

Modernization is just as important as layout because it is part of being competitive with other stores. As a rule, retailers will attract steady customers if their buildings are air-conditioned, well lighted, attractively designed, and generously staffed.

But even beyond this, retailers invest large sums of money in modernization or even in building a new store because in the long run they will save money. For example, a store manager may decide to shift departments around and

install new fixtures so that clerks may sell in two departments instead of one. Or another manager may install a bank of self-service elevators to cut down staff expenses. In very large stores, management may decide that a costly computer system for billing and account records will improve its accounting methods and provide fast and useful sales and trend information for buyers.

Change costs money. But no manager would overlook its benefit. Change is the key to successful business management because spending current profits wisely ensures future growth. In fact, the most successful retailers anticipate change, rather than imitate their competitors, when they make improvements. Perhaps the most demanding and interesting aspect of business management is estimating the new business that improvements will bring and determining how long it will take for the new equipment to pay for itself.

THE ELEMENTS OF A STORE PLAN

Store planning is very complex and almost never easy. From the customer's viewpoint, the store is simply a showroom to display and sell merchandise. But the retailer knows that careful planning must support the nonselling or sales-related activities. A large store that purchases its merchandise from hundreds of suppliers and offers many customer services, such as credit, delivery, and alterations, could easily devote up to 50 percent of its area to sales-supporting activities.

Merchandise is handled in stages over a wide area. It is checked, price-marked, stored, moved to sales floors, sometimes repaired or altered, packed, and delivered to customers' homes. Sometimes it is returned to suppliers. In addition, stores must keep business records, audits, and analyses. They must pay suppliers and bill their customers. A staff is needed to interview credit applicants and prospective employees. Then new employees must be trained, and during their employment they will need rest and recreation rooms. Some very large stores have well-equipped doctors' offices to handle employee health needs. And, of course, there must be space for preparing and installing window and interior displays, and there must be a place to prepare promotional pieces. All this requires a large working area.

To accommodate these space needs, stores will construct their store plan around three basic elements: layout, design, and engineering. Obviously not every store has the same planning requirements. But in general, both the small retail shop and the big department store apply the same principles of store planning.

The *layout* of a store is the allocation of space to each of the selling departments and each of the sales-supporting activities. The areas must relate to each other productively and efficiently. Also, customers, employees, and merchandise must be able to circulate freely.

Architectural character and decorative style, both inside and out, form the *design* of a store. Style creates a visual impression for the customer. This might be a luxury image, a conventional and reliable image, a bargain image, or a young image. Design includes the methods and facilities that retailers use to display merchandise. Design is important because it gives the store its character. But to be successful, a store's design must be consistent. Merchandise, fixtures, furniture, lighting, wall and floor finishes and coverings, and window and interior displays should all combine to create a comfortable selling atmosphere that expresses the exact image the store wants to project.

Engineering involves the actual construction and facilities that will make the store work: elevators, conveyors, chutes, electrical and plumbing systems, water supply, and air conditioning and heating.

THE PROFESSION OF STORE PLANNING

When a store decides to modernize or build, management usually calls in a store planner, an architect who specializes in retailing. Even the giant retailers that employ staff architects often call in outside specialists to give advice on major projects. Only the small retailers are likely to rough out their plans and work directly with a contractor.

The project can involve any number of plans, from constructing a complete building to remodeling only some parts of the store, such as a floor or the storefront.

If an outside architect handles the planning and follows the project through to completion, the fee is a percentage of construction costs, usually 10 percent. Some architectural firms, however, charge for time and service rather than take a percentage of the cost. Still others charge *per diem,* or by the day, and give advice, draw sketches, make plans, and even develop complete specifications without a formal contract.

To offset the cost of these professional services, the architect often gets trade discounts on supplies that the store wouldn't be able to get on its own. But more important, by hiring an architect the store owner is free to carry on with business instead of studying building codes, shopping for fixtures, and supervising contractors.

The national organization for specialists in store planning is the Institute of Store Planners.

Direct and Indirect Buying
The way retailers buy store-planning services depends on their setup. Some retailers buy services indirectly. For example, single-line and limited-line stores that belong to voluntary chains buy their plans and specifications from their

A store's architecture is designed to project a certain image to the customer. The architecture of this Toronto branch of Hudson's Bay Company conveys an atmosphere of elegance and luxury.
Courtesy *Chain Store Age General Merchandise Group*

STORE MANAGEMENT AND OPERATION FUNCTIONS

sponsoring wholesalers. Naturally, standardized stores imply standardized merchandise and standardized dimensions.

However, other retailers buy their services directly. For example, retailers who belong to trade associations that employ consultants can get their help when they need it.

Most store planners are associated with architectural firms. Some, however, work for fixture manufacturers. Frequently major fixture suppliers offer help in store layout and design, and in some cases their planning service is on a par with that of architectural firms. In general, their services exclude the engineering or construction aspects of a building or modernization job.

The Retailer's Role

During initial talks with the store planners, the retailer must explain sales volume goals, the approximate budget for building and modernization, what the store's image is, and any style preferences. Usually the merchant will illustrate taste in style with photographs and pictures of stores that have a particular appeal. In some cases, the architect will accompany the merchant to nearby stores to take a look at the competition. Their joint evaluation will play a large part in the final plans.

By contrast, large chain organizations maintain their own store-planning staffs, and they will employ outside help only occasionally, if at all.

How Much Planning?

During the past 20 years, certain imaginative pioneers have made store architecture an original and dramatic form, especially in suburban branches of leading department stores. For sure, many branches are cut to a standard pattern, but some are quite original and beautiful. With the approval of their retail clients, architects have designed stores that harmonize with the countryside and reflect the prevailing or traditional styles of their regions.

At the other extreme are the discount stores operating in old factories and in prefabricated buildings. They clearly tell the passing shopper that there are bargains inside, because not one unnecessary penny was spent on decorating the building itself.

STORE LAYOUT

All the details that go into allocating space among the different store departments involve layout and interior design. In every case, retailers will want their store's layout to agree with their merchandising plan. The *merchandising plan* is the store's forecast of its total annual volume. Specifically, it predicts the way this volume will be distributed, first among the selling departments, and then among the different merchandise classifications within the selling departments.

After studying the present figures or, in the case of a new store, the tradewide averages, the store planner may make suggestions to alter the merchandising plan. But once it has been set, the plan is the key to how much space each selling department will receive, what fixtures will be installed, and where each department's space will be in the store.

The merchandising plan and, therefore, layout are highly individual for the multi-line or departmentized store. Even the standardized units of big chain-store companies vary the amount of selling space they allocate to different types of merchandise. Customer preference in different locations and the kind of competition a store has in its shopping district account for the variations.

Since layout is the part of a store plan most frequently changed without the help of a professional store planner, retailers must understand the principles behind good layout. In some cases, only minor changes are possible because of some physical limitation. In others, large-scale change can influence the way customers shop and what they will buy. For example, a merchant may decide to enlarge a department, either at the expense of an adjoining department's space or by narrowing a traffic aisle. Or the merchant may introduce or eliminate aisle tables of special merchandise, possibly changing the whole flow of customer traffic. Someone else might suggest that a fitting room be eliminated to provide extra stock space or office space. A buyer may agree to install a fixture especially designed for one manufacturer's line of merchandise.

Where to Locate the Departments

When large-store retailers are building or modernizing an outlet, their first step in designing the interior is to make tentative plans of department locations. Later on, as they gather information on customer traffic and buying patterns, these plans may change.

In locating departments, merchants aim to satisfy customer needs. This is closely tied to a store's image and personality, which retailers project through the merchandise they carry. For example, a fashion store with strong feminine appeal will stamp its personality on the main floor, using prominent locations for expensive perfumes and jewelry. On the other hand, a discount department store may have no permanent department locations along its main aisle leading from the store entrance. Instead, it may arrange the entire space in bargain squares where merchandise changes all the time.

Although shoppers will notice variations, the location of departments in downtown stores generally follows a broadly standard pattern. Shoppers know, for example, that they can usually find cosmetics, perfumes, shirts and neckties, handbags, and umbrellas on the main floor. Furniture and floor coverings, the restaurant, and the beauty salon will probably be higher up in the multistory building. And in most cases, the various apparel departments and other departments will be somewhere in between.

The Most Profitable Use of Space and Its Cost

Different locations in a retail store have different selling values because some locations receive more traffic than others. The most valuable space in the multistory store is on the main floor, and the most valuable space on the main floor is between an entrance and an escalator or elevator. Customer traffic thins out with each succeeding floor. Therefore, space values decline as you go higher in the store. The basement, on the

other hand, usually gets no through traffic, and so its space value is low, making it the traditional place for bargain merchandise.

Nonselling areas such as offices and credit departments are always located in the least-valuable space—on the top floor or floors. If possible, marking and ticketing rooms are located in the basement, adjoining the receiving docks. Otherwise, they, too, go to the upper floors, even though this means extra expense in the movement of merchandise.

In retail store accounting, departmentized stores allocate charges to each department to cover the rent for each square foot of space it occupies. The department that requires the least space and can attract the highest volume of sales has first claim on a high-rent location. In general, a department whose merchandise is physically small in relation to price and can be sold quickly will produce the highest sales per square foot of selling space. *Sales per square foot of selling space* is a figure retailers calculate by taking the department's total sales and dividing these dollars by the square feet of selling space the department occupies. Hosiery and drug departments are good examples of departments with high sales per square foot of selling space.

This ratio is not the only guide to the profitable use of space. Retailers will also check a department's gross margin. If the gross margin is low, the department cannot afford a high-rent location in the store. A good example of this is a major appliances department selling refrigerators, stoves, and washing machines. Because it sells from a sample stock, this department does not require much space in relation to its dollar volume. Consequently, it produces more sales dollars per square foot than the average department. But it operates on a low gross margin. Therefore, the major appliances department will be located on one of the higher floors or in the basement.

Kind of Merchandise

The most profitable use of space also depends on the merchandise itself. In assigning store locations, retailers think of their merchandise in three broad categories: impulse purchases, convenience purchases, and shopping purchases.

The merchant locates impulse merchandise where the largest amount of customer traffic passes. Ideally, this is near an entrance that customers must pass through twice: when entering the store and leaving it. Convenience merchandise goes on a lower floor, preferably the main floor. Customers will not make a long trip into the upper reaches of a store to get these items, but they will go to the back of the main floor, to the basement, or even one floor up. Shopping merchandise goes above the main floor, sometimes to the top floor. The customer who is buying a winter coat or a sofa is ready to spend time in a store and does not begrudge the extra minutes on an elevator or escalator. Far more important to this shopper is a location that is pleasant and comfortable.

An Attractive Look

Often retailers lavish their attention on interior decoration, but the most noticeable visual element is the merchandise itself. Store planners take this into account when they locate perfume and jewelry departments near the entrance. In some stores, gift shops are at the entrance or in a raised location near the entrance because their assortments of colors and shapes are very appealing.

In general, the departments that carry serviceable merchandise are placed in less-prominent locations. For example, attractive furniture, which lends itself to display, receives high-visibility space near the escalators, while mattresses and bedsprings are usually far from the center of the floor, even though they may be more profitable than furniture.

Convenience for Customers

An important element of customer convenience is the logical relation of departments. Handbags and gloves adjoin each other on the main floor. The lingerie department is near the corset department, just as floor coverings, draperies, and slipcovers are usually close together. Such arrangements follow natural shopping patterns and encourage shoppers to buy related merchandise. These arrangements are also convenient for management. In small stores, departments with related merchandise often employ the same buyer, and in large stores they constitute selling divisions, which fall under the supervision of division managers.

Often retailers discover how difficult it is to reconcile the rules governing the most productive use of space with the idea that related departments should be close together. One way stores solve this problem is by creating selling outposts. An *outpost* is an additional location for selling merchandise from a particular department. It is set up at some distance from the department itself. The outpost may be permanent, or it may be a temporary arrangement. A good example is the outpost of the main-floor handbag department, often set up in the women's shoe department. Retailers know this is a convenience for customers and a stimulus to impulse shopping.

Another way for retailers to modify selling arrangements and increase customer convenience is to open a shop or boutique that stocks coordinated apparel and accessories assembled from several departments. In such an arrangement, the customer may buy a dress, a hat, a handbag, accessories, jewelry, and even a fun-fur coat—all coordinated and all purchased at the same place, and with the help of the same salesperson. More and more, department stores are making room on their floors for these select groupings of merchandise. So far most of them appeal to free-spending, fashion-conscious customers who don't want to hunt through racks and counters of clothes and accessories in several sections of a store.

Retailers can also arrange departments to accommodate seasonal buying patterns. For example, they may place garden supplies, which are in demand in the spring and summer, alongside toys, which have their big selling season in the winter. In this way, each department can take up some of the other's space during its slack season.

Convenience for Management

In general, retailers will also discover that using space profitably is often at odds with the goal of management convenience, as well as the goal of handling merchandise economically. Furniture departments occupy upper floors, although their bulky merchandise could be more conveniently displayed on the same level where it enters a store—on the main floor. China and glassware departments are also on upper floors, although sending this merchandise upstairs by freight elevator increases the chance of breakage. For the multistory department store, these situations are disabilities.

The disabilities are not as great in branch stores, however, because these are usually built on not more than three levels. Typically, the suburban branch of a department store enjoys a better natural distribution of customer traffic than its downtown parent. Its construction is wide and low instead of narrow and tall, with only two or three selling floors. Entrances are on two sides, and sometimes on all four. Many such stores take advantage of site gradation and build entrances on more than one level.

In assigning department locations, suburban managers can organize more easily a complete sequence of related merchandise without resorting to outposts.

Encouraging Impulse Buying

All retailers have one thing in common: they want their customers to do as much impulse buying as possible. Many retailers agree that a large amount of unplanned buying is the key to success. How do retailers create a buying atmosphere? In a typical men's store, for example, clothing will be farthest from the entrance. While on his way to buy a suit, a customer will have to pass all the impulse and convenience merchandise the store carries: neckties, toiletries, jewelry, hats, gloves, belts, shirts, underwear, socks, pajamas, robes, and shoes.

In the variety store everything is convenience or impulse merchandise. As a rule, variety store chains carefully check sales figures by type of merchandise and by store location. Items with the highest sales per square foot get locations nearest the entrances. To draw traffic past as much merchandise as possible, cafeterias are at the rear or side of the store. But supplementary snack bars may be located off a main entrance because they draw regular, quick-lunch business, and also because the impulse merchandise near the counters attracts people as they leave the store. Housewares, hardware, china, and glassware are remote from entrances, or they are on an upper or lower level.

The supermarket layout is the best example of how retailers expose their customers to the most opportunities for impulse buying as they make planned purchases. In the supermarket, space is determined not by square feet of floor area but by linear feet of shelf space. Just as the department store basement is assigned the lowest space value, the lowest shelf in the supermarket aisle is graded least productive. Eye-level shelf space is the most valuable space and is eagerly sought by jobbers who sell to supermarkets. Impulse locations for free-standing displays of specials are at the ends of the aisles. Other impulse locations are at checkout counters.

DEPARTMENT SIZES

Before store planners can decide how large each department will be, they must patiently accumulate a wealth of data. In their search, they depend heavily on whatever information they can get from the management of each department. This is often a long, time-consuming process, but it is a necessary one. Unfortunately for retailers, there is no shortcut.

Enlarging or Reducing Space

In an established store, a clear signal for some adjustment in a department's space allocation is a marked change between dollars-per-square-foot sales and the average figures for stores of its volume. These average figures are published yearly by the Controllers' Congress of the National Retail Merchants Association and other retail trade groups. Every merchant wants to do better than the average, but a figure that is much higher than average often means that the department is overcrowded and may need more space. Conversely, a department that produces sales per square foot well below the average should cut back on space allocation.

Space and Sales Goals

Whether retailers are modernizing or building a new store, they will allocate space according to their merchandise plan. After conferring with management and the store planner, the department buyer sets a departmental sales goal. Then the buyer submits a merchandise plan that shows how this volume will be proportioned among the various merchandise classifications within the department. When management approves the plan, the buyer decides how many units of merchandise the department must have on the selling floor for each classification to achieve the sales goal. This includes the *forward stock*, or the merchandise available for immediate sale, and the *reserve stock* stored away in stock rooms.

The next decision for the planner concerns the method of selling in the department, or what type of fixtures to use and how much space they will need. If a store sells from a sample assortment, less sales space and more reserve stock space is the answer. Open or self-selection selling requires more space for customers to move around than over-the-counter, personal selling. For self-selection, fixtures are needed that will permit the customer to see and handle the merchandise easily.

Next comes the question of what sales-supporting facilities the department needs: fitting rooms, wrapping areas, buyers' office, and the personnel to staff them. If a store uses self-service, the merchandise plan must provide for traffic circulation to the wrapping and checkout stations. The store's promotional techniques are important, too. Are there numerous displays within the departments, or are they scarce?

When store planners have considered all these details, they prepare what is called a block plan for the department. This plan shows the fixtures; how the department will be stocked; its total actual selling space; and the location and space allocation for each fitting room, stock room, wrapping desk, and cash register.

TRAFFIC PLANS FOR CUSTOMERS AND MERCHANDISE

What makes the architectural design of stores unique is that it must accommodate a moving population, as in an airport, while presenting a show designed to keep the viewer's attention, as in a theater. A store's physical design must organize the circulation of customer traffic so that through traffic can move easily, while shoppers who stop to buy are comfortable. There is a secondary circulation, too: the movement of merchandise from the receiving dock to the reserve stock room and from the reserve stock room to the selling station. Planners make every attempt to keep this merchandise movement as far away as possible from the stream of customer traffic.

Two Floor Plans

The two basic types of floor plans are the gridiron and the free-flow plans. Stores using the gridiron plan are divided into sections by straight aisles that run front to back. Supermarkets, variety stores, and discount stores use the gridiron plan, but not many modern department stores do.

In the free-flow plan, it is difficult to identify any aisles. While the gridiron plan determines the exact shape of each department, the free-flow plan leads customers around by indirect routes. Most department store main floors reflect a combination of gridiron and free-flow planning. On the upper floors, either one plan or both are used, depending on the nature of the merchandise.

In the gridiron plan, the selling fixtures can be all the same type and built according to a standard module. In the free-flow plan, the fixtures are many different shapes and sizes, frequently

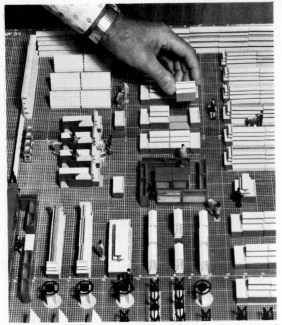

This is a store layout planning board with scale models of showcases, counters, tables, checkouts, and so on. It has been set up as a gridiron floor plan, with standard straight aisles and angular corners.
Courtesy Kidde Merchandising Equipment Group

providing curved turns instead of sharp angles as a customer leaves one aisle for another.

The free-flow plan can be used to suggest quality. But more than that, store planners use the free-flow plan to minimize the proportional flaws of a store's structure. Free-flow planning can make a narrow and deep store look wider or give the customer a clear view of an entire floor from the entrance. For this reason, the merchant must not make design changes later that will defeat the purpose of a free-flow plan. Filling up carefully designated empty space with merchandise tables can counteract a plan that created visibility for a back department. Poor use of space can block a well-planned traffic route.

Planners will also try to consider the relationship between, for example, new fixtures or enlarging a department and the width of traffic aisles. Most store planners like to have main aisles at least seven feet wide and cross aisles four or five feet wide.

Store planners try to place escalators or stairs for easy access from floor to floor. But sometimes the stairway is the only means of exiting from the upper floor of a small store. In this case, fire department regulations may require that the stairway be at a specified place near an exit.

Customer Traffic

One of the key principles of department store layout is that as much merchandise and as many departments as possible should be exposed to passing customers. As you read previously, the location of important departments, such as the fur department, the optical department, and the credit department, on the upper floors helps to draw customers through the store. While going to and from these departments, customers might be encouraged to buy an item on impulse. At the very least, customers grow more familiar with what the store has to offer in all its departments, and this is important to retailers.

Store planners know that customers have a tendency to turn to the right as they enter a store, and so through the merchandise plan they create appropriate traffic patterns. They locate departments where they will profit most from passersby. If managers decide to relocate any departments later on without the store planner's help, they will always keep this fact in mind. To avoid congestion near the entrances and in main aisles, planners will locate departments whose merchandise requires leisurely selection out of the main traffic stream, perhaps against a wall.

There are many other ways for store planners to distribute customer traffic besides strategically locating the departments. Installing appealing fixtures, creating main aisles and feeder aisles, using brighter lights and brighter colors in rear locations, and setting up attractive signs are all familiar techniques for moving traffic past many merchandise displays.

Moving the Merchandise

Retailers use two main plans to move merchandise into their selling areas. In the peripheral plan, reserve stock rooms are located along the

STORE MANAGEMENT AND OPERATION FUNCTIONS

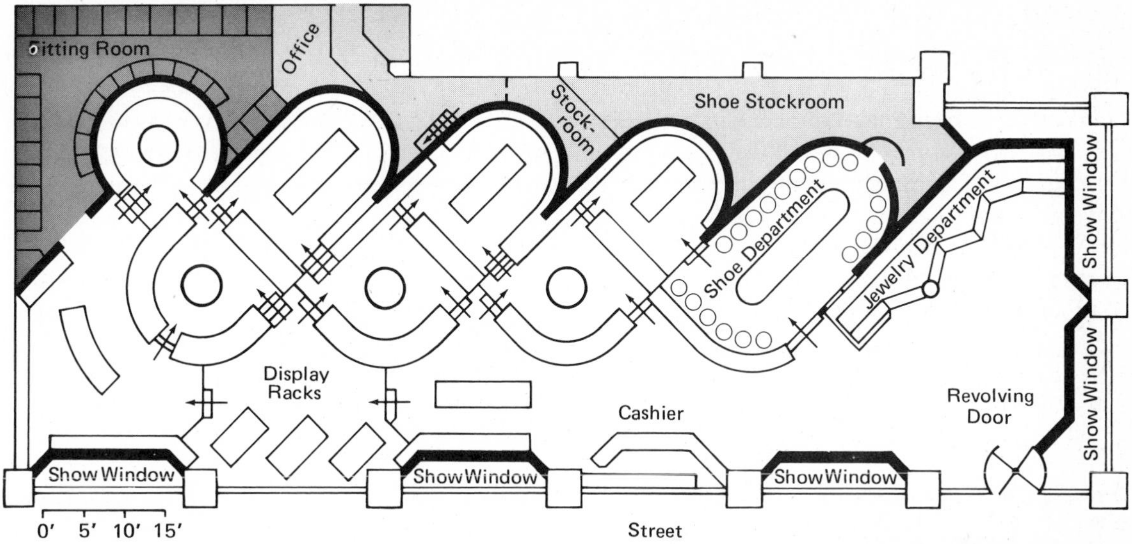

Fitting Room
Office
Stock-
room
Shoe Stockroom
Shoe Department
Jewelry Department
Show Window
Show Window
Display
Racks
Cashier
Revolving
Door
Show Window
Show Window
Show Window
0′ 5′ 10′ 15′
Street

This store (top) has been designed with a free-flow floor plan. Curved aisles, open space, and multi-levels display merchandise attractively and provide a pleasant shopping environment for the customer. Note how the use of mirrors enhances the feeling of spaciousness (bottom).
Courtesy Henry Savady Klein Associates

side walls. Behind them are a corridor and service elevators. In most stores, merchandise commonly travels along this corridor to the stock rooms without ever entering the customer area. Fitting rooms are also placed along this periphery. This plan does not entirely eliminate the movement of merchandise from stock rooms to selling stations. It does, however, reduce the volume of merchandise moving across the selling floor, since the departments with the greatest stock room requirements are along the walls.

In another plan, the service area and its elevators occupy the center of each floor. This service core is completely enclosed, and its walls form the backs of those departments immediately around it. Some large branch stores having two or three levels use this design. There is a disadvantage, however. Although the service core design does create an individual kind of floor plan, it blocks the customer's view of an entire floor. The departments traditionally on the main aisles are now along the perimeter walls, while the centrally located departments may become little individual shops.

TOPICS FOR DISCUSSION

1. Since physical changes in a store can be very costly, how can a retailer justify a program of continuous modernization?
2. Why is it necessary for some large stores to allocate as much as 50 percent of their store space to nonselling activities?
3. Identify and describe the three basic elements of a store plan.
4. Why is it advisable for a retailer to secure the services of a professional store planner when considering changes in store layout?
5. There are several points of information the retailer must provide to a store planner at one of their first meetings. What are two of them, and how might they have a bearing on the architect's plans?
6. Under what circumstances would it be wiser for the retailer *not* to modernize the physical appearance of his or her store?
7. Identify and describe four retailing considerations that have created the traditional placement of departments in urban department stores.
8. How does a retailer judge if a department is "earning its rent"?
9. How do the gridiron and the free-flow floor plans differ? In what type of store is each primarily used? What are the advantages and/or disadvantages, if any, of each?
10. Other than the strategic placement of certain departments, what are some other means of distributing customer traffic around the store?

MATHEMATICS FOR RETAILING

You are the proprietor of "Woman's World," a year-round sportswear shop. You have five departments that take up a total of 900 square feet of selling space. Last year your total sales volume was $200,000, and you want to determine the sales per square foot earned by each department. The square-foot selling space and annual sales figure for each department are given below. On a separate sheet of paper, determine the dollar earnings per square foot of selling space for each department.

Department	Selling Space in sq ft	Total Sales
Accessories	90	$ 8,500
Active sportswear	225	50,000
Blouses and sweaters	185	46,500
Slacks and skirts	100	25,000
Outerwear	300	70,000

COMMUNICATIONS IN RETAILING

Assume you have contracted with a store architect to modernize your pet shop, which, except for periodic repainting, has not undergone any major renovation in ten years. Several of your neighboring stores have been thoroughly redesigned within the last two years, and two large office buildings are being constructed directly across the street from you. You are now preparing for your first official meeting with the architect. You know he will expect you to give him specific information regarding your modernization budget, your sales volume goals, the image you want to present, and your style preferences. On a separate sheet of paper, outline the information you would give to the architect.

MANAGING HUMAN RELATIONS

You have told the pharmacist adjacent to your shop about your desire to renovate your storeroom. The pharmacist wholeheartedly recommended his brother-in-law, an independent carpenter, for the job. You meet with his brother-in-law, and after describing your plans, you ask him for a cost estimate. He tells you that he could do the job for $500, a price that includes the cost of materials and labor, and that he could complete the work in two days. This meets with your approval, and you verbally agree that he could begin work in three weeks. Meanwhile, you hear of a firm in a neighboring town that specializes in store renovations at budget prices, but you are a bit hesitant to contact the company. Though you have not signed an agreement with the carpenter, you wonder if you do have a moral obligation to him. On the other hand, you ask yourself, don't you owe it to your business to get the best deal that you can? Irritating your neighboring retailer, should you not hire his brother-in-law, is another consideration. What would you do in a case like this? Be prepared to explain your answer.

DECISION MAKING

As assistant to the manager of the glassware department, you have been assigned the responsibility of readying your section for repainting. You have been notified that the painters will begin working in your area as soon as the store closes at 6 o'clock Saturday evening, and it is estimated they will complete their job by noon of the next day. Your department has 16 wall shelves, 8 island counters, 4 display tables, and a large U-shaped selling counter. They must all be cleared of merchandise to facilitate the painters' work and then restocked before the store opens at 9:30 on Monday morning. You have on your staff three full-time salespeople, Miss Rivera, Mrs.

Schwartz, and Mr. Gray; one part-time salesperson, Mr. Hanson, who normally works Monday, Wednesday, and Friday evenings and all day Saturday; and a part-time stock clerk, Mr. Malone, who is a daytime college student. These employees are not unionized. Your department manager has turned the entire responsibility over to you and has cautioned that you must not delay the painters in any way, for if they work beyond noon on Sunday, they will demand extra payment, according to their contract. Which people on your staff would you recruit to clear away and restock the merchandise within the designated period? What steps, if any, would you take to impress on your workers the importance of the job ahead? How would you schedule and distribute the work? Be prepared to discuss your answers in class.

chapter 21

TRAFFIC MANAGEMENT FROM VENDOR TO RETAILER

After the wise selection of the right merchandise, the task of getting that merchandise into the store for sale at the right time begins. Part of the profitability of the retailing operation depends upon the efficiency of this movement of goods without waste of money due to delays or loss or damage of merchandise.

Traffic management is the control exercised by the retailer over the transfer of the merchandise from the original vendor to the store or to its warehouse. It includes also sending any merchandise back to the vendor if, for some reason, the products are not satisfactory.

FOUR BROAD RESPONSIBILITIES OF TRAFFIC MANAGEMENT

Traffic management has four main divisions. The first division of work involves proper instructions to the vendor. Through the buyers' order forms, retailers advise vendors of the dates when the merchandise is to be delivered. For most purchases the retailers will pay transportation charges. They therefore instruct the vendors about the method to be used for shipping the merchandise to the store. As necessary, they give the vendor additional instructions about such matters as insurance and packing, and they provide alternative instructions for emergency use.

These instructions are given on the buyer's order form and perhaps in supplements attached to it. Thus, they become part of the store's contract with the vendor. The key document in traffic management is a complete, clear, accurate, and legible order.

The second phase of traffic management is the tracing of delayed shipments.

The third responsibility of traffic management comes after the merchandise has been accepted by the store. It involves the auditing of the freight charges made by vendors and carriers and the filing of claims for overcharges. It also includes the filing of claims for incomplete or erroneous shipments or for merchandise that has arrived damaged. Such merchandise is usually returned, but in some cases—furniture, for example—the store repairs minor flaws in its own workrooms.

The fourth responsibility of traffic management is loss prevention. Making sure all the merchandise moved arrives at its final destination is essential. If merchandise is lost in transit, stolen from cartons or boxes, or carelessly misplaced, the store sustains a loss.

ROUTING AND TRACING MERCHANDISE SHIPMENTS

The buyer's order includes routing instructions. The first decision the retailer makes is whether the merchandise is to travel to the store by premium-rate transportation, in which speed is the chief factor, or by minimum-rate transportation, in which economy is more important.

The retailer tries to achieve a proper balance of speed and economy in shipping instructions to vendors. The owner does this in a small store. In a large store it is the joint responsibility of the buyers and the traffic manager. Money is not saved when merchandise travels inexpensively but so slowly that sales are lost because wanted items are not available in the store when customers ask for them. On the other hand, money is wasted when staple merchandise travels unnecessarily by premium routing, which costs two or three times as much as normal freight transportation. Another source of waste is shipping too many small orders separately instead of consolidating them.

Routings

The premium routings, which are used chiefly for fashion merchandise, are parcel post, air freight, and air express. Small parcel pickup and delivery is practiced by firms such as United Parcel Service. They make weekly or biweekly pickups from manufacturers, bring parcels to distribution centers, and reroute them directly to the stores. Bulk shipments to large stores are normally made by truck and rail, with forwarders, consolidators, and shipping associations combining and expediting shipments and deliveries.

Racks such as the one shown here are a common sight in New York's garment district. They are used to transport apparel from the manufacturer to local retailers or to trucks destined for more distant stores.
Photograph by Jerry Soalt; courtesy ILGWU

Small shipments of valuable merchandise, such as diamonds or other gems, costly art, or antiques, may be sent by registered mail or insured parcel post. Although these methods of shipment are costly, the value of the products is so great that their protection must be assured.

Forwarders. Freight forwarders assemble small shipments—less-than-carload lots—from different shippers into full carload or truckload shipments, which travel at lower rates. While the store that uses the forwarder's services usually pays the higher rate that applies to the small shipment, it gains in two ways: the merchandise is delivered at the store door, and the forwarder's expertise in routing works to the store's benefit. Forwarders function in all three channels of transportation: rail, truck, and air.

Consolidators. In a large city where a store places orders with a number of vendors, the store may arrange with the vendors to deliver shipments to a packing and shipping company in that city, which combines all of them into a single daily shipment to the store. Carriers charge a lower rate for a single large shipment than they do for several small ones.

Shipping Associations. In some areas, stores have combined to form cooperative shipping companies that pool their orders in the major markets into full carloads and then sort and deliver them to the member stores at the destination. This substantially reduces shipping charges.

Other Methods. Chain stores find two methods useful: shipment to a central warehouse from which merchandise for individual stores is then routed, or *drop shipments* that are made to the individual stores directly from the manufacturer.

Routing Guides

All large retailers use routing guides, or shipping instructions, that enable them to choose the best manner of transportation for a given shipment of merchandise.

A routing guide shows all the cities of origin from which a store gets its merchandise and, for each city, a list of the items that are shipped from it. Each item is identified by the freight classification assigned to it by the different types of carriers, and its most desirable routing for economy or speed is also shown.

Uniform Freight Classification Ratings, Rules, and Regulations is the standard book used by the common carriers. This book presents a vast body of technical data, difficult for anyone but trained traffic workers to understand. The routing guide used by a large retail organization is made up and kept up to date by its traffic manager. A smaller store can have one prepared by an outside consultant. In practice, most small stores do not use formal routing guides but, in dealing with a limited number of sources, become familiar with the requirements of either speed or economy transportation. It is probable that they often pay higher rates than necessary, chiefly because of unintentional misclassifications by shippers.

In transmitting shipping instructions to vendors, the store may use either or both of two methods:

- Instructions can be given separately with each buyer's order.

- Each vendor may be supplied with a "permanent routing letter," which covers all the shipments made to the store unless that vendor is informed to the contrary.

Common Shipping Errors

Small-store owners and the individual buyers in larger stores can run up unnecessarily high freight costs by errors such as the following:

- They use too many sources, with the result that many small orders are placed, instead of fewer and larger orders.

- They have the habit of placing orders late, with the result that premium-rate routing must be used. In some cases the trouble is not so much actual lateness in placing the order as not allowing the vendor enough time to fill it.

• When they need merchandise in a hurry, they have a complete large order sent by premium routing instead of instructing the vendor to send the amount required immediately by premium routing and the rest by the more economical route services.

In some large retail organizations, all routing instructions to vendors must be cleared by the traffic manager before the buyer's order goes out. In others, traffic managers carry on an educational program with the buyers. They show buyers how higher-than-necessary freight costs eat into their markups and profits by raising the landed costs of the merchandise. In retailing merchandise, the buyer is required to examine freight charges and figure them into merchandise costs. This often leads to revealing comparisons of total costs of merchandise from different vendors. It may show, for instance, that one has a method of packing merchandise that increases the freight weight. Or it may lead to a decision to look for nearby vendors for certain merchandise instead of doing business routinely with usual sources located farther away.

Tracing of Delayed Shipments

Whether done by a buyer or by a traffic manager, an important part of traffic management is following up on buyers' orders quickly when merchandise is not received on the date specified by the store. Failure to do this promptly can create the most serious of all retail problems: an out-of-stock condition on wanted merchandise. It can also necessitate having the vendor send the delayed merchandise, or a substitute shipment of it, by premium routing, such as air express. In such cases the extra transportation cost must be charged back to the vendor or collected from the carrier, whoever is at fault. Traffic managers in large retail organizations keep a record of carriers and vendors with whom delay is frequently experienced. Unless they are absolutely essential, such vendors and carriers are eliminated from the merchandising and shipping plans of the store.

AUDITS, CHARGEBACKS, AND CLAIMS

Transportation charges for merchandise shipped at the expense of the store are paid on receipt of the shipment or within a limited, prearranged credit period. Where credit arrangements exist with carriers, a detailed audit of the bills may be done before the payment is made. When payments are made on receipt, or when the store prefers to use slack periods for detailed auditing, the auditing occurs after the payment has been made.

Audits

Aside from checking for errors in arithmetic, the chief purposes of auditing are to assure:

• That the vendor shipped as ordered; that there were no extra costs for partial shipments, premium routing, or packing not in accord with the carrier's regulations.

• That the carrier or shipper classified the merchandise correctly. Freight classifications are intricate and not always logical to the inexperienced eye. But slight variations in the description of merchandise can result in considerable differences in transportation costs. If the wrong rate is applied by the carrier, the store can overpay.

Auditing begins with receipt of the merchandise. At this point the shipment should be weighed to make sure there are no discrepancies between weight charged for and actual weight. The succeeding steps may be taken before or after payment of freight charges. First, whether the shipment is complete in one lot, if so ordered, is determined. If an order is received in several shipments, contrary to instructions, the extra transportation cost is the vendor's responsibility. Next, whether the correct rate was applied and the correct routing used is determined. Correct routing includes the use, as instructed on the purchase order, of a freight forwarder, consolidator, or shipping association. Finally, a check is made for any incorrect surcharges—for example, costs for pickups for which the store did not contract.

Even after an audit has been done and overcharge claims have been filed, many big organizations make a practice of having an outside freight audit bureau go over their bills again. Tariff schedules and carrier regulations are so complicated that they offer many opportunities for error, and even experienced traffic managers sometimes overlook errors. The outside bureaus generally charge 50 percent of the overcharges they collect, and they collect enough to make it worthwhile for large stores with full traffic control departments to engage their services.

Chargebacks

If the shipper (vendor) has caused an overcharge by not conforming to the buyer's order instructions, a chargeback is made to the shipper. When a question arises of whether the error was the shipper's or the carrier's, the practice of most retailers is to charge back to the manufacturers, advising them that proper refunds can be obtained from the carrier by filing a corrected bill of lading. The *bill of lading* is the receipt the carrier gives the shipper when the carrier picks up the merchandise.

Damage Claims

The carriers who take the merchandise from the shipper to the store are, in general, liable for any damage that occurs en route unless they can prove that reasonable care was used in handling the merchandise and that the shipper's instructions were carried out. The shippers can be proved liable for damage if they have failed to pack the shipment properly and the failure is not of the kind that is obvious to the carrier. The shippers are also liable if fragile merchandise is not so labeled.

Whether the store or the vendor makes a claim of damage against the carrier depends on which was the legal possessor of the merchandise while it was in transit. If the merchandise was sold FOB destination, the vendor retains title to it until delivery. In that case the stores which have received damaged merchandise report it to the

vendors, who are responsible for filing a claim against the carrier. If the merchandise was sold FOB city of shipment, the store took title when the vendor handed over the merchandise to the carrier. The store therefore will make any damage claims against the carrier. This may require litigation.

Exactly the same principles apply to loss or partial loss of shipments en route.

Damage Prevention

In modern traffic management, much emphasis is placed on educating vendors about the requirements of safe and economical packing. Damaged merchandise represents some loss to the store, even though it collects damage claims. The collection will not compensate for the sales loss that occurs because merchandise is not salable; nor does it compensate for the time that must be spent in filing claims.

GOVERNMENT ADMINISTRATIVE AGENCIES

A *common carrier* is any transportation line whose services are available to all shippers. All common carriers are regulated in the public interest by federal and state agencies. Regulation includes the approval of the rates charged by all carriers. For interstate shipments, the regulating agencies are the Interstate Commerce Commission and the Civil Aeronautics Board. State agencies are concerned with intrastate shipments.

One of the functions of professional traffic managers in retailing is to represent the interests of their stores at hearings before these agencies when proposed rate increases are being considered. They may do this individually or through trade associations.

ASSISTANCE THROUGH TRADE ASSOCIATIONS

The Traffic Group of the National Retail Merchants Association; similar groups in supermarket associations, men's-wear firms, and furniture associations; and regional traffic associations have initiated and improved methods of transporting goods.

The increasingly professional executives who have the title of traffic manager in retail organizations have cooperated with their opposite numbers among the manufacturers, shippers, and carriers to improve transportation. In fact, the whole network of transport and transport methods today is a tribute to the ingenuity and efforts of these people, and the improvements still possible are a challenge to young careerists. They will find that the business of merchandise and materials handling and transportation economics in general is demanding and rewarding.

NEED FOR SUPERVISORY SKILLS

Because they achieve results through other people, traffic managers need to be able to provide leadership for many types of workers. Although traffic managers are not buyers' bosses, they must still get the cooperation and support of the buyers in their firms. Similarly, truckers, railroad personnel, air cargo handlers, and parcel post employees are among the people with whom the traffic managers must work and on whom they must rely for correct handling of goods.

Traffic managers also have personnel in their own departments for whom they must provide leadership.

Knowing how to present ideas effectively, to urge compliance and follow-up, and to see that suggestions are adhered to are all important parts of the traffic managers' job. Only if everyone with whom the traffic managers work is cooperating can high productivity be achieved in the management of moving merchandise into stores. Thus, strong supervisory skills are important to a successful career in this field.

TOPICS FOR DISCUSSION

1. What is the retailer's concern with traffic management?
2. What are the four main responsibilities of traffic management?
3. What role does the buyer's order play in traffic management?
4. What are the primary functions of (a) freight forwarders, (b) consolidators, (c) shipping associations?
5. What are drop shipments?
6. Explain the reason for careful expense control in traffic management.
7. What is the purpose of a chargeback?
8. Who is responsible for any damage that occurs to merchandise in transit?
9. Who is the legal possessor of merchandise while in transit if it is sold (a) FOB shipping point, (b) FOB destination?
10. Explain the statement "When retailers are compensated for shipping losses they still lose money."

MATHEMATICS FOR RETAILING

If purchases for a six-month period amounted to $69,000, and transportation charges were 1.45 percent of purchases:

1. What was the total amount for those transportation charges?
2. What was the total amount for merchandise including transportation charges? Do your figuring on a separate sheet of paper.

COMMUNICATIONS IN RETAILING

On August 14, Mr. Phil Broadstone, owner of Broadstone's Costume Shop, a small store in Ohio, placed an order (Order No. 6460) for 50 assorted Halloween costumes in sizes 4 to 12 to be delivered on October 1. By the 5th of October the costumes had not arrived. Mr. Broadstone decided to send a night letter to the Jackson Novelty Co., 346 Broadway, New York, New York 10003, to check on the shipment.

He asked you to write the message and to keep it within 20 words. On a separate sheet of paper, outline what you would say in the telegram.

MANAGING HUMAN RELATIONS

A shipment of 50 chinaware sets arrived at a variety store one day before the chain's city-wide pre-Thanksgiving sale event was to begin—a sale that had been promoted in all the city and community newspapers. Much to the dismay of the store manager, when the cartons of china were opened, it was discovered that every cup was broken. The manager would have to contact the claims office of the transportation company that delivered the merchandise as well as the buyer at the central buying office. His most immediate concern, however, was what he might do about the customers who would be coming into his store the next morning looking for the advertised sale merchandise. He anticipated seeing some very irate customers during the next few days and was concerned that the disappointment of not being able to buy the dishes might injure the store's image in their eyes. What could he do to improve the situation? Be prepared to discuss your suggestions.

DECISION MAKING

A retail furniture store in a small town had a partial carload shipment of furniture on order. Shipping a less-than-carload lot would cost $2\frac{1}{2}$ percent of the charges for the goods, but the merchandise would arrive at the store by February 1. By pooling the shipment with that of another store and using a common carrier, the transportation charges could be reduced to $1\frac{3}{4}$ percent of the cost, but the goods would not arrive before February 15. Goods worth $5,000 were involved in this decision. What action would you recommend in this matter? Be prepared to discuss your ideas.

chapter 22

INTERNAL MERCHANDISE HANDLING FROM RECEIVING DOCK TO SELLING AREA

The costs of inward transportation of goods from the vendor to the retailer appear as part of the costs of the goods themselves. The costs of moving the merchandise from the store's receiving area to the selling area are part of the expenses of doing business.

When merchandise is received from a vendor, the retailer has seven immediate jobs:

1. Examine the carton for carton damage.

2. Check the contents of the shipment.

3. Verify that the merchandise received is as ordered.

4. Pay the freight charges.

5. Make the merchandise available for sale.

6. Pay the vendor's invoice.

7. Prevent the loss of goods as they move from the receiving area through every stage of handling.

Both the merchandise and the documents that accompany those goods, the records and the invoices, travel through various areas of the store or warehouse and must be checked and rechecked at many points. Receiving, checking, marking, and storing, either in some area of the store or in a warehouse, are involved.

RECEIVING, MARKING, AND CHECKING

In a small store, the processes of receiving, checking, and marking the merchandise and moving it to stock shelves or sales counters are probably all handled by one person. And they are done in such quick succession that they are hardly thought of as separate jobs.

But in a very large retail organization, the merchandise volume is so great that a separate group of specialized workers handles each step, each group working under its own supervisor or manager. In the large organization, furthermore, the areas where the various merchandise handling steps take place and where bills are processed for payment may be widely separated. However, whether a store is large or small, a well-planned system must exist for creating and passing on the documents associated with the merchandise. The system must be carefully followed by all workers involved.

The paper flow and the movement of the merchandise itself are equally important.

The Need for Good Merchandise Handling
Efficient merchandise handling favorably affects store sales and profits. The equipment and talent necessary for a good system are therefore a productive investment. Without it, sales will be lost and markdowns eventually taken because merchandise needed on the selling floor is being held

in the receiving area or in the marking room. If a delay occurs in recording the receipt of ordered merchandise, a delay will also occur in paying bills. The store then loses the cash discount and anticipation the vendor allows for prompt payment. If inadequate equipment or poorly trained manpower results in merchandise damage, the store takes a loss. And should this damaged merchandise get as far as the customer's home, profits are further eroded by the costs of picking up the faulty merchandise and substituting acceptable products. Another result of a poor merchandise handling system is a high rate of inventory shortages, from both theft and bookkeeping errors.

Different Needs and Systems

No two stores, even those of the same size and type, carry out their merchandise handling operations in exactly the same way. The type of store used as an example in the descriptions that follow is a large one with branches. It does the following:

- Receives merchandise of many kinds from many vendors

- Receives it in both large and small shipments

- Distributes it to many departments and usually to more than one store unit

- Typically has two receiving locations: the main store for apparel and other low-bulk merchandise and a warehouse for high-bulk merchandise, such as furniture and appliances, which are sold from samples

- Has a receiving and distribution system that is flexible enough to give priority to fashion merchandise, merchandise bought for special promotions, and merchandise urgently needed on the selling floor for any other reason

- Protects merchandise while it is being processed through the store

These requirements have developed, in the large departmentized store, a comprehensive rather than a highly specialized set of processing problems. In chain stores, such as variety stores and supermarkets, the receiving, checking and marking processes and paper work take place in central or regional warehouses rather than store units. The operations themselves, however, are comparable.

THE RECEIVING PROCESS

The first receiving area is a truck dock at the store or warehouse. The *receiving dock* is a platform built to a convenient height for the level unloading of motor trucks. Unloading is done manually or with the help of lifting or conveyor devices.

In some cases, a large warehouse may be built alongside a railroad siding where rail shipments can be unloaded directly instead of being transferred to motor trucks and then delivered to the warehouse.

The responsibilities of the clerk at the receiving dock are to:

- Examine the cartons or outside wrappings of unopened shipments to note any potential damage to contents

- Compare these shipments with the freight bill presented

- Fill in the receiving record, which will accompany the merchandise through further processing stages

- Route the shipment to the proper area for opening and checking of the contents

Examining the Unopened Shipment

At the point of entry to the store, the purpose of the receiving check is limited to determining that the shipment has arrived as described on the accompanying freight bill or, if it is not as described, preparing a shortage or damage report for follow-up by the traffic manager. Once this is done, the carrier's truck can move out quickly so that another can take its place at the receiving dock.

Comparing Shipment with Freight Bill

Before the receiving clerks sign a receipt for the delivery driver or messenger, they compare the freight bill with the shipment, checking the number of cartons involved and the weight. Most stores do not weigh each shipment but spot-test for correct weight. If visible damage or shortage in the shipment is observed, the receiving clerk notes this on the carrier's receipt and has the delivery driver sign this same notation on the store's copy of the bill. If, as in some cases, transportation charges are to be paid on the spot, the receiving clerk issues a payment voucher to the delivery driver or messenger, who takes it to a payment office to be cashed.

Writing the Receiving Record

After the shipment has been unloaded and accepted, the next step is to fill out an identifying record that will accompany it to the checking area. This record begins a written history of the shipment as it moves through the store.

A receiving record contains the following basic information, all of which is taken from the shipping document and from the receiving clerk's observation of the shipment:

- Name of carrier
- Freight bill number
- Weight
- Number of pieces
- Transportation charges
- Type of merchandise
- Name of vendor
- Purchase order number
- Condition of shipment
- Origin of shipment
- Serial receiving number, which is added by the receiving clerk

Some stores first record this information in the pages of a receiving book, then prepare another form or "apron" to attach to the cartons. Others use multiple-copy forms, of which there are several patented types available. These multiple-copy aprons contain spaces for the addition of further information by the checkers.

Moving the Shipment On

The receiving clerk marks the cartons of each shipment with a serial receiving number, the merchandise department number, and the immediate destination of the shipment within the firm. The receiving clerk then dispatches the shipment to the checking area by conveyor, hand truck, or motorized truck, depending on the type of goods and the available equipment.

CHECKING METHODS

The checker, who receives the cartons or containers after they have been accepted by the receiving clerk, has the following responsibilities:

- Open the shipment.

- Verify that the contents correspond to the store's order or the listing on the vendor's invoice (depending on the system used by the store).

- Check the condition of the merchandise.

- Send the document showing receipt of merchandise to the accounts payable office.

- Move the merchandise on to the markers, who will tag or label it with the price and other required information.

The checking and marking procedures used by stores can be classified into three main types. These are the buyer's order system, the invoice system, and the listing system.

of the retail price at this early stage is called "preretailing." This is in contrast with systems in which the buyer does not give price instructions until the merchandise is actually in the store. If the merchandise ordered is to be distributed to more than one store, the quantities for each store are shown separately on the order form.

The buyer's order form and its several copies are distributed as follows:

1. The original order form is mailed to the vendor.

2. One copy goes to the accounts payable office to be matched later with the invoice for payment.

3. One copy goes to the traffic and receiving departments, where it is filed alphabetically by vendor's name and awaits the shipment.

4. One copy is retained by the buyer for follow-up and the buyer's recordkeeping.

The Checker's Job. When the merchandise arrives, a copy of the order form is pulled from the traffic and receiving department's files and given to the checker, who checks the merchandise descriptions and quantities on the order against the merchandise received. In a special column left open on the form, the checker writes in the actual quantities of each item received next to those specified by the buyer. If the merchandise is as ordered and complete, the checker initials the form that moves with the merchandise to the marking tables. A carbon copy goes to the accounts payable office to be matched with the vendor's bill, or invoice. If the shipment is incomplete, a photocopy only is sent to the accounts payable office, and the regular copy is retained until the balance of the shipment arrives to be checked in.

The Marker's Job. The marker receives with the merchandise the checked copy of the order.

Information from the buyer's original purchase order can be displayed on the screen of this computer terminal. A checker at the receiving dock can then compare the bill of lading to the purchase order to see whether the shipment is complete. The checker can also update the inventory records by keying in new information.
Courtesy IBM Corporation

Checking Against the Buyer's Order

In the buyer's order system, the incoming merchandise is checked against a copy of the order that the buyer placed with the vendor for the merchandise. When writing the order, the buyer must give a complete description of each item ordered, exact quantities, and unit cost. The retail price at which each item is to be sold, if shown on the copies to be retained by the store, is omitted from the vendor's copy. The inclusion

Since this has been "preretailed," it provides the price information the marker puts on the tickets or labels. The marker initials the order copy after completing the marking; the merchandise goes into stock; and the order copy is sent to the buyer.

Advantages. The chief advantage of the buyer's order system is speed. The store's documents give all the information needed to get the merchandise through the processing and on to the sales floor.

A second advantage is that the order copies, which are sent to the buyer's office and the accounts payable office after the merchandise has been processed, give complete information on what has been received in a shipment and what is still to come on the order if the shipment is not complete.

A third advantage is that the invoice is not delayed in reaching the accounts payable office, since it is never required in the receiving room or by the buyer. This means that the store can pay bills promptly and be assured of earning anticipation and cash discounts on invoices.

On the whole, the buyer's order system for checking is generally considered to be the most efficient and tightly controlled. When buyers order for several stores at the same time, and also when merchandise is received at a different location from the buyer's office, such a system is particularly desirable.

Checking Against the Invoice

In the invoice system, it is the manufacturer's invoice rather than the store's buying order that serves as the key document for checkers and markers. This invoice may be received by mail before the shipment arrives, or it may come with the shipment.

The Checker's Job. The checker simply verifies that the contents of the package correspond in kind and amount to the information on the vendor's invoice. The checker records this information on the receiving record or apron attached to the shipment.

The Marker's Job. When the invoice arrives, the buyer "retails" it—that is, writes on it the retail prices at which the merchandise is to be marked. The retailed invoice moves with the checked merchandise to the marking tables. If the buyer's orders have been preretailed, the retail prices may be placed on the invoice by the marker.

Missing Invoices. If the invoice is not received either before or with the shipment, the shipment is held until its arrival. To minimize the pileup of merchandise that can result, stores have devised various methods of moving it, after a specified waiting period, without the invoice. One method is to use a copy of the buyer's order as the checking document. The buyer retails this instead of the missing invoice. Another method is to switch procedures to the listing system described later.

Advantages and Disadvantages. The invoice system is the simplest for checkers to learn and use. Also, the buyer sees the invoice and immediately observes any discrepancy from the initial order. The chief disadvantage is that a missing or delayed invoice will slow up the movement of the merchandise.

Checking by Listing or Blind Checking

The *listing system* is sometimes called the "blind check" system, since the checker is not provided with any document—invoice or order form—against which to compare the shipment.

The Checker's Job. The checker lists the merchandise received on a multicopy form, writing down the kind and count of the contents of the shipment. The original of the checker's form is matched against the vendor's invoice in the accounts payable office. Another copy is given to the buyer for inventory records.

The Marker's Job. Preretailing can be used with this system, the buyer using a copy of the order form for this purpose and sending it to the marking location. Or the buyer can retail a copy of the checker's listing, which will move with the merchandise to the markers.

Advantages. The chief advantage of the listing system is that every shipment can be processed as soon as it arrives, even without an invoice. Invoices are less likely to be lost. "Blind" checking may also lead to a more painstaking count of the merchandise than when the checkers have a document, such as a buyer's order or an invoice, to guide them.

Disadvantages. The checkers' job is more demanding than under the other systems, since they must identify and describe the merchandise without the help of a document prepared elsewhere. In the office, the matching of invoices with the checkers' listings can be a slow process. Merchandise may also be sent to the selling floor before the arrival of the invoice, which may possibly contain a change in cost.

The invoice system is less flexible or speedy than the listing system, and it is not as controlled as the buyer's order system.

MARKING METHODS

Various systems for the marking of goods will be found in most stores. Marking devices include rubber stamps; crayon, pen, or pencil markings; gummed labels; printed tickets; punch-card tickets; and the newest vendor marking for supermarket merchandise—the Universal Product Code. Tickets may be attached by machine or by hand, or they may be folded, flat, or hung from strings or plastic threads. Tickets may have microdots that signal alarms when the merchandise is carried from the store unless they have been demagnetized.

The type of marking to be used with each type of merchandise is determined by the receiving and traffic department manager in accordance with the store policy. Most price tickets carry department identification and coded stock-control information as well as price. A coded ticket for merchandise under a unit-control system would include season letter, classification, department, manufacturer, style, color, size, and price. Universal Product Code marking leaves the price to be manually marked on the goods by the retailer.

Machines are available for typesetting, printing tickets, and attaching tickets. These are located in the marking section of the store or warehouse.

Print-Punch Ticket

On a print-punch ticket, the stock control information is key-punched in the data processing office, while the price and size information the customer must be able to read is printed. A print-punch ticket usually consists of three perforated sections, all carrying identical information. One stub is detached by the salesperson when a sale is made. These stubs are collected daily and electronically sorted and tabulated to provide buyers with reports of sales by type, style, price, color, and size. The other two sections remain with the merchandise. Should it be returned by the customer and placed back into stock, it will not have to be reticketed.

Vendor Marking

Vendor marking—called preticketing, premarking, or source marking—is the attachment of price tickets to merchandise by the vendor before it is delivered to the store. The store, however, may add its own handwritten department number or merchandise classification code.

Some vendors, using print-punch tickets, have established standardized codes for merchandise classification, style, size, and color. Stores that adopt these codes as part of their own classification systems do not have to add any information to the price tickets when the merchandise arrives at the store.

All forms of vendor marking are particularly valuable for fashion merchandise when it is of prime importance to get the merchandise on the selling floor as quickly as possible. The vendor charges extra for such service.

Consolidator Marking

Another premarking service—which is also a prechecking service—is that provided by a few

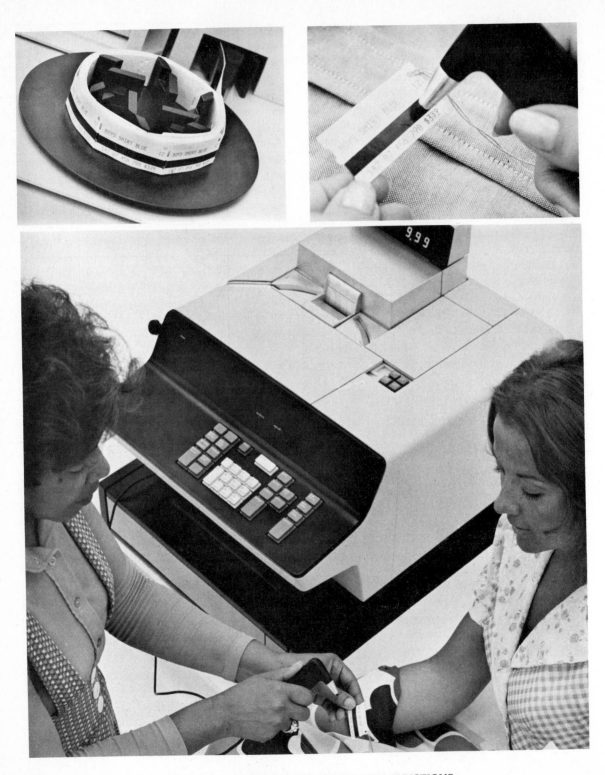

STORE MANAGEMENT AND OPERATION FUNCTIONS

large consolidators, chiefly for apparel. Garments are delivered by the vendors on hangers, checked against copies of the store's retail purchase orders that have been sent to the consolidator, ticketed by the consolidator, hung in trailer trucks, and sent to the store ready for the selling floor. This is a speedier, more efficient process than marking the goods in the marking areas of the store.

Nonmarking

Some low-price merchandise carries too small a profit margin to justify the expense of item marking. Such merchandise is sold from counters under signs carrying the price or from price-marked bins. Another instance of nonmarking is for limited-period price promotions. After the sale is over, the remaining goods are marked, usually by salespeople on the selling floor, at the regular price. This is called *deferred marking*.

RECEIVING, CHECKING, AND MARKING FACILITIES

Location, layout, and equipment for receiving, checking, and marking vary a great deal from store to store. In multistory downtown buildings, the arrangements are seldom ideal from the viewpoint of efficiency engineering. This is because a compromise must be made with the high-priority demands of selling space. As a result the receiving areas at street level are remote from the checking and marking areas, which are located on the lower-rent upper floors or, sometimes, in the basement.

Location of Receiving Area

The best facilities are to be found in recently designed retail service buildings, located away from the store and out of high-rent areas. These buildings combine the functions of merchandise processing and warehouse storage. They also contain workrooms and, in some cases, selling areas for the staging of special warehouse sales.

Generally these service buildings have highly mechanized systems. The merchandise moves in at one side of the building, proceeds by mechanized carriers through checking and marking, is conveyed mechanically to storage areas and stacked mechanically, and eventually moves out on the other side of the building for delivery to store or customer.

Some service building merchandise movement systems are automated; that is, they operate mechanically from remote control instructions provided by an operator at a console. The operator routes the merchandise into particular checking and marking lines.

In a multistory downtown building, the ideal one-level, horizontal movement of merchandise is not possible. Much of the merchandise, however, must be received downtown, even by stores that have outlying service buildings for their high-bulk merchandise.

Layout of Receiving Area

In designing new buildings and modernizing old ones, the following layout principles are taken into consideration and are adhered to as far as possible:

- Truck bays large enough and numerous enough to accommodate modern large trailers, to avoid street congestion, to accommodate future increases in store volume

- Separate locations for inbound merchandise (receiving bays) and outbound merchandise (delivery bays)

- Direct-line flow of inbound shipments to the elevators or conveyors that take them to the checking area; a minimum of cross traffic

The ticket unit (top) is a high-speed ticket encoder and printer. The magnetic stripe down the center of the ticket contains such information as season, classification, department, manufacturer, style, color, size, and price. This information is later read by a wand held by a salesperson (bottom) at the checkout counter.
Courtesy IBM Corporation

INTERNAL MERCHANDISE HANDLING   263

- Adequate and protected storage space for shipments that must be held for some reason before being dispatched to the checking area

- Specially assigned areas for types of merchandise such as carpets and rugs and major appliances that require special types of unloading or moving equipment

- Security provisions designed into the layout to protect the merchandise during processing and when the area is closed

Handling Equipment. Dock levelers are used to connect the truck floor and receiving platform, making it possible to run conveyors into the truck body. Lifting and moving devices include hydraulic platforms; conveyors (gravity-type, roller-type, and powered-type); forklift trucks; hand trucks; and skids, pallets, and dollies of various kinds. The platform equipment includes high-intensity lighting to illuminate the truck interiors.

A wide variety of equipment is available. The aim is to substitute mechanical power for muscle power as far as possible. A governing rule for the selection of equipment is that the devices should be simple to operate, for there are many periods when the receiving platform will be partly staffed by extra, seasonal personnel.

Vertical Transportation. In multistory buildings and warehouses, merchandise is moved from the receiving platform to the checking and marking areas by elevators, chutes or conveyors, or combinations of these. There is a type of vertical lift that connects the receiving platform with mechanized conveyors in the checking area several floors up. It operates on the ferris wheel principle, having a number of self-contained carriers for cartons and parcels. The contents of each carrier are discharged into a conveyor at the checking area, and the conveyor carries the cartons to a checking station.

Besides freight elevators and vertical lifts, there is another type of ascending carrier used by some stores. This is a conveyor on the outside of the building, which rises on a long incline from the receiving dock to the checking area.

When the checking area is in the basement, the other forms of vertical transportation may be supplemented by an ordinary chute down which cartons may slide.

Horizontal Transportation. Merchandise moving on one level goes to and through the checking area in manually moved or motorized trucks, skids, or dollies; on belt conveyors; or (in the case of hanging merchandise) on overhead monorails.

The Checking and Marking Area

The plan of the checking and marking area depends on whether the store follows the principle of moving the merchandise to the workers or has the workers move to the merchandise. In large stores worker movement is minimized, and various methods are used to convey the merchandise to work stations.

Stationary Table Layout. The simplest checking and marking setup is the stationary table plan. Table space is allotted to each department or each type of merchandise. Shipments are wheeled or carried to the tables and are there opened, checked, and marked. As the merchandise is marked, the marker places it on the conveyance by which it will travel to the forward stock or reserve stock areas. In this layout, checking and marking are usually done by the same people.

The tables are usually arranged in twos, parallel to each other. Aisles are wide enough for hand trucks to move between each set of two tables. The tables may be wired for connection with marking machines. Marking machines on portable stands can be moved wherever they are needed.

Movable Table Layout. In the movable table plan, the checking and marking operations are separated. Space, rather than tables, is assigned to the different merchandise departments in both the checking and marking areas. After the merchandise has been checked, the table—usually multishelved—is wheeled to a parking area, if necessary, where the buyer comes to retail the invoice. Then it is wheeled to the marking section. After marking, the table goes into the stock area for shelving and stacking. If some or all of the marked merchandise on the table is to go directly to forward stock, it is wheeled into elevators for transportation to the sales floor.

Conveyor Layouts. The movable table principle has been combined with the conveyor principle. The result is a table with overhead wheels that moves through checking and marking on an overhead track.

Other mechanized systems use a gravity conveyor, and the merchandise travels on pallets. After the merchandise has been opened and checked, it is placed on pallets on the conveyor and directed by a dispatcher to the proper marking line. As the marker finishes each item, he or she transfers it from the incoming full pallet to an empty one. The marker never has to remove a pallet from the conveyor. When the incoming pallet is emptied, the outgoing one is full, and the marker releases the load by means of a switch. The pallet rolls down the conveyor to a collection stop. Here the merchandise is unloaded and sent to the reserve areas on trucks.

Cage Areas. The protection of small but valuable items is usually provided by means of locked cage areas where goods such as fine jewelry, cameras, small radios, and fine giftware can be checked and marked by bonded employees assigned to those areas.

Floor Receipt. Fine jewelry or other small, valuable items may be received in the department by the buyer or other assigned personnel. In this way, safety measures may be carefully controlled.

STORING MERCHANDISE

Marked merchandise has one of three immediate destinations. It may go into (1) forward stock or (2) reserve stock in the same building in which it has been processed, or it may be sent (3) out of the building to another store unit.

Reserve Stock Rooms in Stores

In some stores stock rooms are all located in a single area. This is the centralized stock system. Its advantages are that it saves space and allows for easy and more economical supervision.

The preferred system today uses a *decentralized stock room* for each department which opens directly into the department's selling area. In many well-designed stores, a stock corridor runs behind the stock room so that merchandise can be delivered to the stock room without crossing the sales floor. This type of stock room, situated along the walls, is called a *perimeter stock room.* Another plan is to have a *central stock core,* which runs up through the center of the building.

The advantages of the decentralized stock system are that salespeople can bring stock out to the selling floor themselves whenever it is needed; salespeople become more familiar with what is in stock; and the buyers or department managers have better control of merchandise.

Departmentized Store Warehouses

Major appliances, furniture, floor coverings, large toys, and some smaller staple items, such as housewares, that are bought in large quantities at one time are received and held in remote store warehouses or service buildings.

Besides supervising the receiving, checking, and marking processes, the warehouse manager is responsible for recording additions to inventory, for reporting inventory conditions as required, and for dispatching merchandise on order to either the store or customers.

There are basically two classes of merchandise at the warehouse. *Bulk goods,* which are sold from samples, are delivered directly to the customer and usually require no price marking. *Small goods* require price marking and are delivered periodically to the store to replenish its stocks.

Small Goods. The receiving, checking, and marking procedures are identical to those performed at the store receiving location. The receiving record copy which is sent to the store buyer or store or department manager informs that person of the receipt of the merchandise and provides a record of the inventory which the warehouse is holding for the store or department. When merchandise is required at the store, it is ordered from the warehouse by buyer's or manager's requisition. The merchandise is dispatched to the store by truck. The requisition, receipted by the buyer or store manager, is returned to the warehouse for its records.

Bulk Goods. The checking and marking procedure is somewhat different for bulk goods, which usually do not require price marking but which must be recorded on the buyer's inventory records and identified as to location in the warehouse. For each item received, the warehouse prepares a two-part tag, each part carrying merchandise description, merchandise department number, and inventory control information such as manufacturer's name, style number, and color. One section is attached to the merchandise. To the other section the warehouse adds location information: number of area, section, and bin in the warehouse in which the merchandise has been placed. This second section, the location tag, is sent to the selling department. When the merchandise is sold, it is requisitioned for delivery to the customer's home by sending the sales check and the location tag to the warehouse. After the merchandise has been taken from the warehouse stock and sent to the customer, the location tag is destroyed.

Since the location tag can be in the possession of the selling department only before the merchandise is sold, it provides a satisfactory system of maintaining inventory records.

Other means of requisitioning stock from the warehouse are used by stores—for example, teletypewriter communications. But basically the system is the same: it requires the existence of a document in the selling department that represents a particular item in the warehouse, and the surrender of this document when merchandise is drawn from the warehouse.

Location of Goods in the Warehouse. A warehouse may be zoned into locations for specific types of items—for example, all furniture in one location, all wheel goods in another. Or it may be planned to make the fastest-moving merchandise the most accessible. Or it may simply be divided into areas for merchandise that goes on racks and merchandise that is stored on the same pallets on which it moves. The system that is currently receiving most study is the random-storage system. No kind of merchandise has a rigidly allocated location. Instead, shipments as they arrive are moved into whatever appropriate space is most convenient. The location information is put on punched cards, and when merchandise is requisitioned out of the warehouse, the "address" of the storage cubicle is found electronically in a few seconds. This kind of storage is extremely flexible and saves time and labor. So far it is used mostly in manufacturers' warehouses, but the principle is applicable to all types of reserve storage.

Chain Store Warehouses

The regional warehouse of a chain differs from the warehouse of a departmentized store. First, the chain warehouse is the primary receiver of nearly all the merchandise except perishable products sold by the stores in its region. It therefore stores and distributes greater amounts of both high-bulk and low-bulk goods.

Second, the merchandise in the regional warehouse is part of a central company inventory rather than part of the inventory of an individual store or department. The warehouse receives merchandise orders from the store units just as if it were a wholesaler receiving orders from individual retailers. As a result, the inventory-control procedures are complicated. The chain's regional warehouse maintains records of an overall regional inventory, which must be kept

This warehouse utilizes an automated conveyor system to store clothing. The conveyor makes it easy to sort merchandise and to move it out of the warehouse.
Courtesy Jet Age Systems, Zurich

replenished, as well as records of what has been dispatched to individual stores.

Some large chain store warehouses are highly automated distribution centers. They receive automated sales reports daily from each store they service and match these against predetermined ideal stock levels in each store. Computers signal when stock on an item should be replenished, and in the case of certain staple items a computer will even print out an order for the merchandise to be dispatched. Computers also signal when warehouse stock needs to be replenished. Warehouse buyers are employed to keep these huge stocks of goods on hand.

When dealing with bulk merchandise, these warehouses, like those of the departmentized

stores, dispatch merchandise sold from samples directly to the customer.

Interstore Transfers

Branch stores of department stores receive merchandise from the main store, from other branches, and, of course, from the warehouse.

The practice of the typical large store with a few branches is to have the vendors ship the merchandise either to the main store or to the warehouse, according to its nature (low-bulk or high-bulk). The branch store in this system does not have receiving, checking, and marking facilities.

Merchandise received at the main location but intended for a branch is routed into a special area for checking and marking and then to one of the delivery bays, from which it goes by truck to the branch. This merchandise, marked for each branch store, may be sealed in containers after being checked and marked. These sealed containers are then taken directly to the branch selling floors and opened. The merchandise is ready for sale; no additional checking is needed.

Sometimes merchandise is requisitioned from the main store stocks to fill out the stocks of a branch, or it is requisitioned from one branch for the stocks of another branch. Daily relays of merchandise back and forth between the main store and the branches are necessary in some companies. Others hold to a three-times-a-week schedule, sending emergency stock fill-ins in the private auto shuttles that take buyers and other personnel back and forth between the stores.

Forward Stock

All kinds of stores have some stock areas accessible to salespeople. Where counters are used, the forward stock may be placed in bins under the counters or in covered shelves behind the counters. Where goods are hung on racks or arranged on tables that have no stock drawers, the forward stock may be in stock rooms adjacent to the selling floor.

TOPICS FOR DISCUSSION

1. Discuss the purposes of the receiving process.
2. What is the checker's responsibility in the handling of the merchandise?
3. What is meant by a preretailed order? Why do some buyers preretail orders?
4. Explain what is meant by a blind check.
5. Why is vendor marking used on some merchandise? How does Universal Product Code marking differ from the usual vendor marking?
6. Explain why some firms may use consolidator marking for apparel items.
7. Explain the differences between centralized stock systems and decentralized stock systems. Which is generally preferred? Why?
8. What are the primary functions of a departmentized store warehouse?
9. What are the primary functions of a chain store warehouse?
10. What role is automation playing in merchandise distribution from warehouses?

MATHEMATICS FOR RETAILING

A retailer believed he could speed merchandise to the customer if he had it premarked by the vendor. The vendor's price ticketing was done in round numbers ($2, $3, and so forth), whereas the store used odd endings ($1.98, $2.98, and so forth). The retailer bought 2,000 items from the vendor, who charged him $\frac{1}{2}$ cent apiece for premarking. What was the net gain for the retailer by using the vendor's marking and the vendor's pricing? Do your figuring on a separate sheet of paper.

COMMUNICATIONS IN RETAILING

A vendor, Val Products Co., Fargo, North Dakota, made repeated errors in its invoices to your store over the past five years. Every time a check was run, there was a shortage that required an adjustment in the bill. The store manager requested that the buyer drop the source, but the buyer claimed no other source had equally fine products. What kind of letter should this vendor receive? On a separate sheet of paper, write a letter advising the firm about the delays in payment and extra costs to your store because of this carelessness.

DECISION MAKING

A large store had its stock rooms in the basement and on the top floor of its six-story building. Business justified expanding the store's selling space by enlarging some departments and installing some new ones. A building across the street behind the store could be rented, but the management disliked the idea of having customers divided between the two buildings. Under consideration was the feasibility of using the other building entirely for stock rooms and the original store entirely for selling. Lists were compiled contrasting the possible advantages and disadvantages of both plans. On the basis of facts presented, what decision would you make? Be prepared to explain your reasons.

Results of devoting the entire store to
selling space, with no stock areas

1. Overcrowded conditions. Present vertical transportation systems might slow customer movement from floor to floor.

2. Fewer additional salespeople would be needed. Many more customers could be served by present employees.

3. More customers will be likely to shop in various parts of the store if they do not have to leave the building.

4. If merchandise has to be brought from stock rooms in the annex, movement will take longer, goods will be exposed to weather, and the risk of pilferage might be increased. Sales and profits might suffer.

Results of dividing selling and
storage spaces in two buildings

1. Less overcrowded conditions. Customers would be better distributed. Vertical transportation of customers would be no problem.

2. More help would be needed to serve customers in two separate buildings.

3. Shopping in two buildings might be an inconvenience. Some customers might be lost if they are required to cross the street to get to another part of the store.

4. Having stock rooms in the same building where the merchandise is sold is more convenient for salespeople, department managers, and stock-room workers.

CAREER LADDER

A college student works part-time as a merchandise checker in a large store. What steps would you advise the student to take to reach a middle-management position in that field when working full-time? What might the progression of jobs to the management position be? Be prepared to discuss your answer.

STORE MANAGEMENT AND OPERATION FUNCTIONS

PART SEVEN

SALES PROMOTION FUNCTIONS

---

chapter 23

RETAIL SALES
PROMOTION ACTIVITIES

Every form of Americana merchandise flourished for the Bicentennial. Colonial furniture and ornaments, fabrics designed with Revolutionary War motifs, emblems, flags, mementos, and historic reproductions were featured in stores of all sizes. Window displays, store fixtures, signs, and salespeople dressed in the costumes of 1776 all contributed to the atmosphere that lured customers to the stores to browse and to buy. "Festival, U.S.A." was planned by one store to celebrate this great event.

THE MANY FACETS OF A PROMOTION

The creation of Festival U.S.A. required the planning and coordination of a great many activities. First, store officials had to agree on the desirability of a storewide promotion and specifically on the form that the promotion would take. Then merchandisers and buyers had to be informed so they could make their plans for the necessary purchases of merchandise. Since finding unusual and decorative products that would

be appropriate is time-consuming and must be done many months in advance of the promotion, this event had to be planned six months before its opening date. The display department had to decide upon and create the displays and arrangements both for windows and interior display areas. The advertising department had to schedule the kinds and amount of advertising to be done. Special signs had to be prepared to feature the unusual merchandise. The shopping bags and wrapping paper used throughout the store had Festival U.S.A. motifs and special red, white, and blue coloring to remind people of the celebration. These had to be designed and ordered months before the Festival began.

Salespeople had to be trained, and costumes had to be ordered and fitted for them. The fashion coordinator and the interior decorator needed to arrange for special merchandise for shows and displays.

In addition to its own advertising to tell its customers about the Festival, the store released news stories to the newspapers. Special pictures were taken of unique products that had been borrowed from museums and found in some of the farmhouses that dated back to the 1700s.

The day Festival U.S.A. opened, pictures of the special exhibits and of the memorabilia were shown on the special feature pages of the evening newspaper. Some of the society leaders of the city were also photographed as they lunched amid costumed waiters and waitresses in the store's restaurant. Although this press publicity did not cost the store any money, preplanning had to be done to arrange for the photographers and reporters to be present at the times these events were to occur.

SALES PROMOTION DEFINED

Any activity that attracts customers to a store and results in profitable sales and builds goodwill for the store is *sales promotion*. Sales promotion has as its primary function the encouragement of business through nonpersonal appeals to customers. More narrowly, sales promotion is concerned with the development of ideas, and the coordination of those ideas, to present a story about the store, department, area, or an item. Its aim is to stimulate the customer to seek the merchandise or service being promoted.

Activities Involved

All operations necessary to produce the particular activity and the resulting profitable sales are concerned with sales promotion, but they are not necessarily part of the actual work of the sales promotion division. For example, in the Festival U.S.A. promotion, the merchandise was bought by merchandisers and buyers who are not part of the sales promotion division but who must participate in any storewide promotional activity. Similarly the salespeople are not part of the sales promotion division in most retailing organizations; yet they are essential in most stores to present merchandise successfully to the customer.

Sales promotion may encompass all the work in the store that aids in promoting sales. The function itself, however, refers to the publicity, advertising, display, and special features and events that promote profitable sales in a nonpersonal manner in contrast to salesmanship, which promotes sales on a face-to-face, or personal, basis.

Some stores employ all forms of sales promotion. Some stores have many variations of each type of sales promotion to attract customers. Some stores use only a few sales promotion devices. At the minimum, all stores employ some of the elements of display within the store to attract customers to buy. Most stores use both window and interior displays. Most stores also have special wrapping paper or bags or boxes with their names imprinted for easy identification by customers.

Sales Promotion and Store Image

Every activity and every feature about a store contributes to that store's image in the eyes of its customers. The appearance of the building, the width of the aisles, the color scheme, the types of furnishings and fixtures, the types of merchandise carried, the kinds of services provided, the caliber of employees—all help to form that image. The sales promotion work of the firm is especially devoted to building and maintaining a certain desired image for the store. The function of sales promotion is to attract people to the store. Sales promotion makes the store a place that is considered whenever people have shopping needs and wants that can be satisfied by the firm. Advertising and display (discussed in the following chapters) and special-feature publicity are important parts of this image building.

RETAIL ADVERTISING AND PUBLICITY AND DISPLAY

Sales promotion is divided into three main categories: advertising, publicity, and display.

Advertising

The nonpersonal presentation of information about merchandise, services, or ideas about which a retailing firm wishes to inform its customers is known as *advertising*. The store pays for these presentations, which are made through some form of *media* such as newspapers, magazines, television, radio, bill enclosures, or catalogs. The copy for such advertising is usually prepared by the copywriters and layout artists of the store or by companies that specialize in such activities.

Publicity

Two types of publicity are used by stores: free publicity and special-feature publicity.

Free Publicity. If a store is newsworthy, representatives of newspapers and magazines may write reports, articles, or news stories about a special store activity. Opportunities for executives to appear in person on local radio or television programs are examples of the type of free publicity occasionally available to stores.

Special-Feature Publicity. Special-feature publicity may be obtained through additional or supplemental forms of nonpersonal presentations of merchandise. These may include special exhibits, demonstrations, fashion shows, educational programs, special lectures, visits by celebrities, or giveaways such as stamps, premiums, or contests.

On the outside, some large retailing firms may publicize their stores institutionally by means of parades or other types of general entertainment.

Display

Another form of nonpersonal sales promotion is achieved through visual presentation—store windows, counters, and shelves within the store are used to acquaint customers with the merchandise.

ORGANIZATION FOR SALES PROMOTION

As in all other work in stores, the size of the store and the amount of activity in one area of work will determine the complexity of the sales promotion organization. In a small store, the owner takes charge of all the various sales promotion functions, delegating some of the details to other competent people within the firm. Thus, a small-store owner may plan all the sales promotion activities, buy all the merchandise, and operate the store. That person may not actually trim the windows or the display cases but use

The fashion coordinator is usually responsible for the presentation of fashion shows in the store. These promotional events contribute to the store's fashion image among customers and employees.
Courtesy *Chain Store Age General Merchandise Group.*

salespeople or stock people for those tasks. The owner will decide what merchandise is to be used for the display and what themes or motifs will be developed. In a larger store, the entire function of sales promotion requires specialists who devote their entire time to these varied activities. The various employees who may be needed in large firms have functions as noted below.

- *Sales Promotion Director.* The person who heads sales promotion is known in some firms as the sales promotion director and in other firms as the publicity director. This person's function is to coordinate all the activities pertaining to sales promotion in the store.

- *Advertising Director.* In a large firm the function of advertising is so involved and so important that one specialist is assigned to head the work to be done. This specialist works with the sales promotion director to coordinate all advertising activities into the master plan of the store.

- *Copywriters.* These people, skilled in writing, are charged with the writing of the copy and headlines in advertisements. To do this, they assemble the information needed, develop a copy style, and present the facts about the products, services, or ideas of the firm in as interesting and dramatic a manner as possible, consistent with the overall image or purposes of the firm.

- *Copy Chief.* When a firm has many copywriters, a copy chief who supervises and coordinates the work of all the copywriters may be employed.

- *Layout Artists.* The arrangement and placement of all parts of the advertisements are planned by the layout artists. They are visually skilled people who balance the areas of copy, pictures, and white space to make the advertisements appealing to the readers. If the department is a large one, several layout artists may be employed.

- *Artists or Illustrators.* The artists or illustrators, who specialize in drawing pictures of merchandise, work with copywriters, buyers, or department managers in ascertaining the important features of the products or ideas to portray in their drawings. In a small firm, these artists may report directly to the advertising director. In a large firm, they may be supervised by an art director who is in charge of the work of both the layout artists and the illustrators.

- *Photographers.* Free-lance photographers, who work only when called, or full-time photographers may be employed to take photographs of merchandise. They, too, report either to the art director or to the advertising director for coordination of their work.

- *Production Manager.* The production manager in large firms assembles the copy, illustrations, and layouts and prepares instructions for the printers on the typefaces and type sizes to be used for the various parts of the advertisements. The production manager reports to the advertising director.

- *Proofreaders.* All details on the printed proofs of the advertisements must be checked. Proofreaders are employed in large firms to check the proofs, to correct them, and to see that the executives concerned see the proofs and approve them for release. Proofreaders are responsible for seeing that any suggested corrections are incorporated into the advertisements before they are released.

- *Display Manager.* The display manager, who reports to the sales promotion director, is responsible for both window and interior displays; works with merchandise managers and the store manager to determine how window assignments will be made; and plans backgrounds and placement of decorations and merchandise in windows and in special display areas throughout the store. The display manager coordinates all displays and develops themes to represent the various seasons of the year and the various promotions that the store plans. This manager may be assisted by window trimmers and by interior display specialists.

- *Sign Writers.* Most stores have someone in the organization who prepares by hand or by machine the cards, signs, posters, banners, and other devices used to identify merchandise and to list prices for window and interior displays.

- *Special-Feature Publicity Personnel.* When a store plans many promotional functions in addition to the regular advertising and display, it may have special-feature publicity personnel to coordinate these activities. This person or persons may plan fashion shows both within the store and for outside organizations. The personnel in this department may also be in charge of planning vast publicity schemes, such as annual holiday parades, circuses, lecture series, and other activities that focus the eyes of the public on the store. As with other promotional workers, the personnel in this area report to the sales promotion director.

TYPES OF SPECIAL-FEATURE PROMOTIONS

The amount of special-feature publicity varies with the type and size of the firm, but most organizations find such publicity desirable. These promotions may be meant to sell merchandise directly or to sell the institution and its importance to the community. Most special-feature promotions are one-time occurrences. Some, however, are so successful that they are repeated on a regular basis, becoming traditional store and community events.

Merchandise Promotions

Merchandise promotions are especially important to most retailing firms. Promotions might be developed around a single country or area, such as the Festival U.S.A. mentioned previously. Such promotions may be storewide or may be restricted to just certain divisions of the store.

Special sales may also feature merchandise promotions, such as the annual "white sales" of linens and bedding that customers have come to anticipate every January and August. Special seasonal events—such as Easter, Christmas, and June weddings—may also be the reason for storewide publicity events, as may sporting events for tennis or golf.

Stores located in cities, towns, or shopping centers may band together to have joint promotions to attract people to those areas. Entire streets or centers may be decorated with special lights at Christmastime to impart a festive look to the area and attract people to shop in the stores that line the streets or malls.

Fashion Shows

Fashion shows may be produced for customers, or they may be used for the training and inspiration of store employees. The trend in fashion shows to make them more entertaining by having a plot and musical numbers has increased the popularity of these events. Professional models may be used, or store employees may double as models. Fashion shows may be produced within the store in an area where a runway may be provided for the models and where a sufficient number of chairs can be placed for the viewers to use. Fashion shows may also be given in an auditorium in the store or in a large dining area. Some women's organizations borrow clothes from a store and use their own members to model these clothes at bazaars or luncheons. Some stores take clothes to schools where students model them for an audience composed of their fellow students. Attractive commentators trained to dramatize the new and unique features of merchandise are especially important to the success of the fashion show.

Educational Programs

Stores may aid customers in many ways through educational programs. Some are directly related to the merchandise carried in an area. For example, cooking schools may be formed to teach customers to prepare foods in new types of ovens or to use new refrigerators or freezers or new cooking utensils, cutlery, or gadgets. Educational programs in sewing, rug making, embroidery, needlepoint, knitting, and other handicrafts spur the sales of do-it-yourself kits. Talks on interior decorating, flower arrangement, homemaking, and gardening may also be provided.

Institutional services are sometimes offered through educational programs. For example, some stores may attract people to the firm to learn about investments, or to hear an author discuss a new book, or to meet a world-famous traveler. Such programs are designed to establish goodwill and to make new friends for the store rather than to sell specific items.

Demonstrations

A demonstration is usually staged by the manufacturers' representatives within a merchandise area, and it is designed to dramatize the product and its uses. By demonstrations customers are attracted to the area, and they are instructed in the correct use of the product. Cosmetic items, toys, sporting goods, and household gadgets are commonly sold in this manner. Some demonstrations are brought into the customers' homes. For example, a new type of vacuum cleaner or other appliance may be demonstrated to show the customer its advantages.

Sampling

Especially adapted to the food, cosmetic, and fabric areas within a store, sampling is a frequently used method of sales promotion. Customers are given samples of foods or candies, for example, that they are asked to taste. Similarly, small samples or vials of perfumes, creams, powders, or lotions may be supplied for trial use by customers. Samples of stationery, playing cards, or razor blades and even small samples cut from bolts of material may help customers to decide on a purchase. Samples may be given on the

A store may sponsor a demonstration such as this one to interest customers in buying cookware. The demonstrator, usually a manufacturer's representative, gives instructions and answers questions on the proper use of the product.
Courtesy Bloomingdale's

SALES PROMOTION FUNCTIONS

premises when suitable, or they may be sent through the mail to prospective customers.

Premiums and Contests

Everyone likes to "get something for nothing," and so the premiums that stores and service firms give are often a spur to business, at least until competitors match this giving.

Food stores and gasoline stations have offered such inducements in the past to lure and hold customers. Both stamps and free merchandise have been featured with sales of stipulated amounts. Some firms also offer the customer the chance to buy dishes or cosmetic kits at bargain prices with every purchase at the store.

Some firms offer one-cent sales, allowing the customer to buy two identical articles for the price of one plus one cent. Even dresses have been sold in this manner. The customer buys one product at the regular price in order to obtain the second product for that fractional amount.

Lotteries are provided by some stores, where local laws permit them. Customers receive chances on the prizes with every purchase. Some grand prize, such as an automobile or a trip, is awarded to the top winner, while other winners receive lesser prizes of merchandise.

Contests may be staged by stores for a variety of prizes. Some stores have contests in sewing, knitting, table setting, rug making, or cooking. The person who competes buys needed supplies from the store and then enters the finished product in the contest.

Contests may also be held for employees. They are used as a means of encouraging employees to speed their work or to sell more merchandise.

Institutional Promotions

Some large firms may seek to build their image through community service activities that attract the attention of multitudes of people in the areas they serve. Since many of these retailing firms have appeal beyond their local areas, these activities may focus the eyes of an entire state or even the entire nation upon them. Macy's, T. Eaton's, and Hudson's annual Thanksgiving Day parades, for example, are seen in person by hundreds of thousands of their cities' citizens and by millions more across the nation through the medium of television.

Stores have sponsored events such as circuses, bond drives, celebrity days, scholarship contests, and physical fitness days as a way of serving their communities and informing the communities about their merchandise.

Small stores, although not interested in becoming nationally known, also want to serve their communities and promote goodwill with their customers. They may give merchandise for local contests sponsored by schools, clubs, or religious groups. They may contribute to community activities such as local charity drives. They may provide display space to help publicize the Cub Scouts or Girl Scouts or other local groups. Staging contests for window paintings at Halloween time, offering space for announcements of local events, and providing booths within the store for Red Cross collections are but a few of the thousands of ways local merchants can cooperate with their communities.

Community Rooms. Many stores today plan community rooms as part of their layout. They are used by community groups for various types of meetings, luncheons, parties, and get-togethers. Stores, by providing these rooms, may become the focal point of local community activities. Most stores having such rooms provide low-cost luncheons for the groups meeting there, thus giving local organizations added reasons for making use of such space.

Customer Advisory Boards. Some firms establish customer advisory boards to aid them in providing the goods and services wanted by the local community. The people who make up these boards are usually leaders in local groups who meet with store executives a few times a year to discuss problems of store operation that affect the customers. Many good ideas are obtained from these community leaders, and the store, by indicating its interest in their opinions, builds goodwill for its organization.

Press Publicity

Newspapers often write about stores that are having unusual events run by the local citizens or other events in which the citizens participate. Anything of interest to a newspaper's readers may be printed: articles on new products, stories about unique developments in merchandise, reports on fashion shows, interior decorating tips, introductions of a store's newly decorated model rooms, stories about promotions of employees and contests, and articles about other institutional types of promotions. These are all examples of free publicity for stores in the press. Pictures may accompany the stories, adding even more drama. The stories may result from publicity releases issued by the stores whenever special events are held.

THE SALES PROMOTION BUDGET

Most sales promotion budgets are prepared for a six-month period and adjusted periodically as events necessitate. Budgets include the following items:

- *Sales Promotion Personnel Payroll.* Those expenses that directly apply to sales promotion efforts are the ones that should be charged to the sales promotion budget. These include the payroll for all sales promotion personnel and for free-lance persons hired for special jobs, as well as for consultants who may be called on from time to time for advisory service.

- *Advertising Media Charges.* Charges for newspaper and magazine space, radio and television time, and space in other publications that are used for advertising are part of the sales promotion budget.

- *Cost of Supplies.* Cuts, mats, display materials, paper, art supplies, sign cards, inks, paints, and the countless other materials used by the sales promotion personnel are part of the budget in this division.

- *Postage and Distribution Charges.* Mailing costs and other distribution charges for publicity and for mailing lists are also directly charged to the sales promotion budget.

- *Travel Charges.* The budget includes provisions for travel charges, for membership in professional organizations, and for attendance at functions in line with promotional activities by members of the sales promotion staff.

- *Miscellaneous Charges.* Allowances must be made to cover factors such as merchandise lost or damaged while on loan to the sales promotion department. These costs are covered under the miscellaneous category of the budget.

No average store exists when it comes to determining the size of the budget for sales promotion. Store needs vary, depending on how old or new the store is, how famous or how little known it is, its size, its location, the size of its trading area, the kinds of merchandise carried, the amount and type of competition, the amount and type of advertising and publicity run by the competition, the media costs in the store's area, the traffic the store enjoys, the local business conditions, and other factors of local significance.

Total promotion expenses for most stores do not exceed 4 to 5 percent of net sales. Many stores, however, spend only a fraction of that amount for promotion. Local stores may do little or no advertising and rely almost wholly upon their window and interior displays as their "promotion" effort. Their budget is just a fraction of 1 percent!

THE SALES PROMOTION CALENDAR

When to promote is equally as important as what to promote. Seasonal promotions tend to provide their own calendar, but for all promotions, timing is important. If promotions parallel sales, the promotions are probably not developing

The advertising calendar is a tool for monthly planning of newspaper advertisements. This example ▷ shows the plan for November of a specialty grocery in a small town.

SALES PROMOTION FUNCTIONS

november

newspaper advertising work sheet

Sunday	Monday	Tuesday	Wednesday	Thursday	Friday	Saturday
1	2	3	4 *full page — week's specials*	5 *full page — week's specials*	6	7
8	9	10	11	12	13	14
15	16	17	18	19	20	21 *3 col. ad in women's pages — Thanksgiving greetings*
22	23	24	25 *with holiday banner store closed tomorrow*	26 *Thanksgiving — newspaper not published*	27	28 *3 col. ad in women's pages — Toys for Tots Xmas campaign*
29	30					

Last Year's Weather

Fair Days	Cloudy Days	Rainy Days	Aver. Temp.
10	14	6	40°

This Year's Weather

sufficient interest in advance of sales. Most sales promotion experts therefore recommend that sales promotion efforts should precede sales slightly. Sales promotion should occur enough ahead of the peak in sales to stimulate the extra business that might be attracted early. Sales promotion is less effective when sales are declining.

When the sales promotion budget is planned, an accompanying sales promotion calendar should also be planned. In this manner, the store management can have merchandise and promotion coordinated for maximum impact on sales.

An especially helpful device is a monthly planning chart that lists the important local and national events and special sales promotion activities held the previous year and that has space for planned sales promotion events for the current year. If dollar sales results and dollar anticipated sales are posted on this calendar, comparisons can be made, and the calendar can be used as a guide for developing sales promotion plans.

TOPICS FOR DISCUSSION

1. Discuss the difference between activities essential to successful sales promotion and the work of a sales promotion division.
2. Explain the minimum sales promotion functions performed by even small retail firms.
3. In what ways are the sales promotion efforts of a firm concerned with building a store image?
4. What are the two purposes of special-feature publicity?
5. What are the purposes of fashion shows?
6. What are the purposes of educational programs?
7. Briefly explain the importance of the following promotional devices: (a) demonstrations, (b) samplings, (c) premiums and contests, (d) institutional promotions, (e) community rooms, (f) press publicity.
8. Explain what charges are included in the sales promotion budget.
9. How does the sales promotion budget of a store doing little sales promotion differ in percentage from the budget of a store doing a great deal of promotion?
10. Explain what is meant by the sales promotion calendar.

MATHEMATICS FOR RETAILING

The publicity division placed the following advertising during one month's time:

The Morning Journal, 61,705 lines @ 30 cents a line
The Evening Bugle, 7,224 lines @ 40 cents a line
Local radio station, 125-word announcements, 1 minute a day for 23 days @ $45 per announcement

1. If *The Journal* had an average of 200,000 readers and *The Bugle* an average of 50,000 readers, which paper would be more costly per reader for the month? Do your figuring on a separate piece of paper.
2. If the local radio station had an average of 100,000 listeners, what would the cost per listener be for the month?
3. What would be the total cost for media for that store for the month?

4. What would be the average cost per reader or listener for the month?
5. If the total for advertising represented 2.2 percent of the store's dollar sales volume, how much business did the store do that month?

COMMUNICATIONS IN RETAILING

A fashion coordinator for a small ready-to-wear chain planned a customer fashion show to be presented by each unit of the chain on the Monday evening before Palm Sunday. The directives for the number of models, the clothes to be modeled, the music to be played, and the commentary to accompany the showing were sent to the coordinator of each store. It was also necessary to send general directives to each store manager including the following information:

Time of the show: 6:30 p.m.–7:15 p.m.
Area to be arranged for the show: Ready-to-wear department
Dressing-room area for models: Dressing rooms in department suggested
Platform to be set up and seats arranged for audience
Ushers to show customers to seats
Directives to tell customers the location of the show within the store
Announcements in the windows advertising the show

On a separate sheet of paper, prepare a directive to store managers giving them the necessary information. Include suggested copy for the sign. Use the current calendar for determining the date for the show.

DECISION MAKING

A retailing firm was witnessing a depressingly poor spring season. Prolonged inclement weather had caused business to be off, and the store had lost sales in spite of extensive advertising and other sales promotion activities. Comparison office reports showed customer activity to be poor in all competing stores featuring medium-priced merchandise, but activity was good in stores featuring lower-priced goods.

A large stock of spring suits and coats, which would not be salable in another two weeks, was on hand. The buyer wanted to spend more money on advertising, hoping to move some of this stock at regular prices. As the merchandise manager, what decisions would you make about this matter? Be prepared to give reasons for your suggestions.

CAREER LADDER

A first-year college student, John Partridge, had his heart set on advertising as a career. He wanted to work in a local store as a part-timer while in school, hoping to become a full-time employee upon graduation. For what job should he apply as a beginner if he hopes to progress in the advertising department? What other jobs might he hold on the way to the top advertising job? Be prepared to explain your answers.

chapter 24

ADVERTISING FOR THE RETAIL STORE

Does advertising make a difference in the sales and the profit the store makes? One advertisement stated, "These boots will keep your feet from getting cold." Sales results were carefully observed. After a few weeks had elapsed, the advertisement was run again with reworded copy. "These boots keep feet warm and comfortable," the new ad said. Sales picked up noticeably.

This scene enacted across the country in countless newspapers and magazines by thousands of stores gives one an idea of the importance of advertising. Advertising is one of the basic functions of sales promotion.

The word *advertising* means to notify or to announce publicly. The Definitions Committee of the American Marketing Association defines advertising as "any paid-for form of nonpersonal presentation of goods, services, or ideas to a group."

As our nation has grown in size and complexity, the need for advertising has also grown. Both firms and products, when new, must be introduced publicly, and repeated announcements are necessary to keep the public eye focused on them. Through advertising, initial and repeat patronage are sought, both for the retail stores and for the products and services that they sell.

An advertisement placed in a newspaper or a magazine, heard on radio, or seen on television is an invitation to the customer to visit the particular store advertising the item or service and to look at the merchandise or inquire about the service that is available in that store.

Advertising does more, however, than just notify potential customers about products and services. By its general appearance, it aids in creating the image that customers have of a store. By the advertising copy and by the products or services it advertises, the image is further established in the eyes and minds of the customers. Since the advertisement is seen by all who read or use the media in which it is published, and since this is a larger public than the store itself attracts, the image projected through the advertisement may be the major impact that store has on potential customers.

THE PURPOSE OF RETAIL ADVERTISING

The main purpose of retail advertising is to attract profitable patronage for the store. Advertising achieves this purpose in many ways. It shows products visually and tells about their advantages. Advertising tells customers about services available through the store. It lets customers know how vast the assortments of merchandise and services are. It keeps the customers aware of the excitement represented by the store in the community. Advertising informs customers of the trade and brand names of merchandise carried in the store; it encourages customers to shop first in that particular store for the goods and services that it can supply. Advertising builds a reputation for the store by presenting an image of fashion leadership, large assortments, good service, integrity, and dependability.

To achieve its main purpose and its subsidiary purposes, the advertising that a store does must conform to the policies of the store. It must be carefully planned and executed and must be timed to coordinate with the buying and selling plans of the store.

Stores may be classified as nonpromotional, semipromotional, or promotional depending upon their images and appeals.

Nonpromotional stores appeal to their regular customers through prestige; excellent service; fashionable, high-quality merchandise; regular price lines; and extensive assortments in the merchandise they feature. Advertising is used to inform their customers about the store's unique features.

Semipromotional stores are more aggressive in their advertising policies. Although they offer fashionable merchandise, adequate service, regular price lines, and good assortments, they also appeal frequently to additional customers who respond to special sales events, to bargains, and to clearance sales.

Promotional stores that rely on attracting bargain hunters to buy the off-price goods they provide constantly bombard readers with advertising to remind them of these bargains. Quick turnover of stocks is required to offset the lower prices charged for goods. Heavy customer traffic must therefore be enticed into the store to be exposed to these constant sales. Such stores may feature fashionable merchandise, but they rarely offer many services, and they do not carry complete assortments of all wanted merchandise.

FACETS OF ADVERTISING EXPENSE

Retailing firms must consider the costs of every activity, including advertising. The costs of advertising must be carefully determined before decisions can be made about the amount and kind of advertising to be done.

Factors that will affect the size of the advertising budget include:

• Size of the store

• Location of the store

• Extent of the trading area of the store

• Kinds of merchandise and services the store wishes to feature

• Amount and kind of advertising done by the competitors of the store

• Media available for advertising, their extent of coverage of the trading area of the store, and the cost of advertising in those media

• Results obtained from advertising

• Policies of store about advertising

Expenditures for advertising by various types of stores range from a fraction of 1 percent of sales to about 5 percent. Stores carrying convenience goods (food stores, meat markets, candy and stationery stores, and drugstores) usually spend only small amounts on advertising, while specialty stores, carrying such lines as furniture, may spend up to as much as 5 percent of sales. Department stores have advertising budgets that range from approximately 2 percent to almost 4 percent of sales depending on their size, trading area, location, and competition. These costs include the salaries of personnel who prepare the advertisements, production costs, media charges, and, where necessary, mailing charges.

PLANNING PRODUCTIVE ADVERTISING

Once the advertising expense budget has been planned, steps may be taken to allot that budget for the months ahead. Most planning is done on a six-month basis. The planning steps include:

1. Planning sales goals for the months ahead
   a. Enter the figures for advertising and sales of the previous year on a chart.
   b. Enter the figures anticipated for the current year on the chart.
   c. Determine the amount and kind of advertising needed to achieve those planned sales figures.

d. Compute these figures by months and by types of merchandise or divisions of the store.
  e. Set aside a small percentage of the budget for special events and emergency advertising.

2. Making a master advertising plan
  a. Several weeks ahead of the scheduled advertising period, list all the advertising that will be done.
  b. Include the dates the advertisements are to run, the size of each advertisement, the media to be used, the merchandise or service to be promoted, the overall theme to be used, and information on coordination of merchandise or departments.

3. Planning day-to-day advertising according to the master plan
  a. Allow for changes necessary because of the unavailability of merchandise, weather conditions, special sales, and clearances.

MEDIA USED FOR ADVERTISING

In advertising, media refers to those avenues—either aural or visual or both—through which paid advertising can be projected. These include newspapers and magazines; direct media such as handbills, catalogs, and bill enclosures; signs used on highways, in buses, subways, streetcars, and taxis, or within the store or in windows; and broadcast media such as radio and television.

The retailer decides on the media to use depending on the audience to be reached, the message to be brought to that audience, the cost of the media, and the extent of coverage afforded by those media.

Newspapers and Magazines

Large retailers use newspapers most frequently because they reach a large and varied group of readers at a relatively low cost per reader. Newspapers also can be referred to over and over again in contrast to broadcast messages, which may be missed completely if they are not heard when transmitted.

In addition to city or town papers, foreign language papers, school newspapers, shopping newspapers, and local area newspapers may be used. From time to time the merchant may question the customers to determine what newspapers they read. Sometimes merchants run advertisements in one newspaper but not the others to test response.

Magazines are used mainly by chain store retailers, who reach a regional or national audience that uses their local stores, or by nationally known firms in large cities that can profit by such extensive coverage. Sometimes magazines are used by smaller retail firms that offer mail-order service to readers.

Direct Media

Media that the retailer controls and that go directly to the home of the customer offer several advantages. First, retailers are able to select those people who will receive the advertisement. And second, they can send to as many or as few as they want. Direct media include letters, bill enclosures, circulars, cards, booklets, catalogs, handbills, reprints from newspaper advertisements, and package inserts. These may be sent by direct mail, handed to customers entering the store, handed out on the street, distributed to people's homes, or enclosed in packages.

Many retailers use the telephone as a means of directly presenting sales messages to customers. For example, charge account customers may be notified by phone of private, after-hours sales. Also, customers ordering merchandise by phone may be reminded by the order taker of non-advertised daily specials.

Signs

Highway signs or billboards, posters, and transit cards may be used to tell customers about the store or about special sales events within the store. Since such signs, posters, or cards are directed at a random readership, their effectiveness is difficult to measure.

The retailer's budget will often determine their desirability. When signs, other than those to be used within the store, are costly, the retailer usually plans to use media that have previously provided more tangible results.

Broadcast Media

Retailers who have tried both radio and television advertising have had mixed results. Some, who have had the courage to persist in the use of these media, have been rewarded.

Rarely can a retailer rely totally on broadcast media, but some have found these media satisfactory as supplementary to advertising in newspapers and magazines.

Television advertising necessitates the preparation of visuals as well as the advertising message, and therefore costs are higher. Increasingly, retailers are experimenting with television advertising on a regular basis.

KINDS OF RETAIL ADVERTISING

In addition to a wide choice of media, retailers also have a choice of the types of advertising messages they will present to their audiences. Every advertisement reflects through its total appearance and message the store or institution it promotes. Therefore, all advertisements are institutional in nature.

Advertisements are, however, classified as being institutional, promotional, or a combination of institutional and promotional.

Institutional Advertising

Advertising that provides messages about the store, its relation to the community, its modernization plans, its size, or its reputation is called *institutional advertising*. Such advertising tells about the firm (or institution) instead of telling about its present stock of merchandise for immediate sale or its current offerings of services. Its purpose is to win goodwill for the store.

Institutional advertising is not directed at an audience of shoppers who will rush in the following day to buy. Rather, it is directed at customers whom the store hopes will consider it the place to visit for all future shopping expeditions. The retailer, through institutional advertisements, may wish to impress the customers with the fact that the store has been a good place to shop for many years. Or the ad may emphasize convenient location or pleasant personnel who want to serve the customers. These advertisements may establish in the minds of the customers the fact that this store is noted for its fashion authority, its wide price ranges, its low-price policies, or its services to the individual and to the community.

Institutional advertising may feature local or national current events with which the store wishes to be identified, such as the success of the local baseball team, the opening of a new civic center in the area, or the arrival of a foreign dignitary in this country or the local area. Local school or club activities, famous persons from the area, or national holidays may also serve as themes for institutional advertising.

Promotional Advertising

Advertising that features products or services for immediate selling is known as *promotional advertising*. This type of advertising is used by the majority of retailers, regardless of whether they also use institutional advertising. Promotional advertising may feature regular-priced merchandise or services, special sales on merchandise or services, or clearance merchandise.

Regular merchandise is advertised to inform customers about the products they may buy day in and day out in the store at established prices. Such items are usually part of large assortments and stocks. Consequently, when customers come into the store in response to such advertising, they see varied selections of merchandise from which they can choose. This type of advertising appeals to customers who are seeking new goods or wanted items and who are willing to pay regular prices for these goods.

Advertising of special sales or services informs customers that they can buy certain items at special prices for a limited period of time. These items may have been bought at special prices by

the store to be introduced as new products or services, or they may be items marked down from regular stock. This type of promotional advertising seeks to obtain immediate sales results and to draw large numbers of customers into the store. Customers also see other merchandise while they are in the store, and so other areas may benefit from such sale advertising.

Advertising of clearance merchandise informs customers about bargains available at the end of a month or a season. Since the store wants to sell these goods to release money for the purchase of new merchandise and to free space for exhibiting new merchandise, it usually takes substantial markdowns on such goods. Bargain hunters, particularly, are attracted by such advertising. For the store, this is, however, costly advertising, since customers attracted by clearance sales are not usually the ones who spend money for regular-priced merchandise. Also, end-of-season, marked-down merchandise represents stock surplus or buying errors in merchandise selection. It has to be sold at a loss. Advertising costs to get rid of this merchandise just add to the loss already incurred.

Combination Advertising

Promotional and institutional advertising may be combined in one advertisement. This type of advertisement seeks to establish an image for the store and to promote the sale of merchandise at the same time.

Campaign advertising, which is composed of a series of advertisements with one central theme, frequently employs both promotional and institutional appeals in the sequence of advertisements. Through repetition, the advertisements not only sell the items advertised but also help to create a certain image of the store itself.

Teaser advertising, which stimulates curiosity on the part of readers, may also employ the combination of promotional and institutional advertising. It arouses interest in forthcoming merchandise or service events planned by a store. The teaser advertisements are usually small. They ask questions that are meant to arouse the curiosity of customers. The regular advertisement, when it is finally run, answers the questions the teasers have posed.

THE PSYCHOLOGICAL STEPS IN SUCCESSFUL ADVERTISING

The successful advertisement must appeal emotionally as well as practically and artistically to its readers. All good advertising will attract attention, gain the interest of the reader, and create a desire to purchase the goods or to visit the store. Promotional advertising will also stimulate almost immediate action. The first letters of these four steps—*attention, interest, desire, action*—spell AIDA, which may be used as a mnemonic device for remembering them.

Attracting Attention

Retailers must get the attention of those whom they seek to have enter their stores. Advertisers devise various ways to gain that attention. They may use special type, unusual arrangements, white space, dramatic headlines, unique drawings or photographs, or a combination of these.

Intensifying Interest

Once the attention of the readers has been attracted, the advertiser can tell these readers how the products or services of the store meet their needs or wants.

Developing Desire

Once the customers' attention has been attracted and their interest has been held, the desire to possess the product or service must be aroused. Appeals may be to pride of possession, desire for comfort, interest in what is new or fashionable, concern for safety or ecology, delight in fun and

 An institutional ad provides information about the store such as its pricing policies, its fashion authority, or its services to the individual and to the community.
Courtesy Montgomery Ward and Container Corporation

games, regard for ease of care or use or versatility, and concern for durability or the double-duty use of products.

Advocating Action

The advertisement succeeds when it induces some overt action on the part of the customers. If customers are moved to visit the store, to telephone for goods, to fill out a mail-order form for merchandise, or to inquire about the service offered, the advertisement has achieved its ultimate goal. Both institutional and promotional advertising seek to move the customer to take advantage of the merchandise and services of the store.

Whether advertising does or does not succeed, however, is only partly attributable to the advertising itself. If the merchandise or service advertised is not timely, or if it does not represent a good value, or if it has no appeal, the sales results will be poor, even though the advertisement is well written and illustrated.

The right merchandise or service offered at the right price at the right time and advertised in the right way in the right media will result in profitable sales.

STEPS IN PREPARING ADVERTISING

After the season's advertising plans have been established and the budget has been made, the individual advertisements must be planned. The schedule may vary with some stores, but, in general, the preparations for advertising in newspapers and magazines will include the following steps:

1. The buyer's or manager's request for advertising
2. The planned layout of the advertisement
3. The copy to be used for the advertisement
4. The illustrations or photographs to be used
5. The production of the advertisement

Request for Advertising

Using the advertising plan for the department or store, the managers make their requests a week or more in advance of the date planned for the advertising to run. This ensures getting space in the newspaper in which the advertising is to appear. The requests are submitted to the advertising managers. Most stores have a form calling for the information needed by those who actually compose the advertisement, usually the staff of the store's advertising department.

The manager or the buyer should provide the following information with the request:

- The date of the proposed advertising and suggested selling dates of the products or services being advertised

- The department, store, or area requesting the advertising

- The product or service to be advertised

- The amount of stock on hand and on order, and anticipated dates of receipt of the stock

- The price of the merchandise, with former price, if any, and comparable prices in other stores

- A complete description of the merchandise, including style or design, materials, construction, finish, decoration, colors, sizes, dimensions, special features, and care factors

- Selling features and their benefits to the customer, including the prestige of the merchandise, its fashion importance, its unique properties, ways in which it is better than similar products, and how it will perform in use

---

To run an advertisement in the paper, the buyer must fill out an advertising request form. This form lists information such as how expensive the advertisement can be and where it should be placed, what the special features of the item are, and what the customer benefits of the item are. ▷

MARTELLO'S

ADVERTISING REQUEST FORM

Advertising information and the merchandise to be illustrated must be in the Advertising Department one week prior to the week in which the ad runs in the newspaper.

Item	Regular Price	Sale Price
Saybrooke mattress & spring	$79.95 ea	$59.95 ea

List features in order of importance

1. Firm support for sleeping comfort.
2. Save $40 on each combination of mattress and spring.
3. Save $80 on a twin set.
4. Sturdy, long-lasting construction of foam rubber layer over cotton felt. Features no-sag edge. Tempered steel coil innerspring.
5. Once-a-year event.

Sizes _Twin and full_

Colors _Floral print_

Fabrics _Tufted ticking_

Art Instructions _Show Saybrooke mattress and box spring_

Date Received in Advertising Department _9/13_

Submitted by _J. L. Browker_

Department Name

Home furnishings

Date Ad Runs

9/24/-- (Sunday)

Paper

Star-Herald

Space requested

800 lines (approx.)

Cost of space

$400

Comments

One-week-only sale!

Reason for Advertising

☐ New Line
☐ Season Opening
☑ Sale
☐ Special Purchase
☐ Staple Stock
☐ Clearance

Quantity on Hand Date Ad Runs	Date Merchandise will be in Stock	Amount on order	Use Trade Mark or Label	Is Manufacturer Paying for Ad?	Extra Delivery Charge?	Telephone Orders?	Mail Orders?	Mail Order Coupon?
50 twin 45 full	now	None	Yes ☑ No ☐	Yes ☐ No ☑ % of Payment	Yes ☐ No ☑ Amount?	Yes ☑ No ☐	Yes ☑ No ☐	Yes ☐ No ☑

ADVERTISING FOR THE RETAIL STORE

- Approval signatures of those requesting the advertising and others who must sign such requests

Planned Layout

After the requests for advertising have been submitted and approved, the advertising department has the task of preparing the actual layout for each advertisement. This layout will serve as a master plan. Single-item advertisements are the easiest to lay out. It may be that several different but related items are being advertised, and they will be grouped or arranged together in an advertisement. In *omnibus advertisements,* related and unrelated merchandise are arranged together. Several separate advertisements by one store may be running in the same medium on a given day.

The layout will indicate the media to be used; the size and shape of the advertisement; the placement of the illustrations for the item or items; the space for the headline and copy; the space for the signature cut, called the *logotype* or "logo"; and the arrangement of these components. The logo is a design that gives the name of the firm. The layout also indicates typefaces and type sizes.

Advertising Copy

An effective advertisement does more than simply inform. It moves the public to purchase the product or service being advertised. The copy—for both text and headline—is the heart of the advertisement. Thus, to a large degree, the success or failure of an advertisement depends on the skill of the copywriter employed by the retailer.

Writing Text Copy. Unless the copywriter has all the information necessary about the products or services, copy cannot accurately reflect their desirability. In addition to the information on the advertising request form, the copywriter should, whenever possible, have available for examination:

- The merchandise itself
- Manufacturers' literature, tags, and labels applying to the merchandise
- Books and pamphlets on merchandise information
- Trade papers and journals
- Results of laboratory tests
- Other advertisements concerning this merchandise

Depending on the merchandise or service, the copywriter will determine whether to use "reason why" copy. This uses testimonials, explanations of the performance of the product or service, reports from testing laboratories, or details about the construction of the articles. The copywriter may decide that the product or service has human interest and, therefore, appeals to emotions such as sympathy, affection, or fear or to the senses such as sight, touch, smell, or taste. The copywriter may wish to combine both "reason why" and human-interest copy for dramatic impact.

The copywriter not only is charged with the creative production of appetite-whetting copy but must also include all important details that the customers need to know to make a decision about the purchase. Sizes, colors, dimensions, uses, care, styles, and prices are examples of the facts most advertisers include in the copy.

Writing the Headline. Because most media in which advertisements appear are scanned rather hurriedly by the average reader, the headline in the advertisement is the important attention getter. Its primary function is to attract the potential customer to read about the product or products being advertised. Headlines should also give prospective customers some important information that they may recall when they are ready to buy the product.

- *Identification headlines* tell the customer what the product or service is that is being adver-

for man-sized comfort:
our swivel rocker
and ottoman

Handsome in living room, family room, or
office—a modern swivel rocker with a contoured back high enough for a six-footer,
and an ottoman that invites sprawling out.
No female fussiness about their care either
—black naugahyde plastic looks like leather,
wipes clean. Teak or cafe walnut accents,
polished cast aluminum bases, ball bearing
swivel action. Complete $199. The match-
ing headrest shown, $10.

W & J Sloane, Seventh Floor, Fifth Avenue at 38th

Sloane's masterfully designed

Swivel Rocker

Sloane's modern swivel rocker is skillfully
shaped to achieve supreme comfort and
accent the contemporary styling. The chair
and ottoman have polished cast aluminum
bases and ball bearing swivel mechanisms.
Two striking wood finishes: hand-rubbed
teak or cafe walnut, with serviceable
leather look black naugahyde cover.
complete $199.
(headrest $10.)

W & J Sloane, Seventh Floor. Fifth Avenue at 38th

Only the copy differs in these two newspaper advertisements. Which copy do you think attracted
more customers?
Courtesy W. & J. Sloane

tised. Trade names or article names or classifications of goods are commonly used. "Lenox China Dinnerware," "Men's Suits," or "Toys" are examples of such headlines.

- *Informative headlines* combine identification with the most important fact the reader should know about the article. "Draperies That Never Need Ironing," "Fun Furs That Are Warm and Cuddly," "Coupe Shape Plates with More Space for Food," and "Colorful, No-Iron Tablecloths Brighten Meals" are examples of such headlines.

- *Story headlines* that arouse the reader's curiosity may be used when a copywriter wishes to be provocative. "Are You Well Dressed from the Neck Up?" asks an advertisement for men's hats. "You'll Flip Your Lid," states an advertisement for a stainless-steel pot and pan set. "Is Price per Pound a True Measure of Meat Value?" asks an advertisement for leg of lamb.

- *Selective headlines* are addressed to the specific customers the store is trying to attract for some particular merchandise or service. "Bonus for White-Collar Workers," states an advertisement for men's colored shirts. "Clothes for Co-eds" may be the headline for an advertisement for a campus wardrobe for college-bound girls. "The Beach Bunch" headlines a collection of beachwear being advertised for winter vacationers. These headlines tend to discourage the readership of those other than the people to whom they are specifically directed.

- *Subheadings* are used in some advertisements in addition to the headlines. These are used to explain the headline, to summarize additional selling points, or to divide the copy for ease in reading.

Illustrations

Illustrations in advertisements are useful in gaining the attention of the reader, in showing the merchandise, in highlighting some unique feature of the merchandise, in showing the merchandise in use, or in glamorizing the merchandise.

Line drawings, wash drawings, and photographs are used in retail advertising. Line drawings and wash drawings have several advantages over photographs. They may highlight a particular feature; they may be adjusted to fit any shape of the advertisement; and they may provide individuality. Since they are often less expensive to use than photographs, retailers make extensive use of them. Photographs are usually more costly to use if the retail firm has to pay for models, for the photography, and for the development of the glossy prints that are used. However, if the manufacturer has supplied the glossy prints, photographs in advertisements will be less costly to use than drawings.

Photographs show merchandise as it actually is, and with effective lighting they may highlight or give dramatic effects. Some of the reasons why photographs are, however, less commonly used than artwork in retail advertising are the following: the limitations of reproduction in newspapers; the relatively high cost; the fact that realism is sometimes not as appealing as less-realistic drawings; and the difficulty of getting just the right models.

Improved color photography and improved reproduction of color have made color in advertisements more common than before, but it is still costly.

Production of the Retail Advertisement

After the layout, copy, and illustrations have been assembled and approved, the production of the advertisement can take place. The advertising production specialist indicates the sizes of type and the placement of the various components to conform with the layout. This specialist also provides the newspaper with the information needed regarding the size of the advertisement, where in the newspaper it is to appear, and the number of proofs needed for checking.

The proofs of the advertisement are returned to the store for checking against the original copy and layout. After checking the proof and making any necessary changes, the store returns it to the newspaper. Charges are made by the newspaper for any changes made in the advertisement, with the exception of errors made by the newspaper staff. A second proof incorporating all changes is then sent to the store for final approval.

ANALYZING ADVERTISING RESULTS

The result of the effectiveness of the advertising should be the increased sales. This is, however, not easy to determine. The advertisement itself may have been good, but the weather may have deterred shoppers; or the merchandise may not have been appealing to customers; or the timing of the presentation may not have been right. A local civic event may have claimed the attention of customers that day; or some calamity may have befallen the nation. Even if none of those causes was present, the response of the customers may have been a delayed one and, therefore, difficult to measure. The advertisement may have been institutional in character, and therefore no immediate response could be expected.

In spite of these deterrents to measuring the effectiveness of advertising, the alert store manager will set up standards by which advertising results may be compared from season to season.

Statistics for Measurement

A complete record of each advertisement should be kept. This should include the date of publication, the media used, the size of the advertisement, its cost, and the sales in both dollars and units of the merchandise or service advertised for two or three days to as much as a week following the appearance of the advertisement. By dividing the cost of the space used by the gross sales of the advertised product, the cost percentage for the advertisement can be determined. Thus, if the space cost is $49 and the sales of the advertised merchandise total $700, the cost percentage for the media used is 7 percent.

Cost Percentages

Such cost percentages vary widely. They depend on the store, the kind of advertising it does, and the appeal of the advertisements. Nonpromotional stores that advertise only regularly priced merchandise might get a return only twice the cost of the advertisement. Semipromotional stores that advertise both sale and regular-priced goods might get sales results of five to ten times the cost of the advertisement. Highly promotional stores might expect sales to total ten to twenty times or more the cost of the advertisement for specially priced merchandise.

COOPERATIVE ADVERTISING

Sometimes all or some of the media costs of advertising that are charged to retailers are paid by the manufacturers who supply the products advertised. This is known as *cooperative advertising*. Vendors typically pay 50 percent or more of the charges made by the local papers for such advertising. Vendors may supply copy and pictures or entire mats or matrixes for such advertisements.

Vendors support the retailer's advertising in direct relationship to the amount of purchases made by the retailer. A formula that treats every retailer the same is essential, since the Robinson-Patman Act of 1936 requires that such advertising allowances be made available on proportionally equal terms to all dealers competing in the distribution of the product. Some vendors believe that direct advertising of their products by the retailer to the customers is more effective than national advertising that they might do. Consequently, the budget that the vendors set aside for advertising is distributed on a cooperative basis to the retailers with whom they deal. Some vendors have both national advertising and local part-paid advertising. Other vendors do not make any allowance for cooperative advertising.

Advantages

Since the media used by the retailer are usually less costly to the store than they would be to a national advertiser, the vendors gain the use of the retailers' rates when they supply cooperative advertising money. Because the advertising allowance is made on the basis of volume of business done, the larger purchasers of the manufacturer's goods get more advertising money. Therefore, both the retailer and the manufacturer gain by this plan.

Disadvantages

There are also some disadvantages in the use of vendor money for advertising. The retailer may purchase merchandise because it carries promotional allowances rather than because it represents the best value or is the best product for the customers. Because the vendor money is available, the retailer may be swayed in the development of the promotional program. Consequently, the retailer may advertise products for which cooperative money is available rather than the merchandise that would appeal most to the customers and would draw the largest response from that trading area.

COOPERATIVE MERCHANT ADVERTISING

To reduce costs, merchants in the same line of business may decide to cooperate with each other in advertising. Examples of this type of cooperation would be in voluntary chains, where each member pays part of the costs of the advertising that benefits all members.

In some cases, merchants who carry diversified products but have a common interest, such as a shopping center in which they are located, will benefit by joint advertising. They may cooperate to sponsor special sales-day advertising and special seasonal-event advertising. They may publish a special advertising booklet telling customers

Small stores may use a standard advertisement matrix or mat. The name of the store and the price of the merchandise can be inserted when the advertisement is printed.
Courtesy Metro Associates Services, Inc.

about the values each store is featuring for back-to-school sales, holiday sales, and other events. Through this combined effort, traffic into the shopping center is increased, and all the merchants benefit.

Advertising by Chains

Most variety, drug, and supermarket chains receive advertising assistance from the central office in the form of weekly or monthly pre-planned promotion guides. These guides are usually equipped with layouts and matrixes of the entire advertisements or assorted illustrations with accompanying headlines and text suggestions. It is then the responsibility of the managers of the individual stores in the chains to place the appropriate advertisements in their local papers in accordance with company specifications.

Advertising by Small Independents

Small independent retailers who cannot afford the high cost of original artwork to illustrate their advertisements can obtain the services of companies that specialize in stock merchandise matrixes. Or they can sometimes recruit this service from their local newspapers or from the manufacturers. In these cases, the independent merchants might design and write their own advertisements, select matrixes that illustrate a type of merchandise rather than the actual items, and submit the completed advertisements to the newspapers for production.

DIRECT-MAIL ADVERTISING

Regular newspaper, television, and radio advertising, billboard signs, and other types of advertising discussed previously may attract the eyes or ears of any or all the people who read or listen to those particular media. Direct-mail advertising, however, is addressed to the persons whom the retailer chooses to receive a message. Most stores, therefore, find this a profitable method of advertising. Even small stores frequently use this method of informing their customers about their merchandise or about special sales events.

Lists of Customers' Names

Direct-mail advertising involves, in addition to the preparation of the advertising, getting lists of names of people to whom the advertising will be sent. For firms with charge account customers, the charge account list or any portion of it may be used for direct mail. If firms have only cash sales, they may need to use salespeoples' contacts and names from mail and telephone orders.

Some firms run contests in order to obtain the names and addresses of potential customers. Local clubs, parent-teacher organizations, and civic groups may be good sources for names. The local telephone directories may be used to make up mailing lists. Firms in large cities may buy mailing lists for the distribution of their advertising messages.

Once established, mailing lists must be kept up to date if they are to have any value. Even lists one year old will have many names of people who have moved elsewhere or died, or whose living habits have changed so they are no longer good prospects for certain merchandise. One way lists may be kept up to date is by using postal forms that guarantee return postage for mail that is not delivered. Names are kept on addressograph plates, on special labels, or in computers.

Kinds of Direct-Mail Advertising

In addition to deciding to which persons direct mail should be addressed, the merchant determines how much direct mail will be used during a year and what kinds of direct mail will obtain the best results at the lowest cost. Many types of direct mail may be considered by the merchant. Some are sales letters, mail enclosures, self-mailing envelopes, mailing cards, self-mailing folders with printed messages, booklets, brochures, catalogs, business reply cards and remittance envelopes, flyers, and broadsides.

Sales Letters. Because they are very versatile and because they can be personalized, sales letters often make a good impression on the recipients. The message may be about a special sales event, new merchandise that has arrived, new services available, changes in the location of merchandise, new branch openings, or fashion shows. Not only do sales letters need to be composed to tell the message; envelopes also need to be addressed and mailing charges paid for this one message. This is, therefore, a fairly costly direct-mail method of advertising.

Mail Enclosures or Billing Inserts. Usually colorful single or multifold sheets or circulars are used for mail enclosures, which have been prepared by the manufacturer with the retailer's name imprinted. They usually contain order blanks for the merchandise they portray. These enclosures are made available at a low cost to the retail firm. Since they are included with charge account bills, they cost nothing to distribute as long as they do not raise the total weight of the mailing piece above the minimum weight for first-class mail.

Self-Mailing Envelopes. Other common enclosures, bearing sales messages and having space for the customer's name, address, and order, are self-mailing envelopes. These are generally sent with charge account bills.

Mailing Cards or Postcards. The retailer may wish to send short messages, using selected lists of customers. For this purpose mailing cards or postcards are used. Since these travel at postcard rates, require no folding or closing, and can be read without having to be opened, they are effective devices for transmitting a selling message.

Self-Mailing Folders. The same amount of room for the message as found on the mailing cards described above is found on the self-mailing folders. But they have a second half that can be torn off at the perforations and used as a return mailing piece by the customer who wishes to order the advertised merchandise.

Booklets or Brochures and Catalogs. Though costly to produce, booklets or brochures and catalogs may result in good returns. Most booklets which contain just a few pages feature one category of merchandise, whereas catalogs containing more pages are usually used to present merchandise from the various areas throughout the store. Order blanks that can easily be detached and mailed to the store are enclosed.

Cooperative vendor-paid or part-paid advertising money may be available for such booklets and catalogs, and so these are commonly used for holiday sales, white sales, back-to-school sales, and housewares events. Sometimes small catalogs or booklets are not sent as direct-mail advertising but are distributed to all the readers of the local newspaper as supplements. Then they are not classified as direct mail.

Since catalogs that meet certain postal specifications have a mail rate advantage for direct mail, the retailer planning a catalog should check on the size and other specifications before preparing such a mailing piece.

Business Reply Cards and Remittance Envelopes. Because no stamps are required and the retailer pays postage only if a card or envelope is mailed back by the customer, business reply cards and remittance envelopes are used widely.

Flyers and Broadsides. Larger folded inserts, known as flyers and broadsides, are used by retailers when they wish to make a dramatic impact with large illustrations and large type. These advertising pieces may be folded and sent through the mail, or they may be distributed by hand by messengers.

LEGAL ASPECTS OF ADVERTISING

Most stores that have grown into large organizations have achieved this growth because they have given customers good value in merchandise and the kinds of useful services they desired. Such firms are dedicated to being truthful in all their presentations about merchandise and service. Many maintain comparison shopping offices, which are used to check and compare values, to examine advertising claims, and to make sure that all laws are carefully observed in advertising and selling. Some stores have testing laboratories or use the services of testing laboratories, which check both the contents of products and the advertising for factual accuracy. Some stores also maintain a bureau of standards, which checks sizes, dimensions, and specifications of products to assure that they meet the usual standards acceptable to the firms.

Smaller firms, which cannot afford these laboratories or bureaus or even the outside services, may buy merchandise from manufacturers whose integrity assures that their products will be as labeled and that claims will be accurate.

Retailers may also obtain help from many agencies and government bodies:

• The National Association of Better Business Bureaus, Incorporated, publishes *A Guide to Retail Advertising and Selling*. This publication lists details of what may and may not be said about products in conformance with the laws and with accepted usage. Local better business bureaus are also of service, both to retailers and customers.

• The Federal Trade Commission is empowered in interstate commerce to issue cease and desist orders and to fine advertisers who continually violate any of the many laws and rulings of the government pertaining to truth in advertising, labeling, and selling. Among the laws and rulings under the jurisdiction of the FTC are The Textile Fiber Products Identification Act, The Federal Food, Drug, and Cosmetic Act, The Fur Products Labeling Act, and other Federal Trade Commission rulings that were discussed in Chapter 3.

The Magnuson-Moss Warranty Improvement Act, also known as the Consumer Product Warranty Law, requires disclosures of actual guarantees that consumers can understand when making a purchase. This act, issued in 1975, requires that the consumer be shown a warranty prior to the purchase of goods. The law also distinguishes between full and limited warranties.

Bait and Switch

In addition to issuing specific rulings and laws that apply to certain categories of merchandise, the Federal Trade Commission is empowered to protect consumers, retailers, and other sellers from any unfair competition. The Commission is especially concerned with misleading comparative price advertising and "bait" advertising that lures customers to the store to purchase merchandise that the store does not intend to sell them. Another concern is misleading statements made when products are advertised.

When a customer comes to a store to buy an item featured in a "bait" advertisement, the salesperson may say, "You really don't want that advertised item—we have a much better article for just a few dollars more. This one will serve your needs much better." Thus, the customer is switched away from the product that was used to bait him or her.

Other Laws and Agencies

The following are other laws and agencies that affect advertising:

• The Wheeler-Lea Act of 1938 is directed against false or misleading advertising other than labeling.

• The Robinson-Patman Act of 1936 requires manufacturers to provide services for all retailers on a proportionately equal basis.

• The Miller-Tydings Act of 1937 permits resale price maintenance among retailers when permitted by state law.

• Underwriters' Laboratories (UL) provides protection for consumers who purchase electrical equipment.

• The American Gas Association (AGA) provides protection for consumers who purchase gas appliances.

The Retailer's Role

Not only does the good-citizen retailer observe all the rules and regulations pertaining to the advertising of products. That retailer also reports the unfair trade practices of other retailers to help keep advertising and selling honest.

TOPICS FOR DISCUSSION

1. What are some of the advantages of advertising?
2. Explain the differences in advertising policies among the following types of stores: nonpromotional, semipromotional, and promotional.
3. Retailers have many media among which to choose for their advertising. Explain some of the reasons to be considered in selecting newspapers as the media to be used.
4. Differentiate between institutional and promotional advertising.
5. Explain the psychological steps in successful advertising.
6. Explain why an advertisement may have all the desired features and yet fail to achieve its goal.
7. Discuss the steps taken by the advertising staff to prepare advertising for the local newspaper.
8. (a) What is meant by cooperative advertising?
   (b) What are the advantages of cooperative advertising for the retailer?
   (c) What precautions should the retailer take concerning cooperative advertising?
9. (a) What are the differences between direct-mail advertising and newspaper advertising in reaching customers?
   (b) What are the differences in procedures between those two types of advertising?
   (c) Which type would probably be more effective for a small store in a large city? Why?
10. What laws affect what is said in advertising?

MATHEMATICS FOR RETAILING

A merchant was not satisfied with the volume of business his store was doing. His sales for the previous year had been $150,000, but his net profit of 3.3 percent of that volume amounted to only $4,950. He decided to spend some money on advertising and to be more aggressive in trying to build his business. Following are the comparative figures for the years before and after advertising:

		Before Advertising		After Advertising	
Income	Net sales	$150,000	100.0%	$225,000	100.0%
	Cost of goods sold	80,000	53.3	120,000	53.3
	Gross margin	$ 70,000	46.7%	$105,000	46.7%
	Advertising	—	—	$ 7,000	3.1%
	Other expenses	$ 65,050	43.4	90,000	40.0
Expenses	Total expenses	65,050	43.4%	$ 97,000	43.1%
	Net profit (before taxes)	$ 4,950	3.3%	$ 8,000	3.6%

1. What was the percent of increase in his profit?
2. What was the dollar increase achieved in net profit over the previous year? Do your figuring on a separate sheet of paper.

MANAGING HUMAN RELATIONS

Although the store you work for is semipromotional in its merchandising policies, its advertising for the past several years has been highly promotional. Every advertisement was for "sale" goods. The policy has now been changed by a new president. However, the buyers persist in wanting that word in every advertisement, even though they have been informed that only one advertisement a month may feature reduced-price merchandise. As the manager of the advertising department, what plans would you make to change this concept of advertising among the buyers? Be prepared to discuss your suggestions.

DECISION MAKING

A buyer in the inexpensive-fur department of a fine, century-old, fashionable specialty store did not receive the photographs from the manufacturer for the modestly priced fur stole she wanted to advertise. The policy of the store was always to use at least one picture in fur advertising. When the advertisement was prepared, the buyer remembered that the better-fur department had run an advertisement two weeks earlier on similar stoles at three times the price. She suggested that the advertising department use the same photograph for the stole her department was advertising. She had 50 stoles to sell, and without advertising and an effective photograph, she anticipated that only one or two stoles would be sold.

When the merchandise manager saw the proof for the advertisement, including a photograph of the costly stole, he asked the fur buyer to bring one of the stoles she was advertising to his office. When he compared the rather flat-looking, inexpensive stole with the luxurious-looking photographed stole, he accused the buyer of misrepresenting merchandise. It was too late to substitute another photograph, but the advertisement could be withdrawn from the paper. What action should the merchandise manager take on this matter? Be prepared to give reasons for your decision.

CAREER LADDER

A young college student, Bobbie DeWitt, was interested in a career in the field of retailing. She had been raised on a farm where she had milked cows, raised vegetables, and performed general chores. She loved sports of all kinds—hockey, volleyball, ice skating, skiing, and tennis—and she had even played touch football with an all-boy team.

In addition to having those talents and interests, she was also an avid reader of novels, short stories, and books and articles on business. She dabbled in writing and had received good grades in both composition and poetry writing.

She came to you with a dilemma. "With all those varied interests," she asked, "how can a person decide on a career path?" What facts might you tell her about the field of retailing? Be prepared to discuss them in class.

chapter 25

VISUAL MERCHANDISING

Some experts believe that people learn more from seeing than from all their other senses combined. The old saying "Seeing is believing" tells a great deal about the importance of strong visual display in the retail business. Today more than ever before, retailers spend large amounts of money on displays to presell their merchandise and attract customers into their stores.

TWO TYPES OF DISPLAY

More than any spoken or written word, the sight of attractively arranged merchandise sparks the customer's desire to buy. Using this psychology, retailers have developed the combined art and science of *visual merchandising.* Retailers use two types of visual merchandising: promotional display and institutional display. Though they differ greatly in content, they have a common purpose: to create in the customer either directly or indirectly a desire to buy the store's merchandise.

The *promotional display* presents merchandise dramatically. Promotional displays are usually elaborate. For example, a store may arrange a window like a classroom, with student desks and chalkboards, and use child mannequins dressed in fall apparel to promote back-to-school wear. Other promotional displays might rely on lighting, color, or stark simplicity. However, regardless of theme, the promotional display is strong and quite dramatic.

By contrast, an *institutional display* does not promote store merchandise. Instead, it publicizes an event or theme of public interest that is usually noncommercial. Typical of institutional display themes are those that support a local charity drive, commemorate the anniversary of the local library, or highlight the arts and crafts of a community group. Obviously, the purpose of offering display space to community groups is to create goodwill between the store and its patrons. Establishing institutional displays is also a subtle but effective way of improving sales. Because they project the image of the entire store, institutional displays are usually restricted to windows.

Occasionally, both promotional and institutional displays appear in high-traffic exterior spaces such as booths and glassed-in cases in shopping-center malls and parking lots. Promotional displays may appear in store windows or in various interior locations. One kind of interior promotional display is *selection display.*

Selection display is the showing of a complete assortment of merchandise so that customers can examine and handle the items for sale. Instead of asking for the merchandise, customers wait on themselves. This type of display is also referred to as "open selling," "self-selection selling," and "self-service."

Selection displays are arranged on stationary or mobile fixtures that range in size. Fixtures may be small counter-top units or huge compartmentalized wall or island units. Fixtures contain full selections of merchandise arranged by size, color, and pattern. The allotment of space in the store for these open fixtures and within each fixture for items of specific colors and sizes requires constant merchandise research.

Lighting for selection display requires special attention. The customer must be able to read size and price markers on the shelves and product information on packages and labels. Also, colors and textures of the merchandise should be clearly visible.

As in every other form of successful display, good housekeeping is essential. Retailers must replenish their displays constantly.

DISPLAY PLANNING

Every type of store uses display. Department stores and large specialty stores employ staffs of specialists to design and construct displays. Chain store companies maintain similar staffs at headquarters. The owners of small and medium-size limited-line stores employ free-lance display specialists or do their own displays with the help of assistant managers and staff employees. Managers of branches or units of chain stores may also employ display specialists.

In large departmentized stores and in the central office of chain stores, the display department is part of the sales promotion division (see Chapter 8). In a large store, the display director is likely to head an executive staff consisting of an assistant display manager, one or more window display managers, one or more interior display managers, a display manager for branch stores, and a sign shop manager. These executives may supervise a staff of trimmers, assistants, copywriters, letterers, sign press operators, clerks, carpenters, painters, and porters.

In a Departmentized Store
Departmentized stores may plan the general nature of their promotional displays month by month for a year in advance. This is part of the entire sales promotion program. The schedule itself is based largely on recurring seasonal events, such as Christmas, back-to-school time, and Mother's Day. The basic promotional events automatically preempt all or most of the window and interior display efforts for certain weeks of the year. Then there are major special events, such as import promotions and anniversaries. These events involve all or many of the mer-

chandise departments together and are called *storewide promotions*. The schedule is completed by planning promotions, including displays, for individual departments.

Window space is valued for its visibility in stores that have pedestrian traffic. Therefore, this space is often assigned to the merchandise categories that have the highest gross margins—those that can afford high promotion costs in their budgets. But also, displays that get priority are those that are likely to be on the customer's mind during a particular season. Stores featuring costly merchandise seldom use their windows for displaying convenience goods. However, variety stores and some specialty stores may feature convenience items.

In a Chain Store
Displays for chain stores are designed months ahead at company headquarters. They may be installed in the individual stores by roving display specialists who cover a regional circuit. Or the store manager may be responsible for the installation. In this case, the store manager receives complete instruction sheets and sketches, along with the required window signs.

Store unit design is standardized within a chain company because of the need to control store displays. Generally there are only two or three types of units. But in an old and large chain, there may be as many as six. Each store unit receives a display plan tailored to the shape and size of its windows. The step-by-step directions specify the merchandise, theme, background colors, and props to be used. This helps keep the image of the chain organization uniform and precise.

In a Small Store
In a small store, interior display areas may be limited to a few display cases, counter tops, and shelves on which the staff can install simple displays. The small store usually has only one or two windows, and most of the display plan focuses on them.

BASIC LIST FOR A DEPARTMENT STORE DISPLAY PROGRAM FOR ONE YEAR

January	Rainwear	Camping Equipment	Columbus Day
January White Sale	Flower Show	Travel	**November**
Resort	Career Women's Salute	June Specials	Import Sale
Travel	**April**	**July**	Thanksgiving
February	Baseball	Independence Day	Toy Department
Lincoln's Birthday	Cherry Blossoms	Institutional Events	Christmas:
Valentine's Day	California Fashions	Light Summer Dresses	Windows
Washington's Birthday	**May**	**August**	Interior
Model Rooms	Mother's Day	Back to School	Trim-a-Tree
Designer's Event	May Sale	Back to College	Santa Claus
Automobile Show	Graduation	**September**	Nativity Scene
Boat Show	Camp	Labor Day	Outside Decorations
March	Armed Forces Day	Football	Occasional Tables & Chairs
Easter:*	Memorial Day	Model Rooms	**December**
Main Aisle	**June**	**October**	Christmas and New Year
Windows	Bridal	Men's Event	Festivities
Easter Flowers	Father's Day	Harvest Sale	Cosmetics
Men's Event	Bathing Wear	Halloween	Furs

*Depending on date of Easter

Convenience stores and other types of stores that stock mainly small items often engage independent window trimmers who specialize in arranging mass displays of merchandise. Typical examples of such stores are drugstores, stationery stores, and hardware stores. In many cases, the mass displays are changed only a few times a year. On the other hand, managers of shops that sell fashion merchandise recognize the importance of changing their displays weekly.

Because of their size, small stores have no space available for full-scale institutional displays, but often they encourage community organizations to place announcements and posters in their windows.

THE ATTENTION-GETTING POWER OF DISPLAY

Promotional display is an extremely demanding form of staging or theatrics. It resembles stage production, but with one important difference: merchandise display must stop and impress a *moving* audience. Some members of this moving audience are shoppers who will purposely look into a window display to see what the store is offering. Others might be just window-shopping and have no intention of buying. Still others might be passing by. The display has only seconds to gain the attention of any one of them. So in order to be a success, the display must be striking as well as understandable. What display qualities attract the customer's attention and encourage a closer look? These are some: recognition value, novelty, storytelling, timeliness, striking aesthetic appeal, and competitive character.

Recognition Value

If a shopper has seen very recently an ad featuring the same theme and merchandise in a store display, the display has a double chance of catching and holding that shopper's attention. This is why print advertising and interior displays are parts of a unified sales campaign. Store displays repeat the message carried in a newspaper ad, but with the actual merchandise on view.

For the same reason, manufacturers of national brands urge stores to give display space to their products at the time they introduce a major selling campaign in print or on television. The manufacturers supply stores with reproductions of their ads to back up displays and to use on sales counters. Thus customers might see a manufacturer's advertisement for a new cold-water detergent in the evening paper or on late-night television, and while shopping the next day they will find a display of the product in the local supermarket. For the customer, recognition of a product is psychologically satisfying.

Novelty Value

Novelty is another attention getter. Novelty may be part of the merchandise, the promotion theme, or the materials and construction of the display. The display artist may create the illusion of a rain shower in the window to show raincoats and umbrellas. People are attracted to the display, stop to examine it, and wonder how it all works. Special effects are very striking. For example, a chair suspended from the ceiling by invisible wires seems to float in the air. This is novel. But the device only has meaning if the display demonstrates that the chair weighs very little. The selling message on the display sign must make this point.

A novelty that usually attracts attention in apparel displays is the "invisible mannequin." The clothes—dress, hat, accessories—are arranged over papier-mâché forms, which are suspended by invisible wires. The items are hung in the same relationship to each other as if worn by an actual person. The only open space is where uncovered portions of a mannequin would be, such as face and forearms. This is an effective device for displaying the coordinated look in fashion.

Storytelling

Most displays tell a story. Some do it by suggestion, while others give full details. For example, a store displaying daytime clothes for young women may decide to relate the clothes to the career women's activities. This may be done in several ways, for example, with a sign or with a blown-up photograph of a busy office used as a backdrop.

The most elaborate storytelling windows are those created for Christmas. The windows may feature Hansel and Gretel; ballet dancers performing Swan Lake; busy Santa Claus workshops; and families celebrating a Victorian-style Christmas holiday. Display manufacturers create most of these attractions and sell them to big

stores for as much as $40,000 and $50,000. People bring their children to see such displays. Thus, although such Christmas displays do not promote merchandise, they attract many customers to the store.

Timeliness

Timing is important to effective displays. Just as the seasons determine what categories of merchandise will go on display, current trends dictate the particular item. Timeliness has a special magnetic appeal, not only because it adds excitement to a display but also because it tells shoppers that the store sells the latest merchandise.

Current events often help create mood. Relying on the public's interest in newsmaking events, such as baseball's World Series or the arrival of the circus, creative display people can tap the power of these occasions for eye-catching display themes.

Another aspect of timeliness is that it is often better exploited by display than by newspaper advertising. Placing an ad takes at least 24 hours, but a display can go up in a couple of hours.

Striking Aesthetic Appeal

Aesthetic appeal—or the natural visual appeal of a display—starts with attractive merchandise. The creation of an artistic environment for such merchandise requires the skillful selection and arrangement of lighting, backgrounds, and props.

Competitive Character

Quality merchandise does not attract customers nearly as much as price specials or sales. Promotional stores use their displays to advertise daily or weekly bargain offerings. Supermarkets, discount stores, and some variety chains do this regularly. They rely on signs and mass displays of sale merchandise. Usually such displays require little creative energy. They are preplanned by the central office and assembled by a display specialist who handles several stores. In some cases a member of a store's staff will set up displays.

SALES PROMOTION FUNCTIONS

THE SELLING POWER OF DISPLAY

So far, the attention-getting elements of display have been described, but other qualities and elements transform attention getting into selling power. Among them are a clear selling purpose, a strong selling theme, the ability to satisfy customer needs, good merchandise selection, informative signs, and an attractive arrangement of goods.

A Clear Selling Purpose

Display managers should know the exact purpose of a display before its planning and construction begin. "It's time to change the window" is not a statement of selling purpose. Neither is "Let's have a display of shirts." But "Next week we will promote permanent-press shirts for men and boys" *is* a statement of selling purpose. Managers must plan with a purpose in mind.

A Strong Selling Theme

The statement of a selling purpose describes what the *store* wants. The selection of a selling theme indicates what the *customer* wants. By emphasizing price or fashion or by featuring the advantage to customers of owning the merchandise, the display creates a strong selling theme.

To dramatize the advantage of owning a permanent-press shirt, the display might show the shirt against a background of travel gear—a half-packed suitcase and golf clubs, for example—with a sign reading: "For the Traveler: The Shirt That Never Needs Ironing." While the purpose of the store is to sell permanent-press shirts, the display theme emphasizes convenience for traveling.

In most apparel displays, the selling theme appeals to the customer's desire for change. A theme would therefore not be just "New Shirt Styles for Spring and Summer" but "The Newest Season-Spanning T-Shirts for 24-Hour Dressing." Thus the display communicates to the customer an important piece of fashion information.

Appropriateness

In selecting selling themes for displays, store managers have to know the interests of their customers. If the men's-wear shop, which is featuring permanent-press shirts, has customers who are middle-income business people, the convenience theme—relating, for example, to traveling—is a good one. But if the shop is in a working-class neighborhood, the theme is the labor-saving feature of the material and the ultimate economy that justifies the shirt's higher price. "You Can Put Away the Iron" or "Save Two Dollars a Week on Your Laundry Bill" are blunt statements that have selling power for this particular audience.

Another aspect of appropriateness relates to the store's own image. Promotional stores may use flashing lights, traffic-stopping color combinations, and exclamatory signs. Prestige stores usually use subtle color schemes, lushly carpeted flooring in window displays, and sophisticated mannequins. By featuring particular merchandise, every display tells the customers the kind and quality of goods the store sells.

Merchandise Selection

After stating the selling purpose and creating the selling theme, display managers must decide exactly what items to show.

The first rule of merchandise selection is that every item on display should be stocked sufficiently to meet the expected demand. This rule applies not only to the main merchandise feature of the display but also to the accessories, which suggest related purchases. Customers are annoyed when displayed merchandise is not available on the selling floor. They may not want to return to the store.

The second rule of merchandise selection is never distract the viewer from the primary selling theme. Here is an example. A window display of shirts has as its theme the convenience and the economy of permanent press. The buyer and the person who sets up the display should not fill the window with pink shirts just because of their new-color interest. That would introduce a secondary theme and confuse the message.

The third rule of merchandise selection is that items for display should harmonize with each other and the environment should harmonize with the merchandise. Harmonious combinations of colors, textures, shapes, and sizes provide unity in a display.

THE DESIGN OF DISPLAY

The way items are grouped and the way the groups relate to each other, to the display area, and to the props is called *merchandise arrangement*. The arrangement must please the eye and guide it to the selling message for easy comprehension. A good merchandise arrangement is a good design, that is, a pleasing combination of line and mass.

The Power of Color
Color is the element in visual selling that stirs people's emotions directly and instantly. Size, shape, direction of lines, space, and texture are all important considerations. But of all the factors in display, color is the most powerful "stopper," the one most likely to gain the shopper's attention and provoke a positive or negative reaction. To combine colors effectively, retailers need to use more than just their eyes, imagination, and instinct. They must have a knowledge of basic colors and the way these colors can be used together to create atmosphere.

Color Terminology
Hue is another word for color. Thus, red, yellow, and orange are hues. *Value* is the lightness or darkness of a color, produced by adding white or black. Light values, obtained by adding white, are called *tints*. Dark values, obtained by adding black, are called *shades*.

Intensity refers to the brightness or dullness of a color. The purer the color, the more intense it is.

The Color Wheel
When sunlight is dispersed by a glass prism, six hues are revealed: red, orange, yellow, green, blue, and violet. Three of these colors—red, yellow, and blue—are *primary colors*. By mixing

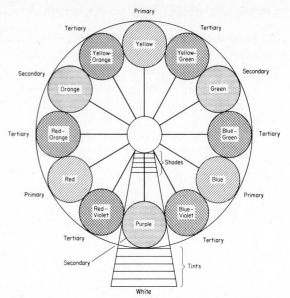

Of all factors in a display, color is the one most likely to attract a shopper's attention. Retailers must have a basic knowledge of colors and of how they can be used together effectively. The color wheel is a convenient reference in planning displays.

them, we obtain all other colors. Orange, green, and violet are *secondary colors*. Orange is a mixture of red and yellow; green, a mixture of yellow and blue; violet, a mixture of blue and red. Mixtures of primary and secondary colors produce another group of six called *tertiary colors*. These are red-orange, yellow-green, blue-green, yellow-orange, red-violet, and blue-violet. All the colors may be arranged in a circle to produce the color wheel.

Black and white are called "achromatic." They do not show any of the hues in the color wheel.

Color Combinations
The color wheel acts as a guide to color combinations. There are three basic color schemes, identified by the relation that colors bear to each other on the wheel. They are the one-color or monochromatic color scheme, the adjacent-color or analogous-color scheme, and the complementary color scheme. Three other schemes, involving more colors, are the split-complement

scheme, the double split-complement scheme, and the triadic scheme.

In the *monochromatic scheme,* different shades or tints of only one color are used, such as red, pink, and maroon; or blue, pale blue, and navy blue. Black, white, and gray may be used with any single color, but the scheme remains monochromatic.

In the *analogous scheme,* the colors used are the ones adjacent to each other on the color wheel, such as yellow, yellow-green, and green. In the basic *complementary color scheme,* on the other hand, the colors used are the two that are exactly opposite each other on the color wheel, such as yellow and violet, or orange and blue.

The *split-complement scheme* is a three-color scheme in which a color is combined with the two colors on each side of its complement. For example, yellow is combined with red-violet and blue-violet; blue, with yellow-orange and red-orange.

The *double split-complement scheme* is a four-color scheme using the two colors on either side of two complements—for example, blue-violet, blue-green, red-orange, and yellow-orange. Last, the *triadic scheme* uses any three colors that form the points of an equilateral triangle—for example, blue, yellow, and red.

With so many color combinations available, there is plenty of room for variety and interest in every display. To a great degree, success depends on the amount of each color used. A display that uses colors in equal proportions is, at best, monotonous. The proportions of the colors in the scheme should be chosen to highlight the dominant color of the merchandise.

DISPLAY PROPS AND EQUIPMENT

The props and equipment in a particular store's displays may range from a few simple fixtures to a vast assortment of custom-made devices. Mannequins and forms are common props in apparel stores, and even in small specialty stores. Informational signs and lighting fixtures are also basic display supplies.

Mannequins and Forms

The display-manufacturing industry provides specially designed stands and forms for every type of merchandise. One of the most versatile pieces of equipment is the *tee stand.* A rod, adjustable to different lengths, with a weighted base is fitted with a straight or curved crossbar. The tee stand is suited for displaying such items of apparel as blouses and lingerie.

Mannequins are a major expense in the display budget. In addition to the initial purchase price, there is the cost of refinishing the mannequins periodically to keep up with cosmetic fashion trends. Wigs must also be changed to reflect the latest hair styles. Mannequins are a worthwhile investment, however, because they show the shopper how the apparel looks on a human figure.

Display specialists handle mannequins only with clean gloves or with tissues held in each hand. When not in use, mannequins are stored carefully, and special protection is provided for the wigs.

Forms are also available in the shapes of parts of the human body. There are feet and legs used to display shoes and hosiery, hands for displaying gloves and jewelry, millinery heads, and jacket forms.

Informational Signs

The display indicates the selling theme visually by showing merchandise in a certain setting, while the sign states the theme in words. If the displayed merchandise has appeared in the newspaper, the sign should repeat the message of the advertisement.

Sign copywriters take suggested copy from the merchandise buyer and rework it for informational signs that state the selling theme. Sign messages should be brief and uncomplicated. A good sign does not just identify the merchandise; it carries a message that appeals to the customer's self-interest or provides some useful information. "Portable Typewriters to Take Back to School" is merely an identifying sign. But

Millinery heads are suitable for displaying wigs and hats.
Photograph by Victoria Wong

"Improve Your Grades with a Portable Typewriter" is a selling sign.

Stores have different policies about the use of price cards in their displays. Whatever the policy, it should be consistent. Those who favor price cards point to studies which show that customers are notoriously poor at guessing prices and more likely to underestimate than overestimate. What some stores do is leave price cards out of their window displays but use them in interior displays.

Lighting
Display lighting varies with the type of store, the merchandise sold, and the design and location of the display. Interior displays generally rely on the overall illumination of the selling floor, although

Forms are commonly used in apparel stores to show the customer how the merchandise looks in use.
Photograph by Victoria Wong

shadow boxes and display cases may be equipped with their own lighting fixtures. The lighting for windows, especially closed-back windows, can be tailored to display purposes. The stock-filled window of a popular-price store may use only fluorescent lights, installed horizontally across the top front and vertically at the sides. A window that is very well equipped and that is in a high-priced store may have facilities that resemble stage lighting. Such an installation allows great flexibility in directing lights, grading their intensity, and creating shadows as part of the composition. This window might have a track installation of incandescent spotlights in directional sockets across the front below the ceiling, a shielded fluorescent lamp at floor level to provide diffused illumination, and a lighting grille below the ceiling as a further source of directional spotlighting. Color screens are sometimes clipped over the lights to create a background color. The display specialist must be very cau-

tious with colored lights, however, because they may distort the color of the merchandise.

Display experts generally use a combination of fluorescent and incandescent lighting. Fluorescent lamps use less electricity than incandescent lamps and are useful for overall or *wash* lighting. Incandescent lamps are used for spotlights because of their intensity.

The light source should be concealed, as far as possible. No light should dazzle the viewer's eyes, and reflections should be minimal. Excessive lighting in a window may fade the merchandise.

WINDOW DISPLAYS

Architecturally, there are two types of store windows, open-back windows and closed-back windows.

The customer sees through the *open-back window* to the store's interior. Because the store becomes a display of merchandise visible to the passerby, its interior must be arranged to face the window. This way, the passerby sees an inviting view of merchandise, not blank backs of selling fixtures or stacks of cardboard boxes.

The open-back window is popular in suburban stores, which do not have much pedestrian traffic, as well as in all types of small stores, since it enlarges the selling and stock area.

The *closed-back window* is like a stage, with a wall of glass where the theater stage is open to the audience. In small stores, the back wall of the window area may be only a half-wall, permitting a partial view of the store interior and also making it easy to get merchandise from the display.

An architectural consideration is the location of the windows. Most display windows are *straight windows,* placed along the wall of the store. Only the front of each window is covered by glass, and the shopper looks at the display from a front view only. *Corner windows* present two or possibly three viewpoints. They may be located at the corner of a building or on either side of a recessed entrance. Some stores have *island windows,* independent structures that the shopper can walk around and view from all sides. Like a set designer, the display specialist must take into account whether the audience will observe the presentation head on or in the round.

In general, designers use two types of window display: the stock-filled window and the window that uses space as well as merchandise.

The Stock-Filled Window

In a stock-filled window, or *mass display,* merchandise covers the entire area and is arranged in compact units in a close-order style. This type of display is common in most variety stores, drugstores, and other types of convenience stores; in chain shoe stores; and in the promotional or discount department stores, apparel stores, and home-furnishings stores. While typical of price-appeal retailing, the stock-filled window also lends itself to sophisticated interpretations in talented hands.

The advantages of the "stocky" window for certain types of retailing are obvious. The passerby will know that the store has a good selection of certain kinds of merchandise.

The stock-filled window also has some disadvantages. For one thing, it is difficult to achieve good proportion and balance and a strong focal point when a window is filled with merchandise. Display specialists must use skill and patience to create a well-proportioned display. Second, the actual trimming of such a window is time-consuming. As a result, stock-filled windows are not changed often, and therefore novelty and timeliness are sacrificed.

The Open-Trim Window

Most department stores limit the amount of merchandise in a window to a few items and leave plenty of space around them. Windows not filled entirely with merchandise are called *open-trim windows.* They give the display specialist the greatest opportunity to create original and beautiful displays. At the same time, open-trim windows are simplest for nonprofessionals to set up, if they observe basic rules of unified arrangement, select attractive merchandise, and use a pleasing color scheme. Another advantage of

open-trim windows is that display managers can change them on very short notice. In general, windows on a weekly or semiweekly change schedule are the open-trim type.

INTERIOR DISPLAYS

Interior displays add life and personality to the store and perform several practical promotion jobs. First, they help to identify departments. A wall display or a display at the entrance of a department guides the customer across the floor. Also, main-floor displays of merchandise carried in upper-floor departments help move customers upstairs to see larger selections. Thirdly, displays of related items suggest additional purchases to the customer. And finally, spot displays anywhere in the store highlight new merchandise and give the customer new buying ideas.

Interior displays are seldom as elaborate as window displays. But often they utilize a seasonal theme and require careful planning and an artistic arrangement of merchandise.

Display Location

Designers may set up interior displays in a number of places in the store—for example, in glassed-in showcases, on selling counters, on ledges of back-of-counter fixtures, in wall cases and shadow boxes, and often in lobby entrances. Displays can be set up on special display tables (for example, in the millinery and shoe departments), and in open floor areas.

Displays in open floor areas require platforms to help set them off from customer traffic and to keep them from being damaged. Merchandise and fixtures are fastened firmly, so as not to fall.

Display Selection

Interior displays allow customers to see the merchandise for sale. If customers want to buy something, they can point it out to the salesperson or select it themselves from the rack, bin, shelf, or table.

In stores that feature self-selection or self-service, displays are carefully planned to showcase the articles and also to make them readily available for customers. More and more service stores are following the lead of the self-service stores in making their merchandise visible and handy for the customer. Valuable merchandise, which must be protected, is usually behind glass for total visibility, even though this makes it less accessible. When displaying samples of small items, such as greeting cards, small hardware, notions, drugs, and cosmetics, just one of each type or color may be on view. Reserves are arranged in drawers where they can be found quickly. Sometimes, to prevent stealing, only one item of a pair of products, such as shoes, gloves, or skates, may be displayed. A salesperson or a stock room worker serves customers and fills their requests.

DISPLAY INSTALLATION

Display professionals plan a display with sketches scaled to size. One sketch is the floor plan, a bird's-eye view. The second is a front-view sketch showing how the display will look to the passerby. The sketch includes notes on the color scheme, the props to be obtained or constructed, and, for window displays, wall and floor backgrounds and lighting. Time spent at this stage with the sketching pad and notebook saves time and physical labor later on.

Whether simple or elaborate, the window display must shine with cleanliness and newness to be a complete success. Nothing looks so unattractive as dirty window glass, dust on the merchandise, or a sign that has fallen over. Everything prepared for a display—merchandise and props—should be inspected, cleaned, polished, or pressed as necessary.

The first step in setting up a window display is to wash the window and give the floor the cleaning treatment it needs: vacuum cleaning for carpeting and polishing for wood or tile. To keep the floor clean and unmarred while they are working, display specialists wear socks. Windows and interior display areas get a housekeeping inspection each day. The outside of the window is washed frequently, if not daily. Frequent restocking, dusting, and cleaning are necessary to keep displays attractive and merchandise ready for sale.

TOPICS FOR DISCUSSION

1. What are the two types of display? What purpose do they have in common? How do they differ from each other?
2. Why does a chain organization prefer to use a standard display plan in its units?
3. Name and explain three qualities of a window display that might attract the customer's attention and cause the customer to take a closer look.
4. Identify and describe four elements that contribute to the selling power of a window display.
5. Explain the three rules of merchandise selection.
6. Draw a color wheel showing the correct locations of the primary, secondary, tertiary colors.
7. When planning their main color combinations, window display specialists are guided by the principles of six color schemes. What are three of them, and how do they differ from each other?
8. Why are mannequins worth having for display purposes if it costs so much to maintain and refinish them?
9. What are the four promotional advantages offered by interior displays?
10. The distinctions between window and interior displays are obvious. Name and explain five elements that they have in common.

MATHEMATICS FOR RETAILING

The merchandise that had been displayed in the window has been returned to your department. As assistant buyer you are to sort through the items and return to stock the merchandise that is in perfect condition. You must also mark down those items that are soiled, faded, or damaged and hold aside any item that is not salvageable at all for selling. The policy of your store regarding display merchandise specifies rules for evaluating and coding damaged goods as follows:

A. Perfect condition—return to stock
B. Slightly damaged—mark down 20 percent of retail price
C. Totally damaged—mark down 100 percent of retail price

When you complete your evaluation and count of the merchandise, your tally sheet reveals the following:

Item	Number	Evaluation Code	Retail Price
Dress shirts	5	A	$6.95
Dress shirts	3	B	6.95
Dress shirts	7	C	5.95
Dress shirts	3	B	5.95
Neckties	6	A	3.95
Neckties	5	B	3.95
Neckties	2	C	2.95
Neckties	5	B	2.95
Dress hose	3	A	1.50
Dress hose	5	B	1.50
Dress hose	2	C	1.50
Dress hose	3	B	1.50

In preparation for a report you must submit to your buyer, compute the following:

1. Total retail value of merchandise returned to stock
2. Total markdown on all damaged merchandise
3. Total retail loss on unsalvageable merchandise
4. Total cost of the display in terms of loss of retail value on all merchandise that had been shown in the window

Do your figuring on a separate sheet of paper.

MANAGING HUMAN RELATIONS

You are the proprietor of a very successful hobby shop that specializes in items of interest to every member of the family. You have scheduled a free-lance display specialist to change your current window display in three weeks. Since this will be just before Memorial Day, you plan to display handicraft kits that would be of interest to boys and girls on school vacation. You get requests for display space from representatives of three different community groups. One request is from the Boy

Scouts of America. The organization would like to place a couple of recruitment posters in your window. Another request is from the local library, which would like to display children's books for summer reading. The third request is from the community amateur theater group, which wishes to display its summer production program. How might you handle this situation so that nobody is offended and so that your own promotional plans for summertime hobby enthusiasts are not jeopardized? Be prepared to discuss your ideas.

DECISION MAKING

You manage a fairly busy unit in a variety chain, which also has three other stores in towns near yours. All four stores are serviced by a roving display specialist. The specialist visits each store weekly to change window displays. In accordance with central plans, the specialist is scheduled to install a massive array of glassware in your front window that will completely deplete your current stock. Though you are reluctant to do so, you allow the display specialist to use as much of the glassware as he needs. The result is a truly eye-catching window display, but a stock of only one complete set of glassware. Throughout the entire week before the sale is to begin, customer reaction to the display gives you reason to anticipate a great run on the glassware and a great problem if the balance of the shipment does not arrive on time. At 4 p.m. on the day before the sale, the glassware still has not arrived. You have several plans in mind, but you must get permission from the central office before you go through with any one of them. Following are possible actions you might take, but each has inherent problems.

1. Borrow half of the glassware stock of each nearby store.
2. Remove most of the glassware from the window display and return it to stock, leaving a small display in the window.
3. Place a sign in the window—either serious or humorous—explaining that there is a stock shortage because of a delivery delay or because all the stock was used up for the display.
4. Set up a special counter displaying the one remaining set of glassware, and assign a special salesperson to take customer orders.

Which plan would you decide upon before calling the central office? What would you say to the central buyer to support your decision? Be prepared to discuss your answers.

CAREER LADDER

You are the manager of the display department of a departmentized women's apparel store. You have narrowed your choice for a new display assistant to two applicants. Arnold is an art school graduate who majored in sculpture. His retailing experience consists of working as a cashier in an art supply store after school hours and on weekends and being a waiter in a resort hotel dining room for two summers.

Stan, who was a merchandising major at a community college, has taken courses in advertising and fashion merchandising and a general studio art course. His retailing experience began when he was assigned to a men's apparel store in his high school cooperative work experience program. He continued to work there part-time and summers while attending the community college. He was also an usher in a movie theater.

Which of these two applicants would you select? Be prepared to discuss your reasons in class.

chapter 26
PUBLIC RELATIONS IN RETAILING

Is the store you are most familiar with a place where customers return again and again to purchase goods? Is that store a place where adjustments are based on the customers' views of the way the products have served? Is that store a place that is concerned primarily with the customers' welfare? Is that store a place where "just-looking" customers are welcome? A store that is interested in pleasing customers offers services graciously and courteously. The result is constant increases in business and profits.

Any person or any firm dealing with the public establishes what has come to be known as *public relations*. Public relations in retailing differs from sales promotion primarily in its focus. Sales promotion is concerned with promoting the sales of merchandise or services, whereas public relations is primarily concerned with developing a desirable image of the store in the eyes of the public.

Public relations may be defined as "doing the thing that is right—at the right time, in the right way, and for the greatest number of people concerned." Since public relations involves doing things "right," everything the retailer does becomes part of the total public relations effect. Each store develops a store personality, and this makes the store individual and unique in the eyes of the public it serves.

ESTABLISHING A GOOD PUBLIC RELATIONS PROGRAM

Good public relations are the result of careful planning and effective work on the part of both management and employees in the firm.

The first step in developing an effective public relations program is to establish a policy whereby all efforts of the firm will be directed toward creating good public acceptance. Once the policy is established, all activities of the store and of the employees of the store must be directed toward carrying out that policy. The managers must inform all employees about the policy and be sure that every employee understands his or her role in cooperating to carry out the policy. The managers must also constantly evaluate the activities and actions of the employees to see that they conform to the policy.

In a small store, the owner or manager is usually in charge of public relations. In large stores, one individual may be placed in charge of public relations. Except in very large firms, this person may also have other duties and responsibilities.

First, the manager of public relations has to decide what activities should be planned and what services should be provided. Next, that manager determines what responsibility each employee should have for establishing a worthy public relations program. The public relations director should be so enthusiastic about the program that every person in the entire organization continuously considers the public relations effect of each action taken.

Those directly charged with the responsibility of making public relations effective should review those relations critically and frequently. Customers, vendors, employees, and the community as a whole must be considered in making this review. Questioning people, observing their interests and reactions, and constantly testing new approaches should all be part of developing and maintaining a good public relations program.

THE RETAIL STORE AND ITS PUBLIC

The retailer is a part of and serves many public groups. These different public groups judge, consciously or subconsciously, the effects of the retailer's public relations.

- The retailer serves the store's customers. The customers seek satisfaction in their purchasing activities. They look for acceptable prices, wide assortments and selections, services, an attractive general appearance, a pleasant atmosphere, ease in finding needed and wanted products, fair treatment, and, most of all, amiable relations with the employees.

- The retailer serves the store's employees and their families. The employees want appreciation and fair play, both in pay and in commendation, in return for their contributions of time and labor.

- The retailer serves the store's vendors or suppliers by ordering regularly, by anticipating customers' needs so that orders can be filled without undue pressure, and by paying bills promptly. Retailers showcase vendors' products attractively and consult with vendors when complaints occur or when returns of goods are necessary.

- The retailer is a part of the neighborhood in which the store is located. Therefore, the retailer needs to be cooperative with the civic, professional, educational, and other groups organized for the betterment of the local area. Most cooperative merchants are members of local better business bureaus, chambers of commerce, local Kiwanis Clubs, or other businesspeople's organizations. Retailers also belong to local and perhaps even state and national merchants associations. The good-neighbor retailer provides space, whenever possible, for club meetings, educational groups, and charity drives and contributes to community activities. The interested retailer also cooperates with local labor groups.

- The retailer is a good citizen. In this role, the merchant cooperates with community leaders and officials and abides by all government rulings and laws. Streets and walkways around the store are kept attractive and clean. Customers can find receptacles for throwing away containers or packages. And the outside of the store adds to the overall attractive appearance of the area where it is located.

The total effort the retailer puts forth in dealing with customers, employees, vendors, other retailers, local community groups, and government will produce the public relations image of the store in its community.

ACTIVITIES THAT MAKE PUBLIC RELATIONS EFFECTIVE

Some stores are world famous; some, famous in just the United States; some, known in their own states or cities; and some, known only to the people who live in the immediate vicinity. Size is not always connected with fame or the lack of fame. The effective work the firm does to build its public relations and to make itself known determines its fame to a considerable extent.

Publicity

Stores have many ways to inform the public about their existence. First, a store can tell its message through the available media. Newspapers and magazines may print articles about the executives in the firm if they are doing interesting things. The executives may be unique because of background, philanthropic activities, extensive travel, and unusual ideas, or by virtue of participation in community events. When a store initiates affairs that are newsworthy—such as parades, circuses, and fund-raising drives for local hospitals or charities—or when a store fosters unique promotions or supports museum collections, articles often appear in local, state, or sometimes national publications. Interviews on radio or coverage of events on television may also highlight the merchant or store.

Institutional Advertising

A store that is contributing in unusual ways to its community may wish to inform its public of such activities. Institutional advertising that tells about the special features or contributions of the store is part of the method of building good public relations. The store may also wish to tell about its convenient location, its unusual services, its new branch stores about to be opened, the new charge policy it is instituting, the employees it is honoring, or the vendors with whom it does business.

Educational Programs

Many stores participate in educational activities in their communities in a variety of ways. Small stores may cooperate by having educational displays within the store. Local jewelers, for example, might show table-setting ideas or have progress displays showing how expensive items are made. One jewelry firm displayed replicas of famous diamonds and also used a progress board showing the various steps necessary in mining diamonds, grading and sorting them, cutting them, and setting them. Men's-wear and women's-wear stores may produce fashion shows in schools or clubs, explaining new fashion trends, new materials, new construction details, or wardrobe ideas. Fur stores may show the progressive steps in fashioning fur garments, while tire shops may show halves of tires to illustrate the plies, the tread, and the shape of the tires. Specialty shops may feature blue jeans, so popular among young people, in a variety of sizes and styles and with decorative motifs as a service to this age group.

Merchants may be available for talks in school assemblies or in classes about retailing or marketing. Such talks may be newsworthy, and the store executive giving the talk may be interviewed for a newspaper story about the retailing field.

Window space may be made available for school displays that publicize student awards or student classroom activities.

The store windows may also be used for local educational exhibits or for award-winning tro-

phies. The merchant may sponsor scholarships in local competitions. If the retailer solicits the aid of local governing officials or local school-board officials in making the scholarship awards, the appeal to those groups may be increased. A firm may give a dinner to which all participants in a scholarship contest are invited, together with town and school officials and guidance counselors. The scholarship awards are made at the dinner.

Merchants may also help with local schools by placing cooperative work experience students or by letting classes visit to learn about the behind-the-scenes work in stores. Some stores have run clinics for investment, banking, and even job-getting techniques.

Civic Betterment Programs

When communities are interested in beautification programs, in rehabilitating areas, or building new areas, retailers usually find many ways to cooperate. They may have their own buildings cleaned or refurbished to meet the town's new image. They may sponsor the planting of trees or flowers or the preservation of historical community landmarks. They may aid in the development of a downtown mall, or they may work to establish parking areas that will enable customers to come downtown with greater ease. Some stores use sprays that eject perfume to scent the atmosphere around the store.

Industrial Progress

Since retailers directly benefit from the economic health of their community, anything that adversely affects that economy is of concern to them. Programs for industrialization will bring workers to the area or will keep the local workers employed. Such programs are of interest to the retailer. As an example, one large chain establishes factories whenever possible in its trading areas to employ residents and to supply the stores with needed products. The alert retailer is therefore delighted to serve on committees to study existing conditions and to recommend potential additions or improvements for the town or local area.

One store in the South, famous for its philanthropy, provided clothing and household goods for dispossessed people when a tragic fire swept through an area of the city. On another occasion, it bought the products of the community to stall economic collapse. Citizens look upon a store that endears itself to its community as "their" store.

Agricultural Progress

In agricultural areas, retailers may work with local 4-H clubs. Merchants may help to raise money to improve livestock or crops. Store representatives may contribute to research that seeks new methods of combating crop damage. Stores may feature new agricultural techniques and achievements in their windows and in their advertising.

Cooperation with Local Government

The community spirit of an area also greatly affects the retailers in that area. If the crime rate is high, people will hesitate to go out after dark. If agitators are given to burning or looting, people will stay away from the area. If derelicts or other undesirables congregate in the nearby streets, people will avoid going to that area. If streets are congested and movement by car or on foot is difficult, people will go elsewhere to shop. Poorly lighted streets will deter nighttime shopping. Littered streets will discourage shoppers from strolling through the area. Fast-food shops may attract those who like such service, but the litter that results may repel regular shoppers. The retailers therefore work with civic groups to make the streets safe, attractive, well lighted, and pleasant for all who wish to shop there. Street safety, free flow of traffic, cleanliness, and adequate police protection are goals that retailers seek and support.

To help to attain these goals, retailers volunteer to serve on local boards; cooperate in having studies made of the highways, traffic, and local crime conditions; and work to ease tensions among community groups. Retailers also encourage their employees to participate in local politics, to join local groups working for the betterment of the community, and to be leaders in youth groups, such as Boy Scouts or Girl Scouts.

In-Store Services and Events

To make the store a focal point of the community, the merchant may offer many services and provide many activities. Store events are ways of attracting customers. Special "meet Santa Claus days," featuring a costumed Santa who talks with young children, are examples of special events that attract large numbers of customers at Christmastime. Similarly, the Easter Bunny may attract people during the Easter season. Special exhibits, lectures, or displays to feature national holidays may make the store a center of holiday activity.

Art shows, book and author lecture series, movie star introductions, bond drives, and charity drives are additional events that interest the community and attract newcomers to the store.

Full-service stores offer many services—such as delivery, charge accounts, time payments, telephone and mail order, and will-calls (retail sales in which items are reserved by a deposit, with full payment to be made when the merchandise is called for at a later date). Special services—such as travel bureaus, a post office, telephones, wrapping service, an information center, foreign language translators, and special shoppers—are additional aids to shopping that attract customers. Some stores even run special buses to their doors from outlying areas to accommodate shoppers who have no easy access to the stores.

Attractive, cheerful rest rooms, places to sit and relax during or after shopping, and pleasant eating places also serve to bring customers to the store and to keep them in the store during their shopping expeditions. Some stores have found it desirable to serve coffee to early-morning shoppers to make them feel welcome.

Money-back adjustment policies, employees who are courteous to all people who enter the store, and pleasant telephone answering services

A store may sponsor a special event to attract new customers. For example, Korvette's recently invited ballet dancer Rudolf Nureyev to sign record albums at one of their store units.
Photograph by Fern Logan

will help to determine the public image of the firm and attract and hold customers for that firm.

Employee Services

Employees are also customers of the store. Their morale is transmitted to customers in every action and statement. Employees are heard and observed by customers even when they are off duty, as they ride elevators or escalators, or walk through the aisles. Reasonably happy employees project their attitude and help to make customers enjoy their shopping. Unhappy employees may antagonize customers or project their unhappiness and make customers who shop in a store feel uneasy while there. Successful management, therefore, is concerned about the store image projected through the attitudes of the employees.

To win the respect and cooperation of the employees, the employer must reward them fairly for their efforts and be concerned with their welfare. The employer may gain employee satisfaction in several ways—for example, by providing stated payment and promotion policies, vacation periods, attractive lunchrooms, and well-kept employee rest rooms. Stores that have the space may provide additional activity rooms for employee libraries, for reading, for card playing, and for games such as table tennis, billiards, and pool. Some large stores have sun roofs for lounging during warm weather. In very large retailing firms, hospital rooms completely equipped for emergency medical care, for health examinations, and for dental care may be available.

Store activities for employees such as the following are also good for employee morale and for good employee relations: store shows that permit talented employees to perform; store parties that permit social mingling; and award programs that set goals and provide incentives for ambitious employees. In-store classes enable employees to upgrade their skills and add to their knowledge. A policy of refunding tuition encourages employees to take courses in local colleges. These are all morale builders and are good for public relations.

Modern Methods of Friendliness

When the majority of Americans lived in rural areas and small towns, the official or salesperson who served in the local store could greet each customer by name as he or she entered that store. As retailing firms and the communities in which they are located have become larger, they have also become more impersonal, and this individual, friendly greeting has disappeared. However, stores have attempted to retain some vestige of this friendliness in various ways.

Telephone clerks greet callers with a courteous "Good morning" or "Good afternoon" before using the store name for identification. Telephone clerks also convey season's greetings at holiday time to callers. Frequently, store employees use similar friendly greetings.

Stores also make use of nonpersonal methods of greeting customers to let them know they are welcome as they enter the store. Many stores use a sign at the entrance that carries a message such as "Welcome. We are pleased that you are visiting us." As the customer leaves, another sign on the other side of the door may say, "Thank you for your visit. Please come again."

Wrapping paper and paper bags may have greetings. Even sales checks and cash register

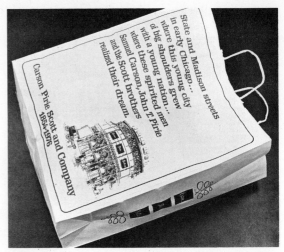

This store issued a shopping bag to celebrate the U.S. bicentennial. Stores often use bags printed with messages conveying seasonal greetings or recognizing special events to create a friendly, neighborly image.
Photograph by Fern Logan

receipts may have "Thank you for your patronage" printed across the face or on the back.

Decorations and displays, in windows and inside the store, may convey season's greetings to customers. Small boutiques and special selling areas may attempt to individualize attention for the customer.

Thus the store is attempting, through signs, sales slips, wrappings, merchandise groupings, and displays, to convey the warmth of a greeting that was previously given in person.

ADVANTAGES OF GOOD PUBLIC RELATIONS

Many benefits result when a store is highly regarded—when it is well known because people talk about it, think about it, and plan to visit it when they are in the area. A store that is talked about and thought about has a great deal of traffic. Some of this traffic may be developed by the many community services provided by the store or by events held in the store.

If a store is well known and well thought of, manufacturers and wholesalers will try to showcase their products in that store. Such a store, therefore, obtains larger selections of goods, which it can offer to its customers. This, in turn, brings additional customers who seek these particular products.

If the store is known as a lively, attractive place to visit, it may also be known as a good place in which to work, and so prospective employees are attracted to apply for jobs. If the displays are dramatic and frequently changed, if new merchandise is constantly coming into the store, and if there is an aura of excitement, customers will go out of their way just to walk through the store to see what is new and interesting. A customer walking through a store is often tempted to do some impulse buying, or that customer may see some item that whets the appetite for a future purchase.

If the store is providing special events for the community, free publicity may be available through local newspapers, on radio, or on television. This further keeps the store name in the minds of its customers, vendors, and employees. The appeal the store has is influenced by the total activity occurring in the store and by the store's appearance. A store that is doing things of interest is a store that is talked and thought about.

TOPICS FOR DISCUSSION

1. Explain how public relations differs from sales promotion.
2. What steps must be taken in a retailing firm to establish an effective public relations program?
3. Discuss the different public groups the retailer serves.
4. What are the advantages to the store of good public relations with each of those different groups?
5. In what ways may a store become known for good public relations?
6. Explain in what manner a store may contribute to civic betterment programs.
7. Why does local government affect retailers' public relations?
8. What role do customer services play in establishing good public relations for a store?
9. What role do employee services play in developing good public relations?
10. What do large stores do to maintain a friendly, personal approach?

COMMUNICATIONS IN RETAILING

Assume you are the public relations director of The Treasure House, a small chain of boutiques that feature imported and domestic art objects. This firm prides itself on its courteous, knowledgeable treatment of customers. On a separate sheet of paper, write a short paragraph for new employees telling them of this policy and advising them about specific actions desirable on their part to achieve the favorable public relations image.

MANAGING HUMAN RELATIONS

As a department head you hired a black college graduate who had majored in accounting. Within six months it became obvious that he was an outstanding employee. You have promoted him about as far as he can go in the department without his having field experience. During the time he has been with the department, he has

PUBLIC RELATIONS IN RETAILING

321

become a specialist in one phase of accounting that is particularly adaptable to one of your branches that is having considerable problems. The store is located in the South and is staffed largely by white Southerners who you believe may resist being supervised by a black manager. There is another employee in the department who could not handle the problems of the Southern store as well but who you feel might be able to get along with the people better. If you do not promote the black employee, he will probably leave the company, and you wish to keep him. The other employee has been with the company a shorter time, and the black employee would resent your not promoting him first. How would you handle the situation? Be prepared to discuss your ideas.

DECISION MAKING

A store in a suburban location had put on a Christmas show each year for the townspeople. This event appealed to people of all ages and was warmly received in the town. Expenses for the show, however, had mounted annually. This year, because of a serious downturn in volume and a resulting profit squeeze, the store manager realized that the show was too costly to stage. She called in several of the store's department heads to discuss this dilemma. If you were a department head, what advice would you give the store manager? Be prepared to explain your ideas.

CAREER LADDER

Assume you are the employment manager in a retailing firm that wishes to establish the position of public relations director. This will be a part-time job, and the director will spend half the time doing public relations work and the rest of the time doing other tasks in the store. You have been asked to draw up a list of desirable characteristics to look for in the person who is to be selected for this position. What are the characteristics you would seek in such a person? Be prepared to discuss them in class.

THE POWER OF PERSONAL SELLING

chapter 27

PRINCIPLES OF EFFECTIVE SELLING

"Selling merchandise that won't come back to customers who will"—that's how a famous salesperson once defined success in his profession. Today successful sales depend very much on this principle. In our competitive markets, no retail store can survive if customers do not return regularly to buy the merchandise they need.

Equally important to successful sales is the selling atmosphere. Today's customers do not tolerate high-pressure techniques. They buy the things they require for comfortable living, and good salespeople recognize the customers' motivations. Very simply, their objective is to satisfy the customers' needs.

For the moment and for the foreseeable future, no vending machine or self-selling fixture exists or will exist that can replace the persuasive and helpful selling job of a competent salesperson. Vending machines may eliminate the order taker or clerk who simply hands customers the specific items they request. Real selling, however, needs a sales story, especially when, as often happens, the store does not have the exact item the customer has seen or perhaps imagined. For example, a woman may want a low boot with a side zipper, but a well-informed salesperson can per-

suade her to try a style without a zipper and see for herself that it is just as easy to put on, comfortable, and good-looking.

Retail salespeople who do a good job perform an important economic and social service. They benefit, their store benefits, and the customer benefits. People in sales can accomplish several important tasks: they can raise their own earnings; move along the promotion path to a buying or supervisory position; and gain the satisfaction of being busy and productive on the job. Also, by using psychology to understand customer needs, successful salespeople can help customers make purchasing decisions and, at the same time, develop for themselves the quality of tactful leadership, so valuable in all social relations.

THE VALUE OF A GOOD SALESPERSON

If all the stores in the United States were staffed with efficient salespeople, the cost of retail distribution would drop, and customers could use their purchasing power more effectively. How is this so? Let's look at three examples.

- An ordinary salesperson can spend up to 20 minutes selling a customer a shirt for $6.50. A good salesperson who has won the customer's respect will convince the customer that it is worthwhile to spend $18 and take advantage of the special price on the purchase of three shirts—not only to save $1.50, but also to save future shopping time and to have three shirts to rotate, thus saving wear and extending the durability of each shirt.

- The order-taker salesperson will sell one pair of stockings. The customer adviser reminds the shopper that there is more wear and value to be gained from buying three pairs of an identical type and color.

- The mechanical salesperson who is selling discounted 12-inch portable televisions will show a set to an interested customer and hope for a quick sale. But the salesperson who knows how to establish good contact with customers will ask a few pertinent questions. Because in one instance the set is for a 25-foot-long recreation room, the salesperson advises the customer that a 21-inch set would give more viewing pleasure in a room of that size.

A good salesperson will suggest purchase of related merchandise before closing the sale.

THREE THEORIES OF SALES

Many theories of good sales exist, but three in particular are most common among professional salespeople: the steps-of-a-sale theory, the full-circle theory, and the problem-solving theory.

Theory One

According to the steps-of-a-sale theory, a customer's decision making follows easily identifiable steps. Any salesperson who recognizes these steps can take the customer through each of them rapidly and successfully. Basically, the seller must know on what step the customer is operating at any given time during the sale. With skillful handling, the salesperson can move the customer to the next step and eventually close the sale. Salespeople use the steps of the AIDA theory that have already been discussed in conjunction with advertising.

Another popular version of Theory One is also identified by an acronym. The ANPOCS method includes the following steps: *approach* the customer correctly; determine the customer's *needs*; *present* the merchandise effectively; *overcome* the customer's objections; *close* the sale; *suggest* additional merchandise.

Both versions of Theory One enjoy wide acceptance because of their simplicity.

Theory Two

According to the full-circle theory, customers will react to certain stimuli when making a decision. If the salesperson can encourage the customer to make each decision in order, the seller completes a circle and closes the sale. This theory draws heavily from the psychology of behaviorism, which dates back to Pavlov and his experiments. Pavlov proved that one can predict the response to a specific and repeated stimulus. Salespeople who use the full-circle theory stimulate the customer with a sales message, watch the response, and stimulate again for another response until the sale is completed.

The success of the full-circle theory depends on the salesperson's ability to recognize and satisfy the specific needs and desires of the customer. By uncovering the right stimuli to engage the customer, the salesperson gets the desired response and makes a sale.

Theory Three
According to the problem-solving theory, all customers have a problem on their mind when they shop. Sometimes this problem is the same as a need. The good salesperson must understand and sense the customer's problem. By relating product knowledge to a specific need, the salesperson can explain how an item can solve the problem. Part of successfully applying this theory is guiding customers to the point where they feel buying a piece of merchandise honestly answers their need.

No matter which theory is used, the salesperson will not be successful without a well-conceived presentation based on how the customer thinks and acts. (Review Chapter 3, which describes in greater detail consumer buying motives and habits.)

SOME CUSTOMER TYPES

One of the interesting by-products of a selling career is the ability salespeople develop to adjust manner and style to different types of customers. This enables them to get a job done smoothly and quickly, as well as to deal effectively with fellow employees and supervisors.

Following are descriptions of twelve customer types salespeople learn to recognize, along with some tried and proven selling suggestions. These types include both males and females, young and old, and people of all races and nationalities.

1. The *decisive customer* knows what he or she wants, is confident of being right, and will not tolerate another opinion. The salesperson

must remember that the purpose of selling is to win a sale, not an argument. The salesperson tries to let the customer make the sale, tactfully using the customer's wants and opinions as part of the sales presentation. This type of customer respects brevity.

2. The *technical customer* wants a factual, detailed explanation of the product and watches for any inaccuracies or hesitations in the salesperson's description. The salesperson should give as technical a presentation as possible, emphasizing laboratory tests, construction, materials, and the manufacturing process. For this customer, it is important to show the content label or any other tag attached to the merchandise. It is also important to volunteer information on caring for the product.

3. The *argumentative customer* may take issue with any statement, tends to disbelieve selling claims, and is cautious. The salesperson needs much skill in overcoming objections, because this type of customer will try to catch the seller in an error. The salesperson carefully avoids personality conflicts and, in general, overcomes the customer's wariness with a strong knowledge of the merchandise. In dealing with this type of customer, the "yes, but . . ." method is more productive than outright disagreement.

4. The *procrastinating customer* likes to postpone the buying decision until another day. Procrastinators are insecure and lack confidence in their own judgment, but they are usually willing to listen. The salesperson must help this customer decide, reinforce his or her judgment by agreeing firmly that a particular choice is right, or offer a positive suggestion. An alert salesperson will try to narrow the selection by putting away the merchandise in which the customer shows least interest. If the customer still wants to "think it over," the salesperson might indicate the problems of a further delay. For

example, the seller might say, "The 10-percent-off sale on furniture will be over in a week." The statement should always be true.

5. The *angry customer* arrives in a bad mood. The salesperson must tread softly because this type of customer becomes indignant at the slightest provocation and may act as if deliberately baited. The professional salesperson won't threaten this customer's ego but will back away from arguments and confine comments to the simple facts, cheerfully displaying a good assortment of merchandise.

6. The *suspicious customer* simply does not trust sales talk, hates the feeling of being "managed," and reaches decisions cautiously. Whenever possible, the salesperson should back up statements about merchandise and demonstrate its use and features.

7. The *impulsive customer* decides quickly but is impatient and could easily cancel the whole transaction if it drags. Because the sale should close as fast as possible, the experienced salesperson will not spend time overselling or overtalking.

8. The *buck-passing customer* most likely wants to talk a purchase over with a spouse or other member of the family. By using agreements and opinion to close a sale, the salesperson helps the customer make his or her own decision.

9. The *wavering customer* is unable to decide easily and is afraid of making a mistake. To help this customer, the salesperson emphasizes the merits of an item and bases the sales message on the customer's needs and doubts.

10. The *silent customer* will not talk, but he or she does think. The salesperson can draw out this customer by asking some direct questions and by emphasizing a knowledge of the product. Sometimes the sales worker can catch the buying signal by watching the customer's eyes for a reaction.

11. The *shopping customer* is not interested in buying today necessarily. This customer looks around, perhaps to get an idea of the merchandise the store is offering this season. The salesperson should show merchandise with courtesy and enthusiasm and keep alert for any buying signals.

12. The *timid customer* is ill at ease, inhibited, and sensitive. Sometimes this customer is shopping in a price range higher than usual and may be unsure of his or her judgment. Very often the friendly approach encourages the customer to express particular wants and needs. In this way, the timid customer is led toward a decision.

TECHNIQUES FOR IMPROVING SALES

Part of anyone's success in retailing is knowing how to handle the twelve basic types of customers. But just as important to the selling process is knowing yourself first and then trying to apply that knowledge to your customers' buying habits, preferences, and personal tastes. Following is a description of seven techniques that make good salespeople even better.

See the World Through the Customer's Eyes
Salespeople must be careful to recognize that they are selling merchandise *to* customers rather than just selling merchandise. The professionals put themselves in their customers' place and see the merchandise not as sellers would but as purchasers. The salesperson asks, "Why would I buy what I am trying to convince my customers to buy?" The answers become part of an *effective* sales presentation.

Good salespeople also ask themselves, "Would I buy this merchandise from someone no more convincing than I am?" Sometimes this question helps sellers to adjust their enthusiasm

A good salesperson finds out what customers need, how they will use the product, and why they want it.

and make sure that their reply is "yes." A third query is "What kind of salesperson would it take to make me buy?" Again, the answers help salespeople to improve their selling abilities. They must consider how customers will use a product, why they want it, and what special problems the item will solve. These are all the things you as a customer would want to know if you were buying yourself. Salespeople must anticipate all the objections and study ways to overcome them.

Adjust the Selling Pace to the Customer

Not all customers decide in the same way and at the same pace. Some are slow thinkers, while others make decisions quickly. Sell to customers individually and at their own pace. A guide might be the study of one customer who always returned to a particular salesperson when she had to buy a new car. When the sales manager asked her why she continuously bought from the same salesperson, she replied, "Because he lets me decide slowly. That's the way I decide best."

Sell What the Merchandise Will Do— Not What It Is

A salesperson once said, "I never sell a vacuum cleaner, just the machine itself. I sell what it will do: pick up dirt and make the house dust-free." Good salespeople always sell what the merchandise will do for the customer. For example, a salesperson will not sell only perfume to a customer; he or she will sell an exotic scent, the ability to attract people of the opposite sex, or the scent that reflects luxury. In order to sell the product successfully, salespeople must sell the results of the product's use.

Believe in the Product

Sellers must learn as much as possible about their merchandise. They ask buyers why they bought certain items and what selling features will make customers want to spend their money. Then the salespeople present a sales story based on these positive points, believing themselves in the product and in their store. A salesperson who thinks that the competition has better merchandise and a better store cannot sell effectively.

Anticipate Objections

A television announcer once asked a famous major league shortstop about his secret of success in playing the infield. The athlete's reply was, "I think of where I will throw the ball even before the pitcher pitches. When it comes to me, I don't have to waste a few seconds thinking what to do with it. That few seconds makes the difference between a safe and an out."

This is a lesson salespeople could apply on the job. A good salesperson learns to analyze the merchandise from all points of view before the customer asks any questions. Anticipating objections can make the difference between success and failure in sales. No matter what point the customer brings up, the seller has already prepared the answers, and the sale moves along quickly. This kind of approach assures a smooth-flowing transaction.

Listen and Comprehend

In the final analysis, selling is an act of communication. Frequently, when the seller has communicated thought, feeling, and some conclusions about the merchandise—most important, what it will do for the customer—a sale is made. Too often communication breaks down, causing misunderstanding instead of understanding. The basis for real communication is listening. Better listening requires both salespeople and customers to make sure of what they hear. A misunderstood statement can result in the failure of a sales effort and the displeasure of a valued customer.

Follow Price With a Selling Point

A good salesperson realizes that price is not the most important part of a sale. The sale should hinge on the product's merits. A professional seller's reply to "How much is this sweater?" would be "That sweater of 100 percent acrylic fiber costs $17.95 and is machine-washable" rather than just "$17.95." The experienced salesperson knows that an attractive selling point always follows the price quotation. The last thought in the customer's mind should be the fact that the sweater is machine-washable, not the cost. Customers usually buy merchandise for its merit and use rather than because of the price, and salespeople are wise to sell on this basis.

TOPICS FOR DISCUSSION

1. Explain what is meant by "selling merchandise that won't come back to customers who will."
2. Explain why, in the long run, a store cannot survive if it doesn't sell merchandise actually wanted and needed by the customers.

3. Discuss the comment "Vending machines may replace a sales clerk, but never a salesperson."
4. Discuss the merits of the steps-of-a-sale theory.
5. How does the steps-of-a-sale theory differ from the full-circle theory?
6. Explain the problem-solving theory.
7. Explain the different methods a salesperson would use in dealing with the decisive customer and the procrastinating customer.
8. Explain the advice "See the world through the customer's eyes."
9. Discuss the statement "Sell what the merchandise will do, not what it is."
10. How can a salesperson learn to anticipate objections?

MATHEMATICS FOR RETAILING

Salespeople Brett and Cripps sold automobiles for King Cars, Inc. Brett sold a car for $2,500, and Cripps sold a car for $3,200. Each one received a commission of 5 percent of net sales, and the company received a margin of 35 percent.

1. What commission did each salesperson receive?
2. How much did the retail price differ from the cost of these sales?

Do your calculations on a separate sheet of paper.

COMMUNICATIONS IN RETAILING

Assume you have just received a report from your city's chamber of commerce entitled "A Survey of Retail Selling." Some of the facts and figures in the report are as follows: Stores in your city lose about $5,000 in retail sales a day because customers are dissatisfied with salespeople's behavior. Sales of $25,000 and more are lost weekly because salespeople fail to suggest merchandise to customers. An average increase of $50 in retail sales per salesperson could be realized weekly if retailers enforced a policy of suggested selling in their stores.

As store manager, you decide to share this important study with your sales staff by distributing a memo to each salesperson. On a separate sheet of paper, compose a brief memo emphasizing the impressive figures from the survey. Do not sound too preachy, yet do get your message across. Originality and creativity in how you handle your message might gain the best results.

DECISION MAKING

You are the assistant manager of a suburban family clothing store that is open every evening until 9. You actually manage the store from 6 to 9 each evening. There are 8 departments in the store, and 4 part-time salespeople are assigned to each one. The evening employees work from 5:30 until 9. Because business is always heavy, they tend to leave merchandise disarranged and sometimes they misplace items, since they have little time to keep merchandise in order. Complaints to the manager by the daytime employees have caused you to come up with a solution. Select one of the following alternatives as an answer to the problem, and be prepared to explain why you decided on it.

1. Extend evening work hours to 9:15 or 9:30, thus giving the evening workers the needed time to clean up the stock.
2. Assign two people from each department to stop selling at 8:30 or 8:45 and straighten up their sections.
3. Get the daytime staff to accept the responsibility of good housekeeping on the basis that the last hour in the evening is far busier than the first hour in the morning. Explain that the daytime people have more time and opportunity to put their departments in order.

THE POWER OF PERSONAL SELLING

chapter 28

THE SELLING CONTINUUM AND THE FORMULA FOR VALUE

Depending upon the location of the store, the kinds of merchandise it carries, the policies of the store, and the customers the store attracts, merchandise may be sold by self-service, by self-selection, by novice salespeople, and by experts who serve as consultants for the goods they handle. This represents the *selling continuum*.

FROM SELF-SERVICE TO FULL SERVICE

In a grocery store, a customer may push a grocery cart through aisles filled with colorful, attractively displayed, clearly price-marked goods. At the end of the last aisle, cashiers and wrappers take the customers' money and bag the purchases.

In a variety store, the customer passes rack after rack and counter after counter of carefully arranged and dramatically presented goods. Cashiers take money, make change, and package the goods either at the station or at checkout counters.

In larger discount houses, department stores, and some specialty stores, merchandise is massed for sale on counters, hangers, and stands. Salespeople serve to answer questions, write out sales checks, take the money, or charge the products to the customer's account. These people are also able to help two or three customers simultaneously.

In more exclusive shops, such as jewelry stores, fur salons, or dress or suit stores, mer-

chandise may be dramatized by showing only a limited amount in artistic settings. Sales consultants who have extensive knowledge about the products determine the customers' interests in goods and select the merchandise to show from reserve stock rooms or locked cases. As the merchandise is brought out for examination, detailed explanations of the special values of the goods are given. When the customers have made their selections, clerical employees may be asked to write out the sales checks and handle the wrapping or delivery of the items.

The Importance of Productivity

All resources and every activity of the personnel of a retail store are directed toward furthering one goal: to sell merchandise profitably. When wages and salaries were low, merchants were not too concerned with the actual costs of selling because those costs did not represent a major part of the total overhead of getting the merchandise to the customer. As wages and salaries increased, however, retailers found themselves in a cost squeeze that necessitated their analysis of every phase of their operation. Consequently, new and more efficient methods of packaging and displaying merchandise have been developed.

In addition, both self-selection, which requires only limited service, and self-service, which necessitates merely a checkout area, have been instituted at least in some areas in most retailing firms. At first only groceries were successfully

The selling continuum ranges from self-service (left) to the assistance of expert salespeople (right), whose technical knowledge can help the customer make a wise buying decision.
Left, courtesy Westvāco Corporation; right, photograph by Freda Leinwand

marketed by self-service. Later prepackaged meats were accepted by the consumer for self-service. Then variety stores, drugstores, stationery stores, toy stores, and other firms concerned with the selling of small, easy-to-carry, prepackaged merchandise found self-service a profitable way of moving goods. Even traditional, full-service stores began to put more merchandise on the tops of counters and on racks where customers could select items without a salesperson's aid. Stores found that hosiery, handbags, gloves, costume jewelry, men's shirts and accessory items, housewares, sporting goods, cameras, tobacco supplies, and a host of other small items could be marketed effectively in that manner.

Dress shops, men's slacks and suit stores, and junior clothing stores are often arranged so that people can browse by themselves through the racks and select merchandise at their leisure.

Selling Titles and Responsibilities
Since selling ranges on a continuum from little or no service to a great deal, surely just "salesperson" is not sufficient as the title for the people engaged in selling activities.

Cashiers and Wrappers. Checkout stores employ cashiers and wrappers who are not classified as salespeople but who provide virtually the same services performed in other stores by so-called

THE POWER OF PERSONAL SELLING

sales clerks. They simply take the money for a purchase, do the necessary recordkeeping, and wrap the package. The word "cashier" comes from the Latin word *cassa,* meaning box. *Casse,* a French word, means "money box." Later, this word came to mean "money." The English word "cash" stemmed from the French word.

Sales Attendants. Some self-service stores may employ sales attendants who help customers to find merchandise and who direct customers to various areas in the store. They do not handle money, do recordkeeping, or wrap packages.

Sales Clerks. Some stores display merchandise for selection by the customer and also have employees nearby to ring up sales on the cash register and to wrap the customers' packages.

Salespeople. In addition to performing the tasks of the sales attendants and cashiers and wrappers, salespeople may also perform additional services, such as finding the item in a different color or a different size or showing the customer some product in direct response to a request. In still other stores or departments, salespeople must know a considerable amount about a product and be able to explain how it is to be used.

Sales Consultants. In selling some types of merchandise, such as draperies and curtains, carpets and rugs, diamond jewelry, farm equipment, shop devices, stereophonic record players, sports equipment, and clothing, the salesperson may be an adviser or consultant for the customer. A person buying furniture, for example, may need assistance not only in learning facts about the article but also in determining color harmony, placement of the piece in the room, and use and care of the article. For most costly, seldom-purchased merchandise, the salesperson may be an authority, having studied the various qualities, grades, types, and advantages and disadvantages over a period of many years. This person might technically be called a *sales consultant.*

Demonstrators. Particularly in variety stores and in houseware sections and cosmetic sections of departmentized stores, salespeople are employed by manufacturers to create customer buying interest by demonstrating and explaining qualities and functions of merchandise. They may perform the duties described under "salespeople."

SALESMANSHIP

Authorities do not agree on any one definition of *salesmanship.* There are as many definitions as there are books and articles on the subject. Salesmanship is variously called a process, an ability, a practice, an art, a science, or an art and a science. According to the definitions, salesmanship persuades, influences, helps, or leads people to accept, to buy, or to take a course of action that results in the purchase of goods and services. This purchase gives satisfaction, is mutually beneficial, meets the customer's needs, or provides the best solution to the customer's problem. Some definitions also include the fact that this sale is made to customers "who return." One succinct definition, mentioned in Chapter 27, is that "salesmanship is the art of selling goods that do not return to customers who do."

The customer's willingness to put the value of a product or service above the price asked for that product or service is essential in making any sale.

Although the wording of the definitions given above varies, the authors are in agreement that the product or service must satisfy the customer if the sale is to be successful. Nowhere, however, in the definitions is there a reference to the salesperson as a necessity in the selling act.

Nonpersonal Selling

Some selling is successfully done without the aid of a salesperson. Such selling is called *nonpersonal selling.* This kind of selling has proved so effective that there are constantly increasing efforts to make use of it. Nonpersonal selling concentrates on the product and its appeal for the customer. Some of the silent selling devices that help to distribute goods and, in some cases, services such as selling insurance, taking photos, or reproducing forms are the following:

- Well-written copy
- Attractive colors
- Eye-catching displays
- Packages with selling messages on them
- Tags and labels that answer customers' questions
- Vending machines that show the product, accept the money, give small amounts of change as needed, and dispense the product
- Catalogs with dramatic color photographs and detailed copy
- Circulars sent to the homes of customers
- Bill enclosures in full color with accompanying order forms
- Posters placed in well-traveled areas
- Open displays that invite examination of the merchandise

Some retailers have found these nonpersonal methods of selling more effective in moving merchandise than disinterested, uninformed salespeople. As one retailer remarked, "The most expensive employee in your store is the untrained, disinterested salesperson."

Personal Selling

In contrast to the ineffective salesperson, there is no substitute for the good salesperson in situations where the sale requires more than the routine handling of the product and the necessary recordkeeping. Good salespeople develop a customer following, build respect for the retail firm, create the concept of service, expand the interest and knowledge of their customers in the products they sell, and become known as authorities.

No matter how effectively mechanized our retailing organizations become, there is no substitute for interpersonal relations between salesperson and customer. Even mechanical marvels that show merchandise, explain its virtues, take money, dispense the product, and make change for the customer cannot replace the interested salesperson who thinks in response to a statement or question by the customer, who listens intently, and who interprets the customer's expressed wishes in terms of the merchandise or services available. In addition to handling personal selling within the store, salespeople may do door-to-door selling and in-home selling. In door-to-door selling, the merchandise is brought directly from the manufacturer or producer to the customers in their homes. In in-home selling, samples or the actual merchandise is brought from the retail store to the customers' homes so the customers can see the products in the setting in which those goods will be used. Both of these methods provide a service that is valued by the customers. Enormous volumes of merchandise may be distributed through such personal at-home service.

THE SALARY CONTINUUM FOR SALESPEOPLE

The wide range of selling talents and the variations in the demands for ability in selling result in extensive differences in salaries for salespeople. Those who act primarily as sales clerks and cashiers in handling transactions are usually paid the minimum salaries when they begin their jobs. Their subsequent increments, as long as they remain in these same positions, are also minimal. These people need little training, have only moderate educational requirements for these positions, and are easily replaced, since their jobs make few demands on their skill or ability. For these reasons, the salary scale for such positions continues to be near the minimum range.

The Salaries of Sales Consultants

As the knowledge required for the job increases, as the training necessary to do a good job is extended, as the skills and abilities the people acquire make them more able to do a good job, and as the people move into the ranks of sales consultants, salaries are also increased. Salespeople may be paid straight hourly or weekly salaries. Salary plus commission, straight commission, or salary plus bonus are other forms of payment. These were discussed in Chapter 10. The salaries for retail selling jobs range on a continuum from the minimum to as much as $25,000 or more yearly for commissioned salespeople in specialized areas where knowledge and consultation ability are needed. Women who sell ready-to-wear in fine specialty stores, men who sell men's clothing in fine men's-wear stores, special cosmetics demonstrators, and furniture, carpet, major appliance, automotive, jewelry, shoe, and fur salespeople are examples of those who may make such sizable salaries. In between the two extremes are those salespeople who receive salaries in the intermediate range—from $5,000 to $20,000 per year. They sell all categories of merchandise and service.

Retail selling, therefore, may be highly remunerative for those who wish to make a career in the field and who have the background knowledge and talents needed to become truly able sales consultants.

The Salary Percent

The productivity of the salesperson is rated by his or her *salary percent,* also called the selling cost percent. This is an objective measure of the person's selling ability. Other objective factors are also considered in the overall rating.

The selling cost percent is derived by dividing the total salary by the net sales. *Net sales* in this case means the total dollar amount of all the salesperson's transactions minus customers' returns of merchandise for credit. Thus, if a salesperson sold $2,500 worth of goods in one week and that person's returns equaled $500, the net sales for that period would be $2,000. If the salary for that week was $165, the salary percent would be 8.25: $165 ÷ $2,000 = 8.25%.

Salary percent ranges from around 2 to a high of about 20. The average salary percent in department stores of all sizes is about 8.5. Usually lower percents are maintained in stores that feature only limited service, while larger percents are characteristic of full-service stores. However, types of merchandise also affect the percents. Clothing patterns, which take a great deal of knowledge and time to sell but which have a low unit sale, usually have high selling percents, while furs, which are, individually, fairly sizable purchases, may have relatively low percents. Junior coordinates and coats also are in the lower percentage ranges.

SALESPEOPLE AND MERCHANDISE KNOWLEDGE

Since the turn of the century the need for unskilled labor and farm labor has decreased while the demand for skilled technicians and professional workers has increased. Women have won the right to vote and have invaded the work force of the nation in unparalleled numbers. Workdays and workweeks have been shortened, and vacation periods have been lengthened, providing for more leisure-time activities. Automobiles have provided mobility for a growing population and changed the places of living, working, and vacationing. Americans of all ages have increased their knowledge through formal and informal education.

The triumvirate of producers, distributors, and consumers has made possible standards of living undreamed of at the turn of the century. Producers have spent billions of dollars in research to make products that the retailers have distributed to their customers. Consumers have enthusiastically accepted the products of test-tube research and technology in such varied fields as clothing and accessories, household goods, foods, and automobiles and their components.

The efforts of the producer and retailer are needed to bring the merchandise marvels to the consumer. Retailers are the purchasing agents for their communities. They provide the showcases for the products. Through the retailers' efforts the consumers are informed of the potential of the products that are available. The entire success of these efforts, however, resides at the point of sale where the customer and the merchandise meet.

The merchants who are concerned about the quality of the products they sell are the best safeguards for the customer. Store-owned testing laboratories for large firms or independent testing services used by small firms are the means alert merchants use to check manufacturers' qualities and standards claims. Constant vigilance keeps merchandise safe to use and statements either in advertising or in selling reliable.

THE IMPORTANCE OF MERCHANDISE KNOWLEDGE

Whether products are sold to the customer through nonpersonal selling methods or through personal salesmanship, knowledge of merchandise is essential if the seller is to impart to the customers the values of the products among which they have to choose. A successful sale depends almost entirely on the significance of the selling message in terms of the customer's needs and wants.

Knowing the Facts

All facts about merchandise are technical. Some of these facts become familiar to customers through use of the products themselves, through the advertising about the products, or through the opportunity to see the products or to read about them. The vast bulk of facts about products, however, are esoteric. This means that those facts are known to the select few who process the raw materials or who manufacture the merchandise. An examination of any newspaper advertising will reveal some of these facts.

Explaining the Facts

Facts tell what the product itself is. For any product the following listing of basic facts could be given:

- The style or design of the product
- The materials from which the product is made

- The construction of the product
- The finish given to the product or its components
- The decoration, if any, applied to the surface
- Unusual handling or care properties

Additional information such as the size of a product or a set, the number of pieces in the set, and the capacity also makes up the list of basic facts.

Since few customers are sophisticated in their knowledge of these and other technical facts, the facts must be explained in language the customer can understand through personal or nonpersonal selling.

Using the Formula for Value

The facts, or "is" information, must also be interpreted in customer language to tell the "does" information or benefits of the product. This interpretation is the most important part of any selling message. Fact information may be of interest and importance in some instances, but if one type of information is to be omitted, the fact information can most successfully be left out. The "does" information should be incorporated as needed in any selling message. A successful *formula for value* must explain the benefits the customer is to derive from ownership and use of the merchandise.

Contrast the following sales talks by two salespeople selling the identical children's shoes to two different customers:

Salesperson A

This a blucher oxford.

Salesperson B

This blucher oxford is built so that the laces across the instep may be as loose or as snug as desired. This shoe will adapt exactly to your child's feet. At the same time, it will offer the necessary support and be completely comfortable.

By using the formula for value that tells the customer the benefits of the product, Salesperson B assured the customer that the shoes would be a good buy for a young child. Salesperson A, by contrast, did not make the sale.

HOW TO OBTAIN MERCHANDISE KNOWLEDGE

There are many sources of merchandise information. Anyone who wants to know about merchandise can seek the facts in a variety of ways.

People Are a Valuable Source

The store buyer and the merchandise manager who decided to buy the merchandise usually have detailed information about the products. This information may be imparted to employees at periodic staff meetings or, in the case of central buyers, on information sheets sent to the store managers or department managers, who then meet with the store personnel. Fashion coordinators who advise buyers and who give fashion shows for customers need such knowledge and can impart it to other employees.

Training department members, although not familiar with each article of merchandise in each department, have broad, general knowledge about merchandise. They may impart this knowledge at departmental, division, or store meetings or when special employee fashion shows are held; in classroom sessions; or through training manuals distributed to new personnel.

Other salespeople in the department and in related departments may be knowledgeable about the merchandise and may be of considerable help in answering questions and providing a model for demonstration.

Customers may have knowledge about certain products and their uses. By listening to their questions, statements, and complaints, salespeople may learn many interesting facts about the products they sell. Also, by knowing their customers' interests, salespeople know what questions to ask when seeking information about the products.

Manufacturers' representatives who visit the store are a valuable source of merchandise information. Sometimes these representatives will hold special meetings to inform salespeople about new products or to explain advantages and limitations of merchandise. Some representatives will actually take over sales so that sales personnel can observe special selling techniques developed by the manufacturers for certain products.

Tours of the manufacturing plant may be arranged by some manufacturers' representatives for store employees. This is one of the most interesting and informative ways to learn about products. Substitutes for such trips in the form of films and sound-slide presentations are made by some manufacturers. These may be shown in the store either before it opens for business or during the day when employees can be spared from their work.

For those stores that maintain testing laboratories, store testing personnel can provide valuable technical information about products. The chemists and laboratory workers—who actually test the items for their durability, their care features, their dimensional stability, and other characteristics—have firsthand knowledge that they can impart to other store personnel.

Comparison shoppers who visit competing stores to check prices and assortments may also be able to provide salespeople with some product selling points.

Publications Are a Valuable Source

Publishing firms, manufacturers, trade associations, and federal, state, and local governments all produce materials containing knowledge important for those handling merchandise.

Books may be found on almost every type of merchandise. These are available through school and public libraries and bookstores. They may be found by looking in the catalog files under the product itself, such as furs, leather, textiles, wallpaper, porcelains, automotive products, or paints. Some books, such as *Know Your Merchandise: for Retailers and Consumers, Fourth Edition* are used as textbooks and cover entire areas of subject matter.

Magazines and newspapers, for both consumers and the trade, abound in information about products for the customer.

Women's Wear Daily, Homefurnishings Daily, and *Supermarket News* are just three examples of the hundreds of trade magazines and papers that carry information in every issue about products. *Consumer Reports* is a publication that explains comparative tests of products and warns of dangers in the use of hazardous products.

Every major industry also has trade journals containing information about products being developed and produced. Some of these trade journals also contain training manuals. Training manuals may also be published by trade associations and manufacturers and distributed to stores that carry their goods. Large stores may also develop training manuals for the use of their own personnel. These are usually concise and easy to read and pertain specifically to the products carried in those stores.

The local, state, and federal government publications especially produced for consumers are often excellent sources of merchandise information. Lists of these are available through the Commerce Department or the Consumer's Bureau of the government.

Unions, such as the ILGWU (International Ladies' Garment Workers' Union), also produce training manuals on the products their workers make.

In addition to the above, organizations such as Better Business Bureaus, the National Retail Merchants Association, the National Manufacturers Association, and trade associations for each category of merchandise have some materials of interest.

The Merchandise Is a Valuable Source

Careful examination of the merchandise itself will often aid in selling the product. Labels and tags placed on the goods by the manufacturer can be

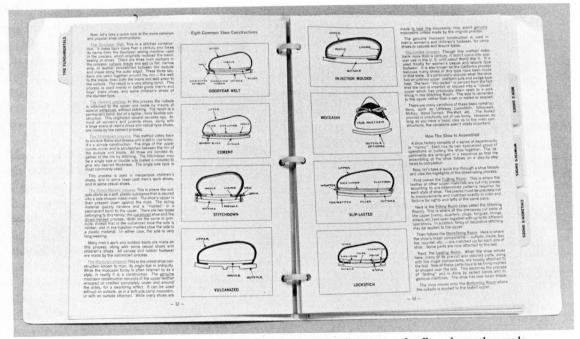

This manual is published by the National Shoe Retailers Association. It offers shoe salespeople helpful information such as how shoes are made, what materials are used in shoe construction, and how to fit shoes.
Photograph by Fern Logan

used as sources of information. Labels often contain information about the ingredients or components and also about the special uses and care needed for the product.

The salesperson's own experience and that of friends and customers may also provide valuable clues about the product. Complaints from customers and returns may be analyzed for information about the product.

Schools Are a Valuable Source

Technical and vocational schools may offer courses for those who need to know about merchandise. Interior decoration, fashion, textiles, nontextiles, color and design, and food preparation are some examples.

CONSTANT CHANGE IS A CHALLENGE

There is nothing static in the world of merchandise. Daily the wizards with their test tubes are bringing out new marvels. No store personnel can therefore ever feel content with their product knowledge. The salespeople may be called upon to use only small amounts of their total knowledge about the product, but the broad base of knowledge that they have serves to give them confidence and assurance as they sell. The customers, in turn, sense this vast reservoir of knowledge and put their faith in the information given by such well-informed advisers. A good slogan for a store to use is "Know your merchandise if you would sell your merchandise successfully!"

CHARACTERISTICS OF SELLING PERSONNEL

Many tests have revealed that successful salespeople have abilities and traits that are different from those of salespeople who are not so successful. Some salespeople with the same amount of training who are selling in the same department, handling the same merchandise, and waiting on the same customers consistently have higher total sales at the end of the day than other

salespeople. Through analysis of the characteristics of these outstanding salespeople, certain traits have been identified as the ones that make them successful. Success-producing characteristics may be classified under three headings: human relations, personal, and mental.

Human Relations Traits

One of the most important characteristics of any person who deals with other people is his or her liking to be with people. Hand in hand with this is the ability to get along well with people.

- *Objectivity* is one important trait. The person who is objective, who sees a problem from the other person's point of view, and who is able to understand the customer's interests and needs is the person who can best present merchandise appealingly.

- *Courtesy, friendliness, and enthusiasm* are all desirable characteristics of salespeople in their interrelationships with other people. These traits make customers feel welcome and make them enjoy their shopping experiences.

- *Ability to listen* is a crucial characteristic needed by the salesperson who has good interpersonal relations. The salesperson who listens attentively selects goods according to the customer's wishes.

- *Emotional maturity* is another desirable characteristic of good salespeople. When problems arise, they handle them as tactfully as possible. They treat others with consideration because they understand that emotions have no place on the selling floor in front of customers.

Personal Traits

Certain personal characteristics such as a pleasant appearance, good grooming, good health, cleanliness, a pleasing general expression, and good posture are also important features of the successful salesperson. The first impression the salesperson, as the representative of the firm, makes on customers is important. If the store is a fashion store, the salesperson must impart a fashion image. Clothes, hair styles, and accessories must be correct and appropriate for that first good impression.

- *Good grooming,* including cleanliness, is noticeable almost immediately.

- *Health* is also a most significant personal characteristic. A person who is not healthy would be unable to stand retailing's pace very long. Good health is a requisite for doing the job successfully.

- A *pleasant expression* is important for a salesperson. The face mirrors the thoughts of most individuals. The person who enjoys the job usually looks pleasant. A happy person projects such feelings to others.

- *Good posture* reflects a person's assurance and pride. A person who stands erect and who has good bearing radiates confidence and helps to reassure the customer about the ability to be of assistance. By contrast, the person who slouches or slumps looks unsure and appears inadequate as an adviser.

Mental Traits
Retailing is a dynamic, fast-moving business requiring mental alertness, a good memory, accuracy, creativity, and imagination.

- *Mental alertness* is necessary for people who succeed in retailing. They must always be alert to what is going on around them. Their minds must be attuned like radar to everything they see and hear.

- A *good memory* for faces and names is important also. Customers like to be remembered, and the able salesperson tries, whenever possible, to remember customers' names and to call them by name. A good memory helps the salesperson to know what merchandise is in stock, where it is located, what orders are outstanding, and when merchandise may be expected. It also enables the salesperson to retain countless merchandise facts; to remember

terms, laws, and rulings; and to relate desirable information to the customers.

- *Accuracy* is an indispensable characteristic for salespeople. Since every transaction involves merchandise or services as well as the money paid for those items, accurate recordkeeping is essential.

- *Creativity and imagination* are both helpful traits for the salesperson who must interpret the customer's needs and wants in terms of the merchandise available. Developing sales talks, answering customer's objections intelligently, and handling queries from all kinds of people require creativity and imagination.

The Effective Salesperson
The salesperson who does a good job really enjoys selling. This person considers the job challenging and is rewarded when products or services that satisfy the needs and desires of the customers are sold.

The traits mentioned above are those any well-educated, able person could develop. The person who likes selling, who has an aptitude for it, and who enjoys helping other people is the person who will be best suited for a career as a salesperson.

THE SALESPERSON'S JOB

The primary work of the person employed to sell to customers is the face-to-face contacts with customers. No salesperson, however, is kept busy during the entire working day in such contacts. Customers are often scarce during morning and late afternoon hours. Therefore, additional tasks related to selling are performed by salespeople during those slack times. These often prepare the salesperson to know the merchandise and its location better than otherwise would be possible.

Stockkeeping
Most salespeople have certain responsibilities for stockkeeping in their assigned sections. They may arrange the merchandise neatly and see that

THE POWER OF PERSONAL SELLING

all sizes, colors, and styles of the various items are in forward stock and, whenever possible, also visible to customers. Many managers ask their salespeople to advise them about the products customers ask for that are not in stock. Some also ask salespeople for their advice on what products they think could profitably be added to the department.

Housekeeping

Salespeople are responsible not only for seeing that the stock in their assigned sections is neat and complete but also for dusting cases, dusting merchandise that is exposed, and generally cleaning the counter areas where their work is concentrated. They may have large covers to throw over the merchandise at night to protect it from soil. These covers are removed in the morning and neatly stacked out of sight.

Clerical Work

Certain clerical work in recording sales is done directly by salespeople who may be responsible for both a cash register or terminal and a sales book. Those with registers or terminals must obtain their allotted change in a cash box each morning from the control department, count the money, and record the amount. At the end of the working day, they return to the control department both the money taken in from customers during that day and the amount they received in the morning cash box.

The salesperson must know how to handle and record all types of sales, including charge, COD, will-call, layaway, part payment, and hold. The salesperson must also know how to give customers receipts for these various transactions. All these sales, in addition to being recorded, must be tallied. Buyers or department managers want totals of all the day's sales handed in at the close of the salesperson's day.

In addition to keeping records of money handled and sales made, some salespeople make exchanges of goods for customers, and some handle customer complaints and returns. Salespeople may also be asked to make counts of merchandise on hand periodically for order purposes. Some may even write out order forms for buyers' signatures. Some salespeople may check incoming merchandise and mark the prices on those goods. Filling out want slips, counting goods for staple stock lists, filling telephone and mail orders, and following up on reorders to manufacturers may also be tasks performed by some salespeople.

Protection

Salespeople provide a valuable protection service for the merchandise for which they are responsible. Just their physical presence deters most shoplifters. Their alertness to people in the area and their care in showing merchandise also help prevent theft. In addition, salespeople can assure that merchandise being handled by customers will not be abused. This is a valuable form of protection that saves costly markdowns for the firm.

Direction of Customers

In large stores salespeople offer a directory service for customers. They can help customers not only to locate merchandise areas but also to find service areas and learn where to go for the products and services they seek. Customers dislike having to ask several times how to find a particular item. The more precise the first direction, the more likely the customer is to find the item and to purchase it in that store.

TOPICS FOR DISCUSSION

1. Explain what the trends in selling have been over the past two decades, and give the reasons for these trends.
2. What is meant by limited selling service?

3. Contrast the work of a sales clerk with that of a sales consultant.
4. Discuss what is meant by nonpersonal selling, and give examples of such selling.
5. Discuss the statement frequently heard that "salespeople's salaries are always low."
6. Explain how a salesperson's salary percent would be determined.
7. Explain what is meant by the "formula for value," and describe in what manner it might be used as an effective tool in selling.
8. Human relations traits are considered important for successful selling. List and explain what these traits include for salespeople.
9. What personal traits help a salesperson to be effective, and why are they important?
10. What mental traits help a salesperson to be effective, and why are they important?

MATHEMATICS FOR RETAILING

You are considering a salary increase of $5 per week for one of your salespeople. Using the formula "total salary divided by net sales equals selling cost percent," work out the following problems. Do your calculations on a separate sheet of paper.

1. What is the salesperson's selling cost percent if $975 worth of goods is sold by this person, there are no returns, and the present salary is $95 per week?
2. If the salary was increased by $5 and the weekly sales remained the same, what would the selling cost percent be?
3. If the weekly salary is $100, approximately how much would the salesperson need to sell to match the selling cost percent at the previous salary level?

MANAGING HUMAN RELATIONS

One salesperson in a ready-to-wear department was known by her co-workers as a "sales grabber." If a customer returned to buy something she had been shown previously, she would invariably be approached by Miss Sales Grabber. This salesperson frequently told customers that she was assigned to take care of them, even though they asked for other salespeople. Since the salespeople were paid a salary plus commission, this sales grabbing caused a great deal of bickering. As department manager, what steps would you take to correct this situation? Be prepared to discuss your suggestions.

DECISION MAKING

A store was situated in the heart of the office district of a large city. Three salespeople were in the hosiery department of the store. Ms. Ace was a part-time salesperson who came to work at 11 a.m. and left at 3 p.m. daily. She consistently sold a great deal of merchandise and was frequently highly commended by the department manager. Ms. Bray and Ms. Charles were full-timers. Each worked from 10 a.m. until 6 p.m. daily. Ms. Bray went to lunch from 11 a.m. to 12 p.m., and Ms. Charles had lunch from 12:30 to 1:30 daily.

The great rush of customers was during the lunch-hour period from 11 a.m. until 2 p.m. Virtually no one was ever in the store to buy from 10 to 11 a.m., and only a few customers were in the store from 2:15 until 5 p.m. From 5 until 5:30 p.m., when the offices let out, a few people shopped on occasion.

Ms. Ace had a selling cost percent of 6. She did no other work in the department because she was kept busy with customers. Ms. Bray and Ms. Charles had selling cost percents of 11 and 12 respectively. Each of them did stockkeeping, took stock counts, answered telephones, filled mail and telephone orders, and helped ticket merchandise occasionally. Each was responsible for display and arrangement at her own counters. Ms. Bray and Ms. Charles were unhappy because they did not think Ms. Ace merited so much praise.

1. Was the manager justified in commending Ms. Ace so highly for her selling ability?
2. Do you have any recommendations for improving this situation?

Be prepared to discuss your answers.

CAREER LADDER

Assume a young person entered retailing during the time he or she was still a student in high school. The student worked in a supermarket as a cashier or bagger at a minimum salary. On a separate sheet of paper, list what paths that person might take over the next five years to become a sales consultant at a salary of $10,000 to $15,000 per year.

CUSTOMER OPERATIONS FUNCTIONS

chapter 29

CONSUMER CREDIT

People who eat out; who travel by rail, plane, or bus; who purchase at local or central city stores; who order goods by telephone; who rent cars or other articles; who "pay as they go" for education; or who need identification often find that credit cards make all these activities possible. Charge cards have become a familiar possession of most people in the United States.

CHANGING NATURE OF CREDIT SELLING

Charge or *credit selling* is a method of giving customers present purchasing power, with payment permitted at a later, stated period of time. Credit selling allows customers to possess and use products while they pay for them or to avail themselves of services for which they pay at a later date.

Initially credit was issued at the customer's request only. Then merchants began to induce affluent customers to shop in their places of business by offering to establish credit to make shopping easier and more convenient. As interest in credit grew, more and more firms began to make this service available to customers. Since World War II, credit selling has swept the nation, and firms that had steadfastly refused to grant credit—such as Macy's, J. C. Penney, Ohrbach's, and, more recently, many discount houses—have succumbed to the trend and initiated this service for their customers.

Today credit selling is promoted by stores, banks, restaurants, hotels, service stations, and credit card companies. Credit is so extensively granted that people in the United States can exist totally on "buy now—pay later" plans.

CHANGING NATURE OF RESTRICTIONS ON CREDIT AND DEBTS

Concurrent with the offering of more extensive credit has been the lowering of bars in other ways. The debtor laws in this country one hundred years ago were brutally severe. A debtor who did not pay his or her bills could be confined to prison for life. Many laws today, however, favor the debtor. Today creditors extend credit at their own risk. Bankruptcy laws favor the debtor; filing lawsuits to collect from the debtor is costly; and garnishment of salaries is outlawed in

Many retailers make a special effort to encourage customers to apply for credit.
Courtesy Montgomery Ward

Fair Credit Reporting Act

Under the Fair Credit Reporting Act of 1970, which became effective April 25, 1971, any store that rejects a credit application or increases the charge for credit on the basis of a private credit agency report must tell the customer involved the name and address of that private agency.

Fair Credit Billing Act

The Fair Credit Billing Act, which became effective October 28, 1975, was created to protect the consumer against inaccurate and unfair billing and credit card practices.

Credit card companies and firms that provide credit have sought in the past to charge the same prices regardless of whether the customer paid in cash or charged the purchase. This new law, initiated by a suit brought by Consumers Union against the American Express Company and other credit card issuers, declares that it is illegal not to allow discounts for cash payments. Further, discounts for cash payments of 5 percent or less do not require disclosure of the annual percentage rates on credit transactions.

Unclaimed Credit Balances

In 1975, many stores were required to refund to customers all unclaimed credit balances exceeding $1. Customers who had credit balances from returns or from excessive charges were to receive a periodic statement of the balance due to them. Further, those customers were to be informed that they could have a cash refund of this balance. Stores were prevented from writing off or deleting credit balances from customers' accounts, even if those accounts were inactive.

Equal Credit Opportunity Act

The Equal Credit Opportunity Act, passed in 1974 and effective in November 1975, banned any bias in granting credit based on the sex of the person concerned—either the borrower or the person applying for credit. After November 1976, women could have credit ratings separate from the ratings of their husbands. Further, if a person is refused credit, the reason for the re-

twenty-three states, and the balance of the states have curbed its use.

Consumer Credit Protection Act

Under the 1968 Consumer Credit Protection Act, which took effect July 1, 1969, finance companies, banks, other lenders, and retailers are required to inform borrowers and credit customers of credit charges. Annual percentage rates and interest charges in dollars and cents on the balance owed must be shown. Exempted from this ruling are installment purchases of items costing $25 up to $75 if the finance charges are less than $5. For purchases costing more than $75, no disclosure of rates and other credit charges is necessary if finance charges are $7.50 or less.

Another provision of the Consumer Credit Protection Act exempts at least $48 of a person's weekly take-home pay from garnishment and permits no more than 25 percent of the remaining take-home pay to be garnisheed.

fusal must be given. This reason, however, may be given orally, and no requirement has been made that it be in writing.

ADVANTAGES OF CREDIT

The advantages of being able to use credit—both for the customers and for the retailers—have made credit selling the important force that it is today in business.

For the Customers
In many cases credit selling allows customers to have more costly products than they would be able to buy if they had to pay cash. It enables them to enjoy the use of the products while they pay for them. It helps them to budget their money, and it is a method of forcing a certain amount of self-restraint, since they must spend their money for the things they have bought rather than on small day-to-day whims or fancies. People who only work seasonally or who have periods of unemployment can still have products they need and want by the use of deferred payments.

For the Retailers
Credit has proved to be very advantageous for retailers. It helps them to sell big-ticket items, which they otherwise might not be able to sell. It builds customer loyalty. Once customers have found a store to be dependable and reliable, they will want to return to that store. The retailers also get to know who their reliable, steady-paying customers are, and they are able to direct their merchandise promotions to those people. Because they can sell higher-priced items and more items, their business volume increases. They also build store traffic and sales, since time-payment customers see products they need and want and purchase them when they come into the store to make their payments.

DISADVANTAGES OF CREDIT

Some disadvantages exist—both for customers and for retailers—in the use of credit.

For the Customers
The trend in legislation to protect consumers will undoubtedly gain momentum as charge selling increases. Flagrant abuses of credit selling, when exposed, have shown that they occurred primarily in areas where disadvantaged persons who could not or did not read contracts were pressured into signing by door-to-door sales agents or unscrupulous merchants. One merchant in a disadvantaged area, for example, had his customers sign a contract that froze their bank savings accounts until their bills were totally paid. Another door-to-door sales agent sold a set of books by misrepresenting himself as being sent by the local board of education. The customer thought the set of books would only cost a total of $400 but had actually paid $1,400 when a suit for nonpayment of balance was instituted.

Customers, lured by easy payment plans, have in some cases overextended themselves. For this reason consumer education has become desirable. Schools are becoming more and more concerned with education for the consumer that will lead to the economic well-being of the individual and that individual's family.

Credit when not planned wisely can be a pitfall for the individual or the family.

For the Retailers
Since customers are more casual in buying on credit, more returns result from charge purchases than from cash purchases. These returns are costly for any store.

A certain amount of bad-debt loss for the retailer is inevitable in any credit selling. While the majority of customers are honest and will pay their bills at least eventually, there are always a few who for various reasons will never pay. Death, divorce, loss of jobs, illness, disaster—many situations may occur to prevent payment. If a store is forced to sue a customer to receive payment, the court costs and time consumed can often be more expensive than the amount of money recovered. Dunning customers also loses the goodwill that the retailer works so hard to establish.

Even with the credit charges that customers pay, stores often lose money on credit operations because of the additional employees needed to handle credit transactions, to keep records, to mail bills, and to record payments.

TYPES OF CREDIT PLANS

As credit buying and selling have increased, various methods of payment have been made available to customers. Most firms use one or more plans to attract customers. These plans include regular charge accounts, also called open-account credit; option credit that varies somewhat from the regular charge account; revolving credit; installment credit; and coupon book plans. In addition, some stores belong to bank or other credit-card plans that permit customers to charge purchases in member stores.

Regular Charge Accounts or Open-Account Credit

The least-costly type of charge account and one of the oldest types of charge plans for the customer is the regular charge account. Once credit is established in opening such an account, there are no extra charges for the customers who pay bills promptly. Bills are issued once a month, and the store usually expects to be paid within 10 days after the billing date. There is no charge, however, even if a customer delays payment beyond that time.

Option-Terms Plan

For customers with regular charge accounts who do not want to pay their bills promptly, an option-terms plan has been instituted by many retailers. Under this plan, the customers sign contracts giving them an option of paying on time with no carrying charge or of delaying payment and paying a service charge for bills past due for 30 or more days. This is a variation on the revolving charge plan discussed next.

Revolving Charge Plans

Revolving credit first appeared on the retail scene in the 1930s, and it zoomed in popularity after World War II. This is the fastest-growing type of credit today.

This newer type of charge plan enables a customer to establish a line of credit with a store. By meeting minimum payment terms, the customer can continue to charge additional amounts indefinitely up to a given credit limit. Carrying charges are assessed on a monthly basis on the unpaid amounts. This type of credit, which made possible extending credit to customers who previously had not been able to obtain merchandise through delayed payments, fixes a credit limit on those purchases. The customer may avoid credit charges by paying the bill in full within 30 days. Balances after that time are subject to service charges.

The retailers can use this method of credit as a promotional device by advising the customers what their "open to buy" is—what the difference is between their upper credit limit and their balance and how much they can charge without changing their monthly payments.

Credit limits for this type of charge plan are usually determined by multiplying by 6 the amount a customer can afford to pay monthly. Thus, if a customer can afford to pay $25 monthly, the credit limit would be set at $150.

Since charges are made only on the balance remaining each month, it is difficult to specify the actual annual rate of interest. Retailers therefore prefer the term "service charge" in referring to this interest. Service charges are usually $1\frac{1}{2}$ percent a month on the unpaid balance. For example, if a customer bought a television set at $158 on revolving credit, there would be no service charge for the first 30 days if at least one-twelfth of the cost was paid in the first month. In the second month, an average charge of 1.5 percent would be made on the unpaid balance. Such a service charge usually averages between 10 and 11 percent a year.

Some states restrict the amounts of service charges that may be made. Pennsylvania, for example, allows a maximum charge of 1.25 percent per month on balances. In New York, 1.5

percent may be charged on balances up to $500; thereafter, the limit is 1 percent.

Under the Consumer Credit Protection Act, both monthly and annual interest rates for revolving charge plans must be stated, unless those charges amount to less than 50 cents per month and were billed as service charges.

Installment Credit

Large expensive items that are durable goods and that can be repossessed if not paid for can be sold on the basis of a different type of credit. This type may be established for just one single sale of a large item. It is known as *installment credit*. The terms of payment are adapted to the customer's ability to make monthly payments. Carrying charges assessed for this method of delayed payment cover the added costs of doing business this way.

Offering this type of credit permits the store to trade up in the selling of big-ticket merchandise. Therefore, this type of credit has been responsible for the sale of merchandise such as pianos, automobiles, furniture, major appliances, jewelry, and furs.

Installment credit necessitates a down payment at the time the merchandise is purchased. The purchaser signs a contract requiring that the remaining payments be made as specified. Furthermore, this contract usually permits repossession of the goods if payments are not made as agreed. The contract also calls for separate carrying charges to be paid for the extension of credit.

Coupon Book Plans

Rather than providing a revolving credit plan, some retailers issue coupon books. The customers' credit limits are established, and books of coupons equal to this credit limit are issued to them. They then use the coupons in this book as money to buy the things they want. The book is paid for on the time-payment plan, and there is a carrying charge for each month until all payments are completed. Customers particularly favor this type of plan when making many small purchases, such as at Christmastime.

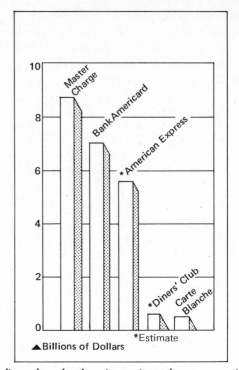

Credit cards make shopping easier and more convenient. This graph illustrates the proportion of credit buying for each of the major national credit card companies.
Reprinted from the August 4, 1975 issue of *Business Week* by special permission. © 1975 by McGraw-Hill, Inc.

Bank Credit Plans and Commercial Credit Plans

Increasingly, banks and commercial credit firms are entering the credit market. A bank or firm arranges with certain stores to charge purchases for customers who are carrying the card issued by the bank or firm. In turn, the bank or firm pays the merchants for the products the customers have charged, deducting a fee of usually 5 to 6 percent for this service. The bank or firm then charges the customers for the purchases made. If a customer pays within 10 days, no service charge is made. If the customer chooses to make payments on a time-payment plan, a service charge is made on the balance that is owed. Many of these credit plans, such as American Express and Master Charge, give the customer credit in stores, transportation firms, hotels, and other retail businesses throughout the world.

Pseudo Credit Plans

Methods of selling that do not involve actually establishing credit for the customer but which give an opportunity to delay payment are provided in most stores. Such methods are known as *layaway plans, deposit plans,* and *will-call plans.* In each case, the customers make a small down payment, usually 10 to 20 percent of the price of the merchandise, and the article or articles are put away for the customers and held until they have completed their payments. Then the merchandise is released.

Although merchants do not risk the actual loss of the goods by this method of selling, they do risk losing the sale if the customers do not complete their payments or if they change their mind and want their money back. Thus, customers who "lay away" winter coats with a small down payment and who later change their mind may have cost the store the opportunity to sell those coats to other customers at the time when such coats were in demand.

Deposit Accounts

On occasion a store may serve as a kind of banker for the customer, allowing the customer to deposit money before making any purchases and then deducting the cost of purchases from the customer's account. Under this plan, customers have to be sure not to overdraw their accounts by excessive purchases. If they do, billing is required. If the balance owed is not paid within a certain length of time, it becomes subject to service charges.

A store may credit such deposits with interest if they remain in the store's bank for several months. Accounts of this type necessitate billing procedures similar to those of regular charge accounts.

DETERMINING CREDIT POLICIES AND PROCEDURES

When retailers choose to offer credit, they immediately face many problems. First, they must determine which type or types of credit they will offer their customers. Next, they must set up procedures to obtain applications from customers. Then they must decide how they will check the applicants, how they will set up credit limits, how they will identify their customers, how they will authorize credit sales, how they will bill their customers, and how they will follow up on slow-paying and nonpaying customers.

The Application Blank

Once retailers have determined that they will extend credit to their customers and have established the procedures for granting credit, they will find that they will rely heavily for information upon the credit application form. This form gives the retailers personal information about their customers as well as a financial profile. The form includes spaces for the following facts:

- The name and address of the customer
- Whether the customer owns a home or rents one
- How long the customer has lived at the current address
- Whether the customer is married, single, or divorced
- The number of children, if any
- Where the customer banks
- Where the customer is employed, and for how long
- Other places where the customer has established credit

If the application records are updated from time to time, and if they include information on birth dates of children and others to whom gifts are given, such records can be used as sales promotion files for special mailing pieces.

Character, Capacity, and Capital

Known as the "three Cs," character, capacity, and capital are the factors that a merchant checks to determine whether an applicant is a good credit risk.

Character. The character of applicants may be determined by their willingness to accept responsibility and to pay their debts promptly; by the length of time they have held a job; by the length of time they have lived in their present home; by their record of payment of gas, electric, telephone, and other bills; and by the judgment of those who know them. Investigating character can be done for a fee through the local credit clearinghouse affiliated with the National Retail Credit Association.

Capacity. The applicants' capacity refers to their income and their ability to pay their bills out of that income.

Capital. The assets of the individual, such as property and securities, are referred to as capital. Some wealthy people may have no current income from a job but own a great amount of property, stocks, and bonds that provide income.

Of these three standards, character is considered to be the most important, since people of fine character will pay their bills at some time, even if their income is low and they possess no capital.

STEPS IN ESTABLISHING CREDIT FOR THE CUSTOMER

Although different stores use different methods of establishing accounts, most stores at some point go through several steps, including interviewing the customer, having the customer fill out an application, obtaining information about the customer, approving the application, establishing credit limits for the account, and informing the customer of the acceptance of the account and of its use.

Interview
The information that appears on the application blank is supplemented by an interview with the customer. The interview also gives the store an opportunity to have its credit interviewer advise the customer of the advantages of using the charge account wisely.

Application Check
The local credit bureau usually checks the application, since it has reports from all agencies with which the customer has business dealings. Consequently, reliable information is available about most people, except for newcomers to a community or people who are establishing their first home.

Credit Application Approval
The results of the interview and the check on the information placed on the application determine the credit application approval. Rarely does a retailer have reason to refuse credit allowances to regularly employed persons.

Establishment of Credit Limits
Current income is usually used as a basis for establishing credit limits. There are no set rules about this, but often the limit is about twice the weekly income. If down payments are to be made on merchandise, and if weekly or monthly payments are to be made, the credit limit might be much higher.

Customer Notification
Customers may be informed about acceptance by letter or in person. At the same time, the customers may be told how to use their identification cards, how to safeguard them, and how to report the loss of the cards. The customers should also be informed of the method of billing and the time allotted for the payment of bills.

IDENTIFICATION

Once credit is established for a customer, protection of the customer's account must be provided by the store through some means of identifying the customer. Stores for years have attempted to educate customers to carry their identification plates with them and to use the plates whenever they charge a purchase. Customers in select specialty stores often dislike being asked for identification, but as stores grow larger and more impersonal, as more customers use charge accounts, and as identification for data processing becomes more routine, stores have to become more insistent that their regulations for identification be adhered to. Customers can charge without proper identification in most stores, but there are necessary delays both in granting the permission and later in processing the account.

In addition to the identification in the form of a charge plate, many stores ask for the customer's signature on the sales check. This serves to prove that the customer made the purchase as well as to identify the customer as the person authorized to use the account.

Trends in identification promised by manufacturers of electronic devices include voice identification. Voice profiles, which electronic devices can read instantaneously, are forecast. The customer will simply speak into a machine, and identification will be made immediately by the voice pattern exhibited. This, of course, will make lost cards valueless, since voice patterns are as individual as fingerprints and cannot be exactly duplicated.

AUTHORIZATION

After the customer has been properly identified, the second problem is that of authorizing the amount of the sale that has been made. Most stores set limits, and so salespeople are required to check for authorization for purchases beyond those amounts. For example, purchases under $15 which the customers plan to take with them may need no authorization. Sales over that amount, however, must be checked by the salesperson before the goods can be issued. This is usually done by telephoning the credit office, reading the customer's charge number, and giving the amount being charged. An authorization clerk in the credit office then checks the account and notes if it is all right for the customer to

charge that amount. If not, the customer will be asked to go to the credit office to talk over the planned purchase. This floor check gives the credit office a chance to talk with a customer whose account is overdue, or who has paid bills slowly in the past, or whose credit limit has been exceeded by previous charges.

Electronic data processing has made authorization checks almost instantaneous. The customer's credit card can be put into a machine at the point of sale. This machine is connected to the credit files, and it searches the account and reports back on the authorization within seconds.

Packages to be sent to the customer also have to be authorized. Authorization may be done in the same manner as for charge-take transactions. Or a system of "draw back" can be used. When the sales check reaches the authorization section, the package is retrieved from the delivery section if there is any irregularity, and the customer is contacted before the delivery is made.

TIMING THE BILLING OF CUSTOMERS

Once the customers make use of their charge accounts, billing them is done at regular intervals. Most stores bill customers once a month. When stores had relatively few charge customers, billing occurred usually at the first of each month, but in recent years, because of the large numbers of charge customers, cycle billing has been used.

Cycle billing is done by rotating the billing operation. This permits bills to be mailed as they are prepared. Every working day during a month, a fraction of the store's bills is mailed. In this way the work of billing is staggered, and the work of collecting is similarly staggered. Customers usually prefer to receive their bills at the first of the month, but as more organizations bill according to this plan, customers are becoming used to bills arriving on different days of the month.

KINDS OF BILLING

Two kinds of billing are used by retail stores: country club billing and descriptive billing.

MELLON BANK

AMOUNT ENCLOSED

$ _____ . ____

CLOSING DATE	PAYMENT DUE DATE	ACCOUNT NUMBER	NEW BALANCE	MINIMUM PAYMENT DUE
02-27-__	03-22-__	190-135-246	393.02	19.00

WILLIAM ACKLEY
4347 Franklin Drive
Pittsburgh, PA 15230

TO ASSURE PROMPT CREDIT TO YOUR ACCOUNT, PLEASE RETURN
THIS PORTION WITH YOUR CHECK PAYABLE TO "MASTER CHARGE"

YOUR STATEMENT

YOUR REVOLVING CREDIT LINE (for regular purchases and cash advances)				YOUR FIXED PAYMENT PLAN (for major purchases only)	
TOTAL LINE	UNUSED AT BILLING	CLOSING DATE	ACCOUNT NUMBER	PAYMENT PER MONTH	BALANCE REMAINING
600.00	206.98	02-27-__	190-135-246		

REFERENCE NO.	DATE	NEW TRANSACTIONS	AMOUNT
3700689	02-01	AJAX OIL CO, BETHEL PARK, PA 15102	7.20
4801268	02-02	FAIR BUY DEPT STORE, GREEN VILLAGE	35.80
4100921	02-03	SKYWAY AIRWAYS, PGH, PA 15222	95.50
4601875	02-07	ARCADE RESTAURANT, PGH, PA 15219	22.50
5001346	02-18	PAYMENT - THANK YOU	65.00-
5706192	02-19	FAIR BUY DEPT STORE - CREDIT	10.50-
5204510	02-21	CASH ADVANCE - MELLON BANK, PGH, PA	100.00
5603462	02-23	SKAT OIL, NEW YORK, NY	6.45

YOUR MASTER CHARGE SUMMARY

TOTAL ACTIVITY SINCE YOUR LAST STATEMENT

DESCRIPTION	CASH ADVANCE	FIXED PAY PLAN	REGULAR PURCH.	TOTAL
YOUR PREVIOUS BALANCE	122.32		75.91	198.23
− PAYMENTS	40.11		24.89	65.00
− CREDITS			10.50	10.50
+ ADJUSTMENTS				
+ FINANCE CHARGE	2.02		.82	2.84
+ NEW TRANSACTIONS	100.00		167.45	267.45
= YOUR NEW BALANCE				393.02
				19.00

YOU CAN AVOID ADDITIONAL **FINANCE CHARGE** ON PURCHASES BY PAYING YOUR NEW BALANCE IN FULL
BEFORE 03-22-__ .

INFORMATION ABOUT YOUR FINANCE CHARGE

	CASH ADVANCE	FIXED PAY PLAN	REGULAR PURCH.	NOTICE: See Reverse Side for Important Information.
BALANCE SUBJECT TO FINANCE CHARGE	182.21		65.41	
MONTHLY PERIODIC RATE OF	1%	%	1.25%	
ANNUAL PERCENTAGE RATE	12%	%	15%	

Send Inquiries To: MELLON BANK P.O. BOX 360610 M PITTSBURGH, PA. 15230

CUSTOMER OPERATIONS FUNCTIONS

MASTER CHARGE

CASH ADVANCE TRANSACTIONS 12%	YOUR PREVIOUS BALANCE	CREDITS AND/OR ADJUSTMENTS	NO.	CASH ADVANCES THIS CYCLE	PAYMENTS	BALANCE SUBJECT TO FINANCE CHARGE	FINANCE CHARGE	YOUR NEW CASH ADVANCE BALANCE
	122 32 +	+		100 00 −	40 11 =		2 02 =	184 23

ANNUAL PERCENTAGE RATES

PURCHASE TRANSACTIONS (IF FINANCE CHARGE EXCEEDS 50¢) 15%	YOUR PREVIOUS BALANCE	CREDITS AND/OR ADJUSTMENTS	BALANCE SUBJECT TO FINANCE CHARGE	FINANCE CHARGE	NO.	PURCHASES THIS CYCLE	PAYMENTS	YOUR NEW PURCHASE BALANCE
	75 91 +	10 50 =		82 +	167 45	24 89 =	208 79

ACCOUNT NUMBER	CLOSING DATE
190-135-246	02-27-__

WILLIAM ACKLEY
4347 Franklin Drive
Pittsburgh, PA 15230

TOTAL OF NEW BALANCES
393 02

TO AVOID ADDITIONAL FINANCE CHARGES PAY TOTAL OF NEW BALANCES BEFORE →

MIN. PAYMENT DUE
19 00

03-22-__

MELLON BANK   P.O. BOX 360618M   PITTSBURGH, PA. 15230
PLEASE KEEP THIS STATEMENT FOR YOUR RECORDS

11731

NOTICE: SEE REVERSE SIDE AND ACCOMPANYING STATEMENT(S) FOR IMPORTANT INFORMATION.

UNIVERSAL CREDIT CARD CHARGE FORM

I ACKNOWLEDGE RECEIPT OF TICKET(S) AND/OR COUPONS FOR RELATED CHARGES DESCRIBED HEREON. PAYMENT IN FULL TO BE MADE WHEN BILLED OR IN EXTENDED PAYMENTS IN ACCORDANCE WITH STANDARD POLICY OF COMPANY ISSUING CARD AND AS REFLECTED IN APPLICABLE TARIFFS.

X *William Ackley*

AIRLINE CODE   O I O
02-03-__
DATE OF ISSUE

4. CONTRACTOR INVOICE COPY

IF EXTENDED PAYMENT DESIRED, CIRCLE NO. OF MONTHS
3   6   9   12

DATE AND PLACE OF ISSUE
Skyway Airways
Pittsburgh, PA
Feb 3 __

NAME OF PASSENGER IF OTHER THAN CARDHOLDER		OTATO NO.	
COMPLETE ROUTING	FARE BASIS	CARRIER	

Pittsburgh-Chicago
Chicago-Pittsburgh   VA

CONNECTION OF PASSENGER WITH SUBSCRIBER

APPROVAL CODE
10

TICKETS NOT TRANSFERABLE
NO CASH REFUNDS

AIRLINE FORM SERIAL NO.
302 1412 914

FORM OF CREDIT
Master Charge
CREDIT CARD NAME/CODE

190-135-246
Mr. William Ackley

FARE	92.00	TOTAL	95.50	ROUTE CODE
TAX	3.50			
EQUIV. AMT. PD.				

With the descriptive billing method, the customer receives a comprehensive statement which details place of purchase, date of transaction, and amount owed (left); with the country club billing method, the customer receives a copy of all the original saleschecks for the month plus a statement of the total amount owed (right).
Courtesy Mellon Bank, NA

Country Club Billing

By using microfilm techniques, stores can photograph the customers' sales checks and use them as their permanent record; total customers' purchases; and send them bills together with the originals of their sales checks. Customers usually like to be billed in this manner because they can see the original sales checks and total their bills. This method simplifies the store's billing operation because it requires just totaling the customer's sales checks on the bill itself. It is, however, more costly than other methods, for returning both the bill and sales checks to the customer results in higher postage rates and may necessitate the omission of bill enclosures.

Descriptive Billing

The use of data processing has brought back descriptive billing to those stores that use electronic data processing for their accounts receivable. In this type of billing, the store notes the number of the department or area where the customer did the purchasing, the number and type of items bought, the price plus tax, if any, and the totals. The customer can refer to the back of the bill for a description of the department or area numbers to check on the purchases made. The customer does not, however, receive sales checks to prove that the purchases were made.

Increased use of data processing in the accounts receivable (charge) departments of stores has necessitated the change from country club billing to descriptive billing. A conversion of this type must be planned carefully. The customers must be educated and prepared for the changes that will occur and for the inconveniences that might take place.

THE COLLECTION FUNCTION

The majority of customers whose credit has been properly established and approved pay their bills reasonably on time. There are always some, however, who are negligent, slow to pay, or unwilling to pay. Collecting past-due accounts is a constant problem that many stores face.

Most stores have a series of letters prepared for slow payers. These letters are progressively insistent. The first letter may be just a gentle reminder of a forgotten bill, but succeeding letters become firmer in the request for payment. The final recourse is a threat to sue the customer.

When charge customers fail to pay, their accounts are marked so that authorization for additional purchases will not be given until they have conferred with a representative from the credit office. Although as much as 80 percent of accounts may be delinquent, only about 15 percent of all store accounts receivable require some action by the retailer to enforce payment beyond the routine means of reminders and other nonlegal measures.

Legal Means of Collection

Repossession, when part of the credit contract, is not desirable because of the low value of repossessed goods. *Garnishment* of salaries (withholding of part of the salary by the charge customer's employer) is allowed by some states, but many states restrict the amount below which a salary can be garnisheed, and the Consumer Credit Protection Act also limits the amount of one's salary that can be garnisheed.

About 5 percent of all accounts receivable require garnishment or other formal or legal judgment. This means that 95 percent of the charge customers pay without the store's having to resort to legal methods. The store must, however, finance the costs of the 5 percent who do not pay. In addition, the store faces the costs incurred in the attempts to collect on the accounts.

Evaluation

Stores evaluate their credit operations by comparing the number of new accounts that are opened with the total number of applications during the same period of time. They also base their evaluation on the age of their delinquent accounts. If delinquent accounts are grouped by age, the merchant knows how many accounts have not been paid for 3 to 4 months, 5 to 7 months, 8 to 12 months, and more than one year. Accounts that have not been paid and for which collection efforts have failed for a period of a year or more are usually written off as a loss.

COSTS OF CREDIT

Buying on credit, as has been previously explained, is a costly process. Both the store and the customer incur added charges because credit is available.

Cost of Credit to the Store

In figuring the costs of offering credit, the costs of the sales audit, cashiering, parts of direct-mail advertising, and the addressograph unit must be added to the direct costs of establishing accounts, maintaining accounts, follow-up, collection, credit management, and losses due to bad accounts. Other charges include the cost of borrowing money to finance accounts.

When all these charges are carefully noted in cost control, stores find that offering credit is costly to them. However, the added business developed by charge accounts makes them worth the costs incurred.

Cost of Credit to the Customer

As a result of the interest shown in the Consumer Credit Protection Act, many articles were written about the cost of credit plans to the customer. A formula suggested for finding the true interest rate when money is borrowed at a fixed percentage is as follows:

$$R = \frac{2(MI)}{P(N + 1)}$$

where R = true interest rate
   M = payment periods during a year (namely, 12)
   I = quoted interest charge (for example, 6% or $30)
   P = original amount borrowed, or the original cost of the goods (for example, $500)
   N = number of equal payments made (12)

Therefore, if the interest charge were 6 percent, the true rate of interest would be calculated as follows:

$$R = \frac{2(12 \times \$30)}{\$500(12 + 1)} = \frac{\$720}{\$6,500} = .11 \text{ or } 11\%$$

If the interest charge were 18 percent, or $90, on the same transaction, the figures would be as follows:

$$R = \frac{\$2,160}{\$6,500} = .33 \text{ or } 33\%$$

This formula works only with a fixed interest rate and a fixed charge. It does not work in figuring service charges on revolving accounts where $1\frac{1}{2}$ percent is paid on balances and where new charges may be added from time to time.

PROMOTING SALES THROUGH CREDIT

Credit transactions offer records for stores that may not be obtainable from any other source. Through the use of classification codes, price-range codes, and descriptive billing, a store can maintain a record of each customer's buying habits. At any time, if data-processing equipment is available, the store can run a historical purchase file against the customer's profile and relate what the customer is buying against what the merchandise needs should be. Promotional literature can then be prepared, based on this knowledge of the individual customer's buying habits.

The store can also obtain records from charge accounts on the frequency of shopping, the effects of advertising on charge purchases, the departments or areas the charge-account customers prefer, the average size of purchases made by charge customers, and the relationship of purchases to each other in a similar category. For example, if a woman spends between $25 and $40 for dresses, what price does that customer pay for her winter coat, her suit, her shoes, and other apparel? Such information is helpful to buyers in coordinating their lines of merchandise.

If a customer buys dresses frequently from a store but never purchases a coat in that store, querying the customer might reveal why she does not make such a purchase in that store.

If a man purchases shoes in the store but no other apparel, the buyers might want to know where he purchases his other clothing and accessories.

Charge accounts, therefore, provide a sales promotion tool for the store in addition to convenience for the customers and added business for the merchants.

TOPICS FOR DISCUSSION

1. Explain the trends regarding credit use in the United States, and explain the reasons for those trends.
2. What are the important protections for the consumer provided by the Consumer Credit Protection Act?
3. Why was the Fair Credit Billing Act initiated?
4. What are the advantages to the customer of having a regular charge account in a store?
5. Why do retailers usually provide opportunities for charge accounts?
6. Explain what is meant by an option-terms credit plan.
7. How does granting installment credit differ from granting other types of charge-account credit?
8. What information about customers can be obtained from applications for credit?
9. Discuss the three factors that are used to determine whether a person is a good credit risk.
10. What problems face the retailer in the identification of the credit customer at the point of sale?

MATHEMATICS FOR RETAILING

A woman bought a coat for $250 in January and charged it to her revolving credit account. Beginning with that same month, she paid $25 a month on the principal. The service charge was $1\frac{1}{2}$ percent on the balance of the principal after the first month.

1. How long would it take her to complete the payments? On a separate sheet of paper, make a chart showing this.
2. What would be her total interest charges?

COMMUNICATIONS IN RETAILING

Ms. Foster, a good customer for many years, had disregarded the payment of her regular charge-account bill for the past three months. During that time she had made no additional charges on the bill. As the assistant in the charge-account office, you have been asked to send a personal reminder notice to her. What would you say in such a letter? Be prepared to discuss your points.

CUSTOMER OPERATIONS FUNCTIONS

DECISION MAKING

Casey's was a small chain of select specialty stores that had an elegant decor. The stores in the chain catered to middle- and upper-income customers, most of whom had charge accounts with the stores. The management analyzed its credit costs and decided that since many customers were slow to pay their bills, the chain could no longer afford to finance its large accounts receivable department. However, it did not want to lose its charge-account business. Two alternatives were available:

1. The chain could sell its accounts receivable to a bank that had a credit card plan which was used in many stores. The bank would charge the stores approximately $4\frac{1}{2}$ percent of each charge sale for billing, accounting, and collecting under the bank's name. This plan necessitated that signs be placed throughout the stores announcing the bank's credit card plan. The bank's charge card would be used.
2. The chain could sell its accounts receivable to a credit card firm which would charge 5 percent of each sale and which would maintain the accounts under Casey's name while performing all the other services of billing, accounting, and collecting.

Which plan would you advise the management to accept? Be prepared to give reasons for your answer.

CAREER LADDER

An entry-level position as receptionist was open in the credit department of a large store with branches. The person selected for that position would move, after about six months, to the position of interviewer and be responsible for screening people applying for credit. Then the person could get the position of analyzer and study credit ratings. Finally, the person could become the manager of a branch store's credit office. On a separate sheet of paper, list the qualifications you would look for in a person applying for this entry-level position.

chapter 30

ADJUSTMENTS AND RETURNS

A policy on which stores differ widely concerns how liberal they are with customers on adjustments and returns. Some stores proudly announce that they guarantee customer satisfaction with goods and will exchange goods or return money within a reasonable time. Others are restrictive and will not return money, but they will exchange merchandise that has not been worn or used. Still others make all sales "final" and refuse to accept returns or exchanges of merchandise.

Customers should know store policies regarding adjustments and returns before they buy. Similarly, retailers need to decide how their policies affect the growth and profitability of their businesses. In general, the large chain organizations and the stores that have grown constantly and that have many branches have liberal return and adjustment policies. Some neighborhood stores, some specialty stores, and some "high pressure" stores that use bait-and-switch sales tactics are the ones that have restrictive policies about returns and adjustments.

ADJUSTMENT POLICY CONSIDERATIONS

Guidelines to be considered in determining store return and adjustment policies include the following:

- Establish a general adjustment policy that is fair for all customers.

- Plan exceptions to that policy for certain lines of merchandise, such as special-order mer-

chandise, sanitary goods, and other products such as bedding that cannot be sold once they have been used, and for personalized merchandise that has no resale possibilities.

- Plan exceptions to that policy for low-priced merchandise offered in clearance sales or special sales where little or no profit can be made and where such services cannot be provided without a considerable loss to the store.

- Plan to announce these policy exceptions so that customers know conditions of purchase.

HUMAN RELATIONS AND THE ADJUSTMENT PROCEDURES

In addition to establishing the policies, the retailer must inform the employees of the store about them. Employees are charged with the responsibility of carrying out the policies at all times. Customers returning goods or complaining about goods should be treated just as courteously and graciously as when they are buying goods. Maintaining goodwill can keep these people as customers in the future.

Adjustments and complaints need to be handled with the utmost speed. Taking care of adjustments and complaints immediately, or as soon as possible, keeps customers friendly to the store.

Advising Customers About Variable Policies
Stores that find it advisable to have both a general adjustment policy that is quite lenient for all regular merchandise purchases and more re-

strictive policies for certain lines of merchandise and for sale merchandise should inform customers about the exceptions. Thus, in the millinery department, for example, signs throughout the area may state, "Millinery cannot be returned or exchanged." Similarly, in departments where merchandise is specially ordered or where the goods have been personalized, signs may state, "Specially ordered or personalized merchandise is not returnable for exchange or refund." Customers should also be informed that sanitary goods cannot be returned.

Whenever sale merchandise cannot be returned, large signs should state clearly, "All Sales Final." Some soiled or slightly imperfect or damaged merchandise is marked and sold "as is." This means that the store will not refund money or make exchanges on such goods.

Anticipating Factors That Cause Complaints
Some stores attempt to foresee situations that may cause complaints and to warn the customers about them. For example, a store that sold a large amount of furniture found that customers were returning dining-room and bedroom sets because the wood grain did not match perfectly on all pieces in the sets. The buyer decided to place signs throughout the department stating, "Because wood is a natural product, no two grains on furniture will be identical; therefore, no two pieces of furniture in any set will match perfectly." Returns and complaints on nonmatching wood grains were greatly reduced by these signs.

Knowledgeable salespeople can anticipate objections. They can reduce complaints by forewarning customers about the results of using merchandise. The following are examples of results of wear: minor scratches that will dull the luster of silver, white gold, and platinum; the shedding to be expected with velvet-type rugs or long, shaggy fur garments; the sheen that will appear on fine woolens when they have been worn for a while; the oxidation that occurs on all furs; and the snags that will appear on all loosely woven or knitted fabrics.

METHODS OF CONTROLLING THE USE AND ABUSE OF GOODS

Some promotional stores offer very liberal return policies for goods that have not been used or worn. In order to ensure that goods are not used or worn before they are returned, they ticket the merchandise visibly so that the products are not usable or wearable as long as the price tickets remain intact. Removal of the price ticket mutilates it so that it cannot be replaced. Since the policy of the store states that the original price ticket may not be removed from the merchandise if it is to be exchanged or returned for refund, goods without the ticket are not accepted for return or exchange. In addition, stores usually specify the number of days during which the goods will be accepted for exchange or refund. Usually 7 to 10 days are allowed for returns.

Because the types of price tickets that cannot be replaced after removal from the merchandise are usually unsightly, stores catering to select customers rarely use them. These stores do examine returned merchandise carefully to make sure that there is no evidence of wear or use, but they rely mainly on the integrity of the customers in making refunds or exchanges.

Experience has shown that stores find it most difficult to control their return policies with charge-account customers. Dissatisfied customers simply announce that they will refuse to pay for an unsatisfactory item if a reasonable adjustment is not made. This can mean that a lengthy series of exchanges takes place between the charge-account office and the customer until the case is finally resolved—usually in the customer's favor.

UNSATISFACTORY MERCHANDISE

When merchandise has been worn or used by the customer, it no longer can be returned in the same manner as unused merchandise. If the product has not performed as anticipated, or if it has not functioned properly, the customer may make a complaint about the product. There are a number of ways of handling such complaints.

Justified Complaints

Many complaints are completely justified. For example, a customer may have purchased a new television set that worked for a few minutes when first plugged in and then suddenly blacked out. The customer reports the occurrence immediately, and the store agrees that the complaint is justified. Under such circumstances, the store may

- Replace the used product with a new one, which is assumed not to be defective. The defective product is then returned to the manufacturer to be fixed or replaced.

- Refund the customer's money if the customer does not want to take a chance on a replacement.

- Pick up the product at the customer's home and return it to the manufacturer for repair or have a service helper call at the customer's home to make the necessary repairs or adjustments. In the case of damaged or nonfunctioning furniture or major appliances, the latter method is frequently used. Service helpers are employed for just such emergencies.

- Make an adjustment in the price when the product itself is usable but not as originally specified or as ordered by the customer. This is done when the customer agrees to keep the product in question.

Unjustified Complaints

Some complaints that customers make are not justified in the opinion of store personnel. Under those circumstances the store may pursue one of the following procedures:

- Refuse to take any action

- Offer to have the product repaired free for the customer

- Offer to have the product repaired and charge the customer just what it costs the store to have it repaired

- Provide a full refund or exchange as a gesture of goodwill

CAUSES FOR COMPLAINTS

Analysis of complaints and returns may indicate several important reasons why they occur.

High-Pressure Selling

Certain salespeople may be pressuring customers to buy and these customers later resist such pressures by returning the goods to the store for credit or a refund.

Lack of Information

Sometimes an uninformed customer unintentionally abuses merchandise. For example, one store found an inordinately high return of aluminum pots and pans. Investigation showed that customers were melting the pans by using too much heat on electric stoves. When salespeople were instructed to warn customers to use just low or medium heat, the complaints on melted aluminum pots and pans greatly decreased.

Faulty Merchandise

By analyzing returns and complaints by merchandise classification and then by manufacturer, the store personnel may find that the merchandise itself is not as represented. The merchandise may be sized or labeled incorrectly, or it may be imperfect. Store buyers may inform the manufacturers of these shortcomings, and if they are not corrected in subsequent shipments, the store may select other vendors from whom to obtain such goods.

Merchandise may be faulty in design. For example, spouts of cream pitchers or coffeepots may not pour properly; lids may not fit correctly; or handles may not be easy to hold. Materials used in the merchandise may be too sleazy, or they may not be appropriate for the use of the items. For example, a tea strainer made from a plastic that melted when hot tea was poured through caused a large number of complaints in a variety chain. Construction of merchandise

CUSTOMER OPERATIONS FUNCTIONS

may be faulty: the item may not be held together securely, or its components may not work smoothly. Finishes may be at fault—they may fade, crack, crock, or be uneven. In addition, customers may get short measure when products are bought by weight, or items may be measured incorrectly when purchased by length and width.

A customer is entitled to receive a product that performs as represented or that can be used in the manner in which it was intended to be used. Similarly, a store expects that a customer will use merchandise as it is intended to be used. Thus a store is justified in not making adjustments when customers use table knives to open cans, when they burn holes in fur coats, when they spill chemicals on garments, or when they drop breakable products.

Noncompetitive Price

If customers find identical merchandise at a competing store for less money than they paid for it, they may either return the goods for a full refund or ask for a rebate equal to the difference in price. Stores that have low-price policies then check to verify the accuracy of the customers' claims and make the requested refund. Stores that do not claim to meet the prices of competitors may or may not make such price adjustments.

Some goods may only appear to be the same, and well-informed salespeople should explain the differences between the goods. There may be differences in the materials used, construction, or trim. Some features may be added to some items but not to others.

Unsatisfactory Service

Delayed delivery, delivery of incorrect merchandise, maintenance service available only at limited times, rudeness on the part of employees, failure to call a customer as promised—these and many other problems may cause a customer to complain or to refuse merchandise or to request refunds on merchandise. The services stores do or do not provide are an important influence on customer satisfaction or dissatisfaction.

CUSTOMERS WHO DO NOT COMPLAIN

Although many store personnel believe that most customers take every opportunity to complain about merchandise or service problems, analysis reveals that many customers are "silent complainers." These customers have reasons to complain, but they refrain from doing so. They often, however, stop shopping in the store that was responsible for their problems! This is a hidden type of adjustment that may cost the store many thousands of dollars in lost volume.

A store can check on the proportion of noncomplainers when defective merchandise is sold. One firm sold thousands of tubes of toothpaste in which the substance that prevents hardening had inadvertently been left out. Only a few persons complained about the hardened toothpaste. The thousands who did not complain may just never have purchased articles in that store again. A store must therefore be vigilant in making sure that its merchandise and service are as represented and that it is not developing "silent complainers," who cease to be customers.

HANDLING ADJUSTMENTS— CENTRALIZED OR DECENTRALIZED

Stores may handle complaints and returns by centralized adjustment, by decentralized adjustment, or by a combination of the two methods.

Centralized Adjustment

When a centralized adjustment plan is instituted, every customer who wishes an exchange or a refund or who wishes to make a complaint is directed to the adjustment department of the store. Such a centralized system has several advantages:

- Employees experienced in handling complaints and returns are assigned to talk with the customers. These employees are familiar with the policies of the store, and they know how to handle each problem.

- These knowledgeable adjusters can control all records on returns, complaints, and exchanges.

- Selling and management personnel in the various sections of the store are relieved from handling these details.

The disadvantages of such a system almost balance the advantages:

- The customers receive less personalized service than when they can return to the salesperson who helped them buy the merchandise initially.

- Customers may be delayed in making adjustments by long lines in the adjustment department, especially at such times as after Christmas. The customers, already annoyed because of some problem with the store, are further annoyed by having to wait to be served.

- Customers have no chance to see other merchandise to replace that which is being returned if they do not go to the department for the exchange or refund.

Decentralized Adjustment

Most small stores and some large stores use a decentralized adjustment system. A customer who has a complaint or wishes to obtain a refund is served in the same area of the store where the purchase was made and often by the same person who waited on him or her initially. Even mail and telephone complaints and adjustments are handled by the department or area personnel. There are several advantages to a decentralized system:

- The customer senses the more personalized attention, since the person handling the problem is acquainted with the merchandise and often with the customer, too.

- Since the customer is served in the area where the merchandise was purchased, the sale may be saved by showing other merchandise or by

This enclosed bill adjustment office provides the customer with privacy and personal attention to billing problems.
Photograph by Helena Frost

explaining the proper use and care of the product purchased.

- Sometimes the customer sees other merchandise she or he also wishes to purchase.

- If the merchandise is currently out of stock, the personnel in the selling area can advise the customer when similar merchandise will arrive.

- The face-to-face meeting with customers gives the personnel in the area firsthand information about the customers' reactions to the merchandise or reasons for wanting a return or adjustment.

There are some rather serious disadvantages, however, in a decentralized system:

- The time of the selling and management personnel is taken from their regular work to assist customers in making adjustments.

- Personnel in the various areas of the store may interpret store policies somewhat differently,

CUSTOMER OPERATIONS FUNCTIONS

causing misunderstandings and friction with customers.

- Return goods may not be controlled effectively, since adjustment is not centralized.

Combination Adjustment

Many stores use a combination of the centralized and decentralized systems explained above. Ordinary returns and complaints are handled in the selling department. Those that are complicated are referred to the central bureau. All telephone and mail complaints, complaints about nondelivery or wrong delivery or about incorrect charges, and other complaints are handled by the central bureau. This plan has some of the advantages and disadvantages of each of the other methods.

COST OF CUSTOMER RETURNS AND COMPLAINTS

Every time merchandise must be handled, remarked, restocked, and resold, additional costs are incurred. When customers complain about faulty merchandise that must be taken back as a return or serviced, such complaints become costly. If the wrong merchandise has been delivered, picking up that merchandise and delivering the correct merchandise triple the initial costs of delivery.

Stores have different average costs for returns and complaints. Estimates indicate that complaints average between $1.50 and $3 each! Obviously, stores cannot afford a high percentage of adjustments if they are to make a profit on sales.

The percentage of returns and allowances varies widely by category of merchandise. According to *Departmental Merchandising and Operating Results* (*MOR*) issued by the Controllers' Congress of the National Retail Merchants Association, which reports data for specialty stores and department stores ranging from those with volumes of less than 1 million dollars to those whose volumes are over 50 million dollars, typical returns and allowances as a percentage of sales are as follows:

Foods and groceries	0.6
Apparel fabrics	0.8
Cosmetics and drug sundries	2.1
Books and stationery	2.3
Records and musical instruments	2.9
Children's footwear	4.5
Hosiery and gloves	5.0
Jewelry and watches	5.7
Men's furnishings	6.0
Boys' clothing	6.8
Women's handbags	7.0
Men's shoes	7.6
Sporting goods	8.5
Girls' and teen-agers' clothing	9.0
Women's footwear	9.8
Men's clothing	9.8
Major appliances	10.0
Furniture and beds	11.4
Television	11.5
Dresses	12.5
Women's and misses' coats and suits	13.7

The average return rate in department stores of varying sizes is 8.0 percent. Specialty stores have a slightly higher percentage of returns—8.2 percent.

EFFECTS OF RETURNS AND ADJUSTMENTS ON INVENTORY CONTROL

Returned merchandise must be charged back into the store's stock. The inventory of goods on hand is increased by these returns. Unit control and dollar control figures must be adjusted to account for these returns.

Every piece of merchandise returned to stock must be examined to make sure that it is still salable and also to make sure that the price tag is still on. After the merchandise passes inspection, it may be placed with department stock or with the stock-room stock.

For merchandise that is frequently returned, as in the case of women's apparel, stores try to avoid excess marking operations by the use of three-part price tickets. When an item is initially sold, one part of the ticket is torn off to use for unit-control records. When the item is returned, no new marking is required if the two remaining parts of the ticket are still intact. If the item is resold, the second stub may be detached for recordkeeping. If the item is returned by the second customer, the remaining stub is used as a guide to re-mark the item with a new three-part ticket.

To avoid theft, to maintain accurate records, and to make sure that all employees understand the importance of return goods, most stores have rigid policies about the handling of these goods. When all re-marking is done on the sales floor, however, such rigid controls are hard to maintain.

DATA PROCESSING MAY COMPLICATE CHARGE CUSTOMERS' BILLS

In some instances, the great speed with which records can be processed because of electronic data processing has complicated the adjustment procedure used for charge accounts. For example, charge customers may make special-order purchases and, because of the speed of processing the charges, be billed for the goods before those items actually arrive at their homes. In fact, if the special orders are for articles that won't be delivered for six or more weeks, the customers may even receive reminders of overdue accounts before the merchandise arrives. In such cases, the customers undoubtedly indicate on the form returned to the store that they are awaiting the arrival of the merchandise before they pay for it. The computer, however, is not programmed to read these replies, so it simply issues its regular reminders for payment. Thus, customers become more and more annoyed.

Some stores, aware of this problem, insert a note in the bill that says, "We are aware that some of the merchandise billed herein has not yet been delivered. You may subtract the amount for that item from your bill, and we will bill you again for it next month." Such a communication helps to reduce the customers' annoyance.

In other cases, when customers are protesting about some purchase, the computer relentlessly duns them for payment even while they are corresponding with the adjustment manager or store personnel about the problem. Again, a note in the bills acknowledging the complaints can help to keep the customers aware of the store's attempt to give its accounts individual attention.

If delivery of merchandise is delayed for customers whose accounts bear interest charges, the computer may bill for interest charges on unpaid balances even before the goods have been delivered. Store personnel have to be alert to these billing problems and prepared to adjust customers' bills even before the customers have a chance to complain.

TOPICS FOR DISCUSSION

1. Explain why complaints and adjustments in different stores might vary widely.
2. What are some of the guidelines to be considered in establishing return and adjustment policies for a store?

3. Why must store managers be constantly concerned with the way complaints and adjustments are handled by store personnel?
4. Why should customers be advised about the adjustment and return policies of a store?
5. What means do some stores use to deter the customer from buying goods, using those goods, and then returning them for refund?
6. What should be the store policy about the treatment of customers seeking adjustments or returns because of unsatisfactory goods?
7. Why is it important to analyze complaints and returns?
8. Why must a store be concerned with "silent complainers"?
9. Explain the advantages of centralized adjustment systems and decentralized systems.
10. Analyze the percentage of returns in various classifications of merchandise as shown in the text. What generalizations can you make about returns from those figures?

MATHEMATICS FOR RETAILING

A customer entered a carpet store to make a purchase of 9- by 15-foot carpeting for her living room. The carpeting was advertised at $12.99 per square yard. Binding for the carpet was an additional $10 for the two ends.

1. How much was the total purchase?
2. If the sales tax was 6 percent, what was the total charge on the bill?
3. When the carpeting was delivered, the customer noticed that it was slightly narrower than she had ordered. The store then advised her that she had been sent a remnant. If remnants ordinarily were priced 30 percent less than roll goods, what total price should the customer have been charged, including the sales tax?

Do your calculations on a separate sheet of paper.

MANAGING HUMAN RELATIONS

The customer for the above-mentioned carpeting was annoyed when the carpet firm dunned her for nonpayment of her bill. The firm had charged her the full roll-goods price instead of the discount price for the remnant it acknowledged sending her. The customer wrote the following letter to the adjustment manager of the firm:

Dear Mr. Fargo:

Imagine my dismay to receive a letter from you dated September 27 dunning me for nonpayment of my bill. I have written you previously to claim a reduction in price, since you acknowledge you sent me a remnant, or to have you pick up the remnant and substitute the roll goods that I initially ordered.

I have been a good customer in your store for 15 years. Never before have I been late in paying a bill, and never before have I refused to pay a bill. However, I shall not pay the full price for merchandise that you have misrepresented to me.

Let me hear from you immediately about this matter.

Sincerely,
Ms. Alice Long

As manager of the store, what action would you suggest be taken on this matter? Be prepared to discuss your suggestions.

DECISION MAKING

A large, progressive store in a city was so successful that many branch stores were added in suburban areas. These stores also flourished, and thus there was a constant need for more floor space and remodeling. This constant growth also led to the employment of many people, and promotions became rapid. Although the firm attempted to give thorough training, too many people were needed to assure that each had had sufficient time to learn all the policies and procedures.

The main store's liberal adjustment policies were a feature of each of the branch stores. Complaints began to be heard from one branch, however, about restrictive policies, about resistance to taking goods back, and about customer dissatisfaction. The president, based in the city store, became aware of the complaints in the branch store. When the manager was queried about the complaints, this person said the store's policies were too liberal and customers were taking advantage of the good nature of the store personnel. Therefore, for that branch store, the policies had been changed.

As president of the store, what action would you take about the handling of complaints and adjustments in the branch store? Be prepared to discuss your ideas.

CAREER LADDER

John Flynn and Floyd McCrary, two salespeople, were employed at the same time to work in a store. They were both good workers, but their work interests and habits varied widely. One liked recordkeeping and putting merchandise away neatly, while the other enjoyed helping customers. The department head soon was assigning John to stock work and recordkeeping and Floyd to handling problem customers. An opening occurred in the adjustment department for an adjustment claims clerk. Both men applied for the job. Who do you think should be transferred? Be prepared to give reasons for your choice.

chapter 31

STORE SERVICES THAT SELL THE STORE

Merchandise, employees, and services are the three vital factors in attracting and holding customers.

The management of a store or chain must decide what the policies regarding services are to be. To do this, the executives determine the type of image the firm is to project to its customers, the kinds of customers the firm wishes to attract, the kinds of prices to charge, and the services the firm can offer its customers. If a store wishes to maintain a discount policy, services will need to be kept to a minimum. If a store is catering to customers who can afford prices that reflect a regular markup, many more services will be offered. When services tend to build traffic, their cost may be offset by the added volume of business they create. Other factors also affect the kinds and number of services offered: the location of the store, the competitions' services, the available space and facilities, the character and size of the merchandise carried, and the demands made by the store's customers.

MINIMUM SERVICES

Every store must provide some services. Every store, for example, gives receipts for purchases at least upon request. Every store provides some type of wrapping for merchandise when needed. Every store provides some type of directory service to help customers find merchandise. Every store provides some aisle space and some free areas in which the customer can stand or sit while viewing the merchandise. Every store provides the customer with a method of seeing the merchandise and selecting the goods. Every store is open during some convenient hours to accommodate its customers. Stores may provide delivery service, free or for a charge.

WRAPPING SERVICE

All stores provide paper, sacks, or boxes for customers to carry their purchases from the stores. Stores that deliver also provide wrapping service for the parcels to be delivered to the customers. Some stores also have a gift-wrapping service. In full-service stores, gift wraps may be done free of charge. If the customers want especially fancy gift wrapping, however, special desks may be set up where the customers can select paper, ribbon, and bows at varying prices and have those used to gift wrap the merchandise they have selected. No charge, however, is made for the service of gift wrapping.

Many stores use store wrappings as promotional devices. Special store events may be dramatized by the special wrappings and by the shopping bags that are designed for the promotion. Customers carrying these bags and wrappings help to publicize the event for the store. Most large stores also have special wrappings for Christmas and other holidays or seasons. Flower shops and candy stores as well as general merchandise stores find that these wrappings help to enhance the products they sell.

Shopping bags that can hold many small packages easily at one time are used extensively. Some stores which feature low prices sell these bags for 10 to 25 cents each for the customer's use. Some stores do not charge for the bags but use them whenever a customer has several packages to carry. Other stores may give shopping bags to the customers free only when they make purchases over a certain total amount. Since these bags are costly, each store determines its own policy for providing these customer aids.

Clerk Wrap

When salespeople complete a sale, including making change for the customer or otherwise recording the purchase, they also usually wrap the customer's package. This is the speediest, simplest, most convenient system for the customer.

In this manner, one person handles the entire transaction. The wrapping is usually done by placing the article purchased in a paper sack or in a box designed to fit the majority of products sold in the department. Or, less frequently, the article may be wrapped in paper and the parcel tied with string or taped together.

Central Wrap

The increased use of self-selection has made a central-wrap system common. The customer, after selecting the article, takes it to a nearby station where the transaction is recorded and the package checked and wrapped. This system provides skilled cashiers and wrappers to handle customers' packages and also gives the store greater protection from theft, since fewer people handle cash and customers' packages. In addition, specially trained wrappers can keep packages to a minimum size for ease of carrying or for lower delivery costs.

Checkout counters may be used instead of wrapping stations. These are found in supermarkets; in self-service variety stores, drugstores, and cosmetic stores; and in self-service sections of department and specialty stores. Customers may gather all their selections in baskets or carts and check out everything purchased in the store or area at one time. This is an efficient, timesaving method, but customers do not receive the same personal attention they get with the clerk-wrap method.

Store Packing and Wrapping

Stores have found that overpacking is not necessarily the best way to protect merchandise. Many stores have learned that fragile products that are visible to the handlers might be treated more carefully than items that are completely encased in wrappings. Mirrors, for example, often have packing just across the back and over the edges. Since the face of each mirror shows, there is assurance that the mirrors will be handled as delicate products.

The general trend toward simplicity and visibility in packing extends even to apparel. Instead of folding dresses, suits, and coats and laying them in boxes, some stores use garment bags, dispensed from perforated rolls, to protect the garments without wrinkling them. Garments to be delivered are then hung in trucks, ready for handlers to remove them from the racks at the customers' homes.

Manufacturer Prepacks

In seeking to reduce costs and to minimize the handling of merchandise, manufacturers are increasingly packaging goods that do not have to be examined closely. The manufacturer packages can be used for display, for protection of the merchandise, and for selling. The visibility of merchandise through clear plastic wraps or through windows in boxes or packages has made these types of wrappings popular. Breakable merchandise—such as china, glassware, and mirrors—that is prepackaged by manufacturers usually rides safely to the store, where it can be stacked in stock rooms or on the selling floor without unpacking and later repacking for delivery to the customer. Delivery of such goods can be made directly to the customer with only a label attached by the store. Although these attractive and secure wrappings may raise the cost of packaging slightly, the reduction in subsequent handling necessary in the retail store offsets this initial charge.

DELIVERY OF MERCHANDISE

Stores have a variety of delivery services available, ranging from no delivery to vast trucking industry delivery. Parcel post and railway express may also be used for delivery to distant points. Small stores may deliver an order of any size, but most large stores that provide regular delivery service have a minimum sale on which delivery will be made. The common minimum is $5 for packages to be delivered.

Delivery Processing

In large stores, shipments to customers originate at the store itself or at the warehouse. Each of these has an area for outgoing merchandise where shipments to customers are accumulated, sorted, and loaded. Each delivery truck bay is assigned to a particular route.

At the warehouse, merchandise for delivery is assembled by order pickers, who work from batches of location tags. At the store, merchandise for delivery is picked up from the selling departments or the central-wrap stations.

Sorters in the delivery area match customer addresses with particular delivery routes to assemble the individual truckloads. Small packages may be dispatched from the sorting area to the truck-loading area down a ramp or chute. Larger items and fragile items are brought to the loading area on wheeled trucks or dollies.

A record of each outgoing shipment is made. The record may be a written list that shows what packages, identified by customers' names and addresses, were given to each driver. Another method is to remove a delivery stub from the sales check for each package and file it.

Minimum Delivery Service

Most local stores that carry small items have no need for delivery service. Many local drugstores, grocery stores, and meat stores, however, maintain delivery on call from customers to increase the volume of their business. Usually these stores employ young people with bicycles to make such deliveries. If the store has a discount policy, there may be a charge for deliveries. Since deliveries in small stores are handled only as the need arises, elaborate systems are not necessary to check on such service.

Store-Owned Delivery System

More elaborate and more carefully checked delivery systems are maintained by larger stores, especially when bulky items such as furniture, major appliances, and television sets are sold. If the store owns its own trucks, delivery standards may be high, and customer service may be unusually gracious. One furniture chain, for example, decided to make its delivery service an effective promotion feature of its total store program. The delivery drivers wear white gloves when they deliver furniture. The furniture is removed from its box or crate and set up for the customer in the desired place in the home, even when this means moving other furniture to make room for the new piece. The furniture is then carefully wiped off and checked before the delivery driver leaves the home. Although such a service is more costly than routine delivery, the extra care and checking reduce complaints and returns. The firm therefore believes it has lower overall costs as a result of this fine service. This firm also makes a telephone call to the home of the customer two or three weeks later to check whether the customer is satisfied with the purchase.

If the store is using its own trucks in the store-owned delivery system, the name of the store may be emblazoned on the trucks, and they become traveling advertisements wherever deliveries are made.

Cooperative Delivery System

Owning and maintaining trucks and employing personnel to service and drive the trucks are costly for a store unless it enjoys a steady, large volume of business. In many localities, stores have banded together to share drivers and jointly owned trucks. Thus a truck serving a certain route can deliver merchandise for all the member stores instead of just one. Delivery costs are reduced by avoiding duplication of travel and personnel. Each store pays its share of the costs of maintenance and service under a plan established by all the stores in mutual agreement. Such a system does not advertise individual stores, but it can advertise a group of stores.

Consolidated Delivery System

Under a consolidated delivery plan, retailers in a city or area are contacted by a private, independent delivery organization which offers its delivery personnel and equipment on a contract basis. Each store joining this plan is charged for each package delivered. The rate for each package is established by size and weight. The delivery firm is responsible for all the goods it handles, and it pays all the costs of equipment and maintenance as well as the wages of the delivery and record-keeping personnel. Many large stores in central cities have found this to be the most economical method of handling delivery service.

In addition to having their packages delivered, stores using such a service receive reports on their packaging effectiveness, their efficiency in taking customers' addresses, and their general care in handling transactions. Such reports help the stores to improve their operations.

The consolidated delivery system, of course, provides the least personal delivery service, and there is no advertising for the individual store. Each individual store loses its identity in the delivery service in using this system. Since the delivery firm specializes only in the delivery of goods, however, it becomes highly efficient in that procedure and is able to perform the service with a minimum of complaints and errors.

When either the cooperative or the consolidated method is used, goods must be handled more frequently. The packages must be collected from each store and then brought to a central distribution area where they are sorted and rerouted to the proper truck for delivery as noted by the addresses on the packages.

Parcel Post and Express Shipments

For orders to distant points and for bulk delivery of goods to those points, stores may use parcel post and express shipments. Most stores charge customers for the costs of such deliveries.

Delivery for Nonservice Stores

Stores that feature low prices because they do not offer delivery or other types of special services may arrange for the delivery of bulky goods at a charge to the customer. When full-service stores that sell at regular prices meet the prices of these discount operations for customers, they, too, charge the customers for the delivery of the specific items sold at a discount.

SHOPPING HOURS

Convenient shopping hours to satisfy the needs of customers are a major consideration for a retail store. Some stores find that customers shop mainly from 10 a.m. until 5 p.m. on weekdays and Saturdays. Other stores find their customers shop mainly from 11 a.m. until 2:30 p.m. and again from 5 p.m. until 8 p.m. Suburban stores often find that customers prefer evening shopping hours. Small neighborhood grocery stores may find that customers want to shop until after midnight. Gasoline stations may need to stay open all night long to satisfy the needs of their customers. Increasing numbers of stores are adding holiday and Sunday selling times for customer convenience.

Stores maintain those hours that best serve the interests of their particular customers. However, staffing a store to serve customers for long periods of time daily proves difficult. The staggering of managers' hours and the hours of regular employees to handle the work when a store is open more than eight or nine hours daily, including Sunday, causes many problems in retail firms. Maintaining desirable shopping hours for customers is a challenge that each store must meet.

ADDITIONAL SERVICES

There is no limit to the number of additional services beyond those discussed that stores may offer. Some stores offer virtually unlimited services to keep customers happy. Executives have been known to get out of bed in the middle of the night in response to a request, dash to the store, get an item that a customer needed desperately, and then rush that item to a train or plane for the waiting customer. Sometimes employees take merchandise to customers' homes after work just to keep the customers satisfied with the service provided.

Stores will sew on buttons for customers while they wait, brush their clothes, make minor repairs, and even do their shopping for them at no extra cost if they believe such service is desirable. Some stores employ linguists to aid non-English-speaking customers in their shopping.

Such services may be conveniences for the customer during or after shopping; promotional services to get the customer to visit the store; services to increase the desirability of merchandise; or services that introduce the customer to do-it-yourself products.

Convenience Services

Very small stores may provide only minimum services. They have little need to keep the customers inside beyond the time necessary for them to make purchases. The larger the store and the more extensive the assortment of merchandise, the more reason the store has to want the customers to extend their stay in the store. The managers want the customers to have time to see all the merchandise and to visit all the various areas of the store. Certain additional services therefore become essential, such as rest rooms and drinking fountains, lounges, and even medical departments.

Some stores may also provide lockers for checking parcels or coats while shopping; coat rooms for checking wraps or parcels; parcel-gathering stations where merchandise that the customer has purchased from various areas in the store can be collected and held until the customer has finished shopping; and play areas where children may be left to be entertained while the parent shops.

Promotional Services

Some services are used as extra attractions to draw more customers into the store and to get them to visit the store more frequently.

Post offices are often stationed in drugstores, stationery stores, or large specialty or department stores. Lunchrooms may serve not only to hold customers in the store through the noon period but also to attract customers to come to the well-designed restaurant or snack bar of the store as part of a day's outing or for business or social appointments. Thus the lunchroom becomes a traffic builder for the store.

In a similar manner, beauty parlors and barbershops may serve to attract customers to the store. Watch-repair stations and other merchandise-repair areas, fur storage, and jewelry mounting may all serve as attractions for customers.

As noted in the chapter on promotional events, stores may sponsor art shows, fashion shows, lectures, contests for teen-agers, song fests, and even playlets in addition to consumer clinics to attract customers.

Gift certificates are offered by some stores for those customers who do not know what item to give a friend or relative. These gift certificates, purchased with cash or charged, are good for merchandise or even cash exchange when presented by the recipient.

Whenever service is offered, people are enticed into visiting the store. Some large jewelry stores and department stores keep records of the silver, chinaware, and glassware patterns selected by engaged couples. Friends and relatives wishing to purchase wedding gifts are advised by the store of these patterns and of the articles still not purchased. Thus the customers are aided in their shopping, and the couples receive matching sets of the patterns of their choice.

Value-Added Services

When merchandise that has to fit the individual—such as men's, women's, or children's clothing—is sold, alteration services may be helpful. The customer purchasing a garment may then have it properly fitted in the store. Men's stores generally include alterations in the original cost of the garment. Women's and children's ready-to-wear garments, however, are usually altered on a fee basis. Some firms charge one fee regardless of the amount of alteration needed on women's garments. Others charge a set fee for each job done, such as hemming, adjusting the size of the armholes, fitting the waist, or resetting the zipper. If customers do not sew, or if they are hard to fit, they are likely to purchase their garments at the stores that offer alterations.

Another service that helps to sell large appliances, television sets, and radios is the guarantee that the customers receive with their purchase. If the article in question does not perform as specified, a service person is sent to check the article in the customer's home. After the guarantee period expires, stores may offer customers additional service periods at a fee. The main problem with this plan is the occasional inability of the stores to find personnel who have the skills necessary for servicing different articles. In large cities, some manufacturers may offer repair service directly to the individual customer at a fee after the guarantee period has expired.

Custom order, which refers to products especially made or sized for the purchaser, is another service some stores offer. Thus, draperies, curtains, and carpets may be ordered to fit the customer's windows and floors. Bedspreads may be custom-made. Bridal gowns, suits, coats, and fur garments may be individually created. One store featured an infants' and children's custom-made shop especially for grandparents and other relatives who wanted to have something unusual made for the children in the family.

Special order, which allows out-of-stock merchandise to be ordered for the individual cus-

One of the additional services offered by some apparel stores is alterations. This service encourages customers to buy clothing in a particular store because they are assured the garment will be altered to fit properly.

CUSTOMER OPERATIONS FUNCTIONS

These customers are learning how to use sewing machines in free classes offered by Singer.
Courtesy The Singer Company

tomer, is a service that some customers appreciate. Although this is a costly method of ordering, some stores find they can carry smaller stocks of merchandise by using special orders. If the customer does not mind waiting for the goods, he or she is served individually by this ordering process.

Personalizing merchandise is another service offered by some retailers. Initials may be embroidered, sewn, engraved, or embossed on merchandise. A fee is charged for this service on most items. Merchandise that has been personalized for the individual customer is not returnable. Salespeople who work on commission often find that this service ensures that products will remain sold.

Instructions on do-it-yourself products and the methods of using sports equipment have caused the increased offerings in some stores of handicraft kits and sports equipment. In these stores, one may learn such skills as hooking rugs, doing needlepoint and petit point, embroidering, painting, cooking, applying makeup, and playing golf or tennis.

SERVICES TO PROMOTE THE STORE

That store services can help a firm be successful has been proved by many famous stores over the years. Major retailers in many large cities and in progressive suburban shopping centers have gone far beyond the traditional services already discussed. They may sponsor ticket sales for cultural and sports events, offer ski-condition reports, and provide bulletin boards for posting local news. Because the desire for shopping convenience and excitement is one of the chief characteristics of the American consumer, retailers are constantly challenged to devise more and more imaginative and timely store services that help to attract customers to their doors.

TOPICS FOR DISCUSSION

1. What factors determine the services a retailing firm will offer its customers?
2. Discuss the fact that all stores must give at least minimum services to customers.
3. How can store wrappings be promotional at the same time that they perform a service for customers?
4. Explain the advantages of the clerk-wrap service.
5. Explain the advantages of the central-wrap service.
6. What are the advantages of manufacturer prepacks for breakable merchandise?
7. Explain the differences between consolidated delivery services, store-owned delivery services, and cooperative delivery services.
8. What are the advantages in large stores of convenience services for customers?
9. What promotional services do large stores often provide?
10. What is meant by "value-added services"?

MATHEMATICS FOR RETAILING

A retailer who used a consolidated delivery service averaged his delivery costs during a one-year period. He found that the average delivery cost him 55 cents. He had allowed deliveries on goods selling for $3 or more. In his analysis, he noted that 10 percent of all his deliveries was for merchandise that averaged $3.50 at retail.

1. For goods selling at $3.50, what percentage of the retail price was spent on delivery?
2. If the maintained markup was 42 percent, what amount of money was left after deducting delivery charges to pay all other expenses?
3. If expenses not including delivery amounted to 36 percent for all items sold, would the retailer make money by the delivery of merchandise that averaged $3.50? Show your figuring for this problem on a separate sheet of paper.

MANAGING HUMAN RELATIONS

Mr. Caldwell paid cash for a portable television set. It came prepacked directly from a nationally famous manufacturer. He requested that the carton be opened and the set checked before he carried it home, but the salesperson informed him that the store policy did not permit the carton to be opened in the store. Mr. Caldwell carried the set home, opened the carton, plugged the set in, and was unable to get any picture. He was understandably annoyed. The next day he took the set back to the store. The salesperson offered to replace the set with another manufacturer-prepacked set, which was not to be checked in the store. Mr. Caldwell refused to take the set unless it was tested in the store. He would take his money back if the set could not be tested in the store. You as the store manager have been called to handle this problem. What would you do? Be prepared to give reasons for your answer.

DECISION MAKING

Mr. Ferron, a buyer of housewares, had a new, easy-to-clean, handy-to-handle garbage can that he wanted to promote for $4.99. He found, however, that the consolidated delivery service that served his firm would charge his department $2 for each garbage can delivered. His firm had one main store and four branches. Customers from the main store would generally require delivery on the items, since few people came downtown with their cars. However, most of the customers at the branch stores, which were in shopping centers and suburban areas, would carry the garbage cans to their cars parked nearby. In analyzing his problem, the buyer made the following estimates:

Main store	40% of volume (95% of cans would be delivered)
Branches	60% of volume (10% of cans would be delivered)
Cost of item	$2.25
Expenses (not including delivery)*	1.20
TOTAL	$3.45

Anticipated profit with no delivery $4.99 − $3.45 = $1.54 per garbage can
Anticipated loss with each delivery $4.99 − ($3.45 + $2.00 = $5.45) =
46¢ loss per garbage can

* This includes overhead, handling, storing, and selling plus any promotion necessary to sell the garbage cans.

1. Are there any creative or unusual solutions that could be offered for this problem?
2. Should the buyer consider buying the garbage cans just for the branch stores and not for the main store?
3. Would the buyer be wise to make the purchase? Be prepared to give reasons for your answers.

CAREER LADDER

A store manager decided to change to a consolidated service for the delivery of merchandise. However, before the changeover was to be made, each employee in the store was guaranteed employment either with the consolidated delivery firm or with the store.

Jobs in the store involved checking packages to be sure they were properly wrapped and addressed and recording the sales check stubs so that each package was accounted for. Packages were then sorted in the store according to delivery truck routes.

The consolidated delivery firm's employees gathered the bins full of presorted packages and stacked those bins in each truck so that those in the back would be available first for unloading. Again, records were kept of deliveries and of the condition of the packages when they were given to the customers.

One delivery person drove each truck, and one went to the customer's door with the package.

A young person in the firm asked you which job would offer the more interesting challenges. What would you tell that employee? Be prepared to discuss your answer.

FINANCIAL CONTROL FUNCTIONS

chapter 32

FINANCIAL MANAGEMENT OF RETAILING

The financial management functions of the retailing business are somewhat less obvious to customers than most of the other activities performed. These financial management functions are equally as important, however, as getting the merchandise, providing the employees to sell those products, and offering the services that attract customers to the store.

Everything retailers do in running their businesses costs money. Retailers need money to buy goods, to rent or purchase their stores, to maintain their places of business, to pay their employees, to advertise their wares, to store those wares, to deliver them to customers, and to handle all the recordkeeping necessary for all those processes.

Retailers who are not progressing find they are not really standing still but, rather, that they are regressing. Therefore retailers seek to have their businesses grow and attract still more customers. To accomplish this, they must make money beyond just that needed for the day-to-day running

of their businesses. Buildings age, equipment breaks down, fixtures become inadequate for displaying merchandise, and recordkeeping equipment becomes obsolete unless refurbished, replaced, added to, or expanded. Employees want increased pay, more benefits, and more services. To keep abreast of all these demands, the retailer must be making money above mere costs. To stay in business, therefore, retailers must make a profit from serving their customers. Profit is commonly referred to as the lifeblood of the retailing business.

THE FINANCIAL FUNCTION

The financial function of the retailing business is called the "control" function. Since the financial health of the company is vital to all decisions and actions, the word "control" suggests the scope of this function.

The financial or control function of a retailing firm includes handling and recording all its receipts of money; handling and recording all payments of the money (accounts payable); and handling all credit and collections (accounts receivable). Furthermore, the control function includes providing for needed insurance coverage; recommending uses of any available funds beyond those essential for the running of the business; and suggesting ways of borrowing funds needed for the operation or expansion of the business.

CONTROLLING CASH

In small stores, retailers may use a small box or cash drawer to keep the money they take in from customers in exchange for merchandise or services. Larger stores have cash registers operated by employees or by specially appointed cashiers to record sales. Most cash registers record the sale and issue a receipt for the customer. Larger, more modern cash registers also keep a record of the products or services purchased, of the person who recorded the sale, of the total receipts for the day by merchandise classification, and of the totals of each salesperson assigned to ring on the registers. More sophisticated types are terminals connected to computers that provide unit-control data about merchandise.

Some retail stores use sales checks to record part of their transactions, and others have all sales recorded on sales checks. Some stores have the sales checks inserted into the cash register for sales recording.

Checking Cash Against Records

At the end of each business day, the money in the register or cash drawer should equal the amount the register has recorded, plus any cash initially placed in the register that was used during the day for making change.

At the close of each shift or at the end of the business day, the total money in the cash register is counted and recorded by the individual assigned to handle the money. All the money is then turned over to the financial department, where it is re-counted and checked against the

cash register tapes or the sales check records. Money not needed for the start of the next day's business is deposited in a bank for safekeeping.

Noting Overages and Shortages

If less cash than the records indicate is present, a shortage has occurred. If more cash than the records indicate is present, an overage has occurred. Both overages and shortages of cash are recorded, and those responsible for these conditions are notified of their errors. If these errors persist, the employees concerned may need retraining. Theft may also be a cause of differences from the recorded amounts. This problem is discussed further in Chapter 36.

ACCOUNTS PAYABLE

Bills and invoices that need to be paid are referred to as *accounts payable.*

All money is channeled through the financial office for disbursements. For example, the retail buyers who order merchandise for resale submit the approved bills to the financial office, which pays for the merchandise. In this way, complete control can be maintained. Those contracting to pay money are not the people who actually pay out the money for the firm.

Except for some petty cash disbursements, most retail firms pay their bills by check. Checks serve as proof of payment, offer protection to those disbursing and receiving the money, and facilitate paying bills.

ACCOUNTS RECEIVABLE

The money due from customers for their charge accounts and other amounts owed for merchandise are known as *accounts receivable.*

The financial officer of the company must keep careful records of outstanding customers' accounts and must recommend necessary actions to prevent imbalances between accounts receivable and available cash. The financial section of the firm is responsible for carrying out the policy on credit extension, for careful investigation of customers' credit ratings, for accurate record-keeping of customers' accounts, and for vigilance in the collection of those accounts.

Retailing firms have found extension of credit to be a method of increasing volume. However, extension of credit drains the working funds of the business, since the merchandise and services customers purchase on credit must usually be paid for by the firm before the customers pay their bills. Thus the firm may find itself without sufficient funds to pay for those goods and services if it is unable to collect on its outstanding accounts. This forces the firm to borrow money and to pay interest on that money in order to satisfy its creditors. Borrowing increases the retailer's costs of doing business. If a retailer is unable to pay back the borrowed money, that retailer is forced into bankruptcy. Therefore, retailers at all times try to control the amount of money owed to them.

INSURANCE COVERAGE

To have a measure of protection against the hazards of doing business, the retail firm must carry various types of insurance. Insurance does not prevent accidents, theft, or embezzlement, but it does give some protection against financial loss resulting from them. The financial officer of the company is responsible for seeing that proper steps are taken to assure adequate insurance coverage for the firm. This is discussed in Chapter 36.

FUNDS FOR CONTINUING THE BUSINESS

When a business does not have a surplus of funds beyond its needs, or when improvements in the plant are desirable, the firm may plan to borrow funds. The financial officer is responsible for recommending sources of borrowing to the other executives and to the board of directors. If the money is essential for day-to-day expenses, that officer may recommend that it be obtained from those firms that lend *short-term funds*.

These are funds that are to be used for a period ranging from a few weeks to as long as six months. If, however, money is needed to finance building alterations, a new building, or other permanent installations, funding would have to be obtained from firms willing to extend *long-term funds*.

FUNDS FOR EXPANSION OR IMPROVEMENT OF THE BUSINESS

If a business is successful, profits may provide money for improvements. Improvements may include purchasing new and better merchandise or equipment, refurbishing the building, buying new buildings, extending promotions, expanding, upgrading personnel, hiring additional people, or a combination of all these. The financial officer of the business participates actively in the discussions and recommendations concerning the use of profits for such purposes.

Sources of Short-Term Funds

Several sources of short-term funds are available to meet the financial needs of the retailing business. In small businesses, one of the owners or friends or relatives may make the loan.

A second source of funds is to be had not by actually borrowing money but by receiving *trade credit* from the firms who supply the merchandise. Often manufacturers will arrange to delay collection of their accounts so the retailers may have ready cash until they, in turn, collect on some of their outstanding accounts or until they sell the goods they have purchased. Large firms are often in a position to aid retailers in this manner.

If funds are borrowed, they are most often obtained from a commercial bank. Interest is charged by the bank for the money borrowed. The credit rating of the retailing firm is of primary importance in obtaining such loans. This credit rating is determined by examining the financial statements of the firm. Collateral or security pledged by the firm is usually required for short-term loans. The movable property of the firm, the inventory of merchandise in the store or in the warehouse, or the assignment of the firm's accounts receivable may be used as security for the loan.

Sources of Long-Term Funds

For permanent installations, for new buildings, for the expansion of inventory, or for any debt with a maturity of more than one year, the firm may need to seek long-term funds. Although these may be obtained at a lower cost than the short-term funds, they usually require more involved procedures.

Shares of Stock. If the firm is a corporation, the executives may seek extra funds by issuing additional shares of stock. In this way new investors in the business are obtained who are willing to share the risks of the business. The investors also share in any profits that may result from the improvements made in the business.

Mortgages. Mortgage loans, which represent a promise to pay back the money borrowed with interest, are secured by submitting a deed or transfer of ownership of real estate. This is canceled when the principal and interest on the loan are repaid. Savings banks, commercial banks, loan companies, and insurance companies all make mortgage loans.

Leasebacks. Since the early 1960s, leasebacks have become an important source of long-term funds. These are obtained from the sale and then leasing of a piece of real estate. The sale of a building that a retail firm has owned is made with a "leaseback" agreement, for which the retailer receives money for immediate use. The retailer no longer owns the building the store occupies. The firm continues to stay on the premises, however, under a lease agreement that requires the payment of rent. If a building, for example, were sold for $100,000, the agreement might call for a 30-year lease with an option to renew for 20 more years at a $9\frac{1}{2}$ percent per annum charge. Thus, rent would equal $9,500 per year. Some leases are based on the volume of business rather than on a percentage of the building cost. The

lease under this kind of arrangement might call for $4,000 per year for the first $100,000 of net sales, with 2 percent additional rent for each additional $100,000 or part of that amount. If the firm had a volume of $300,000, the total rent for the year would be $8,000. However, if the volume increased to $400,000, the rent would rise to $10,000 for the year.

The disadvantages of this method of sale and leaseback as a means of long-term funding include capital gains taxes that must be paid on the sale of the property and the subsequent relatively high rent that must be paid annually. The capital gains tax on the sale of buildings cuts into the availability of ready cash received from the transaction and is an important consideration in the sale of property.

The property buyer usually plans to amortize the cost of the property (pay the cost gradually) during the lease contract with the retailer. This makes lease financing more costly than other forms of long-term borrowing.

Senior Notes. Senior notes are another source of long-term funds. *Senior notes* are equal or senior in claim value to all other long-term debts. Companies with a history of successful operation often seek this type of financing. Loans may be secured from institutional investors, such as insurance companies, in exchange for long-term senior notes. Before investing in this way, the insurance company will examine the retailer's balance sheet and income statement. In general, no loan will be made if the total long-term debt exceeds more than 50 percent of the net worth of the firm.

PURPOSES OF ACCOUNTING RECORDS

A firm may have many goals: being of service to customers and the community, developing and presenting outstanding products, leading in fashion, creating an exciting store for the presentation of goods, creating a socially important store for status, providing the lowest prices possible, or a combination of several of these goals. In addition, making a profit must be a goal of all retail businesses. No matter how worthwhile or admirable its other goals, a firm must be successful financially to stay in business and perform the services it offers to its community.

If a business must make money to exist, it needs a method of recordkeeping to register the income and outgo of money. Government requirements for tax purposes since 1913 have made recordkeeping essential. Today every retail firm, regardless of size, must have financial records of its operation. Records are the thermometer of a business to indicate its state of monetary health. Since records are necessary to show the condition of the profit or loss of the business, they may be used also in various ways to provide information on which decisions for improving the business may be based.

Except for very small operations, most retail firms employ full-time or part-time financial specialists to keep their books and to do their end-of-year accounting. All members of management need to know how to interpret the information provided by the financial records of the firm.

WHAT ACCOUNTING RECORDS TELL

Accounting records contain many kinds of valuable information, and they answer many questions retailers have about their businesses.

First, they tell the results of past performance. From these records retailers know:

- What the costs of doing business last year and the year before were

- Where the major expenditures were

- Whether costs exceeded income

- Whether there was a profit after all costs, expenses, and taxes were paid

- Where the points of weakness in the business were

- Where the points of strength in the business were

Second, accounting records tell the present and future potential of the business. Analysis of past records gives retailers a basis for judging their present performance and a basis for determining their future potential. They can determine which activities have been financially advantageous and use this information to make future plans.

Third, accounting records provide information necessary to establish a credit rating. Retailers, in order to buy merchandise, must either have good credit ratings or pay cash. Accounting records showing a solvent, well-managed organization will aid in establishing good ratings.

Fourth, accounting records provide information required by the government. City, state, and federal government income tax records; sales tax records; payments for employees' social security and unemployment insurance; withholding for employees' income taxes; occupational taxes; and real estate taxes are examples of tax information required of business firms. The reports to the government and payments made are based on the records kept by the firm and, in the case of large firms, substantiated by an audit of the firm's books.

Fifth, accounting records provide a basis for comparing business figures. Many associations and consulting firms furnish comparative figures so that the figures of one business can be compared with the averages of other similar businesses. Using similar formats therefore permits the managers of like firms to compare their costs, markups, sales, shortages, and profits.

TOPICS FOR DISCUSSION

1. Why is it mandatory that a firm make a profit?
2. Explain the function of the financial or control section of a firm.
3. What are the functions of an accounts payable section of a firm?

4. Explain the financial functions of the accounts receivable section of a firm.
5. How do retailers make use of short-term funds?
6. Explain the uses of long-term funds by retailers.
7. What is meant by trade credit?
8. What are the usual sources of long-term funds?
9. Explain the disadvantages of the sale and leaseback as a form of long-term funding.
10. Why are accounting records important for a store?

MATHEMATICS FOR RETAILING

A small men's-wear store had the following sales and expenses during a 3-year period:

	First Year	Second Year	Third Year
Sales	$122,000	$126,800	$131,800
Cost of goods sold	74,630	75,470	78,720
Gross margin	$ 47,370	$ 51,330	$ 53,080
Operating expenses	39,337	43,283	45,352
Profit (before taxes)	$ 8,033	$ 8,047	$ 7,728

1. In the second year, what dollar sales increase did the store have over the first year?
2. Using the first year as the basis, what was the dollar increase in sales in the third year?
3. What percentage of sales each year was spent on operating expenses?
4. What percentage of profit based on sales did the store make in each of the three years?

Do your calculations on a separate sheet of paper.

COMMUNICATIONS IN RETAILING

Mr. Ronald Barth, the manager of the men's-wear store in the above exercise, has been asked by the owners to sell the store. Mr. Barth is about to retire, and he has not been well for the past year. He and the owners believe that a young, healthy person can do a better job than is reflected by the figures shown above. On a separate sheet of paper, write a short letter to accompany these figures to Mr. James Forest, a young, experienced retailer who is a prospective buyer for the business. Mr. Barth has been receiving $15,000 a year as his salary for running the business.

MANAGING HUMAN RELATIONS

Ms. Martin bought a long-established music shop. After purchasing the firm, she found that her customers were slow in paying their bills. She wanted to make a rather large purchase of musical instruments for the holiday season, but the distributors of those instruments were unwilling to extend the time for her to pay her bills because she was a newcomer to the field and, as yet, had no favorable credit rating. If she borrowed money to pay for the instruments, she would not be able to do any better than break even on the year's business. She disliked dunning customers when she was just coming into the firm, yet she had to collect on the overdue accounts. How could she persuade the customers to pay without losing their patronage? On a separate sheet of paper, write the proposed letter for her.

DECISION MAKING

You have been assigned as the manager of the candy department in a large store. You have received the report of your store (Store A) comparing your department with that of your store's competitor (Store B). Based on the following figures, what changes and improvements would you consider to be necessary in your operation? Be prepared to discuss your ideas.

	Store A	Store B
Cumulative markup	45.3%	48.6%
Markdowns	2.6%	1.9%
Stock shortage	2.2%	2.1%
Gross margin	40.5%	44.6%
Number of stockturns	11.4	17.6
Salespeople's salaries	10.4%	8.2%
Average gross sale	$1.11	$1.22

chapter 33

THE INCOME STATEMENT AND THE BALANCE SHEET

Suppliers of goods to retailers often point out how much more the retailers charge for those goods than the vendors do. These vendors sometimes forget that retailers buy in quantity but, in turn, sell individual items to individual customers. For the retailers, such transactions are costly and entail an enormous amount of recordkeeping. Records must be kept of every item of merchandise; of the individual charge customers, cash-send customers, and COD customers from whom money must be collected. There must be records of the vendors, of the truckers or others who deliver the merchandise, of the employees who handle the merchandise from the time of its arrival to its departure from the store, and of the employees who perform other tasks within the organization. In addition, records of all taxes and other charges, such as those for advertising, must be kept. Retailers find it difficult to cover all those charges, even with the current markup they charge for the goods.

INGREDIENTS OF PROFIT

The costs of the merchandise and the costs of handling and selling the merchandise are tallied and subtracted from the income received from the sale of those goods and from other activities in which the firm is involved. Some firms rent space, have leased departments, receive interest on money invested for goods sold, or have other

forms of income. All this income is totaled in determining the net income of the firm after costs, expenses of doing business, and taxes have been paid.

If there is a profit above expenses, management has been successful in the running of the business. If there is a loss, management has been unsuccessful. If this loss is severe and cannot be met by obtaining money from some source, the firm goes into bankruptcy. Analysis of the functions and goals of the business may help to determine which activities contributed to the profit or loss.

PROFIT AIDS PROFIT MAKING

The profit a business makes is essential to its present and future health. If a business is making a profit, some of this money can be used further to improve the business. If a business is making a profit, some of the money can be used to pay dividends to investors and thus attract additional funds for expansion and development. If a business is making a profit, the manufacturers of products in demand by consumers may seek to showcase their products in that store. If a business is making a profit, it can get credit and extend its buying power even further. Thus the firm that is making a profit has a potential to make even more profit in succeeding years. Success begets success.

384

HOW PROFIT IS STATED

Profit is most commonly stated as a percentage of sales. Profit may also be stated as a percentage of net worth.

Profit as a Percent of Sales

A profit or loss in retailing is stated as a dollar figure and as a percentage of the sales figure for the period under consideration. If a firm had a $1 million sales volume and a net profit of $25,000, that profit would be stated as 2.5 percent of sales.

This method of stating profits enables retailers to understand clearly what portion of the money they take in is retained as profit. In the example stated above, out of every $1 spent by a customer in a store, 2.5 cents are retained by the store as profit, while 97.5 cents are used to pay for the goods and for the expenses of getting those goods into the hands of the customers.

By stating net profit or loss in terms of percentages, retailers can compare the figures for one year against those of the previous year to determine whether there has been an increase or a decrease in the profit performance. They can also note a trend over a period of years.

The profit on sales has ranged up to as high as 3.6 percent in recent years. This is called *net profit ratio.*

Profit as a Percentage of Net Worth

The *net worth* of a firm is synonymous with ownership interest in the firm. The capital invested by the owners in the firm plus the profits that are added to that capital equal the net worth. The net worth is the difference between the assets owned and the debts owed.

The percentage of change in the capital is an indication of the success of the operation. If a firm has a 10-percent return on net worth, this means that for every dollar invested in the business, 10 cents have been realized as a profit on that investment. Some retailing firms have losses; some have a small percentage of return on net worth; and others have larger returns. This will

be discussed further in the latter part of this chapter.

The return on net worth has averaged as high as 11.8 percent in recent years.

THE INCOME STATEMENT

Profits or lack of profits is determined by the use of an *income statement,* which is also known as a profit and loss statement or an operating statement. This statement summarizes results of the business for a specific period of time. It may be compiled monthly, every six months, or every year depending on the needs of the business and the speed of its operations. It is important to management because it indicates the results of operating efficiency to date.

The income statement is prepared usually once a month using book figures. Once or twice a year, these book figures are adjusted by actual or physical counts of merchandise.

TERMS IN THE INCOME STATEMENT

A simplified income statement is shown on page 386 to acquaint the reader with the various parts and with their importance to the entire report. If this statement is followed step by step, one can see how this retail firm earned its money and what it needs to do to improve its operations.

Net Sales

The first figure, the one for net sales, is derived from *total gross sales.* Total gross sales represent the sum of all the goods and services purchased by customers during a period. The cash sales, charge sales, revolving credit sales, and installment sales are totaled to equal gross sales. Customers, however, may return some merchandise for credit. They may request adjustments on the price of other goods that they have bought. They may exchange goods for other less-expensive goods. Thus they receive a rebate on the original purchase. *Net sales* are the total dollar sales at retail made after subtracting the amount of

INCOME STATEMENT OF ABC STORE

	Amount	Percent of Net Sales
Net sales	$100,000	100.0
Cost of goods sold (*subtract*)	58,000	58.0
Gross margin	$ 42,000	42.0
Expenses (*subtract*)	38,000	38.0
Operating profit	$ 4,000	4.0
Other income (*add*)	500	0.5
Total profit before income taxes		
	$ 4,500	4.5
Provision for federal income taxes		
	1,500	1.5
Net profit	$ 3,000	3.0

money for the returns, allowances, and adjustments made for customers.

Operating statements often may not show gross sales. Those figures are available, however, to the management of the firm. Analysis of the percent differences between gross and net sales during comparable periods can tell the retailer a great deal about the store's operation. If this percent figure is increasing, the retailer may need to determine whether the employees are using high-pressure tactics, whether merchandise quality is satisfactory, or whether values are comparable to those of competitors. If the figure is decreasing, it may indicate that one or more of those conditions have improved since the last analysis was made.

In the example of the income statement for the ABC store, the gross sales and net sales showed the following:

Gross sales	$107,000
Returns and allowances (*subtract*)	7,000
Net sales	$100,000

Cost of Goods Sold

In the income statement for the ABC store, the total cost of goods sold during the period was $58,000. This included the costs shown below.

As can be seen by this example, the total cost of merchandise handled includes all charges for goods on hand and goods ordered, transportation charges, and workroom costs and alterations. Trade or quantity discounts, which the vendor has allowed the retailer, were deducted before entering the costs of merchandise handled.

The freight and express charges make up the transportation costs of getting the goods to the

Opening inventory at cost	$ 49,000
Purchases at cost (less trade and quantity discounts) (*add*)	49,200
Total merchandise handled	$ 98,200
Freight and express charges (*add*)	800
Workroom costs and alterations (*add*)	1,200
Total cost of merchandise handled	$100,200
Closing inventory at cost (*subtract*)	40,000
Gross cost of merchandise sold	$ 60,200
Cash discount and anticipation (*subtract*)	2,200
Total cost of goods sold	$ 58,000

FINANCIAL CONTROL FUNCTIONS

store from the manufacturer or wholesaler. Merchandise is shipped with an FOB point. The incoming parcel post, freight, or express charges are considered by the retailer as part of the cost of the goods themselves. For retailers situated near their sources of supply, these costs may be negligible. If goods are imported, however, or if they travel across the country, these charges may be substantial. Thus if an item costs $1 on the manufacturer's invoice and the shipping charges are 25 cents per item, the retailer considers the cost of that item to be $1.25. Buyers note carefully the distance of comparable vendors from the store, since a saving in transportation charges may reduce the retail price to the customer and allow the store to be more competitive in its offerings.

In addition to shipping charges, other charges are imposed on foreign purchases. These include duty on imports, fees of commissionaires (those who aid in the buying of goods in the foreign market), and brokerage and entry fees. The merchandise, therefore, is charged into the store at a landed cost, which is considerably higher than the vendor's charge for the goods.

Workroom costs and the costs of alterations are those charges necessitated to make certain categories of goods salable. Furniture, for example, may need to be polished, touched up, or assembled. Ready-to-wear clothing may need alterations for customers before it can be worn. Custom-made products such as draperies may need to be measured and installed. Silverware may need buffing or engraving.

These workroom costs, which deal with alterations and repairs of merchandise, include expenditures for labor, supplies, and outside help as needed, less any money paid by customers for such services. A customer may have a dress altered. The total charges for alteration may amount to $7.50, but the customer may have been charged $6, so that the net cost to the store for that job is $1.50. These workroom charges increase the costs of goods sold, and thus they are added to determine the total costs of goods.

The total cost of merchandise handled includes opening inventory, purchases, freight and express charges, and workroom costs. Not all merchandise is sold at the close of a period, however, and so the cost of goods left on hand must be subtracted. Thus, the retailer has a closing inventory at cost, which is subtracted from the total cost of merchandise handled. The cash discount is also subtracted, and the remaining figure represents the total cost of goods sold during a particular period.

Errors in Valuation

The physical inventory of stock, which is taken once or twice a year in well-run stores, determines the actual cost of goods sold when done accurately. If errors are made in the valuation of the goods or in taking inventory, the total cost of goods sold would be stated incorrectly, and the entire statement would reflect a distorted figure. For the months between such inventories, book figures must be used to indicate the direction costs are taking. Consequently, until an actual physical inventory is taken of the stock on hand, the closing inventory is determined from the records. The book figures are adjusted either semiannually or annually after the physical inventory has been computed.

Cash Discount and Anticipation

The money withheld from the vendors' invoices by the retailer because of early payment of bills is deducted separately on the income statement. Since early payment is possible because the financial state of the firm allows it to take advantage of discounts, and since early payment is not due to the astuteness or bargaining ability of the buyer, the discounts are noted separately. The methods of computing cash discount and anticipation were discussed in Chapter 13.

Gross Margin

The *gross margin,* is a figure that indicates to the retailer the state of health of the business. Regardless of the initial markup placed on merchandise, the amount of money actually realized for the sale of those goods is reflected in the gross margin. This total reflects the difference between the sales and the entire cost of goods sold, including transportation charges and workroom costs and alterations, minus cash discounts and anticipation. The formula is as follows:

Net sales —
total cost of goods and services sold =
gross margin

Thus, for the ABC store,

	Amount	Percent of Net Sales
Total net sales	$100,000	100
Total cost of goods sold	58,000	58
Gross margin	$ 42,000	42

The gross margin is a figure that reveals a great deal to the retailer. The amount of money represented by this figure must cover all the expenses of doing business, pay the taxes, and leave some profit for the owners or stockholders and for the improvement or expansion of the business.

Expenses

Once retailers have determined their gross margin, they know how much money they have to cover all expenses in running their business other than those associated with the costs of the goods. Expenses are divided into two types in large stores: direct and indirect. The large stores must allocate expenses to various departments, divisions, or branches. In small stores, all expenses would be direct, since no allocations of expenses among various segments would be necessary.

Direct expenses are those attributable to a particular store or department activity, such as paying salaries or rent, advertising, purchasing selling supplies, and buying new fixtures. *Indirect expenses,* or those that must be allocated, necessitate some judgment for prorating them. In a large store, for example, each department or unit must share administrative expenses and the costs of donations, losses from bad debts, pensions,

insurance, depreciation, and professional services. Since no way exists to assess the exact amount to be charged to each individual unit of the firm, these expenses must be allocated on the basis of judgment.

The expenses of running the business are among the major factors in determining profit. High expenses can eliminate any chance for profit, while low expenses do not use up the entire gross margin. The profit that remains can be used to improve the business and to pay dividends to the owners and investors.

All expenses involved in running a firm must be included if the operating statement is to be accurate. Owners' salaries, rent on owned property, and interest that would be received on money invested are examples of expenses that might be overlooked. Leaving out such expenses might result in the statement of an artificially high profit picture. Allocation and control of expenses are discussed further in Chapter 35.

Operating Profit or Loss

By subtracting the total expenses from the gross margin, one determines the *operating profit* (or loss). Some departments or segments in large firms do not show an operating profit when expenses not directly allocated to them are assigned. This is especially true of departments carrying large, space-consuming goods such as furniture, where space allocations cause costs to rise inordinately high. Yet without the contribution made by such departments to the overall expenses of the firm, the entire operation might be less profitable. Thus even an area showing an operating loss might be making an important contribution to the total profitability of a firm.

Other Income

Although the primary function of a firm is to sell merchandise profitably, other sources of income may exist. These sources help the store to show a profit or aid in offsetting a loss. The additional income may come from a variety of sources, such as dividends and interest on outside investments, leased departments, rentals on fixtures, fur storage or other service areas, and any gains made on the sale or rental of property or other assets.

Many retailers rely on other income to provide a profit for the firm. This other income may be a larger amount than the operating profit.

Total Profit Before Taxes

When other income is added to the operating profit or subtracted from an operating loss, the total profit or loss is obtained before income taxes are paid. This figure is a true measure of how well the business is doing. However, it does not indicate the effectiveness of just the retailing aspects of the business. The overall success is shown by the amount listed under operating profit.

Provision for Federal Income Taxes

The taxes a business pays are levied by municipal, county, state, or federal agencies on the merchandise, fixtures, buildings, land, equipment, and salaries of employees. These taxes are treated as part of the expenses of the business and are deducted as part of the cost of sales. Federal income taxes on the business, however, are figured on the final total net profit, and therefore they are subtracted from the figure on which they are based. If a firm has a loss instead of a profit, no federal income taxes are paid for that year. If that firm subsequently makes a profit, it may subtract the previous year's losses before paying federal income tax on any remaining profit.

Net Profit

How well all the activities of the firm were carried out is told emphatically by the last line on the income statement. If that line shows a profit, the management considers that it has had a measure of success. If that profit has increased over the previous year, the management considers that it has improved its operation. If that profit shows a decrease, management must examine the various facets of the business to see where improvements

are needed. If the final figure shows a loss, every phase of the business activity must be scrutinized. Policies must be reviewed to see if they are driving customers away. Routines must be checked to see if every cost possible is being controlled. Merchandise must be reviewed to determine if the goods customers want are being carried. Markups must be analyzed to determine if they are sufficient to cover the costs of selling the goods. A loss is a signal that the operation of the business is not successful. If a loss persists and is not corrected, the retail firm might ultimately close the unsuccessful branch, or bankruptcy might result for the entire firm.

To stay in business, a retailing firm must make a profit more often than it incurs a loss.

THE IMPORTANCE OF THE BALANCE SHEET

The income statement tells retailers what their sales and cost results were during a given period, usually six months or a year. The *balance sheet* tells them what their financial position is at any given time, and this may then be compared to their financial position at that same time in the previous year. From the balance sheet, retailers can tell how their assets are distributed. Assets include inventory, customers' accounts receivable, fixtures, equipment, cash, and investments. The balance sheet also tells them what their net worth is. The total assets minus the total liabilities of the firm equals the net worth. In turn, this net worth figure may be used to tell how productive the investment in business is. Retailers can figure what percentage of return they are getting on their net worth and compare that with their percentage of net profit on sales—the figure obtained from the income statement.

If a retailer is seeking additional funds for expansion or improvements, the net worth figure, which includes capital and surplus, is the amount that interested investors will analyze.

Following is an example of a balance sheet for a relatively small retailing firm.

CONSOLIDATED BALANCE SHEET

Current assets		Current liabilities	
Cash on hand and in the bank	$ 10,000	Accounts payable	$ 26,000
U.S. government securities	1,000	Loan	500
Accounts receivable (less reserve		Accrued payroll	2,600
for doubtful accounts)	20,250	Accrued taxes and expenses	5,000
Merchandise inventory	40,000	Total current liabilities	$ 34,100
Supply inventory	3,000	**Fixed liabilities**	
Total current assets	$ 74,250	Notes payable	3,000
		Mortgages due 1985	50,000
Fixed assets		Reserve for contingencies	10,000
Land	5,049	**Capital**	
Buildings, less depreciation reserve	50,000	Surplus	
Furniture and fixtures, less		Capital from sale of property in	
depreciation reserve	100,000	excess of stated value	100,000
Goodwill at nominal amount	1	Earned (undistributed) profits	32,200
TOTAL ASSETS	$229,300	TOTAL LIABILITIES AND CAPITAL	$229,300

THE FORM OF THE BALANCE SHEET

The balance sheet is divided into two parts: assets on the left, and liabilities on the right. Under assets are listed the moneys, property, and goods that the company owns or that are owed to it. Under liabilities are listed the moneys the company owes to others plus bonds due and reserves for contingencies. In addition, the capital and surplus that belong to the company are added to these liabilities. The assets always equal the liabilities plus the capital and surplus sections of the balance sheet. Only through careful analysis can the interested reader unravel the important information contained in the balance sheet.

Assets

Cash on hand and in the bank refers to the money held in the store for use in making change and also to the money in the bank that can be obtained whenever needed.

U.S. government securities are those securities that can easily be converted into cash for the amount listed.

Accounts receivable represent the money owed to the retailer by the charge, revolving-account, and installment-account customers. This money is collectible within the following year. Since some customers may default on their payments, however, a reserve of approximately 10 percent has been subtracted, so that the company's assets will not be overstated.

Merchandise inventory refers to the amount either at cost or at the market price, whichever is lower, at which the company values the merchandise it has available for sale to customers.

Supply inventory consists of the merchandise that the store carries in the form of wrapping paper, string, bags, books of forms, paper, display materials, and so forth that will be used during the year by its employees and that will have to be replaced as they are used.

Total current assets reflect the sum of all these goods and moneys, which are easily marketed and which have measurable value.

Fixed assets include the value of the property, plant, and equipment belonging to the firm. Included in this category also is movable equipment such as the trucks, furniture, and tools that are used in the firm. These assets are all listed at their cost value, less a provision for depreciation.

An intangible that may have considerable value is the goodwill that a firm has developed through the years of its existence. By giving good service and good value to its customers, it has established a following that represents an important asset. However, since it is difficult to put a value in actual dollars and cents on this asset, the company chooses to list it at a nominal amount of $1.

Liabilities

The liabilities side of the balance sheet is particularly confusing, for two reasons. First, the liabilities column always has the same total as the assets side of the balance sheet. Second, it includes many listings that are not liabilities but, rather, form the net worth of the firm.

Current Liabilities. All debts of the firm payable during the current year are listed under current liabilities. Thus *accounts payable* refers to bills owed to vendors. A bank loan may be outstanding and due within the year. *Accrued payroll* costs are those moneys due to employees. Taxes and other expenses due during the year are included.

The total current liabilities figure is especially important when it is compared to the total current assets figure shown on the other side of the balance sheet. The *working capital,* or the net current assets of the firm, is what is left after the current liabilities are subtracted from the current assets. On the balance sheet in our example, the current assets, $74,250, minus current liabilities, $34,100, leaves $40,150 in working capital. In general, current assets should be about twice as large as current liabilities. In this balance sheet, there is a slightly better relationship than that between the two amounts.

The current ratio of assets to liabilities can be obtained by dividing the current assets by the current liabilities. In the balance sheet shown, the current ratio is 2.1. This is a rather low ratio in terms of successful merchandising operations. Preferably, ratios should be 3 or higher.

The net quick assets, which is obtained by totaling the merchandise inventory figure from the assets side of the balance sheet and the total current liabilities, should not be as high as the total current assets if a firm is to be considered in a good position. In our example, this would be figured as follows:

Merchandise inventory	$40,000
Total current liabilities	34,100
	$74,100

Total current assets, $74,250, minus $74,100 equals $150. This $150 is a very small difference between those two amounts and calls the attention of management to an area that should be scrutinized with considerable care.

The *notes payable* represent money owed by the firm. Formal notes payable have been signed for the money owed. Banks and equipment vendors are the usual firms to which such money is owed. A *mortgage* similarly represents money loaned on the property of the firm. This money comes due at some time in the future. The reserve for contingencies is essential for any sudden change, catastrophe, or unforeseen occurrence.

Capital and Surplus. The net worth or the owner's equity in the firm is indicated by the capital and surplus portion of the balance sheet. This represents the owner's initial investment plus any net income or minus any net loss since that time.

The capital realized from the sale of any property in excess of the stated value of that property and any surplus from the net profits of the firm that has not been distributed to shareholders form the net worth of the firm or of the owner of the firm.

COMPARISONS WITH PREVIOUS YEARS

Most balance sheets show the figures for the current year and for the previous year. By comparing the current year's figures with those of the previous year, the management of the firm can determine whether or not operations have improved during that period.

If any figures on the sheet are overstated or

FINANCIAL HIGHLIGHTS

ASSOCIATED DRY GOODS CORPORATION AND CONSOLIDATED SUBSIDIARIES

Sales, Earnings, Dividends	52 weeks ended January 31, 1976	52 weeks ended February 1, 1975	Percent change
Net sales	$1,390,966,000	$1,300,190,000	7.0
Earnings before income taxes	84,051,000	72,856,000	15.4
Net earnings	43,078,000	37,361,000	15.3
Total dividends on common stock	18,909,000	18,900,000	—
Earnings retained	24,169,000	18,461,000	30.9
Net earnings per share	3.19	2.77	15.2
Dividends per share	1.40	1.40	—
Balance Sheet Information			
Accounts receivable	$ 152,414,000	$ 191,000,000	(20.2)
Merchandise inventories	217,470,000	203,364,000	6.9
Working capital	237,146,000	227,391,000	4.3
Ratio of current assets to current liabilities	2.35	2.19	7.3
Shareholders' equity	438,824,000	414,477,000	5.9
Shareholders' equity per common share	32.48	30.70	5.8
Number of common shares outstanding	13,509,107	13,500,535	—
Store Information			
Number of stores	156	150	4.0
Square footage at end of year	25,724,000	24,865,000	3.5

Market Price Data and Dividend Information

	1975			1974		
	Market Prices		Dividend	Market Prices		Dividend
Quarter	High	Low	Rate	High	Low	Rate
1st	31¾	21⅛	$.35	31⅜	22⅝	$.35
2nd	31¼	25¾	.35	29¼	22⅜	.35
3rd	35	23	.35	25⅞	13⅜	.35
4th	38½	33⅛	.35	20¼	14	.35

Stock Listing: New York Stock Exchange
(Symbol: DG)

SEC 10-K REPORT

Copies of the Company's Annual Report on Form 10-K to the Securities and Exchange Commission will be made available to shareholders upon written request to:

Associated Dry Goods Corporation
417 Fifth Avenue
New York, New York 10016
Attention: Secretary

This page from the annual report of a large retail corporation summarizes information from the financial statement and balance sheet. By comparing the current year's figures with those of the previous year, management and investors can determine whether or not operations have improved.
Courtesy Associated Dry Goods Corporation

understated, however, a true financial picture is not available. The importance of the merchandise inventory figure must not be overlooked. If the value of the inventory were stated at a figure lower than the real market value, the owner's net worth would be understated. If the inventory were valued at more than it would actually bring in the market, the owner's net worth would be overstated. Inventory valuation, therefore, is important in determining the true fiscal state of any retailing business. This information is discussed in the following chapter.

TOPICS FOR DISCUSSION

1. Explain the statement "Profit aids profit making."
2. What is meant by profit as a percentage of sales?
3. Explain what is meant by profit as a percentage of net worth.
4. What is revealed by the income statement (operating statement) of a firm?
5. Explain the difference between gross sales and net sales.
6. What factors are included under the category of cost of goods sold?
7. Explain what payments may be classified as other income.
8. Explain what changes in profit indicate to the management of a firm.
9. Explain the purpose of the balance sheet.
10. What are the components of the assets of a firm?

MATHEMATICS FOR RETAILING

A small shop open only on weekends has sales for the year of $20,000 and other income of $600. The cost of merchandise sold is $15,000. The shop's operating expenses are $4,000.

1. What is the gross margin?
2. What is the operating profit?
3. What is the net profit?
4. Express the gross margin as a percentage of net sales.
5. Express the operating profit as a percentage of net sales.
6. Express the net profit as a percentage of net sales.

Do your figuring on a separate sheet of paper.

COMMUNICATIONS IN RETAILING

The sales for the previous year for the firm listed above were $25,000; the gross margin was $6,000; the operating profit was $1,200; and the net profit was $1,920. You, as the manager, have been asked to explain the differences between the figures for the two years. On a separate sheet of paper, write a letter to the owner in response to this request.

MANAGING HUMAN RELATIONS

A large chain organization had a policy of promoting managers to larger stores when they had good profit showings, leaving those managers whose showings were average in the stores to which they had been assigned, but demoting to smaller stores those managers whose profit showings were less than they had been in previous years. One manager, Mr. Charles, who had been with the firm 12 years, had consistently improved profit showings annually until this year. However, large sections of homes near his store had been torn down to make room for a new superhighway, and the customers who had lived in those homes had been forced to move to other neighborhoods. Mr. Charles included in his annual report a statement about the changed character of the neighborhood. What action would you recommend the firm take about this manager's assignment for the coming year? Be prepared to discuss your suggestions.

CAREER LADDER

Peter Fouquet and Jocelyn Walters had just received A.A.S. degrees from the local community college. Both of them were employed by a large variety chain as assistant managers. While in school, Peter had majored in marketing and Jocelyn in accounting. On the job, each did good work. The young woman showed considerable creativity, while the young man was particularly good in human relations. Each was now being considered for promotion to the position of manager of a small local store belonging to the chain. The job would involve working during evening hours, ordering goods, watching costs, managing the people working in the firm, and preparing monthly reports showing operating expenses.

What factors should be taken into consideration in deciding which young person to promote to this position? Be prepared to discuss your answer.

chapter 34

VALUATION
OF MERCHANDISE INVENTORY

How much is the merchandise in a store really worth? This question has perplexed retailers through the ages. Today's newspaper, for example, is worth its full price to the person who has not yet read it. Yesterday's newspaper, however, is worthless except as waste paper. Today's television sports event is salable, but last week's has little news value. Stale bread or cake, vegetables that have wilted, last season's styles—how much are they worth to the merchant?

In the early days of retailing, all records were kept at cost, since bargaining was used in determining the retail price. Under that system, the owners considered any amount of money they obtained from the customer above the actual cost of the goods to be their profit. Their inventory (the goods on hand) retained its original cost value in their opinion. But was it really worth what was originally paid for it? This question has arisen throughout the history of retailing. The speedup of manufacturing processes, the increased rate of style changes, and the computer ordering of merchandise that keeps new goods coming in as fast as the old items are sold have made merchandise that sits on the shelf outdated quickly. Once goods are not salable, what value do they represent? An analysis of the various methods of valuing inventory will help to explain this problem.

THE COST METHOD

Some types of retailing firms find that valuing the goods on hand, their *inventory,* by the cost method best meets their needs. Those in businesses such as food retailing and others who have a rapid turnover or who have merchandise for which prices may change several times during a day find that their calculations are simplest when they use the cost method of valuation.

In using the cost method, the unit cost of each item must be marked in code, or a detailed record of the cost of each item must be kept. When an actual count of goods on hand, the physical inventory, is made, the cost is the amount that is recorded for each item.

Application of the Cost Method

The cost method of valuation is satisfactory when merchandise sells rapidly or when it changes little in value from year to year. In the cost method of valuing inventory, losses due to depreciation are deferred until the items are sold. Consequently, the actual value of the goods may be overstated when using this method.

The cost method of valuation may, however, save retailers a considerable amount of paper work and recording detail, especially if they have frequently fluctuating retail prices for their goods. For example, if a firm is selling milk and there is a price fluctuation, the milk may sell at the beginning of the day for 45 cents a quart, be lowered to 44 cents for an hour or two, then return to 45 cents. When other stores are closed, the owner may choose to raise the price to 46 cents to pay for the extra costs of staying open later hours. If the retailer is keeping records at cost only, the basic cost for the milk (in this instance, 38 cents a quart) remains constant. Sales on the cash register tape, however, show the following:

```
10 quarts @ $.45 = $  4.50
18 quarts @ $.44 =     7.92
20 quarts @ $.46 =     9.20
48                   $21.62 Total retail for day
48 quarts @ $.38 =   18.24 Total cost
                     $  3.38 Gross margin
```

The average price the merchant sold the milk for during the day was 45.04 cents a quart. Since the cost of a quart was 38 cents, the retailer had a gross margin of 7.04 cents on each quart and a markup on cost of 18.5 percent.

Items such as vegetables, whose prices are reduced quickly because of spoilage, are also best recorded under the cost method. In stores that perform many services on the products they sell—such as millinery shops that trim hat bodies and add veils or ribbons, or shops that sell baskets of candies or fruits, which they arrange and decorate—the amount of labor and the cost of other materials added make it necessary to operate on the cost basis in pricing goods and valuing goods for inventory purposes.

Limitations of the Cost Method

The cost method of inventory valuation does not provide for automatic depreciation in inventory value. The merchant can calculate the lower cost of goods if prices have decreased since purchases were made and subtract that amount from the total inventory value. Or the merchant may choose to "age" the inventory and reduce its value by the length of time the goods have remained in stock. When inventory is taken, the totals are listed by age of stock. Stock from 1 to 3 months of age would be taken at full cost; stock from 3 to 6 months of age would be valued at 15 to 25 percent less than original cost; stock 6 months to 1 year old would be valued from 25 to 50 percent less than original cost; and stock over a year old would be valued from 50 to 75 percent less than original cost. In this way, inventory would not be overstated.

THE RETAIL METHOD

Retailers found that carrying inventory and charging it on the books at the price initially paid for it, as in the cost method explained above, frequently resulted in overstating the value of those items. It was a laborious task to compute to get a more realistic inventory value. As a result, a newer method known as the *retail method* of inventory valuation came into popular use in large firms. By this method:

- The total value of the merchandise carried is determined by calculating the sum of the current retail prices of the items.

- The cost is determined by applying the cumulative markup percent. *Cumulative markup* is the markup on the beginning inventory plus the markup on purchases. It is the difference between the total cost and the total original retail price of goods before markdowns, discounts, and shrinkage.

- A current market value is given to inventory without the laborious task of recordkeeping necessitated by the cost method.

The following example shows how inventory is affected by the retail method of valuing goods:

Cost Method	Retail Method
12 items @ $.60 = $7.20 cost	12 items @ $.60 = $7.20 cost
	50% markup = $1.20 each or $14.40 a dozen at retail
	Markdown to meet competition, $.20 each 12 items @ $1 = $12 a dozen at retail
	Cost value: $12 retail × 50% (the complement of the 50% markup) = $6 new cost valuation based on current retail price

As this example shows, although $7.20 was initially the cost of the items, their current value in the store based on the relationship to the retail price is only $6. Thus, if those 12 items were inventoried at $7.20 cost, the inventory for them would be overstated by $1.20.

Since determining costs by the retail method can only be done if the original markups are known, and since costs must be determined for merchandise in related groups having similar markups, this system lends itself best to use in stores carrying related items or in stores that are departmentized for recordkeeping purposes.

An example of the computation of stock by using the retail inventory method is shown in the first table below.

Since records are kept throughout the period, the cumulative markup percent of 45.06 may be used to determine the cost value of the inventory as noted in the second table below:

		Cost		Retail	Cumulative Markup Percent
Opening inventory*		$ 5,000		$ 9,500	47.3
Purchases from vendors	$10,000		$18,000		
Less returns & allowances	−1,000		−1,800		
	$ 9,000		$16,200		
Transportation	200				
Total cost of goods purchased		9,200		16,200	43.2
Additional markups				200	
Revisions of retail price downward (not markdowns)				−50	
Total inventory handled		$14,200		$25,850	45.06

*This is the same figure as the closing inventory from the last inventory taken.

	Cost	Retail	Markup Percent
Net sales of goods		$12,000	
Net markdown (markdowns less cancellations)		500	
Discounts to employees		100	
Estimated shortages (1.5%)		180	
Total deductions		$12,780	
Closing estimated inventory at retail			
($25,850 − $12,780) =		$13,070	45.06
Closing estimated inventory at cost			
($13,070 × 100% − 45.06%, the complement of the markup) =	$7,180.65		
Gross cost of merchandise old ($14,200 − $7,180.65) =	$7,019.35		

The net sales of goods refers to the total sales minus customers' returns. The net markdown includes markdowns less any cancellations of markdowns when sale prices are returned to the original prices. Discounts to employees are subtracted, or, in some stores, they may be included as markdowns. A figure for the estimated shortages is included as a reduction from stock. The total retail amount of these deductions is then subtracted from the total retail figure for the stock to arrive at the closing estimated retail value of the inventory. To determine the estimated cost of the goods left in stock, the complement of the cumulative markup is used. The total retail price of the inventory remaining is multiplied by this complement to derive the estimated cost of the inventory on hand. The book inventory at cost is $7,180.65. When this figure is subtracted from the original cost of goods on hand, the remainder is the gross cost of merchandise sold.

When a physical inventory is taken, a comparison will be made between the closing estimated inventory at retail and the actual retail inventory. If the actual inventory is higher, it indicates an overage in comparison to the book figures. This overage may be caused by errors in bookkeeping, omissions in making records of markups, additions to stock, charging customers too much money, or giving them too little change.

Shortages are much more common than overages. Shortages may be due to any of the following: recordkeeping errors; incorrect counts made when merchandise first arrived in the store; errors in recording the physical inventory; failure to count some merchandise, such as items in windows or other displays; theft of money or merchandise by employees or customers. Shortages in excess of those anticipated are signals for careful evaluation of all operations. Excessive shortages indicate the need for greater supervision and control in every phase of the retailing operation.

Advantages of the Retail Method

The retail method of valuing inventory has been adopted by the majority of large stores and by many smaller stores. The advantages of this method make it usable in most stores selling staple goods or merchandise at prices that do not fluctuate frequently. The retail method is also used where the one-price system of pricing merchandise is employed. Where bargaining for price is common, the retail method cannot be used.

Advantages of the retail method are as follows:

- Estimated figures are made available through perpetual book inventory, as needed for merchandising decisions. This permits buyers and merchandisers to make adjustments as needed to correct imbalances during a period rather than wait until the end of a season or a year to make these adjustments. In the case of theft or loss of goods due to other disasters, the book value of goods lost can be determined. Figuring depreciation in the value of goods is a basic part of this retail inventory system, resulting in a realistic evaluation of goods on hand.

- The cost of goods on hand can be determined as reflecting a true cost in relation to the current market value of those goods. The retail method of inventory is accepted by the federal government in determining the true cost.

- Using retail prices is easier for everyone who handles merchandise. Those who sell can easily see the price, and customers can tell the price without asking for assistance. During inventory, prices are readily ascertainable.

- The market price of the goods can be determined easily. The complement of the cumulative markup percent is applied to the total retail price of the goods to ascertain the cost of merchandise sold and the cost of the goods remaining in stock. The correct market price is further assured by the markups or markdowns that have increased or decreased the value of the merchandise in keeping with prices for those goods charged elsewhere. This makes it easy to value the merchandise accurately at cost or at market price—whichever is lower.

Disadvantages of the Retail Method

The disadvantages of the retail method are as follows:

- The main disadvantage of the retail method of keeping and taking inventory is the amount of recordkeeping it necessitates. Under the cost method, the retailers keep records of the costs of their goods. The money in the till is the amount for which those goods have been sold. A cost inventory then tells them what is remaining in their stocks.

  With the retail method, accurate records must be kept of any price changes that occur because of initial markups, additional markups, markdowns, and cancellations of markdowns. Constant supervision and control are necessary to assure that price changes are systematically recorded.

- A second disadvantage is the fact that the costs are not accurately kept but are arrived at by a series of averages that may not be wholly exact. While the cumulative markup, which is used to derive the cost value of goods, has proved to be a satisfactory figure, it does not reflect the fact that goods that cost more and were sold at lower retail prices may have moved out of stock more quickly than goods with a higher markup that might still be in the store. As a result, the inventory could be overvalued at cost and show profits that did not actually exist.

- The retail method operates efficiently only where markups on the merchandise are similar. Departmentized stores or those stores carrying related merchandise can use this method successfully. General merchandise stores carrying goods with vastly different markups and different rates of sale would find this retail method unsuitable.

FIFO AND LIFO METHODS OF INVENTORY VALUATION

The previous discussion about inventory valuation indicates that this is a complicated subject. If prices remained constant, problems about inventory valuation would be nonexistent. If all goods were sold in the exact ratio in which they were initially bought, the problems would not be great. However, with both prices and amounts of goods sold fluctuating with no relationship to initial purchase prices, the retailer has an almost impossible task of valuing inventory at cost or at market price—whichever is lower. Two systems of inventory valuation are commonly used. These are known as the *FIFO* method (first in, first out) and the *LIFO* method (last in, first out).

FIFO Method

Most retailers attempt to sell the goods that they bought first before they sell the newer goods. Thus, "first in, first out" is a commonly agreed upon way of keeping stocks fresh and goods new. The accounting records used also follow this procedure.

FIFO works well in periods when prices are relatively stable. However, when prices are rising, the FIFO method causes higher inventory valuations. Consider the following record of merchandise bought during a year.

February purchases:	24 items @ $1.00
April purchases:	36 items @ $1.03
June purchases:	36 items @ $1.04
August purchases:	48 items @ $1.05
October purchases:	36 items @ $1.06

When inventory was taken the following January, 40 items remained in stock. Under the FIFO method, the assumption would be that all items purchased in February, April, and June had been sold and that all but 4 of the August purchases had been sold. The October purchases of 36 items at $1.06 each and 4 of the items purchased in August at $1.05 each would be the ones considered for inventory valuation. If the actual costs paid throughout the year were figured for each of the 40 items remaining, the total cost would be $41.56 at an average cost of $1.039 each, with some items from each buying period still in stock. By the FIFO method, however, 36 items would carry the October cost and 4 items the August cost for a total cost inventory of $42.36, or an average cost of $1.059 each. Thus the inventory on hand would have a higher valuation, and the goods sold would have a lower cost. In a rising cost market, the FIFO method tends to overstate profits, while it tends to minimize profits when prices are decreasing.

If the inventory is overstated, the "paper" profits of the firm will be overstated, and the firm will be subject to higher taxes and possibly to overpayment of dividends to owners or stockholders.

The first-in, first-out method that values the inventory at the cost or market price of the latest articles bought is difficult for the merchant to use when replacements of goods constantly cost more than goods bought in earlier periods. Replacement costs tend to absorb the paper profits that appear to exist but that in reality have been used to purchase the higher-cost goods.

LIFO Method

In 1941 retailers requested the use of a newer system of valuing inventories used by industries that extract minerals, gas, and oil from the land. This method, known as LIFO (last in, first out), assumes that the goods most recently bought are sold first. In 1947 the LIFO method was approved for retailers' use by the Bureau of Internal Revenue. A firm using this system must do so continuously. The management cannot shift to the FIFO method when costs remain static or start to decrease. This system requires that the total markdown be subtracted from the retail sales figure in calculating the net markup figure.

The FIFO method and the LIFO method may be compared for purchases made when costs are increasing.

Assume that a person bought 5 items at $50 each at the beginning of a period and 5 more items at $60 each later in the period, or a total of 10 items at a total cost of $550. During the period, 5 items were sold, leaving 5 in stock. The 5 items were sold at a retail price of $100 each. The valuations would be as in the table below.

Under the FIFO method, profits before taxes are higher; therefore, taxes are higher. Ending inventory costs are also higher, inflating the value of that merchandise.

Under the LIFO method, profits before taxes are lower. Taxes are therefore lower, and the merchandise valuation for the ending inventory is lower.

When prices are decreasing, the situation shown above is reversed. The LIFO method inflates profits, taxes, and ending inventory values, while the FIFO method shows lower profits before taxes and lower ending inventory values. During a period of steady prices, there is no gain from either the LIFO method or the FIFO method.

The FIFO and LIFO methods are used primarily as accounting devices for corporate statements and for income-tax reporting. Buyers and merchandisers are not affected by these methods of valuing inventory in planning departmental or store operations.

	FIFO	LIFO
Retail sales	(5 @ $100) $500	$500
Cost of goods sold	(5 @ $50) 250	(5 @ $60) 300
Profit before taxes	$250	$200
Ending inventory value	(5 @ $60) $300	(5 @ $50) $250

TOPICS FOR DISCUSSION

1. Why does the value of merchandise fluctuate while goods are in the store?
2. Why do some retailers use the cost method of inventory valuation?
3. What are the main advantages of using the cost method of inventory valuation?
4. What are the main disadvantages of using the cost method of inventory valuation?
5. What is meant by aging the inventory?
6. Why are book inventory and physical inventory figures often different?
7. What are the advantages of the retail method of inventory valuation?
8. What are the disadvantages of the retail method of inventory valuation?
9. What are the characteristics of the FIFO method of inventory valuation?
10. What are the characteristics of the LIFO method of inventory valuation?

MATHEMATICS FOR RETAILING

A tennis shop carried tennis apparel and equipment. Its prices for goods ranged from a few cents for wristlets to $75 for quality tennis rackets. Fast-selling tennis balls and small clothing items carried a 45-percent markup, while more costly and slower-selling items carried a 55-percent markup. All valuations were kept at retail. The total merchandise handled during a six-month period at initial cost was as follows:

Articles	Cost	Retail	Markup
Small items	$5,000		45%
Expensive items	5,000		55%

1. What retail price was obtained on the small items?
2. What retail price was obtained on the expensive items?
3. What was the average markup on merchandise carried by the store during the six-month period?
4. Assume that $6,000 worth of this merchandise was left at the time of the closing inventory. Based on the average markup for the six-month period, what would be the cost of those goods with no markdowns?

Do your calculations on a separate sheet of paper.

MANAGING HUMAN RELATIONS

A middle-sized jewelry firm had been successfully run by Mr. Bartlett for 30 years. He either maintained a small profit margin without increasing volume or added slightly to volume in some years. Mr. Bartlett decided to pass the reins of business to a younger man trained by him over the past 10 years while in high school and college. Mr. Bartlett, however, still planned to have a part in all major decisions. The young man, Mr. Knoll, college-educated and quite knowledgeable, decided it was time to institute many changes. Since the store was departmentized, Mr. Knoll believed they should convert to the retail method of inventory valuation that would eliminate the cost codes used on all jewelry. Mr. Bartlett resisted the idea. If you were Mr. Knoll, what would you do to get Mr. Bartlett to agree to the new idea? Be prepared to discuss your suggestions.

DECISION MAKING

A men's-wear retailer, running his business according to the retail method, believed that he did not need to take inventory annually. He thought his recordkeeping would suffice to tell him what inventory he had on hand and what profits he had for income-tax declarations. As the new manager of his store, what recommendation would you make about inventory taking? Be prepared to give reasons for your recommendation.

CAREER LADDER

You are responsible for the initial employment of personnel and for their assignment to work areas in the store. Two young college graduates were applying for a job. One young woman had been a cheerleader, president of a school club, and a speaker at many youth group meetings. The other young woman, who was equally attractive, had participated in fewer activities in school. But she had been responsible for handling the funds of the groups she had joined. She almost always was elected treasurer of her class, and even in her social groups she was asked to keep records. Which prospective employee would you assign to the financial office of the store? Be prepared to give reasons for your selection.

chapter 35

EXPENSE BUDGETING AND CONTROL

A *budget* is a plan for spending that is made with income in mind. In retailing, most budgets are made twice a year for the following six-month period. The budget is thoughtfully and carefully created by using the previous year's figures; projections of business for the period ahead, based on economic forecasts and new ideas generated within the firm; and expanded plans for advertising or publicizing the firm.

Management by objectives (MBO) may be used effectively in expense budgeting. With the expense budget set, managers have an objective toward which to work, and every decision will be made with that objective in mind. Setting an objective also helps the other people within the organization to direct their activities toward the ultimate goal of profit making.

The retailer's path to profit is over the rugged terrain of the costs of being in business. Every activity generates expenses that prove to be stumbling blocks along the path. Efficient retailers set up budgets for expenses in the same manner as they do for merchandise purchases. They scrutinize those expense budgets and compare them to the actual expenditures made, trying to detect ways of minimizing costs without cutting services.

To be able to control costs, a retailer must take certain actions:

- Classify expenses
- Allocate expenses to those areas that generate the expenses or prorate them by some formula among income-producing areas
- Budget expenses
- Evaluate and compare expenses constantly in order to determine (a) where savings can be obtained through control of unproductive expenses, (b) where increasing expenditures would bring commensurate increases in business that would benefit the company

CLASSIFICATIONS OF EXPENSES

Certain expenses of running a retailing business are paid regularly and are obvious or *explicit costs* of doing business. Wages and salaries, advertising, taxes, and supplies, for example, are paid for regularly. Other expenses, such as depreciation on the building owned by the firm or on the trucks or equipment owned, are not so obvious and are referred to as *implicit costs*. Some owners of retail firms do not charge rentals on the current value of their owned property. Nor do they assign a reasonable sum for their own or their relatives' salaries. Therefore, they do not have a true picture of the total costs they incur in doing business. Since unincorporated businesses are not permitted by the Internal Revenue Service to deduct a salary for the owner, an owner might mistakenly believe that the firm is making a satisfactory profit if a balance of $15,000 over expenses exists at the end of the year. However, if in working for another firm the owner could draw a salary of $15,000, in reality the profit made by the owner's firm was only equal to the salary that could be earned for the year.

All expenses must be provided for. Those expenses that must be paid directly as well as those that are not so pressing because they are not "out-of-pocket" expenses must be included in the budget. For example, a merchant who owns the building that houses the store may not be including a rental charge in the budget. However, a certain amount of depreciation occurs yearly on the building. This amount should be included.

Retailers classify their expenses in various ways: by natural classification, by functional classification, and by the expense-center method.

Natural Classification

In order not to overlook any obvious or explicit expenses, the merchant may use a natural classification of expenses. One proposed by the National Retail Merchants Association's Controller's Congress includes the following categories:

1. *Payroll.* Wages, salaries, commissions, and bonuses of all employees connected with the retail firm are included under payroll.

2. *Property Rentals.* The costs for land, buildings, equipment, and fixtures are included under this expense classification.

3. *Advertising.* Costs incurred for newspaper space, billboards, display materials, mats, direct mail, and other media used are included under the category of advertising.

4. *Taxes.* All taxes paid to federal, city, state, and county agencies for items such as unemployment, social security, real estate, and occupancy—except those charged as income taxes on the profit of the concern—are included under taxes. (Income taxes are subtracted from the total profit and are not entered as an expense of the business in the operating statement.)

5. *Interest.* Payments which must be made on borrowed money and *imputed interest* (the rate of return implied from the use of one's own capital in the business) are included under interest.

6. *Supplies.* All wrapping materials, forms, paper, pencils, and other materials used by the various sections of the firm for administration, accounting, operating, housekeeping, and so forth are included under supplies.

7. *Services.* Any outside services purchased—such as light, power, delivery or collection services—are included under services.

8. *Unclassified.* Other expenses that are difficult to classify are included, such as company-paid dues for company employees, cash shortages, and publications subscriptions.

9. *Travel.* Travel expenses for buying foreign goods, for attending meetings, for supervising branch operations, and so forth are included.

10. *Communications.* Telephone, telegraph, cable, and postage charges incurred by the firm are included under communications.

11. *Pensions.* Payments to retired persons are placed under this heading.

12. *Insurance.* All types of insurance coverage are included in the insurance grouping, such as fire, theft, liability, plate-glass, and damage.

13. *Depreciation.* Under the heading of depreciation, allowance for the depreciation of buildings, fixtures, furniture, and equipment is made. Buildings depreciate from 2 to 4 percent yearly; furniture and fixtures, 10 percent; equipment, 20 percent. Thus buildings would lose their value and be replaceable in 25 to 50 years; furniture and fixtures, in 10 years; and equipment—such as delivery equipment and machines—in 5 years.

14. *Professional Services.* Retailers need and purchase the services of outside specialists for purposes such as accounting and auditing, giving legal advice, buying foreign and some domestic goods, evaluating credit, and giving merchandise and fashion advice.

15. *Donations.* As good citizens, retailers are called upon to donate money to local and national charitable, welfare, and educational organizations. These expenses are charged to the business under the heading of donations.

16. *Losses from Bad Debts.* Checks that are not honored by the bank and accounts receivable and notes that are uncollected are included under the classification of losses from bad debts.

17. *Equipment Rental.* Any equipment rented by the firm, such as data-processing machines, cash registers, and trucks, is included in the category of equipment rental.

While 17 different headings to classify expenses may be used in major department stores, smaller firms and more specialized firms may use somewhat fewer headings. The following natural expense classifications, for example, can accommodate all the above-mentioned categories in only ten groupings:

1. Wages, salaries, and fringe benefits

2. Real estate costs

3. Heat, light, electric power, water, refrigeration

4. Fixture and equipment costs

5. Supplies

6. Advertising, display, direct mail

7. Insurance

8. Taxes

9. Interest

10. Miscellaneous

In this grouping of expenses, the "miscellaneous" category would contain items such as travel expenses, membership dues, communications costs, pensions, charges for professional services, donations, losses from bad debts, and rent for equipment. In a small firm such expenses, which might be negligible in amount, would not need to be classified separately.

Functional Classification
Expenses may be classified according to their purpose or function. Functional groupings include the following:

• Administrative function

• Buying function

• Occupancy function

• Publicity function

• Selling function

When this classification is used, each function is assigned those expenses incurred by it. Thus under the selling function the following would be included:

• Wages and salaries plus commissions, bonuses, and fringe benefits for salespeople, wrappers, packers, and selling supervisors

• Charges for supplies

• Costs of wrapping, packing, and delivering merchandise

Since functional classification complicates both recordkeeping and assigning each item to a function, this method is not as commonly used as the natural classification system.

Expense-Center Method
When expenses are grouped for accounting purposes, the groupings are called *expense centers*. Examples of these centers are as follows:

1. Fixed and policy expenses

2. Control and accounting expenses

3. Accounts receivable and credit expenses

4. Sales promotion costs

5. Superintendency and building operations costs

6. Personnel and employee benefits costs

7. Materials-handling costs

8. Direct and general selling costs

9. Merchandising costs

In small stores, the above categories would be sufficient for classifying expenses. In large stores, however, these nine listings may be subdivided repeatedly until as many as 71 expense centers are created. Since accountants are responsible for keeping records of expenditures, expense-center methods are commonly used.

Each method produces the same end result. However, some merchants prefer to have expenses classified in more detail, while others are satisfied with more general groupings.

NEED FOR ALLOCATING EXPENSES

An examination of the expense groupings by any of the three methods shown above indicates that some expenses can easily be charged to the stores, departments, or areas responsible for incurring them. These are direct expenses. Other expenses cannot be so easily assigned, since they are general expenses that occur because the business itself exists. These are indirect expenses.

COMPARISON OF THREE METHODS OF CLASSIFYING EXPENSES

Natural Classification	Percent of Sales	Functional Classification	Percent of Sales	Expense-Center Method	Percent of Sales
Payroll	18.04	Administrative	8.42	Fixed and policy expenses	6.97
Real property rentals	2.40	Buying	3.98	Control and accounting	1.45
Advertising	3.00	Occupancy	3.43	Accounts receivable and credit	1.98
Taxes	1.18	Publicity	3.72	Sales promotion	3.72
Interest	.03	Selling	16.16	Superintendency and building operations	3.43
Supplies	1.97				
Services purchased	2.14			Personnel and employee benefits	2.63
Unclassified	1.70			Materials handling	1.23
Travel	.46			Direct and general selling	10.32
Communications	.52			Merchandising	3.98
Pensions	.15				
Insurance	1.07				
Depreciation	1.60				
Professional services	.70				
Donations	.07				
Losses from bad debts	.22				
Equipment rental	.31				
Expense transfers	.00				
Outside revenue	.15				
Gross Operating Expense	35.71	Total	35.71	Total	35.71

Direct Expenses

Direct expenses are those that can be assigned to a specific area and that were incurred because of the existence of that area. These expenses include the salaries of the employees who work solely in that area, the cost of the supplies these employees use, the costs of advertising for that area, and buying costs for that area.

Indirect Expenses

The *indirect expenses* incurred by a business are those costs that would exist even without the presence of a certain department or area. General rental for the entire building, charges for heat and light, expenses of running elevators or escalators, office overhead, receiving and marking costs, central office expenses, and the cost of protection would occur even if some departments or areas of merchandise did not exist. Some system therefore must be devised for assigning or prorating these costs for payment. Any method chosen to allocate these costs must be somewhat arbitrary.

METHODS OF ALLOCATING EXPENSES

Direct expenses may be charged directly to the area, department, or store that causes them. Indirect expenses, however, need to be assigned by some formula. They may be allocated on the basis of a percentage of net sales, by the amount of area in the store occupied by a given department, or by some other method, such as a contribution plan.

Percentage of Net Sales Method

Since selling departments are the ones that are making money in any store, those are the departments charged under the net sales plan of distributing expenses. Under this plan, a proration of all expenses of the store is made to each unit on the basis of the percentage of sales. These expenses are subtracted from the gross margin to get the operating profit for each area or department.

Some people, however, object to this method of prorating expenses. For example, if delivery costs are prorated on the basis of the net sales of the notions and stationery departments, which have little need for the delivery of merchandise, these departments would carry a proportionate share of those costs. Yet the furniture department, which may have every item delivered, may pay only a fraction of the actual charges for the delivery of its goods.

Offsetting this reasoning, however, is another argument. Advertising costs might be directly assigned to one area on the basis of the advertising done for that area. Other merchandise categories, or even other stores in the group that did not advertise, might benefit from the additional number of customers attracted through that advertising, yet they would not have to share in the costs.

Contribution Method

Under the contribution method of assigning expenses, expenses that can be assigned directly to a given selling area are charged directly to that area. The selling area or department then reflects a departmental contribution, rather than a profit, since indirect expenses still have not been deducted. When those are subtracted, the operating profit is computed before other income is added and income taxes are subtracted.

Psychological Effect of Charging Expenses

In the example on page 408, the expenses shown, whether charged directly or entirely allocated, resulted in the same total. In actuality, however, this would be unlikely. Psychologically people work harder to reduce expenses if they have control over those expenses. For example, if Ms. Rock, a store manager, has 10 salespeople in her store, she may make a careful analysis of sales during the various hours of the day and discover that 7 full-time salespeople and 3 part-time salespeople could cover the departments equally as well as 10 full-time people. Three half-time salaries could therefore be saved at no lessening of service or effectiveness on the part of the store. If the store manager has no control over expenses, she may not work so hard to reduce them.

EXAMPLES OF ALLOCATION OF EXPENSES BY TWO METHODS

Percentage of Net Sales Method			Contribution Method		
Net sales		$100,000	Net sales		$100,000
Cost of goods sold		58,000	Cost of goods sold		58,000
Gross margin		$ 42,000	Gross margin		$ 42,000
Expenses			Direct expenses		
Administration	$ 5,300		Promotion	$ 1,810	
Occupancy	10,800		Selling supervision	1,230	
Publicity	5,500		Stock maintenance	4,800	
Buying	3,250		Merchandise management	2,200	
Selling	11,150		Direct selling	9,460	
Total expenses	$36,000	36,000	Total direct expenses	$19,500	19,500
Operating profit		$ 6,000	Controllable margin		$ 22,500
			Indirect expenses allocated		16,500
			Operating profit		$ 6,000

Similarly, control over supplies used may result in a more careful and judicious use of those supplies, with resulting savings. For this reason many retailing firms prefer to charge as many costs as possible directly to a merchandising area, department, or store. In that way they can check the sections where costs seem higher than they should be or where costs are actually higher than in comparable areas.

On the other hand, when all costs are allocated on some basis such as net sales, an attitude of indifference to costs results. The people in charge of the areas, departments, or stores believe that their efforts to reduce costs will have little or no effect on the overall charges made against their respective budgets.

FIXED AND VARIABLE EXPENSES

Certain expenses of a firm are set and do not vary with the amount of business done, while other charges are directly affected by volume.

Fixed expenses are those that do not vary with the volume of business. For example, rent remains the same unless the firm is paying the rent as a percentage of the total volume of sales. Taxes in certain categories remain constant, as do charges for light and heat, administrative expenses, insurance premiums, depreciation, office expenses, and equipment expenditures.

The *variable expenses* are those that change as sales increase. These expenses include salaries; charges for selling, wrapping, and packing supplies; delivery expenses; receiving costs; accounts payable; the costs of sales audits, adjustments, and handling cash; telephone order board costs; the cost of returns to stock; charge authorizations; and advertising expenses.

If the fixed expenses in a department are high, increasing the volume of business will aid considerably in reducing total expenses in relation to sales, thus increasing operating profit.

If the fixed expenses in a department or store

HIGH FIXED EXPENSES

	Lower Volume			Higher Volume		
Sales		$1,000	100%		$1,100	100%
Cost of goods sold		650	65%		715	65%
Gross margin expenses		$ 350	35%		$ 385	35%
Variable	$180			$200		
Fixed	150			150		
	$330	330	33%	$350	350	31.8%
Operating profit		$ 20	2%		$ 35	3.2%

FINANCIAL CONTROL FUNCTIONS

	Lower Volume			Higher Volume		
Sales		$1,000	100%		$1,100	100%
Cost of goods sold		650	65%		715	65%
Gross margin expenses		$ 350	35%		$ 385	35%
Variable	$280			$308		
Fixed	50			50		
	$330	330	33%	$358	358	32.6%
Operating profit		$ 20	2%		$ 27	2.4%

are low, increasing the volume of business will make a much smaller change in the profit.

When markups are increased, high fixed expenses will permit a better profit showing, whereas low fixed expenses will not change the profit showing markedly. High variable expenses have just the opposite effect of high fixed expenses on the operating profit.

EXPENSE BUDGETING

Just as merchants must plan the amount of money to be spent for merchandise during a six-month period, they must also plan the amount of money needed to sell those items. If the costs of selling the goods are too high, merchants must plan some way of reducing their costs. If costs are moderate, but the merchants believe the volume could be expanded by more aggressive promotion or by hiring more salespeople, they may wish to increase their expenditures in order to expand the volume of business being done.

Making the necessary plans is the first step toward the goal of expense reduction, if that is desirable, or toward the goal of increased volume, if that is desired. Planning expenses gives merchants the opportunity to examine previous costs and to determine where they might improve their operation.

Since there is a direct ratio of some expenditures to the volume of business in a given area, those planned figures must be meshed with the merchandise plan if the overall plan is to be meaningful. Also, an expense budget must be flexible, since conditions might arise necessitating departures from the planned budget.

The budget is a guide for action. If it is intelligently and carefully made, it should be a reliable guide to expenditures for the period.

Preparing a Budget
Several steps must be taken in preparation for planning a budget for a given period of time.

1. The planned volume of business and the expenses from the previous period must be known.

2. An estimate must be made of the volume of business to be obtained in the forthcoming period.

3. An estimate must be made of the gross margin to be obtained in the planned period.

4. The total expenditure that would permit the firm to achieve its anticipated volume within the limits of the gross margin, with allowance for operating profit, should be developed.

5. This total expenditure should be broken down into budgeted amounts for each major expense classification.

6. The larger amounts should be subdivided for specific expense items for the period under consideration and then further divided by shorter periods, such as months and weeks.

7. When the overall expense figure has been determined, the known fixed expenses, which do not fluctuate or fluctuate only slightly, should be determined.

8. When the fixed expenses are subtracted from the estimated gross margin, the remainder minus the anticipated operating profit will be the amount of money that may be allocated for variable expenses.

Estimating Expenses

Instead of following the steps outlined above—determining the amount of money available for expenses and then translating that into the expenses to be planned—the merchant may wish to estimate expenses in dollars or in percentages based on the costs incurred during the past year or two. The merchant therefore builds up the expense plan and, when it is complete, checks it with the planned increases in sales and the planned profit.

Certain variable expenses may have been fairly constant throughout the past several years. Salespeople's salaries, for example, may have averaged approximately 8 percent of the net sales for the past two or three years. Estimating salespeople's salaries at 8 percent of an increased sales volume, therefore, would probably give an accurate figure for that expense.

Many large firms with branch stores or chains of stores prepare forms on which both fixed and variable expenses are listed. These forms are submitted monthly to the managers for listing estimated expenses. When managers plan expenses, they are likely to try to keep those expenses in line with their own plans. When expense budgets are imposed by the top management, the store or department manager is less likely to consider the planned budget to be a reasonable one.

ZERO-BASE BUDGETING

A new concept in budgeting has helped firms to reanalyze their expenditures to determine which are essential, which contribute to the expansion or betterment of the business, and which are expendable. *Zero-base budgeting* is budgeting by reduction. The purpose is to determine what would result from sharply reducing or eliminating

a department or a part of a department or firm. It requires two basic steps:

1. *Developing Decision Packages.* This means that each activity must be analyzed and described in detail.

2. *Ranking These Decision Packages.* This means that every step must be carefully evaluated, either from the experience of the manager or by careful cost/benefit analysis.

An example of zero-base budgeting is shown in the following case: A department had five full-time employees. The manager decided to analyze what would happen if the personnel were reduced. These are the facts with which the manager worked:

- The five salespeople sold $10,000 worth of merchandise per week.

- This business was done primarily between the hours of 12 noon and 4 p.m. daily.

- One or two people could cover the department from 10 a.m. until noon and from 4 p.m. until closing at 6 p.m.

- Each person was paid $4 per hour (including fringe benefits). The total salary per day for the five workers was $160. This represented a salary cost of 8 percent.

Number of People	Daily Salary per Person	Daily Volume	Total Daily Salary Cost	Salary Percent
5	$32	$2,000	$160	8.0
4½	32	2,000	144	7.2
4	32	1,900	128	6.7
3½	32	1,700	112	6.5
3	32	1,600	96	6.0
2½	32	1,200	80	6.6
2	32	900	64	7.1
1½	32	600	48	8.0
1	32	300	32	10.6

From these figures, the manager deduced that if selling cost were the only consideration, the most desirable budget would be for three employees selling an anticipated $1,600 worth of merchandise daily. However, the loss of volume might affect other operations of the business. Therefore, to retain the $2,000 volume, the manager could call for the reduction of one-half time for one person. This would result in a percentage savings on salary without any change in volume or other noticeable effect on the department. Undoubtedly, the person could be assigned for one-half day of work daily to another task in the store, thus benefiting another area without affecting volume in the present department.

EXPENSE COMPARISON AND EVALUATION

Analyzing expenses is a complicated job. Some expenses may lend themselves to careful scrutiny with resulting savings. For example, the use of paper bags of a certain size may be found to be wasteful because certain selling areas are supplied with bags that are too large. Or too many bags may be used because each bag is not large enough to accommodate all the purchases a customer makes in an area at one time. A careful examination of the goods and the buying habits of customers may therefore result in supplying bags of the correct size, with consequent savings in costs.

Sometimes, however, expenses are guarded so carefully that the merchants become "penny-wise and pound foolish." For example, they may be paying minimum salaries and obtaining personnel of only marginal quality. By paying higher salaries, the merchants may be able to secure more competent people who would build their sales and, therefore, their profits. Or merchants may be trying to save money by doing less advertising. Through their advertising, however, they might be able to attract many additional customers to their stores to purchase merchandise. Thus cutting costs is not always the answer to increasing profits and improving the operation.

Merchants should get some idea of costs in other similar businesses. They should compare their expenses against those of other firms as well as against their own previous expense figures. By carefully checking and comparing expense figures, merchants may notice areas where money is being wasted or where spending additional funds might result in desired sales increases.

Merchants will find trade associations, buying offices, manufacturers, and trade papers good sources for comparative expense figures.

TOPICS FOR DISCUSSION

1. Explain why merchants sometimes purposely increase their expenses.
2. Explain the differences between natural expense groupings and functional groupings.
3. Explain the meanings of direct and indirect expenses.
4. What are the advantages of allocating expenses directly to a department or branch store?
5. When fixed expenses are low, how is profit affected by an increased sales volume?
6. Why is it desirable to budget for expenses?
7. In a chain organization, should the central administration or the store manager plan the expense budget? Why?
8. How does zero-base budgeting show the value of an activity or the people in a store or a department?
9. Explain why too careful control of expenses may not lead to increased sales.

10. If a merchant wanted to compare expenses with those of other firms of comparable size, where could he or she obtain such data?

MATHEMATICS FOR RETAILING

Sales in a small firm were $5,000 in one year and $5,200 in the second year. Each year the cost of goods sold was 62%, and the gross margin was 38%. On a separate sheet of paper, figure the operating profit in dollars and percent if fixed costs were $750 each year and variable costs were $900 the first year and $1,000 the second year.

COMMUNICATIONS IN RETAILING

Carelessness in the use of supplies, especially paper sacks, has resulted in an increase of costs in the supermarket you manage. The senior officers of your firm have asked you to write a memo to all employees informing them of this carelessness. Before you prepare this memo, you investigate and find that double sacks are being used when a single one would suffice to hold the merchandise and that large sacks are being used unnecessarily for small items. On a separate sheet of paper, write the memo as requested.

MANAGING HUMAN RELATIONS

The notions department on the main floor of a large store had an excellent profit showing when all direct expenses were deducted. However, when indirect expenses, including prorated charges for elevator and escalator service, delivery costs, and costs for special services, were deducted, the department's profit was almost nonexistent. The department manager, Mr. O'Keefe, whose salary was partly dependent on the profitability of the operation, objected to the large amount of indirect expenses charged to his department. He argued that by being on the main floor his department should not be charged for elevator and escalator service and that delivery costs were negligible for his department. Also, special services, such as workroom services and special order, were nonexistent for his department. He therefore appealed for a substantial reduction of these charges. What action would you consider to be fair in this matter? Be prepared to discuss your ideas.

CAREER LADDER

Phil Zabalone, who had just received his A.A.S. degree in marketing with a specialization in retailing, was placed in the training program of a large variety chain. He was assigned to a store where he could become an assistant manager if he did a good job. He observed that the two young men in charge of receiving sat around most of the morning. They had nothing to do until about 11 a.m., when merchandise deliveries began to come in. The young men were then quite busy until 3:30 p.m., when deliveries tapered off. However, they did have to move some goods after that time, and they also filed some of the copies of the receiving records. Since both were not kept busy at these tasks, a lot of boisterous play resulted that was sometimes heard on the selling floor.

Phil wrote a report in his training manual and recommended a careful review of the assignments of personnel in the receiving area. He suggested that one person be assigned part-time to the stock room.

Do you think Phil would be promoted in this store? Be prepared to give reasons for your answer.

chapter 36

PROTECTION AND INSURANCE FOR RETAILING

"From 70 to 80 percent of total shortages in retail stores is due to employee theft." "Awards Offered to Reduce Stealing." "Lie Test to Curb Shrinkages." "Most Shoplifters are Teens and Housewives." Such headlines in newspapers and trade papers indicate the great extent of the theft problem in stores. Dishonest employees, shoplifters, robbers, and burglars all contribute to the over-two-billion-dollar loss that retail firms suffer yearly. There are also losses due to fires, water damage, accidents to customers and employees, and injuries sustained from some products.

Retailers must make their operations profitable if they are to remain in business. Profit is possible only if customers and employees are properly protected while they are in the store, if the products the stores sell are kept safe, and if the property that houses the goods is also guarded.

Protection of customers involves accident prevention, careful attention to their charge accounts, and safety for them and their possessions while they are in the store.

Protection of employees involves accident prevention, provision for illness while on the job, care in the event of any unusual disturbance, and insurance such as workmen's compensation and unemployment insurance.

The protection of merchandise and cash is the most difficult responsibility. This involves store security, including policing; the use of alarm systems; special housing for goods; protection of cash; supervision of charge accounts and sales checks; and insurance against loss due to fire, crime, or disasters.

Protection in a store includes security. This entails planning and implementing ways to prevent problems from occurring and being prepared to handle problems when they do occur. Protection also includes insurance. This provides compensation when problems do occur. Both types of protection are essential for the well-run store.

SECURITY

Temptations abound in retail stores. The very appeals the retailers develop to attract customers to the stores are the same appeals that may cause people to want to steal the merchandise if they cannot afford to pay for it. Occasionally, dishonest employees, surrounded by attractive merchandise and drawers full of cash, also are tempted, if security is not carefully organized, to help themselves to money or merchandise not rightfully theirs. Retailers must be alert to pilferage from light-fingered customers and from employees who cannot resist temptation.

Adequate Policing

Shoplifting, according to the Federal Bureau of Investigation, has increased over 220 percent in the past 10 years. A large percentage of shoplifting is done by teen-agers who think such a crime is a lark to be bragged about to their friends. They should know that it is "stealing" and that it is punishable in ways that may affect them for the rest of their lives!

The management of a well-run store will take a

matching bracelets?

You really won't like this kind of jewelry. It's the kind you get when you're picked up for
shoplifting. That isn't all. When you get caught, you'll also get a criminal record.
Consider also Nevada's new law on shoplifting. It's tough and you should know about it.
In addition to existing criminal penalties and the sheer embarrassment of it all,
Mom and Dad (or you, if you are 18 or over) will have to shell out an additional $100-$250,
payable to the merchant over and above the value of the item wrongfully taken.
In Nevada, shoplifting is stealing and stealing is a serious crime.
Matching bracelets? Don't risk it.

SHOPLIFTING
IN NEVADA IS A
**HANDFUL OF
TROUBLE**

**don't
risk it !**

PREPARED BY THE NEVADA ANTI-SHOPLIFTING COMMITTEE, ATTORNEY GENERAL ROBERT LIST, STATE CHAIRMAN

**Shoplifting has increased at such a rapid pace in recent years that retailers have undertaken a media
campaign to try to discourage theft.**
Courtesy the Nevada Anti-Shoplifting Committee

number of precautions to keep customers from shoplifting. Large stores employ detectives who circulate among the departments dressed like customers. These trained people observe the actions of shoppers whom they suspect of not being ordinary customers. These detectives are particularly observant in areas where costly merchandise is sold. Fine jewelry, cameras, radios, television sets, silverware, furs, better dresses, coats, and accessories are all merchandise categories of concern to these detectives.

Employees in the store are alerted to watch that all goods are paid for when removed from a given area by customers. Salespeople in an area act as deterrents to the person bent on stealing.

Supplementing the sales personnel are floorwalkers, section managers, or department managers whose job is to keep alert to those people who appear suspicious. Mirrors, hidden television cameras, and wall peepholes are devices used by management to observe the selling floor and to watch both questionable customers and questionable employees.

Some firms, particularly discount houses and highly promotional stores, keep uniformed guards at each store exit. These uniformed employees also prove to be deterrents to shoplifters, since they check to see that each package being taken from the store has the appropriate sales

Closed circuit television systems are used by many retailers to discourage burglaries, shoplifting, and vandalism. Courtesy Safeguard Security Systems

check stapled to it to indicate that the contents have been duly paid for. However, stores catering to well-to-do customers believe that such uniformed personnel are offensive to their customers, and therefore they prefer to rely on the private detectives who, as they stroll around the store, are indistinguishable from regular customers.

Electronic devices such as microwave scanners are increasingly used by stores. These are pillar-like stands that are placed at exits of departments or stores. Some are activated by a tiny dot on the price tag that is punched out by the cashier when goods are paid for. The dot may be embedded in the merchandise itself and must be neutralized by the cashier. Other goods have plastic clamps on them that can be removed only with special clamp openers kept at the cashier's desk. Although these clamps have "inventory control" marked on them, they are, in fact, controls to prevent theft. The scanners beep when a person with goods containing these dots or clamps walks past them. Guards can then check to see that the person is not leaving the store with goods that are not paid for.

Adequate Protection of the Merchandise

Using price tickets that are not easily removed from merchandise; securely anchoring displays of costly goods; using clothes hangers on the selling floor only when filled; protecting boxed merchandise; and arranging merchandise so it cannot easily be removed from its display stand are a few safeguards used by the merchant to keep pilferage at a minimum. Keeping costly goods in a protected or supervised area, keeping "try-on" merchandise restricted to certain places designated for trying on, and not permitting goods to be carried to lounge rooms until purchased further protect those goods. Pairs of goods are protected by displaying only one of a pair. Hangers hung backward are harder to remove from racks. Minor appliances may have cords tied together to prevent their being stolen from display racks.

Items that are small but appealing are usually

kept under glass covers or in glass cases where they can easily be seen, but where they can be handled only in the presence of a store employee. Other goods kept on top of the cases may be arranged on fixtures that prevent easy removal yet allow the customers to examine the merchandise they seek to buy. Some merchandise is packaged in plastic "bubble" containers. Toys, notions, and other small wares are thus protected, yet they are wholly visible.

Not only does merchandise have to be protected from theft; it must also be protected from rough handling and soil. Women's dresses, for example, may get lipstick smears when being tried on if facial tissues are not provided to cover the lips of the customers. Clothes carelessly handled when customers step out of them may also be soiled or damaged. Dropping goods on the floor, opening packages and strewing the contents, trying to remove the premium on the outside of the package, tearing the container, or ripping the plastic bag holding the product are some other ways in which customers or employees can lessen the value of goods. Employees who watch customers deter such mutilation of goods.

Miscellaneous Protective Devices

Additional protective measures taken by some retail firms include one or more of the following:

Night Guards. Employed almost exclusively by large firms, these people make periodic rounds through stores and warehouses after hours. They may be accompanied by guard dogs. In addition to scaring intruders by their mere presence, dogs may be trained to detect people who hide in the store until closing.

Safes. These are used to store small but costly items such as jewelry or antiques when they are not being displayed. Furs may be stored in vaults. Only the store managers have the combinations for the safes.

Alarm Systems. Electric burglar alarms wired around windows and doors can protect property from forced entry. An alarm may sound at the

site where it is installed, or it may be wired to alert employees in the office of the installing firm. These employees then notify the police.

Folding Steel Gates. Liquor stores, jewelry stores, clothing stores, drugstores, and camera shops are among the kinds of stores that use folding steel gates, especially in high crime areas. The gates are locked in front of doors and windows when the store is closed.

Adequate Protection of Cash

For change-making purposes, stores need cash at every cashier's station at the beginning of the day. During the day, there is a constant buildup of cash at these stations. To limit the temptation to steal and rob, collections may be made throughout the day by the department or store manager or by a representative from the control office. The amounts collected are noted on a form kept at the cashier's station, and those

When a counterfeit bill is placed under the black light in this counterfeit bill detector, the bill glows, alerting the salesperson.
Courtesy Safeguard Security Systems

amounts are subtracted from the cash register tape at the end of the business period to determine the accuracy of the remaining cash. Cash drawers are locked when the cashier leaves the station and unlocked only when someone is present to use the register.

In a well-run firm, everyone handling cash is trained properly to keep the bills received from the customer on the outside ledge of the cash register while the change is being taken from the register. Only when the price charged for the merchandise plus the change equals the amount of money that the customer handed the cashier is the customer's money put into the till. Careful counting by the cashier of the customer's change as it is handed to the customer is a further check on the accuracy of the change-making process.

If a store takes in a substantial amount of cash, safes may be used during the day for protection of the money. Money not needed for change making is usually deposited daily in a bank.

To ensure that employees are handling cash properly, recording sales accurately, and giving receipts for purchases, stores often employ special "shoppers." These people are trained to watch all the actions of the employee and to check that the handling of both merchandise and money is done according to the company's rules.

Sometimes outside firms, which specialize in such detective work, are employed to make periodic checks on the correct handling of merchandise and money by employees throughout the store. If a store suspects the actions of an employee, such a firm may be asked to make an honesty check on that employee and report back to the retailer. Knowledge that ordinary-looking customers may be detectives in disguise is a deterrent to any attempts by employees to steal.

Adequate Protection of Charge Accounts

Stores must be alert in permitting charges only by those authorized to charge to a given account. Asking for signatures of customers making charge purchases is one method of protecting charge-account holders. Authorizations of charges over given amounts also help to protect charge holders against misuse of their accounts.

Lost credit cards and credit-card frauds are a problem for store management. These situations may involve employees who may have stolen the cards or who had been negligent in handling cards, or they may involve thieves who had obtained the cards fraudulently. To offset the abuse of credit cards, stores have to tighten authorization and security measures and watch particularly for "buildup" accounts, or a situation where a sudden large amount of buying has taken place against a particular account in a short time span. Computers record transactions instantaneously and help to trap fraudulent users of credit cards or personal checks.

Tamper-Proof Sales Checks

To assure that changes of price are not made on sales checks or that descriptions of merchandise are not changed by customers returning goods for cash, tamper-proof sales checks have been devised showing erasures just as bank checks do. A "protecto-tint" background on the sales check provides safety from price or product description alterations. All erasure marks are clearly visible. Stores using such sales checks can reduce the "theft through returns" that some unscrupulous people attempt.

Protection Through Management Personnel

Merchants must provide protection for both customers and employees while they are in the store. Thus retailers take precautions to see that they have adequate staffs of store management employees placed at strategic points throughout the store in case of a disturbance or an accident of any type during the hours the store is open to the public.

Adequate Accident Prevention

Cleaning and checking the building, repairing damaged areas, being sure there are no slippery spots on floors or stairs, and seeing that all walk

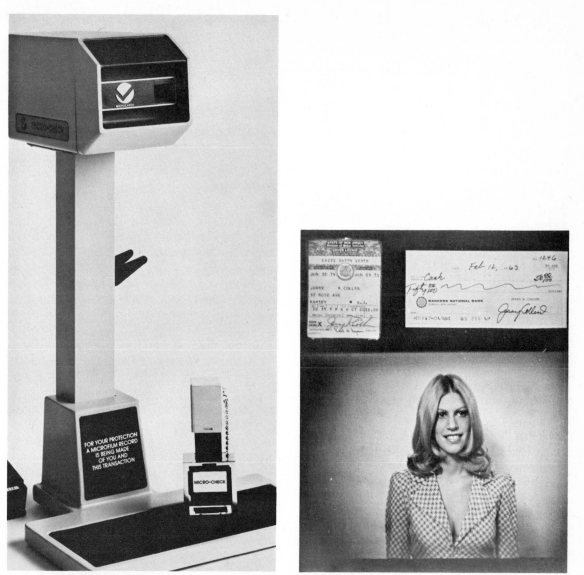

The Micro-Check camera unit takes a photograph of the customer's check, some additional required identification, and the customer, all in one step. When a check bounces, the person's photograph is given to other stores in the area and to the local police. Use of this photo system discourages bad check fraud.
Courtesy Micro-Check

areas are well lighted and clear and that fire-fighting equipment is close by and in working condition are a few of the ways of protecting buildings and people. Making waste disposal containers available for use, maintaining unclut-tered aisles, and removing cartons and debris promptly are ways of protecting both customers and employees. Proper caution signs about the use of escalators, stairs, and self-service elevators also reduce accidents.

PROTECTION AND INSURANCE FOR RETAILING

INSURANCE

Court cases initiated by people who tripped on projections, tore their clothing, ate food containing some foreign substance, stumbled on stairs, or were hurt on escalators or in elevators while in a store are evidence of the problem of protecting people and of insuring against loss. Fires, floods, and riots, which have resulted in widespread damage to stores, are additional proof of the need for protection and insurance for the plant, the products, and the people. Without such protection, there can be no profits. In addition, retailers may wish to insure against liability for both customers and employees, against unemployment for their employees, against interruption of business, and against incidents such as breaking and entering.

Carrying all those types of insurance may be too costly, however. Retailers must therefore determine the minimum insurance they can afford that will give them adequate protection from major losses that might ensue or for which they might be liable. Following are the major types of insurance considered by retailers.

Property Insurance

The retailers' buildings, fixtures, and movable equipment and merchandise make up the tangible property that they must protect if they are to remain in business. The insurance for this property may take many forms. Fire insurance, use and occupancy insurance, and plate glass insurance are examples of insurance protecting their property.

Fire Insurance. Fire insurance that provides compensation for loss or damage due to fire or lightning is one of the most common types of insurance to be carried by retailers. Loss due to smoke and water damage resulting from a fire is also covered under such policies.

The rates for fire insurance vary according to:

- The construction of the building. Those made from fireproof materials receive lower rates.

- The occupancy and fire hazards within a building.

- The availability of protective devices. Automatic sprinkler systems lower the insurance rates.

- Protection of the building from fires in adjacent buildings or structures.

If a fire occurs, the value of the property is usually determined from the books and records of the company. It is therefore important that those records be saved, if possible. If the records are destroyed, an estimate of loss must be made by an outside appraiser, unless the retailer has filed records on a regular basis with the insurance company.

Coinsurance clauses in property insurance provide a method of saving money for the firm. Since it is rare that a place of business is totally damaged by fire, the retailer may take out insurance on a stipulated percentage of the value of the property, usually 80 percent. Thus if the property were valued at $100,000 and a coinsurance clause were included, the retailer would be covered up to $80,000 for loss by fire. If the retailer had insured for only $40,000, however, and a partial loss occurred, he or she would be covered for just $4/8$ or $1/2$ of the loss. In this case, if the damage amounted to $20,000, the retailer would receive only $10,000 against the loss from the insurance company.

Riders or *endorsements,* known as extended coverage endorsements on fire insurance policies, permit coverage of losses due to wind or water damage from storms, cyclones, tornadoes, and hail and also allow for compensation for damages caused by explosions, riots, aircraft, smoke, and vehicles. Through these riders, additional insurance is obtained at minimum charges.

Self-Insurance. Some large, multi-store retailing firms prefer to be self-insured rather than carry fire insurance with a commercial company. The amount these firms would normally pay in premiums to protect each store is put into a reserve account to be used in case of a fire in any unit of the firm.

Use and Occupancy Insurance. A type of insurance to protect the retail firm against interruption of business and consequent loss of money to pay salaries and other expenses is available. Depending on the amount of insurance coverage desired, this insurance may protect a retailer for all expenses incurred, plus assuring a profit that would have been made without the business interruption. Or if reduced coverage is sought, it might pay just the expenses or only a stipulated portion of those expenses.

Insurance Against Burglary, Robbery, and Other Crime Hazards. Insurance against burglary (breaking and entering), robbery (theft during the hours the store is open), and other crimes that may be committed is available to the retailer. Accurate and detailed records are necessary to prove claims of loss from these crimes. In recent years excessive numbers of these types of offenses have made these types of insurance coverage more costly and more difficult to obtain than they once were.

Plate Glass Insurance. Since most retail stores have large plate glass windows that may be broken easily, firms often find insurance against such breakage desirable. While small retail firms may have to use insurance companies for such coverage, large firms with many separate stores often find self-insurance less costly.

Sprinkler Leakage Insurance. Firms that have sprinkler systems to help prevent excessive damage from fires may wish to carry insurance against sprinkler leakage, since leaking water can damage merchandise.

Protection of Goods in Transit. The retailer may wish to insure goods while they are being transported by rail or truck or over waterways from a variety of hazards such as fire, theft, or damage. Parcel post shipments may also be insured under a blanket policy rather than insuring each parcel individually.

Customer and Employee Insurance

Various types of insurance are available to protect customers and employees while they are in the retailer's place of business.

Liability Insurance. Retailers need protection for their customers, who may slip, be hurt in elevators or on escalators, or be hit by hand carts or trucks within the stores. They also need protection against suits brought by customers for injuries sustained from the use of some item purchased in the store. For example, a child's cowboy suit, which was highly flammable, caused the death of a child wearing it. The family sued the store that sold the suit and the manufacturer who made it and was awarded $60,000 for the tragic death of the child.

Separate liability policies may be secured to cover injuries caused by elevators and escalators. If retailers sell products such as drugs, foods, cosmetics, or mechanical devices that might be harmful if imperfect, they especially need to be insured. Comprehensive policies including all these causes of injury may be obtained. Even though the retailers have not manufactured an item, customers may sue them for damages resulting from its use or malfunction. Retailers also need liability insurance to protect them against charges of false arrest, which may be brought by persons accused of shoplifting.

Workmen's Compensation. For employees who are hurt during working hours, most states require that retailers carry workmen's compensation insurance or be self-insured, with bonds posted with the state to ensure payment if a claim is made. This type of insurance guarantees the payment of medical expenses and salary for workers who are injured on the job, except in cases where the injury was willful or the person injured was intoxicated at the time of the accident. Weekly benefits are set at a fraction of the regular wage of the employee, and there is a waiting period before benefits can be obtained to prevent claims for minor accidents. Both temporary and permanent disabilities are covered by this insurance. In the case of the accidental death of a worker on the job, workmen's compensation insurance provides for payments for dependents for a specified period of time.

Unemployment Insurance. A nationwide system of unemployment insurance was provided as part of the Social Security Act passed in 1935. Under this insurance plan, weekly benefits are paid to workers who have been laid off and have been unable to find other jobs. To assure that money to pay these people is available, the government collects approximately 3 percent of payrolls from those firms employing four or more people. This money is paid by the individual states in stipulated amounts and for designated periods of time. The tax may be lowered for individual firms that have a record of minimum unemployment among their regular employees. This makes employers particularly careful in their hiring and firing practices.

Employee Bonding. The retailer may wish to be insured against dishonesty on the part of em-ployees who hold positions of trust and who handle large amounts of money. Through fidelity bonds the retailer is reimbursed for losses up to the amount specified in the policy if an employee leaves with any of the firm's money.

MANAGEMENT POSITIONS IN PROTECTION

In small stores, the owners or managers and the store personnel supervise the protection of property, people, products, and profits. They also decide what types of insurance the store should carry. In larger firms, however, store protection personnel are part of the store team. Protection managers, assistant managers, guards, detectives, and office personnel are employed. Shoppers are employed to check on sales personnel. Specialists in the field of insurance also are needed in large firms.

Since theft of goods has increased so markedly, new career opportunities for theft deterrence have been developed.

TOPICS FOR DISCUSSION

1. Explain the purpose of store security.
2. What are some important steps that management can take in providing store security for customers?
3. What steps can management take to police a firm adequately?
4. What steps can management take to protect merchandise?
5. What can management do to protect cash?
6. What important decisions must a retailer make concerning the amounts and kinds of insurance to carry?
7. What coverage is provided by property insurance?
8. What are the problems of establishing the value of property if a fire occurs that destroys merchandise and records?
9. What protection do riders or endorsements on fire insurance policies offer the retailer?
10. What protection does liability insurance offer the retailer?

COMMUNICATIONS IN RETAILING

The Arden Clothing Store carried employee liability insurance (policy no. 32-6419) to protect its small staff of salespeople and office personnel. One year ago the manager of the store had bought that policy and paid $650. The policy provided coverage for three years. The insurance broker now suggested that the store should have a comprehensive liability policy to cover customers as well as employees. The store manager agreed to take the new comprehensive policy. The manager also canceled the old limited liability policy, which had two more years to run.

When the new policy (no. 61-555-34) arrived, however, the bill was for the full price, with no deduction for the two years remaining on the previous policy. The manager asked you to write a letter explaining the situation and requesting a corrected bill. On a separate sheet of paper, write this letter.

MANAGING HUMAN RELATIONS

You are the manager of a variety store, and you have advertised for a stock clerk. The local parole board officer contacted you and asked you to hire a one-time offender who needed a job. The officer explained that the young man had been a member of a gang of delinquents who had been caught shoplifting, but he had received a suspended sentence on the stipulation that he avoid the gang and get a job. Several other merchants had refused to take a chance on him. Assuming that you were to hire him, what precautions would you consider? Be prepared to discuss your ideas.

DECISION MAKING

A store that had carried only clothing and variety goods decided to add a lunch counter. What additional insurance coverage should the store plan as a result of this new addition? Be prepared to give reasons for your suggestions.

CAREER LADDER

A "Guys and Gals" shop for teen-agers featuring jeans and other sportswear had grown rapidly, and now the owners were planning to add branches. Mr. Jimenez, a young man hired one year ago, wanted to be promoted. He came to you, the personnel officer, to talk about a more responsible job.

He had a particularly good record for deterring shoplifters, and several of his ideas for mirrors, placement of merchandise, and free aisle space had resulted in reduced shortages from theft.

What position might you suggest the owners consider for Mr. Jimenez? Be prepared to discuss your reasons.

PART ELEVEN

SYSTEMATIC RESEARCH FOR RETAILING

chapter 37

FACT-FINDING AND PROBLEM SOLVING

Retailers are constantly puzzled by problems that need to be solved. In general merchandise stores, retailers are perplexed by such questions as whether moving displays cause more purchases than still displays. Does merchandise sell better when it is placed adjacent to related items? How are customers best served by size and color arrangements of merchandise? What are the patterns of traffic throughout a store? What policies are most effective in attracting and holding customers?

For the food merchant, similar questions need to be answered. Where would the fresh vegetables look best, be most readily available, and have the best chance of being selected by the customer? What items will customers stoop to select from bottom shelves? How many employees are needed at the various hours of the day at the checkout counters? What are the optimum store hours? Should the store be open on Sunday if laws permit?

These are a few of the questions confronting any merchant in any type of retail store. How? Why? When? Where? How much? How many? Who? Since so many questions must be answered, one of the important jobs of every store manager is research that requires fact-finding and problem solving.

DETERMINING THE NEED FOR FACT-FINDING RESEARCH

How do merchants determine that they need to search for facts about their business? Every activity within the business may present a challenge for fact-finding, yet some merchants will be much more active in searching for information than others. Retailers rarely seek special facts about areas of the store or organization that are running smoothly. In most cases the problem spots are the ones for which fact-finding efforts are expended. A merchant's mind must therefore be like radar in detecting these trouble zones. The following are typical concerns:

- Sales slump

- Fewer customers

- Disgruntled salespeople

- Greater success by competition

- Slow-turning merchandise

- Drab-looking windows or store interior

- Departmental friction

- Unsuccessful promotions

- High personnel turnover

- High percentage of walkouts

- Lower average sales than previously

- Inadequate sales per square foot

- Low number of qualified job applicants

- Slow collection of accounts receivable

- Decreasing charge-account sales

Merchants who are alert will be just as interested in unusually good reports as they are in the trouble spots. If sales suddenly increase beyond expectations, the retailers will want to know the reason. If morale among employees improves noticeably, they will again search for the reasons for the change. Thus fact-finding is a constant activity triggered in most cases by a desire to know why situations differ from normal and to resolve problems or apply solutions to those sections in need of help.

The purpose of fact-finding through research is not only to analyze what is better or worse than normal but also to find new ways, better ways, less costly ways, more efficient ways, or easier ways of accomplishing what has to be done. Fact-finding is the merchants' way of trying to improve their operations. Since retailing is a constantly changing and growing field, every retailer must be alert at all times to ideas that will improve business and thus permit the firm to serve customers better.

Research for Large or Small Retail Firms

In large retail firms, a research team may be employed full-time for gathering data. In small jewelry firms, shoe stores, and millinery shops and in other types of small retail operations, the owner or manager may be responsible for research.

Fact-finding research helps to explain the reasons for a certain situation. It does not, however, present solutions. It does permit the management of the firm to draw conclusions based on evidence rather than on hunches or guesses. Then creative solutions to the problems may be sought.

Every executive in a store, regardless of its size, must search constantly for facts and must analyze those facts. This is true whether the facts are needed to know what to order, how to improve the displays in a window, how to increase responses to advertising, or what to do to alter the image of the store.

The Cost of Fact-Finding Research

If merchants do their own fact-finding, the cost may be only the time they or their employees spend on this activity. If a firm hires a team of investigators, the cost may run to thousands of dollars. Between these two extremes, fact-finding may vary in cost depending on the number of people needed and the time used to ascertain the facts and to suggest solutions. However, the application of the results may bring about considerable savings, and so research over the years may reduce rather than raise costs.

WHO IS INVOLVED IN RESEARCH?

Research in retailing is a constant activity involving all employees who handle or promote merchandise, who do recordkeeping, who handle personnel, or who deal with vendors or customers. No one—from the person who checks the supplies for cleaning needs to the president who bases decisions on facts—can work in a retail store without being involved in fact-finding. The results of fact-finding are analyzed and used as a basis for conclusions and recommendations.

The Retail Research Department

In large retailing organizations, a special department assigned to do research may be established. Such a department does not attempt to supervise regular fact-finding activities in the various areas throughout the store. Instead, its duty is to investigate situations involving the entire store, or those not previously explored, or those so vast in scope that knowledgeable and trained researchers are needed for the investigation. A central research department may also be available to help with fact-finding activities where the department or manager has been unable to resolve a situation.

Central research departments can keep records and maintain controls to help the top executives obtain needed information almost immediately. For example, customer counts may be taken at regular intervals and comparisons made to show trends in promotional effectiveness. The number of people passing the store can be compared to the number entering. Other facts that can be gathered include the number of customers who carry packages from the store, the average ages of customers entering the store, and traffic patterns within the store. In addition, central research offices may study the merchandise mix, personnel turnover, merchandise-handling techniques, and population shifts. And they may conduct customer interviews.

Other studies carried out by research departments include analyses of vendors to determine which ones sell goods in more than one area of the store. The studies may also examine the profitability of lines by vendor, and a check of customers' returns and complaints may be made according to vendor lines. Analyses may also be made of the comparative costs of selling similar goods in different parts of the store. For example, silver gift items for infants may be carried both in the silverware department and in the infants' department. Comparative analyses of all the costs in the two areas will reveal which department sells infants' silver items more profitably.

Research departments also conduct studies of a general nature. They compare competitive organizations' activities with those of the home store, and they keep records of nationwide trends in areas of concern to their store. They analyze financial records published by the Federal Reserve Bank, by the National Retail Merchants Association, and by local business groups. Population trends, income groups, urban and suburban growth, traffic patterns, buying habits of customers across the nation, the development and acceptance of new products, data-gathering systems, and cultural trends are some of the concerns investigated by research departments. They use national and local government reports, trade association information, and professional publications.

Outside Research Agencies

Some firms with or without a research department of their own may find occasional need for special investigations by outside experts. Fashion specialists may be called on to analyze the stocks of ready-to-wear and accessories for style rightness. Accounting experts may be called upon to investigate the books and records and methods of accounting. If a retailer is planning to build a new store, firms that specialize in the analysis of new sites for businesses may be called upon to gather important data about one or more proposed areas. These data may include population figures, income levels, information about whether people own or rent homes in the areas, ages of inhabitants, the number and kinds of retail outlets already in the areas or proposed, and the projected growth in the areas. Access roads, the amount of traffic on those roads, ethnic groups in the areas, the amount and kind of employment, and leisure potential are also of concern in such investigations.

This is a questionnaire used by a market research firm to evaluate the performance of salespersonnel. ▷
Courtesy Dale Systems Incorporated

PROFICIENCY PROFILE

SERVICED BY DALE SYSTEM Inc

STORE NAME Martello's
CITY Avon

ADDRESS 1501 Main Street
STATE New York
DATE June 2, 19--
TIME 3:15 (P.M.) A.M.

QUAN.	MDSE. PURCHASED	PRICE
1	turntable	
1	receiver	
2	speakers	
	TAX	
	TOTAL	

DESCRIPTION OF SALESPERSON

SEX	APPR. AGE	HEIGHT	BUILD	HAIR
M	25	5'10"	Average	brown

WEARING GLASSES		S.P.'S NO. OR LETTER	DEPT.	FLOOR
YES	NO ✓	362	16	7

SPECIAL FEATURES

APPROACH

	YES	NO
Dep't. Busy? Yes ✓ No..... Was Approach Prompt		✓
Were You Recognized As Waiting Customer		✓
Were You Greeted By Salesperson......................	✓	
Was Salesperson Pleasant	✓	

APPEARANCE

	YES	NO
Was Salesperson Free of Offending Odors	✓	
Satisfactorily Dressed	✓	

NOTES:

	YES	NO
Hair Neat	✓	
Fingernails, Hands Clean	✓	
Satisfactory Business Conduct: Check "NO" for CHEWING GUM, SMOKING, OTHER OBJECTIONAL BEHAVIOR ..	✓	

DEPARTMENT APPEARANCE

	YES	NO
Was Floor Clean .... ANSWER ONLY IF S.P.'S RESPONSIBILITY		✓
Merchandise Clean		✓
Merchandise Neatly Arranged		✓

SALE CLOSING

	YES	NO
If Necessary, Was Mdse. Wrapped Properly	✓	
Did S. P. Thank You	✓	
Were You Asked To Come Back Again..................	✓	
Was Closing Transaction Effected Promptly	✓	

FINAL IMPRESSION

	YES	NO
S. P. Courteous Throughout Transaction	✓	
Was S. P. Patient	✓	
S. P. Interested in Making Sale	✓	
As Customer, Would You Seek Out This S. P. Next Time	✓	

EACH NEGATIVE ITEM SCORED ABOVE (−2%) −10%

MERCHANDISE PRESENTATION

	YES	NO
Mdse. In Stock, Yes ..✓..... No...... Substitute Offered		
Did S. P. Offer To Order Item		
NAME OF ITEM NOT IN STOCK — Familiar With Prices	✓	
Familiar With Stock	✓	
Mdse. Gotten Quickly ...	✓	
Did S. P. Help in Selection	✓	

EXPLOITATION OF MERCHANDISE

	YES	NO
Quality Of Mdse. Stressed	✓	
Questions Answered Properly	✓	
Did S. P. Show Enough Merchandise	✓	
Was S. P. Patient in Showing Merchandise	✓	
Refrained From Showing Too Much Mdse	✓	

SUGGESTIVE SELLING

	YES	NO
Did S. P. Suggest Increased Quantity	✓	
Were Related Purchases Suggested	✓	
Did S. P. Display Suggested Item(s)	✓	
Did S. P. Avoid "High-Pressure" Selling	✓	

STORE RULES

	YES	NO
If Required, Was Receipt Issued	✓	
Was Receipt Made Out Properly..............	✓	
If Register Used, Was Drawer Closed		✓
Did S. P. Call Back Amount Tendered	✓	
Was Sale Recorded Correctly	✓	

EACH NEGATIVE ITEM SCORED ABOVE (−3%) −3%

REMARKS:

Personnel experts may be called in to make morale studies for a firm or to analyze the personnel needs of the firm. Advertising experts may be asked to study the advertisements and customer responses and to make recommendations. Firms that specialize in time and motion studies may be asked to check the efficiency of the business operation. Merchandise-handling techniques may be analyzed by outside experts to determine more efficient ways of moving merchandise. In fact, every area of concern may be investigated by an outside firm, even the personalities, characteristics, and capabilities of the executives. The outside agency may recommend actions to be taken to improve the internal workings of the top management branch of the organization.

THE IMPORTANCE OF RESEARCH

If retailers have a constant need to improve their operations, they must regularly seek the information they need for these improvements. Such activity is commonly called *research*. Research is a broad term used in exact sciences as well as in the social sciences, and it ranges in meaning depending on the field to which it is applied. For the retailer, *research* means fact-finding to decrease costs, to improve sales, and to increase profits.

Research is based on the use of the scientific method of fact-finding and analysis. If a retailer merely guesses or has an idea that a certain amount of goods is in stock or thinks that more salespeople might be needed at certain times of the day, that retailer is not being scientific. Guessing is based only on the person's general knowledge or impressions, not on actual facts. Through the scientific method, by contrast, retailers seek to examine information systematically or to use experiments that keep human error and bias at a minimum.

Research is based on facts. Facts are pieces of substantiated evidence, as opposed to hunches, guesses, thoughts, or isolated examples. In a store, for example, buyers may need to order coats for the coming season. If they guessed the number they thought they could sell, they would probably be understocked or overstocked on coats. If, however, they checked their records to see how many coats were sold last year during the same period, if they obtained weather forecasts for the current year, and if they compared the amounts of sales in their departments this year with the amounts of the previous year, their estimate of the number of coats they could sell would be more reliable. Decisions based on facts are much more dependable than those based on guesswork. Through research, the probability of error is reduced. Decisions based on facts will be:

- Rational rather than emotional
- Unbiased rather than biased
- Current rather than dated
- Objective rather than subjective
- Knowledgeable rather than opinionated
- Dependable rather than doubtful

Facts About Things

Retailers constantly seek statistics about various facets of their businesses. They get reports on the number of items they buy, the number of inches of newspaper advertising copy they run, the number of customers who enter their stores, the number of customers who have charge accounts, the number of employees in each segment of the firm, and the number of packages delivered.

If retailers have established good recordkeeping systems, either manual systems or electronic data processing systems, many of these facts will be available on a moment's notice. Sometimes physical counts are required to provide facts. Even these physical counts can often be made rather quickly, and they are usually reliable. This would be a form of physical research.

Facts About People

In addition to knowing about the merchandise they sell or the records they keep, retailers also want to know about their customers, their employees, and their vendors. Obtaining facts about people is usually more difficult and less reliable than obtaining facts about things. Retailers generally cannot gather all the facts about the people in whom they are interested. They must therefore be highly selective in gathering facts and obtain primarily those facts that are pertinent to the problem at hand.

For example, a retailer may want to know how many customers would shop at a store in a shopping center in a particular area. The retailer might want to know many things about the customers in addition to their interest in the proposed store. However, customers may resent answering too many questions, and they may deny the retailer their goodwill. Retailers are therefore selective in their attempts to get facts about customers and their families. Obtaining information about people's interests, wants, and needs is a form of social research.

THE SAMPLING THEORY

When retailers have the information they seek in their own records, they can use all the facts about the problem. If, however, they seek information beyond what is available within their own stores, they may have to be satisfied with only a small part of the total information desired. For example, if a retailer wanted to question customers about their interest in having a suburban store in a given area, it would be costly and time-consuming to attempt to get every person in the area to respond to the question. In most cases only a portion of the total number of people in the community would be interviewed.

Since the majority of research performed uses this "part" method, it is based on set rules that rely on the fact that the part gives results that reflect the whole.

The Universe
The total population of people or things for any given study is called the *universe*. If a retailer wanted to know whether the firm's employees would like to have a group insurance plan, for example, the universe would be all the employees in the firm. By polling every employee, the retailer would obtain information from *every* person included in this universe, and the response would be representative of all employees. If, however, the retailer wanted to find out what hours customers would like to have the store open, it would be costly and time-consuming to attempt to get answers from all the customers. Some would not be available or willing to answer. By interviewing just those who entered the store during a given period, a large and important group would be omitted, and the information would not be representative of the universe of the firm's customers.

Since most research cannot be done using the entire universe, sampling techniques have been established that make it possible to get a limited number of respondents to mirror the total universe accurately.

The Sample
Using a sample instead of the entire universe is based on the theory of chance. If the sample is obtained by methods that assure a proportional representation of the entire universe, the results of the research will be virtually the same as if the entire universe had been investigated, but these results will be obtained at a greatly reduced cost and in a considerably shorter time. If the selection of the sample is done improperly, however, the sample will not mirror the universe of the study. For example, if you want information from a certain population and you use the telephone book to obtain names, people who have privately listed numbers, those who live in hotels or rooming houses, and those who do not have telephones will not be included in your sample. It is therefore possible that your sample will not mirror the universe and that this will negate the results of your study.

One study showing such a sample bias was made of the effect of stamp plans upon the cost of grocery items. The entire study was based on the results analyzed in one store in a relatively small community. Since stamp plans flourish in large metropolitan areas, the one store was not representative of the universe of stamp-issuing firms and therefore could not be relied upon to provide dependable information.

The two most common methods of obtaining samples that will adequately reflect the universe are known as random sampling and stratified sampling. A *random sample* means that a selection is made by chance and that *every* person or object in the universe has the same opportunity to be chosen. If, for example, numbers were assigned to *every* individual in a given universe and these numbers were then placed in a barrel where they were thoroughly mixed and then drawn by a blindfolded person, one number in the barrel would have the same opportunity to be selected as every other number. If a sufficient number of these sample numbers were selected, the sample should adequately reflect the universe. Researchers, however, do not use such an old-fashioned technique. Instead of drawing numbers from a barrel, they use a table of random numbers to obtain the sample.

In *stratified sampling,* the fact finders choose the participants on a predetermined basis. For example, if retailers were sampling opinions about their organizations and wanted to be sure that every ethnic group, every income group, and every social group were represented, they would plot the proportion of responses they would need from each segment of the community to be representative of the whole, and they would plan to obtain data by selecting a certain number of customers from each area. Shopping-center retailers want to know how far customers travel to reach their stores. After obtaining addresses from charge accounts, telephone orders, and cash customers, they divide the area surrounding their stores by distances of 10 miles. Then, at random, they select customers' house and apartment numbers from those blocked sections. They find that some customers live as much as 50 to 60 miles from the stores but that the majority live within a radius of a few blocks from the store.

An Adequate Sample

An adequate sample that can be relied upon when doing research is one that represents the universe accurately. A sizable number of responses is preferable to just a few. Costs mount rapidly, however, as the sample size increases. If absolute accuracy is not too important, a small sample at low cost might give sufficient information to be usable. For a really reliable sample, however, participants should continue to be added at random until there is no change in the results as more responses are included. At that point, the sample should mirror the universe.

For interviews, or for studies that involve lengthy questionnaires, small samples selected through stratified sampling are considered to be quite reliable.

COOPERATIVE EFFORT IS NEEDED FOR RESEARCH

Total commitment by everyone in the store is the ideal situation for effective research. The manager or head of the firm must encourage all employees to be aware of the importance of the research. The employees should learn how important it is to have available facts that are needed for decision making. Some decisions in retailing are still based on hunches and guesswork. These methods are rarely used, however, by progressive, successful firms. Decisions based on known facts and resulting conclusions and recommendations are more likely to be productive than those based on a person's intuition. Since facts constantly change, every person holding a responsible position must be a researcher and must seek, record, and analyze a variety of facts daily to keep up with the dynamics of retailing.

TOPICS FOR DISCUSSION

1. Why is fact-finding important to retail managers?
2. Why do costs for fact-finding vary so much?
3. What kinds of research are done by a retail research department?
4. For what kinds of research might outside agencies be employed?
5. Explain the advantages of the scientific method of gathering data.
6. Why is obtaining facts about people more difficult for the retailer than obtaining facts about things?
7. What is meant by the sampling theory?
8. Explain the reasons why a retailer would select a sample rather than use the universe for a study of the customers of the store.
9. What is an adequate sample?
10. Why is it important that all people holding responsible positions in a firm do some amount of research?

COMMUNICATIONS IN RETAILING

Mr. Comer, the manager of The Jewel Case, a jewelry store in a city of 10,000 inhabitants, wanted to encourage more high school girls to patronize his store. He thought of running a contest in which he would offer a $25 prize to the winner. He wanted to be sure that the contest would attract the participants to the store. Think of a type of contest that he might run, and on a separate sheet of paper rough out the initial advertisement or mailer he might use to promote the event.

MANAGING HUMAN RELATIONS

A store manager, Ms. Walker, believed that customers were requesting items that were not carried in her store and that the salespeople were not bothering to tell her about this. She decided to establish a "want slip" system. Each salesperson would have some simple forms on which to list the merchandise requested by customers. The forms would have spaces in which the colors, sizes, and other pertinent details of the merchandise could be recorded. The salespeople objected to taking the time to fill out these forms. What steps could the manager take to get their cooperation? Be prepared to discuss your suggestions.

DECISION MAKING

Mr. Chin, a store manager, wanted to increase the number of his charge-account customers. He was not sure, however, that the cost of sending people out to solicit new accounts would be warranted. He therefore wanted to test his idea by stratified sampling before investing too heavily in such a campaign. He decided on an initial sample of 100 interviews. An analysis of the statistics for his area revealed the following: (a) 40 percent of the population was under 25 years of age; (b) 80 percent of the households represented married couples; (c) 70 percent of the households had children.

What numerical breakdown would you suggest for the sampling of 100 households? Be prepared to explain your answer.

CAREER LADDER

A college student was employed in a store's basement shoe department for his cooperative work assignment. The buyer was out sick, and the assistant buyer was trying to do both the buyer's job and his own. He therefore told the college student to make himself busy and try to learn the business without the help he would normally get from the management of the department. The college student first examined the stock in the department. He then observed the customers coming through the store, and he noticed that very few stopped in the shoe department. He immediately asked himself why that was so. Then he began to notice the shoes of the people who entered the store. He went outside the store and observed the shoes of the passersby. He made careful counts of what he saw. When he compared what people were wearing with what was carried in stock, he began to think that sales must be poor in comparison to other stores' sales of shoes. A check of figures in comparable stores showed that he was correct. At the first opportunity he showed his report to the assistant buyer. Should the college student be considered for a job in the department if an opening occurred? Be prepared to give reasons for your answer.

chapter 38

THE SEQUENCE FOR FACT-FINDING ACTIVITY

A young man had just finished the manager training program with the variety store chain he had joined. He was transferred to a store in a nearby city where he was to become the manager when the present one left. The retiring manager explained to the young man, "Since I shall be retiring in a couple of months, you will have a good chance while I am still here to get the store rearranged as you want it. Feel free to do whatever you think best to improve the profitability of the store."

With this authorization, what are the things this young man needs to do?

ASCERTAINING NEEDS

How does the prospective manager know what needs improvement in the store? Managers get ideas from every conceivable source. They may notice many customers walking out without buying; they may see many customers at a counter with no free salesperson to help them; they may receive complaints from customers; they may see that their competitors are underselling them. These are just samples of the types of problems that may be transmitted to them. From this array, they can isolate one problem at a time for which they hope to find a solution.

Stating the Problem
Once a merchant has determined what problem needs solving, the fact-finding activity can begin. The first need is to state the problem in a clear and forthright manner. Thus, the merchant attempting to find out whether brand "x" jams and jellies always sold best or whether the position on the shelf affected sales might state the problem as follows: To determine whether shelf placement affects sales of brand "x" jams and jellies.

A merchant with too large an inventory of men's-wear merchandise might state the problem as follows: To determine whether classification controls and twice-yearly inventory can aid in the reduction of stock with no loss of sales volume.

Once the problem is succinctly stated, the merchants know what their fact-finding goals are going to be, and they should be able to direct their energies toward the goals they have established.

Developing the Hypothesis
The electric clock in the store was not running one Monday morning. The first reaction of the assistant manager who opened the store was one of annoyance at not knowing the time. The second reaction was to ask why a usually perfect timekeeper was suddenly not functioning. The problem was to get the clock running again as quickly as possible.

What, the manager wondered, could be the reason it had stopped?

• A vital part of the mechanism of the clock could have worn out.

• There could be an electric power failure.

- The cord attached to the wall outlet could have been loosened or pulled out.

- The electricity could be turned off.

If the mechanism were faulty, a clock repairer would need to be called, and the repairs would be time-consuming and costly. It would therefore be wise to check other solutions first. Since the lights went on when the electric switch was flipped, there could be no power failure. The cord attached to the wall outlet was secure. The assistant manager therefore assumed that the master switch for the wall outlet had been shut off. Acting on that assumption, the electrician was asked if all the master switches had been turned on. This assumption proved to be correct—a master switch had inadvertently been turned off by a new employee. This story illustrates the way problems are resolved and how priority is determined for the reasons for any solution. The assumption or *hypothesis,* the term used by professional researchers, is the tentative theory adopted about a situation. Further investigation then proves the truth or falsity of this assumption.

GATHERING FACTS BY SURVEY

After a problem has been isolated and the hypothesis developed, the managers decide what facts they need, where they can get the information, how they can get those facts, and what use they can make of those data when they have collected them. They may use the survey method, the observation method, or the experimental method to obtain facts; or they may use information gathered from outside sources that is reported by various government agencies or in professional or trade publications.

All facts are important, whether they are gathered by the retailers or by outside agencies. Let us examine the methods by which merchants may gather facts by themselves or with the aid of other members of their organization.

The simplest fact-gathering method is known as the *survey.* This is a question-and-answer method that uses either a personal interview or a written questionnaire. Developing a set of questions is relatively easy. The value of the survey, however, is in having a sufficient sample of people who will provide accurate, usable answers. The questions the retailers may ask are those of fact, of opinion, or of interpretation.

Factual Surveys

When retailers want to find the answers to questions such as where people live, where they shop, what price they pay for certain items, what papers they read, what radio or TV programs they hear, or what their incomes are, the easiest method is to ask direct questions, either in person or by mailing questionnaires.

Although replies to such questions should be entirely accurate, there are, in fact, many errors that may occur in answers. Some respondents may deliberately give false information. Some people may answer incorrectly in the hope of making a good impression. Questions about age, income, or the price paid for products, for example, may elicit responses that are inaccurate.

Another type of error that creeps into answers in factual surveys is due to forgetting. In one study, several people were asked to list the television programs they had watched the previous evening. Unaided, they were able to recall about one-third of the programs. Aided by a list of programs, they were able to recall 30 percent more of the programs they had watched. Black media representatives hold that black people exposed to black media have a higher percentage of commercial recall than the general market control sample. For example, the Center for Research in Marketing reports that black radio listeners could recall 50 percent more products advertised than those who listen to general radio. The agency further indicates that radio advertising has the greater appeal among black customers.

A third problem that may affect the accuracy of the responses to direct questions is the indifference of the respondent. If the person is not interested in helping the questioner by answering truthfully, he or she may toss off any answer just to be finished with the business. One customer, for example, emerging from a store with a newly made purchase, refused, when approached, to admit that he had made any purchase.

In spite of difficulties in getting correct answers, asking direct questions that request facts is still one of the most reliable methods of getting information. Through a well-developed and well-administered questionnaire, many bits of important information may be obtained.

Opinion Surveys
A second method of obtaining information is conducting an opinion survey. This is the method retailers use to find out which styles customers prefer, in which store they like best to shop, what colors they will buy this season, or what they think of a particular fad. Expressions of opinion, however, are less reliable than expressions of fact.

A group of college students was asked which of several proposed chinaware designs they preferred. After the researcher left, the students said that to be polite they had chosen a few of the designs. Actually, they reported, none of the designs appealed to them enough to make them want to buy. From this illustration, anyone can see that the retailer needs to be cautious in accepting opinion surveys as a basis for merchandise selection.

Panel groups are sometimes used by the merchant to obtain ideas and opinions. Students, club members, and other groups of people may be invited to meet with a store executive to express opinions about merchandise or services offered by the store. The value of such opinions, however, has never been established. These groups often are more important for their publicity value than for their advice on store activities.

Interpretive Surveys
In the third type of survey, customers are asked to evaluate or to give a judgment on their reasons for making certain purchases or performing certain acts. Or employees may be asked to tell why

they reacted in a certain way. The type of question asked will help to determine the value of the answer. For example, if you ask customers why they bought a particular suit or pair of shoes, they may rationalize their answers. If, however, you ask what features of the product appealed most to them, you will probably get more reliable responses. The more specific the questions are, the more likely it is that the responses will be usable.

GATHERING FACTS BY OBSERVATION
Watching people, observing activities, or seeing what products customers buy are more reliable methods of gathering data than the survey method. Observation is, however, a slower and a more costly method, since observers have to be specially trained for this work. If, for example, a firm wishes to know how many customers leave the store without carrying their purchases with them, the manager has observers stand at the exit and count those customers emerging with packages and those customers emerging without packages. If some of the customers have shopping bags or large handbags, pockets, or briefcases, the count may not be entirely accurate. Similarly, rather than asking people how old they are, a researcher might estimate the ages of the people entering or leaving the store. If the ages are grouped by decades, the observers' estimates may be more accurate than the responses given by some of the customers who dislike such personal questions.

Through observation, retailers also obtain information about other retailers' activities, their stocks of goods, and the response to their advertising, their window displays, and other promotional devices they use. Comparison shoppers frequently perform this observation of competitors' goods, prices, services, and customer responses to advertised products.

Observation may be extended beyond just recording facts to determine why customers act as they do. For example, one may observe how many customers stop at a display when it is shown in one type of environment as opposed to the number who respond to the same display in a different environment.

Observation may be used by the manager to note the selling techniques of a salesperson in order to determine what causes success or lack of success in dealing with customers. The manager can also observe the flow of traffic through the store, the hours at which customers prefer to shop, the kinds of merchandise to which they are attracted, the response of customers to advertising, and the acceptance by customers of new ideas in presenting merchandise. If this observation is done in a planned, organized manner, and if accurate records are kept on which decisions may be based, observation becomes a helpful form of fact-finding research.

GATHERING FACTS BY EXPERIMENTATION

The most valuable method of fact-finding is the experimental method. It is, however, the most difficult, the most costly, and the most time-consuming method in use. The experimental method requires developing situations where controls can be established so that the only variable is the one factor being tested. For example, one manager wanted to test the power of a sign to attract customers to buy merchandise. He had one sign made reading "BELTS, $1.99." A second sign read, "BRIGHTEN YOUR DRESS WITH A NEW BELT, $1.99." To make sure that each sign had the same exposure to the public, the signs were changed every hour. The sign used for the opening hour one day was replaced on the next day by the other sign, and the hourly sign switching continued. A tally was kept of the sales by hour for the belts. At the end of one six-day week, the results were analyzed. During the time the second sign was up, sales were 40 percent higher than for the same period of time when the less-informative sign was in place. Since the merchandise, the price, the amount of time, the salespeople, and the display of the merchandise were all the same, and the only difference was in the wording on the sign, the manager concluded that the selling message of the second sign was responsible for the increase in belt sales.

Similarly, tests may be made on sales presentations, the height of displays, merchandise shown in windows, moving versus motionless displays, the placement of merchandise on counters or in bins, the wording in advertising, and training methods. The experimental method necessitates careful recordkeeping as well as careful controls to ensure that the varied methods are being analyzed accurately; however, its results are dependable. Consequently, retailers find this the most desirable fact-finding method.

AREAS OF INVESTIGATION

Although the primary concerns of store managers are those activities within their own organizations, they know that outside sources may also provide help. They therefore look within their organizations and outside to other firms and services for areas of investigation.

Within the Organization

Store managers have unlimited store activities to analyze. Their main problem is to decide which area needs investigation most. Let us observe a manager, Ms. Wittek, at work. She has noticed, in comparing last year's figures with this year's, that she has not had good business in the ladies' coat department. First she checks the weather records. If the weather was noticeably warmer this year than last, she could conclude that weather was responsible for a certain proportion of the sales lag. However, if a check of the weather records showed that this year's weather was as cold as or colder than last year's, she would have to look for other reasons for the sales decline. She might then turn to the want slips filled out daily by the salespeople. These might indicate reasons for the decline. If the want slips showed many colors, sizes, and styles not on hand, the manager would have considerable evidence that the improper stock assortment had caused the decrease in sales. If, however, carefully kept want slips had shown only sporadic calls for goods not on hand, she would need to look still further for answers to her problem. Next she might check her advertising to compare the size and frequency of advertising to that of the previous year. If she found the amount and size of advertising to be comparable, she might want to check the quality of the advertising itself to see if there were noticeable differences in customer appeal.

Thus, the manager would proceed to analyze all the activities of the department to determine what could have caused the overall drop in sales. Since fact-finding may extend into every conceivable store activity, a few in-store experiences will serve as illustrations of the potential areas for this research.

Customer Traffic Counts. To show how many customers enter the store at various entrances and at various times during the day, customer counts may be taken at specified intervals and compared with previous counts taken at similar times of the day at those same entry points.

Some counts are made of the total number of customers who pass the store in addition to those who enter. Such counts, when compared with similar counts taken previously, may reveal increasing or decreasing proportions of customers who are attracted to enter the store.

Where Customers Live. Information about where charge customers live is readily ascertained by examining their accounts. If a retail firm has electronic data-processing equipment, the proportions of charge customers from various areas may be determined quickly by checking the charge-account records. Cash customers, however, cannot be so easily categorized. Those who

have packages delivered supply certain information of value, but those who pay cash and carry their packages must be asked where they live.

Such data may be used, for example, to determine where advertising dollars might best be spent, what communities should receive special services such as fashion shows, what newspapers to use for publicity releases, or what schools to canvass for college board members. The data may also indicate how the characteristics of customer shopping are changing.

Frequency of Shopping. How often customers shop in a given store is another factor of interest to the store manager. For a questionnaire study in one store, 319 customers were interviewed in one day. Each customer was asked two questions; the responses were as shown below.

Through this analysis, the store manager learned that the majority of customers did not have a charge account and that over 50 percent of those customers shopped at least once a month in the store. Over one-third, however, shopped less frequently than once a month in the store. As a result of this survey, the store manager decided to promote charge accounts and to extend "special sale invitations" to get customers into the store more often.

Weather Records. To ascertain what effect weather has on the number of people who pass by and enter the store during certain hours of the day, carefully detailed records must be kept of weather conditions. Just the word "snow," for example, next to the day's receipts is of little help in analyzing the impact of the snow on the business for the day. Good records might reveal facts such as shown on the next page.

Questions	Responses	Percent
Do you have a charge account here?	No Yes	82.5 17.5
When did you last visit the store?	Last week 1–2 weeks ago 2–4 weeks ago Over one month ago No response	14.5 14.0 27.2 38.2 6.1

Day	Time	Temperature	Weather	Business
Feb. 2	9 a.m.–12 p.m.	30°–40°	Skies overcast.	Fair
	12 p.m.–6 p.m.	32°	Snow beginning— 4-inch accumulation.	Poor
Feb. 3	9 a.m.–12 p.m.	25°	Bright, sunny day. Snow accumulation slowed traffic.	Moderate

Outside the Organization

In addition to the surveys that can be done within a firm, outside fact-finding may also prove to be beneficial. Reports may be available through the government, universities, colleges, high schools, independent organizations, manufacturers, publishers, and trade organizations.

A professor and his class queried 1,400 customers about their reasons for shopping in areas other than their local neighborhood. The responses they tabulated are shown below.

Information of this type would make the local merchants aware of customers' attitudes and help them to make changes and improvements that would attract customers to do their shopping in the local area.

Government reports offer a great deal of helpful information. In 1975, the U.S. Census Bureau said that the average household consisted of less than three people for the first time in history. Fewer marriages and the increasing number of divorces were the reasons for the lower birthrate, and thus for the smaller size of households on the average. Such data are important for the retailers' planning.

Best Selling Seasons for Merchandise. Every product sold in stores has a peak selling season. This is reflected not only by the figures of individual stores but also by industry studies. The U.S. Department of Commerce publishes industry figures such as the following, which retailers find useful:

PEAK MONTHLY SELLING SEASONS

Month	Percent Carpet Sales	Percent Men's-wear Sales
January	7.9	8.0
February	8.0	5.0
March	7.6	6.0
April	7.4	6.0
May	7.7	8.0.
June	7.2	8.0
July	6.0	7.0
August	8.0	7.0
September	8.0	8.0
October	11.5	9.0
November	11.4	9.0
December	8.4	19.0

Only two types of merchandise have been reported above. Figures are available, however, for all classifications of goods. Although these figures vary slightly from year to year, they indicate the

Reason for Shopping Beyond Local Area	Percent
The local stores carry too few articles.	58
Local stores are not as exciting.	43
Local store prices are higher.	39
Local store merchandise quality is not as good.	28
Salespeople in local stores are not as knowledgeable.	20
Parking is difficult in the streets around the local stores.	19
Local store hours are inconvenient.	16
Local stores are not as attractive.	12

Note: Respondents made multiple replies, and so figures do not add up to 100 percent.

RETAIL STORES SELLING HOUSEWARES*

	Cookware and Bakeware (Percent)	Small Electrical Appliances (Percent)
Department stores	41	32
Discount houses	39	52
Hardware and appliance stores	14	13
Variety chains	6	3

*Stores, December 1974, pp. 14 and 15.

Influence on Choice of Personal Clothing	Rating	Influence on Choice of Sports Equipment	Rating
Parents	1.87	Store personnel	2.45
Friends	2.21	Friends	2.66
Newspapers and magazines	3.29	Parents	2.67
Store personnel	3.33	Newspapers and magazines	3.22
Television	4.34	Television	4.09

months in which peaks of business occur. Notice, for example, that October and November are the best selling months for carpets, while December far outstrips any other month in men's-wear sales.

Industry Surveys. Although somewhat less meaningful for the individual store manager, industry surveys may show trends in customer buying habits or may indicate the importance of various types of stores in handling certain lines of merchandise. One such survey was conducted among retail stores carrying housewares. The results indicated that business in housewares was divided among retailers as shown in the first table above.

Customers' tastes in food have changed, and the high cost of some foods has caused buying changes. Steaks and chops have been supplanted by hot dogs, hamburgers, cheese, and peanut butter; frozen cakes by packaged flour; TV dinners by frozen pizzas; and soft drinks by coffee, tea, and milk. People who buy dog food have changed from dog meat to dry dog food.

Customer Buying Influences. Who influences teen-agers in their buying? Retailers need an-

swers to such questions in planning their advertising and merchandise presentations. One study in Denver, Colorado,[1] of 500 unmarried teen-agers (aged 16 to 19) reported the teen-agers' beliefs about who influenced their selections. Ratings ranged from 1, a great deal of influence, to 5, very little if any influence. The results were as shown in the second table above.

Using these data, merchants could plan self-selection areas for clothing while providing knowledgeable sales help in sporting goods departments.

Style Survey. Publications may take surveys to aid the industries that they represent. A national newspaper serving discount houses and mass merchandising firms reported a survey on men's and boys' wear. Changing fashions and interest in fashion, the newspaper explained, was making men's and boys' wear almost as volatile as ladies' ready-to-wear. Private-label merchandise, it stated, was used in some form by 70 percent of the discount firms answering the questionnaire.

Best-selling items, it concluded from the sur-

[1] Paul Gilkison, "What Influences the Buying Decisions of Teen-Agers?" *Journal of Retailing,* Fall 1965, pp. 33–48.

vey's results, were sport shirts, underwear, hosiery, and slacks.

Armed with such information, store managers can check their stock and their sales of merchandise to compare their best-selling items with the ones on the list. They can determine if they are getting results comparable to those reported in the study.

Competitors' Advertising. Although a superficial examination of competitors' advertising may give some idea of the scope and details of the copy, an analysis that specifies details is beneficial. One such analysis was made by a store manager of advertising for women's shoes. The analysis revealed the following:

100% of competitors' advertising pictured the shoes.

84% mentioned the types of materials used in the shoes.

78% was for regular-priced merchandise.

78% specified the style or design of the shoes.

75% mentioned the colors of the shoes.

54% listed the size range of the shoes.

50% mentioned nothing about the construction of the shoes.

32% referred to the comfort or the good fit of the shoes.

30% mentioned special features, such as finish, decorations, and heel shapes and heights.

22% was for sale-priced or specially priced goods.

14% mentioned the wearing qualities of the shoes.

Having found the omissions in the competitors' advertising, the manager was able to improve the advertising and increase the response to the advertising for the store.

COMPILING FACTS

The managers who have gathered the facts must compile them into usable form. Data gathering for retailing is often quantitative as opposed to being qualitative. The retailers may want to know which are their best-selling price lines, their best-selling styles or their most profitable departments or lines. They may want to identify their most efficient salespeople, the vendors who supply products that contribute the most profit, or their advertising costs as a ratio to sales.

After such quantitative data are obtained, they must be analyzed and reported in a manner that is accurate and helpful. A few commonly used methods of analyzing and reporting data are presented here. Frequently used terms are defined, and applications of the methods are described.

Determining the Central Tendency

Retailers frequently use the word "average" when they refer to factors such as sales, the amount of stock on hand, the salary of employees, the cost per sale, and markup.

The word "average" implies the central tendency or the middle or most popular group of numbers. Since there are three common ways of determining this central tendency, one must know which method has been employed when the term "average" is used. Is the average the *mean*, the *median*, or the *mode?* While each may represent the same or similar numbers, they can differ quite widely from one another.

The Mean. The mean is determined by simple arithmetic. If retailers want to know the average price among a group of prices, they simply add the prices and divide by the total number in the list. Thus, five articles priced at $2, $2, $3, $5, and $8 would give an average price of $4. The total of all the prices, $20, is divided by the total number of prices, which is 5 in this case.

The Median. The median differs from the mean in that it is the middle number in a group of numbers arranged in ascending or descending order. Among the prices listed above, the middle price is $3. Therefore, the median price and the mean price in this example are not the same. If there were an even number of prices instead of an uneven number as in the example given above, the median would still be in the middle— but this time in between two numbers. For example, if the prices were $2, $3, $4, and $5, the middle price would be between $3 and $4—it would be $3.50.

The Mode. The mode refers to the most popular item in a list. In the first list of prices above, three prices—$3, $5, and $8—each appear only once. Therefore, none of the three is more "popular" than the other. The $2 price, however, appears twice and is, therefore, the popular or mode price. Longer lists may be bimodal (have two sets of the most popular numbers) or trimodal.

The Average. As this example has shown, the term "average" may mean different things. From the short list of prices—$2, $2, $3, $5, $8—three different averages may be quoted: the mean average, $4; the median average, $3; and the mode average, $2.

This illustrates the need to understand which method has been used to determine the "average" when this term is used. Although this example showed three different figures depending on the method used to determine the average, in many normal distributions the mean, mode, and median all fall at the same point.

Rating by Ranking

Retailers have many opportunities to rate merchandise, services, and people. Knowing how to rank a list of numbers or the qualities or achievements of people is therefore helpful. For example, a retailer who wanted to know how the store's salespeople ranked in sales might arrange their dollar amounts for a given period as follows:

Salesperson	Sales
A	$1,000
B	950
C	900
D	850
E	800
F	750

These six salespeople would then be ranked from number 1 to number 6.

If, however, two of the salespeople had the same amounts—for example, if salesperson D and salesperson E both had $800 in sales—the ranking in this descending order would show that A was first, B ranked second, and C ranked third but that D and E had the same amounts and would have to share the fourth and fifth places, while F would rank sixth. When ranking two or more having equal value, the middle ranking is always used. Thus D and E would rank neither fourth nor fifth but $4\frac{1}{2}$, and F would still rank sixth.

Similarly, if three of the salespeople had the same amount of sales, the middle ranking number would be assigned to each as follows:

Salesperson	Sales	Rank
A	$1,000	1
B	950	2
C	800	4
D	800	4
E	800	4
F	750	6

Ranking permits each person or number to receive a value in comparison to other people or numbers on the list. Ranking may be used for salary comparisons or for raises for the most able persons.

Grouping by Quartiles, Deciles, and Percentiles

Grouping numbers of cases in reporting simplifies and condenses the information available.

Quartiles. If large groupings will provide sufficient detail, the whole may be divided into fourths, known as *quartiles.* The lowest fourth is known as the first quartile, and the ranking progresses to the top grouping, which would be the fourth quartile.

Deciles. If retailers wanted a more detailed breakdown of the data they sought, they might ask to have the information submitted by deciles. Deciles are obtained by dividing the whole into tenths. The lowest tenth is the first decile.

Percentiles. Dividing the entire group by 100 to report by percentiles is the most common method used by retailers. The figuring of all costs and markups and analyses of costs are done by using percentages. This permits detailed reporting such as the following:

A 1-percent shortage figure has been provided for, and 60 percent of the retail price is the cost of the goods. Another 37 percent is the cost of overhead and personnel. Therefore, only a 2-percent net profit may be realized if all costs are watched carefully.

For reporting, retailers use the breakdown that will give the most accurate information for their particular purpose. Suppose, for example, they were reporting salaries of employees and made the following statement: "Fifty percent of our employees made $6,250 or more last year." Little would be revealed about the salary range. If, however, they reported by percentiles, fairly detailed knowledge would be available:

Percent	Salary
10	$ 5,000 or less
10	5,200
9	5,500
11	6,000
12	6,250
9	6,500
8	7,000
11	7,500
7	10,000
6	15,000
5	20,000
1	30,000
0.5	40,000
0.5	45,000 or more

DRAWING CONCLUSIONS

When the retailer has obtained the facts and analyzed those facts, conclusions may be drawn. One store manager noticed that her competitors advertised sales on women's coats for October 12. She had run no such advertisements. She decided to check the results of their sales. Comparison shoppers were sent to four competitors' stores to count the customers in the coat departments. They compared the figures with customer counts in their own store and then reported their findings. After compiling the results, the manager concluded that the sale advertising attracted many customers to her competitors' firms and that their volume of business in coats on that date was many times the volume of her own women's coat department.

MAKING AND ACTING ON RECOMMENDATIONS

After the managers have analyzed their data, they make recommendations based on their findings. In the case of the coat advertising mentioned above, the manager recommended that her firm institute advertising in succeeding years for October 12 coat sales.

Research is of value only if it improves the activities of the firm. Once a recommendation has been made, therefore, it must be carried out if it is to enable the firm to do a better job. The manager did try advertising coats in October of the following year, and the results indicated that her analysis and recommendations had been entirely correct. The store continued each year to advertise sales on women's coats for October 12 as a result of the fact-finding. Through this activity, the store was able to increase sales, decrease costs, and improve profits—the goal of all fact-finding activity in retailing.

SOME PRACTICAL USES OF RETAIL RESEARCH

For successful fact-finding activity, more is needed than just the ability to gather, interpret, and analyze facts, draw conclusions, and make recommendations. The attitude of the top management of the retail firm will largely decide the effectiveness of such work. If the management is progressive and not fearful of trying new techniques or methods, fact-finding can be profitable and rewarding. If, however, top management does not believe in deviating from the previous methods used, the fact-finding activity will result in wasted effort. Therefore, the support and flexibility of the top executive personnel are essential to success in this phase of the business. If the top management is willing to support new activities, substantial success can be achieved through research.

Customer File

If managers want to send direct-mail announcements to customers, or if they want to telephone customers when certain kinds of merchandise are in stock, a customer file is necessary. This should include the following:

- The name and address of the customer and, if possible, names and addresses of family members and their approximate ages

- The styles of products he or she prefers, and the preferences of family members

- The sizes the customer wears, and those worn by family members

- The names of the salespeople who usually serve that customer

Managers have various ways of compiling a customer file. Some names may be recorded on the sales checks at the time the sales are made. To get names of potential customers, however, other methods must be used. One store manager enticed students from the nearby high schools and college into his store by offering to give away pairs of socks to all visitors during a given period of time. A card file was then built from the names and addresses of the students who received the 1,200 pairs of socks. During the year direct-mail advertising was sent to these students. In this manner, for a low cost, the manager acquired names of potential customers, and the resulting sales proved the value of building this student file.

One manager of a family shoe store learned that to "sell the children first" would help to sell the entire family. He therefore sends birthday greetings to all the child customers of the store. This necessitates his keeping a record of each child's name, address, and birth date. He mails out 4,000 birthday cards yearly. However, this mailing is much less costly than newspaper advertising, and it often brings not only the child but also the entire family to his store to buy shoes.

Advertising

One retailer was curious about the effectiveness of advertising a product in newspapers as opposed to advertising the same product on the radio. As a test, he ran advertising concurrently on radio and in the newspapers for the same merchandise. As customers came in to purchase, each was asked, "Where did you learn of this sale?" The responses showed a ratio of 38 customers who had seen the advertisement in the newspapers to 1 who had heard it on the radio. Although this does not prove the superiority of one medium over another, the store manager did conclude that for single-item sale advertising, his dollars were better spent on newspapers than on radio.

Window Display

One store manager wanted to know how many customers observed the merchandise exhibited in the windows. To determine this, she conducted a survey for a three-day period. During that period, 491 customers were questioned, and the results were as follows:

41.3% of the people interviewed could describe an item seen in the windows.

17.1% said they entered the store because of the merchandise they saw in the windows.

5.5% went to a particular department only because they had seen that department's merchandise in the windows.

36.1% could not remember seeing merchandise in the windows or made no response to the question.

Interior Display

Point-of-purchase displays are excellent areas for fact-finding. One store manager experimented with stocks of infants' shoes. Instead of leaving them in the manufacturer's cardboard boxes, she displayed them in clear plastic containers on the tops of counters. Because baby booties and shoes are impulse items and are so tiny and cute that customers who can see them cannot resist them, sales increased noticeably. By comparing current sales with the previous year's sales, the manager discovered that the new display method had increased sales by 42 percent. Thus, experimentation proved to be a real sales booster, and this was confirmed by fact-finding.

In another study, dresses were displayed during a two-week period

- With a plain background and no sign

- With a plain background and a descriptive sign

- With an embellished background and a descriptive sign

The results of this study showed that the most elaborate display caused 78.6 percent more customers to stop and take notice as opposed to the ones with the plain background. The study also revealed that over 75 percent of the customers could remember the price of the merchandise in the displays where the informative signs were used.

In still another display test, specially built racks were used to show fast-selling men's slippers in an eye-catching manner. As a result, sales of the merchandise tripled for the department. The newly built stand allowed for examination and self-selection of the items and freed salespeople to sell more costly shoes and slippers.

Redesigning the box that houses merchandise can also lead to increased sales. One slipper manufacturer increased sales tenfold by changing his polyethylene soft package to a see-through, reusable carryall box with an attached carrying cord.

Customer Complaints

The New York Better Business Bureau made a study of customer complaints. The most significant findings showed that common complaints were caused by errors resulting in nondelivery or partial delivery of goods, in the loss of merchandise, in unsatisfactory workmanship, and in faulty installation or service. Only 1.9 percent of the complaints were about misleading advertising, 1.1 percent about nonavailability of advertised items, and 3.6 percent about failure to include oral representations in the contract. For this survey, 2,928 complaint letters received during a month's time were analyzed.

Sales Training

Finding the best way to make salespeople work as efficiently and accurately as possible is a problem constantly confronting the retailer. One firm prepared a programmed sales-training course to be studied by salespeople individually at their own rate of speed. An analysis of the sales of the salespeople involved in the test was made before these employees took the course and again after they completed the course. The results are indicated on the next page.

In this case, the same number of customers was involved in the selling before and after the course. But because the skills and knowledge of the salespeople were improved and expanded through the programmed instruction, there was a substantial increase in sales results. Research proved that the programmed course was well worth its cost.

Floor Arrangement

Mr. Ashby, the manager of a large department store in a Western city, believed his main floor was not providing the fashion image that he

	Before Taking the Course	After Taking the Course	Difference	
			Number	Percent
Number of customers greeted	200	200	0	0
Number of customers who made purchases	140	173	33	+23.6
Number of multiple sales of item	43	57	14	+32.6
Number of other goods sold	33	59	26	+78.7

sought for the store. Aisle tables scattered throughout the main floor featured bargain prices on goods. A large quantity of this low-markup merchandise was sold through these tables.

Mr. Ashby decided to experiment with an area that occupied about one-tenth of the main floor's space. All aisle tables were removed, and cosmetics counters were highlighted with dramatic displays replacing the bargain tables. Volume dropped slightly, but in place of inexpensive, low-markup goods, fashionable, high-markup goods were sold. After a three-month trial period, it was evident that customers wanted better goods and would buy them when they were featured and given adequate selling space. Volume slowly built up in the cosmetics area, and profits for that one-tenth of the main floor's space jumped.

Mr. Ashby then redid the rest of the main floor, removing the bargain-table goods and placing them in areas within the departments where customers were attracted to shop. This caused customers to travel throughout the store, brought more customers to each department seeking bargains, and resulted in more sales at higher markups. Although the revitalization of the store was costly, improved markups over three years paid for the refurbishing and left better profits for the firm.

RESEARCH IMPROVES RETAILING

The examples of research both inside and outside the retail store reveal that every store manager must be involved in such activity to some degree. Since fact-finding research is time-consuming, some retailers believe they do not have time for more than is required for day-to-day business transactions. Those retailers usually find that their stores are less progressive and less appealing to customers as the years roll by. Research not only pinpoints problems; it also encourages solutions. When retailers are seeking answers to problems, they are forced to be progressive. Progressive retailers keep abreast of the newest developments, and this progress is always reflected in their stores. Wherever you find good retailing practices, you will also find store managers who seek the facts about problems and who act on the suggested solutions.

TOPICS FOR DISCUSSION

1. Explain how a manager uses fact-finding to determine what he or she needs to improve in the operation of the store.
2. Why is an accurate statement of the problem desirable?
3. What is the function of the hypothesis or assumption in fact-finding?
4. Which is most likely to provide accurate responses—the factual survey, the opinion survey, or the interpretive survey? Give reasons for your answer.
5. Explain the advantages of gathering facts by observation.

6. What are the advantages of the experimental method of fact-finding? Give reasons for your answers.
7. Explain which fact-finding methods you would suggest for the following:
   a Determining what your competitors are advertising during a given week
   b Checking on the length of high school girls' school skirts and dresses
   c Determining how many customers would shop at your store if you moved it to another location some blocks away from its present site
   d Determining how often customers request merchandise that you do not carry
   e Determining the response to a competitor's advertisement in a local newspaper for a certain item
8. What are some areas of fact-finding within a retail organization?
9. What are some areas outside a retail organization that the manager might wish to investigate to help his or her store improve?
10. What should a customer file include?

MATHEMATICS FOR RETAILING

The salespeople in a large department had the following approximate weekly net sales.

A. $3,000	D. $ 4,500	G. $4,000	J. $9,000
B. 9,000	E. 8,500	H. 8,000	K. 4,500
C. 8,500	F. 10,000	I. 8,500	L. 4,000

1. Place the sales in descending order—from the highest to the lowest.
2. Rank the salespeople according to their sales, assigning first place to the salesperson with the highest sales.
3. Determine which salespeople were in the upper quartile in sales.

Do this exercise on a separate sheet of paper.

MANAGING HUMAN RELATIONS

A store manager had a college work-experience student acting as department manager while a regular department manager was on a month's leave of absence. After the regular manager had returned, the store manager noticed that the sales of the department were consistently lower than they had been during the time the college student had run the department. He did a little fact-finding by questioning the regular salespeople. He learned that the college student had instituted little contests among the salespeople, had commended them for their suggestions, had been enthusiastic in explaining new merchandise, and had readily accepted suggestions made by department members. The regular department manager did none of those things. What would you suggest the store manager do to restore the level of sales achieved under the college student's management? Be prepared to discuss your suggestions.

DECISION MAKING

A chain organization selling family clothing and accessories planned to open a store near a new housing development. Since the space available for the store was limited in size, and there would be no space to carry slow-moving merchandise, the retail firm needed to know what merchandise would be bought by the people living in the nearby community. Be prepared to suggest what steps the store management should take in deciding what sizes and types of garments to carry.

CAREER LADDER

A young trainee in a women's ready-to-wear chain had a choice of two assignments in stores in adjacent towns when she finished her internship. Both jobs carried the title "department manager," and the salary was the same for both. She could easily commute to either store from her home in a half hour.

Store A was a large store that had many problems. It had old fixtures, an old-fashioned decor, and sales personnel who had been on the job for many years. It also had a very good profit showing.

Store B was a smaller, fairly new store. It had new fixtures and a modern look. The staff had been on the job only a short time. High personnel turnover, excessive shortages, and a poor profit showing characterized this store. Which should the trainee choose for her first assignment? Be prepared to give reasons for your answer.

chapter 39

RETAILING
HAS A CAREER FOR YOU!

Retailing has a career for virtually any person who wishes to devote time to this field. Buying merchandise and reselling it is done everywhere throughout the world, and it flourishes in all types of economies and under all varieties of political movements. Retailing abounds at crossroads, in vacant lots, in small towns, and in large cities. Retailing is found to exist in the form of street vending, in door-to-door selling, in barter and exchange, or in buying goods at established firms. Licensing is needed for selling only a certain few products, and so retailing is open without test or license to most people who wish to join its ranks. Almost 14 million of the more than 95 million people employed in the United States are employed in some form of retailing!

Although retailing ranges through all types of buying and selling, young people who study to enter the field usually have limited their interests. They may join a family-run business, become an entrepreneur (a person who creates his or her own opportunities), or work up through the ranks of a larger firm that may or may not have branches or be part of a chain organization. One's life will depend upon which choice is made. Some people begin with one choice and shift to another. Some shift back again after a trial period. Retailing may be entered at many points, and a person may then progress in any direction. For our pluralistic society, retailing offers multifaceted opportunities, and it does have a career for you!

MANAGEMENT OPPORTUNITIES IN RETAILING

A variety of management opportunities exists in retailing. One may choose to open a store of one's own. Usually, such a business initially is small and involves a limited amount of capital invested. One may choose to open a franchised type of business where help both in financing and running the business is available. One may wish to start with a "flea market" type of operation—

simply an outdoor stand side-by-side with other outdoor stands in a vacant lot or vacant building. Or one may choose to enter a larger firm and work through the ranks to a management position.

If one decides to work through the ranks in a large organization, eventually there are many opportunities to move into management positions. Retailing has long led all businesses in the ratio of management employees to nonmanagement employees. In a typical large departmentized general or specialty store, the ratio of executives to nonexecutives is 1 to 10. Therefore, 10 out of every 100 people employed have management responsibilities and earn management salaries. No other field of employment can boast so high a ratio.

Store Hours Affect Management Jobs
Retailing increasingly offers the 6-day, 12-hours-a-day week to match store hours to customer convenience. Some stores are even open on Sundays. This trend toward longer store hours does not affect the working hours for individuals. However, these longer store hours do mean that many stores have two or even three complete sets of managerial employees in both selling and nonselling areas.

Regular management employees and management trainees usually work some Saturdays and some evenings on a rotation system. Young careerists may find their promotions dependent upon their willingness to take an evening shift initially and then to accept such assignments thereafter from time to time. Anyone to whom regular nine-to-five hours and free weekends are extremely important will not be happy in the retail business.

Technology Affects Retail Management Jobs
Computer technology and improved mechanical devices have, during the past ten years, lessened the detail and routine work for managerial personnel in retailing. More sophisticated techniques of buying and selling and general management were also responsible for changes. Retailing has entered upon the era of scientific controls and automation. This has created new middle-management jobs for systematizers and specialists without reducing the number of existing management jobs. For example, specialists assist retail buyers by providing computerized inventory control and more line-by-line market research. In addition, merchandise handling has been speeded by automation and scientific productivity measurement and control. This has increased the need for college-trained managers in the non-merchandising areas of retailing.

Employment Security Affects Retail Management Jobs
Stores are in style! Even in economically bad times, historians record that retail businesses—and retail employment—survive with fewer losses than in other types of businesses.

The retailing experience one gains in a store is always transferable, and this is another aspect of security. The experience and the skills gained enable the trained retail management worker to find employment in other stores anywhere. The employment history of many of the top-ranking retailing managers shows that they have held jobs in many parts of the country. The experience gained in one firm could easily be transferred to another firm.

Not only are people experienced in retailing able to find jobs in other retailing firms; they can also transfer their experience to marketing management in manufacturing, and wholesaling, or even to jobs with consumer and trade publications firms. The knowledge that retail managers gain of consumer wants and behavior is valuable to other businesses that deal in consumer goods and advertising.

Automation, while it is clearly invading retailing, is no threat to the security of jobs at the middle- and upper-management levels. It is, in fact, creating a demand for new kinds of skills and training that have not previously been much utilized in retailing. In addition, automation will not displace the career salesperson. The increasingly sophisticated and rapidly changing products of the late 1970s and the 1980s will require high-quality personal selling.

Starting Salaries Affect Retail Management Jobs

Given equal education, management trainees in retailing receive salaries about equal to those received by beginners in journalism, career civil service, the administrative and selling areas of the manufacturing industries, and even, in some areas, teaching.

Management trainees in retailing are recruited chiefly from among graduates of two- and four-year colleges. The only possible obstacle to recruitment for graduates of two-year colleges who are otherwise qualified would be their age. Those graduates who are under 20 years old might be required to wait a year or two before being placed in a management training program. Meanwhile, they could be acquiring experience by working as salespeople or as juniors in non-selling departments.

Retailing, like most businesses, bases starting salaries on years of education and experience. The possession of a degree usually means a higher starting salary, and a graduate degree commands a premium for the management trainee. However, some stores admit qualified high school graduates to their management training programs after they have demonstrated ability in nonmanagerial jobs.

Salaries in larger stores in metropolitan areas are usually higher than in comparable stores in smaller places. Lower living costs and greater convenience compensate, however, for the somewhat lower salaries in those smaller places.

Retailing is generally not regarded as a field in which the starting salary itself is a strong attraction. The industry is one in which management responsibility and resulting high salaries are frequently achieved while a person is still quite young. This is chiefly because of the rapid rate at which retail companies expand. By and large, except in times of national economic depression, stores are always short of competent managerial personnel.

Those who have ability and training usually move ahead rapidly in retailing. Within two years, most ambitious college-educated people have attained beginning management jobs. Even top management jobs may be reached in about 11 to 17 years. Middle management positions usually take about five years to attain.

Management Salaries Affect Retailing Jobs

Middle management and top management personnel in retailing earn salaries equal to, or better than, the salaries of their counterparts in other businesses. When retailing is compared with other fields requiring a comparable education, it is found that although the beginning salaries in retailing may be somewhat lower, the middle management and top management salaries are usually somewhat higher. This is because retailing demands not only ability but also stamina and stick-to-it-iveness.

Some Special Fringe Benefits in Retailing Affect Management Salaries

Those entering retailing, in both management and nonmanagement positions, should consider, besides their salaries, the value of the employee discount, which is 10 or 20 percent or more in most stores.

Vacation policies, pension plans, health plans, and other benefits approximate those of other businesses of the same size. Usually, the larger the organization, the more highly developed the plans.

The Demands of Retailing Affect Management Jobs

Retailing is a demanding and an exciting business. The most persistent and characteristic elements in the retailing environment are competitiveness and pressure in all jobs that are involved with getting merchandise into or out of the store. Those who find "beating last year's figures" or "beating yesterday's figures" a challenge will enjoy retailing. Those who have the self-confidence to be evaluated almost daily on their production and results will find the retailing environment rewarding. Retailing is a fast-paced, innovative field, besides being very competitive. Retailing's fast pace even affects parts of the business that are not so intimately associated with merchandise, such as personnel management and accounting.

RETAIL MANAGEMENT REQUIRES A WIDE RANGE OF TALENTS AND ABILITIES

Except for the entrepreneurs who start their own businesses, the road to a management job in a large retailing firm will lead through one of the specialized functional divisions mentioned earlier in this book—merchandising, operations, finance and control, sales promotion, and personnel. In a smaller firm, moving to a management position may involve doing general tasks to assist the owner or manager.

Management Training Programs in Large Firms

Management training is designed to develop generalists to the extent that they understand thoroughly how every segment of the business operates. To be a good buyer, one needs a knowledge of the routing and rate problems of the traffic manager, of the receiving and marking and stocking problems of those operating parts of the business, and of the advertising and copy-writing problems of the advertising or sales promotion division. Similarly, one cannot be an efficient controller or a productive sales promotion manager without firsthand knowledge of selling, stock control, and actual buying in the markets.

Beginners who aim to reach managerial levels must recognize that their early months in retailing should be spent learning about all the functions and operations of the firm. The most progressive retail organizations usually provide an opportunity for training in their management development programs, or they pay all or part of the tuition for courses that their potential management personnel take at local colleges or universities.

Management Training Opportunities in Small Firms

A second way to acquire an all-around knowledge of retailing is to go into a small store under the sponsorship of the owner or manager. Such a person may be looking for a general assistant, or someone to train for a branch store opening, or someone to become the owner in the future. To be trained under such a person is an assurance of being involved in every phase of a retail business. For the beginner whose goal is the all-around management or ownership of a small business, training in a small store could well be the most advisable route to take. Since such training involves all activities in retailing, it could also be transferred at a later time to a larger firm, if the person wanted a new opportunity.

Management training programs offer the individual an opportunity to learn how every segment of the business operates. Such programs can include courses given at local colleges or by the firm and on-the-job training under the sponsorship of the owner or manager.
Courtesy Thom McAn Shoe Company and Friendly Ice Cream Corporation

Training Opportunities in Franchised Departments or Stores

Firms that franchise merchandise for individual departments or that franchise entire stores offer training for the management personnel of those operations. Since franchisers' routines are usually carefully worked out and detailed, the person seeking to manage a franchised department or firm receives excellent training. In addition, franchise operators usually oversee the franchise to make sure that all practices are being carried out as detailed. A franchised operation, then, is a worthwhile training ground for prospective management personnel.

Varied Job Goal Opportunities

In seeking a job, the young applicant needs to think about the future as well as the present. Asking oneself about job goals five years and ten years in the future will help provide direction to job seeking. Usually, in addition to deciding upon small or large stores, franchised stores or chains, and mass or class stores, the individual needs to decide upon the area of work most desirable, both now and in the future. Will it be merchandising, operations control, promotion, personnel, or store unit management?

FOR THOSE WHO WANT TO REMAIN SPECIALISTS

Not everybody wants to take on administrative responsibilities, and not everybody is qualified to do so. For outstanding achievement in a creative line, some people may find themselves rewarded by being assigned to a managerial job. They may find themselves supervising—instead of actually doing—the work they love.

For example, many people prefer selling as a career instead of the buying job, with its management anxieties and mounds of paper work. There are many salespeople—for example, those who sell furniture, high-fashion and custom-made clothing, and other big-ticket items—who earn over $20,000 a year in retail stores.

Plenty of people who go into the sales promotion division as managers would rather build reputations as outstanding copywriters or window trimmers. Many who go into merchandising wish to establish themselves as fashion authorities or interior decorators, not as buyers or merchandise managers.

If one is in favor of being a specialist rather than a generalist, retailing offers a number of opportunities to earn a manager's salary without taking on the responsibilities of individual department or store management. Here are some examples of specialists:

Accountants	Laboratory personnel
Architects	Labor specialists
Artists	Management engineers
Building operators	Market researchers
Copywriters	Personnel specialists
EDP system designers	Quality control
Fashion coordinators	personnel
Interior decorators	Real estate experts

For these people the road to a good reputation and high earnings may not be so much upward through one organization as sideways to bigger and bigger companies.

DOING RESEARCH ON THE PROSPECTIVE EMPLOYER

The young person planning a career in retailing should know his or her prospective employer. To learn about the firms to which they are applying, young people should do some serious fact-finding.

Asking Questions

First, the candidate should talk to friends who work in the firm under consideration or who know people who do. How does the firm treat its employees? How well does it pay the employees? What hours do they work? What promotions do they get? Are promotions from within the firm, or are people brought in from outside to fill choice positions?

Recruiters from various firms may be asked such questions when they set up meetings on college campuses. They should also be asked about training programs for new employees and about promotion calendars—for both salary increases and movement into other jobs.

Taking the Initiative

With the aid of friends in retailing, campus recruiters, and retailers' advertisements in local and city papers, trade journals, and the students' own teacher of retailing or marketing, a list of stores can be compiled for study. Much depends on whether or not the student wants to stay in the home community or go afield. This is a personal decision.

Study the list, and get acquainted with the background, the image, and the probable future of the stores on it. Check how many branches or units each company has, as well as their locations. Choose stores that are growing. Fairchild's *Financial Manual of Retail Stores* is a good reference book. It lists all the publicly owned retail companies in the United States and describes their business, their volume compared with previous years, and their growth in number of units or branches compared with previous years.

At the end of a few weeks of research, students will have compiled two lists: one of stores in which, because of their growth record and location, they would like to be interviewed, and one of stores known to be recruiting. They should not be tempted to follow the line of least resistance by taking the job most easily available, for their research about executive opportunities is not complete until they have learned more about what several companies offer. That requires personal interviews.

APPLYING FOR A JOB

After a list of prospective employers has been drawn up, there are four steps in applying for a job: preparing a résumé, writing a letter of appli-cation, going to an interview, and following up the interview. The student who hopes for executive responsibilities in retailing must handle each of these steps well, for the ability to communicate effectively is a necessary aptitude in this field.

The Résumé

The student's faculty adviser, teacher of retailing or marketing, or college placement bureau will be able to provide standard résumé forms to be used as a guide. A résumé should be short and informative and should stress the accomplishments of the applicant. It should contain the following information:

Name	Extracurricular
Address	activities
Telephone number	Career goal
Marital status	Previous job
Position wanted	experience
Schooling	References

The Letter of Application

A résumé should be accompanied by a covering letter. The letter should be addressed to the personnel manager or employment manager of the company by name. The name of the executive can be obtained by calling the store.

The letter should be short, since it is accompanying a detailed résumé, but it should make it clear that the applicant's goal is executive training and that the applicant has prepared for store work while still at school. The letter should specify a time when the applicant will call to make an appointment.

Both the letter and the résumé should be neatly typed with a new ribbon on good-quality paper. Attention should be given to clarity, grammar, punctuation, spelling, and spacing. Résumés are often mechanically reproduced.

The Interview

The applicant should dress for a job interview as he or she would expect to dress as a manager in the store. The applicant expresses in appearance and clothing his or her sense of what is fitting for

LISA CHAVEZ

358 Fairlawn Road
Tulsa, Oklahoma 47000
(405) 555-2634

P E R S O N A L   I N F O R M A T I O N

Birth Date: February 14, 19--
Social Security Number: 102-03-0405
Health: Excellent

P O S I T I O N   D E S I R E D

Assistant Buyer

E D U C A T I O N

Graduate of Glenoaks High School, June, 19--
A.A., June, 19-- Tulsa Community College, Marketing Major

W O R K   E X P E R I E N C E

* Part-time junior apparel salesperson and college board member at Sanders'
Department Store, Tulsa, while attending community college
* Salesperson-trainee at Carla's Boutique, Tulsa, during senior year of
high school through distributive education cooperative program
* Part-time cashier, The Burger Stop, Tulsa, during junior year of high
school

A C T I V I T I E S   A N D   I N T E R E S T S

Coordinator for Freshman Fashion Luncheon, Tulsa Community College,
September, 19--
Member of High School and Junior College Divisions of DECA
Hobbies and Sports: pottery, folk dancing, swimming

R E F E R E N C E S

* Ms. Sharon McGuire, Assistant Buyer for junior sportswear, Sanders'
Department Store, 2300 Main Street, Tulsa
* Ms. Carla Brown, Owner and Manager, Carla's Boutique, 264 Bristol
Avenue, Tulsa
* Mr. Steven Glass, Associate Professor of Distributive Education and
DECA chapter advisor, Tulsa Community College, 112 College Drive, Tulsa

the occasion, and this is an important part of the management personality.

The applicant should bring to the interview whatever documents may be needed, such as classroom or work samples, if these are relevant.

Remember that the interview is a two-way affair. It is sensible and correct to ask questions and gather as much information as possible. The probability is that the first interview will end with no commitment on either side, since the number of positions in an executive training program is limited, and the interviewer is seeing many people. The applicant, too, will have the opportunity later to compare the advantages offered by different stores.

When making appointments for interviews, allow enough time for each. Sometimes the applicant will be required to take a written test or a physical examination.

The Follow-Up

Follow up the interview, whatever its outcome, with a letter expressing appreciation for the interview. Include in the letter any additional information that has been requested or that you think might help affect the outcome favorably. If you have been given a firm offer, and you have asked for time to consider it, send your acceptance or refusal promptly. If you are sending a refusal, express it courteously. Remember that you may be applying to this store again sometime in the future. Accept only when you are sure you are going to take the job.

THE ROAD AHEAD

The first year or two with a store will give the beginning careerist the opportunity to make an on-the-spot appraisal of the many different positions that retailing has to offer.

It is not unusual for executive trainees to change their ambitions during this period as they discover aptitudes and interests somewhat different from those that seemed most important to them at the beginning. That is, indeed, part of the purpose of the management training period. The personnel specialists who keep track of the potential manager's progress will be alert to observe any special aptitudes or deficiencies he or she displays. The initial period in the store is a time during which the potential manager is under continuous appraisal. It is a testing as well as a training time, during which his or her qualities as a manager are thoroughly analyzed.

DESIRABLE MANAGEMENT CHARACTERISTICS

What are the desirable qualities one should possess to be considered for management positions? These qualities include good personal attributes, human relations skills, intelligence, and interest in a retailing career.

Personal Attributes

The seven personal attributes most frequently sought as characteristic of the promotable manager are good work habits, a pleasant personality, emotional stability and confidence, enthusiasm, interest, physical stamina, and integrity and loyalty.

Human Relations Skills

A friendly attitude is characteristic of all who are skilled in human relations. Successful managers have, in addition, good leadership qualities and the ability to sell their ideas. The people who are chosen for management training programs have generally been tested during the initial interview for their friendly attitude.

Leadership Qualities. The leadership qualities of the recruits are judged largely by the record of extracurricular activities at school. On the job—and to some degree in the store's classroom—the leadership qualities of the potential managers will

◁ The information on this résumé gives the potential employer a clear presentation of the applicant's qualifications.

be judged according to the attitude their fellow employees adopt toward them.

The Ability to Sell an Idea. The development of the ability to sell an idea will help during management training to bring the young recruits to the attention of their supervisors. Later this ability will be equally useful when dealing with manufacturers, other vendors, newspapers, and the entire community in which the store operates.

Intelligence

Under the general heading "intelligence," retailers include general intelligence, mental alertness, decision-making ability, organizing ability, flexibility, shrewdness, and a desirable educational background.

Although some of these characteristics are brought to the job, certain aspects can be continuously improved on the job.

Interest in Retailing

Interest in retailing is shown by retailing career-mindedness, retailing work experience, an aptitude for retailing, and creative ability in the field of retailing.

Creativity is an element that makes the retailing career interesting and rewarding. Those who get to the top in sales promotion, in merchandising, or in management and control have all exhibited creativity in reaching that position.

The creative sense can be developed by being aware of the world around you—particularly the retailing world. Young managers in retailing should make a point of visiting other stores whenever they have the opportunity. To the person interested in retailing, the opening of a new shopping center anywhere in the vicinity should mean an early visit to see what the designers, planners, merchandisers, and promoters have done. Interest in the theater, museum exhibitions, art shows, the ballet, travel, and sports encourages the development of a creative sense. To one who is absorbed in a retail enterprise, every sight and experience suggests ideas that contribute to merchandising or selling efforts.

THE FUTURE OF MINORITY GROUPS IN RETAILING

Persian rugs sold by dealers from Iran, exotic jewelry and accessories sold by Indians and Pakistanis, African art objects sold by natives of Africa, and Mexican stones and jewelry sold by Mexicans are but a few examples of merchandise from other lands that has been accepted in the United States. There has been a growing patronage in businesses run by members of minority groups from other countries who import such products.

However, members of minority groups who were born in this country have not always moved into retailing and up the management ladder in the proportions that they represent in the population. Women, for example, have long been employed in retailing. Women as salespeople, as clerks, and as fashion coordinators, buyers, and even department managers have been rather frequently observed. Women in top management positions, however, are rare except in small stores that they own. Few women have ever been presidents of large retailing firms, and few are members of the boards of directors of large firms. Similarly, blacks, Puerto Ricans, Mexicans, and other minority groups have had relatively little representation in top management positions in retailing. Franchising has provided opportunities for training and advancing people of minority groups, but even that effort has not attracted large numbers of these people.

Both education and the desire to succeed in retailing must be present before the minority groups can take their rightful place in the hierarchy of retailing. Schools, colleges, universities, and retailers must work together to help people in these groups get the proper background and training so that they can progress through the ranks to the top-level jobs. Retailing does offer the opportunity and the challenge. The competition is keen, but members of minority groups can compete on an equal footing once they receive the proper education and once their interest is sparked.

THE EXCITEMENT OF RETAILING

To those in retailing who enjoy their work, no other field is as exciting or as rewarding. A retail store is like a theater. Each morning the stage is set, the doors open, the audience arrives, and the drama of merchandising unfolds. Plots and subplots complicate the activities and spur the behind-the-scenes personnel to improvise and to be creative. Each day a new drama is presented—with different audiences, varied settings, and extemporaneous dialogue. To those who enjoy such drama, challenge, suspense, and commotion, no other work is as dynamic and exhilarating as retailing.

METRIC CONVERSION CHART

In the coming years the United States will convert from its conventional system of measurement to the metric system. Although a complete changeover will not take place for some time, retailers should become familiar with metric measurements. The following table shows how to obtain the metric equivalent for the conventional measurements used throughout this book.

Multiply	by	to obtain
LENGTH		
inches	25.4	millimeters
feet	.305	meters
yards	.914	meters
miles	1.609	kilometers
AREA		
square inches	6.45	square centimeters
square feet	.092	square meters
square yards	.836	square meters
VOLUME		
cubic inches	16.387	cubic centimeters
quarts	.946	liters
gallons	3.785	liters
cubic yards	.765	cubic meters
WEIGHT		
ounces	28.35	grams
pounds	.45	kilograms
tons	.91	metric tons

INDEX